ELEVENTH ESSENTIALS EDITION

We the People

AN INTRODUCTION TO AMERICAN POLITICS

THE PRESIDENTIAL ELECTION OF 2016

Hillary Clinton (Democrat) margin of victory

Total electoral votes: 232

<5%   5–10%   >10%

Donald Trump (Republican) margin of victory

Total electoral votes: 306

<5%   5–10%   >10%

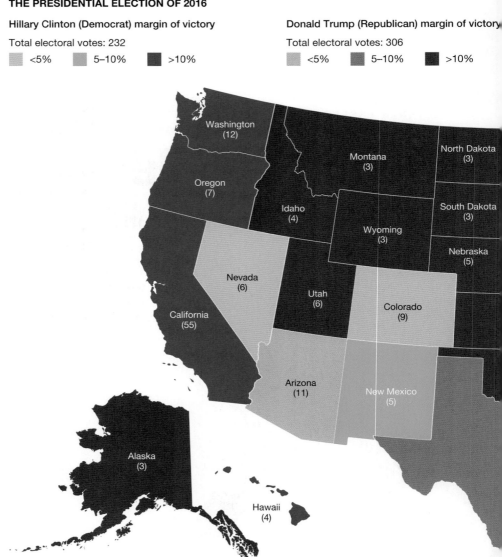

NOTE: Donald Trump won the electoral college with 304 votes to Hillary Clinton's 227. Seven electors voted for someone other than their party's candidate.

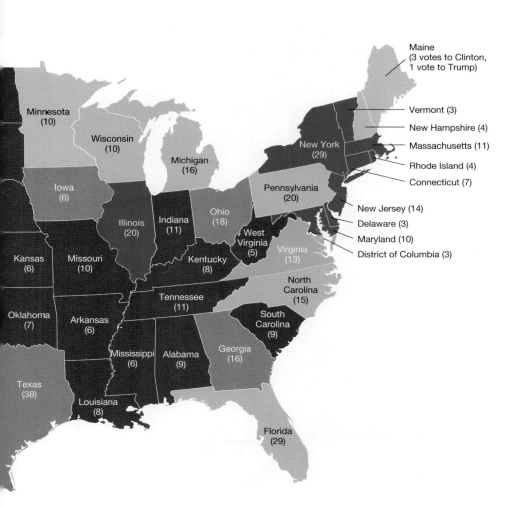

Maine
(3 votes to Clinton,
1 vote to Trump)

Vermont (3)

New Hampshire (4)

Massachusetts (11)

Rhode Island (4)

Connecticut (7)

New Jersey (14)

Delaware (3)

Maryland (10)

District of Columbia (3)

New York
(29)

Pennsylvania
(20)

Minnesota
(10)

Wisconsin
(10)

Michigan
(16)

Iowa
(6)

Illinois
(20)

Indiana
(11)

Ohio
(18)

West
Virginia
(5)

Virginia
(13)

Kentucky
(8)

Kansas
(6)

Missouri
(10)

North
Carolina
(15)

Tennessee
(11)

South
Carolina
(9)

Oklahoma
(7)

Arkansas
(6)

Mississippi
(6)

Alabama
(9)

Georgia
(16)

Texas
(38)

Louisiana
(8)

Florida
(29)

ELEVENTH ESSENTIALS EDITION

We the People

AN INTRODUCTION TO AMERICAN POLITICS

Benjamin Ginsberg
THE JOHNS HOPKINS UNIVERSITY

Theodore J. Lowi
CORNELL UNIVERSITY

Margaret Weir
BROWN UNIVERSITY

Caroline J. Tolbert
UNIVERSITY OF IOWA

Robert J. Spitzer
SUNY CORTLAND

 W. W. NORTON & COMPANY
NEW YORK   LONDON

W. W. Norton & Company has been independent since its founding in 1923, when William Warder Norton and Mary D. Herter Norton first published lectures delivered at the People's Institute, the adult education division of New York City's Cooper Union. The firm soon expanded its program beyond the Institute, publishing books by celebrated academics from America and abroad. By mid-century, the two major pillars of Norton's publishing program—trade books and college texts—were firmly established. In the 1950s, the Norton family transferred control of the company to its employees, and today—with a staff of four hundred and a comparable number of trade, college, and professional titles published each year—W. W. Norton & Company stands as the largest and oldest publishing house owned wholly by its employees.

Editor: Ann Shin
Associate Editor: Emily Stuart
Project Editor: Christine D'Antonio
Editorial Assistant: Shannon Jilek
Manuscript Editor: Andrew Pachuta
Managing Editor, College: Marian Johnson
Managing Editor, College Digital Media: Kim Yi
Production Manager, College: Ashley Horna
Media Editor: Spencer Richardson-Jones
Associate Media Editor: Michael Jaoui
Media Editorial Assistant: Ariel Eaton

Marketing Manager, Political Science: Erin Brown
Art Director: Rubina Yeh
Text Design: Lissi Sigillo
Photo Editor: Catherine Abelman
Photo Researcher: Elyse Rieder
Permissions Manager: Megan Schindel
Permissions Clearing: Elizabeth Trammell
Information Graphics: Kiss Me I'm Polish LLC, New York
Composition: Graphic World, Inc.
Manufacturing: TransContinental

Permission to use copyrighted material is included in the credits section of this book, which begins on page A97.

The Library of Congress has cataloged the full edition as follows:

Library of Congress Cataloging-in-Publication Data

Ginsberg, Benjamin, author. | Lowi, Theodore J., author. | Weir, Margaret,
    1952- author. | Tolbert, Caroline J., author.
We the people : an introduction to American politics / Benjamin
    Ginsberg, the Johns Hopkins University, Theodore J. Lowi, Cornell
    University, Margaret Weir, Brown University, Caroline J. Tolbert,
    University of Iowa.
Eleventh Edition. | New York : W.W. Norton & Company, [2017]
    Tenth edition: 2015.
    Includes bibliographical references and index.
LCCN 2016050517 | ISBN 9780393283624 (hardcover)
LCSH: United States—Politics and government—Textbooks.
LCC JK276.G55 2017 | DDC 320.473—dc23 LC record available at https://lccn.loc
.gov/2016050517

This edition:
ISBN: 978-0-393-28364-8 (pbk.)

W. W. Norton & Company, Inc., 500 Fifth Avenue, New York, N. Y. 10110
www.wwnorton.com

W. W. Norton & Company Ltd., 15 Carlisle Street, London W1D 3BS

3 4 5 6 7 8 9 0

To Teresa Spitzer

Sandy, Cindy, and Alex Ginsberg

Angele, Anna, and Jason Lowi

Nicholas Ziegler

David, Jackie, Eveline, and Ed Dowling

contents

PART II Politics

5 ● Public Opinion 142

6 ● The Media 174

7 ● Political Parties, Participation, and Elections 202

PART III Institutions

9 ● Congress 272

PART IV Policy

preface

his book has been and continues to be dedicated to developing a satisfactory response to the question more and more Americans are asking: Why should we be engaged with government and politics? Through the first ten editions, we sought to answer this question by making the text directly relevant to the lives of the students who would be reading it. As a result, we tried to make politics interesting by demonstrating that students' interests are at stake and that they therefore need to take a personal, even selfish, interest in the outcomes of government. At the same time, we realized that students needed guidance in how to become politically engaged. Beyond providing students with a core of political knowledge, we needed to show them how they could apply that knowledge as participants in the political process. The "Who Participates?" sections in each chapter help achieve that goal.

As events from the last several years have reminded us, "what government does" inevitably raises questions about political participation and political equality. The size and composition of the electorate, for example, affect who is elected to public office and what policy directions the government will pursue. Hence, the issue of voter ID laws became important in the 2016 election, with some arguing that these laws reduce voter fraud and others contending that they decrease participation by poor and minority voters. Other recent events have underscored how Americans from different backgrounds experience politics. Arguments about immigration became contentious during the 2016 election as the nation once again debated the question of who is entitled to be an American and have a voice in determining what the government does. And charges that the police often use excessive violence against members of minority groups have raised questions about whether the government treats all Americans equally. Reflecting all of these trends, this new Eleventh Edition shows more than any other book on the market (1) how students are connected to government, (2) why students should think critically about government and politics, and (3) how Americans from different backgrounds experience and shape politics. These themes are incorporated in the following ways:

- **Chapter introductions focus on "What Government Does and Why It Matters."** In recent decades, cynicism about "big government" has dominated the political zeitgeist. But critics of government often forget that governments do a great deal for citizens. Every year, Americans are the beneficiaries of billions of dollars of goods and services from government programs. Government "does" a lot, and what it does matters a great deal to everyone, including college students. At the start of each chapter, this theme is introduced and applied to the chapter's topic. The goal is to show students that government and politics mean something to their daily lives.

- **A twenty-first-century perspective on demographic change** moves beyond the book's strong coverage of traditional civil rights content with expanded coverage of contemporary group politics.

- *New* **"Who Participates?" infographics at the end of every chapter** show students how different groups of Americans participate in key aspects of politics and government. Each concludes with a "What You Can Do" section that provides students with specific, realistic steps they can take to act on what they've learned and get involved in politics.

- **"America Side by Side" boxes** in every chapter use data figures and tables to provide a comparative perspective. By comparing political institutions and behavior across countries, students gain a better understanding of how specific features of the American system shape politics.

- **Up-to-date coverage**, with more than 10 pages and numerous graphics on the 2016 elections, including a five-page section devoted to analysis of the 2016 elections in Chapter 8, as well as updated data, examples, and other information throughout the book.

- **Built-in study guides at the end of each chapter offer valuable learning tools.** A practice quiz and glossary definitions help students review the chapter material. Each chapter also includes a list of recommended readings to help students get started on research projects.

- **"Politics and Your Future" chapter conclusions** give students direct, personal reasons to care about politics. These sections focus on the political opportunities and challenges that students will face in their lives as a result of emerging social, political, demographic, and technological change. The conclusions reprise the important point made in the chapter introductions that *government matters* and prompt students to consider how political change will impact their futures.

- **This Eleventh Edition is accompanied by InQuizitive**, Norton's award-winning formative, adaptive online quizzing program. The InQuizitive course for *We the People*, Essentials Edition, guides students through questions organized around the text's chapter learning objectives to ensure mastery of the core information and to help with assessment. More information and a demonstration are available at digital.wwnorton.com/wethepeople11ess.

We continue to hope that our book will itself be accepted as a form of enlightened political action. This Eleventh Edition is another chance. It is an advancement toward our goal. We promise to keep trying.

acknowledgments

We are especially pleased to acknowledge the many colleagues who had a direct and active role in criticism and preparation of the manuscript. Our thanks go to:

First Edition Reviewers

Sarah Binder, Brookings Institution
Kathleen Gille, Office of Representative David Bonior
Rodney Hero, University of Colorado at Boulder
Robert Katzmann, Brookings Institution
Kathleen Knight, University of Houston
Robin Kolodny, Temple University
Nancy Kral, Tomball College
Robert C. Lieberman, Columbia University
David A. Marcum, University of Wyoming
Laura R. Winsky Mattei, State University of New York at Buffalo
Marilyn S. Mertens, Midwestern State University
Barbara Suhay, Henry Ford Community College
Carolyn Wong, Stanford University
Julian Zelizer, State University of New York at Albany

Second Edition Reviewers

Lydia Andrade, University of North Texas
John Coleman, University of Wisconsin at Madison
Daphne Eastman, Odessa College
Otto Feinstein, Wayne State University
Elizabeth Flores, Delmar College
James Gimpel, University of Maryland at College Park

Jill Glaathar, Southwest Missouri State University
Shaun Herness, University of Florida
William Lyons, University of Tennessee at Knoxville
Andrew Polsky, Hunter College, City University of New York
Grant Reeher, Syracuse University
Richard Rich, Virginia Polytechnic
Bartholomew Sparrow, University of Texas at Austin

Third Edition Reviewers

Bruce R. Drury, Lamar University
Andrew I. E. Ewoh, Prairie View A&M University
Amy Jasperson, University of Texas at San Antonio
Loch Johnson, University of Georgia
Mark Kann, University of Southern California
Robert L. Perry, University of Texas of the Permian Basin
Wayne Pryor, Brazosport College
Elizabeth A. Rexford, Wharton County Junior College
Andrea Simpson, University of Washington
Brian Smentkowski, Southeast Missouri State University
Nelson Wikstrom, Virginia Commonwealth University

Fourth Edition Reviewers

M. E. Banks, Virginia Commonwealth University
Lynn Brink, North Lake College
Mark Cichock, University of Texas at Arlington
Del Fields, St. Petersburg College
Nancy Kinney, Washtenaw Community College
William Klein, St. Petersburg College
Dana Morales, Montgomery College
Christopher Muste, Louisiana State University
Larry Norris, South Plains College
David Rankin, State University of New York at Fredonia
Paul Roesler, St. Charles Community College
J. Philip Rogers, San Antonio College
Greg Shaw, Illinois Wesleyan University
Tracy Skopek, Stephen F. Austin State University
Don Smith, University of North Texas
Terri Wright, Cal State, Fullerton

Fifth Edition Reviewers

Annie Benifield, Tomball College
Denise Dutton, Southwest Missouri State University
Rick Kurtz, Central Michigan University
Kelly McDaniel, Three Rivers Community College
Eric Plutzer, Pennsylvania State University
Daniel Smith, Northwest Missouri State University
Dara Strolovitch, University of Minnesota
Dennis Toombs, San Jacinto College–North
Stacy Ulbig, Southwest Missouri State University

Sixth Edition Reviewers

Janet Adamski, University of Mary Hardin–Baylor
Greg Andrews, St. Petersburg College
Louis Bolce, Baruch College
Darin Combs, Tulsa Community College

Sean Conroy, University of New Orleans
Paul Cooke, Cy Fair College
Vida Davoudi, Kingwood College
Robert DiClerico, West Virginia University
Corey Ditslear, University of North Texas
Kathy Dolan, University of Wisconsin, Milwaukee
Randy Glean, Midwestern State University
Nancy Kral, Tomball College
Mark Logas, Valencia Community College
Scott MacDougall, Diablo Valley College
David Mann, College of Charleston
Christopher Muste, University of Montana
Richard Pacelle, Georgia Southern University
Sarah Poggione, Florida International University
Richard Rich, Virginia Tech
Thomas Schmeling, Rhode Island College
Scott Spitzer, California State University–Fullerton
Robert Wood, University of North Dakota

Seventh Edition Reviewers

Molly Andolina, DePaul University
Nancy Bednar, Antelope Valley College
Paul Blakelock, Kingwood College
Amy Brandon, San Jacinto College
Jim Cauthen, John Jay College
Kevin Davis, North Central Texas College
Louis DeSipio, University of California–Irvine
Brandon Franke, Blinn College
Steve Garrison, Midwestern State University
Joseph Howard, University of Central Arkansas
Aaron Knight, Houston Community College
Paul Labedz, Valencia Community College
Elise Langan, John Jay College
Mark Logas, Valencia Community College
Eric Miller, Blinn College
Anthony O'Regan, Los Angeles Valley College
David Putz, Kingwood College
Chis Soper, Pepperdine University
Kevin Wagner, Florida Atlantic University
Laura Wood, Tarrant County College

Eighth Edition Reviewers

Brian Arbour, John Jay College, CUNY
Ellen Baik, University of Texas–Pan American
David Birch, Lone Star College–Tomball
Bill Carroll, Sam Houston State University
Ed Chervenak, University of New Orleans
Gary Church, Mountain View College
Adrian Stefan Clark, Del Mar College
Annie Cole, Los Angeles City College
Greg Combs, University of Texas at Dallas
Cassandra Cookson, Lee College
Brian Cravens, Blinn College
John Crosby, California State University–Chico
Scott Crosby, Valencia Community College
Courtenay Daum, Colorado State University, Fort Collins
Peter Doas, University of Texas–Pan American
John Domino, Sam Houston State University
Doug Dow, University of Texas–Dallas
Jeremy Duff, Midwestern State University
Heather Evans, Sam Houston State University
Hyacinth Ezeamii, Albany State University
Bob Fitrakis, Columbus State Community College
Brian Fletcher, Truckee Meadows Community College
Paul Foote, Eastern Kentucky University
Frank Garrahan, Austin Community College
Jimmy Gleason, Purdue University
Steven Greene, North Carolina State University
Jeannie Grussendorf, Georgia State University
M. Ahad Hayaud-Din, Brookhaven College
Alexander Hogan, Lone Star College–CyFair
Glen Hunt, Austin Community College
Mark Jendrysik, University of North Dakota
Krista Jenkins, Fairleigh Dickinson University
Carlos Juárez, Hawaii Pacific University
Melinda Kovács, Sam Houston State University
Boyd Lanier, Lamar University
Jeff Lazarus, Georgia State University
Jeffrey Lee, Blinn College
Alan Lehmann, Blinn College
Julie Lester, Macon State College
Steven Lichtman, Shippensburg University
Fred Lokken, Truckee Meadows Community College
Shari MacLachlan, Palm Beach Community College
Guy Martin, Winston-Salem State University
Fred Monardi, College of Southern Nevada
Vincent Moscardelli, University of Connecticut
Jason Mycoff, University of Delaware
Sugumaran Narayanan, Midwestern State University
Anthony Nownes, University of Tennessee, Knoxville
Elizabeth Oldmixon, University of North Texas
John Osterman, San Jacinto College–Central
Mark Peplowski, College of Southern Nevada
Maria Victoria Perez-Rios, John Jay College, CUNY
Sara Rinfret, University of Wisconsin, Green Bay
Andre Robinson, Pulaski Technical College
Susan Roomberg, University of Texas at San Antonio
Ryan Rynbrandt, Collin County Community College
Mario Salas, Northwest Vista College
Michael Sanchez, San Antonio College
Mary Schander, Pasadena City College
Laura Schneider, Grand Valley State University
Subash Shah, Winston-Salem State University
Mark Shomaker, Blinn College
Roy Slater, St. Petersburg College
Debra St. John, Collin College
Eric Whitaker, Western Washington University
Clay Wiegand, Cisco College
Walter Wilson, University of Texas at San Antonio
Kevan Yenerall, Clarion University
Rogerio Zapata, South Texas College

Ninth Edition Reviewers

Amy Acord, Lone Star College–CyFair
Milan Andrejevich, Ivy Tech Community College

Steve Anthony, Georgia State University

Phillip Ardoin, Appalachian State University

Gregory Arey, Cape Fear Community College

Joan Babcock, Northwest Vista College

Evelyn Ballard, Houston Community College

Robert Ballinger, South Texas College

Mary Barnes-Tilley, Blinn College

Robert Bartels, Evangel University

Nancy Bednar, Antelope Valley College

Annie Benifield, Lone Star College–Tomball

Donna Bennett, Trinity Valley Community College

Amy Brandon, El Paso Community College

Mark Brewer, The University of Maine

Gary Brown, Lone Star College–Montgomery

Joe Campbell, Johnson County Community College

Dewey Clayton, University of Louisville

Jeff Colbert, Elon University

Amanda Cook-Fesperman, Illinois Valley Community College

Kevin Corder, Western Michigan University

Kevin Davis, North Central Texas College

Paul Davis, Truckee Meadows Community College

Terri Davis, Lamar University

Jennifer De Maio, California State University, Northridge

Christopher Durso, Valencia College

Ryan Emenaker, College of the Redwoods

Leslie Feldman, Hofstra University

Glen Findley, Odessa College

Michael Gattis, Gulf Coast State College

Donna Godwin, Trinity Valley Community College

Precious Hall, Truckee Meadows Community College

Sally Hansen, Daytona State College

Tiffany Harper, Collin College

Todd Hartman, Appalachian State University

Virginia Haysley, Lone Star College–Tomball

David Head, John Tyler Community College

Rick Henderson, Texas State University–San Marcos

Richard Herrera, Arizona State University

Thaddaus Hill, Blinn College

Steven Holmes, Bakersfield College

Kevin Holton, South Texas College

Robin Jacobson, University of Puget Sound

Joseph Jozwiak, Texas A & M–Corpus Christi

Casey Klofstad, University of Miami

Samuel Lingrosso, Los Angeles Valley College

Mark Logas, Valencia College

Christopher Marshall, South Texas College

Larry McElvain, South Texas College

Elizabeth McLane, Wharton County Junior College

Eddie Meaders, University of North Texas

Rob Mellen, Mississippi State University

Jalal Nejad, Northwest Vista College

Adam Newmark, Appalachian State University

Stephen Nicholson, University of California, Merced

Cissie Owen, Lamar University

Suzanne Preston, St. Petersburg College

David Putz, Lone Star College–Kingwood

Auksuole Rubavichute, Mountain View College

Ronnee Schreiber, San Diego State University

Ronald Schurin, University of Connecticut

Jason Seitz, Georgia Perimeter College

Jennifer Seitz, Georgia Perimeter College

Shannon Sinegal, The University of New Orleans

John Sides, George Washington University

Thomas Sowers, Lamar University

Jim Startin, University of Texas at San Antonio

Robert Sterken, University of Texas at Tyler

Bobby Summers, Harper College

John Theis, Lone Star College–Kingwood

John Todd, University of North Texas

Delaina Toothman, The University of Maine

David Trussell, Cisco College

Ronald Vardy, University of Houston

Linda Veazey, Midwestern State University

John Vento, Antelope Valley Community College

Clif Wilkinson, Georgia College

John Wood, Rose State College

Michael Young, Trinity Valley Community College

Tyler Young, Collin College

Tenth Edition Reviewers

Stephen P. Amberg, University of Texas at San Antonio
Juan F. Arzola, College of the Sequoias
Thomas J. Baldino, Wilkes University
Christina Bejarano, University of Kansas
Paul T. Bellinger, Jr., University of Missouri
Melanie J. Blumberg, California University of Pennsylvania
Matthew T. Bradley, Indiana University Kokomo
Jeffrey W. Christiansen, Seminole State College
McKinzie Craig, Marietta College
Christopher Cronin, Methodist University
Jenna Duke, Lehigh Carbon Community College
Francisco Durand, University of Texas at San Antonio
Carrie Eaves, Elon University
Paul M. Flor, El Camino College Compton Center
Adam Fuller, Youngstown State University
Christi Gramling, Charleston Southern University
Sally Hansen, Daytona State College
Mary Jane Hatton, Hawai'i Pacific University
David Helpap, University of Wisconsin–Green Bay
Theresa L. Hutchins, Georgia Highlands College
Cryshanna A. Jackson Leftwich, Youngstown State University
Ashlyn Kuersten, Western Michigan University
Kara Lindaman, Winona State University
Timothy Lynch, University of Wisconsin–Milwaukee
Larry McElvain, South Texas College
Corinna R. McKoy, Ventura College
Eddie L. Meaders, University of North Texas
Don D. Mirjanian, College of Southern Nevada
R. Shea Mize, Georgia Highlands College
Nicholas Morgan, Collin College
Matthew Murray, Dutchess Community College
Harold "Trey" Orndorff III, Daytona State College
Randall Parish, University of North Georgia

Michelle Pautz, University of Dayton
Michael Pickering, University of New Orleans
Donald Ranish, Antelope Valley College
Glenn W. Richardson, Jr., Kutztown University of Pennsylvania
Jason Robles, Colorado State University
Ionas Aurelian Rus, University of Cincinnati–Blue Ash
Robert Sahr, Oregon State University
Kelly B. Shaw, Iowa State University
Captain Michael Slattery, Campbell University
Michael Smith, Sam Houston State University
Maryam T. Stevenson, University of Indianapolis
Elizabeth Trentanelli, Gulf Coast State College
Ronald W. Vardy, University of Houston
Timothy Weaver, University of Louisville
Christina Wolbrecht, University of Notre Dame

Eleventh Edition Reviewers

Maria J. Albo, University of North Georgia
Andrea Aleman, University of Texas at San Antonio
Juan Arzola, College of the Sequoias
Ross K. Baker, Rutgers University
Lauren Balasco, Pittsburg State University
Daniel Birdsong, University of Dayton
Phil Branyon, University of North Georgia
Camille D. Burge, Villanova University
Matthew DeSantis, Guilford Technical Community College
Sheryl Edwards, University of Michigan–Dearborn
Lauren Elliott-Dorans, University of Toledo
Heather Evans, Sam Houston State University
William Feagin, Jr., Wharton County Junior College
Glen Findley, Odessa College
Heather Frederick, Slipper Rock University
Jason Ghibesi, Ocean County College
Patrick Gilbert, Lone Star–Tomball
Rebecca Herzog, American River College
Steven Horn, Everett Community College

Demetra Kasimis, California State University, Long Beach

Eric T. Kasper, University of Wisconsin–Eau Claire

Jill Kirkham, Brigham Young University–Idaho

Mary Linder, Grayson County College

Johnson Louie, California State University, Stanislaus

Phil McCall, Portland State University

Patrick Novotny, Georgia Southern University

Carolyn Myers, Southwestern Illinois College–Belleville

Gerhard Peters, Citrus College

Michael A. Powell, Frederick Community College

Robert Proctor, Santa Rosa Junior College

Allen K. Settle, California Polytechnic State University

Laurie Sprankle, Community College of Allegheny County

Ryan Lee Teten, University of Louisiana at Lafayette

Justin Vaughn, Boise State University

John Vento, Antelope Valley College

Aaron Weinschenk, University of Wisconsin–Green Bay

Tyler Young, Collin College

We are also grateful to Melissa Michelson, of Menlo College, who contributed to the "Who Participates?" infographics for this edition; Holley Hansen, of Oklahoma State University, who contributed to the "America Side by Side" boxes; and Gabrielle Ellul for research assistance.

Perhaps above all, we thank those at W. W. Norton. For its first five editions, editor Steve Dunn helped us shape the book in countless ways. Lisa McKay contributed smart ideas and a keen editorial eye to the Tenth Edition. Ann Shin carried on the Norton tradition of splendid editorial work on the Sixth through Ninth Editions and on the current Eleventh Edition. As associate editor, Emily Stuart brought intelligence and dedication to the development of this Eleventh Edition. For our InQuizitive course, Coursepack, and other instructor resources, Spencer Richardson-Jones has been an energetic and visionary editor. Ashley Horna, Michael Jaoui, Shannon Jilek, and Ariel Eaton also kept the production of the Eleventh Edition and its accompanying resources coherent and in focus. Andrew Pachuta copyedited the manuscript, and our superb project editor Christine D'Antonio devoted countless hours to keeping on top of myriad details. We thank Elyse Rieder for finding new photos and our photo editor Catherine Abelman for managing the image program. Finally, we thank Roby Harrington, the head of Norton's college department.

Benjamin Ginsberg
Theodore J. Lowi
Margaret Weir
Caroline J. Tolbert

October 2016

ELEVENTH ESSENTIALS EDITION

We the People

AN INTRODUCTION TO AMERICAN POLITICS

Most Americans share the core political values of liberty, equality, and democracy and want their government and its policies to reflect these values. However, people often disagree on the meaning of these values and what government should do to protect them.

1

Introduction: The Citizen and Government

WHAT GOVERNMENT DOES AND WHY IT MATTERS Americans sometimes appear to believe that the government is an institution that does things
to them and from which they need protection. Students may wonder why they
have to fill in long, often complicated forms to apply for financial assistance.
They may frown when they see the payroll tax deducted from their small pay-
check. Like Americans of all ages, they may resent municipal "red-light" cameras designed to photograph traffic violators—and send them tickets.

Although most people complain about something that government does
to them, most everyone wants the government to do a great deal *for* them.
Some of the services that people expect from government are big-ticket items,
such as providing national security and keeping the nation safe from terrorist
attacks. We all know that government pays for and directs the military. Students attending a state university know that state and federal public dollars
help support their education.

Yet many of the other services that government provides are far less visible,
and often it is not even clear that government plays a role at all. For example,
students grabbing a quick bite to eat between classes take it for granted that
their hamburger will not contain bacteria that might make them sick. Without federal inspection of meat, however, chances of contracting food-borne

illnesses would be much higher and the everyday task of eating would be much riskier. Driving to school would not be possible if not for the tens of billions of dollars spent each year on road construction and maintenance by federal, state, and municipal governments. Like most Americans, young people expect to get reliable information about the weather for the week ahead and warnings about dangerous events such as hurricanes. The National Weather Service and the National Hurricane Center both provide reliable forecasts for such simple calculations as whether to bring an umbrella to more significant calculations made by airlines and air traffic control to get travelers safely where they need to go. These daily decisions don't seem to involve government, but in fact they do. Indeed, most Americans would not be here at all if it were not for federal immigration policies, which set the terms for entry into the United States and for obtaining citizenship.

Government is the term generally used to describe the formal institutions through which a land and its people are ruled. As the government seeks to protect its citizens, it faces the challenge of doing so in ways that are true to the key American political values of liberty, equality, and democracy. *Liberty* means personal freedom and a government whose powers are limited by law. *Equality* is the idea that all individuals should have the right to participate in political life and society on equivalent terms. *Democracy* means placing considerable political power in the hands of ordinary people. Most Americans find it easy to affirm all three values in principle. In practice, however, matters are not always so clear. Policies and practices that seem to affirm one of these values may contradict another. Americans, moreover, are sometimes willing to subordinate liberty to security and have frequently tolerated significant departures from the principles of equality and democracy.

chaptergoals

- Explore Americans' attitudes toward government (pp. 5–8)
- Describe the role of the citizen in politics (pp. 8–9)
- Define government and forms of government (pp. 9–12)
- Show how the social composition of the American population has changed over time (pp. 12–19)
- Analyze whether the U.S. system of government upholds American political values (pp. 19–21)

Government Affects Our Lives Every Day

Explore Americans' attitudes toward government

Since the United States was established as a nation, Americans have been reluctant to grant government too much power, and they have often been suspicious of politicians. But over the course of the nation's history, Americans have also turned to government for assistance in times of need and have strongly supported the government in periods of war. In 1933 the power of the government began to expand to meet the crises created by the stock market crash of 1929, the Great Depression, and the run on banks. Congress passed legislation that brought the government into the businesses of home mortgages, farm mortgages, credit, and relief of personal distress. More recently, when the economy fell into a recession in 2008 and 2009, the federal government took action to shore up the financial system, oversee the restructuring of the ailing auto companies, and inject hundreds of billions of dollars into the faltering economy. Today, the national government is an enormous institution with programs and policies reaching into every corner of American life. It oversees the nation's economy, it is the nation's largest employer, it provides citizens with a host of services, it controls the world's most formidable military establishment, and it regulates a wide range of social and commercial activities.

Much of what citizens have come to depend on and take for granted—as, somehow, part of the natural environment—is in fact created by government. Take the example of a typical college student's day, throughout which that student relies on a host of services and activities organized by national, state, and local government agencies. The extent of this dependence on government is illustrated by Table 1.1.

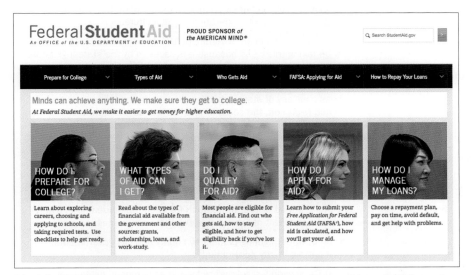

The federal government maintains a large number of websites that provide useful information to citizens on such topics as loans for education, civil service job applications, the inflation rate, and how the weather will affect farming. These sites are just one way in which the government serves its citizens.

TABLE 1.1

The Presence of Government in the Daily Life of a Student at "State University"

TIME OF DAY	SCHEDULE
7:00 A.M.	Wake up. Standard time set by the national government.
7:10 A.M.	Shower. Water courtesy of local government, either a public entity or a regulated private company. Brush your teeth with toothpaste whose cavity-fighting claims have been verified by a federal agency.
7:30 A.M.	Have a bowl of cereal with milk for breakfast. "Nutrition Facts" on food labels are a federal requirement, pasteurization of milk required by state law, recycling the empty cereal box and milk carton enabled by state or local laws.
8:30 A.M.	Drive or take public transportation to campus. Air bags and seat belts required by federal and state laws. Roads and bridges paid for by state and local governments, speed and traffic laws set by state and local governments, public transportation subsidized by all levels of government.
8:45 A.M.	Arrive on campus of large public university. Buildings are 70 percent financed by state taxpayers.
9:00 A.M.	First class: Chemistry 101. Tuition partially paid by a federal loan (more than half the cost of university instruction is paid for by taxpayers), chemistry lab paid for with grants from the National Science Foundation (a federal agency).
Noon	Eat lunch. College cafeteria financed by state dormitory authority on land grant from federal Department of Agriculture.
2:00 P.M.	Second class: American Government 101 (your favorite class!). You may be taking this class because it is required by the state legislature or because it fulfills a university requirement.
4:00 P.M.	Third class: Computer Lab. Free computers, software, and Internet access courtesy of state subsidies plus grants and discounts from IBM and Microsoft, the costs of which are deducted from their corporate income taxes; Internet built in part by federal government.
6:00 P.M.	Eat hamburger for dinner. Meat inspected by federal agencies.
7:00 P.M.	Work at part-time job at the campus library. Minimum wage set by federal, state, or local government; books and journals in library paid for by state taxpayers.
8:15 P.M.	Check the status of your application for a federal student loan (FAFSA) on the Department of Education's website at studentaid.ed.gov.
10:00 P.M.	Go home. Street lighting paid for by county and city governments, police patrols by city government.
10:15 P.M.	Watch TV. Networks regulated by federal government, cable public-access channels required by city law. Weather forecast provided to broadcasters by a federal agency.

Trust in Government Has Declined

Ironically, even as popular dependence on government has grown, the American public's view of government has turned more sour. Public trust in government has declined, and Americans are now more likely to feel that they can do little to influence the government's actions. Different groups vary somewhat in their levels of trust: African Americans and Latinos express more confidence in the federal government than do whites. But even among the most supportive groups, more than half do not trust the government.[1] These developments are important because politically engaged citizens and public confidence in government are vital for the health of a democracy.

By 2015, only 19 percent of Americans reported trusting the government in Washington "to do what is right" all or most of the time, down from 75 percent in the early 1960s.[2] Several factors contributed to the decline in trust. Revelations about the faulty information that led up to the war in Iraq and ongoing concern about the war had increased Americans' mistrust of government. In March 2007, 54 percent of those surveyed believed that the Bush administration had deliberately misled the American public about whether Iraq had weapons of mass destruction. By 2012, the government's inability to get the economy moving had further undermined trust in government. When political differences over the Affordable Care Act, President Obama's program to reform the American health care system, led to a two-week partial government shutdown in 2013 and the second dramatic showdown over raising the national debt limit in two years (usually a routine matter), public trust once again dipped to historically low levels.[3] Distrust of government greatly influenced the presidential primary elections in 2015 and 2016, when a number of "outsider" candidates—most notably Donald Trump and Bernie Sanders—who were critical of government and eager to depart from business as usual in Washington, attracted wide support.

Does it matter if Americans trust their government? For the most part, the answer is yes. As we have seen, most Americans rely on government for a wide range of services and laws that they simply take for granted. But long-term distrust in government can result in public refusal to pay the taxes necessary to support such widely approved public activities. Low levels of confidence may also make it difficult for government to attract talented and effective workers to public service.[4] The weakening of government as a result of prolonged levels of distrust may ultimately harm the capacity of the United States to defend its national interest in the world economy and may jeopardize its national security. Likewise, a weak government can do little to assist citizens who need help in weathering periods of sharp economic or technological change.

Political Efficacy Means People Can Make a Difference

Another important trend in American views about government has been a declining sense of **political efficacy**, the belief that ordinary citizens can affect what government does, that they can take action to make government listen to them. In 2015, 74 percent of Americans said that elected officials do not care what people like them think; in 1960, only 25 percent felt so shut out of government.[5] Accompanying this sense that ordinary people cannot be heard is a growing belief that government is not run for the benefit of all the people. In 2015, 76 percent of the public disagreed with the idea that the "government is really run for the benefit of all the people."[6] These views are widely shared across the age spectrum.

This widely felt loss of political efficacy is bad news for American democracy. The feeling that you can't affect government decisions can lead to a self-perpetuating cycle of apathy, declining political participation, and withdrawal from political life. Why bother to participate if you believe it makes no difference? Yet the belief that you can be effective is the first step needed to influence government. Not every effort of ordinary citizens to influence government will succeed, but without any such efforts, government decisions will be made by a smaller and smaller circle of powerful people. Such loss of broad popular influence over government actions undermines the key feature of American democracy: government by the people.

● Citizenship Is Based on Political Knowledge and Participation

Describe the role of the citizen in politics

Beginning with the ancient Greeks, citizenship has meant membership in one's community. In fact, the Greeks did not even conceive of the individual as a complete person. The complete person was the public person, the *citizen*; a noncitizen or a private person was referred to as an *idiōtēs*. Participation in public affairs was virtually the definition of citizenship.

Today, voting is considered the building block of **citizenship**—informed and active membership in a political community—as it is the method by which Americans choose their elected leaders. Citizens can influence their government in many ways, including serving on a jury, lobbying, writing a letter to the editor of a local newspaper, and engaging in a public rally or protest. The point of these activities is to influence the government.

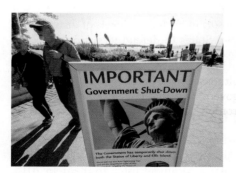

Citizens need political knowledge to figure out how best to act in their own interests. To take a simple example, if the garbage is not collected from in front of people's homes, people need to know that this job is the responsibility of their local government, not the national government. Americans often complain that government does not respond to their needs, but sometimes the failure of government to act may simply result from citizens lacking the information necessary to present their problems to the correct government office or agency. To put the matter more simply, effective

When the federal government partially shut down in October 2013, millions of citizens were affected, including visitors who were turned away from the Statue of Liberty.

participation requires knowledge. (It should come as no surprise, then, that people who have less knowledge of politics vote at lower rates than those with more knowledge.) Knowledge is the first prerequisite for achieving an increased sense of political efficacy.

"Digital Citizenship" Is the Newest Way to Participate

As more and more of our social, workplace, and educational activities have migrated online, so too have opportunities for political knowledge and participation, creating a new concept of "digital citizenship." *Digital citizenship* is the ability to participate in society online, and it is increasingly important in politics. A 2015 Pew survey found that over the previous year, 65 percent of Americans had used the Internet to find data or information about government. These include visiting a local, state, or federal government website.[7] Digital citizenship benefits individuals, but it also provides advantages to society as a whole. Digital citizens are more likely to be interested in politics and to discuss politics with friends, family, and coworkers than individuals who do not use online political information. They are also more likely to vote and participate in other ways in elections. Individuals without Internet access or the skills to participate in politics and the economy online are being left further behind. Exclusion from participation online is referred to as the "digital divide." Lower-income and less educated Americans, racial and ethnic minorities, those living in rural areas, and the elderly are all less likely to have Internet access.

Greater political knowledge increases the ability of people to influence their government. It is to the nature of government that we now turn.

● Government Is Made Up of the Institutions and Procedures by Which People Are Ruled

Define government and forms of government

Government refers to the formal institutions and procedures through which a territory and its people are ruled. To govern is to rule. A government may be as simple as a tribal council that meets occasionally to advise the chief or as complex as the vast establishments—with their forms, rules, and bureaucracies—found in the United States and the countries of Europe. A more complex government is sometimes referred to as "the state." In the history of civilization, governments have not been difficult to establish. There have been thousands of them. The hard part is establishing a government that lasts. Even more difficult is developing a stable government that promotes liberty, equality, and democracy.

Different Forms of Government Are Defined by Power and Freedom

Governments vary in their structure, in their size, and in the way they operate. Two questions are of special importance in determining how governments differ: Who governs? And how much government control is permitted?

In some nations, government power is held by a single individual, such as a king or dictator, or by a small group of powerful individuals, such as military leaders or wealthy landowners. Such a system of government normally pays little attention to popular preferences; it tends to hold power by violence or the threat of violence and is referred to as an **authoritarian** system, meaning that the government recognizes no formal limit but may nevertheless be restrained by the power of other social institutions. A system of government in which the degree of control is even greater is a **totalitarian** system, where the government recognizes no formal limits on its power and seeks to absorb or eliminate other social institutions that might challenge it. Nazi Germany under Adolf Hitler and the Soviet Union under Joseph Stalin are classic examples of totalitarian rule.

In contrast, a **democracy** is a political system that permits citizens to play a significant part in the governmental process, where they are vested with the power to rule themselves, usually through the election of key public officials. Under such a system, **constitutional government** is the norm, in that formal and effective limits are placed on the powers of the government. At times, an authoritarian government might bend to popular wishes, and democratic governments do not automatically follow the wishes of the majority. The point, however, is that these contrasting systems of government are based on very different assumptions and practices.

Americans have the good fortune to live in a nation in which limits are placed on what governments can do and how they can do it. By one measure, just 40 percent of the global population (those living in 86 countries) enjoy sufficient levels of political and personal freedom to be classified as living in a constitutional democracy.[8] And constitutional democracies were unheard of before the modern era. Prior to the eighteenth and nineteenth centuries, governments seldom sought (and rarely received) the support of their ordinary subjects.[9]

Beginning in the seventeenth century, in a handful of Western nations, two important changes began to take place in the character and conduct of government. First, governments began to acknowledge formal limits on their power. Second, a small number of governments began to provide the ordinary citizen with a formal voice in public affairs—through the vote. Obviously, the desirability of limits on government and the expansion of popular influence were at the heart of the American Revolution in 1776. "No taxation without representation" was hotly debated from the beginning of the Revolution through the adoption of the modern Constitution in 1789. But even before the Revolution, a tradition of limiting government and expanding citizen participation in the political process had developed throughout western Europe. Thus, to understand how the relationship between rulers and the ruled was transformed, we must broaden our focus to take into account events in Europe as well as in America. We will divide the transformation into its two separate parts. The first is the effort to put limits on government. The second is the effort to expand the influence of the people through access to government and politics.

Limits on Governments Encouraged Freedom

The key force behind the imposition of limits on government power was a new social class, the bourgeoisie. *Bourgeoisie* is a French word for "freeman of the city," or *bourg*. Being part of the bourgeoisie later became associated with being "middle class" and with involvement in commerce or industry. In order to gain a share of control of government, joining or even displacing the kings, aristocrats, and gentry who had dominated government for centuries, the bourgeoisie sought to change existing institutions—especially parliaments—into instruments of real political participation. Parliaments had existed for centuries but were generally controlled by the aristocrats. The bourgeoisie embraced parliaments as means by which they could exert the weight of their superior numbers and growing economic advantage against their aristocratic rivals. At the same time, the bourgeoisie sought to restrain the capacity of governments to threaten these economic and political interests by placing formal or constitutional limits on governmental power.

Although motivated primarily by the need to protect and defend their own interests, the bourgeoisie advanced many of the principles that became the central underpinnings of individual liberty for all citizens—freedom of speech, freedom of assembly, freedom of conscience, and freedom from arbitrary search and seizure. It is important to note here that the bourgeoisie generally did not favor democracy as we know it. They were advocates of electoral and representative institutions, but they favored property requirements and other restrictions so as to limit political participation to the middle and upper classes. Yet once these institutions of politics and the protection of the right to engage in politics were established, it was difficult to limit them to the bourgeoisie.

Expansion of Participation in America Changed the Political Balance

In America, the expansion of participation to ever-larger segments of society, seen mostly in the expansion of voting rights, occurred because competing segments of the bourgeoisie sought to gain political advantage by reaching out and mobilizing the support of working- and lower-class groups that craved the opportunity to take part in politics—"lining up the unwashed," as one American historian put it.[10] To be sure, excluded groups often agitated for greater participation. But seldom was such agitation, by itself, enough to secure the right to participate. Usually, expansion of voting rights resulted from a combination of pressure from below and help from above.

This pattern of suffrage expansion by groups hoping to derive some political advantage has been typical in American history. After the Civil War, one of the chief reasons that the Republican Party moved to enfranchise newly freed slaves was to use the support of the former slaves to maintain Republican control over the defeated southern states. Similarly, in the early twentieth century, upper-middle-class Progressives advocated women's suffrage because they believed that women were likely to support the reforms espoused by the Progressive movement.

The Goal of Politics Is Having a Say in What Happens

Expansion of participation means that more and more people have a legal right to take part in politics. *Politics* is an important term. In its broadest sense, it refers to conflicts over the character, membership, and policies of any organization to which people belong. As Harold Lasswell, a famous political scientist, once put it, politics is the struggle over "who gets what, when, how."[11] Although politics is a phenomenon that can be found in any organization, our concern in this book is narrower. Here, **politics** will be used to refer only to conflicts and struggles over the leadership, structure, and policies of governments. The goal of politics, as we define it, is to have a share or a say in the composition of the government's leadership, how the government is organized, or what its policies are going to be. Having a share is called **power** (influence over a government's leadership, organization, or policies) or influence.

Politics can take many forms, including blogging and posting opinion pieces online, voting, sending emails to government officials, lobbying legislators on behalf of particular programs, and participating in protest marches and even violent demonstrations. A system of government in which the populace selects representatives, who play a significant role in governmental decision making, is usually called a **representative democracy**, or **republic**. A system that permits citizens to vote directly on laws and policies is often called a **direct democracy**. At the national level, America is a representative democracy in which citizens select government officials but do not vote on legislation. Some states and cities, however, have provisions for direct legislation through ballot initiative and popular referendum. In 2016, 165 initiatives appeared on state ballots.

● The Identity of Americans Has Changed over Time

> **Show how the social composition of the American population has changed over time**

While American democracy aims to give the people a voice in government, the meaning of "we the people" has changed over time. Who are Americans? Over the course of American history, politicians, religious leaders, prominent scholars, and ordinary Americans have puzzled over and fought about the answer to this fundamental question. It is not surprising that such a simple question could provoke so much conflict: the American population has increased over eighty-fold, from 3.9 million in 1790, the year of the first official census, to 323 million in 2016. As the American population has grown, it has become more diverse in nearly every dimension imaginable.[12]

At the time of the Founding, when the United States consisted of 13 states arrayed along the Eastern Seaboard, 81 percent of Americans counted by the census traced their roots to Europe, mostly England and northern Europe; nearly one in five were of African origin, the vast majority of whom were slaves.[13] There was also an unknown number of Native Americans, not counted by the census because the government did not consider them Americans.[14]

Fast-forward to 1900. The country, now stretched out across the continent, had a sharply altered racial and ethnic composition. Waves of immigrants, mainly from Europe, had boosted the population to 76 million. The black population stood at 12 percent. Residents who traced their origins to Latin America or Asia each accounted for less than 1 percent of the entire population.[15] Although principally of European origin, the American population had become much more ethnically diverse as immigrants, first from Germany, then from Ireland, and finally from southern and eastern Europe, made their way to the United States. The foreign-born population of the United States reached its height at 14.7 percent in 1910.[16]

Immigration and Increasing Ethnic Diversity Have Long Caused Intense Debate

As the population grew more diverse, anxiety about Americans' ethnic identity mounted, and much as today, politicians and scholars argued about whether the country could absorb such large numbers of immigrants. The debate encompassed such issues as whether immigrants' political and social values were compatible with American democracy, whether they would learn English, and what diseases they might bring into the United States.

Immigrants' religious affiliations also aroused concern. The first immigrants to the United States were overwhelmingly Protestant, many of them fleeing religious persecution. The arrival of Germans and Irish in the mid-1800s meant increasing numbers of Catholics, and the large-scale immigration of the early twentieth century threatened to reduce the percentage of Protestants significantly: many eastern European immigrants pouring into the country were Jewish, while the southern Europeans were mostly Catholic. A more religiously diverse country challenged the implicit Protestantism embedded in many aspects of American public life.

After World War I, Congress responded to the fears swirling around immigration with new laws that sharply limited the number of immigrants who could enter the country each year. Congress also established a new National Origins Quota System based on the nation's population in 1890 before the wave of immigrants from eastern and southern Europe arrived.[17] The new system set up a hierarchy of admissions: northern European countries received generous quotas for new immigrants, whereas eastern and southern European countries were granted very small quotas. These restrictions ratcheted down the numbers of immigrants so that by 1970 the foreign-born population in the United States reached an all-time low of 5 percent.

Official efforts to use racial and ethnic criteria to restrict the American population were not new. The very first census, as we have seen, did not count Native Americans; in fact, Native Americans were not granted

In the 1900s, many immigrants entered the United States through New York's Ellis Island, where they were checked for disease before being admitted.

the right to vote until 1924. Most people of African descent were not officially citizens until 1868, when the Fourteenth Amendment to the Constitution conferred citizenship on the freed slaves.

In 1790 the federal government had sought to limit the nonwhite population with a law stipulating that only free whites could become naturalized citizens. Not until 1870 did Congress lift the ban on the naturalization of nonwhites. Restrictions applied to Asians as well. The Chinese Exclusion Act of 1882 outlawed the entry of Chinese laborers to the United States, and additional barriers enacted after World War I meant that virtually no Asians entered the country as immigrants until 1943, when China became our ally in World War II and these provisions were lifted. People of Hispanic origin do not fit simply into the American system of racial classification. In 1930, for example, the census counted people of Mexican origin as nonwhite, but it reversed this decision a decade later. Not until 1970 did the census officially begin counting persons of Hispanic origin, noting that they could be any race.[18] As this history suggests, American citizenship has always been tied to "whiteness" even as the meaning of "white" shifted over time.

Today the Country Still Confronts the Question "Who Are Americans?"

Race and Ethnicity By 2000, immigration had profoundly transformed the nation's racial and ethnic profile once again. The primary cause was Congress's decision in 1965 to lift the tight immigration restrictions of the 1920s, a decision that resulted, among other things, in the growth of the Latino population (see Figure 1.1). Census figures for 2014 show that the total Hispanic proportion of the population is now 17.4 percent, while the black, or African American, population is 13.2 percent of the total population. Asians make up 5.4 percent of the population. European Americans account for less than two-thirds of the population—their lowest share ever. Moreover, about 2.5 percent of the population now identifies itself as of "two or more races," a new category added to the census in 2000.[19] Although it is only a small percentage of the population, the multiracial category points toward a future in which the lines separating the traditional labels of racial identification may be blurring.

In 2014, 13.3 percent of the population was born outside the United States, a figure comparable to the rates of foreign-born at the turn of the previous century. Over half of the foreign-born population came from Latin America, with nearly 4 in 10 from Central America (including Mexico). Those born in Asia constituted the next largest group, making up over one-quarter of foreign-born residents. By 2014, just 11.2 percent of those born outside the United States came from Europe.[20] These figures represent only legally authorized immigrants, while estimates put the number of undocumented immigrants at almost 12 million, the majority of whom are from Mexico and Central America.[21]

Religion The new patterns of immigration combined with a number of other factors to alter the religious affiliations of Americans. In 1900, 80 percent of the population was Protestant; by 2014, only 46.6 percent of Americans identified

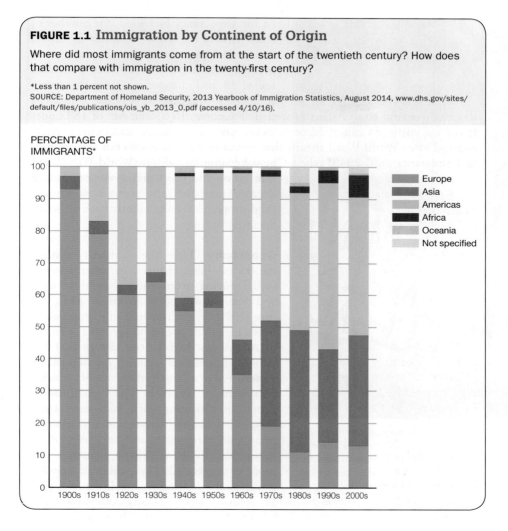

FIGURE 1.1 Immigration by Continent of Origin

Where did most immigrants come from at the start of the twentieth century? How does that compare with immigration in the twenty-first century?

*Less than 1 percent not shown.
SOURCE: Department of Homeland Security, 2013 Yearbook of Immigration Statistics, August 2014, www.dhs.gov/sites/default/files/publications/ois_yb_2013_0.pdf (accessed 4/10/16).

PERCENTAGE OF IMMIGRANTS*

Legend:
- Europe
- Asia
- Americas
- Africa
- Oceania
- Not specified

X-axis: 1900s 1910s 1920s 1930s 1940s 1950s 1960s 1970s 1980s 1990s 2000s

themselves as Protestants.[22] Catholics made up 20.8 percent of the population, and Jews accounted for 1.9 percent. A small Muslim population had also grown, to nearly 1 percent of the population. One of the most important changes in religious affiliation during the latter half of the twentieth century was the percentage of people who professed no organized religion. In 2014, 28.8 percent of the population was not affiliated with an organized church. These changes suggest an important shift in American religious identity: although the United States thinks of itself as a "Judeo-Christian" nation—and indeed was 95 percent Protestant, Catholic, or Jewish from 1900 to 1968—by 2014 the numbers had fallen to 72.5 percent of the adult population.[23]

Age As America grew and its population expanded and diversified, the country's age profile shifted with it. In 1900 only 4 percent of the population was over 65.

As life expectancy increased, the number of older Americans grew with it: by 2014, nearly 14.5 percent of the population was over 65. The number of children under the age of 18 also changed; in 1900 this group comprised 43 percent of the American population; by 2014, children 18 and under had fallen to about 25 percent of the population.[24] An aging population poses challenges to the United States. As the elderly population grows and the working-age population shrinks, questions arise about how we will fund programs for the elderly such as Social Security.

Geography Over the nation's history, Americans have changed in other ways as well, moving from mostly rural settings and small towns to large urban areas. Before 1920, less than half the population lived in urban areas; today 80.7 percent of Americans do.[25] Critics charge that the American political system, created when America was a largely rural society, underrepresents urban areas. The constitutional provision allocating each state two senators, for example, overrepresents sparsely populated rural states and underrepresents urban states, where the population is far more concentrated. The American population has also shifted regionally. In the past 50 years, especially, many Americans have left the Northeast and Midwest and moved to the South and Southwest. As congressional seats have been reapportioned to reflect the population shift, many problems that particularly plague the Midwest and Northeast, such as the decline of manufacturing jobs, receive less attention in national politics.

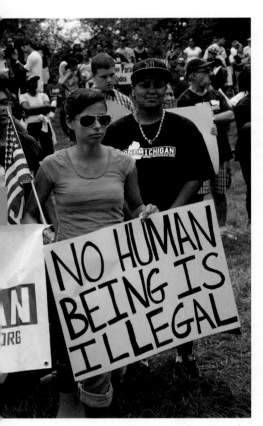

Immigration remains a controversial issue in the United States. While many believe we should do more to protect our borders, others call for comprehensive immigration reform, including an easier pathway to citizenship.

Socioeconomic Status Americans have fallen into diverse economic groups throughout American history. For much of American history most people were relatively poor working people, many of them farmers. A small wealthy elite, however, grew larger in the 1890s, in a period called "the gilded age." By 1928, nearly 25 percent of the total annual income went to the top 1 percent of earners; the top 10 percent took home 46 percent of total annual income. After the New Deal in the 1930s, a large middle class took shape, and the share going to those at the top dropped sharply. By 1976, the top 1 percent took home only 9 percent of the national annual income. Since then, however, economic inequality has once again

Global Diversity

In this chapter, we learned that the United States has become an increasingly diverse country over time. One way that the American population is diverse is in its racial and ethnic make-up. How does the racial and ethnic diversity of the United States compare to that of other countries around the world?

Racial and ethnic diversity is related not only to immigration rates but also to geography, historical legacies, and whether the government has favored certain groups over others. Many western European and Asian countries have histories of past conflict and strong state-building efforts, resulting in less diversity. For example, Japan's geographic isolation has created a racially homogeneous society, which was reinforced by the government's use of isolationism as a means to consolidate power.[a] Modern policies limiting immigration continue these historic trends. To take another example, France has historically pursued both political and cultural assimilation, using its schools as tools to socialize its citizens into a common "republican" identity. More recent waves of immigrants, however, have highlighted potential problems with this policy.[b]

As a "nation of immigrants," the United States is more diverse than many Western countries, but some former colonies are even more diverse than the United States. Many countries in sub-Saharan Africa were colonized by multiple empires, whose governments often drew borders that encompassed multiple ethnic groups in the region. State-building and nationalism are also very new to these regions, meaning that local identities remain stronger than national ones.

How might the degree of diversity shape political values in specific countries? What types of values and policies would we expect to see in countries with a high degree of diversity versus those with less diversity?

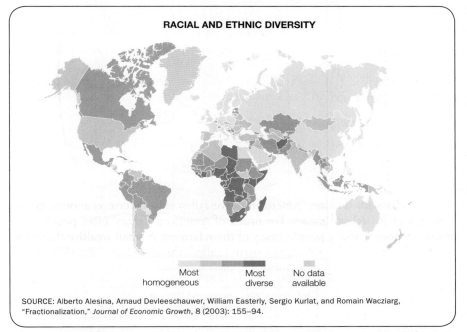

RACIAL AND ETHNIC DIVERSITY

Most homogeneous — Most diverse — No data available

SOURCE: Alberto Alesina, Arnaud Devleeschauwer, William Easterly, Sergio Kurlat, and Romain Wacziarg, "Fractionalization," *Journal of Economic Growth*, 8 (2003): 155–94.

[a]Benedict Anderson, *Imagined Communities: Reflections on the Origin and Spread of Nationalism* (London: Verso, 2006), 94–99.
[b]John R. Bowen, *Why the French Don't Like Headscarves: Islam, the State, and Public Space* (Princeton, NJ: Princeton University Press, 2007).

widened as a tiny group of super-rich has emerged. By 2014, the top 1 percent earned 21.2 percent of annual income, and the top 10 percent took home almost 50 percent of the total national income, the highest ever recorded, except for 2012.[26] At the same time, the incomes of the broad middle class have largely stagnated (see Figure 1.2).[27] And 14.8 percent of the population remains below the official poverty line. As the middle class has frayed around the edges, the numbers of poor and near poor have swelled to nearly one-third of the population.[28]

FIGURE 1.2 Income in the United States

The graph shows that while the income of most Americans has risen only slightly since 1950, the income of the richest Americans (the top 5 percent) has increased dramatically. What are some of the ways that this shift might matter for American politics? Does the growing economic gap between the richest groups and most other Americans conflict with the political value of equality?

*Dollar values are given in constant 2014 dollars, which are adjusted for inflation so that we can compare a person's income in 1950 with a person's income today.
SOURCE: U.S. Census Bureau, Current Population Survey, www.census.gov/hhes/www/income/data/historical/inequality/index.html (accessed 1/18/16).

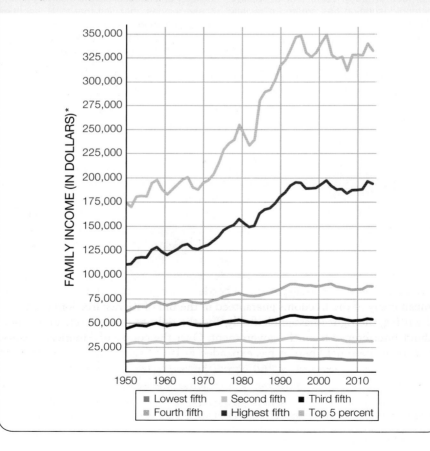

Population and Representation The shifting contours of the American people have regularly raised challenging questions about our politics and governing arrangements. Population growth has spurred politically charged debates about how the population should be apportioned among congressional districts and has also transformed the close democratic relationship between congressional representatives and their constituents envisioned by the framers. For example, the framers stipulated that the number of representatives in the House "shall not exceed one for every thirty Thousand" constituents; today the average member of Congress represents 721,641 constituents.[29] Immigration and the cultural and religious changes it entails provoked heated debates 100 years ago and still do today. The different languages and customs that immigrants bring to the United States trigger fears among some that the country is changing in ways that may undermine American values and alter fundamental identities. Yet a changing population has been one of the constants of American history.

America Is Built on the Ideas of Liberty, Equality, and Democracy

Analyze whether the U.S. system of government upholds American political values

A few fundamental values underlie the American system. These values are reflected in such Founding documents as the Declaration of Independence, the Constitution, and the Bill of Rights. The three values on which the American system of government is based are liberty, equality, and democracy.

Liberty Means Freedom

No ideal is more central to American values than liberty. The Declaration of Independence defined three inalienable rights: "Life, Liberty and the pursuit of Happiness." The preamble to the Constitution likewise identified the need to secure "the Blessings of Liberty" as one of the key reasons for which the Constitution was drawn up. For Americans, **liberty** means freedom from government control as well as economic freedom. Both are closely linked to the idea of **limited government**, meaning that powers are defined and limited by a constitution.

The Constitution's first 10 amendments, known collectively as the Bill of Rights, above all preserve individual personal liberties and rights. In fact, liberty has come to mean many of the freedoms guaranteed in the Bill of Rights: freedom of speech and writing, the right to assemble freely, and the right to practice religious beliefs without interference from the government. Over the course of American history, the scope of personal liberties has expanded as laws have become more tolerant and as individuals have successfully used the courts to challenge restrictions on their individual freedoms. Far fewer restrictions exist today on the press, political speech, and individual moral behavior than in the early years of the nation. Even so, conflicts persist over how personal liberties should be extended and when personal liberties violate community norms.

In addition to personal freedom, the American concept of liberty means economic freedom. Since the Founding, economic freedom has been linked to capitalism, free markets, and the protection of private property. Free competition, the unfettered movement of goods, and the right to enjoy the fruits of one's labor are all essential aspects of economic freedom and American capitalism.[30] In the first century of the Republic, support for capitalism often meant support for the doctrine of laissez-faire (literally, "let do" in French), an economic system in which the means of production and distribution are privately owned and operated for profit with minimal or no government interference. **Laissez-faire capitalism** allowed very little room for the national government to regulate trade or restrict the use of private property, even in the public interest. Americans still strongly support capitalism and economic liberty, but they now also endorse some restrictions on economic freedoms to protect the public. Federal and state governments now deploy a wide array of regulations in the name of public protection. These include health and safety laws, environmental rules, and workplace regulations. Not surprisingly, fierce disagreements often erupt over what the proper scope of government regulation should be. What some people regard as protecting the public, others see as an infringement of their own freedom to run their businesses and use their property as they see fit.

Equality Means Treating People Fairly

The Declaration of Independence declares as its first "self-evident" truth that "all men are created equal." As central as it is to the American political creed, however, equality has been a less well-defined ideal than liberty because people interpret "equality" in different ways. Most Americans share the ideal of **equality of opportunity** wherein all people should have the freedom to use whatever talents and wealth they have to reach their fullest potential. Yet it is hard for Americans to reach an agreement on what constitutes equality of opportunity. Must a group's *past* inequalities be remedied in order to ensure equal opportunity in the *present*? Should inequalities in the legal, political, and economic spheres be given the same weight? In contrast to liberty, which requires limits on the role of government, equality implies an *obligation* of the government to the people.[31]

Americans do make clear distinctions between political equality and social or economic equality. **Political equality** refers to the right to participate in politics equally, based on the principle of "one person, one vote." Beginning from a very restricted definition of political community, which originally included only propertied white men, the United States has moved much closer to an ideal of political equality. Broad support for this ideal has helped expand the American political community and extend the right to participate to all. Although considerable conflict remains over whether the political system makes it harder for some people to participate and easier for others and about whether the role of money in politics has drowned out the public voice, Americans agree that all citizens should have an equal opportunity to participate and that government should enforce that right.

In part because Americans believe that individuals are free to work as hard as they choose, they have always been less concerned about social or economic inequality. Many Americans regard economic differences as the consequence of individual choices, virtues, or failures. Because of this, Americans tend to be less supportive than most Europeans of government action to ensure economic equality.

Democracy Means That What the People Want Matters

The essence of democracy is the participation of the people in choosing their rulers and the people's ability to influence what those rulers do. In a democracy, political power ultimately comes from the people. The principle of democracy in which political authority rests ultimately in the hands of the people is known as **popular sovereignty**. In the United States, popular sovereignty and political equality make politicians accountable to the people. Ideally, democracy envisions an engaged citizenry prepared to exercise its power over rulers. As we noted earlier, the United States is a representative democracy, meaning that the people do not rule directly but instead exercise power through elected representatives. Forms of participation in a democracy vary greatly, but voting is a key element of the representative democracy that the American Founders established.

American democracy rests on the principle of **majority rule** with **minority rights**, the democratic principle that a government follows the preferences of the majority of voters but protects the interests of the minority. Majority rule means that the wishes of the majority determine what government does. The House of Representatives—a large body elected directly by the people—was designed in particular to ensure majority rule. But the Founders feared that popular majorities could turn government into a "tyranny of the majority" in which individual liberties would be violated. Concern for individual rights has thus been a part of American democracy from the beginning. The rights enumerated in the Bill of Rights and enforced through the courts provide an important check on the power of the majority.

American Political Values
and Your Future

Americans express mixed views about government. Almost everyone complains about government, and general trust in government has declined significantly. Despite mounting distrust, when asked about particular government activities or programs, a majority of Americans generally support the activities that government undertakes. These conflicting views reflect the tensions in American political culture: there is no perfect balance between liberty, equality, and democracy. In recent years, finding the right mix of government actions to achieve these different goals has become especially troublesome. Some charge that government initiatives designed to promote equality infringe on individual liberty, while others point to the need for government to take action in the face of growing inequality. Sharp political debate over competing goals alienates many citizens, who react by withdrawing from politics. Yet, in contrast to totalitarian and authoritarian forms of government, democracy rests on the principle of popular sovereignty. No true democracy can function properly without knowledgeable and engaged citizens.

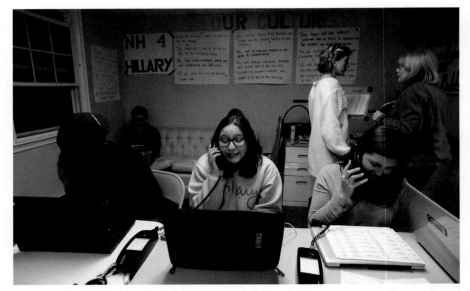

While levels of participation in politics are relatively low for young Americans, the presidential primary campaigns of 2008 and 2016 saw the highest levels of youth turnout—to volunteer and to vote—in decades. What factors might have energized young people to become involved in these particular campaigns?

The "**Who Participates?**" feature on the following page shows various ways Americans were engaged with and participated in the 2012 presidential election.

The remarkable diversity of the American people represents a great strength for American democracy as well as a formidable challenge. The shifting religious, racial and ethnic, and immigration status of Americans throughout history has always provoked fears about whether American values could withstand such dramatic shifts. The changing face of America also sparks hopes for an America that embodies its fundamental values more fully.

Demographic changes will continue to raise tough new questions. For example, as the American population grows older, programs for the elderly will take up an increasing share of the federal budget. Yet to be successful, a nation must invest in its young people. And, as any college student knows, the cost of college has risen in recent years. Many students drop out as they discover that the cost of college is too high. Or they graduate and find themselves saddled with loans that will take decades to pay back. Yet, in a world of ever-sharper economic competition, higher education has become increasingly important for individuals seeking economic security. Moreover, an educated population is critical to the future prosperity of the country as a whole. Are there ways to support the elderly and the young at the same time? Is it fair to cut back assistance to the elderly, who have worked a lifetime for their benefits? If we decrease assistance to the elderly, will they stay in the labor market and make the job hunt for young people even more difficult? As these trade-offs suggest, there are no easy answers to these demographic changes.

Who Participated in the 2012 Presidential Election?

Percentage of Each Age Group Who...

	17–24	25–44	45–65	65+
Voted	58.3%	74.6%	83.3%	89.9%
Displayed a campaign button, lawn sign, or bumper sticker	12.5%	13.5%	16.6%	20.5%
Gave money to a candidate, party, or other group	9.9%	13.1%	23.6%	35.0%
Talked about voting for or against a candidate or party	32.0%	34.6%	44.4%	50.4%
Went to political meetings, rallies, or speeches	6.8%	4.3%	6.4%	8.8%

SOURCE: American National Election Study 2012 Time Series,
The American National Election Studies,
www.electionstudies.org (accessed 9/25/15).

WHAT YOU CAN DO ➡

WHAT YOU CAN DO

Register to Vote

 In most states you can register to vote using the National Mail Voter Registration Form found at **www.eac.gov**. The Election Assistance Commission website also includes various tips about registering and voting.

 Find out when you need to register in order to vote in the next election. Visit **www.usa.gov/register-to-vote** for a list of registration deadlines.

 Many states allow online registration. Go to **www.ncsl.org** and search "online voter registration" to find a list of these states with links to their websites.

 If you've moved to attend college or for another reason, you can register with your new address.

chapterstudyguide

Practice Quiz

1. Americans' trust in their government *(p. 7)*
a) has risen steadily since the 1960s.
b) has declined significantly since the 1960s.
c) has remained the same over the last 50 years.
d) has never been studied.
e) is unimportant because Americans do not rely on government for many services.

2. *Political efficacy* is the belief that *(pp. 7–8)*
a) government operates efficiently.
b) government has grown too large.
c) government cannot be trusted.
d) ordinary citizens can influence what government does.
e) government is wasteful and corrupt.

3. What is digital citizenship? *(p. 9)*
a) a new government initiative to expand online voter registration
b) the ability to vote online
c) an online certification program that allows immigrants to become American citizens
d) the ability to participate in society online
e) a new government initiative to provide daily legislative updates online

4. What is the difference between a totalitarian government and an authoritarian government? *(p. 10)*
   a) Authoritarian governments require popular participation while totalitarian governments do not.
   b) Totalitarian governments are generally based on religion, while authoritarian governments are not.
   c) Authoritarian governments are often restrained by the power of social institutions, while totalitarian governments are not.
   d) Totalitarian governments acknowledge strict limits on their power, while authoritarian governments do not.
   e) There is no difference between these two kinds of government.

5. In a constitutional government *(p. 10)*
   a) the government recognizes no formal limits on its power.
   b) presidential elections are held every four years.
   c) governmental power is held by a single individual.
   d) formal and effective limits are placed on the powers of government.
   e) the government follows the wishes of the majority.

6. Although not present at the national level, a number of states and cities permit citizens to vote directly on laws and policies. What is this form of rule called? *(p. 12)*
   a) representative democracy
   b) direct democracy
   c) pluralism
   d) laissez-faire capitalism
   e) a republic

7. The percentage of foreign-born individuals living in the United States *(p. 13)*
   a) has increased significantly since reaching its low point in 1970.
   b) has decreased significantly since reaching its high point in 1970.
   c) has remained the same since 1970.
   d) has never been less than the percentage of native-born individuals living in the United States.
   e) has not been studied since 1970.

8. Which of the following statements best describes the history of income inequality in the United States? *(pp. 16–18)*
   a) The top 1 percent has never earned more than 10 percent of the nation's annual income.
   b) The top 1 percent has never earned less than 10 percent of the nation's annual income.
   c) Income inequality has remained fairly constant since the late 1970s.
   d) Income inequality has increased considerably since the late 1970s.
   e) Income inequality has decreased considerably since the late 1970s.

9. Latinos now make up *(p. 14)*
   a) more than 65 percent of the American public.
   b) more than 50 percent of the American public.
   c) more than 33 percent of the American public.
   d) more than 25 percent of the American public.
   e) more than 15 percent of the American public.

10. Which of the following statements best describes the changes in America's age profile since 1900? *(pp. 15–16)*
    a) The percentage of adults over the age of 65 has declined dramatically.
    b) The percentage of adults over the age of 65 has increased dramatically.
    c) The percentage of adults over the age of 65 has remained constant.
    d) The percentage of children under the age of 18 has increased dramatically.
    e) The percentage of children under the age of 18 has remained constant.

11. What percent of Americans live in urban areas today? *(p. 16)*
    a) less than 10 percent
    b) about 20 percent
    c) about 40 percent
    d) about 60 percent
    e) about 80 percent

12. Which of the following is *not* related to the American conception of liberty? *(pp. 18–19)*
   a) freedom of speech
   b) economic liberty
   c) freedom of religion
   d) freedom of assembly
   e) All of the above are related to the American conception of liberty.

13. Which of the following is *not* part of the core values that underlie the American political system? *(pp. 19–20)*
   a) belief in economic equality
   b) belief in political equality

   c) belief in personal freedom
   d) belief in economic freedom
   e) belief in democracy

14. The principle of political equality can be best summed up as *(pp. 19–20)*
   a) "equality of results."
   b) "equality of opportunity."
   c) "one person, one vote."
   d) "equality between the sexes."
   e) "leave everyone alone."

Key Terms

authoritarian government *(p. 10)* a system of rule in which the government recognizes no formal limit but may nevertheless be restrained by the power of other social institutions

citizenship *(p. 8)* informed and active membership in a political community

constitutional government *(p. 10)* a system of rule in which formal and effective limits are placed on the powers of the government

democracy *(p. 10)* a system of rule that permits citizens to play a significant part in the governmental process, usually through the election of key public officials

direct democracy *(p. 12)* a system of rule that permits citizens to vote directly on laws and policies

equality of opportunity *(p. 20)* a widely shared American ideal that all people should have the freedom to use whatever talents and wealth they have to reach their fullest potential

government *(p. 4)* institutions and procedures through which a territory and its people are ruled

laissez-faire capitalism *(p. 20)* an economic system in which the means of production and distribution are privately owned and operated for profit with minimal or no government interference

liberty *(p. 19)* freedom from government control

limited government *(p. 19)* a principle of constitutional government; a government whose powers are defined and limited by a constitution

majority rule/minority rights *(p. 21)* the democratic principle that a government follows the preferences of the majority of voters but protects the interests of the minority

political efficacy *(p. 7)* the ability to influence government and politics

political equality *(p. 20)* the right to participate in politics equally, based on the principle of "one person, one vote"

politics *(p. 12)* conflict over the leadership, structure, and policies of governments

popular sovereignty *(p. 21)* a principle of democracy in which political authority rests ultimately in the hands of the people

power *(p. 12)* influence over a government's leadership, organization, or policies

representative democracy (republic) *(p. 12)* a system of government in which the populace selects representatives, who play a significant role in governmental decision making

totalitarian government *(p. 10)* a system of rule in which the government recognizes no formal limits on its power and seeks to absorb or eliminate other social institutions that might challenge it

For Further Reading

Dahl, Robert. *How Democratic Is the American Constitution?* New Haven, CT: Yale University Press, 2002.

Dalton, Russell. *The Good Citizen: How a Younger Generation Is Reshaping American Politics.* 2nd ed. Washington, DC: CQ Press, 2015.

Delli Carpini, Michael X., and Scott Keeter. *What Americans Know about Politics and Why It Matters.* New Haven, CT: Yale University Press, 1996.

Hochschild, Jennifer L. *Facing Up to the American Dream: Race, Class, and the Soul of the Nation.* Princeton, NJ: Princeton University Press, 1995.

Lasswell, Harold. *Politics: Who Gets What, When, How.* New York: Meridian Books, 1958.

McCarty, Nolan, Keith T. Poole, and Howard Rosenthal. *Polarized America: The Dance of Ideology and Unequal Riches.* Cambridge, MA: MIT Press, 2008.

Mettler, Suzanne. *The Submerged State: How Invisible Government Policies Undermine American Democracy.* Chicago: University of Chicago Press, 2011.

Nye, Joseph S., Jr., Philip D. Zelikow, and David C. King, eds. *Why People Don't Trust Government.* Cambridge, MA: Harvard University Press, 1997.

Page, Benjamin I., and Lawrence R. Jacobs. *Class War? What Americans Really Think about Economic Inequality.* Chicago: University of Chicago Press, 2009.

Tocqueville, Alexis de. *Democracy in America.* Translated by Phillips Bradley. New York: Knopf, Vintage Books, 1945. First published 1835.

When the framers of the Constitution met in 1787, they set out to establish a political system that would protect liberty and place limits on government. They also believed a powerful government required a broad popular base. However, they debated how best to protect liberty and how to balance democracy with other concerns.

2

The Founding and the Constitution

WHAT GOVERNMENT DOES AND WHY IT MATTERS The framers of the U.S. Constitution knew why government mattered. In the Constitution's preamble, the framers tell us that the purposes of government are to promote justice, to maintain peace at home, to defend the nation from foreign foes, to provide for the welfare of the citizenry, and, above all, to secure the "Blessings of Liberty" for Americans. The remainder of the Constitution spells out a plan for achieving these great objectives. This plan includes provisions for the exercise of legislative, executive, and judicial powers and a recipe for the division of powers among the federal government's branches and between the national and state governments.

Americans often become impatient with the Constitution as the constitutional separation of powers seems to be a recipe for inaction and "gridlock" when America's major institutions of government are controlled by opposing political forces. This has led to bitter fights that sometimes prevent government from delivering important services. In October 2013, for instance, the federal government partially shut down for 16 days when the House and Senate could not reach agreement on a budget. As a result, permit offices across the country no longer took in fees, contractors stopped receiving checks, research projects stalled, and 800,000 federal employees were sent home on unpaid leave—at a cost to the economy of 2–6 billion.[1]

The framers, however, believed that a good constitution not only created a government with the capacity to act forcefully but also promoted compromise and deliberation, sometimes delaying action until tempers cooled and a variety of viewpoints could be heard. The cost of compromise and deliberation encouraged by such constitutional arrangements as the separation of powers might sometimes be gridlock, but the benefit may be a government compelled to take many interests and viewpoints into account when it formulates policies.

America's long-standing values of liberty, equality, and democracy were all major themes of the Founding period and are all elements of the U.S. Constitution. However, the Constitution was a product of political bargaining and compromise, formed in very much the same way political decisions are made today. As this chapter will show, the Constitution reflects high principle as well as political self-interest. It also defines the relationship between American citizens and their government.

chaptergoals

- **Describe the events that led to the Declaration of Independence and the Articles of Confederation (pp. 31–36)**

- **Analyze the reasons many Americans thought a new Constitution was needed, and assess the obstacles to a new Constitution (pp. 36–41)**

- **Explain how the Constitution attempted to improve America's governance, and outline the major institutions established by the Constitution (pp. 41–49)**

- **Present the controversies involved in the struggle for ratification (pp. 49–52)**

- **Trace how the Constitution has changed over time through the amendment process (pp. 54–57)**

The First Founding: Ideals, Interests, and Conflicts

Describe the events that led to the Declaration of Independence and the Articles of Confederation

The government created by the country's Founders was the product of British legal and political traditions, colonial experience, and new ideas about governance that gained currency in the century before America broke with Britain. While America's leaders were first and foremost practical politicians, they also read political philosophy and were influenced by the important thinkers of their day, including Hobbes, Locke, and Montesquieu.

The seventeenth-century British philosopher Thomas Hobbes (1588–1679) was no advocate of democratic government, but he wrote persuasively in *Leviathan* about the necessity of a government authority as an antidote to human existence in a government-less state of nature, where life was "solitary, poor, nasty, brutish, and short." He also believed that governments should have limits on the powers they exercised and that political systems are based on the idea of "contract theory"— that the people of a country voluntarily give up some freedom in exchange for an ordered society. The monarchs who rule that society derive their legitimacy from this contract, not from a God-given right to rule.

Another British political thinker, John Locke (1632–1704), advanced the principles of republican government by arguing not only that monarchical power was not absolute but that such power was dangerous and should therefore be limited. In a break with Hobbes, Locke argued that the people retain rights despite the social contract they made with the monarch. Preserving safety in society is not enough; people's lives, liberty, and property also require protection. Further, Locke wrote in his *Second Treatise of Civil Government* that the people of a country have a right to overthrow a government they believe to be unjust or tyrannical. This key idea shaped the thinking of the Founders, including Thomas Jefferson, the primary author of the Declaration of Independence, who said that the document was "pure Locke." Locke advanced the important ideas of limited government and consent of the governed.

Baron de la Brède et de Montesquieu (1689–1755) was a French political thinker who advocated the idea that power needed to be balanced by power as a bulwark against tyranny. The way in which this could be achieved was through the separation of governing powers. This idea was already in practice in Britain, where legislative and executive powers were divided between Parliament and the monarch. In *The Spirit of the Laws*, Montesquieu argued for the separation and elevation of judicial power, which in Britain was still held by the monarch. Montesquieu did not argue for a pure separation of powers; rather, basic functions would be separated, but there would also be some overlap of functions. These ideas were central in shaping the three-branch system of government that America's Founders outlined in the Constitution of 1787.

Narrow Interests and Political Conflicts Shaped the First Founding

The American Revolution and the U.S. Constitution were outgrowths of a struggle among competing economic and political forces within the colonies. Five sectors of society had interests that were important in colonial politics: (1) the New England merchants; (2) the southern planters; (3) the "royalists"—holders of royal lands, offices, and patents (licenses to engage in a profession or business activity); (4) shopkeepers, artisans, and laborers; and (5) small farmers. Throughout the eighteenth century, these groups were in conflict over issues of taxation, trade, and commerce. For the most part, however, the southern planters, the New England merchants, and the royal office and patent holders—groups that together made up the colonial elite—were able to maintain a political alliance that held in check the more radical forces representing shopkeepers, laborers, and small farmers. After 1760, however, by seriously threatening the interests of New England merchants and southern planters, British tax and trade policies split the colonial elite, permitting radical forces to expand their political influence, and set in motion a chain of events that culminated in the American Revolution.[2]

British Taxes Hurt Colonial Economic Interests

During the first half of the eighteenth century, Britain ruled its American colonies with a light hand. Evidence of British rule was hardly to be found outside the largest towns, and the enterprising colonists had founds ways of evading most of the taxes nominally levied by the distant British government. Beginning in the 1760s, however, the debts and other financial problems faced by the British government forced it to search for new revenue sources. This search rather quickly led to the Crown's North American colonies, which, on the whole, paid remarkably little in taxes to their parent country. Much of Britain's debt arose from the expenses it had incurred in defense of the colonies during the recent French and Indian War (1756–63), as well as from the continuing protection that British forces were giving the colonists from Indian attacks and that the British navy was providing for colonial shipping. Thus, during the 1760s, Great Britain sought to impose new, though relatively modest, taxes on the colonists.

Like most governments of the period, the British regime had limited ways in which to collect revenues. In the mid-eighteenth century, governments relied mainly on tariffs, duties, and other taxes on commerce; and it was to such taxes, including the Stamp Act, that the British turned during the 1760s.

The Stamp Act and other taxes on commerce, such as the Sugar Act of 1764, which taxed sugar, molasses, and other commodities, most heavily affected the two groups in colonial society whose commercial interests and activities were most extensive—the New England merchants and the southern planters. United under the famous slogan "No taxation without representation," the merchants and planters sought to organize opposition to these new taxes. In the course of the struggle against British tax measures, the planters and merchants broke with their royalist allies and turned to their former adversaries—the shopkeepers, laborers, artisans, and small farmers—for help. With the assistance of these groups, the merchants and planters organized demonstrations and a boycott of British goods that ultimately forced the Crown to rescind most of its hated new taxes.

From the perspective of the merchants and planters, this was a victorious conclusion to their struggle with the parent country. They were anxious to end the unrest they had helped to arouse, and they supported the British government's efforts to restore order. Indeed, most respectable Bostonians supported the actions of the British soldiers involved in the Boston Massacre (1770), when those soldiers killed five colonists while attempting to repel an angry mob moving against a government building. In their subsequent trial, the soldiers were defended by John Adams, a pillar of Boston society and a future president of the United States. Adams asserted that the soldiers' actions were entirely justified, provoked as they were by "a motley rabble of saucy boys, negroes and mulattoes, Irish teagues and outlandish Jack tars." All but two of the soldiers were acquitted.[3]

Yet political strife persisted. The more radical forces representing shopkeepers, artisans, laborers, and small farmers, who had been mobilized and energized by the struggle over taxes, continued to agitate for political and social change. These radicals, whose leaders included Samuel Adams, a cousin of John Adams, asserted that British power supported an unjust political and social structure within the colonies and began to advocate an end to British rule.[4]

Political Strife Radicalized the Colonists

The political strife within the colonies was the background for the events of 1773–74. In 1773 the British government granted the politically powerful but ailing East India Company a monopoly on the export of tea from Britain, eliminating a lucrative form of trade for colonial merchants. To add insult to injury, the East India Company sought to sell the tea directly in the colonies instead of working through the colonial merchants. Tea was an extremely important commodity in

The British helped radicalize colonists through bad policy decisions in the years before the Revolution. For example, Britain gave the East India Company a monopoly on the tea trade in the American colonies, which colonists feared would hurt colonial merchants' business.

the 1770s, and these British actions posed a serious threat to the New England merchants. Together with their southern allies, the merchants once again called upon the radicals for support. The most dramatic result was the Boston Tea Party of 1773, when anti-British radicals, led by Samuel Adams (some of them "disguised" as Mohawk Indians), boarded three vessels anchored in Boston Harbor and threw the entire cargo of 342 chests of tea into the harbor.

This event was of decisive importance in American history. The merchants had hoped to force the British government to rescind the Tea Act, but they did not support any demands beyond this one. They certainly did not seek independence from Britain. Samuel Adams and the other radicals, however, hoped to provoke the British government to take actions that would alienate its colonial supporters and pave the way for a rebellion. This was precisely the purpose of the Boston Tea Party, and it succeeded. By dumping the East India Company's tea into Boston Harbor, Adams and his followers goaded the British into enacting a number of harsh reprisals that closed the port of Boston to commerce, changed the provincial government of Massachusetts, provided for the removal of accused persons to Britain for trial, and, most important, restricted movement to the West—further alienating the southern planters, who depended upon access to new western lands. These acts of retaliation confirmed the worst criticisms of British rule and helped radicalize Americans. Radicals such as Samuel Adams had been agitating for more violent measures against the British. But ultimately it was Britain's political repression that fanned support for independence.

Thus, the Boston Tea Party set in motion a cycle of provocation and retaliation that in 1774 resulted in the convening of the First Continental Congress—an assembly of delegates from all parts of the colonies that called for a total boycott of British goods and, under the prodding of the radicals, began to consider the possibility of independence from British rule. The eventual result was the Declaration of Independence.

The Declaration of Independence Explained Why the Colonists Wanted to Break with Great Britain

In 1776, more than a year after open warfare had commenced in Massachusetts, the Second Continental Congress appointed a committee consisting of Thomas Jefferson of Virginia, Benjamin Franklin of Pennsylvania, Roger Sherman of Connecticut, John Adams of Massachusetts, and Robert Livingston of New York to draft a statement of American independence from British rule. The Declaration of Independence, written by Jefferson and adopted by the Second Continental Congress, was an extraordinary philosophical and political document. Philosophically, the Declaration was remarkable for its assertion that certain rights, called "unalienable rights"—including life, liberty, and the pursuit of happiness—could not be abridged by governments. In the world of 1776, a world in which some kings still claimed to rule by divine right, this was a dramatic statement. As discussed earlier in this chapter, colonial political thought was heavily influenced by the works of the philosopher John Locke, who asserted that all individuals were equal and possessed a natural right to defend their lives, liberties, and possessions. Individuals created governments to help them protect these rights but, if a government failed in its duties, the citizenry had the right to alter or abolish it. It is easy to see why the colonists found inspiration in Locke's writings as they contemplated altering their relationship to the British Crown.

Politically, the Declaration was remarkable because it focused on grievances, aspirations, and principles that might unify the various colonial groups that were otherwise divided economically, philosophically, and by region. The Declaration was an attempt to identify and articulate a history and set of principles that might help to forge national unity.[5] It also explained to the rest of the world why American colonists were attempting to break away from Great Britain.

The purpose of the Declaration of Independence was to explain to the world why the colonists had rebelled against the British and sought self-government. Every year, Americans celebrate the signing of the Declaration on the Fourth of July.

The Articles of Confederation Created America's First National Government

Having declared their independence, the colonies needed to establish a governmental structure. In November 1777 the Continental Congress adopted the **Articles of Confederation**, the United States' first written constitution. Although it was not ratified by all the states until 1781, it was the country's operative constitution for almost 12 years, until March 1789.

The Articles of Confederation were concerned primarily with limiting the powers of the central government. The central government, first of all, was based entirely in a Congress. Since it was not intended to be a powerful government, it was given no executive branch. Execution of its laws was to be left to the individual states. Second, the Congress had little power. Its members were not much more than delegates or messengers from the state legislatures. They were chosen by the state legislatures, their salaries were paid out of the state treasuries, and they were subject to immediate recall by state authorities. In addition, each state, regardless of its size, had only a single vote.

The Congress was given the power to declare war and make peace, to make treaties and alliances, to coin or borrow money, and to regulate trade with the Native Americans. It could also appoint the senior officers of the U.S. Army. But it could not levy taxes or regulate commerce among the states. Moreover, the army officers it appointed had no army to serve in because the nation's armed forces were composed of the state militias. And in order to amend the Articles, all 13 states had to agree—a virtual impossibility. Probably the most unfortunate part of the Articles of Confederation was that the central government could not prevent one state from discriminating against other states in the quest for foreign commerce.

The relationship between the Congress and the states under the Articles of Confederation was much like the contemporary relationship between the United Nations and its member states, a relationship in which the states retained virtually all governmental powers. It was properly called a **confederation** (a system of government in which states retain sovereign authority except for the powers expressly delegated to the national government) because, as provided under Article II, "each state retains its sovereignty, freedom and independence, and every Power, Jurisdiction and right, which is not by this confederation expressly delegated to the United States, in Congress assembled." Not only was there no executive, there also was no judicial authority and no other means of enforcing the Congress's will. If there was to be any enforcement at all, the states would do it for the Congress.[6]

● The Failure of the Articles of Confederation Made the "Second Founding" Necessary

Analyze the reasons many Americans thought a new Constitution was needed, and assess the obstacles to a new Constitution

The Declaration of Independence and the Articles of Confederation were not sufficient to hold the new nation together as an independent and effective nation-state. From almost the moment of armistice with the British in 1783, moves were afoot to reform and strengthen the Articles of Confederation.

Competition among the states for foreign commerce posed a special problem to the new country because it allowed the European powers to play the states against one another, which not only made America seem weak and vulnerable abroad but also created confusion on both sides of the Atlantic. At one point during the winter of 1786–87, John Adams of Massachusetts, a leader in the independence struggle, was sent to negotiate a new treaty with the British, one that would cover disputes left over from the war. The British government responded that, because the United States under the Articles of Confederation was unable to enforce existing treaties, it would negotiate with each of the 13 states separately.

At the same time, well-to-do Americans—in particular the New England merchants and southern planters—were troubled by the influence that "radical" forces exercised in the Continental Congress and in the governments of several of the states. The colonists' victory in the Revolutionary War had not only ended British rule but also significantly changed the balance of political power within the new states. As a result of the Revolution, one key segment of the colonial elite—the royal land, office, and patent holders—was stripped of its economic and political privileges. In fact, many of these individuals, along with tens of thousands of other colonists who considered themselves loyal British subjects, left for Canada after the British surrender. And while the pre-Revolutionary elite was weakened, the pre-Revolutionary radicals were better organized than ever and now controlled such states as Pennsylvania and Rhode Island, where they pursued economic and political policies that struck terror into the hearts of the pre-Revolutionary political establishment. Of course, the central government under the Articles of Confederation was powerless to intervene.

The Annapolis Convention Was Key to Calling a National Convention

The continuation of international weakness and domestic economic turmoil led many Americans to consider whether their newly adopted form of government might not already require revision. In the fall of 1786, many state leaders accepted an invitation from the Virginia legislature for a conference of representatives of all the states, to be held in Annapolis, Maryland. Delegates from only five states actually attended, so nothing substantive could be accomplished. Still, this conference was the first step toward what is now known as the second founding. The one positive thing that came out of the Annapolis convention was a carefully worded resolution calling on the Congress to send commissioners to Philadelphia at a later time "to devise such further provisions as shall appear to them necessary to render the Constitution of the Federal Government adequate to the exigencies of the Union."[7] But the resolution did not necessarily imply any desire to do more than improve and reform the Articles of Confederation.

The government under the Articles did enact some important measures, including the Land Ordinance of 1785 and the Northwest Ordinance of 1787. The Land Ordinance established the principles of land surveying and landownership that governed America's westward expansion, and under the Northwest Ordinance the states agreed to surrender their western land claims, which opened the way for the admission of new states to the Union. Still, the young nation's political and economic position deteriorated during the 1780s, and something had to be done.

Shays's Rebellion Showed How Weak the Government Was

It is quite possible that the Constitutional Convention of 1787 in Philadelphia would never have taken place at all except for a single event that occurred during the winter following the Annapolis convention: Shays's Rebellion.

Daniel Shays, a former army captain, led a mob of farmers in a rebellion against the government of Massachusetts, which had levied heavy taxes against them. The purpose

In the winter of 1787, Daniel Shays led a makeshift army against the federal arsenal at Springfield to protest heavy taxes levied by the Massachusetts legislature. The rebellion proved the Articles of Confederation too weak to protect the fledgling nation.

of the rebellion was to prevent foreclosures on farmers' debt-ridden land by keeping the county courts of western Massachusetts from sitting until after the next election. The state militia dispersed the mob, but for several days in February 1787, Shays and his followers terrified the state government by attempting to capture the federal arsenal at Springfield, provoking an appeal to the Congress to help restore order. Within a few days, the state government regained control and captured 14 of the rebels. (All were eventually pardoned.) Later that year, a newly elected Massachusetts legislature granted some of the farmers' demands.

George Washington summed up the effects of this incident: "I am mortified beyond expression that in the moment of our acknowledged independence we should by our conduct verify the predictions of our transatlantic foe, and render ourselves ridiculous and contemptible in the eyes of all Europe."[8]

The Congress under the Confederation had been unable to act decisively in a time of crisis. This provided critics of the Articles of Confederation with precisely the evidence they needed to push the Annapolis resolution through the Congress. Thus, the states were asked to send representatives to Philadelphia to discuss constitutional revision. Delegates were eventually sent by every state except Rhode Island.

The Constitutional Convention Didn't Start Out to Write a New Constitution

The delegates who convened in Philadelphia in May 1787 had political strife, international embarrassment, national weakness, and local rebellion fixed in their minds. Recognizing that these issues were symptoms of fundamental flaws in the Articles of Confederation, the delegates soon abandoned the plan to revise the Articles and committed themselves to a second founding—a second, and ultimately successful, attempt to create a legitimate and effective national system of government. This effort would occupy the convention for the next five months.

A Marriage of Interest and Principle For years, scholars have disagreed about the motives of the Founders in Philadelphia. Among the most controversial views of the framers' motives is the "economic interpretation" put forward by historian Charles Beard and his disciples.[9] According to Beard's account, America's Founders were a collection of securities speculators and property owners whose only aim was personal enrichment. From this perspective, the Constitution's lofty principles are little more than sophisticated masks behind which the most venal interests sought to enrich themselves.

The opposing view is that the framers of the Constitution *were* concerned with philosophical and ethical principles. Indeed, the framers did try to devise a system of government consistent with the dominant philosophical and moral principles of the day. But, in fact, these two views belong together; the Founders' interests were reinforced by their principles. The convention that drafted the American Constitution was chiefly organized by the New England merchants and southern planters. Although the delegates representing these groups did not all hope to profit personally from an increase in the value of their securities, as Beard would have it, they did hope to benefit in the broadest political and economic sense by breaking the power of their radical foes and establishing a system of government more compatible with their long-term economic and political interests. Thus, the framers sought to create a new government capable of promoting commerce and protecting property from radical state legislatures and populist forces hostile to the interests of the commercial and propertied classes.

The Great Compromise The proponents of a new government fired their opening shot on May 29, 1787, when Edmund Randolph of Virginia offered a resolution that proposed corrections and enlargements in the Articles of Confederation. The proposal, reflecting the strong influence of James Madison, was no simple motion; rather, it provided for an entirely new government.

The portion of Randolph's motion that became most controversial was called the **Virginia Plan**. This plan provided for a system of representation in the national legislature based upon the population of each state or the proportion of each state's revenue contribution to the national government or both. (Randolph also proposed a second chamber of the legislature, to be elected by the members of the first chamber.) Since the states varied enormously in size and wealth, the Virginia Plan was heavily biased in favor of the large states.

While the convention was debating the Virginia Plan, opposition to it began to mount as more delegates arrived in Philadelphia. William Paterson of New Jersey introduced a new resolution known as the **New Jersey Plan**, which called for equal state representation in the national legislature regardless of population. Its main proponents were delegates from the less populous states, including Delaware, New Jersey, Connecticut, and New York, who asserted that the more populous states, such as Virginia, Pennsylvania, North Carolina, Massachusetts, and Georgia, would dominate the new government if representation were determined by population. The smaller states argued that each state should be equally represented in the new regime regardless of the state's population.

The issue of representation was one that threatened to wreck the entire constitutional enterprise. Delegates conferred, factions maneuvered, and tempers flared. James Wilson of Pennsylvania told the small-state delegates that if they wanted to disrupt the union, they should go ahead. The separation, he said, could "never happen on better grounds." Small-state delegates were equally blunt. Gunning Bedford of Delaware declared that the small states might, if forced, look elsewhere for friends. "The large states," he said, "dare not dissolve the confederation. If they do the small ones will find some foreign ally of more honor and good faith, who will take them by the hand and do them justice." These sentiments were widely shared. The union, as Luther Martin of Maryland put it, was "on the verge of dissolution, scarcely held together by the strength of a hair."[10]

The outcome of this debate was the Connecticut Compromise, also known as the **Great Compromise**. Under the terms of this compromise, in the first chamber of Congress, the House of Representatives, the representatives would be apportioned according to the population in each state. This, of course, was what delegates from the large states had sought. But in the second chamber, the Senate, each state would have equal representation regardless of its population; this provision addressed the concerns of the small states. This compromise was not immediately satisfactory to all the delegates. Indeed, two of the most vocal members of the small-state faction, John Lansing and Robert Yates of New York, were so incensed by the concession that their colleagues had made to the large-state forces that they stormed out of the convention. In the end, however, most of the delegates preferred compromise to the breakup of the Union, and the plan was accepted.

The Question of Slavery: The Three-Fifths Compromise Many of the conflicts that emerged during the Constitutional Convention were reflections of the fundamental differences between the slave and the nonslave states—differences that pitted the southern planters against New England merchants. This was one example of the conflict that would later almost destroy the Republic.

More than 90 percent of the country's slaves resided in five states—Georgia, Maryland, North Carolina, South Carolina, and Virginia—where they accounted for 30 percent of the total population. In some places, slaves outnumbered nonslaves by as many as 10 to 1. For the Constitution to embody any principle of national supremacy, some basic decisions would have to be made about the place of slavery in the general scheme. James Madison observed, "It seemed now to be pretty well understood that the real difference of interests lay, not between the large and small but between the northern and southern states. The institution of slavery and its consequences formed the line of discrimination."[11]

The issue of slavery was the most difficult one faced by the framers, and it nearly destroyed the Union. Although some delegates believed slavery to be

Despite the Founders' emphasis on liberty, the new Constitution allowed slavery, counting only three-fifths of all slaves in apportioning seats in the House of Representatives. In this 1792 painting, Liberty Displaying the Arts and Sciences, *the books, instruments, and classical columns at the left contrast with the kneeling slaves at the right—illustrating the divide between America's rhetoric of liberty and equality and the realities of slavery.*

morally wrong, an evil and oppressive institution that made a mockery of the ideals and values espoused in the Constitution, morality was not the issue that caused the framers to support or oppose the Three-Fifths Compromise. Whatever they thought of the institution of slavery, most delegates from the northern states opposed counting slaves in the distribution of congressional seats. James Wilson of Pennsylvania, for example, argued that if slaves were citizens, they should be treated and counted like other citizens. If, on the other hand, they were property, then why should not other forms of property be counted toward the apportionment of representatives? But southern delegates made it clear that if the northerners refused to give in, they would never agree to the new government. William R. Davie of North Carolina heatedly asserted that the people of North Carolina would never enter the Union if slaves were not counted as part of the basis for representation. Without such agreement, he asserted ominously, "the business was at an end." Even southerners such as Edmund Randolph of Virginia, who conceded that slavery was immoral, insisted on including slaves in the allocation of congressional seats. Eventually the North and South compromised on the issue of slavery and representation. Indeed, northerners even agreed to permit a continuation of the odious slave trade until 1808 in order to keep the South in the Union. But eventually, the disparate interests of the North and the South could no longer be reconciled, and a bloody civil war was the result.

Northerners and southerners eventually reached agreement through the **Three-Fifths Compromise**. The seats in the House of Representatives would be apportioned according to a "population" in which only three-fifths of slaves would be counted. The slaves would not be allowed to vote, of course; but the number of representatives would be apportioned accordingly.

● The Constitution Created Both Bold Powers and Sharp Limits on Power

Explain how the Constitution attempted to improve America's governance, and outline the major institutions established by the Constitution

The political significance of the Great Compromise and the Three-Fifths Compromise was to reinforce the unity of the mercantile and planter forces that sought to create a new government. The Great Compromise reassured those in both groups who feared that this new governmental framework would reduce the importance of their own local or regional influence. The Three-Fifths Compromise temporarily defused the rivalry between the merchants and planters. Their unity secured, members of the alliance supporting the establishment of a new government moved to fashion a constitutional framework consistent with their economic and political interests.

In particular, the framers sought a new government that, first, would be strong enough to promote commerce and protect property from radical state legislatures such as Rhode Island's. This became the constitutional basis for national control over commerce and finance and for the establishment of national judicial supremacy and the effort to construct a strong presidency. See Table 2.1 for a comparison of the Articles of Confederation to the Constitution. Second, the framers sought to prevent what they saw as the threat posed by the "excessive democracy" of the state and national governments under the Articles of Confederation. This led to such constitutional principles as a **bicameral** legislature (a legislative assembly composed of two chambers or houses), **checks and balances** (mechanisms through which each branch of government is able to

TABLE 2.1

Comparing the Articles of Confederation and the Constitution

MAJOR PROVISIONS	ARTICLES	CONSTITUTION
Executive branch	None	President of the United States
Judiciary	No federal court system. Judiciary exists only at state level.	Federal judiciary headed by the Supreme Court
Legislature	Unicameral legislature with equal representation for each state. Delegates to the Congress of the Confederation were appointed by the states.	Bicameral legislature consisting of Senate and House of Representatives. Each state is represented by two senators, while apportionment in the House is based on state population. Senators are chosen by the state legislatures (changed to popular election in 1913) and House members by popular election.
Fiscal and economic powers	The national government is dependent upon the states to collect taxes. The states are free to coin their own money, print paper money, and sign commercial treaties with foreign governments.	Congress given the power to levy taxes, coin money, and regulate commerce. States prohibited from coining money or entering into treaties with other nations.
Military	The national government is dependent upon state militias and cannot form an army during peacetime.	The national government is authorized to maintain an army and navy.
Legal supremacy	State constitutions and state law are supreme.	National Constitution and national law are supreme.
Constitutional amendment	Must be agreed upon by all states.	Must be agreed upon by three-fourths of the states.

participate in and influence the activities of the other branches), staggered terms in office with longer terms for senators, and indirect election (selection of the president not by voters directly but by an **electoral college**, whereby presidential electors from each state who meet after the popular election cast ballots for president and vice president; senators also were chosen indirectly, by state legislatures). Third, the framers, lacking the power to force the states or the public at large to accept the new form of government, sought to identify principles that would help to secure support. This became the basis of the constitutional provision for direct popular election of representatives and, subsequently, for the addition of the **Bill of Rights** (the first 10 amendments to the Constitution, ratified in 1791; they ensure certain rights and liberties to the people). Finally, the framers wanted to be certain that the government they created did not pose an even greater threat to its citizens' liberties and property rights than did the radical state legislatures they feared and despised. To prevent the new government from abusing its power, the framers incorporated principles such as the **separation of powers** (the division of governmental power among several institutions that must cooperate in decision making) and **federalism** (a system of government in which power is divided, by a constitution, between a central government and regional governments) into the Constitution. Let us assess the major provisions of the Constitution's seven articles to see how each relates to these objectives.

The Legislative Branch Was Designed to Be the Most Powerful

In Article I, Sections 1–7, the Constitution provides for a Congress consisting of two chambers: a House of Representatives and a Senate. Members of the House of Representatives were given two-year terms in office and were to be elected directly by the people. Members of the Senate were to be appointed by the state legislatures (this was changed in 1913 by the Seventeenth Amendment, which instituted direct election of senators) for six-year terms. These terms were staggered so that the appointments of one-third of the senators would expire every two years. The Constitution assigned somewhat different tasks to the House and Senate. Although the approval of each body was required for the enactment of a law, the Senate alone was given the power to ratify treaties and approve presidential appointments. The House, on the other hand, was given the sole power to originate revenue bills.

The structure of the legislative branch reflected the framers' major goals. The House of Representatives was designed to be directly responsible to the people in order to encourage popular consent for the new Constitution and to help enhance the power of the new government. At the same time, to guard against "excessive democracy," the Constitution checks the power of the House of Representatives with that of the Senate, whose members were to be appointed by the states for long terms rather than elected directly by the people. The purpose of this provision, according to Alexander Hamilton, was to avoid "an unqualified complaisance to every sudden breeze of passion, or to every transient impulse which the people may receive."[12] Staggered terms of service in the Senate, moreover, were intended to make that body even more resistant to popular pressure. Since only one-third of the senators would be selected at any given time, the composition of the institution would be protected from changes in popular preferences transmitted by the state legislatures. This would prevent what James Madison called "mutability in the public councils arising from a rapid succession of new members."[13] Thus, the structure of the legislative branch was designed to contribute to governmental power, to promote popular consent for the new government, and at the same time to place limits on the popular political currents that many of the framers saw as a radical threat to the economic and social order.

The issues of power and consent were important throughout the Constitution. Section 8 of Article I specifically listed the powers of Congress, which include the authority to collect taxes, borrow money, regulate commerce, declare war, and maintain an army and navy. By granting Congress these powers, the framers indicated very clearly that they intended the new government to be far more powerful than its predecessor. At the same time, by defining the new government's most important powers as belonging to Congress, the framers sought to promote popular acceptance of this critical change by reassuring citizens that their views would be fully represented whenever the government exercised its new powers.

As a further guarantee to the people that the new government would pose no threat to them, the Constitution seems to say that any powers not listed are not granted at all. Specific powers granted to Congress in the Constitution are **expressed powers**. But the framers intended to create an active and powerful government, so they also included the necessary and proper clause, sometimes known as the **elastic clause**, which declared that Congress could write laws needed to carry out its expressed powers. This clause indicated that the expressed powers could be broadly interpreted as a source of strength for the national government, not a limitation on it. In response to the charge that they intended to give the national government too much power, the framers adopted language in the Tenth Amendment stipulating that powers not specifically granted by the Constitution to the federal government were reserved to the states or to the people. As we will see in Chapter 3, the resulting tension between the elastic clause and the Tenth Amendment has been at the heart of constitutional struggles between federal and state powers.

The Executive Branch Created a Brand New Office

The Articles of Confederation had not provided for an executive branch, and the framers viewed this as a source of weakness, so the Constitution provides for the establishment of the presidency in Article II. As Hamilton commented, the presidential article aimed toward "energy in the Executive." It did so in an effort to overcome the natural tendency toward stalemate that was built into the bicameral legislature as well as into the separation of powers among the three branches. The Constitution affords the president a measure of independence from the people and from the other branches of government—particularly the Congress.

In line with the framers' goal of increased power to the national government, the president is granted the unconditional power to receive ambassadors from other countries—this amounts to the power to "recognize" other countries—as well as the power to negotiate treaties, although their acceptance requires the approval of two-thirds of the Senate. The president is also given the unconditional right to grant reprieves and pardons, except in cases of impeachment, and the powers to appoint major departmental personnel, to convene Congress in special session, and to veto congressional enactments. The veto power is formidable, but it is not absolute since Congress can override it by a two-thirds vote, reflecting the framers' concern with checks and balances.

The framers hoped to create a presidency that would make the federal government rather than the states the agency capable of timely and decisive action to deal with public issues and problems. At the same time, however, the framers sought to help the presidency withstand excessively democratic pressures by creating a system of indirect rather than direct election through an electoral college.

The Judicial Branch Was a Check on Too Much Democracy

In establishing the judicial branch in Article III, the Constitution reflects the framers' preoccupation with nationalizing governmental power and checking radical democratic impulses while preventing the new national government from interfering with liberty and property.

Under the provisions of Article III, the framers created a court that was to be literally a supreme court of the United States and not merely the highest court of the national government. The most important expression of this intention was granting the Supreme Court the power to resolve any conflicts that might emerge between federal and state laws. In particular, the Supreme Court is given the right to determine whether a power is exclusive to the national government, concurrent with the states, or exclusive to the states. In addition, the Supreme Court is assigned jurisdiction over controversies between citizens of different states. The long-term significance of this provision was that as the country developed a national economy, it came to rely increasingly on the federal judiciary, rather than on the state courts, for the resolution of disputes.

Judges are given lifetime appointments in order to protect them from popular politics and from interference by the other branches. This, however, does not mean that the judiciary remains totally impartial to political considerations or to the other branches, for the president is to appoint the judges and the Senate to approve the appointments. Congress also has the power to create inferior (lower) courts, change the jurisdiction of the federal courts, add or subtract federal judges, and even change the size of the Supreme Court.

No explicit mention is made in the Constitution of **judicial review**, the power of the courts to review and, if necessary, declare actions of the legislative and executive branches invalid or unconstitutional. The Supreme Court asserted this power in *Marbury v. Madison* (1803).[14] Its assumption of this power, as we shall see in Chapter 12, was based not on the Constitution itself but on the politics of later decades and the membership of the Court.

National Unity and Power Set the New Constitution Apart from the Old Articles

Various provisions in the Constitution address the framers' concern with national unity and power, including Article IV's provisions for comity (reciprocity) among states and among citizens of all states. Each state is prohibited from discriminating against the citizens of other states in favor of its own citizens, and the Supreme Court is charged with deciding in each case whether a state has discriminated against goods or people from another state. The Constitution restricts the power of the states in favor of ensuring enough power to the national government to give the country a free-flowing national economy.

The framers' concern with national supremacy was also expressed in Article VI, in the **supremacy clause**, which provides that national laws and treaties "shall be the supreme Law of the Land" and superior to all laws adopted by any state or any subdivision. This means that states are expected to respect all laws made under the "Authority of the United States." The supremacy clause also binds the officials of all state and local governments as well as the federal government to take an oath of office to support the national Constitution. This means that every action taken by the U.S. Congress has to be applied within each state as though the action were in fact state law.

The Constitution Establishes the Process for Amendment

The Constitution establishes procedures for its own revision in Article V. Its provisions are so difficult that the document has been successfully amended only 17 times since 1791, when the first 10 amendments were adopted. Thousands of other amendments have been proposed in Congress, but fewer than 40 of them have even come close to fulfilling the Constitution's requirement of a two-thirds vote in Congress, and only a fraction have gotten anywhere near adoption by three-fourths of the states. Article V also provides that the Constitution can be amended by a constitutional convention, but thus far, all the amendments to the U.S. Constitution have been approved first by the Congress and then by the state legislatures. The only exception is the amendment repealing prohibition, which was approved by Congress but ratified by state conventions. No national convention has been called since the Philadelphia convention of 1787.

The Constitution Sets Forth Rules for Its Own Ratification

The rules for the ratification of the Constitution are set forth in Article VII. Nine of the 13 states have to ratify, or agree to, the terms in order for the Constitution to be formally adopted.

The Constitution Limits the National Government's Power

As we have indicated, although the framers sought to create a powerful national government, they also wanted to guard against possible misuse of that power. To that end, the framers incorporated two key principles into the Constitution: the separation of powers and federalism. A third set of limitations, the Bill of Rights, was added to the Constitution in the form of 10 amendments proposed by the first Congress and ratified by the states in 1791. Most of the framers had thought a Bill of Rights to be unnecessary but accepted the idea during the debates over the Constitution's ratification.

The Separation of Powers No principle of politics was more widely shared at the time of the 1787 Founding than the principle that power must be used to balance power. As mentioned earlier in the chapter, Montesquieu believed that this balance was an indispensable defense against tyranny. His writings, especially his major

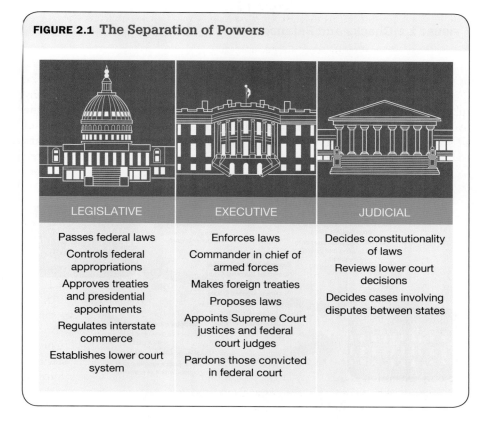

FIGURE 2.1 The Separation of Powers

LEGISLATIVE	EXECUTIVE	JUDICIAL
Passes federal laws	Enforces laws	Decides constitutionality of laws
Controls federal appropriations	Commander in chief of armed forces	Reviews lower court decisions
Approves treaties and presidential appointments	Makes foreign treaties	Decides cases involving disputes between states
Regulates interstate commerce	Proposes laws	
Establishes lower court system	Appoints Supreme Court justices and federal court judges	
	Pardons those convicted in federal court	

work, *The Spirit of the Laws*, "were taken as political gospel" at the Philadelphia convention.[15] Although the principle of the separation of powers is not explicitly stated in the Constitution, the entire structure of the national government is built precisely on Article I (the legislature), Article II (the executive), and Article III (the judiciary; see Figure 2.1).

However, separation of powers is nothing but mere words on parchment without a method to maintain that separation. The method became known by the popular label "checks and balances" (see Figure 2.2). Each branch is given not only its own powers but also some power over the other two branches. Among the most familiar checks and balances are the president's veto as a power over Congress and Congress's power over the president through its control of appointments to high executive posts and to the judiciary. Congress also has power over the president with its control of appropriations (the spending of government money) and the right of approval of treaties (by the Senate). The judiciary has the power of judicial review over the other two branches.

Another important feature of the separation of powers is the principle of giving each of the branches a distinctly different constituency. Theorists such as Montesquieu called this a "mixed regime," with the president chosen indirectly by electors, the House by popular vote, the Senate (originally) by state legislature, and

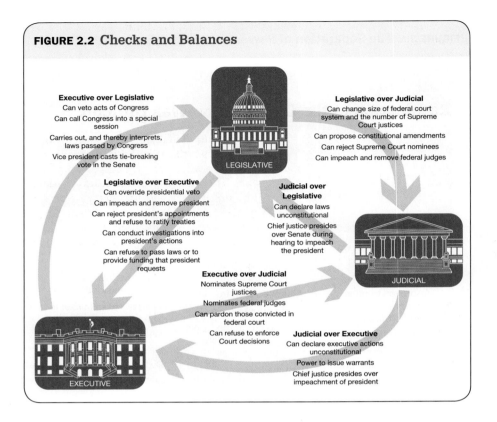

FIGURE 2.2 Checks and Balances

Executive over Legislative
Can veto acts of Congress
Can call Congress into a special session
Carries out, and thereby interprets, laws passed by Congress
Vice president casts tie-breaking vote in the Senate

LEGISLATIVE

Legislative over Judicial
Can change size of federal court system and the number of Supreme Court justices
Can propose constitutional amendments
Can reject Supreme Court nominees
Can impeach and remove federal judges

Legislative over Executive
Can override presidential veto
Can impeach and remove president
Can reject president's appointments and refuse to ratify treaties
Can conduct investigations into president's actions
Can refuse to pass laws or to provide funding that president requests

Judicial over Legislative
Can declare laws unconstitutional
Chief justice presides over Senate during hearing to impeach the president

JUDICIAL

Executive over Judicial
Nominates Supreme Court justices
Nominates federal judges
Can pardon those convicted in federal court
Can refuse to enforce Court decisions

Judicial over Executive
Can declare executive actions unconstitutional
Power to issue warrants
Chief justice presides over impeachment of president

EXECUTIVE

the judiciary by presidential appointment. By these means, the occupants of each branch would tend to develop very different outlooks on how to govern, different definitions of the public interest, and different alliances with private interests.

Federalism Compared to the confederation principle of the Articles of Confederation, federalism was a step toward greater centralization of power. The delegates agreed that they needed to place more power at the national level, without completely undermining the power of the state governments. Thus, they devised a system of two sovereigns—the states and the nation—with the hope that competition between the two would be an effective limitation on the power of both.

The Bill of Rights Late in the Philadelphia convention of 1787, a motion was made to include a list of citizens' rights in the Constitution. After a brief debate in which hardly a word was said in its favor and only one speech was made against it, the motion was almost unanimously defeated. Most delegates sincerely believed that since the federal government was already limited to its expressed powers, further protection of citizens was not needed. The delegates argued that the states should adopt bills of rights because their greater powers needed greater limitations. But almost immediately after the Constitution was ratified, there was a movement to adopt a national bill of rights. This is why the Bill of Rights, adopted in 1791, comprises the first 10 amendments to the Constitution rather than being part of the body of it. (We will have a good deal more to say about the Bill of Rights in Chapter 4.)

● Ratification of the Constitution Was Difficult

Present the controversies involved in the struggle for ratification

The first hurdle facing the proposed Constitution was ratification by state conventions of delegates elected by the people of each state. This struggle for ratification was carried out in 13 separate campaigns. Each involved different people, moved at a different pace, and was influenced by local and national considerations. Two sides faced off throughout the states, however; the two sides called themselves Federalists and Antifederalists (see Table 2.2).

The **Federalists** (who more accurately should have called themselves "Nationalists" but who took their name to appear to follow in the Revolutionary tradition) supported the constitution proposed at the American Constitutional Convention of 1787 and preferred a strong national government. The **Antifederalists** favored strong state governments and a weak national government and opposed the document produced at the Constitutional Convention. They preferred a federal system of government that was decentralized; they took their name by default, in reaction to their better-organized opponents. The Federalists were united in their support of

TABLE 2.2

Federalists versus Antifederalists

	FEDERALISTS	ANTIFEDERALISTS
Who were they?	Property owners, creditors, merchants	Small farmers, frontiersmen, debtors, shopkeepers, some state government officials
What did they believe?	Believed that elites were most fit to govern; feared "excessive democracy"	Believed that government should be closer to the people; feared concentration of power in hands of the elites
What system of government did they favor?	Favored strong national government; believed in "filtration" so that only elites would obtain governmental power	Favored retention of power by state governments and protection of individual rights
Who were their leaders?	Alexander Hamilton, James Madison, George Washington	Patrick Henry, George Mason, Elbridge Gerry, George Clinton

the Constitution, while the Antifederalists were divided over possible alternatives to the Constitution.

During the struggle over ratification of the Constitution, Americans argued about great political principles. How much power should the national government be given? What safeguards would most likely prevent the abuse of power? What institutional arrangements could best ensure adequate representation for all Americans? Was tyranny to be feared more from the many or from the few?

Federalists and Antifederalists Fought Bitterly over the Wisdom of the New Constitution

During the ratification struggle, thousands of essays, speeches, pamphlets, and letters were written in support of and in opposition to the proposed Constitution. The best-known pieces supporting ratification of the Constitution were the 85 essays written, under the name of "Publius," by Alexander Hamilton, James Madison, and John Jay between the fall of 1787 and the spring of 1788—known today as the **Federalist Papers.** They not only defended the principles of the Constitution but also sought to dispel fears of a strong national authority. The Antifederalists published essays of their own, arguing that the new Constitution betrayed the Revolution and was a step toward monarchy. Among the best of the Antifederalist works were the essays, usually attributed to New York Supreme Court justice Robert Yates, that were written under the name of "Brutus" and published in the *New York Journal* at the same time the *Federalist Papers* appeared. The Antifederalist view was also ably presented in the pamphlets and letters written by a former delegate to the Continental Congress and future U.S. senator, Richard Henry Lee of Virginia, using the pen name "The Federal Farmer." These essays highlight the major differences of opinion between Federalists and Antifederalists. Federalists appealed to basic principles of government in support of their nationalist vision. Antifederalists cited equally fundamental precepts to support their vision of a looser confederacy of small republics. Three areas of disagreement were representation, majority tyranny, and governmental power.

Representation The Antifederalists believed that the best and most representative government was that closest to the people, what we would think of as local and state governments. These smaller, more homogeneous governing units would provide "a true picture of the people . . . [possessing] the knowledge of their circumstances and their wants."[16] A strong national government could not represent the interests of the nation as effectively, the Antifederalists argued, because the nation as a whole was simply too large and diverse.

The Federalists, on the other hand, thought that some distance between the people and their representatives might be a good thing because it would encourage the selection of a few talented and experienced representatives to serve in a national legislature who could balance the wishes of the people with their own considered judgment. In James Madison's view, representatives would not simply mirror society; rather, they must be "[those] who possess [the] most wisdom to discern, and [the] most virtue to pursue, the common good of the society."[17]

Tyranny of the Majority Both Federalists and Antifederalists feared **tyranny**, oppressive and unjust government that employs cruel and arbitrary use of power and authority. But each painted a different picture of what kind of tyranny to fear.

The Antifederalists feared that tyranny would arise from the tendency of all governments to become more "aristocratic," wherein a few individuals in positions of authority would use their positions to gain more and more power over the people. For this reason, Antifederalists were sharply critical of those features of the Constitution that limited direct popular influence over the government, including the election of senators by state legislatures, election of the president by the electoral college, and selection of federal judges by the president and the Senate. Judges, who are appointed for life, were seen as an especially dire threat: "I wonder if the world ever saw . . . a court of justice invested with such immense powers, and yet placed in a situation so little responsible," protested Brutus.[18]

For the Federalists, tyranny in a republic was less likely to come from aristocrats and more likely to come from the majority. They feared that a popular majority, "united and actuated by some common impulse of passion, or of interest, adverse to the rights of other citizens," would attempt to "trample on the rules of justice."[19] Those features of the Constitution opposed by the Antifederalists were the very ones that the Federalists defended as the best hope of avoiding tyranny. The sheer size and diversity of the American nation, as represented in the two houses of Congress, would provide a built-in set of balances that would force competing interests to moderate and compromise.

Governmental Power A third difference between Federalists and Antifederalists was over the matter of governmental power. Both sides agreed on the principle of **limited government**, meaning a government whose powers are defined and limited by a constitution; but they differed on how best to limit the government.

Antifederalists wanted the powers of the national government to be carefully specified and limited. Otherwise, the federal government would "swallow up all the power of the state governments." Antifederalists bitterly attacked the supremacy clause and the elastic clause of the Constitution, saying that these provisions gave the national government dangerously unlimited grants of power. They also insisted that a bill of rights be added to the Constitution to place limits on the government's power over citizens.

Federalists favored a national government with broad powers to defend the nation from foreign threats, guard against domestic strife and insurrection, promote commerce, and expand the nation's economy. Federalists agreed that such power could be abused but believed that the best safeguard against such abuse was through the Constitution's internal checks and controls, not by keeping the national government weak. As Madison put it, "The power surrendered by the people is first divided between two distinct governments [federal and state], and then the portion allotted to each subdivided among distinct and separate departments. Hence, a double security arises to the rights of the people. The different governments will control each other, at the same time that each will be

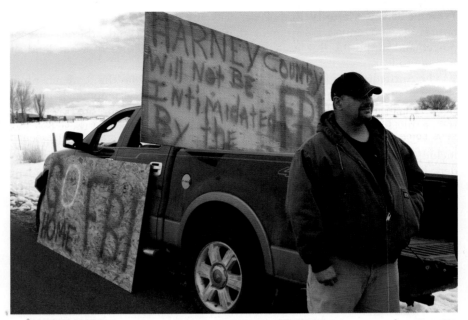

Debates over how much power the national government should have continue today. Here, a man protests the presence of the FBI in Harney County, Oregon, after an antigovernment group seized a U.S. wildlife refuge building.

controlled by itself."[20] The Federalists considered a bill of rights to be unnecessary, although this Antifederalist demand was eventually embraced by Federalists, including Madison.

Both Federalists and Antifederalists Contributed to the Success of the New System

In general, the Federalist vision of America triumphed. The Constitution adopted in 1789 creates the framework for a powerful national government that for more than 200 years has defended the nation's interests, promoted its commerce, and maintained national unity. In one notable instance, the national government fought and won a bloody war to prevent the nation from breaking apart. And despite this powerful government, the system of internal checks and balances has functioned reasonably well, as the Federalists predicted, to prevent the national government from tyrannizing its citizens.

Although they were defeated in 1789, the Antifederalists present us with an important picture of a road not taken and of an America that might have been. Would Americans in the eighteenth century have been worse off if they had been governed by a confederacy of small republics linked by a national administration with severely limited powers? Were the Antifederalists correct in predicting that a government given great power in the hope that it might do good would, through "insensible progress," inevitably turn to evil purposes?

Comparing Systems of Government

There is tremendous variation across the world's democracies. All democracies possess some form of an executive, a legislature, and a judiciary; but the amount of power that each branch has varies. Note that in some systems, no one branch has very much power. In the United States, that is because of the system of checks and balances among the branches. Israel and the United Kingdom, which lack written constitutions, have branches with even less power than in the United States.

Country	Written Constitution?	Year Enacted	Length (in Words)	Federal or Unitary System
Brazil	Yes	1988	64,488	Federal
France	Yes	1958	10,180	Unitary
India	Yes	1949	146,385	Federal
Israel	No	—	—	Unitary
South Africa	Yes	1996	43,062	Unitary
Tunisia	Yes	2014	9,508	Unitary
United States	Yes	1789	7,762	Federal
United Kingdom	No	—	—	Unitary

Country	Strength of Executive	Strength of Legislature	Judicial Independence
Brazil	High	Medium	High
France	High	Low	Low
India	Medium	Low	Medium
Israel	Low	Low	Medium
South Africa	Medium	Low	High
Tunisia	High	Medium	Low
United States	Low	Medium	High*
United Kingdom	High*	Low	Medium

*Although the Comparative Constitutions Project classifies the formal powers of both the American presidency and the judicial branch, as originally provided for in the Constitution, as relatively *weak*, we have classified both here as strong, based on the greater powers that have developed over time.
SOURCE: Comparative Constitutions Project, "CCP Rankings," http://comparativeconstitutionsproject.org/ccp-rankings/ (accessed 7/16/15).

Constitutional Amendments Dramatically Changed the Relationship between Citizens and the Government

Trace how the Constitution has changed over time through the amendment process

The Constitution has endured for more than two centuries as the framework of government because it has changed over time. Without change, the Constitution might have become merely a sacred but obsolete relic of a bygone era.

Amendments: Many Are Called; Few Are Chosen

The inevitable need for change was recognized by the framers of the Constitution, and the provisions for **amendment** (a change added to a bill, law, or constitution) were incorporated into Article V. The Constitution has proven to be extremely difficult to amend. In the history of efforts to amend it, the most appropriate characterization is "many are called; few are chosen." Since 1789, more than 11,000 amendments have been formally offered in Congress. Of these, Congress officially proposed only 29, and 27 of these were eventually ratified by the states.

Four methods of amendment are provided for in Article V:

1. Passage in House and Senate by two-thirds vote, then ratification by majority vote of the legislatures of three-fourths (now 38) of the states.

2. Passage in House and Senate by two-thirds vote, then ratification by conventions called for the purpose in three-fourths of the states.

3. Passage in a national convention called by Congress in response to petitions by two-thirds of the states, then ratification by majority vote of the legislatures of three-fourths of the states.

4. Passage in a national convention, as in method 3, then ratification by conventions called for the purpose in three-fourths of the states.

Figure 2.3 illustrates each of these possible methods. Since no amendment has ever been proposed by national convention, routes 3 and 4 have never been employed. And route 2 has only been employed once (the Twenty-First Amendment, which repealed the Eighteenth Amendment, or Prohibition). Thus, route 1 has been used for all the others.

Now it should be clear why it has been so difficult to amend the Constitution. The requirement of a two-thirds vote in the House and the Senate means that any proposal for an amendment in Congress can be killed by only 34 senators or 136 members of the House. What is more, if the necessary two-thirds vote is obtained, the amendment can still be killed by the refusal or inability of only 13 out of 50 state legislatures to ratify it. Since each state has an equal vote regardless of its population, the 13 holdout states may represent a very small fraction of the total American population.

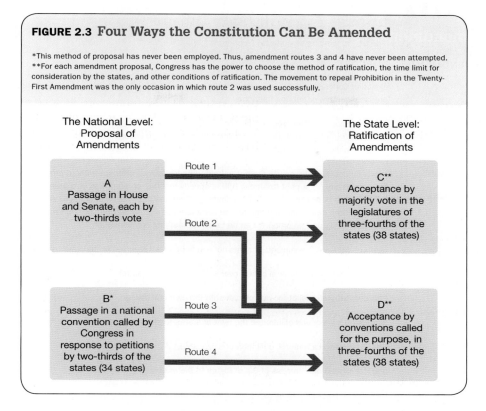

FIGURE 2.3 Four Ways the Constitution Can Be Amended

*This method of proposal has never been employed. Thus, amendment routes 3 and 4 have never been attempted.
**For each amendment proposal, Congress has the power to choose the method of ratification, the time limit for consideration by the states, and other conditions of ratification. The movement to repeal Prohibition in the Twenty-First Amendment was the only occasion in which route 2 was used successfully.

The National Level:
Proposal of
Amendments

The State Level:
Ratification of
Amendments

Route 1

Route 2

Route 3

Route 4

A
Passage in House
and Senate, each by
two-thirds vote

B*
Passage in a national
convention called by
Congress in
response to petitions
by two-thirds of the
states (34 states)

C**
Acceptance by
majority vote in the
legislatures of
three-fourths of the
states (38 states)

D**
Acceptance by
conventions called
for the purpose, in
three-fourths of the
states (38 states)

The Amendment Process Reflects "Higher Law"

The very high failure rate of nearly all amendment attempts suggests that only a limited number of changes can actually be made through the Constitution. Most efforts to amend the Constitution have failed because they were simply attempts to use the Constitution as an alternative to legislation for dealing directly with a specific public problem.

Successful amendments, on the other hand, are concerned with the structure or composition of government (see Table 2.3; the first 10 amendments will be discussed in Chapter 4). This is consistent with the dictionary, which defines *constitution* as the makeup or composition of something. And it is consistent with the concept of a constitution as "higher law" because the whole point and purpose of a higher law is to establish a framework within which government and the process of making ordinary law can take place. Even those who would have preferred more changes to the Constitution have to agree that there is great wisdom in this principle. A constitution ought to enable legislation and public policies to be enacted, but it should not determine what that legislation or those public policies ought to be.

TABLE 2.3

Amendments to the Constitution

AMENDMENT	PURPOSE
I	*Limits on Congress:* Congress is not to make any law establishing a religion or abridging speech, press, assembly, or petition freedoms.
II, III, IV	*Limits on Executive:* The executive branch is not to infringe on the right of people to keep arms (II), is not arbitrarily to take houses for a militia (III), and is not to engage in the search or seizure of evidence without a court warrant swearing to belief in the probable existence of a crime (IV).
V, VI, VII, VIII	*Limits on Courts:** The courts are not to hold trials for serious offenses without provision for a grand jury (V), a petit (trial) jury (VII), a speedy trial (VI), presentation of charges (VI), confrontation of hostile witnesses (VI), immunity from testimony against oneself (V), and immunity from more than one trial for the same offense (V). Neither bail nor punishment can be excessive (VIII), and no property can be taken without just compensation (V).
IX, X	*Limits on National Government:* All rights not enumerated are reserved to the states or the people.
XI	Limited jurisdiction of federal courts over suits involving the states.
XII	Provided separate ballot for vice president in the electoral college.
XIII	Eliminated slavery and eliminated the right of states to allow property in persons.**
XIV	(Part 1) Provided a national definition of citizenship.†
XIV	(Part 2) Applied due process of Bill of Rights to the states.
XV	Extended voting rights to all races.
XVI	Established national power to tax incomes.
XVII††	Provided direct election of senators.
XIX	Extended voting rights to women.
XX	Eliminated "lame-duck" session of Congress.
XXII	Limited presidential term.
XXIII	Extended voting rights to residents of the District of Columbia.
XXIV	Extended voting rights to all classes by abolition of poll taxes.
XXV	Provided presidential succession in case of disability.
XXVI	Extended voting rights to citizens aged 18 and over.†
XXVII	Limited Congress's power to raise its own salary.

* These amendments also impose limits on the law-enforcement powers of federal (and especially) state and local executive branches.
** The Thirteenth Amendment was proposed January 31, 1865, and adopted less than a year later, on December 18, 1865.
† In defining *citizenship*, the Fourteenth Amendment actually provided the constitutional basis for expanding the electorate to include all races, women, and residents of the District of Columbia. Only the "18-year-olds' amendment" should have been necessary since it changed the definition of citizenship. The fact that additional amendments were required following the Fourteenth suggests that voting is not considered an inherent right of U.S. citizenship. Instead, it is viewed as a privilege.
†† The Eighteenth Amendment, ratified in 1919, outlawed the sale and transportation of liquor. It was repealed by the Twenty-First Amendment, ratified in 1933.
† The Twenty-Sixth Amendment holds the record for speed of adoption. It was proposed on March 23, 1971, and adopted on July 5, 1971.

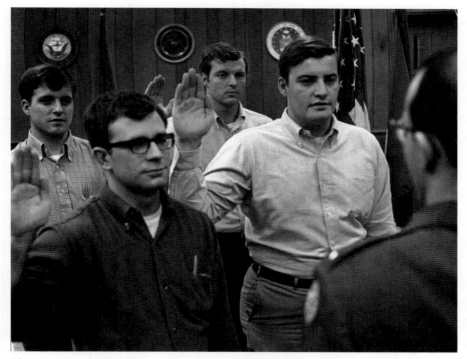

The Twenty-Sixth Amendment addressed an issue of representation that came to the fore when 18-, 19-, and 20-year-olds were drafted to serve in the Vietnam War but could not vote for Congress or the president who enacted the policies that affected their lives and deaths.

For those whose hopes for change center on the Constitution, it must be emphasized that the amendment route to social change is, and always will be, extremely limited. Through a constitution it is possible to establish a working structure of government and basic rights of citizens by placing limitations on the powers of that government. Once these goals have been accomplished, the next problem is how to extend rights to those people who do not already enjoy them. Of course, the Constitution cannot enforce itself. But it can and does have a real influence on everyday life because a right or an obligation set forth in the Constitution can become a cause of action in the hands of an otherwise powerless person.

Private property is an excellent example. Property is one of the most fundamental and well-established rights in the United States, but it is well established not because it is recognized in so many words in the Constitution but because legislatures and courts have made it a crime for anyone, including the government, to trespass or to take away property without compensation.

A constitution is good if it produces the cause of action that leads to good legislation, good court decisions, and appropriate police behavior. A constitution cannot eliminate power. But its principles can be a citizen's dependable defense against the abuse of power.

The Constitution
and Your Future

The Constitution's framers placed individual liberty ahead of all other political values, a concern that led many of the framers to distrust both democracy and equality. They feared that democracy could degenerate into a majority tyranny in which the populace, perhaps led by rabble-rousing demagogues, trampled on liberty. As for equality, the framers were products of their time and place; our contemporary ideas of racial and gender equality would have been foreign to them. The basic structure of the Constitution—separated powers, internal checks and balances, and federalism—was designed to safeguard liberty, and the Bill of Rights created further safeguards for liberty. At the same time, however, many of the Constitution's other key provisions, such as indirect election of senators and the president and the appointment of judges for life, were designed to limit democracy and, hence, the threat of majority tyranny.

By championing liberty, however, the framers virtually guaranteed that democracy and even a measure of equality would sooner or later evolve in the United States. Where they have liberty, more and more people, groups, and interests will almost inevitably engage in politics and gradually overcome whatever restrictions might have been placed on participation. Indeed, this is precisely what happened in the early years of the American Republic. During the Jeffersonian period, political parties formed. During the Jacksonian period, many state suffrage restrictions were removed and popular participation greatly expanded. The "**Who Participates?**" feature on the following page traces the expansion of the United States from the founding to today. Over time, liberty is conducive to democracy.

Who Gained the Right to Vote through Amendments?

Adult Citizens Eligible to Vote in National Elections*

1789
The Founding:
White men of property, age 21+ (27.9%)

1869
Fifteenth Amendment:
All men, age 21+ (31.7%)

1920
Nineteenth Amendment:
All men and women, age 21+ (92.6%)

1971
Twenty-Sixth Amendment:
All men and women, age 18+ (99.9%)

*Percentages are of the adult (18+) population. These figures are
approximate for 1789 and 1869. The voting rights of convicted
felons are restricted in some states, and of noncitizens in all states.
SOURCES: U.S. Census of Population and Housing, 1790–2010,
www.census.gov/prod/www/decennial.html (accessed 9/28/15);
United States Elections Project, www.electproject.org/national
-1789–present (accessed 9/27/15).

WHAT YOU CAN DO ➡

WHAT YOU CAN DO

Know Your Constitutional Rights

 Review your rights as outlined in the Constitution, a copy of which is reproduced in the appendix of this book.

 Find out what voting rights are retained by individuals who have been convicted of a felony. Go to **www.ncsl.org** and search "felon voting rights" for more information.

 Find out what voting rights are retained by individuals with mental illness. Go to **www.bazelon.org** and search "voting" for more information.

Should noncitizens (such as longtime permanent legal residents) have the right to vote? Go to **www.latimes.com/citizenship** to read more and to join the conversation online.

chapterstudyguide

Practice Quiz

1. In their fight against British taxes such as the Stamp Act and the Sugar Act of 1764, New England merchants and southern planters allied with which of the following groups? *(p. 32)*
   a) shopkeepers, small farmers, laborers, and artisans
   b) shopkeepers only
   c) laborers only
   d) artisans only
   e) shopkeepers and laborers only

2. How did the British attempt to raise revenue in the North American colonies? *(p. 33)*
   a) income taxes
   b) tariffs, duties, and other taxes on commerce
   c) expropriation and sale of Native American lands
   d) licensing fees for the mining of natural resources
   e) requests for voluntary donations

3. The first governing document in the United States was *(p. 35)*
   a) the Declaration of Independence.
   b) the Articles of Confederation.
   c) the Constitution.
   d) the Bill of Rights.
   e) the Virginia Plan.

4. Where was the execution of laws conducted under the Articles of Confederation? *(p. 35)*
   a) the presidency
   b) the Congress
   c) the states
   d) the federal judiciary
   e) the federal bureaucracy

5. Which event led directly to the Constitutional Convention by providing evidence that the government created under the Articles of Confederation was unable to act decisively in times of national crisis? *(p. 37)*
   a) the Boston Massacre
   b) the Boston Tea Party
   c) Shays's Rebellion
   d) the Annapolis Convention
   e) the War of 1812

6. Which state's proposal embodied a principle of representing states in the Congress according to their size and wealth? *(p. 39)*
   a) Connecticut
   b) Maryland
   c) New Jersey
   d) Rhode Island
   e) Virginia

7. The agreement reached at the Constitutional Convention that determined that every five slaves would be counted as three free persons for the purposes of taxation and representation in the House of Representatives was called the *(p. 40)*
   a) Virginia Plan.
   b) New Jersey Plan.
   c) Connecticut Compromise.
   d) Three-Fifths Compromise.
   e) Great Compromise.

8. What mechanism was instituted in the Congress to guard against "excessive democracy"? *(p. 40)*
   a) bicameralism
   b) staggered terms in office

c) appointment of senators for long terms
d) indirect election of the president
e) all of the above

9. Which of the following best describes the Supreme Court as understood by the Founders? *(p. 45)*
   a) the body that would choose the president
   b) the principle check on presidential power
   c) arbiter of disputes within the Congress
   d) a figurehead commission of elders
   e) the highest court of both the national government and the states

10. Theorists such as Montesquieu referred to the system of giving each branch of government a distinctly different constituency as *(p. 47)*
    a) a mixed regime.
    b) a confederation.
    c) a bicameral structure.
    d) a limited government.
    e) a federalist arrangement.

11. Which of the following were the Antifederalists most concerned with? *(pp. 50–52)*
    a) interstate commerce
    b) the protection of property
    c) the distinction between principles and interests
    d) the potential for tyranny in the central government
    e) abolishing slavery

12. Which of the following best describes the process of amending the Constitution? *(p. 54)*
    a) It is difficult and has rarely been used successfully to address specific public problems.
    b) It is difficult and has frequently been used successfully to address specific public problems.
    c) It is easy and has rarely been used successfully to address specific public problems.
    d) It is easy and has frequently been used successfully to address specific public problems.
    e) It is easy, but it has never been used for any purpose.

Key Terms

amendment *(p. 54)* a change added to a bill, law, or constitution

Antifederalists *(p. 49)* those who favored strong state governments and a weak national government and were opponents of the constitution proposed at the American Constitutional Convention of 1787

Articles of Confederation *(p. 35)* America's first written constitution; served as the basis for America's national government until 1789

bicameral *(p. 42)* having a legislative assembly composed of two chambers or houses; distinguished from *unicameral*

Bill of Rights *(p. 43)* the first 10 amendments to the Constitution, ratified in 1791; they ensure certain rights and liberties of the people

checks and balances *(p. 42)* mechanisms through which each branch of government is able to participate in and influence the activities of the other branches. Major examples include the presidential veto power over congressional legislation, the power of the Senate to approve presidential appointments, and judicial review of congressional enactments

confederation *(p. 36)* a system of government in which states retain sovereign authority except for the powers expressly delegated to the national government

elastic clause *(p. 44)* Article I, Section 8, of the Constitution (also known as the *necessary and proper clause*), which declares that Congress can write laws needed to carry out its expressed powers, providing Congress with the authority to make all laws "necessary and proper" to do so

electoral college *(p. 43)* the electors from each state who meet after the popular election to cast ballots for president and vice president

expressed powers *(p. 44)* specific powers granted by the Constitution to Congress

(Article I, Section 8) and to the president (Article II)

federalism *(p. 43)* a system of government in which power is divided, by a constitution, between the central (national) government and regional (state) governments

Federalist Papers *(p. 50)* a series of essays written by James Madison, Alexander Hamilton, and John Jay supporting the ratification of the Constitution

Federalists *(p. 49)* those who favored a strong national government and supported the constitution proposed at the American Constitutional Convention of 1787

Great Compromise *(p. 39)* the agreement reached at the Constitutional Convention of 1787 that gave each state an equal number of senators regardless of its population but linked representation in the House of Representatives to population

judicial review *(p. 45)* the power of the courts to review and, if necessary, declare actions of the legislative and executive branches invalid or unconstitutional. The Supreme Court asserted this power in *Marbury v. Madison* (1803)

limited government *(p. 52)* a principle of constitutional government; a government whose powers are defined and limited by a constitution

New Jersey Plan *(p. 39)* a framework for the Constitution, introduced by William Paterson, that called for equal state representation in the national legislature regardless of population

separation of powers *(p. 43)* the division of governmental power among several institutions that must cooperate in decision making

supremacy clause *(p. 46)* Article VI of the Constitution, which states that laws passed by the national government and all treaties "shall be the supreme law of the land" and superior to all laws adopted by any state or any subdivision

Three-Fifths Compromise *(p. 41)* the agreement reached at the Constitutional Convention of 1787 that stipulated that for purposes of the apportionment of congressional seats only three-fifths of slaves would be counted

tyranny *(p. 51)* oppressive and unjust government that employs cruel and unjust use of power and authority

Virginia Plan *(p. 39)* a framework for the Constitution, introduced by Edmund Randolph, that called for representation in the national legislature based on the population of each state

For Further Reading

Ackerman, Erin, and Benjamin Ginsberg. *A Guide to the United States Constitution*. 2nd ed. New York: W. W. Norton, 2011.

Beard, Charles. *An Economic Interpretation of the Constitution of the United States*. New York: Macmillan, 1913.

Beeman, Richard. *Plain, Honest Men: The Making of the American Constitution*. New York: Random House, 2009.

Chernow, Ron. *Alexander Hamilton*. New York: Penguin Books, 2005.

Ellis, Joseph. *The Quartet: Orchestrating the Second American Revolution*. New York: Knopf, 2015.

Hamilton, Alexander, James Madison, and John Jay. *The Federalist Papers*. Edited by Isaac Kramnick. New York: Viking, 1987.

Jensen, Merrill. *The Articles of Confederation*. Madison: University of Wisconsin Press, 1963.

Rossiter, Clinton. *1787: Grand Convention*. New York: Macmillan, 1966.

Storing, Herbert, ed. *The Complete Anti-Federalist*. 7 vols. Chicago: University of Chicago Press, 1981.

Wood, Gordon S. *Empire of Liberty: A History of the Early Republic*. New York: Oxford University Press, 2011.

Federalism is at the center of a national debate over marijuana policy: while marijuana remains illegal under federal law, some states permit marijuana for medicinal or recreational use. Colorado legalized recreational use of marijuana in 2012, and participants in this 2015 Denver rally called for national legalization.

3

Federalism

WHAT GOVERNMENT DOES AND WHY IT MATTERS In 1996, voters in California approved a new law legalizing the cultivation, possession, and use of marijuana for medical purposes. As the idea spread, other states followed suit. By 2016, 26 states and the District of Columbia had approved medical marijuana. In these states, medical clinics selling marijuana have popped up in many cities. With a doctor's prescription, patients can purchase marijuana for personal use. Some states have gone even further. In 2012, voters in Washington state and Colorado approved measures to legalize the recreational use of marijuana. The laws gave adults over the age of 21 the right to buy limited amounts of marijuana. And in the 2014 and 2016 elections, ballot measures in Alaska, California, Maine, Massachusetts, Nevada, Oregon, and Washington, D.C., also legalized recreational use of marijuana.

States routinely devise their own laws on a wide variety of topics. But the marijuana laws passed over the past two decades are extraordinary because marijuana remains a controlled substance under federal law, making it illegal to grow, sell, or possess marijuana for medical or recreational purposes. States began to legalize marijuana in defiance of clear federal prohibitions.

The federal response to the states has shifted over time. As state laws began to loosen marijuana restrictions, the federal government at first sought to assert its authority. The federal Drug Enforcement Agency staged raids on marijuana clinics and even searched individual homes to enforce the federal law prohibiting marijuana. In 2005, the Supreme Court ruled that these federal actions were constitutional. The Court affirmed the federal government's right to prohibit marijuana even as a growing number of state laws moved in the opposite direction. By 2013, however, the Justice Department, bowing to the states, announced a change of course. The department stated that it would not challenge state laws so long as the states maintained a close watch over their marijuana markets. Instead the federal government would focus its enforcement efforts on specific issues, including trafficking by gangs, sales to minors, and selling across state lines. Washington state's governor, Jay Inslee, issued a joint statement with the state's attorney general noting that the decision "reflects a balanced approach by the federal government that respects the states' interests in implementing these laws and recognizes the federal government's role in fighting illegal drugs and criminal activity."[1]

The debates about marijuana policy engage some of the oldest questions in American government: What is the responsibility of the federal government, and what is the responsibility of the states? And when should there be uniformity across the states, and when is it better to let the states adopt their own laws based on the preferences of their population, which may result in a diverse set of laws across the nation? The United States is a federal system, in which the national government shares power with lower levels of government. Throughout American history, lawmakers, politicians, and citizens have wrestled with questions about how responsibilities should be allocated across the different levels of government. Some responsibilities, such as foreign policy, clearly lie with the federal government. Others, such as divorce laws, are controlled by state governments. Many government responsibilities are shared in American federalism and require cooperation among local, state, and federal governments. The debate about "who should do what" remains one of the most important discussions in American politics.

chaptergoals

- Describe what the Constitution says about the powers of the national government and of the states (pp. 67–70)
- Trace developments in the federal framework leading to a stronger national government (pp. 71–82)
- Analyze the developments in the federal framework since the 1970s (pp. 83–88)

Federalism Shapes American Politics

Describe what the Constitution says about the powers of the national government and of the states

The Constitution has had its most fundamental influence on American life through **federalism**. Federalism can be defined as the division of powers and functions between the national government and the state governments. Governments can organize power in a variety of ways. One of the most important distinctions is between unitary and federal governments. In a **unitary system**, the central government makes the important decisions and lower levels of government have little independent power. In such systems, lower levels of government primarily implement decisions made by the central government. In France, for example, the central government was once so involved in the smallest details of local activity that the minister of education boasted that by looking at his watch he could tell what all French schoolchildren were learning at that moment because the central government set the school curriculum. In a **federal system**, by contrast, the central government shares power or functions with lower levels of government, such as regions or states. Nations with diverse ethnic or language groupings, such as Switzerland and Canada, are most likely to have federal arrangements. In federal systems, lower levels of government often have significant independent power to set policy in some areas, such as education and social programs, and to impose taxes. Yet the specific ways in which power is shared vary greatly: no two federal systems are exactly the same.

Federalism Comes from the Constitution

The United States was the first nation to adopt federalism as its governing framework. With federalism, the framers sought to limit the national government by creating a second layer of state governments. American federalism thus recognized two sovereigns in the original Constitution by granting a few "expressed powers" to the national government and reserving the rest to the states.

The Powers of the National Government As we saw in Chapter 2, the **expressed powers** granted to the national government are found in Article I, Section 8, of the Constitution. These 17 powers include the powers to collect taxes, coin money, declare war, and regulate commerce. Article I, Section 8, also contains another important source of power for the national government: the **implied powers** that enable Congress "to make all Laws which shall be necessary and proper for carrying into Execution the foregoing Powers." Such powers are not specifically expressed but are *implied* through the expansive interpretation of delegated powers. Not until several decades after the Founding did the Supreme Court allow Congress to exercise the power granted in this **necessary and proper clause**, but as we shall see later in this chapter, this doctrine allowed the national government to expand considerably the scope of its authority, although the process was a slow one.

Aside from these powers, the federal government operates with one other advantage over the states: as mentioned in the last chapter, Article VI of the

Constitution says that whenever there is a conflict between a national law and a state law, the national law shall prevail. This doctrine of *national supremacy* says that "[t]his Constitution, and the Laws of the United States . . . and all Treaties made . . . shall be the supreme Law of the Land," even extending to state courts and constitutions.

The Powers of State Government One way in which the framers sought to preserve a strong role for the states was through the Tenth Amendment to the Constitution. The Tenth Amendment states that the powers that the Constitution does not delegate to the national government or prohibit to the states are "reserved to the States respectively, or to the people." The Antifederalists, who feared that a strong central government would encroach on individual liberty, repeatedly pressed for such an amendment as a way of limiting national power. The Federalists agreed to the amendment because they did not think it would do much harm, given the powers of the Constitution already granted to the national government. The Tenth Amendment is also called the "**reserved powers** amendment" because it aims to reserve powers to the states.

The most fundamental power that the states retain is that of coercion—the power to develop and enforce criminal codes, to administer health and safety rules, and to regulate the family via marriage and divorce laws. The states have the power to regulate individuals' livelihoods; if you're a doctor or a lawyer or a plumber or a hair stylist, you must be licensed by the state. Even more fundamentally, the states have the power to define private property—private property exists because state laws against trespass define who is and is not entitled to use a piece of property. If you own a car, your ownership isn't worth much unless the state is willing to enforce your right to possession by making it a crime for anyone else to drive your car without your permission. These laws are essential to citizens' everyday lives, and the powers of the states regarding such domestic issues are much greater than the powers of the national government.

A state's authority to regulate the health, safety, and morals of its citizens is commonly referred to as the **police power** of the state. Policing is what states do—they coerce you in the name of the community in order to maintain public order. And this was exactly the type of power that the Founders intended the states, rather than the federal government, to exercise.

In some areas, the states share **concurrent power** (authority possessed by *both* state and national governments) with the national government, whereby they retain and share some power to regulate commerce and to affect the currency—for example, by being able to charter banks, grant or deny corporate charters, grant or deny licenses to engage in a business or practice a trade, and regulate the quality of products or the conditions of labor. Wherever there is a direct conflict of laws between the federal and the state levels, the issue will most likely be resolved in favor of national supremacy.

States' Obligations to One Another The Constitution also creates obligations among the states. These obligations, spelled out in Article IV, were intended to promote national unity. By requiring the states to recognize actions and decisions taken in other states as legal and proper, the framers aimed to make the states less like independent countries and more like parts of a single nation.

Article IV, Section 1, establishes the **full faith and credit clause**, stipulating that each state is normally expected to honor the "public Acts, Records, and judicial Proceedings" that take place in any other state. So, for example, if a person has a restraining order placed on a stalker or batterer in one state, the other states are required to enforce that order as if they had issued it.

Previously a state-level policy, same-sex marriage was declared a fundamental right nationwide by the Supreme Court in 2015. The decision prompted a brief backlash when clerks in some states refused to issue marriage licenses to same-sex couples.

Until recently, the full faith and credit clause was embroiled in the controversy over same-sex marriage. In 2004, Massachusetts became the first state to legalize gay marriage. By 2015, 37 states plus the District of Columbia had legalized gay marriage, and 13 states had either state constitutional amendments or laws that barred same-sex marriage.[2] The principle of full faith and credit would seem to suggest that states without gay marriage would be obliged to recognize such unions in their states, just as they would recognize heterosexual marriages performed in other states. But to forestall this possibility, in 1996, Congress passed the Defense of Marriage Act (DOMA), which declared that states did not have to recognize same-sex marriage even if it were legal in other states. DOMA also said that the federal government would not recognize gay marriage, even if legal in some states, and that same-sex partners were not eligible for federal benefits such as Medicare and Social Security. In 2013, however, the Supreme Court in *United States v. Windsor* struck down part of the DOMA, ordering that same-sex married couples receive equal treatment on issues relating to taxes, inheritance, and other federal laws.[3] It also opened the door for same-sex couples to receive federal social benefits on the same terms as heterosexual married couples. The court did not rule on whether states have to recognize same-sex marriages in other states.

In 2015, however, the Supreme Court ruled that the Fourteenth Amendment guaranteed a fundamental right to same-sex marriage. The case, *Obergefell v. Hodges*, combined four lawsuits by same-sex couples challenging their home states' refusals to grant same-sex marriage licenses or recognize same-sex marriages performed out-of-state. While 37 states recognized same-sex marriage on the eve of the *Obergefell* announcement, the Court's 5–4 decision immediately required that all 50 states must offer marriage licenses to two people of the same sex and recognize same-sex marriages licensed out of state. In one stroke, same-sex marriage turned from a state-level policy choice to a nationally recognized right. In the aftermath of the *Obergefell* decision, several of the 13 states that were mandated to lift their bans on same-sex marriage protested the ruling. Ken Paxton, the attorney general of Texas, for example, called the decision "unlawful" and pledged to provide legal assistance to local officials who refused to carry out the new law.[4] However, such resistance ebbed as it became clear that the courts would enforce the constitutional right to same-sex marriage.

Article IV, Section 2, known as the "comity clause," also seeks to promote national unity. This clause provides that citizens enjoying the "**privileges and immunities**" of one state should be entitled to similar treatment in other states. What this has come to mean is that a state cannot discriminate against someone from another state or give special privileges to its own residents. For example, in the 1970s, when Alaska passed a law that gave residents preference over nonresidents in obtaining work on the state's oil and gas pipelines, the Supreme Court ruled the law illegal because it discriminated against citizens of other states.[5] The comity clause also regulates criminal justice among the states by requiring states to return fugitives to the states from which they have fled. Thus, in 1952, when an inmate escaped from an Alabama prison and sought to avoid being returned to Alabama on the grounds that he was being subjected to "cruel and unusual punishment" there, the Supreme Court ruled that he must be returned according to Article IV, Section 2.[6]

Local Government and the Constitution Local government occupies a peculiar but very important place in the American system. In fact, the status of American local government is probably unique in world experience. First, local government has no status in the U.S. Constitution and is therefore an authority or function under the control of the states. *State* legislatures created local governments, and *state* constitutions and laws permit local governments to take on some of the responsibilities of the state governments. Most states amended their constitutions to give their larger cities **home rule**, powers delegated by the state to a local unit of government to manage its own affairs. But local governments enjoy no such recognition in the federal Constitution. Local governments have always been creatures of the states.[7]

Local governments became administratively important in the early years of the Republic because the states relied on local governments (cities and counties) to implement the laws of the state. Local government was an alternative to a statewide bureaucracy (see Table 3.1).

TABLE 3.1

90,107 Governments in the United States

TYPE	NUMBER
National	1
State	50
County	3,031
Municipal	19,519
Townships	16,360
School districts	12,880
Other special districts	38,266

SOURCE: U.S. Census Bureau, www2.census.gov/govs/cog /g12_org.pdf (accessed 11/02/13).

The Definition of Federalism Has Changed Radically over Time

Trace developments in the federal framework leading to a stronger national government

Many of the fiercest political controversies in American history have revolved around competing views of federalism. The best way to understand these disputes, and how federalism has been redefined throughout American history, is to examine how its conception has changed over time. During the "traditional system" in America, from 1789 to 1937, the political scales clearly favored the states over the federal government. (We call it the "traditional system" because it covered much of American history and because it closely approximated the intentions of the framers of the Constitution.) Then, from the New Deal period of the 1930s to the present, some important limits were placed on state governments and the federal government exerted far more power than it had under the traditional system, despite efforts to roll back national government powers in recent decades.

Federalism under the "Traditional System" Gave Most Powers to the States

The prevailing view of national government–state government relations under the traditional system was one of **dual federalism**, in which most fundamental governmental powers were shared between the federal and state governments. During this time, the states possessed a vast amount of governing power, and virtually all of the important policies affecting the lives of Americans were made by the state governments. For evidence, look at Table 3.2, which lists the major types of public policies by which Americans were governed for the first century and a half under the Constitution. Under the traditional system, the national government was quite small by comparison both with the state governments and with the governments of other Western nations. It was not only smaller than most governments of that time but also very narrowly specialized in the functions it performed. The national government built or sponsored the construction of roads, canals, and bridges (internal improvements). It provided cash subsidies to shippers and shipbuilders and distributed free or low-priced public land to encourage western settlement and business ventures. It placed relatively heavy taxes on imported goods (tariffs), not only to raise revenues but also to protect "infant industries" from competition from the more advanced European enterprises. It protected patents and provided for a common currency, which encouraged and facilitated enterprises and helped to expand markets.

What do these functions of the national government reveal? First, virtually all the national government's functions were aimed at assisting commerce. It is quite appropriate to refer to the traditional American system as a "commercial republic." Second, virtually none of the national government's policies directly coerced citizens. The emphasis of governmental programs was on assistance, promotion, and encouragement—the allocation of land or capital to meet the needs of economic development.

TABLE 3.2

The Federal System: Specialization of Governmental Functions in the Traditional System, 1789–1937

NATIONAL GOVERNMENT POLICIES (DOMESTIC)	STATE GOVERNMENT POLICIES	LOCAL GOVERNMENT POLICIES
Internal improvements	Property laws (including slavery)	Adaptation of state laws to local conditions
Subsidies		
Tariffs	Estate and inheritance laws	Public works
Public land disposal	Commerce laws	Contracts for public works
Patents	Banking and credit laws	
Currency	Corporate laws	Licensing of public accommodation
	Insurance laws	Zoning and other land-use regulation
	Family laws	
	Morality laws	Basic public services
	Public health laws	
	Education laws	
	General penal laws	
	Eminent domain laws	
	Construction codes	
	Land-use laws	
	Water and mineral laws	
	Criminal procedure laws	
	Electoral and political party laws	
	Local government laws	
	Civil service laws	
	Occupations and professions laws	

Meanwhile, state legislatures were also actively involved in economic regulation during the nineteenth century. In the United States, then and now, private property exists only in state laws and state court decisions regarding property, trespass, and real estate. American capitalism took its form from state property and trespass laws and from state laws and court decisions regarding contracts, markets, credit, banking, incorporation, and insurance. Laws concerning slavery were a subdivision of property law in states where slavery existed. The practice of important professions, such as law and medicine, was (and is) illegal except as provided for by state law. To educate or not to educate a child has been a decision governed more by state laws than by parents. It is important to note also that most criminal laws, from trespass to murder, have been state laws. Thus, most of the fundamental governing in the United States was done by the states.

Ultimately, the fundamental impact of federalism on the way the United States is governed comes not from any particular provision of the Constitution but from the framework itself, which has determined the flow of government functions and, through that, the political development of the country. By allowing state governments to do most of the fundamental governing, the Constitution saved the national government from many policy decisions that might have proved too divisive for a large and very young country. There is little doubt that if the Constitution had provided for a unitary system rather than a federal system, the war over slavery would have come in 1789 or not long thereafter; and if it had come that early, the South might very well have seceded and established a separate and permanent slaveholding nation.

In helping the national government remain small and apart from the most divisive issues of the day, federalism contributed significantly to the political stability of the young nation, even as the social, economic, and political systems of many of the states and regions of the country were undergoing tremendous, profound, and sometimes violent change.[8] As we shall see, some important aspects of federalism have changed, but the federal framework has survived over two centuries and through a devastating civil war.

The Supreme Court Paved the Way for the End of the "Traditional System"

As the nation grew, disputes arose about the powers of the federal government versus the powers of the states. In the first several decades after the Founding, the Supreme Court decided several critical cases that expanded federal powers and facilitated trade across the states. These decisions removed barriers to trade in the new nation and laid the groundwork for a national economy. However, by the end of the nineteenth century, as reformers began to enact laws regulating businesses through such measures as child labor restrictions, the Court took a much more restrictive view of federal power. Not until well into the New Deal, in 1937, did the federal government gain the expansive powers it exercises today.

Article I, Section 8, of the Constitution delegates to Congress the power "to regulate Commerce with foreign Nations, and among the several States and with the Indian Tribes." For most of the nineteenth century, the Supreme Court consistently interpreted this **commerce clause** in favor of national power over the economy. The first and most important such case was *McCulloch v. Maryland* (1819), which involved the question of whether Congress had the power to charter a national bank as such an explicit grant of power was nowhere to be found in Article I, Section 8.[9] Chief Justice John Marshall answered that this power could be "implied" from other powers that were expressly delegated to Congress, such as the "powers to lay and collect taxes; to borrow money; to regulate commerce; and to declare and conduct a war."

By allowing Congress to use the necessary and proper clause to interpret its delegated powers expansively, the Supreme Court created the potential for an unprecedented increase in national government power. Marshall also concluded that whenever a state law conflicted with a federal law (as in the case of *McCulloch v. Maryland*), the state law would be deemed invalid since the Constitution states that "the Laws of the United States . . . shall be the supreme Law of the Land." Both parts of this great case are pro-national, including the verification of the principle of "national supremacy," yet Congress did not immediately seek to expand the policies of the national government.

Another major case, *Gibbons v. Ogden* (1824), reinforced this nationalistic interpretation of the Constitution. The important but relatively narrow issue was whether the state of New York could grant a monopoly to Robert Fulton's steamboat company to operate an exclusive service between New York and New Jersey. Chief Justice Marshall argued that New York state did not have the power to grant this particular monopoly. In reaching this decision, Marshall had to define what Article I, Section 8, meant by "commerce among the several states." He insisted that the definition was "comprehensive," extending to "every species of commercial intercourse." However, this comprehensiveness was limited "to that commerce which concerns more states than one." *Gibbons* is important because it established the supremacy of the national government in all matters affecting what later came to be called "interstate commerce."[10] But the precise meaning of interstate commerce would remain uncertain during several decades of constitutional discourse.

Backed by the implied powers and national supremacy decision in *McCulloch* and by the broad definition of "interstate commerce" in *Gibbons*, Article I, Section 8, was a source of power for the national government as long as Congress sought to facilitate commerce through subsidies, services, and land grants. Later in the nineteenth century, though, the Supreme Court declared any effort of the national government to *regulate* commerce in such areas as fraud, the production of substandard goods, the use of child labor, or the existence of dangerous working conditions or long hours to be unconstitutional as a violation of the concept of interstate commerce. Such legislation meant that the federal government was entering the factory and the workplace—local areas—and was attempting to regulate goods that had not yet passed into interstate commerce. To enter these local workplaces was to exercise police power—a power reserved to the states. No one questioned the power of the national government to regulate businesses that intrinsically involved interstate commerce, such as railroads, gas pipelines, and waterway transportation. But well into the twentieth century, the Supreme Court used the concept of interstate commerce as a barrier against most efforts by Congress to regulate local conditions.

This interpretation of federalism gave the American economy a freedom from federal government control that closely approximated the ideal of free enterprise. The economy was never entirely free, of course; in fact, entrepreneurs themselves did not want complete freedom from government. They needed law and order. They needed a stable currency. They needed courts and police to enforce contracts and prevent trespass. They needed roads, canals, and railroads. But federalism, as interpreted by the Supreme Court for 70 years after the Civil War, made it possible for business to have its cake and eat it, too. Entrepreneurs enjoyed the benefits of national policies facilitating commerce but were shielded by the courts from policies that regulate commerce by protecting the rights of consumers and workers.[11] In addition, the Tenth Amendment was used to bolster arguments about **states' rights**, the principle that the states should oppose the increasing authority of the national government. This principle was most popular in the period before the Civil War.

In the early twentieth century, however, the Tenth Amendment appeared to lose its force as reformers began to press for national regulations to limit the power of large corporations and to protect the health and welfare of citizens, as we shall see next.

FDR's New Deal Remade the Government

The New Deal of the 1930s marked a major change in how the courts interpreted national power. The door to increased federal action opened when states proved unable to cope with the demands brought on by the Great Depression. Before the depression, states and localities took responsibility for addressing the needs of the poor, usually through private charity. But the extent of the need created by the depression quickly exhausted local and state capacities. By 1932, 25 percent of the workforce was unemployed. The jobless lost their homes and settled into camps all over the country, called "Hoovervilles" after President Herbert Hoover. Elected in 1928, the year before the depression hit, Hoover steadfastly maintained that there was little the federal government could do to alleviate these people's misery caused by the depression. It was a matter for state and local governments, he said.

Yet demands mounted for the federal government to take action. When Franklin Delano Roosevelt took office in 1933, he energetically threw the federal government into the business of fighting the depression through a number of proposals known collectively as the New Deal. He proposed a variety of temporary measures to provide federal relief and work programs. Most of the programs he proposed were to be financed by the federal government but administered by the states. In addition to these temporary measures, Roosevelt presided over the creation of several important federal programs designed to provide future economic security for Americans. The New Deal signaled the rise of a more active national government.

For the most part, the new national programs that the Roosevelt administration developed did not directly take power away from the states. Instead, Washington

John C. Calhoun, one of the most prominent advocates of states' rights, argued that states should have the right to veto any federal law they found to be unconstitutional.

The New Deal expanded the scope of the federal government. One of the largest and most effective New Deal programs, the Works Progress Administration, employed millions of Americans in public-works projects such as constructing highways, bridges, and public parks.

typically redirected states by offering them **grants-in-aid**, programs through which Congress provided money to state and local governments on the condition that the funds be employed for purposes defined by the federal government.

Franklin Roosevelt did not invent the idea of grants-in-aid, but his New Deal vastly expanded the range of grants-in-aid to include social programs, providing grants to the states for financial assistance to poor children. Congress added more grants after World War II, creating new programs to help states fund activities such as providing school lunches and building highways. Sometimes the national government required state or local governments to match the national contribution dollar for dollar, but in some programs, such as the development of the interstate highway system, the congressional grants provided 90 percent of the cost.

These types of federal grants-in-aid are called **categorical grants** because they are given to states and localities by the national government on the condition that expenditures be limited to a problem or group specified by law. For the most part, the categorical grants created before the 1960s simply helped the states perform their traditional functions.[12] In the 1960s, however, the national role expanded and federal funding in the form of categorical grants increased dramatically (see Figure 3.1). For example, during the 89th Congress (1965–66) alone, the number of categorical grant-in-aid programs grew from 221 to 379.[13] The *value* of categorical grants also has risen dramatically, from $2.3 billion in 1950 to an estimated $667 billion in 2016. The grants authorized during the 1960s addressed national purposes much more strongly than did earlier grants. One of the most important—and expensive—was the federal Medicaid program, which provides states with grants to pay for medical care for the poor, the disabled, and many nursing home residents.

Changing Court Interpretations of Federalism Helped the New Deal While Preserving States' Rights

In a dramatic change beginning in 1937, the Supreme Court threw out the old distinction between interstate and intrastate commerce on which it had relied in the late 1800s and early 1900s. It converted the commerce clause from a source of limitations to a source of power for the national government. The Court began to refuse to review appeals that challenged acts of Congress protecting the rights of

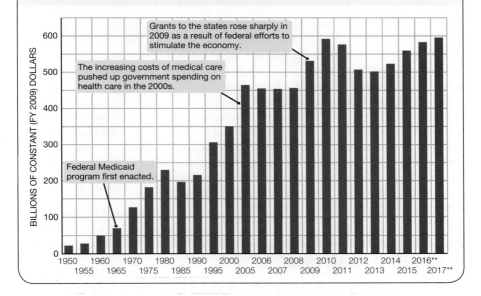

FIGURE 3.1 Historical Trend of Federal Grants-in-Aid,* 1950–2017

Spending on federal grants-in-aid to the states and local governments has grown dramatically since 1990. These increases reflect the growing public expectations about what government should do. What has been the most important cause of the steady increase in these grants?

*Excludes outlays for national defense and international affairs.
**Data for 2016 and 2017 are estimated.

SOURCE: Office of Management and Budget, U.S. Budget for Fiscal Year 2017, "Historical Tables: Table 12.2—Total Outlays for Grants to State and Local Governments, by Function and Fund Group: 1940–2021" and "Table 10.1—Gross Domestic Product and Deflators Used in the Historical Tables: 1940–2021," www.whitehouse.gov/omb/budget /Historicals (accessed 4/12/16).

employees to organize and engage in collective bargaining, regulating the amount of farmland in cultivation, extending low-interest credit to small businesses and farmers, and restricting the activities of corporations dealing in the stock market; it upheld many other laws that contributed to the construction of the modern "welfare state."[14]

The Court also reversed its position on the Tenth Amendment, which it had used to strike down national laws as violations of state power. Instead, the Court approved numerous expansions of national power, to such an extent that the Tenth Amendment appeared irrelevant. In fact, in 1941, Justice Harlan Fiske Stone declared that the Tenth Amendment was simply a "truism" that had no real meaning.[15]

Yet the idea that some powers should be reserved to the states did not go away. Indeed, in the 1950s, southern opponents of the civil rights movement revived the idea of states' rights. In 1956, 96 southern members of Congress issued a "Southern Manifesto" in which they declared that southern states were not constitutionally bound by Supreme Court decisions outlawing racial segregation. They believed that states' rights should override individual rights to liberty and formal equality. With the triumph of the civil rights movement, the slogan of "states' rights" became tarnished by its association with racial inequality.

The 1990s saw a revival of interest in the Tenth Amendment and important Supreme Court decisions limiting federal power. Much of the interest in the Tenth Amendment stemmed from conservatives who believe that a strong federal government encroaches on individual liberties. They believed such freedoms were better protected by returning more power to the states through the process of **devolution**, whereby a program is removed from one level of government by delegating it or passing it down to a lower level of government, such as from the national government to the state and local governments. In 1996, Republican presidential candidate Bob Dole carried a copy of the Tenth Amendment in his pocket as he campaigned, pulling it out to read at rallies.[16] The Supreme Court's 1995 ruling in *United States v. Lopez* fueled further interest in the Tenth Amendment. In that case, the Court, stating that Congress had exceeded its authority under the commerce clause, struck down a federal law that barred handguns near schools.[17] This was the first time since the New Deal that the Court had limited congressional powers in this way. In 1997 the Court again relied on the Tenth Amendment to limit federal power in *Printz v. United States*.[18] The decision declared unconstitutional a provision of the Brady Handgun Violence Prevention Act that required state and local law-enforcement officials to conduct background checks on handgun purchasers. The Court declared that this provision violated state sovereignty guaranteed in the Tenth Amendment because it required state and local officials to administer a federal regulatory program.

Cooperative Federalism Pushes States to Achieve National Goals

The growth of categorical grants, along with favorable court rulings, created a new kind of federalism. If the traditional system of two sovereigns performing highly different functions could be called dual federalism, historians of federalism suggest that the system since the New Deal could be called **cooperative federalism**, in which grants-in-aid have been used strategically to encourage states and localities to pursue nationally defined goals, with national and state governments sharing powers and resources via intergovernmental cooperation. One political scientist, Morton Grodzins, characterized this as a move from "layer cake federalism" to "marble cake federalism,"[19] in which intergovernmental cooperation and sharing have blurred a once-clear distinguishing line, making it difficult to say where the national government ends and the state and local governments begin (see Figure 3.2).

For a while in the 1960s, it appeared as if the state governments would become increasingly irrelevant to American federalism. Many of the new federal grants bypassed the states and instead sent money directly to local governments and even to local nonprofit organizations. The theme heard repeatedly in Washington was that the states simply could not be trusted to carry out national purposes.[20]

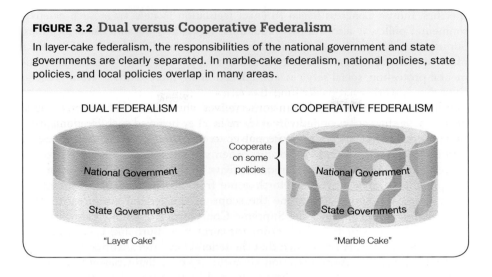

FIGURE 3.2 Dual versus Cooperative Federalism

In layer-cake federalism, the responsibilities of the national government and state governments are clearly separated. In marble-cake federalism, national policies, state policies, and local policies overlap in many areas.

One of the reasons that Washington distrusted the states was the way African American citizens were treated in the South. The southern states' forthright defense of segregation, justified on the grounds of states' rights, helped tarnish the image of the states as the civil rights movement gained momentum. The national officials who planned the War on Poverty during the 1960s pointed to the racial exclusion practiced in the southern states as a reason for bypassing state governments. Political scientist James Sundquist described how the "Alabama syndrome" affected the War on Poverty: "In the drafting of the Economic Opportunity Act, an 'Alabama syndrome' developed. Any suggestion within the poverty task force that the states be given a role in the administration of the act was met with the question, 'Do you want to give that kind of power to [then–Alabama governor] George Wallace?'"[21] (Wallace at the time was nationally known for his virulent opposition to the civil rights movement.)

Yet even though many national policies of the 1960s bypassed the states, other new programs, such as Medicaid, relied on state governments for their implementation. In addition, as the national government expanded existing programs run by the states, states had to take on more responsibilities. These new responsibilities meant that the states were now playing a very important role in the federal system.

National Standards Have Been Advanced through Federal Programs

Over time, the Supreme Court has pushed for greater uniformity in rules and procedures across the states. In addition to legal decisions, the national government uses two other tools to create similarities across the states: grants-in-aid and regulations.

Grants-in-aid, as we have seen, are incentives: Congress gives money to state and local governments if they agree to spend it for the purposes Congress specifies. But as Congress began to enact legislation in new areas, such as environmental policy, it also imposed additional *regulations* on states and localities. Some political scientists call this a move toward regulated federalism.[22] The effect of these national standards is that state and local policies in the areas of environmental protection, social services, and education are more uniform from coast to coast than are other nationally funded policies.

Some national standards require the federal government to take over areas of regulation formerly overseen by state or local governments. Such **preemption** (the principle that allows the national government to override state or local actions in certain policy areas) occurs when state and local actions are found to be inconsistent with federal requirements. If this occurs, all regulations in the preempted area must henceforth come from the national government. In many cases, the courts determine the scope of the federal authority to preempt. For example, in 1973 the Supreme Court struck down a local ordinance prohibiting jets from taking off from the airport in Burbank, California, between 11 P.M. and 7 A.M. It ruled that the federal Civil Aeronautics Act granted the Federal Aviation Administration all authority over flight patterns, takeoffs, and landings and that local governments could not impose regulations in this area. As federal regulations increased after the 1970s, Washington increasingly preempted state and local action in many different policy areas. This preemption has escalated since 1994, when Republicans gained control of Congress. Although the Republicans came to power promising to grant more responsibility to the states, they reduced state control in many areas by preemption. For example, in 1998, Congress passed a law that prohibited states and localities from taxing Internet access services. The 1996 Telecommunications Act reduced local control by giving broadcasters and digital companies broad discretion over where they could erect digital television and cellular phone towers even if local citizens objected.[23]

In 2009, after only a few months in office, President Obama reversed the Bush administration's use of federal regulations to limit state laws. Under the new policy, federal regulations should preempt state laws only in extraordinary cases. The president directed agency leaders to review the regulations that had been put in place over the past 10 years and consider amending them if they interfered with the "legitimate prerogatives of the states."[24] But as we will see later in this chapter, the Obama administration did use its power of preemption to challenge state immigration laws, charging that states were making laws in a domain reserved for federal authority.

The growth of national standards has created some new problems and has raised questions about how far federal standardization should go. One problem that emerged in the 1980s was the increase in **unfunded mandates**—regulations or new conditions for receiving grants that impose costs on state and local governments for which they are not reimbursed by the national government. The growth of unfunded mandates was the product of a Democratic Congress, which wanted to achieve liberal social objectives, and Republican presidents who opposed increased social spending. Between 1983 and 1991, Congress mandated standards in many policy areas, including social services and environmental regulations, without providing additional funds to meet those standards. Altogether, Congress enacted

Government Spending in Federal and Unitary Systems

A key difference between unitary and federal systems of government is in the amount of power that is reserved for state and local governments. In federal systems, subnational units are given considerable taxation and spending power, whereas the federal (or central) government carries out most of these tasks in unitary systems.

The graph here shows the percentage of total government expenditures by the central government and by the state and/or local governments. The central governments of France, the United Kingdom, and New Zealand, all unitary countries, spend a larger percentage than federal countries such as Mexico and the United States.

South Korea is a unitary country where local governments operate under a great deal of autonomy, carrying out many of the country's administrative functions. Local government spending in South Korea is thus higher than in many unitary countries, and, as a result, its spending behavior falls somewhere in the middle of the federal–unitary divide. This example shows that while the distinction between federalism and unitary systems is important, it is not the only factor in determining who holds power in a country.

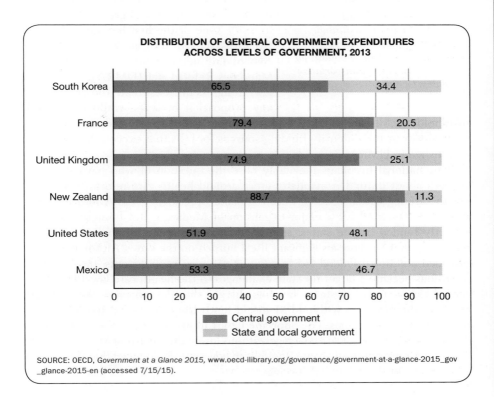

DISTRIBUTION OF GENERAL GOVERNMENT EXPENDITURES ACROSS LEVELS OF GOVERNMENT, 2013

Country	Central government	State and local government
South Korea	65.5	34.4
France	79.4	20.5
United Kingdom	74.9	25.1
New Zealand	88.7	11.3
United States	51.9	48.1
Mexico	53.3	46.7

SOURCE: OECD, *Government at a Glance 2015*, www.oecd-ilibrary.org/governance/government-at-a-glance-2015_gov _glance-2015-en (accessed 7/15/15).

The federal government frequently passes laws that impose mandates on the states, such as the 1990 Americans with Disabilities Act, which protects against discrimination based on disability. States were required to pay for changes to meet federal standards for accessibility in public transportation and public facilities.

27 laws that imposed new regulations or required states to expand existing programs.[25] For example, the 1973 Rehabilitation Act prohibited discrimination against the disabled in programs that were partly funded by the federal government. The new law required state and local governments to make public transit accessible to disabled people with wheelchair lifts in buses, elevators in train stations, and special transportation systems where needed. These requirements were estimated to cost state and local governments $6.8 billion over 30 years.[26] But Congress did not supply additional funding to help states meet these new requirements; the states had to shoulder the increased financial burden themselves. States complained that mandates took up so much of their budgets that they were not able to set their own priorities.[27]

These burdens became part of a rallying cry to reduce the power of the federal government—a cry that took center stage when a Republican Congress was elected in 1994. One of the first measures the new Congress passed was an act to limit the cost of unfunded mandates, the Unfunded Mandates Reform Act (UMRA). Under this law, Congress must estimate the expense for any proposal it believes would exceed the threshold established in UMRA ($76 million in 2014, adjusted for inflation). Congress must then identify funding sources for bills that exceed the threshold established in UMRA.

New national problems inevitably raise the question of who pays. Recently, concern about unfunded mandates arose around health care reform. The major health care legislation enacted during Obama's presidency, the Affordable Care Act of 2010, called for a major expansion of Medicaid. But because Medicaid is partly funded by the states, any major increase in the number of Medicaid recipients could impose a significant fiscal burden on the states. Although the law provided additional federal aid to support the new requirements, the Medicaid provisions became a target for state challenges to the health care law. One of the central claims in the 26 states' lawsuits charged that the federal government did not have the power to withhold Medicaid funds from states that did not implement the new expansions. The Supreme Court ultimately ruled that states could decline to expand Medicaid coverage without losing their existing Medicaid funds. After the Court's decision, some Republican governors announced that they would not implement the expanded coverage.

New Federalism Means More State Control

Analyze the developments in the federal framework since the 1970s

Since the 1970s, as states have become more capable of administering large-scale programs, the idea of devolution—transferring responsibility for policy from the federal government to the states and localities—has become popular.

Proponents of more state authority have looked to **block grants** as a way of reducing federal control. Block grants are federal grants-in-aid that allow states considerable discretion in how the funds are spent. President Richard Nixon led the first push for block grants in the early 1970s. Nixon's approach consolidated programs in the areas of job training, community development, and social services into three large block grants. These grants imposed some conditions on states and localities as to how the money should be spent but avoided the narrow regulations contained in the categorical grants discussed earlier. In addition, Congress approved a fourth block grant called **general revenue sharing**, whereby the federal government provided money to local governments and counties with no strings attached; localities could spend the money as they wished. In enacting revenue sharing, Washington acknowledged both the critical role that state and local governments play in implementing national priorities and their need for increased funding and enhanced flexibility in order to carry out that role (see Figure 3.3). Ronald Reagan's version of **New Federalism**

The debate over national versus state control of speed limits arose in 1973, when gas prices skyrocketed and supplies became scarce. Drivers nationwide were forced to wait in long lines at gas stations. The federal government responded to the gas crisis by instituting a national 55-mile-per-hour speed limit.

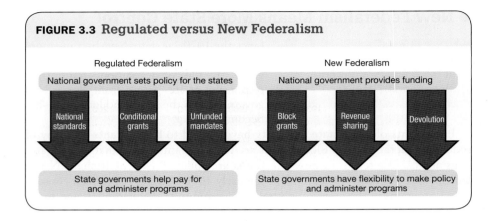

FIGURE 3.3 Regulated versus New Federalism

Regulated Federalism

National government sets policy for the states

| National standards | Conditional grants | Unfunded mandates |

State governments help pay for and administer programs

New Federalism

National government provides funding

| Block grants | Revenue sharing | Devolution |

State governments have flexibility to make policy and administer programs

(returning power to the states through block grants) similarly aimed to reduce the national government's control. In all, Congress created 12 new block grants between 1981 and 1990.[28]

But this new approach, like those that preceded it, has not provided magic solutions to the problems of federalism. For one thing, there is always a trade-off between accountability—that is, whether the states are using funds for the purposes intended—and flexibility. If the objective is to have accountable and efficient government, it is not clear that state bureaucracies are any more efficient or more capable than national agencies. In Mississippi, for example, the state Department of Human Services spent money from the child care block grant for office furniture and designer salt and pepper shakers that cost $37.50 a pair. As one Mississippi state legislator said, "I've seen too many years of good ol' boy politics to know they shouldn't [transfer money to the states] without stricter controls and requirements."[29] Even after block grants were created, Congress reimposed regulations in order to increase the states' accountability.

At times the federal government has also moved to limit state discretion over spending in cases where it thinks states are too generous. For example, in 2007, President Bush issued regulations that prevented states from providing benefits under the State Child Health Insurance Program (SCHIP) to children in families well above the poverty line. The Bush administration also barred states from providing chemotherapy to illegal immigrants, who are guaranteed emergency medical treatment under Medicaid.[30]

There Is No Simple Answer to Finding the Right National–State Balance

As Figure 3.4 indicates, federalism has changed dramatically over the course of American history, even over just the past several decades. Finding the right balance among states and the federal government is an evolving challenge for American democracy. In recent years, many of the most controversial issues in American politics—including the appropriate size of public social spending, the rights and benefits of immigrants (legal as well as undocumented), what government should

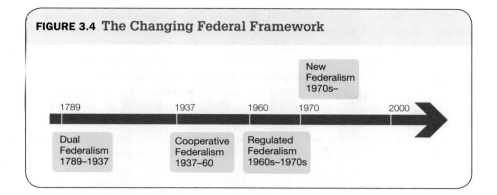

FIGURE 3.4 The Changing Federal Framework

New Federalism 1970s–

1789   1937   1960   1970   2000

Dual Federalism 1789–1937

Cooperative Federalism 1937–60

Regulated Federalism 1960s–1970s

do in response to climate change, and whether and how government should regulate business and moral behavior—have been fought out through the federal system. Politicians of all stripes regularly turn to the federal government to override decisions made by states. Likewise, when the federal government proves unable or unwilling to act, activists and politicians try to achieve their goals in states and localities. In many cases, it is up to the courts to decide which level of government should have the final say.

Although conservatives proclaim their preference for a small federal government and their support for more state autonomy, in fact, they often expand the federal government and limit state autonomy. President George W. Bush, for example, expanded federal control and increased spending in various policy areas. The 2001 No Child Left Behind Act, passed with Democratic support, introduced unprecedented federal intervention in public education, traditionally a state and local responsibility. New detailed federal testing requirements stipulating how states should treat failing schools were major expansions of federal authority in education. When a number of states threatened to defy some of the new federal requirements, Bush's Department of Education relaxed its tough stance and became more flexible in enforcing the act. But the administration did not back down entirely, leading to several legal challenges to different aspects of the law.

In the Supreme Court, too, many decisions supported a stronger federal role over the states. Decisions to uphold the federal Family and Medical Leave Act and the Americans with Disabilities Act asserted federal authority against state claims of immunity from the acts. In one important 2005 case, the Court upheld the right of Congress to ban medical marijuana, even though 11 states had legalized its use. Overturning a lower court ruling that said Congress did not have authority to regulate marijuana when it had been grown for noncommercial purposes in a single state, the Supreme Court ruled that the federal government did have the power to regulate use of all marijuana under the commerce clause. Even so, as we have seen, by 2016, 26 states and the District of Columbia had legalized medical marijuana, and a few states have now gone further to legalize its recreational use. Although the federal government has not endorsed these laws, it has made prosecution of marijuana in these states a low priority.

In other policy areas, states and localities have forged their own policies because the federal government has not acted. One of the most controversial of these issues is immigration legislation. In the first half of 2013, for example, state legislatures enacted 377 laws and resolutions related to immigration.[31] Many state and local laws that govern immigration are not controversial, but some raise critical questions about the federal government's role as opposed to the responsibilities of state and local governments. In 2010, Arizona enacted an extremely controversial immigration measure requiring immigrants to carry identity documents and requiring police to ask about immigration status when they stop drivers they suspect of being illegal immigrants. The federal Department of Justice joined several other groups in challenging the law. In the words of then–attorney general Eric Holder, "It is clearly unconstitutional for a state to set its own immigration policy."[32] In 2012 the Supreme Court ruled that Arizona's law did not preempt federal authority to make immigration law.[33] The court's decision in *Arizona v. United States* did overturn three of four provisions in Arizona's law, but it ruled in favor of the most controversial provision, which allows state police to check the immigration status of anyone stopped or arrested.

Immigration policy once again became embroiled in federal–state conflict after 2014. Frustrated by congressional inaction on immigration, President Obama issued an executive order that would provide temporary legal status to those who had been brought to the United States as children and would extend legal status to the parents of U.S. citizens and legal residents. Approximately 5 million undocumented immigrants could receive work permits under the new program.

The federal government brought Arizona to court over law SB1070, which imposed strict requirements on immigrants. The Supreme Court found that three provisions of the law were preempted by federal law, meaning Arizona did not have the authority to make the regulation. However, the controversial "show me your papers" provision of the law was upheld.

However, led by Texas, 26 states challenged the executive order in court, charging that it exceeded executive authority and would impose unreasonable costs on states. The program was never implemented because the Supreme Court, in the wake of the death of Justice Antonin Scalia, deadlocked in a 4–4 decision, leaving in place lower-court decisions that sided with the states.[34]

Obama also announced the termination of the controversial Secure Communities program in 2014. Initially launched in 2008, Secure Communities required state and local authorities to check the fingerprints of people being booked into jail against a Homeland Security database. The policy led to a record number of deportations, leading several states and localities to pull out of the agreement with the federal government on the grounds that the law was detaining too many undocumented immigrants who had never committed a crime. The administration softened its deportation policy in 2011, but sustained opposition as well as federal court decisions that challenged the constitutionality of elements of the policy ultimately led the government to end the program in late 2014. In its place, the Obama administration launched the Priority Enforcement Program in July 2015, which adopts a more limited deportation policy than the one formerly mandated by Secure Communities.[35]

In some ways, the Obama White House signaled that it would allow the states more leeway for action than they had under the Bush administration. This was particularly true in the domains of social policy and the environment when states sought to enact laws more stringent than those of the federal government. In the memo reversing the Bush policy of preemption, the White House noted, "Throughout our history, State and local governments have frequently protected health, safety, and the environment more aggressively than has the national Government."[36]

The most significant Obama law to affect the states was the 2010 health care overhaul. One controversial part of that legislation required states to expand their Medicaid programs to cover more low-income residents and to offer them additional services. As we saw earlier, the Supreme Court's 2012 ruling in *National Federation of Independent Business v. Sebelius* that the federal government could not impose all-or-nothing conditions on the states—implement the expansion or lose all Medicaid funding—represented a new limit on the national government's power. The ruling mostly upheld the law but also gave the states more leeway. The other controversial provision of the Affordable Care Act was the "individual mandate," the requirement that individuals without health care insurance be required to purchase such insurance. The 26 states suing the federal government charged that Congress had no power to force individuals to purchase a product and that it had exceeded its power under the commerce clause. In defending the law, the federal government argued the opposite: that the complex interactions of the health care market made the individual mandate constitutional under the commerce clause.[37] From the moment a person is born, he or she is part of the health care economy. Even if a person does not have health insurance, federal law requires that hospitals provide treatment in an emergency. Those costs are borne by all of the people who do pay for health insurance.

Taking a more narrow view of the health care market, the Court rejected this argument on the grounds that the federal government cannot regulate economic *in*activity, that is, the failure to purchase health insurance. Instead, it found that the Affordable Care Act was constitutional based on Congress's power to tax. The law requires individuals who do not receive insurance from their employers or their parents and are not eligible for Medicaid to purchase insurance or pay a penalty. The Court reasoned that the penalty could be considered a tax and, in that sense, passed constitutional muster. The Court placed limits on two of the key powers that have expanded the reach of the federal government since the New Deal—the power to regulate commerce and the power to spend for the general welfare.

The Affordable Care Act survived another challenge in 2015 when the Supreme Court ruled that federal subsidies to help pay for insurance should be available to residents in states that offered insurance only through the federal exchange as well as in states that had formed their own state insurance marketplaces. The outcome of *King v. Burwell* ensured that subsidies would be available in all states.[38]

Federalism
and Your Future

The connections between federalism and our fundamental national values have made federalism a focus of political contention throughout our nation's history. In recent years, sharp differences in Americans' views on many economic and social issues have been reflected in the federal system. More than half of the 50 states have legalized medical marijuana, while eight have gone further and legalized recreational marijuana. Until 2015, when the Supreme Court ruled that state-level bans on same-sex marriage were unconstitutional, 37 states allowed same-sex marriage. Some states actively welcome immigrants and seek to opt out of restrictive federal laws; other states go beyond the federal government in enacting restrictive immigration laws. Yet, while states have the authority to devise their own laws on a variety of important issues, Americans' participation in state and local politics remains low (see the "**Who Participates?**" feature on p. 89).

For young people, differences across the states provoke important questions about the future. Is the federal government endangering people by allowing states to legalize marijuana? Is it fair that a transgender person in California can legally change the sex on her birth certificate but a transgender person in Tennessee would be denied the same? Each generation confronts a different set of questions about how much variation across the states is appropriate. Are some of the issues on which the states differ fundamental rights that should be uniform across the country? As today's youth help to answer these questions in the coming decades, they will be remaking American federalism.

Who Participates in State and Local Politics?

Turnout in 2014 Election, by State

Percentage of Voting-Eligible Population*

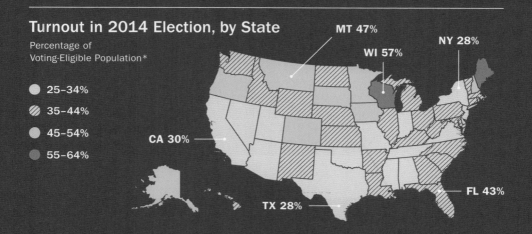

- 25–34%
- 35–44%
- 45–54%
- 55–64%

MT 47%

WI 57%

NY 28%

CA 30%

FL 43%

TX 28%

Turnout in Most Recent Municipal Election

Percentage of Voting-Age Population in Selected Cities*

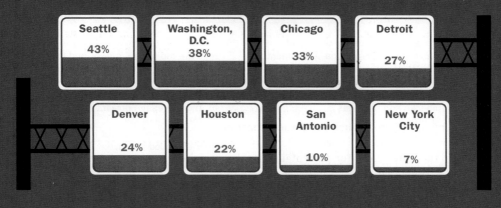

Seattle	Washington, D.C.	Chicago	Detroit
43%	38%	33%	27%

Denver	Houston	San Antonio	New York City
24%	22%	10%	7%

* The voting-eligible population excludes noncitizens and people who are institutionalized or not allowed to vote in some states because they are ex-felons. The voting-age population includes everyone over 18. SOURCES: 2014 November General Election Turnout Rates, United States Election Project, www.electproject.org/2014g (accessed 9/27/15); Voting Age Population by Citizenship and Race (CVAP), U.S. Census American Community Survey, www.census.gov/rdo/data/voting_age_population_by_citizenship_and_race_cvap.html (accessed 9/27/15).

WHAT YOU CAN DO →

WHAT YOU CAN DO

Get Involved in State and Local Politics

 Attend a board of supervisors, city council, planning commission, or other local government meeting. Agendas and minutes will usually be available on county and city websites.

 Visit the state capitol. If you make an appointment, you might be able to meet with your local representative. Committee meetings and hearings are generally open to the public, as are meetings of the legislature.

 Attend a session of your local or state judiciary. Cases on the docket are available online, as are rules for attendance and behavior when the court is in session.

chapterstudyguide

Practice Quiz

1. Which term describes the division of powers between the national government and the state governments? *(p. 67)*
   a) separation of powers
   b) federal system
   c) checks and balances
   d) expressed powers
   e) implied powers

2. Which amendment to the Constitution stated that the powers not delegated to the national government or prohibited to the states were "reserved to the states"? *(p. 68)*
   a) First Amendment
   b) Fifth Amendment
   c) Tenth Amendment
   d) Fourteenth Amendment
   e) Twenty-Sixth Amendment

3. A state government's authority to regulate the health, safety, and morals of its citizens is frequently referred to as *(p. 68)*
   a) the reserved power.
   b) the expressed power.
   c) the police power.
   d) the concurrent power.
   e) the implied power.

4. Which constitutional clause requires that states normally honor the public acts and judicial decisions of other states? *(p. 69)*
   a) privileges and immunities clause
   b) necessary and proper clause
   c) interstate commerce clause
   d) preemption clause
   e) full faith and credit clause

5. Many states have amended their constitutions to guarantee that large cities will have the authority to manage local affairs without interference from state government. This power is called *(p. 70)*
   a) home rule.
   b) preemption.
   c) devolution.
   d) states' rights.
   e) New Federalism.

6. The relationship between the states and the national government from 1789 to 1937 is known as *(p. 71)*
   a) dual federalism.
   b) regulated federalism.
   c) states' rights.
   d) cooperative federalism.
   e) New Federalism.

7. In which case did the Supreme Court create the potential for increased national power by ruling that Congress could use the necessary and proper clause to interpret its delegated powers broadly? *(p. 73)*
   a) *United States v. Lopez*
   b) *Printz v. United States*
   c) *Loving v. Virginia*
   d) *McCulloch v. Maryland*
   e) *Gibbons v. Ogden*

8. Which of the following tools has the federal government used in the past to create similarities across the states? *(p. 79)*
   a) states' rights
   b) general revenue sharing
   c) grants-in-aid
   d) eminent domain
   e) home rule

9. The process of returning more of the responsibilities of governing from the national level to the state level is known as *(p. 78)*
   a) dual federalism.
   b) devolution.

c) preemption.
d) home rule.
e) incorporation.

10. The principle that allows the federal government to take over areas of regulation formerly overseen by states or local governments is called *(p. 80)*
    a) categorical grants.
    b) devolution.
    c) formula grants.
    d) preemption.
    e) project grants.

11. When state and local governments must conform to costly regulations or conditions in order to receive grants but do not receive reimbursements for their expenditures from the federal government it is called *(p. 80)*
    a) a reciprocal grant.
    b) an unfunded mandate.
    c) general revenue sharing.
    d) a counterfunded mandate.
    e) a concurrent grant.

12. To what does the term *New Federalism* refer? *(pp. 83–84)*
    a) the era of federalism initiated by President Roosevelt during the late 1930s
    b) the national government's regulation of state action through grants-in-aid
    c) the type of federalism that uses categorical grants to influence state action
    d) efforts to return more policy-making discretion to the states through the use of block grants
    e) the recent emergence of local governments as important political actors

Key Terms

block grants *(p. 83)* federal grants-in-aid that allow states considerable discretion in how the funds are spent

categorical grants *(p. 76)* congressional grants given to states and localities on the condition that expenditures be limited to a problem or group specified by law

commerce clause *(p. 73)* Article I, Section 8, of the Constitution, which delegates to Congress the power "to regulate Commerce with foreign Nations, and among the several States and with the Indian Tribes"; this clause was interpreted by the Supreme Court in favor of national power over the economy

concurrent powers *(p. 68)* authority possessed by both state and national governments, such as the power to levy taxes

cooperative federalism *(p. 78)* a type of federalism existing since the New Deal era in which grants-in-aid have been used strategically to encourage states and localities (without commanding them) to pursue nationally defined goals; also known as "intergovernmental cooperation"

devolution *(p. 78)* a policy to remove a program from one level of government by delegating it or passing it down to a lower level of government, such as from the national government to the state and local governments

dual federalism *(p. 71)* the system of government that prevailed in the United States from 1789 to 1937 in which most fundamental governmental powers were shared between the federal and state governments

expressed powers *(p. 67)* specific powers granted by the Constitution to Congress (Article I, Section 8) and to the president (Article II)

federal system *(p. 67)* a system of government in which the national government shares power with lower levels of government such as states

federalism *(p. 67)* a system of government in which power is divided, by a constitution, between the central (national) government and regional (state) governments

full faith and credit clause *(p. 69)* provision from Article IV, Section 1, of the Constitution requiring that the states normally honor the public acts and judicial decisions that take place in another state

general revenue sharing *(p. 83)* the process by which one unit of government

yields a portion of its tax income to another unit of government, according to an established formula; revenue sharing typically involves the national government providing money to state governments

grants-in-aid *(p. 76)* programs through which Congress provides money to state and local governments on the condition that the funds be employed for purposes defined by the federal government

home rule *(p. 70)* power delegated by the state to a local unit of government to manage its own affairs

implied powers *(p. 67)* powers derived from the necessary and proper clause of Article I, Section 8, of the Constitution; such powers are not specifically expressed but are implied through the expansive interpretation of delegated powers

necessary and proper clause *(p. 67)* provision from Article I, Section 8, of the Constitution providing Congress with the authority to make all laws necessary and proper to carry out its expressed powers

New Federalism *(p. 83)* attempts by presidents Nixon and Reagan to return power to the states through block grants

police power *(p. 68)* power reserved to the state government to regulate the health, safety, and morals of its citizens

preemption *(p. 80)* the principle that allows the national government to override state or local actions in certain policy areas; in foreign policy, the willingness to strike first in order to prevent an enemy attack

privileges and immunities clause *(p. 70)* provision, from Article IV, Section 2, of the Constitution, that a state cannot discriminate against someone from another state or give its own residents special privileges

reserved powers *(p. 68)* powers, derived from the Tenth Amendment to the Constitution, that are not specifically delegated to the national government or denied to the states

states' rights *(p. 75)* the principle that the states should oppose the increasing authority of the national government; this principle was most popular in the period before the Civil War

unfunded mandates *(p. 80)* regulations or conditions for receiving grants that impose costs on state and local governments for which they are not reimbursed by the federal government

unitary system *(p. 67)* a centralized government system in which lower levels of government have little power independent of the national government

For Further Reading

Dye, Thomas R. *American Federalism: Competition among Governments.* Lexington, MA: Lexington Books, 1990.

Elazar, Daniel. *American Federalism: A View from the States.* 3rd ed. New York: Harper & Row, 1984.

Gerston, Larry N. *American Federalism: A Concise Introduction.* Armonk, NY: M. E. Sharpe, 2007.

Johnson, Kimberly S. *Governing the American State: Congress and the New Federalism, 1877–1929.* Princeton, NJ: Princeton University Press, 2007.

Kettl, Donald. *The Regulation of American Federalism.* Baltimore: Johns Hopkins University Press, 1987.

Mettler, Suzanne. *Dividing Citizens: Gender and Federalism in New Deal Public Policy.* Ithaca, NY: Cornell University Press, 1998.

Peterson, Paul E. *The Price of Federalism.* Washington, DC: Brookings Institution, 1995.

Pierceson, Jason. *Same-Sex Marriage in the United States: The Road to the Supreme Court.* Lanham, MD: Rowman and Littlefield, 2013.

Robertson, David Brian. *Federalism and the Making of America.* New York: Routledge, 2011.

Van Horn, Carl E. *The State of the States.* 4th ed. Washington, DC: CQ Press, 2005.

Zimmerman, Joseph. *Contemporary American Federalism.* 2nd ed. Albany: SUNY Press, 2009.

Though the black civil rights movement of the 1960s addressed civil and political rights, many people worry that African Americans still face structural racism in the United States. The Black Lives Matter movement gained momentum in response to a number of incidents of excessive police force against African Americans.

BLACK · LIVES · MATTE

4

Civil Liberties and Civil Rights

WHAT GOVERNMENT DOES AND WHY IT MATTERS Today in the United States, we often take for granted the liberties contained in the first 10 amendments to the Constitution, known as the Bill of Rights. In fact, few people in recorded history, including American citizens before the 1960s, have enjoyed such protections. And as we shall see in this chapter, guaranteeing the liberties articulated in the Bill of Rights to all Americans required a long struggle. As recently as the early 1960s, many of the freedoms we have today were not guaranteed. At that time, criminal suspects in state cases did not have to be informed of their rights, some states required daily Bible readings and prayers in their public schools, and some communities regularly censored material they deemed to be obscene.

Since the early 1960s the Supreme Court has expanded considerably the scope of **civil liberties**, defined as individual rights and personal freedoms with which governments may not interfere; that is, they are protections for Americans *from* the government. These liberties are constantly subject to judicial interpretation, and their provisions need to be safeguarded vigilantly, especially during times of war or a threat to national security, such as in the aftermath of the terrorist attacks of September 11, 2001.

Civil rights—protections of citizen equality provided *by* the government—have also expanded dramatically since the middle of the twentieth century, when the African American struggle for equal rights took center stage. Many goals of the civil rights movement that once aroused bitter controversy are now widely accepted as part of the American commitment to equal rights. But even today the question of what is meant by "equal rights" is hardly settled. To what extent can states mandate racial preferences in college admissions? Do transgender individuals have the right to use a public restroom based on their gender identification rather than their physical characteristics? What rights do undocumented immigrants possess? Although the United States was founded on the ideals of liberty, equality, and democracy, its history of civil rights reveals a gap between these principles and actual practice. This history also demonstrates how the struggle to attain those ideals has helped narrow this gap. The election of Barack Obama as the nation's first black president was a testament to the successes of those struggles but did not alter persistent social and economic differences across racial lines.

chaptergoals

- Explain the origins and evolution of the civil liberties in the Bill of Rights as they apply to the federal government and the states (pp. 97–100)

- Describe how the First Amendment protects freedom of religion (pp. 101–3)

- Describe how the First Amendment protects free speech and freedom of the press (pp. 103–9)

- Explore whether the Second Amendment means people have a right to own guns (pp. 109–11)

- Explain the major rights that people have if they are accused of a crime (pp. 111–15)

- Assess whether people have a right to privacy under the Constitution (pp. 116–18)

- Trace the legal developments and social movements that expanded civil rights (pp. 118–26)

- Describe how different groups have fought for and won protection of their civil rights (pp. 126–34)

- Contrast arguments for and against affirmative action (pp. 134–35)

The Origin of the Bill of Rights Lies in Those Who Opposed the Constitution

Explain the origins and evolution of the civil liberties in the Bill of Rights as they apply to the federal government and the states

When the first Congress under the newly ratified Constitution met in April 1789, the most important item of business was the proposal to add a bill of rights to the Constitution. Such a proposal had been turned down with little debate in the waning days of the Philadelphia Constitutional Convention in 1787, not because the delegates were against rights but because—as the Federalists, led by Alexander Hamilton, later argued—such a bill was "not only unnecessary in the proposed Constitution but would even be dangerous."[1] First, according to Hamilton, a bill of rights would be irrelevant to a national government that was given only delegated powers in the first place. To put restraints on "powers which are not granted" could provide a pretext for governments to claim more powers than were in fact granted: "For why declare that things shall not be done which there is no power to do?"[2] Second, the Constitution was to Hamilton and the Federalists a bill of rights in itself, containing provisions that amounted to a bill of rights without requiring additional amendments (see Table 4.1). For example, Article I, Section 9, included the right of **habeas corpus**, a court order demanding that an individual in custody be brought into court and shown the reason for detention. This prohibits the government from depriving a person of liberty without explaining the reason before a judge.

Despite the power of Hamilton's arguments, when the Constitution was submitted to the states for ratification, Antifederalists, most of whom had not been delegates in Philadelphia, picked up on the argument of Thomas Jefferson

TABLE 4.1

Rights in the Original Constitution (Not in the Bill of Rights)

CLAUSE	RIGHT ESTABLISHED
Article I, Section 9	Guarantee of habeas corpus
Article I, Section 9	Prohibition of **bills of attainder**
Article I, Section 9	Prohibition of **ex post facto laws**
Article I, Section 9	Prohibition against acceptance of titles of nobility, etc., from any foreign state
Article III	Guarantee of trial by jury in state where crime was committed
Article III	Treason defined and limited to the life of the person convicted, not to the person's heirs

(who also had not been a delegate) that the omission of a bill of rights was a major imperfection of the new Constitution. The Federalists conceded that for the document to gain ratification they would have to make an "unwritten but unequivocal pledge" to add a bill of rights.

The Bill of Rights might well have been titled the "Bill of Liberties" because the provisions that were incorporated in it were seen as defining a private sphere of personal liberty, free from governmental restrictions.[3] As Jefferson put it, a bill of rights "is what people are entitled to against every government on earth." Note the wording: *against* government. Civil liberties are *protections of citizens from* improper government action. Some of these restraints are substantive liberties, which put limits on *what* the government shall and shall not have power to do—such as establishing a religion, quartering troops in private homes without consent, or seizing private property without just compensation. Other restraints are procedural liberties, which are restraints on *how* the government is supposed to act. These procedural liberties are usually grouped under the general category of **due process of law**, which is the right of every citizen to be protected against arbitrary action by national or state governments. It first appears in the Fifth Amendment provision that "no person shall be . . . deprived of life, liberty, or property, without due process of law." For example, even though the government has the substantive power to declare certain acts to be crimes and to arrest and imprison persons who violate criminal laws, it may not do so without meticulously observing procedures designed to protect the accused person. The best-known procedural rule is that an accused person is presumed innocent until proven guilty. This rule does not question the government's power to punish someone for committing a crime; it questions only the way the government determines who committed the crime. Substantive and procedural restraints together identify the realm of civil liberties.

In contrast, civil rights are the obligations imposed on government to *take positive action* to protect citizens from any illegal actions by government agencies and by other private citizens. Civil rights did not become part of the Constitution until 1868, with the adoption of the Fourteenth Amendment, which sought to provide for each citizen "the equal protection of the laws."

The Fourteenth Amendment Nationalized the Bill of Rights through Incorporation

In the first 70 years of the country's history, the Bill of Rights was understood to apply only to the national government and not to the states. In fact, the Supreme Court said this in a decision in 1833, *Barron v. Baltimore*.[4] But the Civil War cast new light on the large question of state versus national governmental power. After the war, the Fourteenth Amendment was added to the Constitution. Part of the amendment reads as though it were meant to tell the states that they must now adhere to the Bill of Rights:

> No State shall make or enforce any law which shall abridge the privileges or immunities of citizens of the United States; nor shall any State deprive any person of life,

liberty, or property, without due process of law; nor deny to any person within its jurisdiction the equal protection of the laws.

This language sounds like an effort to extend the Bill of Rights to all citizens, wherever they might reside.[5] Yet this was not the Supreme Court's interpretation of the amendment for nearly 100 years. Within five years of ratification of the Fourteenth Amendment, the Court was making decisions as though the amendment had never been adopted.[6]

The first change in civil liberties following the adoption of the Fourteenth Amendment came in 1897, when the Supreme Court held that the due process clause of the Fourteenth Amendment did in fact prohibit states from taking property for a public use without just compensation (a protection found in the Fifth Amendment), overruling the *Barron* case.[7] However, the Supreme Court had selectively "incorporated" under the Fourteenth Amendment only the property protection provision of the Fifth Amendment and no other clause of the Fifth or any other amendment of the Bill of Rights. In other words, although according to the Fifth Amendment "due process" applied to the taking of life and liberty as well as property, only property was incorporated into the Fourteenth Amendment as a limitation on state power.

No further expansion of civil liberties via the Fourteenth Amendment occurred until 1925, when the Supreme Court held that freedom of speech is "among the fundamental personal rights and 'liberties' protected by the due process clause of the Fourteenth Amendment from impairment by the states."[8] In 1931 the Court added freedom of the press to that short list protected by the Bill of Rights from state action; by 1939 it had added freedom of assembly and petitioning the government for redress of grievances.[9] But that was as far as the Court was then willing to go.

As Table 4.2 shows, **selective incorporation**—the process by which different protections in the Bill of Rights were incorporated or applied to the states, part by part, using the Fourteenth Amendment, thus guaranteeing citizens' protection from state as well as national government—continued to occur gradually, up until 2010. The final provision of the Bill of Rights to be incorporated by the Supreme Court was the Second Amendment, which protects the right to bear arms.[10] (Incorporation is also sometimes referred to as the "absorption" or the "nationalizing" of the Bill of Rights.)

To make clear that "selective incorporation" should be narrowly interpreted, Justice Benjamin Cardozo, writing for an 8–1 majority in 1937, asserted that although many rights have value and importance, some rights do not represent a "principle of justice so rooted in the traditions and conscience of our people as to be ranked as fundamental." So, until 1961, only the First Amendment and one clause of the Fifth Amendment had been clearly incorporated into the Fourteenth Amendment as binding on the states as well as on the national government.[11]

The best way to examine the Bill of Rights today is the simplest way: to take each of the major provisions one at a time. Some of these provisions are settled areas of law; others are not.

TABLE 4.2

Incorporation of the Bill of Rights into the Fourteenth Amendment

SELECTED PROVISIONS AND AMENDMENTS	INCORPORATED	KEY CASE
Eminent domain (V)	1897	Chicago, Burlington, and Quincy R.R. v. Chicago
Freedom of speech (I)	1925	Gitlow v. New York
Freedom of press (I)	1931	Near v. Minnesota
Free exercise of religion (I)	1934	Hamilton v. Regents of the University of California
Freedom of assembly (I) and freedom to petition the government for redress of grievances (I)	1937	DeJonge v. Oregon
Freedom of assembly (I)	1939	Hague v. CIO
Nonestablishment of state religion (I)	1947	Everson v. Board of Education
Freedom from unnecessary search and seizure (IV)	1949	Wolf v. Colorado
Freedom from warrantless search and seizure (IV; "exclusionary rule")	1961	Mapp v. Ohio
Freedom from cruel and unusual punishment (VIII)	1962	Robinson v. California
Right to counsel in any criminal trial (VI)	1963	Gideon v. Wainwright
Right against self-incrimination and forced confessions (V)	1964	Malloy v. Hogan; Escobedo v. Illinois
Right to counsel and remain silent (V)	1966	Miranda v. Arizona
Right against double jeopardy (V)	1969	Benton v. Maryland
Right to bear arms (II)	2010	McDonald v. Chicago

The First Amendment Guarantees Freedom of Religion

Describe how the First Amendment protects freedom of religion

Congress shall make no law respecting an establishment of religion, or prohibiting the free exercise thereof; or abridging the freedom of speech, or of the press; or the right of the people peaceably to assemble, and to petition the Government for a redress of grievances.

The Bill of Rights begins by guaranteeing freedom of religion, and the First Amendment provides for that freedom in two distinct clauses: "Congress shall make no law (1) respecting an establishment of religion, or (2) prohibiting the free exercise thereof." The first clause is called the "establishment clause," and the second is called the "free exercise clause."

Separation between Church and State Comes from the First Amendment

The **establishment clause** and the idea of "no law" regarding the establishment of religion can be interpreted in several ways. One interpretation, which probably reflects the views of many of the First Amendment's authors, is that the government is prohibited from establishing an official church. Official state churches, such as the Church of England, were common in the eighteenth century and were viewed by many Americans as inconsistent with a republican form of government. Indeed, many American colonists had fled Europe to escape persecution for having rejected state-sponsored churches. A second interpretation is the view that the government may not take sides among competing religions but may provide assistance to religious institutions or ideas as long as it shows no favoritism. The United States accommodates religious beliefs in a variety of ways, from the reference to God on U.S. currency to the prayer that begins every session of Congress. These forms of establishment have never been struck down by the courts.

The third view regarding religious establishment, the most commonly held today, is the idea of a "wall of separation" between church and state—Jefferson's formulation—that cannot be breached by the government. For two centuries, Jefferson's words have had a powerful impact on our understanding of the proper relationship between church and state in America.

Despite the seeming absoluteness of the phrase "wall of separation," there is ample room to disagree on how high or strong this wall is. For example, the Court has been consistently strict in the area of public education in cases of school prayer, striking down such practices as Bible reading,[12] nondenominational prayer,[13] reading prayers over a public address system during a football game,[14] and even a moment of silence for meditation.[15] In each of these cases, the Court reasoned that school-sponsored religious observations, even if nondenominational, are highly suggestive of school sponsorship and therefore violate the prohibition against establishment of religion. On the other hand, the Court has been quite permissive (and some would say inconsistent) about the public display of religious symbols, such as city-sponsored

Nativity scenes in commercial or municipal areas.[16] And although the Court has consistently disapproved of government financial support for religious schools, even when the purpose has been purely educational and secular, it has permitted certain direct aid to students of such schools in the form of busing, for example.

The difficulty in defining what religious establishment means is evident from two cases in 2005 involving government-sponsored displays of religious symbols. In *Van Orden v. Perry*, the Court decided by a 5–4 margin that a display of the Ten Commandments at the Texas State Capitol did not violate the Constitution.[17] However, in *McCreary v. ACLU of Kentucky*, decided at the same time and also by a 5–4 margin, the Court determined that a display of the Ten Commandments inside two Kentucky courthouses was unconstitutional.[18] Justice Stephen Breyer, the swing vote in the two cases, said that the displays in *Van Orden* had a secular purpose, whereas the displays in *McCreary* had a purely religious purpose. The key difference between the two cases is that the Texas display had been exhibited in a large park for 40 years with other monuments related to the development of American law without any objections raised until this case, whereas the Kentucky display was erected much more recently and initially by itself, suggesting to some justices that its posting had a religious purpose. But most observers saw little difference between the two cases. Clearly, the issue of government-sponsored displays of religious symbols has not been settled.

Does it violate the free exercise of religion if a private business does not allow its employees to wear religious headscarves to work? In 2015, the Supreme Court ruled in favor of Samantha Elauf, declaring that Abercrombie and Fitch could not make an applicant's religious practice a factor in employment decisions.

Free Exercise of Religion Means You Have a Right to Your Beliefs

The **free exercise clause** protects the citizen's right to believe and to practice any religion; it also protects the right to choose not to practice a religion. The precedent-setting case involving free exercise is *West Virginia State Board of Education v. Barnette* (1943), which involved the children of a family of Jehovah's Witnesses who refused to salute and pledge allegiance to the American flag on the grounds that their religious faith did not permit it. Three years earlier, the Court had upheld such a requirement and had permitted schools to expel students for refusing to salute the flag. But the entry of the United States into a war to defend democracy, coupled with the ugly treatment to which the Jehovah's Witnesses children had been subjected, induced the Court to reverse itself and to endorse the free exercise of religion even when it may be offensive to the beliefs of the majority.[19]

In recent years, the principle of free exercise has been bolstered by statutes prohibiting religious discrimination by public and private entities in a variety of realms including hiring, land use, and the treatment of prison inmates. Two recent cases illustrating this point are *Holt v. Hobbs* and *Equal Employment Opportunity Commission v. Abercrombie and Fitch Stores, Inc.*[20] The *Holt* case involved a Muslim prisoner in an Arkansas jail. The prisoner, Gregory Holt, asserted that his religious beliefs required him to grow a beard. Thus, according to Holt, an Arkansas prison policy prohibiting beards was a violation of his ability to exercise his religion. The Court held that the prison policy was a violation of the free exercise clause and violated a federal statute designed to protect the ability of prisoners to worship as they pleased. In the second case, the Equal Employment Opportunity Commission (EEOC) brought suit against Abercrombie for refusing to hire a Muslim woman who wore a head scarf in violation of the company's dress code. The Court held that the store's actions amounted to religious discrimination in hiring—a violation of Title VII of the U.S. Code.

● The First Amendment and Freedom of Speech and of the Press Ensure the Free Exchange of Ideas

> **Describe how the First Amendment protects free speech and freedom of the press**

Congress shall make no law . . . abridging the freedom of speech, or of the press.

Freedom of speech and of the press have a special place in American political thought. To begin with, democracy depends upon the ability of individuals to talk to one another and to disseminate information. A democratic nation could not function without free and open debate. Such debate, moreover, is seen as an essential mechanism for determining the quality or validity of competing ideas. As Justice Oliver Wendell Holmes said, "The best test of truth is the power of the thought to get itself accepted in the competition of the market . . . that at any rate is the theory of our Constitution."[21] What is sometimes called the "marketplace of ideas" receives a good deal of protection from the courts. In 1938 the Supreme Court held that any legislation that attempts to restrict these fundamental freedoms "is to be subjected to a more exacting judicial scrutiny . . . than are most other types of legislation."[22] This higher standard of judicial review came to be called **strict scrutiny**.

The doctrine of strict scrutiny places a heavy burden of proof on the government if it seeks to regulate or restrict speech. Americans are assumed to have the right to speak and to broadcast their ideas unless some compelling reason can be identified to stop them. But strict scrutiny does not mean that speech can never be regulated. According to the courts, although virtually all speech is protected by the Constitution, some forms of speech are entitled to a greater degree of protection than others.

Political Speech Is Consistently Protected

Over the past 200 years, the courts have scrutinized many different forms of speech and constructed different principles and guidelines for each. And of all forms of speech, political speech is the most consistently protected.

Political speech was the activity of greatest concern to the framers of the Constitution, even though some found it the most difficult provision to tolerate.

Within seven years of the ratification of the Bill of Rights in 1791, Congress adopted the infamous Alien and Sedition Acts (long since repealed), which, among other things, made it a crime to say or publish anything that might tend to defame or bring into disrepute the government of the United States. Quite clearly, the acts' intentions were to criminalize the very conduct given absolute protection by the First Amendment. Fifteen violators, including several newspaper editors, were indicted; and a few were actually convicted before the relevant portions of the acts were allowed to expire.

The first modern free speech case arose immediately after World War I. It involved persons who had been convicted under the federal Espionage Act of 1917 for opposing U.S. involvement in the war. The Supreme Court upheld the Espionage Act and refused to protect the speech rights of the defendants on the grounds that their activities—appeals to draftees to resist the draft—constituted a **"clear and present danger"** to national security.[23] This is the first and most famous, though since discarded, "test" for when government intervention or censorship can be permitted.

It was only after the 1920s that real progress toward a genuinely effective First Amendment was made. Since then, the courts have consistently protected political speech even when it has been deemed "insulting" or "outrageous."

Symbolic Speech, Speech Plus, Assembly, and Petition Are Highly Protected

The First Amendment treats the freedoms of religion and political speech as equal to the freedoms of assembly and petition—speech associated with action. Freedom of speech and freedom of assembly are closely related by the "public forum doctrine." In the 1939 case of *Hague v. Committee for Industrial Organization*, the Court declared that the government may not prohibit speech-related activities such as demonstrations or leafleting in public areas traditionally used for that purpose, though, of course, the government may impose rules designed to protect the public safety so long as these rules do not discriminate against particular viewpoints.[24]

Generally, the Supreme Court has protected actions that are designed to send a political message. Thus, the Court held unconstitutional a California statute making it a felony to display a red Communist flag "as a sign, symbol or emblem of opposition to organized government."[25]

Another example is the burning of the American flag as a symbol of protest. In 1984, at a political rally held during the Republican National Convention in Dallas, Texas, a political protester burned an American flag, thereby violating a Texas law that prohibited desecration of a venerated object. The Supreme Court declared the Texas law unconstitutional on the grounds that flag burning was expressive conduct protected by the First Amendment.[26]

In the 2011 case of *Snyder v. Phelps*, the Court continued to protect symbolic speech. Members of the Westboro Baptist Church had frequently demonstrated at military funerals, claiming that the deaths of soldiers were a sign that God disapproved of acceptance of homosexuality in the United States. They carried signs that included slogans like "Thank God for dead soldiers." The father of a soldier

Should the First Amendment's protection of free speech apply even when that speech is seen as offensive? The Supreme Court ruled that members of the Westboro Baptist Church had a right to picket soldiers' funerals to demonstrate what they take as a sign of God's disapproval of homosexuality.

killed in Iraq brought suit against the church and its pastor claiming that the demonstrators had caused him and his family severe emotional distress. The Supreme Court ruled, however, that the First Amendment protected this form of speech in a public place against such suits.[27]

Closer to the original intent of the assembly and petition clause is the category of "speech plus"—speech accompanied by conduct or physical activity such as sit-ins, picketing, and demonstrating; protection of this form of speech under the First Amendment is conditional, and restrictions imposed by state or local authorities are acceptable if properly balanced by considerations of public order. Courts consistently protect such assemblies under the First Amendment; state and local laws regulating such activities are closely scrutinized and frequently overturned. But the same assembly on private property is quite another matter and can in many circumstances be regulated. For example, the directors of a shopping center can lawfully prohibit an assembly protesting a war or supporting a ban on abortion. Assemblies in public areas can also be restricted in some circumstances, especially when the assembly or demonstration jeopardizes the health, safety, or rights of others. This condition was the basis of the Supreme Court's decision to uphold a lower-court order that restricted the access abortion protesters had to the entrances of abortion clinics.[28]

Speech by Public School Students One group that seems to enjoy only a limited right of free speech is public school students. In 1986 the Supreme Court upheld the punishment of a high school student for making sexually suggestive speech. The Court opinion held that such speech interfered with the school's goal of teaching students the limits of socially acceptable behavior.[29] Two years later, the Supreme Court restricted student speech and press rights even further by defining them as part of the educational process, not to be treated with the same standard as adult speech in a regular public forum.[30] In the 2007 case of *Morse v. Frederick*, the Court held that a principal did not violate a student's free speech rights by suspending him for displaying a banner proclaiming, "BONG HiTS 4 JESUS."[31] The decision affirmed that school officials can censor student speech that advocates or celebrates the use of illegal drugs.

Freedom of the Press Is Broad

For all practical purposes, freedom of speech implies and includes freedom of the press. With the exception of the broadcast media, which are subject to federal regulation, the press is protected under the doctrine against **prior restraint** (efforts by a governmental agency to block the publication of material it deems libelous or harmful in some other way; otherwise known as "censorship"). Beginning with the landmark 1931 case of *Near v. Minnesota*, the U.S. Supreme Court has held that, except under the most extraordinary circumstances, the First Amendment of the Constitution prohibits government agencies from seeking to prevent newspapers or magazines from publishing whatever they wish.[32] In the case of *New York Times v. United States* (1971), the so-called *Pentagon Papers* case, the Supreme Court ruled that the government could not block publication of secret Defense Department documents given to the *New York Times* by an opponent of the Vietnam War who had obtained the documents illegally.[33]

Another press freedom issue is the question of whether journalists can be compelled to reveal their sources of information. Journalists assert that if they cannot promise to keep the confidentiality of their sources, the flow of information will be reduced and press freedom effectively curtailed. Government agencies, however, assert that the names of news sources may be relevant to criminal or even national security investigations. Nearly all states have "shield laws" that to varying degrees protect journalistic sources. There is, however, no federal shield law, and the Supreme Court has held that the press has no constitutional right to withhold information in court.[34] In 2005, Judith Miller, a *New York Times* reporter, was jailed for contempt of court for refusing to tell a federal grand jury the name of a confidential source in a case involving the leaked identity of the CIA analyst Valerie Plame. Plame's husband, Joseph Wilson, had been critical of the Bush administration's Iraq policies.

Some Speech Has Only Limited Protection

At least four categories of speech fall outside the guarantees of the First Amendment and therefore outside the realm of absolute protection: (1) libel and slander, (2) obscenity and pornography, (3) fighting words, and (4) commercial speech. It should be emphasized once again that these types of speech still enjoy considerable protection by the courts.

Libel and Slander If a written statement is made in "reckless disregard of the truth" and is considered damaging to the victim because it is "malicious, scandalous, and defamatory," it can be punished as **libel**. If an oral statement of such a nature is made, it can be punished as **slander**.

Today, most libel suits involve freedom of the press, and the realm of free press is enormous. Historically, newspapers were subject to the law of libel, which provided that newspapers that printed false and malicious stories could be compelled to pay damages to those they defamed. In recent years, however, American courts have greatly narrowed the meaning of libel and made it extremely difficult, particularly for politicians or other public figures, to win a libel case against a newspaper. In the important 1964 case of *New York Times v. Sullivan*, the Court held that to be deemed libelous, a story about a public official not only had to be untrue but also had to result from "actual malice" or "reckless disregard" for the truth.[35] In other words, the newspaper had to print false and malicious material *deliberately*. In practice, this is a very difficult legal standard to meet.

With the emergence of the Internet as an important communications medium, the courts have had to decide how traditional libel law applies to Internet content. In 1995 the New York courts held that an online bulletin board could be held responsible for the libelous content of material posted by a third party. To protect Internet service providers, Congress subsequently enacted legislation absolving them of responsibility for third-party posts. The federal courts have generally upheld this law and declared that service providers are immune from suits regarding the content of material posted by others.[36]

Obscenity and Pornography If libel and slander cases can be difficult because of the problem of determining the truth of statements and whether those statements are malicious and damaging, cases involving pornography and obscenity can be even trickier. Not until 1957 did the Supreme Court confront these issues, and it did so with a definition of *obscenity* that may have caused more confusion than it cleared up. Justice William Brennan, in writing the Court's opinion, defined *obscenity* as speech or writing that appeals to the "prurient interest"—that is, whose purpose is to excite lust as this appears "to the average person, applying contemporary community standards." Even so, Brennan added, the work should be judged obscene only when it is "utterly without redeeming social importance."[37] In 1964, Justice Potter Stewart confessed that, although he found *pornography* impossible to define, "I know it when I see it."[38]

An effort was made to strengthen the restrictions in 1973, when the Supreme Court expressed its willingness to define *pornography* as a work that (1) as a whole, is deemed prurient by the "average person" according to "community standards"; (2) depicts sexual conduct "in a patently offensive way"; and (3) lacks "serious literary, artistic, political, or scientific value." This definition meant that pornography would be determined by local rather than national standards. Thus, a local bookseller might be prosecuted for selling a volume that was a best-seller nationally but that was deemed pornographic locally.[39] This new definition of standards did not help much either, and not long after 1973 the Court began again to review all such community antipornography laws, reversing most of them.

In recent years, the battle against obscene speech has targeted "cyberporn," pornography on the Internet. Opponents of this form of expression argue that it should be banned because of the easy access children have to the Internet. The first major effort to regulate the content of the Internet occurred in 1996, when Congress passed the Communications Decency Act (CDA), designed to regulate the online transmission of obscene material. The constitutionality of the CDA was immediately challenged in court by a coalition of interests led by the American Civil Liberties Union (ACLU). In the 1997 Supreme Court case of *Reno v. ACLU*, the Court struck down the CDA, ruling that it suppressed speech that "adults have a constitutional right to receive," saying that "the level of discourse reaching the mailbox simply cannot be limited to that which would be suitable for a sandbox." Supreme Court justice John Paul Stevens described the Internet as the "town crier" of the modern age and said that the Internet was entitled to the greatest degree of First Amendment protection possible.[40] By contrast, radio and television are subject to more control than the Internet. In 2008, the Supreme Court upheld a law that made it a crime to sell child pornography on the Internet.[41]

In 2000, the Supreme Court extended the highest degree of First Amendment protection to cable (not broadcast) television. In *United States v. Playboy Entertainment Group*, the Court struck down a portion of the 1996 Telecommunications Act that required cable TV companies to limit the broadcast of sexually explicit programming to late-night hours. In its decision, the Court noted that the law already provided parents with the means to restrict access to sexually explicit cable channels through various blocking devices. Moreover, such programming could come into the home only if parents decided to purchase such channels in the first place.[42]

Closely related to the issue of obscenity is the matter of violent broadcast content. Here, too, the Court has generally upheld freedom of speech. For example, in the 2011 case of *Brown v. Entertainment Merchants Association* the Court struck down a California law banning the sale of violent video games to children, saying that the law violated the First Amendment.[43]

Fighting Words Speech can also lose its protected position when it moves toward the sphere of action. "Expressive speech," for example, is protected until it moves from the symbolic realm to the realm of actual conduct—to direct incitement of damaging conduct with the use of so-called **fighting words**. In 1942 a man called a police officer a "goddamned racketeer" and "a damn Fascist" and was arrested and convicted of violating a state law forbidding the use of offensive language in public. When his case reached the Supreme Court, the arrest was upheld on the grounds that the First Amendment provides no protection for such offensive language because such words "are no essential part of any exposition of ideas."[44] This decision was reaffirmed in the important 1951 case of *Dennis v. United States*, in which the Supreme Court held that there is no substantial public interest in permitting certain kinds of utterances: the lewd and obscene, the profane, the libelous, and the insulting or "fighting" words—those which by their very utterance inflict injury or tend to incite an immediate breach of the peace.[45] Since that time, however, the

Supreme Court has reversed almost every conviction based on arguments that the speaker had used "fighting words."

Commercial Speech Commercial speech, such as newspaper or television advertisements, has only partial First Amendment protection because it cannot be considered political speech. Initially considered to be entirely outside the protection of the First Amendment, commercial speech is subject to regulation, although it is also recognized and protected for the part it plays in the free flow of information. For example, prohibition of false and misleading advertising by the Federal Trade Commission is an old and well-established power of the federal government. The Supreme Court long ago approved the constitutionality of laws prohibiting electronic media from carrying cigarette advertising.[46] It has also upheld city ordinances prohibiting the posting of all signs on public property (as long as the ban is total so that there is no hint of censorship).[47]

However, the gains outweigh the losses in the effort to expand the protection of commercial speech under the First Amendment. For example, in 1996 the Court struck down Rhode Island laws and regulations banning the advertisement of liquor prices,[48] and in 2001 the Court overturned a Massachusetts ban on all cigarette advertising as violations of the First Amendment.[49] These instances of commercial speech indicate the breadth and depth of the freedom today to direct appeals to a large public, to sell goods and services, and to mobilize people for political purposes.

● The Second Amendment Now Protects an Individual's Right to Own a Gun

Explore whether the Second Amendment means people have a right to own guns

The Second Amendment was included in the Bill of Rights to provide for "well-regulated" militias to enforce the "security of a free State," which were to be the backing of the government for the maintenance of local public order. *Militia* was understood at the time of the Founding to be a military or police resource for state governments; militias were specifically distinguished from professional armies, which came within the sole constitutional jurisdiction of Congress. While the right of the people "to keep and bear Arms" was linked to citizen service in militias, many have argued that the Second Amendment also establishes an individual right to bear arms, aside from militia service.

A 1939 Supreme Court case upheld a federal gun law in which the Court concluded that the Second Amendment pertained to "the preservation or efficiency of a well regulated militia,"[50] but the Court made no further Second Amendment decisions for nearly 70 years. Thus, states and localities across the country have very different gun ownership standards. For instance, in Wyoming there is no ban on any type of gun, there is no waiting period to purchase a firearm, and no permit is required for carrying a concealed weapon. In California, by contrast, the possession of assault weapons is banned, there is a 10-day waiting period to purchase a firearm, and a permit is required to carry a concealed weapon. Figure 4.1 shows the percentage of adults in each state who own guns.

The Court's silence on the application of the Second Amendment ended in 2008, when it made the first of two rulings in favor of expansive rights of gun ownership by individuals. The case of *District of Columbia v. Heller* challenged a strict Washington, D.C., law that banned handguns. In a 5–4 decision, the Court ruled that the Second Amendment provides a constitutional right to keep a loaded handgun at home for self-defense. The Court also said that the decision was not intended to cast doubt on most existing gun laws. The dissenting opinion asserted that the Second Amendment only protects the rights of individuals to bear arms as part of a militia force, not in an individual capacity.[51] Because the District of Columbia is an entity of the federal government, the ruling did not apply to state firearm laws. However, in the 2010 case of *McDonald v. Chicago*, the Court applied the Second Amendment to the states, making this decision the first new incorporation decision by the Court in 40 years (see Table 4.2). The case concerned a Chicago ordinance that made it extremely difficult to own a gun within city limits, and the Court's ruling had the effect of overturning the law.[52]

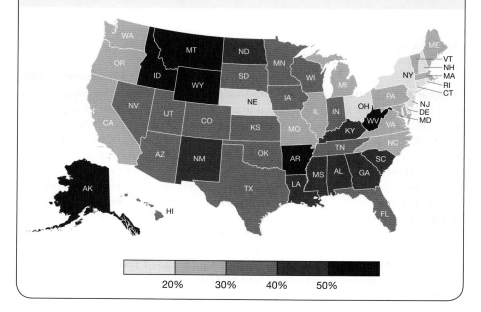

FIGURE 4.1 Gun Ownership by State

Although state gun laws must conform to the Second Amendment as interpreted by the U.S. Supreme Court, laws concerning gun sales and ownership vary widely from state to state. It is much more difficult to buy a gun in, say, New York or California than in Texas or Kentucky. This map shows the percentage of the adult population in each state owning a gun in 2013.

SOURCE: Bindu Kalesan, Marcos D. Villarreal, Katherine M. Keyes, and Sandro Galea, "Gun Ownership and Social Gun Culture," June 29, 2015, http://injuryprevention.bmj.com/content/early/2015/06/09/injuryprev-2015-041586 .full.pdf?keytype5ref&ijkey5doj6vx0laFZMsQ2 (accessed 6/13/16).

Despite these rulings, the debate over gun control continues to loom large. A series of tragic shootings in recent years—including the killing of 20 elementary school students in Newtown, Connecticut; 9 parishioners at a Charleston, South Carolina, church; 14 people at a San Bernardino, California, office building; and, in the worst mass shooting in U.S. history, 50 people at a gay nightclub in Orlando, Florida—has kept the issue of gun laws firmly on the national agenda.

● Rights of the Criminally Accused Are Based on Due Process of Law

Explain the major rights that people have if they are accused of a crime

Except for the First Amendment, most of the battle to apply the Bill of Rights to the states was fought over the various protections granted to individuals who are accused of a crime, who are suspects in the commission of a crime, or who are brought before the court as a witness to a crime. The Fourth, Fifth, Sixth, and Eighth amendments, taken together, are the essence of the due process of law, even though this key phrase does not appear until the very last words of the Fifth Amendment.

The Fourth Amendment Protects against Unlawful Searches and Seizures

The right of the people to be secure in their persons, houses, papers, and effects, against unreasonable searches and seizures, shall not be violated, and no Warrants shall issue, but upon probable cause, supported by Oath or affirmation, and particularly describing the place to be searched, and the persons or things to be seized.

The purpose of the Fourth Amendment is to guarantee the security of citizens against unreasonable (that is, improper) searches and seizures. In 1990 the Supreme Court summarized its understanding of the Fourth Amendment brilliantly and succinctly: "A search compromises the individual interest in privacy; a seizure deprives the individual of dominion over his or her person or property."[53] But how are we to define what is reasonable and what is unreasonable?

The 1961 case of *Mapp v. Ohio* illustrates one of the most important principles that has grown out of the Fourth Amendment: the **exclusionary rule**, which is the ability of courts to exclude evidence obtained in violation of the Fourth Amendment, such as barring evidence obtained during an illegal search from being introduced in a trial. Acting on a tip that Dollree Mapp was harboring a suspect in a bombing incident, several police officers forcibly entered Mapp's house claiming they had a warrant to look for the bombing suspect. The police did not find the bombing suspect but did find some materials connected to the local numbers racket (an illegal gambling operation) and a quantity of "obscene materials," in violation of an Ohio law banning possession of such materials. Although no warrant was ever produced, the evidence that had been

Under what circumstances can the police search an individual's car? The Fourth Amendment protects against "unreasonable searches and seizures," but the Supreme Court has had to interpret what is unreasonable.

seized was admitted by a court; and Mapp was convicted for illegal possession of obscene materials.

By the time Mapp's appeal reached the Supreme Court, the question was whether any evidence produced under the circumstances of the search of her home was admissible. The Court's opinion affirmed the exclusionary rule: under the Fourth Amendment (applied to the states through the Fourteenth Amendment), "all evidence obtained by searches and seizures in violation of the Constitution . . . is inadmissible."[54] This means that even people who are clearly guilty of the crime of which they are accused must not be convicted if the only evidence for their conviction was obtained illegally. This idea was expressed by future Supreme Court justice Benjamin Cardozo nearly a century ago when he wrote that "the criminal is to go free because the constable has blundered."[55]

The exclusionary rule is the most dramatic restraint imposed by the courts on police behavior because it rules out precisely the evidence that produces a conviction; it frees those people who are *known* to have committed the crime of which they have been accused because the evidence was obtained improperly, though few convictions are actually lost because of excluded evidence. Because it works so dramatically in favor of persons known to have committed a crime, the Court has since softened the application of the rule. In recent years, the federal courts have relied upon a discretionary use of the exclusionary rule, whereby they make a judgment as to the "nature and quality of the intrusion." It is thus difficult to know ahead of time whether a defendant will or will not be protected from an illegal search under the Fourth Amendment.[56] Several recent cases have imposed strict interpretations of a reasonable search. In 2013, the Court held that the use of a drug-sniffing dog on the front porch of a home constituted an improper search in the absence of consent or a warrant. The decision rested on "traditional property notions."[57]

Changes in technology have also had an impact on Fourth Amendment jurisprudence. In the 2012 case of *United States v. Jones*, the Court held that prosecutors violated Jones's rights when they attached a Global Positioning System device to his Jeep and monitored his movements for 28 days.[58] On the other hand, in *Maryland v. King*, the Court upheld DNA testing of arrestees without the need for individualized suspicion. The Court characterized DNA testing as an administrative tool for identifying the arrestee and thus as legally indistinguishable from photographing and fingerprinting.[59] In the 2014 case of *Riley v. California*, the Court held that the police were constitutionally prohibited from seizing and searching the digital contents of a cell phone during an arrest.[60] As new technologies develop, the Court will continue to face the question of what constitutes a reasonable search. In 2016, the Federal Bureau of Investigation (FBI) sought to compel the Apple Corporation to unlock the cell phone used by Syed Farook, an alleged terrorist who, along with his wife Tashfeen Malik, killed 14 people in San Bernardino, California. Apple asserted that creating a new software to enable the FBI to unlock the phone would allow the agency to invade the privacy of millions of iPhone users. The case became moot when the FBI was able to unlock the phone without Apple's help.

Finally, the Fourth Amendment places limits on government surveillance of individuals, an ongoing and controversial issue in the United States today. For example, a federal judge in Washington, D.C., recently ruled that a National Security Agency (NSA) program that collected millions of records of telephone calls was impermissible under the Fourth Amendment.[61]

The Fifth Amendment Covers Court-Related Rights

No person shall be held to answer for a capital, or otherwise infamous crime, unless on a presentment or indictment of a Grand Jury, except in cases arising in the land or naval forces, or in the Militia, when in actual service in time of War or public danger; nor shall any person be subject for the same offence to be twice put in jeopardy of life or limb; nor shall be compelled in any criminal case to be a witness against himself, nor be deprived of life, liberty, or property, without due process of law; nor shall private property be taken for public use, without just compensation.

Grand Juries The first clause of the Fifth Amendment sets forth the right to a **grand jury** (a jury that determines whether sufficient evidence is available to justify a trial; grand juries do not rule on the accused's guilt or innocence) to determine whether a trial is warranted. Grand juries play an important role in federal criminal cases. However, the provision for a grand jury is the one important civil liberties provision of the Bill of Rights that was not incorporated by the Fourteenth Amendment to apply to state criminal prosecutions. Thus, some states operate without grand juries. In such states, the prosecuting attorney simply files a "bill of information," affirming that there is sufficient evidence available to justify a trial. If the accused person is to be held in custody, the prosecutor must take the available information before a judge to determine that the evidence shows probable cause.

Double Jeopardy "Nor shall any person be subject for the same offence to be twice put in jeopardy of life or limb" is the constitutional protection from **double jeopardy**, a protection to prevent a person from being tried more than once for the same crime. The protection from double jeopardy was at the heart of the *Palko v. Connecticut* case in 1937. In that case, a Connecticut court had found Frank Palko guilty of second-degree murder and sentenced him to life in prison. Unhappy with the verdict, the state of Connecticut appealed the conviction to its highest state court, won the appeal, got a new trial, and then succeeded in getting Palko convicted of first-degree murder. Palko appealed to the Supreme Court on what seemed an open-and-shut case of double jeopardy. Yet, although the majority of the Court agreed that this could indeed be considered a case of double jeopardy, they decided that double jeopardy was not one of the provisions of the Bill of Rights incorporated in the Fourteenth Amendment as a restriction on the powers of the states.[62] It took more than 30 years for the Court to nationalize the constitutional protection against double jeopardy, when the court overruled *Palko* and declared that double jeopardy now applied to the states (see Table 4.2). Palko was eventually executed for the crime, because he lived in Connecticut rather than in a state whose constitution included a guarantee against double jeopardy.

Self-Incrimination Perhaps the most significant liberty found in the Fifth Amendment, and the one most familiar to many Americans who watch television crime shows, is the guarantee that no citizen "shall be compelled in any criminal case to be a witness against himself." The most famous case concerning self-incrimination involved 23-year-old Ernesto Miranda, who was sentenced to between 20 and 30 years in prison for the kidnap and rape of an 18-year-old woman. The woman had identified him in a police lineup, and, after two hours of questioning, Miranda confessed, subsequently signing a statement that his confession had been made voluntarily, without threats or promises of immunity. This confession was admitted into evidence and served as the basis for Miranda's conviction. After his conviction, Miranda argued that his confession had not been truly voluntary and that he had not been informed of his right to remain silent or his right to consult an attorney. The Supreme Court agreed and overturned the conviction.[63] Following one of the most intensely and widely criticized decisions ever handed down by the Supreme Court, Miranda's case produced the rules the police must follow before questioning an arrested criminal suspect. The reading of a person's "*Miranda* rights" became a standard scene in every police station and on virtually every dramatization of police action on television and in the movies. *Miranda* advanced the civil liberties of accused persons not only by expanding the scope of the Fifth Amendment clause covering coerced confessions and self-incrimination but also by confirming the right to counsel (discussed later). Subsequent Supreme Courts considerably softened the *Miranda* restrictions, but the **Miranda rule** (as set out in *Miranda v. Arizona*) that persons under arrest must be informed prior to police interrogation of their rights to remain silent and to have the benefit of legal counsel, still stands as a protection against egregious police abuses of arrested persons. However, in the 2010 case of *Berghuis v. Thompkins*, the Supreme Court introduced an important qualification to the Miranda rule, deciding that statements made by suspects who did not expressly waive their rights (usually by signing a form) could be used against them.[64]

Eminent Domain The other fundamental clause of the Fifth Amendment is the "takings clause," which extends to each citizen a protection against the "taking" of private property by the government "without just compensation." The power of any government to take private property for public use is called **eminent domain**. The Fifth Amendment puts limits on that inherent power through procedures that require a showing of a public purpose and the provision of fair payment for the government's taking of someone's property.

The Sixth Amendment's Right to Counsel Is Crucial for a Fair Trial

> In all criminal prosecutions, the accused shall enjoy the right to a speedy and public trial, by an impartial jury of the State and district wherein the crime shall have been committed, which district shall have been ascertained by law, and to be informed of the nature and the cause of the accusation; to be confronted with the witnesses against him; to have compulsory process for obtaining witnesses in his favor, and to have the Assistance of Counsel for his defence.

Like the exclusionary rule of the Fourth Amendment and the self-incrimination clause of the Fifth Amendment, the "right to counsel" provision of the Sixth Amendment is notable for sometimes freeing defendants who seem to the public to be guilty as charged. Other provisions of the Sixth Amendment, such as the right to a speedy trial and the right to confront witnesses before an impartial jury, are not very controversial.

Gideon v. Wainwright (1963) is the perfect case study because it involved a disreputable person who seemed patently guilty of the crime of which he was convicted. In and out of jails for most of his 51 years, Clarence Earl Gideon received a five-year sentence for breaking and entering a poolroom in Panama City, Florida. While serving time in jail, Gideon became a fairly well-qualified "jailhouse lawyer," made his own appeal on a handwritten petition, and eventually won the landmark ruling on the right to counsel in all felony cases. After the Supreme Court's decision, Gideon was granted a new trial. This time, represented by an attorney, he was found not guilty.[65] The right to counsel was later expanded, beyond just serious crimes, to any trial, with or without a jury, that holds the possibility of imprisonment.

The Eighth Amendment Bars Cruel and Unusual Punishment

> Excessive bail shall not be required, nor excessive fines imposed, nor cruel and unusual punishment inflicted.

Virtually all the debate over Eighth Amendment issues focuses on the last clause of the amendment: the protection from "cruel and unusual punishment." One of the greatest challenges in interpreting this provision consistently arises over the death penalty. In 1972, the Supreme Court overturned several state death penalty laws, not because they were cruel and unusual but because they were being applied unevenly—that is, blacks were much more likely than whites to be sentenced to death, the poor more likely than the rich, and men more likely than women.[66] Very soon after that decision, a majority of states revised their capital punishment provisions to meet the Court's standards, and the Court reaffirmed that the death penalty could be used if certain standards were met.[67] Since 1976, the Court has consistently upheld state laws providing for capital punishment, although it also continues to review death penalty appeals each year.

Between 1976 and October 2016, states executed 1,439 people. Most of those executions occurred in southern states, with Texas leading the way at 538. As of 2016, 31 states had statutes providing for capital punishment for specified offenses, a policy supported by a majority of Americans, according to polls. On the other hand, 19 states bar the death penalty; and since the end of the 1990s, both the number of death sentences and the number of executions have declined annually.[68]

Many death penalty supporters assert its deterrent effects on other would-be criminals. Although studies of capital crimes usually fail to demonstrate any direct deterrent effect, this failure may be due to the lengthy delays (typically years and even decades) between convictions and executions. A system that eliminates undue delays might enhance deterrence.

Opponents argue that the death penalty constitutes cruel and unusual punishment. In recent years, the use of lethal injection drugs including Midazolam has come under scrutiny after troubling executions where the process was drawn out and painful. In 2015 the Supreme Court upheld the use of lethal injection.

Death penalty opponents are quick to counter that the death penalty has not been proven to deter crime, either in the United States or abroad. In fact, America is the only Western nation that still executes criminals. If the government is to serve as an example of proper behavior, say foes of capital punishment, it has no business sanctioning killing when incarceration also protects society. Furthermore, execution is time-consuming and expensive—more expensive than life imprisonment—precisely because the government must make every effort to ensure that it is not executing an innocent person. Curtailing legal appeals would increase the possibility of a mistake. Race also intrudes in death penalty cases: people of color are disproportionately more likely than whites charged with identical crimes to be given the ultimate punishment.

In recent years, the Court has issued a number of death penalty opinions, declaring that death was too harsh a penalty for the crime of raping a child[69] and invalidating a death sentence for a black defendant when the prosecutor had improperly excluded African Americans from the jury.[70] In 2015, the Court upheld lethal injection as a mode of execution, despite arguments that this form of execution was likely to cause considerable pain.[71]

● The Right to Privacy Means the Right to Be Left Alone

Assess whether people have a right to privacy under the Constitution

Although the word *privacy* never appears in the Bill of Rights, there is general agreement that a right to privacy emanates from the first 10 amendments—even though judges and legal scholars continue to disagree about where the right comes from. The idea behind the right to privacy is simple: people have a right to be left alone from government or other persons' interference in certain personal areas.

The sphere of privacy was drawn by the Supreme Court in 1965, when it ruled that a Connecticut statute forbidding the use of contraceptives violated the right of marital privacy. Estelle Griswold, the executive director of the Planned Parenthood League of Connecticut, was arrested by the state of Connecticut for providing information, instruction, and medical advice about contraception to married couples. She and her associates were found guilty as accessories to the crime and fined $100 each. The Supreme Court reversed the lower-court decisions and declared the Connecticut law unconstitutional because it violated "a right of privacy older than the Bill of Rights—older than our political parties, older than our school system."[72] Justice William O. Douglas, author of the majority decision in the *Griswold v. Connecticut* case, argued that this right of privacy is also grounded in the Constitution because it fits into a "zone of privacy" created by a combination of the Third, Fourth, and Fifth amendments. A concurring opinion, written by Justice Arthur Goldberg, attempted to strengthen Douglas's argument by adding that "the concept of liberty . . . embraces the right of marital privacy though that right is not mentioned explicitly in the Constitution [and] is supported by numerous decisions of this Court . . . and *by the language and history of the Ninth Amendment* [emphasis added]."[73]

The right to privacy was confirmed and extended in 1973 in an important but controversial privacy decision: *Roe v. Wade*. This decision established a woman's right to seek an abortion and prohibited states from making abortion a criminal act prior to the point at which the fetus becomes viable, which, in 1973, was the twenty-seventh week.[74] It is important to emphasize that the preference for privacy rights and for their extension to include the rights of women to control their own bodies was not something invented by the Supreme Court in a vacuum. Most states did not regulate abortions in any fashion until the 1840s, at which time only 6 of the 26 existing states had any regulations governing abortion. In addition, many states had begun to ease their abortion restrictions well before the 1973 *Roe* decision. In recent years, a number of states have reinstated some restrictions on abortion, including lowering the viability standard to 20 weeks (Texas), 12 weeks (Arkansas), and 6 weeks (North Dakota). While the Supreme Court has continued to affirm a woman's right to seek an abortion, it has limited the right, approving restrictions as long as they do not pose an "undue burden."

Like any important principle, once privacy was established as an aspect of civil liberties protected by the Bill of Rights through the Fourteenth Amendment, it took on a life of its own. In a number of important decisions, the Supreme Court and the lower federal courts sought to protect rights that could not be found in the text of the Constitution but could be

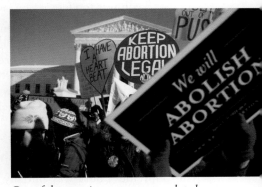

One of the most important cases related to the right to privacy was Roe v. Wade, *which established a woman's right to seek an abortion. However, the decision has remained highly controversial, with opponents arguing that the Constitution does not guarantee this right.*

discovered through a study of the philosophic sources of fundamental rights. Right-to-privacy claims have been made by those attempting to preserve the right to obtain legal abortions, by those seeking to obtain greater rights for gay people, and by supporters of physician-assisted suicide (also known as the "right-to-die" movement). In the case of gay people, the Supreme Court extended privacy protections to them in 2003 when it ruled that they are "entitled to respect for their private lives" in the case of *Lawrence v. Texas*.[75] The case overturned a Texas law banning certain sexual acts among same-sex partners. The Court concluded, "Petitioners are entitled to respect for their private lives. The State cannot demean their existence or control their destiny by making their private sexual conduct a crime." For the first time, gay men and lesbians could claim right-to-privacy protection.

● Civil Rights Are Protections by the Government

Trace the legal developments and social movements that expanded civil rights

With the adoption of the Fourteenth Amendment in 1868, civil rights became part of the Constitution, guaranteed to each citizen through "equal protection of the laws." Together with the Thirteenth Amendment, which abolished slavery, and the Fifteenth Amendment, which guaranteed voting rights for black men, it seemed to provide a guarantee of civil rights for the newly freed black slaves. But the general language of the Fourteenth Amendment meant that its support for civil rights could be even more far-reaching. The very simplicity of the **equal protection clause** of the Fourteenth Amendment left it open to interpretation:

> No State shall make or enforce any law which shall . . . deny to any person within its jurisdiction the equal protection of the laws.

This provision of the Fourteenth Amendment guarantees citizens "the equal protection of the laws." These words launched a century of political movements and legal efforts to press for racial equality. The African American quest for civil rights in turn inspired many other groups, including members of other racial and ethnic groups, women, the disabled, and gay men, lesbians, and transgender individuals, to seek new laws and constitutional guarantees of their civil rights.

Plessy v. Ferguson Established "Separate but Equal"

The Supreme Court was initially no more ready to enforce the civil rights aspects of the Fourteenth Amendment than it was to enforce the civil liberties provisions. Resistance to equality for African Americans in the South led Congress to adopt the Civil Rights Act of 1875, which attempted to protect blacks from discrimination by proprietors of hotels, theaters, and other public accommodations. But the Court declared the Civil Rights Act of 1875 unconstitutional on the grounds that it sought to protect blacks against

The 1896 Supreme Court case of Plessy v. Ferguson *upheld legal segregation and created the "separate but equal" rule, which fostered national segregation. Overt discrimination in public accommodations was common.*

discrimination by *private* businesses, while the Fourteenth Amendment, according to the Court's interpretation, was intended to protect individuals only from discrimination that arose from actions by *public* officials of state and local governments.

In the infamous case of *Plessy v. Ferguson* (1896), the Court went still further by upholding a Louisiana statute that *required* segregation of the races on trolleys and other public carriers (and, by implication, in all public facilities, including schools). Homer Plessy, a man defined as "one-eighth black," had violated a Louisiana law that provided for "equal but separate accommodations" on trains and a $25 fine for any white passenger who sat in a car reserved for blacks or any black passenger who sat in a car reserved for whites. The Supreme Court held that the Fourteenth Amendment's "equal protection of the laws" was not violated by laws requiring segregation of the races in public accommodations as long as the facilities were equal, thus establishing the **"separate but equal" rule** that prevailed through the mid-twentieth century.[76] People generally pretended that segregated accommodations were equal as long as some accommodation for blacks existed. Thus, racial inequality in the guise of the separate but equal doctrine persisted for decades.

Lawsuits to Fight for Equality Came after World War II

The Supreme Court had begun to change its position on racial discrimination before World War II by being stricter about the criterion for equal facilities in the "separate but equal" rule. In 1938, for example, the Court rejected Missouri's

"Massive resistance" among white southerners attempted to block the desegregation efforts of the national government. For example, at Little Rock Central High School in 1957, an angry mob of white southerners prevented black students from entering the school.

policy of paying the tuition of qualified blacks to out-of-state law schools rather than admitting them to the University of Missouri Law School.[77] Similar rulings in the 1940s and '50s began to chip away at "separate but equal."

Although none of those pre-1954 cases confronted "separate but equal" and the principle of racial discrimination head-on, they gave black leaders encouragement to believe that recent legal precedent might change the constitutional framework itself. Much of this legal work was done by the Legal Defense and Educational Fund of the National Association for the Advancement of Colored People (NAACP). Formed in 1909 to fight discrimination against African Americans, the NAACP was the most important civil rights organization during the first half of the twentieth century.

In the fall of 1952 the Court had on its docket cases from Delaware, the District of Columbia, Kansas, South Carolina, and Virginia challenging the constitutionality of school segregation. Of these, the case filed in Kansas became the chosen one by the NAACP. It seemed to be ahead of the pack in its district court, and it had the special advantage of being located in a state outside the Deep South, which would minimize local opposition to a favorable decision.[78] Oliver Brown, the father of three girls, lived "across the tracks" in a low-income, racially mixed Topeka neighborhood. Every school day morning, Linda Brown took the school bus to the Monroe School for black children about a mile away but had to walk through a dangerous railroad switchyard to get to the stop—all this, even though a white school was closer to their home. In September 1950, Oliver Brown took Linda to the closer all-white Sumner School to enter her into the third grade in defiance of state law and local segregation rules. When they were refused, Brown took his case to the NAACP; and soon thereafter **Brown v. Board of Education** was born.

In deciding the *Brown* case, the Court, to the surprise of many, rejected as inconclusive all the learned arguments about the intent and the history of the Fourteenth Amendment and committed itself instead to considering only the consequences of segregation:

> Does segregation of children in public schools solely on the basis of race, even though the physical facilities and other "tangible" factors may be equal, deprive the children of the minority group of equal educational opportunities? We believe that it does. . . . We conclude that in the field of public education the doctrine of "separate but equal" has no place. Separate educational facilities are inherently unequal.[79]

The *Brown* decision altered the constitutional framework in two fundamental respects. First, after *Brown*, the states no longer had the power to use race as a criterion of discrimination in law. Second, the national government from then on had the power (and eventually the obligation) to intervene with strict regulatory policies against the discriminatory actions of state or local governments, school boards, employers, and many others in the private sector.

The Civil Rights Struggle Escalated after
Brown v. Board of Education

Brown v. Board of Education withdrew all constitutional authority to use race as a criterion for exclusion, and it signaled more clearly the Court's determination to use the strict scrutiny test in cases related to racial discrimination. This meant that the burden of proof would fall on the government to show that the law in question *was* constitutional—not on the challengers to show the law's *un*constitutionality.[80] But the historic decision in *Brown v. Board of Education* was merely a small opening move. First, most states refused to cooperate until sued, and many ingenious schemes were employed to delay obedience (such as states paying the tuition for white students to attend newly created "private" academies). Second, while school boards began to cooperate by eliminating legally enforced school segregation (what is referred to as de jure segregation, meaning literally "by law" or legally enforced practices), extensive actual segregation remained (what is referred to as de facto segregation, meaning literally "by fact," wherein races are still segregated even though the law does not require it). Thus, school segregation in the North as well as in the South remained as a consequence of racially segregated housing patterns that were untouched by the 1954–55 *Brown* principles. Third, discrimination in employment, public accommodations, juries, voting, and other areas of social and economic activity was not directly touched by *Brown*.

Social Protest and Congressional Action Ten years after *Brown*, fewer than 1 percent of black school-age children in the Deep South were attending schools with whites.[81] A decade of frustration made it fairly obvious to all observers that adjudication alone would not succeed. The goal of "equal protection" required positive, or affirmative, action by Congress and by federal agencies. And given massive southern resistance and a generally negative national public opinion toward racial integration, progress would not be made through courts, Congress, or federal agencies without intense, well-organized support. Organized civil rights demonstrations began to mount slowly but surely after *Brown v. Board of Education*. Only a year after Brown, black citizens in Montgomery, Alabama, challenged the city's segregated bus system with a yearlong boycott. The boycott began with the arrest of Rosa Parks, who refused to give up her bus seat for a white man. A seamstress who worked with civil rights groups, Parks eventually became a civil rights icon, as did one of the ministers leading the boycott: Martin Luther King, Jr. After a year of private carpools and walking, Montgomery's bus system desegregated but only after the Supreme Court ruled the system unconstitutional.

By the 1960s the many organizations that made up the civil rights movement had accumulated experience and built networks capable of launching massive direct-action campaigns against southern segregationists. The Southern Christian Leadership Conference, the Student Nonviolent Coordinating Committee, and many other organizations had built a movement that stretched across the South, using the media to attract nationwide attention and support. The image of protesters being beaten, attacked by police dogs, and set upon with fire hoses did much to win broad sympathy for the cause of black civil rights and to discredit state and local governments in the South. In the massive March on Washington in 1963, the Reverend Martin Luther King, Jr., staked out the movement's moral claims in his famous "I Have a Dream" speech.

Protests against discriminatory practices toward African Americans did not end in the 1960s. Beginning in 2012, a variety of protests coalesced under the banner Black Lives Matter to focus attention on allegations of police misconduct directed at African Americans. The movement took off after the shooting of an unarmed black teenager by a white police officer in Ferguson, Missouri, in 2014 and spread across the nation as the media carried reports, photos, and videos of police violence against blacks around the country. African Americans have long asserted that they are often victims of racial profiling and more likely than whites to be harassed or arrested by the police. Police departments have always replied that blacks are more likely than whites to be engaged in criminal activity. Reports and even film footage of killings, however, proved difficult for the police to justify and seemed likely to lead to new rules governing police behavior.

The Civil Rights Acts Made Equal Protection a Reality

The right to equal protection of the laws could be established and, to a certain extent, implemented by the courts. But after a decade of very frustrating efforts, the courts and Congress ultimately came to the conclusion that the federal courts alone were not adequate to the task of changing the social rules and that legislation and administrative action would be needed.

Congress used its legislative powers to help make equal protection of the laws a reality by passing the Civil Rights Act of 1964, prohibiting major forms of discrimination against racial, ethnic, national and religious minorities, and women in voting registration, schools, public accommodations, and the workplace. The act seemed bold at the time, but it was enacted 10 years after the Supreme Court had declared racial discrimination "inherently unequal" and long after blacks had demonstrated that discrimination was no longer acceptable.

Public Accommodations After the passage of the 1964 Civil Rights Act, public accommodations quickly removed some of the most visible forms of racial discrimination. Signs defining "colored" and "white" restrooms, water fountains, waiting rooms, and seating arrangements were removed and a host of other practices that relegated black people to separate and inferior arrangements were ended. In addition, the federal government filed more than 400 antidiscrimination suits in federal courts against hotels, restaurants, taverns, gas stations, and other "public accommodations."

Many aspects of legalized racial segregation, such as using separate Bibles to swear in black and white witnesses in the courtroom, seem like ancient history today. But the issue of racial discrimination in public settings is by no means over. In 1993, six African American Secret Service agents filed suit after a Denny's restaurant in Annapolis, Maryland, failed to serve them. Similar charges citing discriminatory service at Denny's restaurants surfaced across the country. Faced with evidence of a pattern of systematic discrimination and numerous lawsuits, Denny's paid $45 million in damages to plaintiffs in Maryland and California in what is said to be the largest settlement ever in a public accommodation case.[82] In addition to the settlement, the chain vowed to expand employment and management opportunities for minorities in Denny's restaurants.

School Desegregation The 1964 Civil Rights Act also declared discrimination by private employers and state governments (school boards, etc.) illegal, then went further by providing for administrative agencies to help the courts implement these laws. The act, for example, authorized the executive branch, through the Justice Department, to implement federal court orders to desegregate schools and to do so without having to wait for individual parents to bring complaints. The act also provided that federal grants-in-aid to state and local governments for education be withheld from any school system practicing racial segregation.

In recent years, a series of court rulings have slowed race-based integration efforts. In 2007, the Supreme Court's ruling in *Parents Involved in Community Schools v. Seattle School District No. 1* limited the measures that can be used to promote school integration.[83] The case involved school assignment plans voluntarily initiated by the cities of Seattle, Washington, and Louisville, Kentucky. By making race one factor in assigning students to schools, the cities hoped to achieve greater racial balance across the public schools. The court ruled that these plans, even though they were voluntarily adopted by cities, were unconstitutional because they discriminated against white students on the basis of race. Many observers described the decision as the end of the Brown era because it eliminated one of the few public strategies left to promote racial integration.[84]

Outlawing Discrimination in Employment The federal courts and the Justice Department also fought employment discrimination through the Civil Rights Act of 1964, which outlawed job discrimination by all private and public employers, including governmental agencies (such as fire and police departments) that employed more than 15 workers.[85] The 1964 act makes it unlawful to discriminate in employment on the basis of color, religion, sex, or national origin, as well as race.

In order to enforce fair employment practices, the national government could revoke public contracts for goods and services and refuse to engage in contracts with any private company that could not guarantee that its rules for hiring, promotion, and firing were nondiscriminatory.

But one problem was that the complaining party had to show that deliberate discrimination was the cause of the failure to get a job or a training opportunity. Rarely, of course, does an employer explicitly admit discrimination on the basis of race, sex, or any other illegal reason. Recognizing this, the courts have allowed aggrieved parties (the plaintiffs) to make their case if they can show that an employer's hiring practices had the *effect* of exclusion, even if they cannot show the *intention* to discriminate.

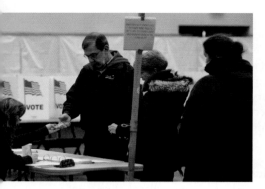

One of the most contentious areas of voting rights today is voter ID laws. Proponents say ID requirements prevent fraud, while opponents argue the rules purposely keep the poor and minorities, who are less likely to have picture IDs, from the polls.

Voting Rights Although 1964 was the *most* important year for civil rights legislation, it was not the only important year. In 1965, Congress significantly strengthened legislation protecting voting rights by barring literacy and other tests as a condition for voting in six southern states,[86] by making it a crime to interfere with voting, and by providing for the replacement of local registrars with federally appointed registrars in counties designated by the attorney general as significantly resistant to registering eligible blacks to vote. The right to vote was further strengthened with ratification in 1964 of the Twenty-Fourth Amendment, which abolished the poll tax, and later with legislation permanently outlawing literacy tests and mandating bilingual ballots or oral assistance for speakers of Spanish, Chinese, Japanese, Korean, and Native American languages. This 1965 law finally broke the back of voting discrimination, meaning that it took almost 100 years to carry out the Fifteenth Amendment.

In the long run, the laws extending and protecting voting rights could prove to be the most effective of all the great civil rights legislation because the progress in black political participation produced by these acts has altered the shape of American politics. In 1965, in the seven states of the Old Confederacy covered by the Voting Rights Act, 29.3 percent of the eligible black residents were registered to vote, compared with 73.4 percent of the white residents (see Table 4.3). In 1967, a mere two years after implementation of the voting rights laws, 52.1 percent of the eligible blacks in the seven states were registered. By 1972 the gap between black and white registration in the seven states was only 11.2 points.

A new area of controversy in the realm of voting rights concerns so-called voter ID laws. Some 34 states have enacted legislation requiring voters to show positive identification at the polls. As of 2016, seven of these states required photo ID, like a driver's license, in order to vote. Republicans generally support such laws, arguing that they deter voter fraud. Democrats generally oppose such laws, countering that they are particularly burdensome to poor, young, and minority voters, who they say are less likely than others to possess such IDs. Critics also note that virtually no documented cases of voter ID fraud exist, despite intensive efforts to uncover them. Several studies of whether such laws suppress voter turnout have been conducted but have produced inconclusive results.

Housing The Civil Rights Act of 1964 did not address housing, but in 1968, Congress passed another civil rights act specifically to outlaw housing discrimination. Called the Fair Housing Act, the law prohibited discrimination in the sale or rental of most housing, eventually covering nearly all of the nation's housing.

TABLE 4.3

Registration by Race and State in Southern States Covered by the Voting Rights Act (VRA)

The VRA had a direct impact on the rate of black voter registration in the southern states, as measured by the gap between white and black voters in each state. Further insights can be gained by examining changes in white registration rates before and after passage of the VRA and by comparing the gaps between white and black registration. Why do you think registration rates for whites increased significantly in some states and dropped in others? What impact could the increase in black registration have had on public policy?

	BEFORE THE ACT*			AFTER THE ACT* 1971–72		
	WHITE (%)	BLACK (%)	GAP** (%)	WHITE (%)	BLACK (%)	GAP (%)
Alabama	69.2	19.3	49.9	80.7	57.1	23.6
Georgia	62.6	27.4	35.2	70.6	67.8	2.8
Louisiana	80.5	31.6	48.9	80.0	59.1	20.9
Mississippi	69.9	6.7	63.2	71.6	62.2	9.4
North Carolina	96.8	46.8	50.0	62.2	46.3	15.9
South Carolina	75.7	37.3	38.4	51.2	48.0	3.2
Virginia	61.1	38.3	22.8	61.2	54.0	7.2
TOTAL	73.4	29.3	44.1	67.8	56.6	11.2

*Available registration data as of March 1965 and 1971–72.
**The gap is the percentage-point difference between white and black registration rates.

SOURCE: U.S. Commission on Civil Rights, Political Participation (1968), Appendix VII: Voter Education Project, attachment to press release, October 3, 1972.

Housing was among the most controversial of discrimination issues because of deeply entrenched patterns of residential segregation across the United States.

Although it pronounced sweeping goals, the Fair Housing Act had little effect on housing segregation because its enforcement mechanisms were so weak. Individuals believing they had been discriminated against had to file suit themselves. The burden was on the individual to prove that housing discrimination had occurred, even though such discrimination is often subtle and difficult to document. Although local fair-housing groups emerged to assist individuals in their court claims, the procedures for proving discrimination created a formidable barrier to effective change. These procedures were not altered until 1988, when Congress passed the Fair Housing Amendments Act. This new law put more teeth in the enforcement procedures and allowed the Department of Housing and Urban Development to initiate legal action in cases of discrimination.[87]

Another kind of discrimination, related to discriminatory home mortgage–lending practices, remained significant. So-called predatory lending—offering loans with interest rates that are higher than prevailing market rates, including "subprime mortgages"—led to charges that such loans were offered to African Americans and Latinos, while whites with similar incomes were offered loans with lower interest rates. These charges received extensive national attention when the economic downturn of 2008–09 led to widespread mortgage defaults, with many people losing their homes.[88] Lawsuits over these practices have resulted in the largest financial settlements ever issued for lending discrimination.

● The Civil Rights Struggle Was Extended to Other Disadvantaged Groups

Describe how different groups have fought for and won protection of their civil rights

Even before equal employment laws began to have a positive effect on the economic situation of blacks, something far more dramatic began to happen: the universalization of civil rights. The right not to be discriminated against was being successfully claimed by the other groups listed in the 1964 Civil Rights Act (those defined by sex, religion, or national origin) and eventually by still other groups (defined by age or sexual orientation). This extension of civil rights became the new frontier of the civil rights struggle, and women emerged with the greatest prominence in this new struggle.

Americans Have Fought Gender Discrimination

In many ways the Civil Rights Act fostered the growth of the women's movement (although critics noted that this movement largely benefited white women). The first major campaign of the National Organization for Women (NOW) involved picketing the EEOC for its refusal to ban sex-segregated employment advertisements. NOW also sued the *New York Times* for continuing to publish such ads after the passage of the act. Another organization, the Women's Equity Action League, pursued legal action on a wide range of sex-discrimination issues, filing lawsuits against law schools and medical schools for discriminatory admission policies, for example.

Building on these victories and the growth of the women's movement, feminist activists sought to add an "Equal Rights Amendment" (ERA) to the Constitution. The proposed amendment was short; it stated that "equality of rights under the law shall not be denied or abridged by the United States or by any State on account of sex." The amendment's supporters believed that such a sweeping guarantee of equal rights was a necessary tool for ending all discrimination against women and for making gender roles more equal. Opponents charged that it would be socially disruptive and would introduce changes (such as unisex restrooms) that most Americans did not want. The amendment easily passed Congress in 1972 and won quick approval in many state legislatures, but it fell 3 states short of the 38 needed to ratify it by the 1982 deadline.[89]

Despite the failure of the ERA, efforts to stop gender discrimination expanded dramatically as an area of civil rights law. In the 1970s the conservative

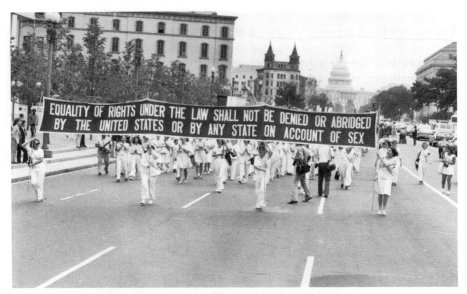

Political equality did not end discrimination against women in the workplace or in society at large. African Americans' struggle for civil rights in the 1950s and '60s spurred a parallel equal rights movement for women in the 1960s and '70s.

Burger Court (under Chief Justice Warren Burger) helped establish gender discrimination as a major and highly visible civil rights issue. Although the Supreme Court refused to treat gender discrimination as the equivalent of racial discrimination,[90] it did make it easier for plaintiffs to file and win suits on the basis of gender discrimination.

Courts began to find sexual harassment a form of sex discrimination during the late 1970s. Most of the law on sexual harassment has been developed by courts through interpretation of Title VII of the Civil Rights Act of 1964. In 1986, the Supreme Court recognized two forms of sexual harassment: the quid pro quo type, which involves an explicit or strongly implied threat that submission is a condition of continued employment, and the hostile environment type, which involves offensive or intimidating employment conditions amounting to sexual intimidation.[91]

Another major step was taken in 1992, when the Court decided in *Franklin v. Gwinnett County Public Schools* that violations of Title IX of the 1972 Education Act could be remedied with monetary damages.[92] Title IX forbade gender discrimination in education, but it initially sparked little litigation because of its weak enforcement provisions. The Court's 1992 ruling that monetary damages could be awarded for gender discrimination opened the door for more legal action in the area of education. The greatest impact has been in the areas of sexual harassment (the subject of the *Franklin* case) and in equal treatment of women's athletic programs. The potential for monetary damages has made universities and public schools take the problem of sexual harassment more seriously.

In 1996, the Supreme Court made another important decision by putting an end to all-male schools supported by public funds. It ruled that the policy of the Virginia Military Institute (VMI) not to admit women was unconstitutional.[93] Along with The Citadel, an all-male military college in South Carolina, VMI had never admitted women in its 157-year history. VMI argued that the unique educational experience it offered—including intense physical training and the harsh treatment of freshmen—would be destroyed if women were admitted. The Court, however, ruled that the male-only policy denied "substantial equality" to women. Two days after the Court's ruling, The Citadel announced that it would accept women.

Women have also pressed for civil rights in employment. In particular, women have fought against pay discrimination, which occurs when a male employee is paid more than a female employee of equal qualifications in the same job. In the 1960s, pay discrimination was common. After the Equal Pay Act of 1963 made such discrimination illegal, women's pay slowly moved toward the level of men's pay. In 2007, this movement received a setback when the Supreme Court ruled against a claim of pay discrimination. The case, *Ledbetter v. Goodyear Tire and Rubber Co.*, involved a female supervisor named Lily Ledbetter, who learned late in her career that she was being paid up to 40 percent less than male supervisors, including those with less seniority. Ledbetter filed a grievance with the EEOC, charging sex discrimination.[94] The Supreme Court denied her claim, ruling that, according to the law, workers must file their grievance 180 days after the discrimination occurs. Many observers found the ruling unfair because workers often do not know about pay differentials until well after the initial decision to discriminate has been made. In 2009, the Lily Ledbetter Fair Pay Act became the first bill that President Obama signed into law, giving workers expanded rights to sue in cases, such as Ledbetter's, when an employee learns of discriminatory treatment well after it has started.

In recent years, laws and court decisions designed to deal with discrimination against women have been used by groups representing transgender individuals to press for equal rights, especially in the realm of employment. For example, Title VII of the 1964 Civil Rights Act makes it unlawful to discriminate in employment on the basis of color, religion, sex, national origin, or race. Pressed by groups representing transgender workers, in 2015, President Obama issued an executive order prohibiting federal contractors from discriminating against workers based on their sexual orientation or gender identity. Two months later, the EEOC filed its first ever lawsuits to protect transgender workers under Title VII of the Civil Rights Act. Later that year, Attorney General Eric Holder announced that, going forward, the Justice Department would consider discrimination against transgender people as covered by the Civil Rights Act's prohibition of sex discrimination.[95] Nonetheless, attempts have been made to pass legislation requiring transgender individuals to use public bathrooms that correspond to the gender designated on their birth certificates. In 2016, North Carolina enacted such a law. After the federal Department of Justice warned the state that the law violated the Civil Rights Act, the state and the department filed opposing lawsuits over the issue. As the legal standoff continued, many companies pulled conventions and other events out of the state, costing North Carolina's economy millions of dollars. In the midst of this battle, in June 2016, the U.S. military dropped its ban against openly transgender people serving in the uniformed services.

Latinos and Asian Americans Fight for Rights

Although the Civil Rights Act of 1964 outlawed discrimination on the basis of national origin, limited English proficiency kept many Asian Americans and Latinos from full participation in American life. Two developments in the 1970s, however, established rights for language minorities. In 1974 the Supreme Court ruled in *Lau v. Nichols*, a suit filed on behalf of Chinese students in San Francisco, that school districts have to provide education for students whose English is limited.[96] It did not mandate bilingual education, but it established a duty to provide instruction that the students could understand. And the 1970 amendments to the Voting Rights Act permanently outlawed literacy tests in all 50 states and mandated bilingual ballots or oral assistance for those who speak Spanish, Chinese, Japanese, Korean, or Native American languages.

Asian Americans and Latinos have also been concerned about the impact of immigration laws on their civil rights. Many Asian American and Latino organizations opposed the Immigration Reform and Control Act of 1986 because it imposed sanctions on employers who hire undocumented workers. Such sanctions, they feared, would lead employers to discriminate against Latinos and Asian Americans. These suspicions were confirmed in a 1990 report by the General Accounting Office that found employer sanctions had created a "widespread pattern of discrimination" against Latinos and others who appear foreign.[97]

Young adults demonstrate their support for the DREAM Act by staging a sit-in protest on the floor of Senator John McCain's headquarters in Tucson, Arizona. The DREAM Act would provide a path to permanent residency via military service or college attendance for individuals who were brought to the United States illegally as children by their parents.

As we saw in Chapter 3, a number of states, including Arizona, Utah, South Carolina, Georgia, and Alabama, have recently passed very strict immigration laws. Civil rights groups have contested the laws in court, and the federal Justice Department has instituted its own legal challenges. Arizona's 2010 law provided the inspiration for these far-reaching state measures. Arizona's law required immigrants to carry identity documents with them at all times, made it a crime for an undocumented immigrant to apply for a job, gave the police greater powers to stop anyone they suspected of being an unauthorized immigrant, and required the police to check the immigration status of a person they detain if they suspect that person is an unauthorized immigrant. The Justice Department challenged the law on the grounds that the federal government was responsible for making immigration law, not the states. In 2012, the Court struck down three parts of the Arizona law on the grounds that they preempted federal responsibility. These included the provision that immigrants carry identity papers, that undocumented immigrants cannot apply for jobs, and that police can stop persons they suspect of being undocumented immigrants. But the Court let stand the provision that required local police to check the immigration status of an individual detained for other reasons, if they had grounds to suspect that the person was in the country illegally.[98]

In 2014, President Obama issued executive orders granting quasi-legal status and work permits to millions of individuals who entered the United States illegally as children or who have children who are American citizens. The Supreme Court challenged Obama's authority to issue the executive order, and in 2016, with only eight members on the Court after the death of Justice Scalia, the Court issued a 4–4 tie.[99] The stalemate let stand a lower-court decision striking down Obama's order. The lower-court decision, however, did not establish a binding national precedent and the administration seemed likely to ignore it.

Native Americans Have Sovereignty but Still Lack Rights

As a language minority, Native Americans were affected by the 1975 amendments to the Voting Rights Act and the *Lau* decision. The *Lau* decision established the right of Native Americans to be taught in their own languages. This marked quite a change from the period when Native American children attended boarding schools run by the Bureau of Indian Affairs, where they were forbidden from speaking their own languages. In addition to these language-related issues, Native Americans have sought to expand their rights on the basis of their sovereign status. Since the 1920s and '30s, Native American tribes have sued the federal government for illegally seizing land, seeking monetary reparations and land as damages. Both types of damages have been awarded in such suits but only in small amounts. Native American tribes have been more successful in winning federal recognition of their sovereignty. Sovereign status has, in turn, allowed them to exercise greater self-determination. Most significant economically was a 1987 Supreme Court decision that freed Native American tribes from most state regulations prohibiting gambling. The establishment of casino gambling on Native American lands has brought a substantial flow of new income into some desperately poor reservations.

Disabled Americans Won a Great Victory in 1990

The concept of rights for the disabled began to emerge in the 1970s as the civil rights model spread to other groups. The seed was planted in a little-noticed provision of the 1973 Rehabilitation Act, which outlawed discrimination against individuals on the basis of disabilities. As in many other cases, the law itself helped give rise to the movement demanding rights for the disabled.[100] Modeling it on the NAACP's Legal Defense Fund, the disability movement founded the Disability Rights Education and Defense Fund to press its legal claims. The movement achieved its greatest success with the passage of the Americans with Disabilities Act of 1990, which guarantees equal employment rights and access to public businesses for the disabled and bars discrimination in employment, housing, and health care. The EEOC is a body that considers claims of discrimination in violation of this act. The impact of the law has been far-reaching as businesses and public facilities have installed ramps, elevators, and other devices to meet the act's requirements.[101]

Gay Men and Lesbians Have Gained Significant Legal Ground

In less than 50 years, the lesbian, gay, bisexual, transgender, and queer (LGBTQ) movement has become one of the largest civil rights movements in contemporary America. For much of the country's history, any sexual orientation other than heterosexuality was considered "deviant" and many states criminalized sexual acts considered to be "unnatural." Gay people were often afraid to reveal their sexual orientation for fear of reprisals, including being fired from their jobs; and the police in many cities raided bars and other establishments where it was believed that gay people gathered. While no formal restrictions existed on their political participation, gay people faced the possibility of ostracism, discrimination, assault, and even prosecution.[102]

The contemporary gay rights movement began in earnest in the 1960s, growing into a well-financed and sophisticated lobby. But until 1996, there was no Supreme Court ruling or national legislation explicitly protecting gays and lesbians from discrimination. The first gay rights case that the Court decided, *Bowers v. Hardwick* (1986), ruled against a right to privacy that would protect consensual homosexual activity.[103] After the *Bowers* decision, the gay and lesbian rights movement sought suitable legal cases to test the constitutionality of discrimination against gay men and lesbians, much as the black civil rights movement did in the late 1940s and '50s. As one advocate put it, "lesbians and gay men are looking for their *Brown v. Board of Education*."[104] In 1996, the Supreme Court, in *Romer v. Evans*, explicitly extended fundamental civil rights protections to gays and lesbians by declaring unconstitutional a 1992 amendment to the Colorado state constitution that prohibited local governments from passing ordinances to protect gay rights.[105] In its decision, the Court highlighted the connection between gay rights and civil rights as it declared discrimination against gay people unconstitutional.

The gay community won another major victory in the 2003 case of *Lawrence v. Texas*, in which the Supreme Court overturned *Bowers* and struck

Edith Windsor (left center) won her case in 2013 when the Supreme Court struck down the portion of the Defense of Marriage Act denying federal benefits to married same-sex couples. This decision paved the way for the Court decision two years later legalizing same-sex marriage nationwide. The Obama administration showed its support by illuminating the White House in rainbow light (right).

down a Texas law that made certain sexual conduct between consenting partners of the same sex illegal. Extending the right-to-privacy umbrella to lesbians and gay men, the Court said that "petitioners are entitled to respect for their private lives. The State cannot demean their existence or control their destiny by making their private sexual conduct a crime."[106]

While the ruling in *Lawrence* struck down laws that made homosexual acts a crime, it did not change federal and state laws that deprived gay people of full civil rights, including the right to marry. In 2013 the Supreme Court struck down a federal law (the Defense of Marriage Act, or DOMA) that barred benefits to married same-sex couples and let stand a California law recognizing same-sex marriage. Invoking several constitutional protections, the cases significantly strengthened the rights of married gay couples.[107] The federal government subsequently expanded recognition of same-sex marriages for the purpose of federal benefits and legal proceedings, such as survivor benefits, bankruptcies, tax purposes, and immigration.

In 2015 the Supreme Court clarified the law concerning same-sex marriage. In the landmark case of *Obergefell v. Hodges*, the Court ruled that the Constitution's equal protection clause and the Fourteenth Amendment's due process clause guarantee same-sex couples the right to marry in all states and required states to recognize same-sex marriages performed in other jurisdictions.[108] Though deemed controversial, the Court's decision actually reflected a shift in public opinion on same-sex unions, with a majority of Americans now favoring the right of same-sex couples to wed.

Another significant victory at the national level occurred in 2009, when new legislation extended the definition of hate crimes to include crimes against gays and transgender people. Such legislation had been sought since the 1998 murder of Matthew Shepard, a Wyoming college student who was brutally slain because of his sexual orientation. The new law allows for tougher penalties when a crime is designated a hate crime. In another important victory for the gay rights movement,

Same-Sex Marriage around the World

When the U.S. Supreme Court legalized same-sex marriage in 2015, the United States joined the roughly 20 countries in the world that allow gay marriage. As the map shows, most of these countries are in Western Europe and the Americas, and we see in the time line that most have only legalized same-sex marriage in the past several years.

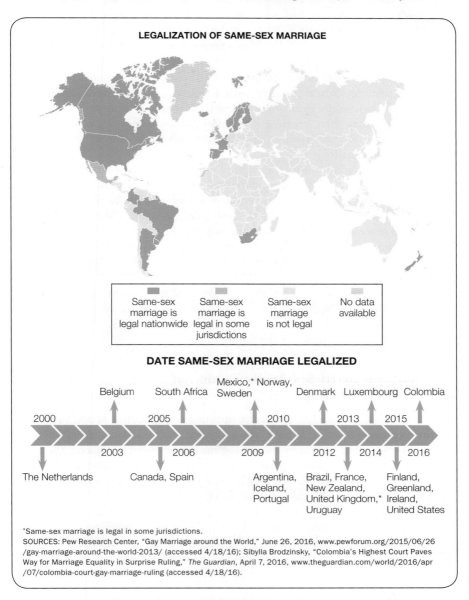

LEGALIZATION OF SAME-SEX MARRIAGE

- Same-sex marriage is legal nationwide
- Same-sex marriage is legal in some jurisdictions
- Same-sex marriage is not legal
- No data available

DATE SAME-SEX MARRIAGE LEGALIZED

Year	Countries (above line)	Countries (below line)
2000		
2003		The Netherlands
Belgium	Belgium	
2005		
South Africa	South Africa	
2006		Canada, Spain
Mexico,* Norway, Sweden	Mexico,* Norway, Sweden	
2009		Argentina, Iceland, Portugal
2010		
Denmark	Denmark	
2012		Brazil, France, New Zealand, United Kingdom,* Uruguay
2013	Luxembourg	
2014		Finland, Greenland, Ireland, United States
2015		
Colombia	Colombia	
2016		

*Same-sex marriage is legal in some jurisdictions.
SOURCES: Pew Research Center, "Gay Marriage around the World," June 26, 2016, www.pewforum.org/2015/06/26/gay-marriage-around-the-world-2013/ (accessed 4/18/16); Sibylla Brodzinsky, "Colombia's Highest Court Paves Way for Marriage Equality in Surprise Ruling," *The Guardian*, April 7, 2016, www.theguardian.com/world/2016/apr/07/colombia-court-gay-marriage-ruling (accessed 4/18/16).

an executive order signed by President Obama in 2011 repealed the U.S. military's "Don't Ask, Don't Tell" policy, a 20-year-old rule that expelled gays and lesbians from the military if they made their sexual orientation known. The new policy allows gays to serve openly in the military.

● Affirmative Action Attempts to Right Past Wrongs

Contrast arguments for and against affirmative action

Over the past half-century, the relatively narrow goal of equalizing opportunity by eliminating discriminatory barriers developed toward the far broader goal of **affirmative action**, government policies or programs that seek to redress past injustices against specified groups by making special efforts to provide members of these groups with access to educational and employment opportunities. An affirmative action policy uses two novel approaches: (1) positive or benign discrimination in which race or some other status is counted as a positive rather than negative factor and (2) compensatory action to favor members of the disadvantaged group who themselves may never have been the victims of discrimination.

Affirmative action also took the form of efforts by the agencies in the Department of Health, Education, and Welfare to shift their focus from "desegregation" to "integration."[109] Federal agencies required school districts to present plans for busing children across district lines, for closing certain schools, and for redistributing faculties as well as students or face the loss of aid from the federal government. The guidelines constituted preferential treatment to compensate for past discrimination, leading to a dramatic increase in the numbers of black children attending integrated classes.

Affirmative action was also initiated in the area of employment opportunity. The EEOC has often required plans whereby employers must attempt to increase the number of minority employees, and the Department of Labor has used the threat of contract revocation for the same purpose.

The Supreme Court Shifts the Burden of Proof in Affirmative Action

Efforts by the government to shape the meaning of affirmative action today tend to center on one key issue: What is the appropriate level of review in affirmative action cases—that is, on whom should the burden of proof be placed: the plaintiff, to show that discrimination has not occurred, or the defendant, to show that discrimination has occurred? Affirmative action was first addressed formally by the Supreme Court in the case of Allan Bakke. Bakke, a white male, brought suit against the University of California at Davis Medical School on the grounds that it denied him admission on the basis of his race. (That year the school had reserved 16 of its 100 available slots for minority applicants.) Bakke argued that his grades and test scores had ranked him well above many students who had been accepted at the school and that the only possible explanation for his rejection was that he was white, whereas those others accepted were black or Latino. In 1978, Bakke won his case before the Supreme Court and was admitted to the medical school, but he did not succeed in getting affirmative action declared unconstitutional. The Court accepted the argument that achieving "a diverse student body" was "a compelling public purpose," but it ruled that the method of a rigid quota of student slots assigned on the basis of race was incompatible with the Fourteenth Amendment's equal protection clause. Thus, the Court permitted universities and other hiring authorities to continue to take minority status into consideration but barred the use of quotas.[110]

The Supreme Court's 1995 ruling in *Adarand Constructors v. Peña* further weakened affirmative action. This decision stated that race-based policies must survive strict scrutiny, placing the burden on the government to show that such affirmative action programs serve a compelling government interest and are narrowly tailored to address identifiable past discrimination.[111]

This betwixt-and-between status of affirmative action was how things stood in 2003, when the Supreme Court took two cases against the University of Michigan. In *Grutter v. Bollinger*, the Court upheld the "holistic" and "individualized" affirmative action program used by Michigan's law school, finding it in keeping with the standard set in the *Bakke* case.[112] Michigan's undergraduate affirmative action program was declared unconstitutional, however, in *Gratz v. Bollinger* because its ranking system for admissions gave specific points (20 out of 150) to African American, Latino, and Native American applicants.[113] This approach was barred for resembling too closely the specific numerical quota system struck down by *Bakke*. In 2013 the Court indicated in *Fisher v. University of Texas* that a school's affirmative action program of admissions that seems to discriminate in favor of black students must be subjected to the same "strict scrutiny" as a program that seems to discriminate against black students and sent the case back to the lower courts for consideration.[114] The Court heard the case again in 2016, and declared that some intrusion on equal protection was warranted by the importance of creating a diverse student body.[115]

Civil Liberties, Civil Rights,
and Your Future

Government surveillance of its citizens—encompassing their communications, travel, and personal conduct—is among the major civil liberties questions facing Americans today. Revelations in 2013 of extensive electronic surveillance by the NSA of Americans' phone and Internet communications caused an uproar in Congress and in the country.

While many expressed concerns about citizens' privacy, NSA officials declared in 2013 congressional testimony that the agency's eavesdropping program had averted dozens of potential terrorist attacks. But since the matters were highly classified, no actual proof of these assertions was proffered, and many members of Congress expressed doubts about the agency's claims. Later, the NSA conceded that its domestic surveillance programs had possibly thwarted only one terrorist plot, rather than the dozens initially claimed. Are worries about privacy overblown, or are the actual threats exaggerated? How have new technologies affected the government's ability to monitor its citizens? These issues, along with questions about the right to bear arms, the use of the death penalty, and religious freedom (see the "**Who Participates?**" feature on the facing page) are unlikely to go away anytime soon.

For the past several decades, the civil rights revolution has broadened to include not only women and Latinos but sexual orientation and immigration status. As our nation becomes more and more diverse, equal protection of the laws will become more and more important. What civil rights battles now appear on the country's horizon? And how does a country based on the democratic principle of majority rule ensure that the civil rights of minorities are protected?

Know Your First Amendment Rights

 Learn more about freedom of religion from a variety of legal scholars at **www.constitutioncenter.org**.

 Share your opinion about the First Amendment and religion on campus with your school newspaper. Find information about students' religious rights at **www.thefire.org**.

 Learn more about your other First Amendment rights, such as free speech on the Internet, at **www.eff.org**.

chapterstudyguide

Practice Quiz

1. Which of the following rights was *not* included in the original Constitution? *(p. 97)*
   a) prohibition of bills of attainder
   b) prohibition of ex post facto laws
   c) guarantee of habeas corpus
   d) guarantee of trial by jury in state where crime was committed
   e) prohibition of warrantless search and seizure

2. When did civil rights become part of the Constitution? *(p. 98)*
   a) in 1789 at the Founding
   b) with the adoption of the Fourteenth Amendment in 1868
   c) with the adoption of the Nineteenth Amendment in 1920
   d) in the 1954 *Brown v. Board of Education* case

   e) with the passage of the 1964 Civil Rights Act

3. The process by which some of the liberties in the Bill of Rights were applied to the states (or nationalized) is known as *(p. 99)*
   a) selective incorporation.
   b) judicial activism.
   c) civil liberties.
   d) establishment.
   e) preemption.

4. The judicial doctrine that places a heavy burden of proof on the government when it seeks to regulate or restrict speech is called *(p. 103)*
   a) judicial restraint.
   b) judicial activism.
   c) habeas corpus.

Religious Affiliation and Freedom of Religion

Percentage of American Adults in Each Religious Tradition

Under the First Amendment, Americans enjoy the freedom to practice (or not practice) the religion of their choice. Most Americans identify with and participate in some form of religion.

- Protestant **46.5%**
- Catholic **20.8%**
- Other Christian **3.3%**
- Jewish **1.9%**

- Muslim **0.9%**
- Buddhist **0.7%**
- Hindu **0.7%**
- Other faiths **1.7%**

- Nothing in particular **15.8%**
- Agnostic **4%**
- Atheist **3.1%**
- Don't know **0.6%**

SOURCE: Pew Research Center, "America's Changing Religious Landscape." www.pewforum.org/2015/05/12/americas-changing-religious-landscape, (accessed 9/20/15).

WHAT YOU CAN DO ➡

d) prior restraint.

e) strict scrutiny.

5. Which of the following protections are *not* contained in the First Amendment? *(pp. 103–9)*
   a) the establishment clause
   b) the free exercise clause
   c) freedom of the press
   d) the right to peaceably assemble
   e) freedom from unlawful searches and seizures

6. In *McDonald v. Chicago*, the Supreme Court ruled that *(p. 110)*
   a) states can require citizens to own firearms.
   b) federal grants can be used to support the formation of state militias.
   c) felons can be prevented from purchasing assault rifles.
   d) the Second Amendment applies to states as well as the federal government.
   e) the Second Amendment applies only to the federal government and not to states.

7. The Fourth, Fifth, Sixth, and Eighth amendments, taken together, define *(p. 111)*
   a) due process of law.
   b) free speech.
   c) the right to bear arms.
   d) civil rights of minorities.
   e) freedom of religion.

8. In *Mapp v. Ohio*, the Supreme Court ruled that *(pp. 111–12)*
   a) evidence obtained from an illegal search could not be introduced in a trial.
   b) the government must provide legal counsel for defendants who are too poor to provide for themselves.
   c) persons under arrest must be informed prior to police interrogation of their rights to remain silent and to have the benefits of legal counsel.
   d) the government has the right to take private property for public use if just compensation is provided.
   e) a person cannot be tried twice for the same crime.

9. In which case did the Supreme Court rule that state governments no longer had the authority to make private sexual behavior a crime? *(p. 118)*
   a) *Webster v. Reproductive Health Services*
   b) *Gonzales v. Oregon*
   c) *Lawrence v. Texas*
   d) *Bowers v. Hardwick*
   e) *Texas v. Johnson*

10. Which of the following was *not* a way the Twenty-Fourth Amendment of 1964 and the Voting Rights Act of 1965 significantly extended and protected voting rights? *(p. 124)*
    a) barring literacy tests as a condition for voting in six southern states
    b) requiring all voters to register two weeks before any federal election
    c) making it a crime to interfere with voting
    d) abolishing the poll tax
    e) providing for the replacement of local registrars with federally appointed registrars in counties designated as significantly resistant to registering eligible black voters

11. The Supreme Court's decision in *Bakke v. Board of Regents* was significant because *(pp. 134–35)*
    a) it stated that race can never be used as a factor in university admissions.
    b) it stated that achieving diversity was a "compelling public purpose" but a rigid quota system based on race was incompatible with the Fourteenth Amendment's equal protection clause.
    c) it permitted quotas and separate university admission standards for members of minority groups.
    d) it upheld the constitutionality of mechanical point systems that favor minority applicants in university admissions.
    e) it declared that affirmative action policies would no longer be subject to strict scrutiny from the courts.

Key Terms

affirmative action *(p. 134)* government policies or programs that seek to redress past injustices against specified groups by making special efforts to provide members of these groups with access to educational and employment opportunities

bill of attainder *(p. 97)* a law that declares a person guilty of a crime without a trial

Brown v. Board of Education *(p. 120)* the 1954 Supreme Court decision that struck down the "separate but equal" doctrine as fundamentally unequal; this case eliminated state power to use race as a criterion for discrimination in law and provided the national government with the power to intervene by exercising strict regulatory policies against discriminatory actions

civil liberties *(p. 95)* areas of personal freedom constitutionally protected from government interference

civil rights *(p. 96)* obligation imposed on government to take positive action to protect citizens from any illegal action of government agencies and of other private citizens

"clear and present danger" test *(p. 104)* test to determine whether speech is protected or unprotected, based on its capacity to present a "clear and present danger" to society

double jeopardy *(p. 113)* the Fifth Amendment right providing that a person cannot be tried twice for the same crime

due process of law *(p. 98)* the right of every citizen against arbitrary action by national or state governments

eminent domain *(p. 114)* the right of government to take private property for public use

equal protection clause *(p. 118)* provision of the Fourteenth Amendment guaranteeing citizens "the equal protection of the laws"; this clause has served as the basis for the civil rights of African Americans, women, and other groups

establishment clause *(p. 101)* the First Amendment clause that says that "Congress shall make no law respecting an establishment of religion"; this law means that a "wall of separation" exists between church and state

exclusionary rule *(p. 111)* the ability of courts to exclude evidence obtained in violation of the Fourth Amendment

ex post facto laws *(p. 97)* laws that declare an action to be illegal after it has been committed

fighting words *(p. 108)* speech that directly incites damaging conduct

free exercise clause *(p. 102)* the First Amendment clause that protects a citizen's right to believe and practice whatever religion he or she chooses

grand jury *(p. 113)* jury that determines whether sufficient evidence is available to justify a trial; grand juries do not rule on the accused's guilt or innocence

habeas corpus *(p. 97)* a court order demanding that an individual in custody be brought into court and shown the cause for detention

libel *(p. 107)* a written statement made in "reckless disregard of the truth" that is considered damaging to a victim because it is "malicious, scandalous, and defamatory"

Miranda rule *(p. 114)* the requirement, articulated by the Supreme Court in *Miranda v. Arizona* (1966), that persons under arrest must be informed prior to police interrogation of their rights to remain silent and to have the benefit of legal counsel

prior restraint *(p. 106)* an effort by a governmental agency to block the publication of material it deems libelous or harmful in some other way; censorship; in the United States, the courts forbid prior restraint except under the most extraordinary circumstances

selective incorporation *(p. 99)* the process by which different protections in the Bill of Rights were incorporated into the Fourteenth Amendment, thus guaranteeing citizens protection from state as well as national governments

"separate but equal" rule *(p. 119)* doctrine that public accommodations could be segregated by race but still be considered equal

slander *(p. 107)* an oral statement made in "reckless disregard of the truth" that is considered damaging to the victim because it is "malicious, scandalous, and defamatory"

strict scrutiny *(p. 103)* a test used by the Supreme Court in racial discrimination cases and other cases involving civil liberties and civil rights that places the burden of proof on the government rather than on the challengers to show that the law in question is constitutional

For Further Reading

Abraham, Henry J., and Barbara A. Perry. *Freedom and the Court: Civil Rights and Liberties in the United States*. 8th ed. Lawrence: University Press of Kansas, 2004.

Barendt, Eric. *Freedom of Speech*. 2nd ed. New York: Oxford University Press, 2007.

Chen, Anthony S. *The Fifth Freedom: Jobs, Politics, and Civil Rights in the United States, 1941–1972*. Princeton, NJ: Princeton University Press, 2009.

Eisgruber, Christopher. *Religious Freedom and the Constitution*. Cambridge, MA: Harvard University Press, 2010.

Friedman, Barry. *The Will of the People: How Public Opinion Has Influenced the Supreme Court and Shaped the Meaning of the Constitution*. New York: Farrar, Straus and Giroux, 2009.

Greenberg, Jack. *Crusades in the Courts: How a Dedicated Band of Lawyers Fought for the Civil Rights Revolution*. New York: Basic Books, 1994.

King, Desmond, and Rogers M. Smith. *Still a House Divided: Race and Politics in Obama's America*. Princeton, NJ: Princeton University Press, 2011.

Lee, Sonia Song-Ha. *Building a Latino Civil Rights Movement*. Chapel Hill: University of North Carolina Press, 2014.

Lewis, Anthony. *Freedom for the Thought that We Hate: A Biography of the First Amendment*. New York: Basic Books, 2010.

Nichols, Walter. *The Dreamers: How the Undocumented Youth Movement Transformed the Immigrant Rights Debate*. Stanford, CA: Standford University Press, 2013.

Orth, John. *Due Process of Law: A Brief History*. Lawrence: University Press of Kansas, 2003.

Richards, Neil. *Intellectual Privacy: Rethinking Civil Liberties in the Digital Age*. New York: Oxford University Press, 2015.

Solove, Daniel. *Nothing to Hide: The False Tradeoff between Privacy and Security*. New Haven, CT: Yale University Press, 2011.

Spitzer, Robert J. *Saving the Constitution from Lawyers: How Legal Training and Law Reviews Distort Constitutional Meaning*. New York: Cambridge University Press, 2008.

What accounts for changing public opinion? Before 2011, most Americans did not think income inequality was a problem, whereas today the issue is at the forefront of the political agenda. The recent movement to increase the minimum wage to $15 an hour has continued the national discussion on wealth distribution in the United States.

Public Opinion

WHAT GOVERNMENT DOES AND WHY IT MATTERS We expect government to pay attention to the people, and research has shown that public opinion does indeed have a significant impact on public policy. There are debates among scholars, however, about whether the public is sufficiently informed about politics, as well as whether elected officials represent the interests of all Americans or only some Americans.

Consider public opinion on certain economic policies. Economic inequality—a growing gap in income between the very richest Americans and everyone else—is a striking condition of contemporary America. Political scientist Larry Bartels has shown that the gap between the super-rich and everyone else has increased since the 1980s and continues to grow.[1] Between 1993 and 2013, the income of the top 1 percent of Americans grew 62.4 percent, while the income of the other 99 percent grew 7.3 percent. While the average household income in the United States was $56,516 in 2015, the top 5 percent of earners had an income of at least $214,463.[2] The United States has some of the highest economic inequality in the world.[3]

Are Americans aware of this growing economic inequality? Public opinion polls have shown that while most Americans acknowledge the large gap between the rich and the poor in the United States, only 47 percent thought it was a serious problem in 2013.[4] But public opinion on inequality of wealth has shifted in recent years, becoming more in line with the reality of economic conditions. A 2015 survey found that 67 percent of Americans believed the "gap between the rich and the poor in the United States is getting larger," a major increase from two years prior. Six in 10 Americans now say that it is mainly just a few people at the top who have a chance to get ahead.[5]

Today large majorities of Americans favor a variety of proposals aimed at strengthening workers' rights, including paid sick leave and paid family leave, and raising taxes on the wealthy. A recent movement to increase the minimum wage to $15 an hour has sparked rallies and strikes in many cities round the country as organized labor and antipoverty groups worked to draw attention to income inequality. Furthermore, partisanship appears to have a big effect on people's opinions. While 89 percent of Democrats agreed that money and wealth in the United States should be more evenly distributed among more people, just 44 percent of Republicans agreed.[6] Still, concern about inequality is growing on both sides and challenges long-held beliefs about economic opportunity.

What caused this shift in public opinion on economic inequality? Will policy makers in government respond to these changing opinions and if so, how? As we will see in this chapter, an informed public is crucial in order for citizens to have their voices heard, and what people think about politics matters. In the first four chapters, we have examined the development of the American government. With this chapter, we turn to American politics as it operates in society. We begin with public opinion.

chaptergoals

- Define public opinion, and identify broad types of values and beliefs Americans have about politics (pp. 145–50)

- Explain the major factors that shape specific individual opinions (pp. 150–55)

- Explore when and why public opinion changes and the role that political knowledge plays (pp. 156–58)

- Describe the major forces that shape public opinion (pp. 158–61)

- Describe basic survey methods and other techniques researchers use to measure public opinion (pp. 161–67)

● Public Opinion Represents Attitudes about Politics

Define public opinion, and identify broad types of values and beliefs Americans have about politics

The term **public opinion** refers to the attitudes citizens have about political issues, leaders, institutions, and events. It is useful to distinguish between values and beliefs, on the one hand, and attitudes and opinions, on the other. **Values (or beliefs)** are the basic principles that shape a person's opinions about political issues and events. They constitute a person's basic orientation to politics. Values underlie deep-rooted goals, aspirations, and ideals that shape an individual's perceptions of political issues and events. Liberty, equality of opportunity, and democracy, for example, are basic political values held by most Americans.

An **attitude (or opinion)** is a specific preference on a particular issue. An individual may have an attitude toward American policy in the Middle East or an opinion about economic inequality in the United States. The attitude or opinion may have emerged from a broad belief about the purpose of military intervention or about the role of government in the economy, but the opinion itself is very specific. Some attitudes may be short-lived and can change based on changing circumstances or new information.

Factors such as race, gender, income, age, religion, and region—which not only affect individuals' interests but also shape their experiences and upbringing—influence Americans' beliefs and opinions. For example, individuals whose incomes differ substantially have correspondingly different views on the desirability of any number of important economic and social programs. In general, the poor—who are the chief beneficiaries of these programs—support them more strongly than do those who are wealthier and pay more of the taxes that fund the programs. Blacks and whites have different views on issues that touch upon civil rights and race relations, such as affirmative action, presumably reflecting differences of interest and historical experience. In recent years, many observers have begun to take note of various differences between the views expressed by men and those expressed by women, especially on foreign policy questions, where women appear to be much more concerned with the dangers of war. Political attitudes are also strongly influenced by partisanship (e.g., Republican versus Democrat) and ideology (e.g., conservative versus liberal).

Opinions about issues and politics have emotional underpinnings as well.[7] Emotional responses to candidates or policies run the gamut from strongly positive to strongly negative, and these emotions are traditionally measured by survey questions asking if a candidate (or individual, event, or issue) makes the respondent feel fearful, anxious, angry, or enthusiastic. Contrary to the idea that public opinion is purely rational, feelings are complicated and often irrational; once individuals become emotionally attached to particular beliefs, they tend to hold on to those beliefs even in the face of contradictory information. Using emotions as a guide, individuals form opinions quickly in response to current events.[8]

Take, for example, public opinion about foreign policy and global terrorism. When President Obama entered the White House in 2008, Americans had tired

Emotional responses to events can have a substantial effect on public opinion. The fear and anger that many Americans felt following the 2015 terrorist attacks on Paris by ISIS contributed to increased public support for military intervention in the Middle East.

of the Iraq War (begun in 2003), and large majorities wanted the United States to withdraw troops from the region. But in 2015, most Americans again favored military intervention in the Middle East. Why? Emotions may be part of the answer. Viral news spread rapidly beginning in 2014 when an extremist militia group calling itself the Islamic State of Iraq and Syria (ISIS) used the web to distribute gruesome videos of beheadings of foreign journalists, soldiers, and Christians. ISIS gained momentum quickly, taking over large swaths of Iraq and Syria, including key cities, trade routes, and oil fields. Media coverage of the militant group fueled emotions of fear, and by 2015 more than twice as many people approved as disapproved of the military campaign against ISIS.[9]

Americans Share Common Political Values

Most Americans share a common set of values, including a belief in the principles, if not always the actual practice, of liberty, equality, and democracy. The United States was founded on the principle of individual **liberty**, or freedom. Since the birth of our nation, Americans have always voiced strong support for the idea of liberty and typically support the notion that governmental interference in individuals' lives and property should be kept to a minimum.

Similarly, **equality of opportunity** has always been an important theme in American society. Most Americans believe that all individuals should be allowed to seek personal and material/economic success. Moreover, Americans generally believe that such success should be the result of individual effort and ability, rather than family connections or other forms of special privilege. Quality public education is one of the most important mechanisms for obtaining equality of opportunity in that it allows individuals, regardless of personal or family wealth, a chance to get ahead. Today, the Internet is an important example of equality of opportunity by providing online access to news, politics, jobs, and other benefits of digital citizenship.[10]

Most Americans also believe in **democracy**. They believe that every citizen should have the opportunity to take part in the nation's governmental and policy-making processes and to have some say in determining how he is governed, including the right to vote in elections.[11] Figure 5.1 shows there is consensus among Americans on fundamental values.

Obviously, the principles that Americans espouse have not always been put into practice. For 200 years, Americans embraced the principles of individual liberty and equality of opportunity while denying them in practice to generations of African Americans. Yet the strength of the principles ultimately helped overcome practices that deviated from those principles.

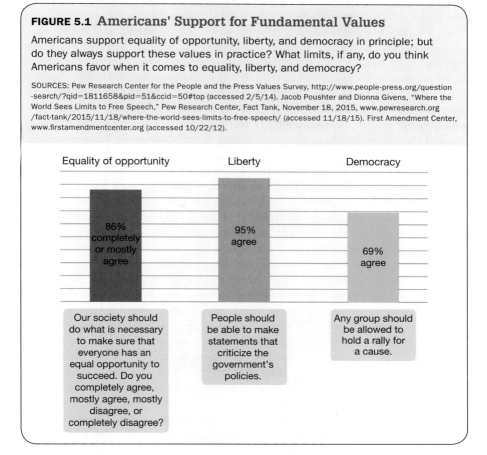

FIGURE 5.1 Americans' Support for Fundamental Values

Americans support equality of opportunity, liberty, and democracy in principle; but do they always support these values in practice? What limits, if any, do you think Americans favor when it comes to equality, liberty, and democracy?

SOURCES: Pew Research Center for the People and the Press Values Survey, http://www.people-press.org/question -search/?qid=1811658&pid=51&ccid=50#top (accessed 2/5/14). Jacob Poushter and Dionna Givens, "Where the World Sees Limits to Free Speech," Pew Research Center, Fact Tank, November 18, 2015, www.pewresearch.org /fact-tank/2015/11/18/where-the-world-sees-limits-to-free-speech/ (accessed 11/18/15). First Amendment Center, www.firstamendmentcenter.org (accessed 10/22/12).

Equality of opportunity — Liberty — Democracy

86% completely or mostly agree

95% agree

69% agree

Our society should do what is necessary to make sure that everyone has an equal opportunity to succeed. Do you completely agree, mostly agree, mostly disagree, or completely disagree?

People should be able to make statements that criticize the government's policies.

Any group should be allowed to hold a rally for a cause.

America's Dominant Political Ideologies Are Liberalism and Conservatism

As we noted in the previous section, Americans share broadly in their fundamental political values. However, the application of these values to specific policies varies quite a bit. The set of underlying orientations, ideas, and beliefs through which we come to understand and interpret politics is called a **political ideology**. In the United States today, a variety of ideologies compete for attention and support, but two are dominant: liberalism and conservatism.

Liberalism In classical political theory, a *liberal* was someone who favored individual initiative and was suspicious of governments and their ability to manage economic and social affairs—a definition akin to that of today's libertarian. The proponents of a larger and more active government called themselves *progressives*. In the early twentieth century, many liberals and progressives coalesced around the doctrine of "social liberalism," which represented recognition that government action might be needed to preserve individual liberty. Today's liberals are social liberals rather than classical liberals.

In contemporary politics being **liberal** has come to imply supporting political and social reform; extensive government intervention in the economy and progressive taxation; workers' rights; the expansion of federal social services; more vigorous efforts on behalf of the poor, minorities, and women; and greater concern for consumers and the environment. Liberals generally support abortion rights and rights for gays and lesbians and are concerned with protecting the rights of people accused of crime. In international affairs, liberals often support arms control, aid to poor nations, and international organizations such as the United Nations; liberals generally oppose the development and testing of nuclear weapons and are suspicious of the use of American troops to influence the affairs of developing nations.

Conservatism By contrast, **conservatives** generally support the social and economic status quo and are suspicious of efforts to introduce new political formulae and economic arrangements. They believe strongly that a large and powerful government poses a threat to the freedom of individual citizens. Ironically, today's conservatives support the views of classical liberalism. Today, in the domestic arena, conservatives generally oppose the expansion of governmental activity, asserting that solutions to social and economic problems can and should be developed in the private sector. Conservatives particularly oppose efforts to impose government regulation on business and the environment, maintaining that regulation frequently leads to economic inefficiency, is costly, and can ultimately lower the entire nation's standard of living. In terms of social policy, many conservatives support school prayer and traditional family arrangements and are concerned about law and order; conservatives generally oppose abortion, same-sex marriage, and the use of mandatory school busing to achieve the racial integration of schools. In international affairs, conservatism has come to mean support for military intervention and the maintenance of American military power as well as a desire to restrict immigration.

Other political ideologies also influence American politics. **Libertarians**, for example, argue that government interferes with freedom of expression, free markets,

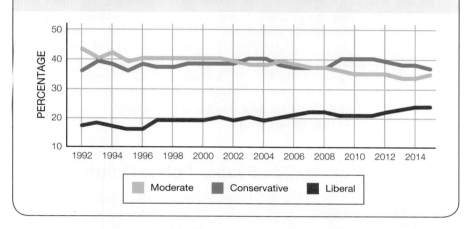

FIGURE 5.2 Americans' Ideology

More Americans identify themselves as "conservatives" than "liberals." During the period shown in this figure, however, Americans have had two Democratic presidents and have several times elected Democratic majorities to a house of Congress. What might account for this apparent discrepancy? What role do moderates play in the electorate? How stable is Americans' ideology over time?

SOURCE: Lydia Saad, "Conservatives Hang On to Ideology Lead by a Thread," Gallup, January 11, 2016, www.gallup .com/poll/188129/conservatives-hang-ideology-lead-thread.aspx (accessed 10/3/16).

and society and thus should be limited to as few spheres of activity as possible (national defense being a notable exception). Libertarians prefer government to be even smaller than that favored by conservatives. While libertarians believe in less government intervention in economic and social realms, **socialists** argue that more government is necessary to promote justice and to reduce economic inequality.

Americans' Ideologies Today Although many Americans subscribe to libertarianism, socialism, or other ideologies in part, most describe themselves as either liberals, conservatives, or moderates. Figure 5.2 shows that the percentage of Americans who consider themselves moderates, liberals, or conservatives has remained relatively constant since the 1990s. Gallup surveys indicate that as of 2015, 37 percent of Americans considered themselves conservatives, 35 percent moderates, and 24 percent liberals. Within each ideological group, individual beliefs often vary. Many conservatives support at least some government social programs, and many liberals favor strong national defense or oppose government regulations.

Americans Exhibit Low Trust in Government

One of the most important measures of public opinion in a democracy is trust in government. High levels of political trust create legitimacy for democratic government, whereas very low levels can cause concern. Many scholars and political pundits argue that Americans are becoming more and more disenchanted with traditional political institutions; public approval of Congress reached a low of only 10 percent in 2014. "Critical citizens" are characterized by high expectations of democracy as an ideal and yet low evaluations of the actual performance of government.[12]

Why does public opinion in the form of trust matter? Declining trust has been linked to declines in political participation and voting. Low confidence in government and elected officials is related to the perception that the government is unable to solve problems, spend money in an effective or efficient way, or represent the interests and policy preferences of average voters.[13]

The Pew Research Center has tracked trust in the federal government from 1958 to 2015 by asking this question on national surveys: "How much of the time do you trust the government in Washington?"[14] The percentage of Americans who indicate they trust the government "just about always or most of the time" has fallen from 73 percent in 1960 to just 19 percent in 2015. These trends span party lines. In 2015 only 11 percent of Republicans indicated they trusted government all or most of the time compared with 16 percent of independents and 26 percent of Democrats. (When Republicans hold the White House, slightly more Republicans trust government than Democrats.)

● Political Socialization Shapes Public Opinion

Explain the major factors that shape specific individual opinions

People's attitudes about political issues and elected officials tend to be shaped by underlying political beliefs and values. For example, an individual who has negative feelings about government intervention in America's economy and society would probably oppose the development of new social and health care programs. Similarly, someone who distrusts the military would likely be suspicious of any call for the use of U.S. troops. The processes through which these underlying political beliefs and values are formed are collectively called **political socialization**.

Probably no nation, and certainly no democracy, could survive if its citizens did not share some fundamental beliefs. If Americans had few common values or perspectives, it would be very difficult for them to reach agreement on particular issues. In contemporary America, some elements of the socialization process tend to produce differences in outlook, whereas others promote similarities. The **agents of socialization** that shape political beliefs are the family and social networks, social groups and race, political party affiliation, education, and political environment.

The Family and Social Networks Most people acquire their initial orientation to politics from their families. As might be expected, differences in family background tend to produce divergent political perspectives. Although relatively few parents spend much time directly teaching their children about politics, political conversations occur in many households, and children tend to absorb the political views of parents and other caregivers, often without realizing it. Studies find, for example, that political party preferences are initially acquired

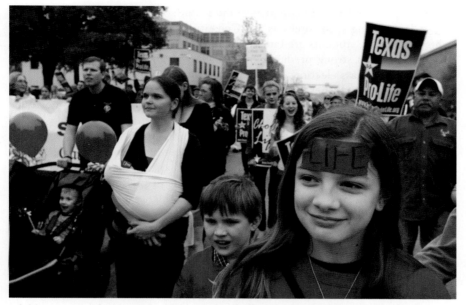

Children are socialized into political environments in ways large and small, from attending political rallies with their parents to hearing offhand comments at the dinner table. What political opinions did you learn from your parents?

at home. Children raised in households in which the primary caregivers are Democrats tend to become Democrats, whereas children raised in homes where their caregivers are Republicans tend to favor the Republican Party.[15] Similarly, children reared in politically liberal households are more likely than not to develop a liberal outlook, whereas children raised in politically conservative settings are likely to see the world through conservative lenses. Family, friends, coworkers, and neighbors are an important source of political orientation for nearly everyone.

Online social networks such as Facebook and Twitter may increase the role of peers in shaping public opinion. For example, after the June 2015 Supreme Court decision legalizing same-sex marriage nationwide, Facebook launched a "Celebrate Pride" tool that enabled users to give their profile pictures a rainbow-tinted background to show their support for gay rights, signaling to friends and family their opinion on this issue. In the 72 hours following the Court's decision, 26 million individuals added this filter to their profile picture.[16] This phenomenon was associated with upticks in public support for same-sex marriage rights; in 2015 a record high of 55 percent of Americans believed marriages between same-sex couples should be recognized by law.[17]

Education Often thought of as a great equalizer, education is also an important source of differences in political perspectives. Governments use public education to try to teach all children a common set of civic values; it is mainly in school that Americans acquire their basic beliefs in liberty, equality, and democracy. In history classes, students are taught that the Founders fought for the principle of liberty. In studying such topics as the Constitution, the Civil War, and the civil rights movement, students are taught the importance of equality. Research finds education to be a strong predictor of tolerance for racial minorities.[18] Through participation in class elections and student government, students are taught the virtues of democracy. These lessons are repeated in every grade and in many contexts. It is no wonder they constitute such an important element in Americans' beliefs.

At the same time, differences in formal education are strongly associated with differences in political outlook. In particular, those who attend college are often exposed to modes of thought that will distinguish them from their friends and neighbors who do not pursue college diplomas. One of the major differences between college graduates and other Americans is that higher levels of education are associated with greater involvement in politics. College graduates are more likely to vote, join campaigns, take part in protests, and generally make their voices heard.[19]

Social Groups and Public Opinion Another important source of political values is the social groups to which individuals belong. Social groups include those that individuals haven't chosen (national, religious, gender, and racial groups, for example) and those they join willingly (such as political parties, labor unions, the military, and environmental, educational, and occupational groups). Group membership gives individuals experiences and perspectives that shape their view of political and social life.

Race and Ethnicity Among the most important of these is race. The experiences of blacks and whites, for example, can differ significantly. Blacks are a minority and have been victims of persecution and discrimination throughout American history. Blacks and whites also have different occupational opportunities, often live in separate communities, and may attend separate schools. Such differences tend to produce distinctive political outlooks. That black and white Americans have different views is reflected in public perception of fair treatment across racial groups in the United States (see Figure 5.3).

For example, blacks and whites differ significantly in views of the role of race in the criminal justice system. In 2009, 80 percent of African Americans said blacks and other minorities do not get equal treatment under the law; the number of whites giving this response was just

A majority of Latinos has supported Democratic candidates in recent elections. Here, Hillary Clinton poses with Janet Murguia, president and CEO of the National Council of La Raza, the largest Latino advocacy organization in the country.

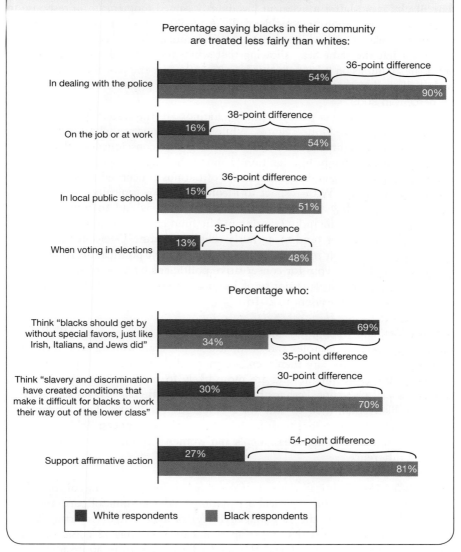

FIGURE 5.3 Perception of Fair Treatment across Racial Groups

In the United States, racial groups may not perceive race relations in precisely the same way. How, according to the data in this figure, do blacks and whites differ in their views on race relations? Which group is more likely to think that race relations are good? What factors help to account for these differences in perception?

SOURCE: Brakkton Booker, "How Equal Is American Opportunity? Survey Shows Attitudes Vary by Race," National Public Radio, September 21, 2015, www.npr.org/sections/thetwo-way/2015/09/21/442068004/how-equal-is-american-opportunity-survey-shows-attitudes-vary-by-race (accessed 3/11/16).

Percentage saying blacks in their community
are treated less fairly than whites:

In dealing with the police
54%
90%
36-point difference

On the job or at work
16%
54%
38-point difference

In local public schools
15%
51%
36-point difference

When voting in elections
13%
48%
35-point difference

Percentage who:

Think "blacks should get by without special favors, just like Irish, Italians, and Jews did"
69%
34%
35-point difference

Think "slavery and discrimination have created conditions that make it difficult for blacks to work their way out of the lower class"
30%
70%
30-point difference

Support affirmative action
27%
81%
54-point difference

■ White respondents   ■ Black respondents

40 percent.[20] In the past few years, however, widely publicized incidents of excessive use of police force against African Americans around the country have begun to cause a shift in public opinion on this issue. The activist movement Black Lives Matter took off in 2014 after the killing of Michael Brown, an unarmed, 18-year-old African American, by a police officer in Ferguson, Missouri. Protests erupted across the nation when the officer, Darren Wilson, was not indicted. One month after that verdict, a police officer in New York was not indicted despite video evidence that he had used a chokehold and other means of force on Eric Garner, an African American man heard repeatedly asserting that he could not breathe. The Black Lives Matter movement has quickly gained momentum in response to the growing number of these incidents. By 2015, 90 percent of African Americans agreed that blacks and whites are not treated equally by police and 54 percent of whites felt the same way, showing that while there is still a racial divide on this issue, opinions on it have changed significantly over the past few years.[21] Strikingly, half of all Americans now agree that racism is a big problem, compared to only 26 percent in 2009.[22]

Ethnicity also affects policy attitudes. Latinos are the fastest-growing minority population in the United States. While most Latinos are white in race, their shared Hispanic ethnicity contributes to a group consciousness that shapes opinions. Unsurprisingly, immigration is one of the most important policy issues among Latinos, with significant majorities of Latinos concerned about restrictive immigration politics. With respect to ideology, Latinos typically are supportive of government policy to improve the lives of citizens and to reduce prevailing inequality, which includes favoring public funding for education, health, and welfare. While Latinos tend to be fairly religious, Latino Decision surveys find they do not allow their religious beliefs to dictate their political decisions—they are thus less likely to vote for conservative politicians because of social issues.[23] This helps explain why a majority of Latinos supported Democratic candidate Hillary Clinton for president in 2016.

Gender Men and women have important differences of opinion as well. Reflecting differences in social roles and occupational patterns, women tend to oppose military intervention more than men, are more likely than men to favor policies to protect the environment, and are more likely to support government education and social programs. Perhaps because of these differences on issues, women are more likely than men to vote for Democratic candidates. This tendency of men's and women's opinions to differ is known as the **gender gap**. Table 5.1 shows that across different policy areas, men's and women's opinions vary from a 5- to 20-point difference.

Party Affiliation Political party membership or loyalty is one of the most important factors affecting political orientation.[24] We can think of partisanship as red-tinted (referring to the Republican Party) or blue-tinted (referring to the Democratic Party) glasses that color opinion on a vast array of issues. Partisans tend to rely on party leaders and the media for cues on the appropriate positions to take on major political issues.[25] Walter Lippmann, an influential political

TABLE 5.1

Disagreements among Men and Women on Public Policy Issues

On many policy issues, there is an approximately 5- to 20-point gap between the opinions of men and women. What might explain this consistent difference?

POLICY	MEN	WOMEN	GENDER GAP
Support cutting defense spending	38	43	5 points
Support cutting domestic spending	43	34	9 points
Favor raising the minimum wage	68	81	13 points
Favor background checks to purchase guns	82	92	10 points
Support banning assault rifles	51	71	20 points

SOURCE: Brian Schaffner and Stephen Ansolabehere, "CCES Common Content, 2014," Harvard Dataverse, V2, http://dx.doi.org/10.7910/DVN/XFXJVY (accessed 5/4/16).

commentator of the mid-twentieth century, argued that public opinion is but an echo of elite positions on policy issues; and many others studying public opinion agree.[26]

According to recent studies, differences between Democratic and Republican partisans on a variety of political and policy questions are greater today than during any other period for which data are available. For example, 72 percent of Republicans oppose granting legal citizenship to immigrants with jobs in the United States, but only 34 percent of Democrats do. Seventy-six percent of Democrats strongly favor government policies to protect the environment compared to 30 percent of Republicans.[27] Wide differences in public opinion exist based on partisanship involving energy, income inequality, infrastructure, job creation, immigration, climate change, national defense, budget deficit, taxes, terrorism, trade, and much more. Democrats and Republicans also have different policy priorities.

Political Environment The conditions and events that exist when individuals and groups enter political life shape their political attitudes and values. Although political beliefs are influenced by family background and group membership, the content and character of these views are, to a large extent, determined by political circumstances. For example, the baby-boom generation that came of age in the 1960s was exposed both to the Vietnam War and to widespread antiwar protests, which has made that generation suspicious of foreign wars. The September 11, 2001, terrorist attacks and the war on terrorism helped shape the political lives of those who came of age during that time, making them more concerned about security and safety and less opposed to foreign wars.

● Political Knowledge Is Important in Shaping Public Opinion

Explore when and why public opinion changes and the role that political knowledge plays

What best explains whether citizens are generally consistent in their political views or inconsistent and open to the influence of others? In general, knowledgeable citizens are better able to evaluate new information and determine if it is relevant to and consistent with their beliefs and opinions.[28] As a result, better-informed individuals can recognize their political interests and act consistently to further those interests. But political knowledge is generally low in America. In one widely reported survey, 71 percent of Americans could not name their own member of Congress.[29]

This raises the question of how much political knowledge is necessary for one to act as an effective citizen. In an important study of political knowledge in the United States, the political scientists Michael X. Delli Carpini and Scott Keeter found that the average American exhibits little knowledge of political institutions, processes, leaders, and policy debates.[30] Does this ignorance of key political facts matter? Delli Carpini and Keeter also found that political knowledge is not evenly distributed throughout the population. Those with higher education, income, and occupational status and who are members of social or political organizations are more likely to know about and be active in politics. An interest in politics reinforces an individual's sense of political efficacy (the belief that their actions and opinions matter) and provides an incentive to acquire additional knowledge and information about politics. As a result, individuals with higher income and education also have more knowledge and influence and thus are better able to get what they want from government.

Shortcuts and Cues Because being politically informed requires a substantial investment of time and energy, most Americans seek to acquire political information and to make political decisions "on the cheap," making use of shortcuts for political evaluation and decision making rather than engaging in a lengthy process of information-gathering. Researchers have found that individuals rely on cues and information from party elites and the media to aid them in attitude formation.[31] Other "inexpensive" ways to become informed include taking cues from trusted friends, social networks and social media, relatives, colleagues, or religious leaders.[32] By means of these informational shortcuts, average citizens can form political opinions that are, in most instances, consistent with their underlying preferences. Studies show that even individuals with low levels of political knowledge are able to make relatively informed political choices by relying on these voter cues. Scholars agree that people rely on shortcuts when forming their opinions on politics and public policy.[33]

The public's reliance on elite cues has taken on new significance in today's era of party polarization. As the political parties and elected officials have become increasingly polarized, has this change affected the way that citizens arrive at their opinions? Political scientists James Druckman, Erik Peterson, and Rune Slothuus have found stark evidence that polarized political environments fundamentally change how citizens make decisions and form opinions. Notably, polarization between the parties means that party endorsements (such as of an issue or candidate) have a larger impact on public opinion formation than they used to. At the same time, polarization decreases the impact of other information on public opinion—that is, party polarization may actually reduce levels of political knowledge. Thus, elite polarization may have negative implications for public-opinion formation.[34]

Skim and Scan Another factor affecting political knowledge is the *form* in which people consume information. The transformation of political information in the digital era has had a profound effect on the way the news is reported and how citizens learn about politics. A 2012 survey found that 36 percent of social networking site users say those sites are important for their political information and that more than three in four Americans read the news online or seek political information online.[35] Recent research also indicates a trend in journalism toward shorter articles and flashier headlines. Americans today are likely to read the news by scanning and skimming multiple headlines online, in bits and bytes, rather than by reading long news articles.[36]

To illustrate how political knowledge matters, consider tax policy. As discussed in the introduction to this chapter, the United States has one of the largest gaps between the rich and the poor of any nation in the world. But rather than raise taxes, over the past several decades the United States has substantially reduced the rate of taxation levied on its wealthiest citizens. Most recently, tax cuts signed into law by George W. Bush in 2001 and extended by President Obama provided a substantial tax break mainly for the top 1 percent of the nation's wage earners. Political scientist Larry Bartels has shown that, surprisingly, most Americans favored the tax cuts, including millions of middle- and lower-middle-class citizens who did not stand to benefit from the tax policy. Additionally, 40 percent of Americans had no opinion at all regarding the Bush tax cuts.[37] The explanation for this odd state of affairs appears to be a lack of political knowledge. Millions of individuals who were

Following the death of conservative Supreme Court justice Antonin Scalia in 2016, the public was exposed to competing messages from political elites as Senate Republicans and Democrats vehemently argued opposing points of view about how and when his successor should be named.

unlikely to derive benefit from President Bush's tax policy thought they would. Since most Americans think they pay too much in taxes, they favored the policy, even if the wealthy benefited much more than the middle class.

Upper-bracket taxpayers, who are more informed and knowledgeable, are more likely to see to it that their economic self-interest is supported by government policy. This example illustrates that basic political knowledge matters in American politics.

Costs to Democracy? If political scientists are correct in their findings that many citizens base their opinions (and votes) on inadequate knowledge and an overreliance on cues from political elites, this raises a critical question: If political knowledge is necessary for effective citizenship, how does a general lack of such knowledge affect the way we govern ourselves?

Although understandable and perhaps inevitable, low levels of political knowledge and engagement weaken American democracy in two ways. First, those who lack political information cannot effectively defend their own political interests and can easily become losers in political struggles. The presence of large numbers of politically inattentive or ignorant individuals means that political power can more easily be manipulated by political elites, the media, and wealthy special interests. But other research has shown that individuals are quite stable and rational in their policy formation. Notice that even when public opinion has shifted, as in the case of same-sex marriage, the shifts have been relatively steady; we don't see dramatic jumps up and down.

Second, if knowledge is power, then a lack of knowledge can contribute to growing political and economic inequality. When individuals are unaware of their interests or how to pursue them, it is virtually certain that political outcomes will not favor them.

● The Media and Government Mold Opinion

Describe the major forces that shape public opinion

When individuals attempt to form opinions about particular political issues, events, or personalities, they seldom do so in isolation. Typically, they are confronted with— sometimes bombarded by—the efforts of a host of individuals and groups seeking to persuade them to adopt a particular point of view. During the 2016 presidential election, someone trying to decide what to think about Hillary Clinton or Donald Trump could hardly avoid an avalanche of opinions expressed through the media, in meetings, or in conversations with friends. The **marketplace of ideas** is the interplay of opinions and views that occurs as competing forces attempt to persuade as many people as possible to accept a particular position on a particular issue. Given this constant exposure to the ideas of others, it is virtually impossible for most individuals to resist some modification of their own beliefs. Three forces that play important roles in shaping opinions in the marketplace are the government, private groups, and the news media.[38]

The Government Leads Public Opinion

All governments try to influence, manipulate, or manage their citizens' beliefs. But the extent to which public opinion is actually affected by governmental public relations can be limited. Often, governmental claims are disputed by the media, by interest groups, and at times even by opposing forces within the government itself.

This hasn't stopped modern presidents from focusing a great deal of attention on shaping public opinion to boost support for their policy agendas. Franklin Delano Roosevelt promoted his policy agenda directly to the American people through his famous "fireside chat" radio broadcasts. The George W. Bush administration developed an extensive public-relations program to bolster popular support for its policies, including its war against terrorism. These efforts included presidential speeches, media appearances by administration officials, numerous press conferences, and thousands of press releases presenting the administration's views.[39] Using the runway of an aircraft carrier as his stage, a confident Commander in Chief Bush, dressed in a flight suit, proclaimed the end of the Iraq War in 2003. His statement was premature by eight years but was effective at maintaining public support for the Iraq War. Like its predecessors, the Obama administration sought to shape public opinion in the United States and abroad, relying on the power of the president's oratorical skills to build support for his administration's initiatives in domestic and foreign policy. But Obama's White House was unique in using social media to promote the president's policy agenda. Hourly posts on Facebook promoted Obama's policies and campaign and served to personalize the president. Obama was especially adept at using Twitter, with 77 million followers on that network.

Private Groups Also Shape Public Opinion

Important political ideas that become prominent in political life are developed and spread not only by government officials but also by important economic and political groups searching for issues that will advance their causes. One especially notable example is the abortion issue, which has inflamed American politics over the past 40 years. The notion of a fetal "right to life," whose proponents seek to outlaw abortion and overturn the Supreme Court's 1973 *Roe v. Wade* decision, was developed by conservative politicians who saw the issue of abortion as a means of uniting Catholic and Protestant conservatives and linking both groups to the Republican Party, along with various right-to-life groups.[40] Catholic and evangelical Protestant religious leaders organized to denounce abortion from their church pulpits and, increasingly, from their television, radio, and Internet pulpits, including the Christian Broadcasting Network. Religious leaders have also organized demonstrations, pickets, and disruptions at abortion clinics throughout the nation.[41] These efforts have helped win the enactment of stricter abortion laws in many states.

The News Media's Message Affects Public Opinion

The media are among the most powerful forces operating in the marketplace of ideas. As we shall see in Chapter 6, the mass media are not simply neutral messengers for ideas developed by others. Instead, they are very much opinion makers in their own right and have an enormous impact on popular attitudes. For example, since the publication of the Pentagon Papers by the *New York Times* and the exposure of the Watergate scandal led by the *Washington Post* in the early 1970s, the national news media have relentlessly investigated personal and official wrongdoing on the part of politicians and public officials. The continual media presentation of corruption in government has undoubtedly contributed to the general attitude of cynicism and distrust that prevails in much of the general public, as discussed above.

At the same time, the ways in which media coverage interprets or "frames" specific events can have a major impact on popular responses and opinions about these events (see Chapter 6). For example, the Bush administration went to great lengths to persuade the media to follow its lead in their coverage of America's response to terrorism in the months following the September 11, 2001, attacks. The media mostly went along, presenting the administration's military campaigns in Afghanistan and Iraq, as well as its domestic antiterrorist efforts, in a positive light. Even supposedly liberal newspapers such as the *New York Times*, which had strongly opposed Bush in the 2000 election, praised his leadership and published articles supportive of the president's bellicose rhetoric against the Iraqi regime prior to March 2003, when President Bush ordered the invasion of Iraq.

Government Policies Also Respond to Public Opinion

Studies generally suggest that elected officials pay attention to the preferences of the public.[42] For example, political scientists Benjamin Page and Robert Shapiro explored the relationship between changes in opinion toward various political issues and the policy outcomes that most closely correspond to the issues.[43] The results show that shifts in public opinion on particular issues do in fact tend to lead to changes in public policy. One such example is in health care. A July 2009 Pew survey found that 65 percent of Americans favored a law "requiring all Americans to have health insurance, and government aid for those unable to afford it."[44] The federal government adopted the Affordable Health Care Act in 2010, which required health insurance for all citizens.

However, there is reason to question whether prevailing public opinion causes politicians to make policies that reflect the general will or whether government policy in fact causes changes in public opinion. The relationship between government policy and opinion may be dynamic, wherein policy responds to opinion

To what extent do political leaders listen to the opinions of their constituents? To what extent should they listen? Is Calvin's father right that leaders should do what they believe is right, not what the public wants?

but opinion also shifts based on new government policies.[45] Studies of whether government policy can affect public opinion have found it to have an effect in various policy areas, such as the environment, health care, welfare reform, the death penalty, and smoking bans.

Of course, sometimes public opinion and policy do not align. At times, officials act on their own preferences if they believe it will benefit government or society, and lawmakers typically do use their own judgment when making policy choices.[46] The bailout of the banks in 2008, for example, was carried out despite polls showing that a majority of Americans opposed this policy. When elected officials pursue policies not aligned with centrist opinion, it is often because they view particular groups of the electorate as more important than others. Inevitably, loyal voting blocs or interest groups that regularly contribute to a candidate may have their interests more closely represented than the general public.[47]

● Measuring Public Opinion Is Crucial to Understanding What It Is

Describe basic survey methods and other techniques researchers use to measure public opinion

Today public officials make extensive use of **public-opinion polls** to help them decide whether to run for office, what policies to support, how to vote on important legislation, and what types of appeals to make in their campaigns. All recent presidents and other major political figures have worked closely with polls and pollsters. In addition, major media outlets and other private organizations make extensive use of polls and polling.

Public-Opinion Surveys Are Accurate If Done Properly

It is not feasible to interview the more than 300 million Americans residing in the United States on their opinions of who should be the next president or what should be done about important policy issues such as how to improve the economy and create jobs. Instead, pollsters take a **sample** of the population and use it to make inferences (e.g., extrapolations and educated guesses) about the preferences of the population as a whole. For a political survey to be an accurate representation of the population, it must meet certain requirements, including an appropriate sampling method, a sufficient sample size, and the avoidance of selection bias.[48]

Representative Samples One way to obtain a representative sample is what statisticians call a **simple random sample (or probability sample)**, in which every individual in the population has an equal probability of being selected as a respondent. Since we don't have a complete list of all Americans, pollsters use census data, lists of households, and telephone numbers to create lists, drawing samples from regions and then neighborhoods within regions. Just as in a simple random sample, everyone has an equal chance of being selected for the survey. Rolls of registered voters are often used in political surveys designed to predict the outcome of an election.

Public Opinion on Climate Change

When it comes to public opinion on climate change, different security or economic interests may influence global attitudes. Some people are opposed to increasing environmental regulations out of fear that they will impose costs on businesses and slow economic growth. People who live in regions particularly susceptible to the effects of climate change and flooding, such as countries with low-lying coastal areas, tend to express greater concern for the environment.

Public opinion surveys also show higher levels of concern in developing countries that are less equipped to deal with the consequences of climate change.

In Latin America and Africa, for example, most of the population considers climate change to be the *most* significant international issue, while other countries rank this concern much lower. What do you think are possible explanations for these global differences?

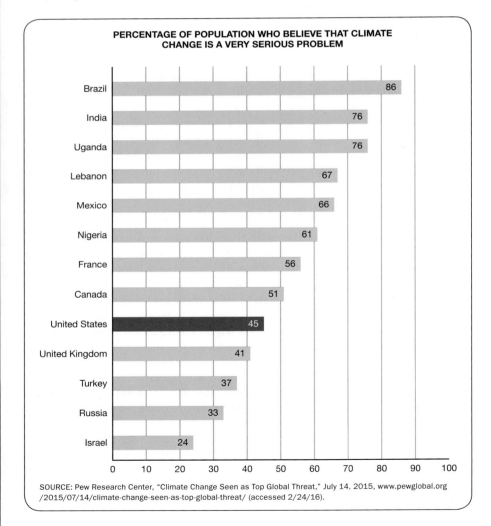

PERCENTAGE OF POPULATION WHO BELIEVE THAT CLIMATE CHANGE IS A VERY SERIOUS PROBLEM

Country	Percentage
Brazil	86
India	76
Uganda	76
Lebanon	67
Mexico	66
Nigeria	61
France	56
Canada	51
United States	45
United Kingdom	41
Turkey	37
Russia	33
Israel	24

SOURCE: Pew Research Center, "Climate Change Seen as Top Global Threat," July 14, 2015, www.pewglobal.org /2015/07/14/climate-change-seen-as-top-global-threat/ (accessed 2/24/16).

Another method for drawing samples of the national population is a technique called **random digit dialing** of landline and cell phone numbers but not business phones or inoperative home telephones. In this method, respondents are selected at random from a list of 10-digit telephone numbers, with every effort made to avoid bias in the construction of the sample. A computer random-number generator is used to produce a list of 10-digit telephone numbers. Given that 98 percent of Americans have telephones (cell phones or landlines), this technique usually results in a random national sample. Telephone surveys are fairly accurate, cost-effective, and flexible in the type of questions that can be asked; but many people refuse to answer political surveys, and response rates—the percent of those called who actually answer the survey—have been falling steadily and average less than 15 percent.[49] Websites such as RealClearPolitics.com list the results of every political survey released each day.

Sample Size A sample must be large enough to provide an accurate representation of the population. Surprisingly, though, the size of the population being measured doesn't matter, only the size of the *sample*. A survey of 1,000 people is just as effective for measuring the opinions of all Texans, a state with 26 million residents, as the opinions of all Americans, with over 314 million residents.

Flipping a coin shows how this works. After tossing a coin 10 times, the number of heads and tails may not be close to 5 and 5. After 100 tosses of the coin, though, the percentage of heads should be close to 50 percent, and after 1,000 tosses, very close to 50 percent. In fact, after 1,000 tosses, there is a 95 percent chance that the number of heads will be somewhere between 46.9 percent and 53.1 percent. This 3.1 percent variation from 50 percent is called the **sampling error (or margin of error)**—a polling error that arises based on the small size of the sample. That is, it is the amount of error we can expect with a typical 1,000-person survey. Normally, samples of 1,000 people are considered sufficient for accurately measuring public opinion through the use of surveys. When the media refer to a "scientific poll" conducted by a highly respected polling firm, they actually mean a poll that has followed the steps just outlined: a poll based on a random (representative) sample of the population that is sufficiently large and avoids selection bias.

Survey Design and Question Wording Even with a good sample design, surveys may fail to reflect the true distribution of opinion within a target population. One frequent source of measurement error is the wording of survey questions. The precise words used in a question can have an enormous impact on the answers that question elicits. The reliability of survey results can also be adversely affected by poor question format, faulty ordering of questions, poor vocabulary, ambiguity of questions, or questions with built-in biases.

Often, seemingly minor differences in the wording of a question can convey vastly different meanings to respondents and, thus, produce quite different response patterns (see Box 5.1). For example, for many years the University of Chicago's National Opinion Research Center has asked respondents whether they think the federal government is spending too much, too little, or about

BOX 5.1

It Depends on How You Ask

THE SITUATION

The public's desire for tax cuts can be hard to measure. In 2000, pollsters asked what should be done with the nation's budget surplus and got different results depending on the specifics of the question.

THE QUESTION

President Clinton has proposed setting aside approximately two-thirds of an expected budget surplus to fix the Social Security system. What do you think the leaders in Washington should do with the remainder of the surplus?

VARIATION 1

Should the money be used for a tax cut, or should it be used to fund new government programs?

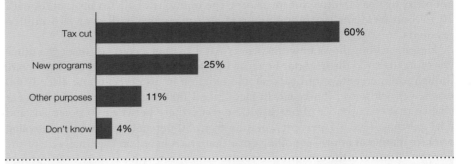

Tax cut	60%
New programs	25%
Other purposes	11%
Don't know	4%

VARIATION 2

Should the money be used for a tax cut, or should it be spent on programs for education, the environment, health care, crime fighting, and military defense?

Tax cut	22%
Programs	69%
Other purposes	6%
Don't know	3%

SOURCE: Pew Research Center, reported in the *New York Times*, January 30, 2000, WK 3.

the right amount of money on "assistance for the poor." Answering the question posed this way, about two-thirds of all respondents seem to believe that the government is spending too little. However, the same survey also asks whether the government spends too much, too little, or about the right amount for "welfare." When the word *welfare* is substituted for *assistance for the poor*, about half of all respondents indicate that too much is being spent.[50] Today, pollsters are increasingly turning to the use of online surveys, often using similar techniques to those of telephone surveys. But while Internet surveys can be more efficient, can be less costly, and can have larger samples, many online surveys do not use probability sampling (random sampling) and thus are not representative of the American population.

Why Are Some Polls Wrong?

The history of polling over the past century contains many instances of getting it wrong and learning valuable lessons in the process. As a result, polling techniques have grown more and more sophisticated, and pollsters have a more and more nuanced understanding of how public opinion is formed and how it is revealed.

Social Desirability Effects Political scientists have found that survey results can be inaccurate when the survey includes questions about sensitive issues for which individuals do not wish to share their true preferences. For example, respondents tend to overreport voting in elections and the frequency of their church attendance. Why? These activities are deemed socially appropriate, so even if the respondents do not vote or attend church regularly, they may feel social pressure to do so and thus may respond inaccurately on a survey. Political scientist Adam Berinsky calls this the **social desirability effect**, whereby respondents report what they expect the interviewer wishes to hear or whatever they think is socially acceptable rather than what they actually believe or know to be true.[51] On other topics, such as questions about income or alcohol and drug use, respondents may feel self-conscious and so choose not to answer.

Questions that ask directly about race or gender are particularly problematic. "Social desirability" makes it difficult to learn voters' true opinions about touchy subjects such as racial attitudes because respondents hide their preferences from the interviewer for fear of social retribution. However, surveys can be designed to tap respondents' latent or hidden feelings about sensitive issues without directly asking them to express overt opinions. For example, one such survey examined support for a generic black presidential candidate; the study was conducted in mid-2007, well before Barack Obama became president. The survey was designed to tap underlying attitudes toward a black candidate, allowing researchers to compare openly expressed support for such a candidate with unvoiced hidden attitudes toward the same candidate. Results show that 30 percent of Americans exhibited reluctance about voting for a generic black presidential candidate, even though, when asked directly, nearly 85 percent had claimed they would support such a candidate.[52]

Selection Bias The importance of accurate sampling was brought home early in the history of political polling when a 1936 *Literary Digest* poll predicted that the Republican presidential candidate, Alf Landon, would defeat the Democratic incumbent, Franklin Delano Roosevelt, in that year's presidential election. The actual election, of course, ended in a Roosevelt landslide. The main problem with the survey was what is called **selection bias** in drawing the sample. This is a polling error that arises when the sample is not representative of the population being studied, which creates errors in overrepresenting or underrepresenting some opinions. The pollsters had relied on telephone directories and automobile registration rosters to produce the survey sample. During the Great Depression, though, only wealthier Americans owned telephones and automobiles. Thus, the millions of working-class Americans who constituted Roosevelt's base of support were excluded from the sample.

Selection bias was also at play in preelection polls in the 2016 presidential election. Although most polls predicted the direction of the popular vote correctly in Hillary Clinton's favor, they failed to predict the size of the vote margin. Clinton won the popular vote by a small margin, but she lost to Donald Trump in the electoral college. Reasons for the polling inaccuracies include the use

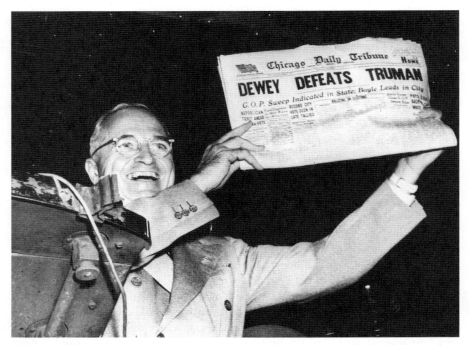

Though public opinion is important, it is not always easy to interpret; polls often fail to predict accurately how Americans will vote. In 1948 election-night polls showed Thomas Dewey defeating Harry S. Truman for the presidency. The Chicago Daily Tribune *trusted the polls and incorrectly printed a banner headline proclaiming Dewey the winner, which a triumphant Truman displayed when he won the election by a margin of approximately 4 percent.*

of "likely voter models," which left out groups that voted at higher-than-usual rates, such as rural and blue-collar voters; social desirability bias in which survey respondents didn't want to admit their support for Trump; and what is referred to as "nonresponse bias," where Trump supporters were less likely to respond to surveys. A combination of these and other missteps led to large inaccuracies in predicting the outcome.

In recent years, the issue of selection bias has been complicated by the fact that growing numbers of individuals refuse to answer pollsters' questions, or they use such devices as answering machines and caller ID to screen unwanted callers. If pollsters could be certain that those who responded to their surveys simply reflected the views of those who refused to respond, there would be no problem. Studies suggest that the views of respondents and nonrespondents can differ, especially along social class lines. Upper-class individuals are often less willing to respond to surveys or less likely to be at home than their working-class counterparts, which can bias telephone surveys. Additionally, women are significantly more likely to answer telephone surveys than men. This can lead to incorrect inferences of public opinion.

Push Polling Push polls are not scientific polls, as just discussed, and are not intended to yield accurate information about a population. Instead, they involve asking a respondent a loaded question about a political candidate designed to elicit the response sought by the pollster and, simultaneously, to shape the respondent's perception of the candidate in question. One of the most notorious uses of push polling occurred in the 2000 South Carolina Republican presidential primary, in which George W. Bush defeated John McCain and went on to win the presidency. Callers working for Bush supporters asked conservative white voters if they would be more or less likely to vote for McCain if they knew he had fathered an illegitimate black child. Because McCain often campaigned with a daughter whom he and his wife had adopted from Mother Teresa's orphanage in Bangladesh, many voters accepted the premise of the "poll." The purpose of such push polls is not to solicit opinions as much as to plant negative ideas about the opposing candidate—to, in this case, "push" McCain voters away from him. Push polls may be one reason Americans are becoming increasingly skeptical about the practice of polling and increasingly unwilling to answer pollsters' questions.[53]

The Bandwagon Effect Sometimes polling can even create its own reality. The so-called **bandwagon effect** occurs when polling results convince people to support a candidate marked as the probable victor. This is especially true in the presidential nomination process, where there may be multiple candidates within one party vying to be the party's nominee. A candidate who has "momentum"—that is, one who demonstrates a lead in the polls—usually finds it considerably easier to raise campaign funds than a candidate whose poll standing is low. And with these additional funds, poll leaders can often afford to pay for television time and other campaign activities that will generate positive media attention and thus cement their advantage.

Public Opinion, Democracy,
and Your Future

A major purpose of democratic government, with its participatory procedures and representative institutions, is to ensure that political leaders will heed the public will. And, indeed, a good deal of evidence suggests that they do.[54] Some political scientists argue, however, that government policy is much less responsive to public opinion on the issues that really count and that when the interests of elites are at stake, government officials are much more likely to represent the opinions of the affluent than the poor.[55] People in lower-income groups, though, are less likely to actively seek out ways to express their political opinions than are wealthier people (see the "**Who Participates?**" feature on the facing page).

New technology may be able to help. The migration of politics online has greatly expanded the amount of information available and the ease of becoming informed. Given this new media environment, we might expect public opinion to be more accurate, even about the nuances of public policy. Digital citizenship offers the promise of a more informed electorate, with citizens having multiple venues in which to translate their opinions into political action and demand improved representation from political leaders.

At the same time, the Internet raises concerns about the accuracy and consistency of public opinion. Some research finds that the gap between the haves and the have-nots in terms of political knowledge actually increases with the availability of more information. The implications are significant, given the explosion of political coverage online. The research suggests that with more information, public opinion may actually be less consistent.[56]

Of course, technological change will continue; the media of 2040 will not be the same as the media of 2016. Young adults will face a changing media environment, just as their parents did. Such technological evolution may bring yet further changes to our understanding of the relationship between public opinion, government, and the media. New media may make it easier than ever for citizens to stay informed about the actions of their elected leaders or for leaders to learn about their constituents' preferences. What can citizens do to stay informed and make their views known amid a changing media and political environment?

Who Expresses Their Political Opinions?

By income group

○ < $20,000   ● $20,000–$39,999   ○ $40,000–$74,999   ○ $75,000+

Attended a town or city council meeting

| 13% | 16% | 21% | 27% |

Signed a petition

| 25% | 30% | 38% | 43% |

Attended a protest march

| 5% | 6% | 7% | 7% |

Tried to contact a member of Congress

| 13% | 15% | 22% | 31% |

SOURCE: American National Election Study 2012 Time Series, www.electionstudies.org (accessed 9/25/15).

WHAT YOU CAN DO ➡

WHAT YOU CAN DO

Be an Informed Consumer of Opinion Polls

 When you encounter information from opinion polls, consider the source of the poll and the question wording and whether individuals were randomly selected to participate. Learn more at **www.umich.edu/~numbers/polls**.

 Go to **www.realclearpolitics.com** to see polls about the same issues from different sources. Note the margins of error, and notice how aggregating polls makes a difference.

☑ If asked, consider responding to an opinion poll—or take the initiative and express your views through one of the actions above.

chapterstudyguide

Practice Quiz

1. The term *public opinion* is used to describe *(p. 145)*
   a) the collected speeches and writings made by a president during his or her term in office.
   b) the analysis of events broadcast by news reporters during the evening news.
   c) the beliefs and attitudes that people have about issues, events, elected officials, and policies.
   d) decisions of the Supreme Court.
   e) any political statement that is made by a citizen outside of his or her private residence or place of employment.

2. Today, the term _____ refers to an ideology that supports social and political reform, greater economic equality, and expansion of government social services. *(p. 148)*
   a) libertarianism
   b) liberalism
   c) conservatism
   d) egalitarianism
   e) authoritarianism

3. A **libertarian** is someone who
   a) believes in social ownership and strong government.
   b) believes in freedom and voluntary association with small government.

c) believes in the need to place strict limitations on voting rights and civil liberties.

d) believes that a single ruler should have total control over every aspect of people's lives.

e) believes that governments are inherently repressive and should be abolished entirely.

4. The process by which Americans learn political beliefs and values is called *(p. 150)*
   a) brainwashing.
   b) propaganda.
   c) indoctrination.
   d) political socialization.
   e) political development.

5. Which of the following is *not* an agent of socialization? *(p. 150)*
   a) the family
   b) social groups
   c) education
   d) the political environment
   e) All of the above are agents of socialization

6. The term *gender gap* refers to *(p. 154)*
   a) differences in the amount of attention elected officials give to men and women in their campaign speeches.
   b) differences in education and income levels for men and women.
   c) differences in voting behavior between men and women.
   d) differences in life expectancy between men and women.
   e) differences in the overall number of constitutional rights granted to men and women.

7. Which of the following are the most important external influences on how political opinions are formed in the marketplace of ideas? *(p. 158)*
   a) the government, private groups, and the news media
   b) the unemployment rate, the Dow Jones Industrial Average, and the NASDAQ composite
   c) random digit dialing surveys, push polls, and the bandwagon effect
   d) the Constitution, the Declaration of Independence, and *The Federalist Papers*

e) the legislative branch, the executive branch, and the judicial branch

8. Which statement best describes the relationship between public opinion and government policy? *(p. 160)*
   a) Public opinion almost never influences government policy.
   b) Government policy almost never influences public opinion.
   c) The relationship between government policy and public opinion is dynamic, wherein government policy responds to public opinion but public opinion also shifts based on new government polices.
   d) Public opinion always influences government policy because lawmakers are legally bound to enact the majority's preferences.
   e) Government policy never influences public opinion because most Americans pay very little attention to politics.

9. Which of the following is the term used in public-opinion polling to denote the small group representing the opinions of the whole population? *(p. 161)*
   a) control group
   b) sample
   c) micropopulation
   d) respondents
   e) median voters

10. A *push poll* is a poll in which *(p. 167)*
    a) the questions are designed to shape the respondent's opinion rather than measure the respondent's opinion.
    b) the questions are designed to measure the respondent's opinion rather than shape the respondent's opinion.
    c) the questions are designed to reduce measurement error.
    d) the sample is chosen to include only undecided or independent voters.
    e) the sample is not representative of the population it is drawn from.

11. A familiar polling problem is the "bandwagon effect," which occurs when *(p. 167)*
    a) the same results are used over and over again.
    b) polling results influence people to support the candidate marked as the probable victor in a campaign.
    c) polling results influence people to support the candidate who is trailing in a campaign.
    d) background noise makes it difficult for a pollster and a respondent to communicate with each other.
    e) a large number of people refuse to answer a pollster's questions.

Key Terms

agents of socialization *(p. 150)* social institutions, including families and schools, that help to shape individuals' basic political beliefs and values

attitude (or opinion) *(p. 145)* a specific preference on a particular issue

bandwagon effect *(p. 167)* a shift in electoral support to the candidate whom public-opinion polls report as the front-runner

conservative *(p. 148)* today this term refers to those who generally support the social and economic status quo and are suspicious of efforts to introduce new political formulae and economic arrangements; conservatives believe that a large and powerful government poses a threat to citizens' freedom

democracy *(p. 147)* a system of rule that permits citizens to play a significant part in the governmental process, usually through the election of key public officials

equality of opportunity *(p. 146)* a widely shared American ideal that all people should have the freedom to use whatever talents and wealth they have to reach their fullest potential

gender gap *(p. 154)* a distinctive pattern of voting behavior reflecting the differences in views between women and men

liberal *(p. 148)* today this term refers to those who generally support social and political reform, governmental intervention in the economy, more economic equality, the expansion of federal social services, and greater concern for consumers and the environment

libertarian *(p. 148)* someone who emphasizes freedom and believes in voluntary association with small government

liberty *(p. 146)* freedom from governmental control

marketplace of ideas *(p. 158)* the public forum in which beliefs and ideas are exchanged and compete

political ideology *(p. 148)* a cohesive set of beliefs that forms a general philosophy about the role of government

political socialization *(p. 150)* the induction of individuals into the political culture; learning the underlying beliefs and values on which the political system is based

public opinion *(p. 145)* citizens' attitudes about political issues, leaders, institutions, and events

public-opinion polls *(p. 161)* scientific instruments for measuring public opinion

push polling *(p. 167)* a polling technique in which the questions are designed to shape the respondent's opinion

random digit dialing *(p. 163)* a polling method in which respondents are selected at random from a list of 10-digit telephone numbers, with every effort made to avoid bias in the construction of the sample

sample *(p. 161)* a small group selected by researchers to represent the most important characteristics of an entire population

sampling error (or margin of error) *(p. 163)* polling error that arises based on the small size of the sample

selection bias (surveys) *(p. 166)* polling error that arises when the sample is not representative of the population being studied, which creates errors in overrepresenting or underrepresenting some opinions

simple random sample (or probability sample) *(p. 161)* a method used by pollsters to select a representative sample in which every individual in the population has an equal probability of being selected as a respondent

social desirability effect *(p. 165)* the effect that results when respondents in a survey report what they expect the interviewer wishes to hear rather than what they believe

socialist *(p. 149)* someone who generally believes in social ownership, strong government, free markets, and reducing economic inequality

values (or beliefs) *(p. 145)* basic principles that shape a person's opinions about political issues and events

For Further Reading

Althaus, Scott. *Collective Preferences in Democratic Politics*. New York: Cambridge University Press, 2003.

Asher, Herbert. *Polling and the Public: What Every Citizen Should Know*. 8th ed. Washington, DC: CQ Press, 2011.

Bartels, Larry. *Unequal Democracy: The Political Economy of the New Gilded Age*. Princeton, NJ: Princeton University Press, 2008.

Berinsky, Adam. *Silent Voices: Public Opinion and Political Participation in America*. Princeton, NJ: Princeton University Press, 2005.

Bishop, George. *The Illusion of Public Opinion*. New York: Rowman and Littlefield, 2004.

Clawson, Rosalee, and Zoe Oxley. *Public Opinion: Democratic Ideals and Democratic Practice*. 2nd ed. Washington, DC: CQ Press, 2012.

Erikson, Robert, and Kent Tedin. *American Public Opinion*. 9th ed. New York: Routledge, 2014.

Fiorina, Morris. *Culture War: The Myth of a Polarized America*. New York: Longman, 2005.

Gallup, George. *The Pulse of Democracy*. New York: Simon and Schuster, 1940.

Ginsberg, Benjamin. *The American Lie: Government by the People and Other Political Fables*. Boulder, CO: Paradigm, 2007.

Jacobs, Lawrence R., Fay Lomax Cook, and Michael X. Delli Carpini. *Talking Together*. Chicago: University of Chicago Press, 2009.

Lee, Taeku. *Mobilizing Public Opinion*. Chicago: University of Chicago Press, 2002.

Lippman, Walter. *Public Opinion*. New York: Harcourt, Brace, 1922.

Norrander, Barbara, and Clyde Wilcox. *Understanding Public Opinion*. Washington, DC: CQ Press, 2009.

Zaller, John. *The Nature and Origins of Mass Opinion*. New York: Cambridge University Press, 1992.

Political candidates who receive positive news coverage gain momentum, which helps them attract campaign contributions and endorsements and eventually win votes. The influence of the media on political campaigns is just one example of its important role in American democracy.

The Media

WHAT GOVERNMENT DOES AND WHY IT MATTERS One area in which our government's role is intended to be minimal is the news media. The Constitution's First Amendment guarantees freedom of the press, and most Americans believe that a free press is an essential condition for both liberty and democratic politics. Today the media play a central role in American politics, not only in setting the agenda of topics Americans think about and discuss but also in swaying opinions on political issues and politicians.

The influence of the media on political candidates is just one example of the media's vitally important role in American democracy. Without the media's investigations, citizens would be forced to rely entirely on the information provided by politicians and the government and would be deprived of an indispensable opportunity to evaluate issues carefully and to form reasoned opinions.

The rise of the Internet has fundamentally altered the media's role in politics and American democracy. In the middle of the 1990s, the majority of Americans got their political news from a daily newspaper, the radio, or the local evening news and the national evening news from one of the three major TV networks (ABC, CBS, and NBC). Today more Americans read the news online than read a print newspaper, and those reading digital news are more likely to vote and participate in politics in other ways.[1] In 2015, 1 in 10 Americans found political news on Twitter, 4 in 10 on Facebook, and 3 in 4 on social media of some sort—platforms that did not exist before 2000. Traditional media such as newspapers and television must also compete with digital-only media that tailor news to their readers and viewers.[2]

Digital media such as Twitter have caused the public's demand for round-the-clock, real-time news to skyrocket. The 2016 presidential candidates used Twitter extensively in their political campaigns. Notably, Donald Trump frequently tweeted provocative attacks on his rivals and even members of his own party. The number of articles written about the 2016 candidates also increased dramatically compared to previous elections. Trump in particular received an extraordinary level of media attention. Was the media capitalizing on Trump's novel campaign style, including his Twitter rants, for profits and traffic? Or was the media simply fulfilling their watchdog role by informing the public?

In Chapter 5, we examined the vital question of how public opinion is related to government actions and decisions. We turn now to the most important way in which Americans learn information about their government, which in turn shapes people's opinions. Because most Americans do not have the time, ability, or opportunity to find out directly what their government does on a day-to-day basis, they must rely on the media to inform them.

chaptergoals

- Describe the role of print and broadcast media in providing political information (pp. 177–82)

- Explain how the Internet has transformed the news media (pp. 182–89)

- Analyze how the media, politicians, and public opinion are influenced by one another (pp. 189–94)

● Traditional Media Have Always Mattered in a Democracy

Describe the role of print and broadcast media in providing political information

It is impossible to imagine democratic politics without vigorous **media**. The public, and therefore public opinion, depends on the news media to publicize and assess the claims of political candidates, to examine government policies and programs, and to reveal wrongdoing by government agencies and public officials. Without the information provided by the media, the public could not possibly know enough to play any role in national politics. The freedom to speak one's mind is one of the most cherished of American political values. As Thomas Jefferson wrote, "The basis of our government being the opinion of the people, the very first object should be to keep that right; and were it left to me to decide whether we should have a government without newspapers or newspapers without a government, I should not hesitate a moment to prefer the latter."[3]

Americans get their news from three main sources: print media (newspapers and magazines), broadcast media (radio and television), and, increasingly, digital media. While television remains the public's top source for news, digital media are now second most important. Among those under 50 years of age, digital media are where the majority get their news. This pattern is found across racial and ethnic groups. The percentage turning to television for news has changed little over the past decade (see Figure 6.1).[4] Online sources, including social media, have become a major source of news for Americans, and today reading news on mobile devices and cell phones is much more common than reading from desktop computers or print newspapers.

Each of these sources has distinctive characteristics. We discuss trends in print and broadcast first, and then we look at online news and how it is changing the media industry and the way Americans get political news.

Print Media

Newspapers, though no longer the primary news source for most Americans, remain important nevertheless because they are influential among the political elite. The broadcast media also rely on leading newspapers such as the *New York Times* and the *Washington Post* to set their news agenda. In fact, the broadcast media engage in relatively little original reporting; they primarily cover stories that have been "broken," or initially reported, by the print media or online media. Print and online media, as written text, also provide more detailed and complete information than radio or television media, offering a better context for analysis. The nation's economic, social, and political elites rely on the detailed coverage provided by the print media to inform and influence their views about important public matters. The print media may have a smaller audience than their cousins in broadcasting, but they have an especially influential audience.

For most traditional newspapers, though, competition from broadcast media and, more recently, from free content online has combined with declining advertising

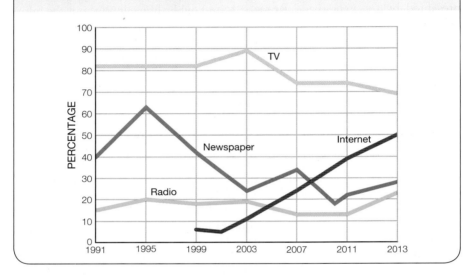

FIGURE 6.1 Americans' Main Sources for News

The media landscape for news has seen remarkable shifts in a short period of time. Twenty years ago, more than 80 percent of Americans watched news on television and more than half read news in a newspaper. Today, fewer Americans watch news on TV and just over one-quarter read the newspaper. What media source has gained rather than lost its audience?

SOURCE: Pew Research Center, "Amid Criticism, Support for Media's 'Watchdog' Role Stands Out," U.S. Politics & Policy, August 8, 2013, www.people-press.org/2013/08/08/amid-criticism-support-for-medias-watchdog-role-stands -out (accessed 4/27/14).

revenue and circulation levels to undermine the traditional business model of newspapers, bringing financial disaster to traditional print media.[5] Daily newspaper print circulation has declined by over 30 percent over the past 30 years.[6] Advertising revenue at print newspapers is half of what it was in 2005.[7] For most newspapers today, non-ad revenue comes mainly from digital subscriptions rather than print circulation. The *New York Times*, for example, reported an average weekday print circulation of less than 650,000 copies in September 2014, but by 2015 the *Times* had 1.4 million paid subscribers.[8] Many of the newspapers with the highest digital traffic are also those with the greatest circulation.

To counter these trends, traditional media organizations have been forced to adapt, and most now have a significant online presence, blurring the distinction between old media and new. Faced with shrinking revenues from their print versions, a few news organizations, such as the *Washington Post*, the *New York Times*, and the *Wall Street Journal*, charge customers for reading the news online, while others, such as the *Seattle Post-Intelligencer* and the *Christian Science Monitor*, are available online only. The success of paid digital news is increasing revenue and improving content. This metered model allows a certain number of free visits before requiring users to pay. On the other hand, newspapers now face the greatest competition from digital-only news outlets, such as Politico, the Drudge Report, and Huffington Post.

The effects of a decade of newsroom cutbacks are most evident in the political sphere. During the 2012 presidential election, a Pew report indicated that campaign reporters were acting primarily as megaphones, rather than as investigators, of the claims made by the candidates. These findings indicate a decline in investigative reporting by journalists to interpret the claims presented by the candidates. Readers, too, noticed this shift: Pew found that nearly one-third of U.S. adults stopped turning to a news outlet because it no longer provided them with the quality of news they were used to receiving.[9] The media were also widely criticized during the 2016 presidential campaign for uneven coverage and a lack of scrutiny of candidates.

The circulation and newsstand sales of traditional newspapers and newsmagazines have fallen in the last decade. However, because the remaining audience includes political elites and politically engaged citizens, they remain important forums in the marketplace of ideas.

Broadcast Media

Television news reaches more Americans than any other single news source. It is estimated that over 95 percent of Americans have a television, and tens of millions of individuals watch national and local news programs every day. Most television news, however, covers relatively few topics and provides little depth of coverage. Television news is more like a series of newspaper headlines connected to pictures. It serves the extremely important function of alerting viewers to issues and events, but, with exceptions such as the Public Broadcasting System (PBS), it provides little more than a series of "sound bites," brief quotes or headlines of the day's events. Because they are aware of the character of television news coverage, politicians and others often seek to manipulate the news by providing the media with sound bites that will dominate news coverage for at least a few days. Twenty-four-hour news stations such as MSNBC and Fox News offer more detail and commentary than the half-hour evening news shows found on the three broadcast news stations—ABC, NBC, and CBS. Yet even these outlets offer more headlines than analysis, especially during their prime-time broadcasts. As more Americans turn online for news and entertainment, cable television has experienced modest declines; but from 2014 to 2015, network television experienced audience growth of 5 percent in evening news and 2 percent in morning news, with an average viewership of roughly 24 million.[10] Americans' reliance on television as a news source does not appear to be going away.

Radio news is essentially a headline service but without pictures. In the short time they devote to news—usually five minutes per hour—radio stations announce the day's major events without providing much detail. In major cities, all-news stations provide more coverage of major stories; but for the most part, these stations fill the day with repetition rather than detail. All-news stations assume that most listeners are in their cars and that, as a result, the people in the audience change throughout the day as listeners reach their destinations. Thus, rather than use their time to flesh out a given set of stories, these stations repeat the same stories each hour to present them to new listeners.

In recent years, radio talk shows and podcasts have become important sources of commentary and opinion. A number of conservative radio hosts such as Rush Limbaugh and Sean Hannity have huge audiences and have helped mobilize support for conservative political causes and candidates. In the political center or left center, National Public Radio (NPR) is a coveted source for moderate talk radio, providing in-depth political reporting.

Comedy talk shows with political content, such as *The Daily Show* and *The Late Show*, attract millions of television viewers. Comedian Stephen Colbert even established a political action committee (PAC) during the 2012 presidential primaries in an effort to draw attention to problems with current campaign finance laws. *The Daily Show* and other late-night talk shows use humor, sarcasm, and social criticism to cover major political events. Yet these talk shows are not just for fun. They have become increasingly important sources of political news, especially for younger viewers. Pew surveys show that many Americans get political news from these shows and that followers of comedic talk shows are well informed about politics.[11]

The broadcast media are also diversifying as the country has become more multicultural. In California and Texas, as well as other states, the Latino-oriented television channels Telemundo, Univision, and MSN Latino attract large audiences by focusing on topics or perspectives of particular interest to their audience. Coverage of the Arizona and Alabama illegal immigration laws, for example, in Latino media outlets was significantly different from that of mainstream media. News outlets aimed at other ethnic groups have also become common in many areas. As the United States has become more multicultural, multiethnic television—a form of niche media—has broadened news media.

More Media Outlets Are Owned by Fewer Companies

The United States boasts nearly 2,000 television stations, approximately 1,400 daily newspapers, and more than 13,000 radio stations (20 percent of which are devoted to news, talk, or public affairs). Despite these substantial numbers overall, the number of traditional news-gathering sources operating nationally is actually quite small—several wire services, four broadcast networks, public radio and television, a few elite newspapers and newsmagazines, and a smattering of other sources such as the national correspondents of a few large local papers and the small independent radio networks. More than three-fourths of the daily newspapers in the United States are owned by large media conglomerates such as the Hearst, McClatchy, or Gannett corporations. Much of the national news published by local newspapers is provided by one wire service, the Associated Press, while additional coverage is provided by services run by several major newspapers, such as the *New York Times* and the *Chicago Tribune*. More than 500 of the nation's television stations are affiliated with one of the four networks and carry that network's evening news programs. Some of the most popular online news outlets are electronic versions of the conventional print or broadcast media.

The trend toward concentration of traditional media ownership became possible in large part as a result of the relaxation of government regulations in the 1980s and '90s. The 1996 Telecommunications Act opened the way for further consolidation in the media industry, and a wave of mergers and consolidations has further reduced independent media across the country, resulting in media monopolies. For example, the Australian press baron Rupert Murdoch owns the Fox network plus a host of radio, television, and newspaper properties around the world, known collectively as News Corporation, the world's second-largest media conglomerate. In 2007, Murdoch won control of the *Wall Street Journal*, consolidating his position as one of the world's most powerful publishers. News Corporation owned 800 media companies before its 2013 split into the new News Corporation and 21st Century Fox. Murdoch remains chair of both. But as more digital-only news sources come online, these trends toward concentration in media ownership may reverse.

One negative consequence of media concentration combined with party polarization may be a growing distrust of mainstream media. The political scientist Jonathan Ladd argues that 50 years ago the political parties were less polarized and were less likely to attack one another in the press.[12] During this period, newspaper editors also had less incentive to attack their competitors. Ladd cites a 1956 study that found 66 percent of Americans thought newspapers were fair. Party polarization increased with the Nixon presidency, and over the past 50 years, political candidates, especially Republican candidates, have made prominent attacks

Though the media generally attempt to remain unbiased, a number of media figures and outlets are distinctly left- or right-leaning, such as Rachel Maddow of MSNBC and Megyn Kelly of Fox News. Consumers are increasingly turning to partisan media, reflecting a tendency to self-select information that already conforms with their beliefs, making it more difficult to objectively evaluate information.

on the mainstream media. Ladd argues that as competition increased in party politics and journalism, the public's distrust of the mass media grew, leading the public to reject the mainstream press's reporting and turn to alternative partisan media sources—those expressly favored by Republicans or Democrats. As a result, public opinion and voting behavior are now increasingly shaped by partisan media, such as Fox News on the right or the Huffington Post on the left. Recently, political fact-checking websites such as Politifact have grown in importance and popularity. In an age of digital media, it is more important than ever for citizens to find and evaluate information (see the "What You Can Do" section at the end of the chapter).

● The Rise of New Media Has Strongly Influenced How Americans Get Their News

Explain how the Internet has transformed the news media

The twenty-first century has already experienced a profound transformation of the media. The impact of the Internet in mass communication parallels that of the printing press in nineteenth-century America, which saw the rise of the penny press and widespread literacy.[13] Today, even as the newspaper business struggles for its life, readership of online news has soared. The Internet has become the medium of choice for all age groups below 50 years to consume entertainment, news, and information about politics. In 2000, just 35 percent of adult Internet users said they looked for news or information about politics or the upcoming campaigns online.[14] As of 2015, that number had risen to over 60 percent.[15] Besides online-only newspapers, new forums for news include websites, blogs, social media, YouTube, and Twitter.

The Internet is particularly convenient for obtaining news, and formats for doing so are becoming more diverse and interactive. For example, it is increasingly common to watch online videos to understand a political issue. In 2012, one in three Internet users reported watching online campaign ads. Presidential addresses are now regularly streamed live, and millions tune in to hear the president in this format.[16]

Rather than merely providing a forum to connect with friends and family, social media (discussed in more detail below) are increasingly places for learning about politics and now a primary source for news—a dramatic change from just a few years prior. A 2016 Pew survey found that 66 percent of Facebook users and 59 percent of Twitter users read the news from these platforms.[17]

The rise of digital media has changed the way that people get information and share it, affecting everything from political activism, campaign organization, and voter mobilization to public opinion. Online media are more diverse and have created a more participatory press, one in which citizens play a prominent role. Readers can now post comments online, upload videos, and participate in a community, providing feedback on almost all online news articles. Digital media, by representing a wider range of political views than traditional media, have created more information and a more vibrant media environment.

The term *digital citizenship* refers to the ability to participate in culture and politics online. In much the same way that education and literacy promoted democracy and economic growth in the nineteenth century, today's Internet has the potential to benefit society as a whole and facilitate political participation by individuals within society. Like education, the Internet helps provide the information and skills needed for democratic engagement and economic opportunity.[18] It facilitates social inclusion through greater access to political information and news.[19]

However, regular and effective use of the Internet requires high-speed access, technical skills, and literacy to evaluate and use information online.[20] Individuals without access or the skills to use the Internet may be increasingly uninformed and excluded from the world of politics online. As of 2014, 8 in 10 Americans were **digital citizens**, individuals with home Internet access, and more than 8 in 10 Americans used the Internet in some location. There are important differences in Internet access rates across race and ethnicity. As of 2015, 75 percent of white non-Hispanics and 75 percent of Asians were online at home compared to 64 percent of blacks and 61 percent of Hispanics.[21] Among Hispanics who only speak Spanish, 43 percent had home access compared to 72 percent of Hispanics who speak at least some English.[22] Access to the Internet is also shaped by income and education. While only half of the working poor (those earning less than $20,000 a year) had home broadband, 85 percent of those earning more than $100,000 a year did. Sixty-three percent of high school graduates have home broadband compared with almost 90 percent of college graduates.[23] This suggests that there are significant inequalities in access to digital media, what is called the *digital divide*.

The rise of digital media has made it easier for Americans to get political news, but one in five Americans still lacks home Internet access. People without high-speed Internet access at home often get free access in public libraries, but access is restricted to certain times.

Online News Takes Many Forms

While many traditional news sources, such as newspapers, now publish online, other web news outlets tend to be smaller and more specialized and have lower personnel and overhead costs than mainstream publishers. The types of online news sources include niche journalism, citizen journalism and blogs, nonprofit journalism, and social media.

Niche Journalism In the gap opened by the decline in traditional print media, the last two decades have seen the rise of **niche journalism** (news reporting devoted to a targeted portion of a journalism market sector or for a portion of readers based on content or ideological presentation) and digital-only publications ranging from Slate.com to Politico.com. Bloomberg News, one of the most successful specialty online sources, has hundreds of thousands of readers who pay a large annual fee for detailed business-related news. In politics, the Huffington Post, Politico, Vice, Gawker, Buzzfeed, the Drudge Report, and others are niche leaders with detailed political reporting. Niche journalism feeds citizens' interest in politics across the full range of the political spectrum. These niche outlets are supplemented by a rich array of international and foreign online news sources.

Social Media Social media, such as Twitter and Facebook, represent the single most important trend in news and political communication. Worldwide, Facebook had over 1.7 billion users in 2016, with 190 million users in the United States. More than 70 percent of Americans use social media.[24] As of 2016, roughly 67 percent used Facebook and 16 percent used Twitter, both of which have high rates of exposure to political news. Figure 6.2 shows the percentage of Americans who use each social networking site as well as the percentage who get news from that site.

Because they are more personalized and interactive than anonymous news organizations, social media allow Americans to learn about politics and political news from each other. Growing use of social media for news is evident across demographic groups, including those under and over 35 years of age, women and men, and groups defined by race, education, and income. Social media tend to be secondary sources for news after television for many Americans but not for the young. A 2015 Pew study found that 61 percent of 18- to 33-year-olds said they got political news from Facebook in a given week compared with 39 percent of 34- to 54-year-olds. The high rate of exposure to political news online is notable since young Americans overall are less engaged in politics—just 35 percent of 18- to 33-year-olds say they talk about politics at least a few times a week. As the Internet becomes an increasingly important source for political news, young people may become more engaged in politics.[25]

Social media also provide a platform for citizens to be directly engaged with political candidates and elected officials, who have been quick to adopt Facebook and Twitter as means of communicating with their supporters and providing them a continual feed of new information. Barack Obama was the first American president to use social media extensively for his 2008 campaign for the Democratic presidential nomination.[26] In 2016 every serious presidential candidate had a Facebook account and Twitter page.

Both Facebook and Twitter possess important features for political mobilization and information sharing. With these virtual social networks, groups of like-minded individuals, or individuals with shared interests, can quickly and easily share information.

Citizen Journalism and Blogs The old media system was dominated by professional journalists, trained in journalism schools, who served as gatekeepers in determining what was front-page news and how political events were to be interpreted. This system had benefits and costs: the quality was high, but the diversity of opinions was relatively low. The media's gatekeeper role continues, but the diversity of online media is changing traditional journalism and the very nature of

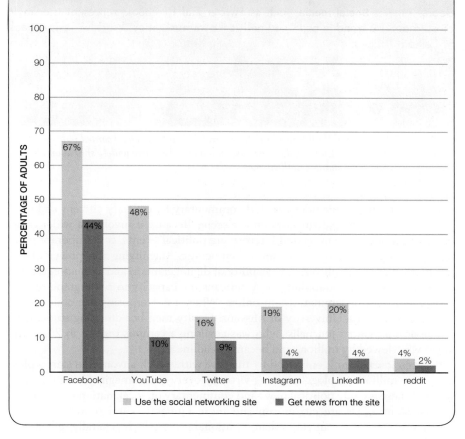

FIGURE 6.2 Social Media as a News Source

Many Americans who use social media use those websites as a way to obtain political news. This graph shows the percentage of American adults who use each social media site compared with the percentage who report getting news from that site. What are the advantages of getting news on social media, and what are some potential drawbacks?

SOURCE: Jeffrey Gottfriend and Elisa Shearer, "News Use across Social Media Platforms 2016," Pew Research Center, May 26, 2016, www.journalism.org/2016/05/26/news-use-across-social-media-platforms-2016 (accessed 6/17/16).

PERCENTAGE OF ADULTS

Site	Use the social networking site	Get news from the site
Facebook	67%	44%
YouTube	48%	10%
Twitter	16%	9%
Instagram	19%	4%
LinkedIn	20%	4%
reddit	4%	2%

Use the social networking site ■ Get news from the site

"news coverage." Just a few years ago most establishment journalists took their cues exclusively from a small handful of outlets, but now many of them use a much more extensive and diversified roster of sources, including blogs, Twitter, and independent political commentators. Online news is creating a new generation of whistleblowers, enhancing the media's traditional role as a watchdog for the people against government corruption; and it is creating new venues for political activism.

A distinguishing feature of the digital media is **citizen journalism**, which is interactive and participatory. *Citizen journalism* refers simply to news reported and distributed by citizens, rather than professional journalists and for-profit news

During the 2011 Occupy Wall Street protests, many ordinary citizens recorded videos—both of the protests themselves and of police responses to them—that were widely shared on the Internet and sometimes made headline news.

organizations. It also includes political commentary by ordinary citizens and even crisis coverage from eyewitnesses on the scene. Because it involves a wider range of voices in gathering news and interpreting political events, contemporary news reporting and commentary are more democratic. Magnifying the power of the Internet is the nearly universal availability of digital cameras and camera-equipped cell phones, which give millions of Americans the capacity to photograph or film events and then disseminate them online. When a citizen using a mobile phone captured video of a University of Missouri faculty member directing students to strong-arm a student journalist who was covering a campus protest in 2015, the video was viewed by millions and became headline news.

Citizen journalism is enhanced by the ease with which anyone can start a blog. There are millions of blogs, covering virtually every topic imaginable; and a large share of these include political news and commentary on local, national, and world events. Many blogs are citizen-run and more interactive and representative of the diversity of American views than traditional news, which generally reflects the priorities of political elites.

To be sure, the open, freewheeling nature of blogging often means that there is little of the quality control employed by traditional media. Because they do not face the burden of fact-checking required for the mainstream media, even well-meaning bloggers can post false information. This could be one reason misinformation about political issues is higher among blog readers than those reading online news from the mainstream press.[27]

Nonprofit Journalism As traditional news organizations have cut budgets and reduced investigative journalism, political information is increasingly emanating from universities, think tanks, nonprofit organizations, and private foundations. Think tanks such as the Brookings Institution, the Cato Institute, the Hoover Institution, the Heritage Foundation, and the Center for American Progress provide information and analysis on current events in order to influence public debate. Universities have expanded their public outreach, encouraging faculty to explain their findings for a general audience; as a result, university faculty are increasingly cited in the mainstream media, and many are bloggers themselves.

New Media Have Many Benefits

Americans may prefer online news for several reasons. Here we look at four advantages of online news.

Convenience Information online is convenient and always available for those who have regular access to the Internet at home or, increasingly, through mobile devices such as smartphones. Pew surveys show that nearly half of those who use online news and political information cite its convenience.[28] Use of online political information is associated with more interest in politics, greater knowledge of politics, and a greater likelihood of discussing politics with friends and family.[29]

Currency Major news stories regularly break first, and immediately, online and are later reported through print newspapers and television. Social media have accelerated even further the speed with which news travels around the globe. For example, news of Osama bin Laden's death in 2011 spread rapidly through text messaging, smartphones, and social media outlets such as Facebook and Twitter even before it could be verified by traditional media.

Depth Online news provides more information than the 60-second sound bites found in television and radio news. By blending detailed treatment of topics with the visual and emotive appeal of streaming videos, the Internet shares qualities both of print media (promoting knowledge) and of the visual aspects of television (promoting interest and engagement).[30]

Diversity Online sources are much more diverse than those found in the traditional media, and this diversity may increase citizens' political knowledge and interest.[31] While major players online certainly do include mainstream outlets, the Internet remains populated by a wide range of information sources. By making foreign media such as the British Broadcasting Company (BBC) easily available, the Internet has reduced the importance of physical proximity and created a truly global shared culture. Millions went online to learn news of the 2016 presidential campaign. Such a vast array of voices, of course, means that online sources also can provide misinformation or outright lies. To verify media reports found in both traditional and online media, new websites, such as FactCheck.org and PolitiFact.com, are devoted exclusively to checking the veracity of political claims.

But New Media Raise Several Concerns

Despite the benefits of new media, changes to the media arising from the rapid proliferation of the Internet have raised a multitude of concerns.

Loss of Investigative Power One such concern is the loss of investigative power. In a democracy, the press is expected to be a watchdog for the people and to inform the citizens of government abuses of power. The greatest challenge for contemporary news organizations is to generate enough revenue to finance traditional investigative journalism.[32] This activity requires more time and resources than other aspects of the news, yet it may be the most important. By breaking apart mainstream news organizations, online news may actually reduce the media's ability to engage in the kind of sustained, in-depth, and expensive reporting that is critical to the media's watchdog role and thus to the health of American democracy. In the 2016 presidential election, the media were criticized for focusing coverage on some candidates, most notably Donald Trump, much more than others and for a lack of more critical reporting.

More Variation in the Quality of News Another concern is the variation in the quality of the news. As already noted, the growing diversity of online news has led to wide variation in the quality of available information. The freewheeling nature of the Internet also means that hate speech, rumors, falsehoods, and outdated information can overwhelm thoughtful, original, factual, and civic-oriented voices. Misinformation and unsubstantiated rumors can substitute for objective truth as claims are widely repeated, especially in anonymous and unedited online forums.

Potential Effects on Knowledge and Tolerance Perhaps the greatest concern about politics in the digital age goes to the heart of modern democracy: Do online media ultimately help or hinder progress toward a well-informed citizenry that can govern itself effectively? One study has found that while readers of online news from major websites (largely offshoots of the traditional print and broadcast media) are more knowledgeable than average citizens, those who get their political news mainly from blogs are actually worse off.[33] And the very diversity of online news, in fact, may actually *lower* tolerance for social and political diversity. Most new media do not abide by traditional media's principle of objective journalism.

Social Media as Propaganda Another concern about the Internet as a source of political information is that its accessibility has enabled violent groups to spread political propaganda more effectively. Social media have been a primary means to distribute the political propaganda of the extremist militia group Islamic State of Iraq and Syria (ISIS), creating headline news worldwide. The group's sophisticated media campaign, including the use of Twitter, YouTube, and other forums, distributes a multitude of social media messages daily and has helped mobilize thousands of people to fight on behalf of its cause. In the most significant terrorist attack on U.S. soil since September 11, 2001, Omar Mateen carried out a mass shooting at a gay nightclub in Orlando, Florida, in 2016. Mateen killed 49 people and wounded dozens more. He took to social media immediately following the killings to pledge his loyalty to ISIS. Just six months earlier, a husband-and-wife team carried out a terrorist attack in San Bernardino, California, leaving more than a dozen Americans dead. According to the Federal Bureau of Investigation (FBI), the couple was inspired, if not directed, by extremists via social media.

ISIS has also used social media to distribute gruesome videos of public executions, beheadings, and burnings of foreign journalists, soldiers, and other individuals. These videos, in combination with mass media coverage of ISIS's actions in the Middle East, have fueled fear and calls for government action in countries around the world.

● The Media Affect Power Relations in American Politics

> **Analyze how the media, politicians, and public opinion are influenced by one another**

The content and character of news and public affairs programming—what the media choose to present and how they present it—can have far-reaching political consequences. The media can shape and modify, if not fully form, the public's perception of events, issues, and institutions. Media coverage can rally support for, or intensify opposition to, national policies on matters as weighty as health care, the economy, and international wars.

The Media Influence Public Opinion through Agenda-Setting, Framing, and Priming

Traditional and digital media influence American politics in a number of important ways.[34] The power of all media collectively, both traditional and online, lies in their ability to shape what issues Americans think about (setting the agenda) and what opinions Americans hold about those issues (framing and priming).

Agenda-Setting and Selection Bias The first source of media power is **agenda-setting**—that is, the power of the media to bring public attention to particular issues and problems. Groups and forces that wish to bring their ideas before the public in order to generate support for policy proposals or political candidacies must secure media coverage. If the media are persuaded that an idea is newsworthy, they may declare it an "issue" that must be confronted or a "problem" to be solved, thus clearing the first hurdle in the policy-making process. If, on the other hand, an idea lacks or loses media appeal, its chance of resulting in new programs or policies is diminished.

For example, in 2008 and 2009, the news agenda was dominated by the global financial crisis and the severe economic recession that ensued. Continuing media attention created enormous pressure for the government to "do something" even as the crisis began to ease, and the new Obama administration's "honeymoon period" was cut short by public frustration over the government's inability to solve the economic problems quickly.

Through agenda-setting, the media have the power to influence which issues the public pays attention to. Although drinking water contamination in Flint, Michigan, began in April 2014, it didn't gain any national media attention until almost a year later. Mass media coverage eventually led to governmental action.

Because the media are businesses and because the media seek to attract the largest possible audiences, they naturally tend to cover stories with dramatic or entertainment value, giving less attention to important stories that are less compelling. News coverage thus often focuses on crimes and scandals, especially those involving prominent individuals. This **selection bias**—the tendency to focus news coverage on only one aspect of an event or issue, avoiding coverage of other aspects—means that the media may provide less information about important political issues. The age-old journalistic instinct for sensational stories to tell often trumps the media's responsibility to inform the public about what really matters—and the public's responsibility to demand that from the media.

What the mainstream media decide to report on and what they ignore have important implications. For example, the mainstream media provided little coverage of the Bush tax cuts of 2001 and 2003 (or their extension under President Obama in 2009), although they dramatically increased the federal budget deficit and widened the gap between the super-rich and most other Americans in terms of wealth.[35] It is not surprising that public-opinion polls showed that 40 percent of Americans had no opinion on whether they favored the massive tax cuts in 2001.

Framing **Framing** is the media's ability to influence how the American people interpret events and policies. Politicians take care to choose language that presents their ideas in the most favorable light possible. Public opinion on politics naturally changes with facts, but few citizens read legislation; so when forming opinions about policy and politics, the public relies on media coverage. This means that arguments made by elected officials and other political actors, or "frames," are critical to the process of forming opinions.

For example, Barack Obama's health care initiative was framed differently by Democrats and Republicans. The Obama administration labeled its health care initiative the Patient Protection and Affordable Care Act, thus framing the proposal as a matter of compassionate responsibility and good economic sense. As the bill was debated in Congress, early press coverage framed it as "health care reform." Sensing that Americans generally approve of the idea of "reform," Republican opponents of the legislation chose language that framed it quite differently: the law's provisions for limiting excessive medical testing were labeled as "health care rationing," for example, and committees that were proposed to advise patients about end-of-life care were called "death panels." The language used by Democrats and Republicans framed the debate in different terms: the Democrats framed it as achieving the positive goal of reform, while the Republicans framed it as achieving the negative outcome of rationing.

Priming Another source of media influence on opinion, related to framing, is **priming**. Priming involves "calling attention to some matters while ignoring others."[36] As a result, the public will be *primed* to use certain criteria when evaluating a politician or an issue and to ignore other criteria. For example, the media's intensive focus on terrorism and security in the wake of the September 11, 2001, terrorist attacks primed the public to evaluate President Bush's performance in office based on his ability to defend the nation from terrorism and not, say, his ability to manage the economy at the time, as people were not primed to be thinking about the economy. This situation was quite different in 2008, when a serious economic recession received much more extensive media coverage than national security. In the 2008 presidential election, the economy was a more important lens through which the public evaluated the candidates rather than national security.

In the case of political candidates, the media have considerable influence over whether a particular individual will receive public attention and whether a particular individual will be taken seriously as a viable contender. Thus, if the media find a candidate interesting, they may treat him or her as a serious contender despite possible weaknesses and shortcomings. As noted earlier, the media were criticized in the 2016 presidential race for covering Donald Trump—a reality TV star known for his inflammatory comments and disdain for political correctness—much more than other candidates. Many people believed that Trump's unexpected victory in the Republican primaries was due in part to widespread media coverage.

News media are not alone in agenda-setting, framing, and priming; elected officials, interest groups, and other political players compete over all three in hopes of influencing public opinion.

Leaked Information Can Come from Government Officials or Independent Sources

The media may also report information that is leaked by government officials. A *leak* is the disclosure of confidential information to the news media. Leaks may emanate from a variety of sources, including whistle-blowers, lower-level officials who hope to publicize what they view as their bosses' improper activities. In 1971, for example, a minor Defense Department staffer named Daniel Ellsberg sought to discredit official justifications for U.S. involvement in Vietnam by leaking top-secret documents to the press. The Pentagon Papers—the Defense Department's own secret history of the war, differing widely from the Pentagon's public pronouncements—were published by the *New York Times* and the *Washington Post* after the U.S. Supreme Court ruled that the government could not block their release.[37] Pentagon credibility was severely damaged, hastening the erosion of public support for the war.

Most leaks, though, originate not with low-level whistle-blowers but rather with senior government officials, prominent politicians, and political activists. These individuals cultivate long-term relationships with journalists, to whom they regularly leak confidential information, knowing that it is likely to be published on a priority basis in a form acceptable to them. In turn, of course, journalists are likely to regard high-level sources of confidential information as valuable assets whose favor must be retained. For example, during the George W. Bush administration, Lewis "Scooter" Libby, Vice President Dick Cheney's chief of staff, was apparently such a valuable source of leaks to so many prominent journalists that his name was seldom even mentioned in the newspapers, despite his prominence in Washington and his importance as a decision maker.[38] Through such tacit alliances with journalists, prominent figures can manipulate news coverage and secure the publication of stories that serve their purposes.

New technology and online media have taken leaks to a new level. WikiLeaks, an independent nonprofit organization dedicated to publishing classified information, posts leaked documents to its website and uses an anonymous drop-box system so that leakers cannot be identified. In recent years, WikiLeaks has released thousands of secret government documents involving instances of government corruption, such as war crimes in Afghanistan and Iraq. During the 2016 presidential campaign, Wikileaks released thousands of hacked emails from Democratic candidate Hillary Clinton's campaign. WikiLeaks shares its treasure trove of leaked government documents with major international papers, including the *New York Times*.

Leaks of classified information have sparked significant debate over what the government should classify as "secret" and what deserves to be public knowledge. After Edward Snowden leaked thousands of classified documents, he fled the United States in order to escape arrest and prosecution. His actions have been both defended and denounced.

In 2013, Edward Snowden, a former employee of the Central Intelligence Agency (CIA) and contractor for the National Security Agency (NSA), disclosed thousands of classified digital documents to journalists and international media in what has been called the most significant leak in U.S. history. The leaks disclosed widespread global surveillance programs by the U.S. government working with telecommunication companies. The world learned the NSA was searching millions of email and instant messaging contact lists and tracking and mapping the locations of cell phones. For revealing the mass surveillance programs, Snowden has been called a hero, a whistle-blower, a dissident, and a traitor. The leaks garnered intense media attention and sparked heated public debate over government surveillance and privacy of information for individuals.

Critics of WikiLeaks and Snowden argue that posting government documents online is not journalism, that governments must have some secrets, and that the release of some government documents may jeopardize American soldiers and their local allies by revealing their identities. The whistle-blower behind the Pentagon Papers, Daniel Ellsberg, defended WikiLeaks in 2010, arguing that it has played a vital role in informing the public of government wrongdoing.

Adversarial Journalism Has Risen in Recent Years

The political power of the news media vis-à-vis the government has greatly increased in recent years through the growing prominence of "adversarial journalism," an aggressive form of investigative journalism that attempts to expose and antagonize the status quo.

The national media's aggressive use of the techniques of investigation, publicity, and exposure allowed them to inform the public about major news stories. Without such aggressive media coverage, would we have known of Bill Clinton's extramarital affair or of Richard Nixon's Committee to Re-elect the President's illegal break-in to the Democratic Party headquarters in the Watergate building? Would we have known that Iraq did not have weapons of mass destruction, despite claims to the contrary by then-president George W. Bush? Without aggressive media coverage, would important questions be raised about the conduct of American foreign and domestic policy, including drone attacks, torture, and civil liberty violations? It is easy to criticize the media for their aggressive tactics, but would our democracy function effectively without the critical role of the press? Independent media are needed as the watchdogs of American politics. Digital technology has provided a new means by which the media can be watchdogs.

Broadcast Media Are Regulated but Not Print Media

In many countries, such as China, the government controls media content. In other countries, the government owns the broadcast media (e.g., the BBC in Britain) but does not tell the media what to say. In the United States, the government neither owns nor controls the communications networks, but it does regulate the content and ownership of the broadcast media.

In the United States, the print media are essentially free from government interference. The broadcast media, on the other hand, are subject to federal regulation. American radio and television are regulated by the Federal Communications Commission (FCC), an independent regulatory agency established in 1934. Radio and TV stations must have FCC licenses, which must be renewed every five years. Licensing provides a mechanism for allocating radio and TV frequencies to prevent broadcasts from interfering with and garbling one another. License renewals are almost always granted automatically by the FCC. Indeed, renewal requests are now filed by postcard.

Through regulations prohibiting obscenity, indecency, and profanity, the FCC has also sought to prohibit radio and television stations from airing explicit sexual and excretory references between 6 A.M. and 10 P.M., the hours when children are most likely to be in the audience. Generally speaking, FCC regulation applies only to the "over-the-air" broadcast media. It does not apply to cable television, the Internet, or satellite radio. As a result, explicit sexual content and graphic language that would run afoul of the rules on broadcast television are regularly available on cable channels.

For more than 60 years, the FCC also sought to regulate and promote competition in the broadcast industry; but in 1996, Congress passed the Telecommunications Act, a broad effort to do away with most regulations in effect since 1934. The act loosened restrictions on media ownership and allowed telephone companies, cable television providers, and broadcasters to compete with one another for telecommunication services. Following the passage of the act, several mergers between telephone and cable companies and among different segments of the entertainment media produced an even greater concentration of media ownership than had been possible since regulation of the industry began in 1934.

After Janet Jackson's "wardrobe malfunction" during a live performance at the Super Bowl in 2004 led to indecent exposure, the FCC increased fines for indecency and profanity violations. In turn, many networks increased their broadcast delays for live performances.

The Telecommunications Act of 1996 also included an attempt to regulate the content of material transmitted over the Internet. This law, known as the Communications Decency Act, made it illegal to make "indecent" sexual material on the Internet accessible to those under 18 years old. The act was immediately denounced by civil libertarians and became the subject of lawsuits. The case reached the Supreme Court in 1997, and the act was ruled an unconstitutional infringement of the First Amendment's right to freedom of speech (see Chapter 4).

Although the government's ability to regulate the content of the electronic media on the Internet has been questioned, the federal government has used its licensing power to impose several regulations that can affect the political content of radio and TV broadcasts. The first of these is the **equal time rule**, under which broadcasters must provide candidates for the same political office equal opportunities to communicate their messages to the public. If, for example, a television station sells commercial time to a state's Republican gubernatorial candidate, it may not refuse to sell time to the Democratic candidate for the same position.

The second regulation affecting the content of broadcasts is the **right of rebuttal**, which requires that individuals be given the opportunity to respond to personal attacks made on a radio or television broadcast. In the 1969 case of *Red Lion Broadcasting Company v. Federal Communications Commission*, for example, the U.S. Supreme Court upheld the FCC's determination that a radio station was required to provide a liberal author with an opportunity to respond to a conservative commentator's attack that the station had aired.[39]

For many years, a third important federal regulation was the **fairness doctrine**. Under this doctrine, broadcasters who aired programs on controversial issues were required to provide time for opposing views. In 1985, however, the FCC stopped enforcing the fairness doctrine on the grounds that there were so many radio and television stations—to say nothing of newspapers and newsmagazines—that in all likelihood many different viewpoints were already being presented without each station's being required to try to present all sides of an argument. Critics of this FCC decision charge that in many media markets the number of competing viewpoints is small.

The rise of online media challenges our thinking about regulation of the media as it is more difficult—some say impossible—to regulate political content online. In 2011, the United Nations (UN) declared that access to the Internet is a human right.[40] While this came in response to threats by authoritarian governments against Internet access, the UN's position demonstrates the significance of information technology in modern life. Many authoritarian countries continue to censor the Internet, sometimes blocking the transmission of stories that contain specific terms or information from specific websites.[41]

Press Freedom around the world

The First Amendment to the U.S. Constitution guarantees that the media are essentially free from government interference. A free press is a necessary component of a functioning democracy, as critical media help hold leaders accountable for their actions. However, many countries limit freedom of the press in at least some ways. For example, in some democratic countries, such as Hungary, rules limiting hate speech or protecting privacy rights can inhibit critical journalism. Some non-democratic governments, such as in China or Cuba, exercise strict control over the media.

When we think about attacks on the freedom of the press, it's often government arrests and even killing of journalists that make the headlines, but threats to media freedom can be more subtle. In Russia, for example, journalists who criticize government officials may find themselves targets of expensive libel or slander lawsuits. In an ideal world, should all media be free from interference? Is there ever a reason to place limits on press freedom?

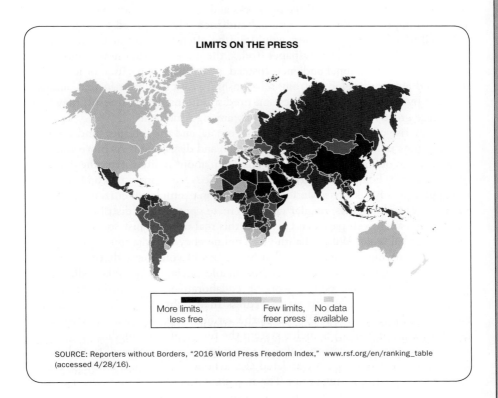

LIMITS ON THE PRESS

More limits, less free — Few limits, freer press — No data available

SOURCE: Reporters without Borders, "2016 World Press Freedom Index," www.rsf.org/en/ranking_table (accessed 4/28/16).

The Media, Democracy,
and Your Future

The free media are essential to democratic government. Ordinary citizens depend on the media to investigate wrongdoing, to publicize and explain governmental actions, to evaluate programs and politicians, and to bring to light matters that might otherwise be known to only a handful of governmental insiders. Without free and active media, democratic government would be virtually impossible. Citizens would have few means through which to know or assess the government's actions—other than the claims or pronouncements of the government itself. Moreover, without active (indeed, aggressive) media, citizens would be hard pressed to make informed choices among competing candidates at the polls.

Today's media are not only adversarial but also increasingly partisan. Debates about the liberalism and conservatism of the mass media make it clear that many readers and viewers perceive more and more bias in newspapers, radio, and television. Blogs, niche media, social media, and other Internet outlets, of course, are often highly partisan. To some extent, increasing ideological and partisan stridency is an inevitable result of the expansion and proliferation of news sources. When the news was dominated by three networks and a handful of national papers, each sought to appeal to the entire national audience. This required a moderate and balanced tone so that consumers would not be offended and transfer their attention to a rival network or newspaper. Today, there are so many news sources that few can aim for a national audience. Instead, many target a partisan or ideological niche and aim to develop a strong relationship with consumers in that audience segment by catering to their biases and predispositions. The end result may be to encourage greater division and disharmony among Americans.

Has the rise of citizen journalism, social media, and the Internet fundamentally changed how political information is gathered and distributed? As more and more Americans go online to read the news and learn about politics, even the definition of "journalist" is being challenged. Are Twitter feeds from protesters on the ground in Egypt or in a Black Lives Matter demonstration examples of citizen journalism? In an era of online news, regular citizens create content and distribute the news through personal web pages and blogs. Is this real news or just social media gossip on a global scale? Wikipedia, the free online encyclopedia founded by Jimmy Wales, has millions of pages compiled by legions of volunteers that provide content on virtually every political topic imaginable. Social media, Wikipedia, and all Wiki-type sites involve people working collaboratively to transmit knowledge. Social media also enable citizens to express their political opinions. (The "**Who Participates?**" feature on p. 197 shows the various ways Americans participate in politics via social media.) Is such a system the future of news media?

In the twenty-first century, political campaigns are covered wall to wall by the Internet; on newspapers' sites updated throughout the day; and on blogs, tweets, social media, and cable television. The new digital media are more diverse, more representative of multiple viewpoints, more interactive and participatory, and, to many, more interesting than traditional news media. Time will tell whether the shift to online news strengthens or harms American democracy.

Who Participates via Social Media?

Percentage of Adults Who Have...

Age group
- 18–29
- 30–49
- 50–64
- 65+

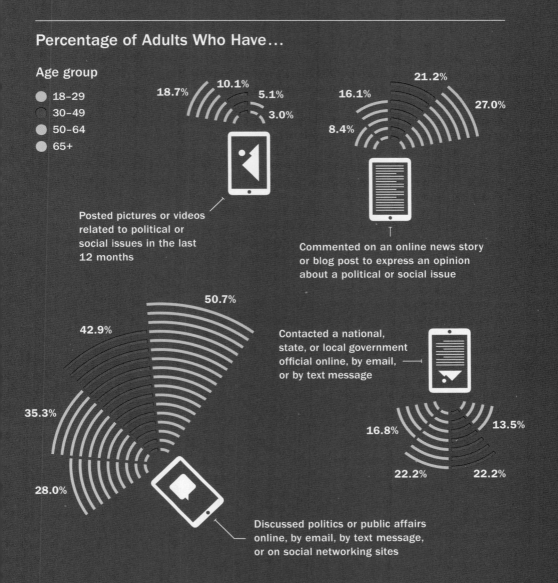

18.7% 10.1% 5.1% 3.0%

Posted pictures or videos related to political or social issues in the last 12 months

21.2% 27.0% 16.1% 8.4%

Commented on an online news story or blog post to express an opinion about a political or social issue

50.7% 42.9% 35.3% 28.0%

Contacted a national, state, or local government official online, by email, or by text message

16.8% 13.5% 22.2% 22.2%

Discussed politics or public affairs online, by email, by text message, or on social networking sites

SOURCE: Pew Research Center, "Civic Engagement in the Digital Age," www.pewinternet.org/2013/04/25/civic-engagement-in-the-digital-age/ (accessed 10/5/15).

WHAT YOU CAN DO ➡

WHAT YOU CAN DO

Be an Informed Consumer of Media

 Gather information from a variety of news sources rather than relying on just one. You can set up a news aggregator with a variety of free downloadable apps, including Flipboard (**www.flipboard.com**) and Feedly (**www.feedly.com**).

 Check media watchdog organizations such as the Columbia Journalism Review (**www.cjr.org**), Fairness & Accuracy in Reporting (**www.fair.org**), and Accuracy in Media (**www.aim.org**) for reports of media bias and censorship.

 For information on the factual accuracy of what is said by political players, go to **www.factcheck.org**. For investigative journalism in the public interest, go to **www.propublica.org**. For reporting on the accuracy of news rumors, go to **www.snopes.com**.

chapterstudyguide

Practice Quiz

1. Which of the following statements is *not* true about newspapers? *(pp. 177–79)*
   a) They typically offer readers a better context for analysis by providing more detailed and complete information than broadcast media.
   b) They are still read on a daily basis by almost all Americans.
   c) They are influential among the nation's economic, social, and political elites.
   d) Broadcast media organizations rely heavily on newspapers to set their news agendas.
   e) Daily newspaper circulation in the United States has declined over the last 20 years.

2. The vast majority of daily print newspapers are owned by *(pp. 180–82)*
   a) large media conglomerates.
   b) the national government.
   c) small local companies.
   d) private individuals.
   e) the employees who run them.

3. Digital citizenship requires *(p. 183)*
   a) a subscription to one or more online newspapers.
   b) high-speed Internet access and the technical and literacy skills to evaluate and use information online.
   c) high-speed Internet access only.
   d) a social media account, such as Facebook or Twitter.
   e) maintaining a political blog.

4. News reporting devoted to a targeted portion of readers based on content or ideological presentation is called *(pp. 183–84)*
   a) nonprofit journalism.
   b) for-profit journalism.
   c) adversarial journalism.
   d) citizen journalism.
   e) niche journalism.

5. Which of the following is *not* a reason that many Americans appear to prefer online news? *(p. 187)*
   a) the depth of the information available online
   b) the diversity of online viewpoints
   c) the convenience of getting news online
   d) the accuracy and objectivity compared to traditional media outlets
   e) the up-to-the-minute currency of the information available online

6. The media's powers to determine what becomes a part of political discussion and to shape how political events are interpreted are known as *(pp. 189–90)*
   a) issue definition and protest power.
   b) agenda-setting and framing.
   c) the illusion of saliency and the bandwagon effect.
   d) the equal time rule and the right of rebuttal.
   e) media consolidation and selection bias.

7. The tendency of the media to focus news coverage on only one aspect of an event or issue is called *(pp. 189–90)*
   a) agenda-setting.
   b) framing.
   c) priming.
   d) adversarial journalism.
   e) selection bias.

8. Most leaks originate with *(p. 191)*
   a) low-level government whistle-blowers.
   b) senior government officials, prominent politicians, and political activists.
   c) members of the public who witness misbehavior.
   d) ambassadors from foreign countries.
   e) members of the media.

9. *Adversarial journalism* refers to *(pp. 192–93)*
   a) the recent shift in American society away from general-purpose sources of information and toward narrowly focused niche sources.
   b) an era in American history when political parties provided all of the financing for newspapers.
   c) an aggressive form of journalism that attempts to expose and antagonize the status quo.
   d) a form of reporting in which the media adopt an accepting and friendly posture toward the government and public officials.
   e) the process of preparing the public to take a particular view of an event or political actor.

10. In general, FCC regulations apply only to *(p. 193)*
    a) cable television.
    b) Internet websites.
    c) over-the-air broadcast media.
    d) satellite radio.
    e) newspapers and magazines.

11. In *Red Lion Broadcasting Company v. Federal Communications Commission*, the Supreme Court ruled that a radio station *(p. 194)*
    a) could not legally charge Democratic and Republican gubernatorial candidates different prices for commercials aired at the same time of day.
    b) could legally charge Democratic and Republican gubernatorial candidates different prices for commercials aired at the same time of day.
    c) was required to provide a liberal author with an opportunity to respond to a personal attack broadcast by one of the station's conservative commentators.

d) was not required to provide a liberal author with an opportunity to respond to a personal attack broadcast by one of the station's conservative commentators.

e) was not required to secure a license from the FCC if it accepted no money in grants or tax credits from the federal government.

12. The now-defunct requirement that broadcasters provide time for opposing views when they air programs on controversial issues was called *(p. 194)*
    a) the equal time rule.
    b) the fairness doctrine.
    c) the right of rebuttal.
    d) the response rule.
    e) the free speech doctrine.

Key Terms

agenda-setting *(p. 189)* the power of the media to bring public attention to particular issues and problems

citizen journalism *(p. 185)* news reported and distributed by citizens, rather than professional journalists and for-profit news organizations

digital citizen *(p. 183)* a daily Internet user with high-speed home Internet access and the technology and literacy skills to go online for employment, news, politics, entertainment, commerce, and other activities

equal time rule *(p. 194)* the requirement that broadcasters provide candidates for the same political office equal opportunities to communicate their messages to the public

fairness doctrine *(p. 194)* a Federal Communications Commission (FCC) requirement for broadcasters who air programs on controversial issues to provide time for opposing views; the FCC ceased enforcing this doctrine in 1985

framing *(p. 190)* the power of the media to influence how events and issues are interpreted

media *(p. 177)* print and digital forms of communication, including television,

newspapers, radio, and the Internet, intended to convey information to large audiences

niche journalism *(p. 183)* news reporting devoted to a targeted portion (subset) of a journalism market sector or for a portion of readers or viewers based on content or ideological presentation

priming *(p. 191)* process of preparing the public to take a particular view of an event or political actor

right of rebuttal *(p. 194)* a Federal Communications Commission regulation giving individuals the right to have the opportunity to respond to personal attacks made on a radio or television broadcast

selection bias (news) *(p. 190)* the tendency to focus news coverage on only one aspect of an event or issue, avoiding coverage of other aspects

social media *(p. 184)* web-based and mobile-based technologies that are used to turn communication into interactive dialogue between organizations, communities, and individuals; social media technologies take on many different forms including blogs, Wikis, podcasts, pictures, video, Facebook, and Twitter

For Further Reading

Boydstun, Amber E. *Making the News: Politics, the Media, and Agenda Setting*. Chicago: University of Chicago Press, 2013.

Campbell, Richard, Christopher Martin, and Bettina Fabos. *Media and Culture*. New York: St. Martin's Press, 2009.

Carr, Nicholas. *The Shallows: What the Internet Is Doing to Our Brains*. New York: W. W. Norton, 2011.

Fenton, Tom. *Bad News: The Decline of Reporting, the Business of News, and the Danger to Us All*. New York: HarperCollins, 2005.

Fox, Richard, and Jennifer Ramos. *iPolitics: Citizens, Elections and Governing in the New Media Era*. New York: Cambridge University Press, 2011.

Graber, Doris, and Johanna Dunaway. *Mass Media and American Politics*. 9th ed. Washington, DC: CQ Press, 2014.

Iyengar, Shanto. *Media Politics: A Citizen's Guide*. 3rd ed. New York: W. W. Norton, 2015.

Iyengar, Shanto, and Donald Kinder. *News That Matters: Television and American Public Opinion*. Chicago: University of Chicago Press, 2010.

Jenkins, Henry. *Convergence Culture: Where Old and New Media Collide*. New York: New York University Press, 2008.

MacArthur, John. *Second Front: Censorship and Propaganda in the 1991 Gulf War*. Berkeley and Los Angeles: University of California Press, 2004.

Spitzer, Robert J., ed. *Media and Public Policy*. Westport, CT: Praeger, 1993.

West, Darrell M. *Air Wars: Television Advertising in Election Campaigns, 1952–2012*. 6th ed. Washington, DC: CQ Press, 2013.

For much of the country's history, large groups of Americans were denied the right to vote. Most restrictions on voting have been eliminated for Americans age 18 and older, but turnout remains relatively low, especially among young voters. Will changes in voting laws increase participation?

POLLING PLACE
投票站 CASILLA ELECTORAL
投票所 LUGAR NG BOTOHAN
투표소 PHÒNG PHIẾU

7

Political Parties, Participation, and Elections

WHAT GOVERNMENT DOES AND WHY IT MATTERS In 2016, the major American political parties faced an unprecedented populist uprising within their ranks during the presidential nomination process, when massive numbers of voters preferred "outsider" candidates. Self-described democratic socialist Bernie Sanders (running for the Democratic nomination) and television celebrity and businessman Donald Trump (running for the Republican nomination) both positioned themselves as outsiders who would better represent ordinary Americans than the "establishment" candidates would. Both were critical of their own parties. Sanders's campaign message directed outrage at Wall Street and the wealthiest 1 percent who have prospered while the wages of average Americans have stalled. His proposals included free college tuition at state schools, single-payer health insurance, increasing the minimum wage to $15 an hour, imposing a tax on financial transactions on Wall Street, and raising taxes on the wealthiest Americans. Republican candidate Donald Trump dominated national media headlines for months with his highly controversial statements and proposals, which included building a wall at the Mexican border to stop illegal immigration and enacting a temporary ban on Muslims entering the United States.

Trump and Sanders represented a radical departure for the political parties, which have generally turned to insiders when choosing political leaders. Both initially received few endorsements from party elites and appealed to working-class white voters, independents, and young voters. Both also challenged the status quo by refusing contributions from big business and outside funding by Super PACs. Sanders's campaign received a record-breaking $206 million in individual contributions, $129 million of which was made up of small contributions.[1] As a businessman who had donated hundreds of thousands of dollars to political candidates, Trump positioned himself as one who could not be bought off as a candidate. He stated, "my whole life I've been greedy, greedy, greedy. I've grabbed all the money I could get. I'm so greedy. But now I want to be greedy for the United States."[2] He claimed he would redirect his competitive capitalist charisma toward the public good. Trump's and Sanders's surprising victories—both won many key state primaries and caucuses and Trump went on to secure the Republican nomination—posed a major challenge to the two major political parties. Revolts against the political parties from within their ranks occur rarely in American history.

Political parties and elections are all about who controls the government; participation is about who gets involved and why. Social forces work through the parties to gain control over government personnel (meaning those who run the government) and policies. Parties are also a means by which those in government try to influence important groups in society.

chaptergoals

- Explain the roles that parties play in American elections and government (pp. 205–9)

- Describe the American party system and how it has changed over time (pp. 209–18)

- Identify the most common forms of political participation (pp. 218–23)

- Examine the factors that influence voters' decisions (pp. 225–27)

- Analyze the strategies, issues, and outcomes of the 2016 elections (pp. 229–35)

- Describe how candidates raise the money they need to run (pp. 235–38)

Parties and Elections Have Been Vital to American Politics and Government

Explain the roles that parties play in American elections and government

Political parties, like interest groups, are organized groups that attempt to influence the government by electing their members to government offices. A party, however, seeks to control the entire government by electing its members to office and thereby controlling the government. Interest groups, by comparison, don't control the operation of government and its personnel but rather try to influence government policies, often through lobbying electoral officials and campaign contributions.

Political Parties Arose from the Electoral Process

Although the Founders did not envision the rise of political parties and George Washington was elected the nation's first president without association with a political party, parties quickly became a core feature of the American political system. Historically, parties form in one of two ways. The first, which could be called "internal mobilization," occurs when political conflicts prompt officials and competing factions within government to mobilize popular support. This is precisely what happened during the early years of the American Republic. Competition in Congress between northeastern merchants and southern farmers led first the southerners and then the northeasterners to attempt to organize their supporters. The result was the foundation of America's first national parties: the Jeffersonians, or Antifederalists, whose primary base was in the South, and the Federalists, whose strength was greatest in the New England states.

The second way that parties form is called "external mobilization," which takes place when a group of politicians outside government organizes popular support to win governmental power. For example, during the 1850s, a group of state politicians who opposed slavery, especially the expansion of slavery in America's territorial possessions, built what became the Republican Party by constructing party organizations and mobilizing popular support in the Northeast and West.

America's two major parties now, of course, are the Democratic Party and the Republican Party. Both trace their roots back over 150 years to the nineteenth century, and both have evolved over time. Since they were formed, the two major parties have undergone significant shifts in their policy positions and their membership. These changes have been prompted both by issues and events (economic change, the civil rights movement, immigration, etc.) and by demographic and social developments in the United States.

Political parties play a traditionally important role in elections. They recruit candidates to run for office, get their loyal party members out to vote, and work in a variety of ways to promote the causes and issues of the party. In earlier times the parties had near total control over the electoral process. In recent decades, however, they have lost their monopoly to candidates who decide not to work within the party, to **political action committees (PACs)** that raise and distribute millions of dollars for candidates, and to direct appeals through the media.

Parties Recruit Candidates

One of the most important party activities is the recruitment of candidates for thousands of local, state, and national offices. Where they do not have an incumbent running for re-election, party leaders attempt to identify strong candidates and to interest them in entering the campaign.

An ideal candidate will have a strong leadership record and the capacity to raise enough money to mount a serious campaign. Party leaders are usually not willing to provide financial backing to candidates who are unable to raise substantial funds on their own. For a U.S. House seat, this can mean several hundred thousand dollars; for a Senate seat, a serious candidate must be able to raise several million dollars. Presidential candidates raise hundreds of millions of dollars, an amount that continues to rise with every election cycle. Often, party leaders have difficulty finding attractive candidates and persuading them to run. Candidate recruitment has become particularly difficult in an era in which **incumbents** (candidates running for re-election to positions that they already hold) are hard to beat, when lengthy political campaigns often involve mudslinging, and when candidates must assume that their personal lives will be intensely scrutinized on social media, in the press, and in negative campaign ads run by their opponents.[3] Over 20 percent of House races are uncontested (meaning there is only one candidate from one party on the ballot) because challenging incumbents in the House and winning is so difficult. Incumbents in the House on average have more than double the money for their political campaigns than challengers, while Senate incumbents have on average 50 percent more.

Parties Organize Nominations

Nomination is the process by which a party selects a single candidate to run for each elective office. Parties want only one candidate on the general-election ballot so that members of the same party do not take votes from one another, allowing the other party's candidate to win. So parties undertake an internal process of nomination to settle on one candidate who will be on the ballot in the general election. The party nomination process varies from state to state and office to office, but it usually involves a primary election among multiple candidates from the same party. Voters in the primary election select just one candidate to go on to general election. Scholars have found that although the nomination process appears democratic in that average citizens have a say, party elites play an outsized role in selecting the candidates nominated by their party for president of the United States. In 2016, however, the Republican Party insiders had less control over the process; businessman and reality-TV star Donald Trump secured the nomination despite the fact that many members of the party emphatically spoke out against him.

Parties Help Get Out the Vote

The general-election period begins immediately after the nominations conclude. Historically, this has been a time of heightened partisanship when popular support for the political parties is high. All the paraphernalia of party committees—from signs, bumper stickers, and buttons to social media slogans and YouTube ads—are on display, and all the committee members are activated into local party workforces.

The first step involves voter registration. Party workers collaborate with nonprofit organizations, local community groups, and other organizations to turn out the vote. The parties and candidate campaigns still mail notices, call voters, organize voter-registration drives on college campuses, and knock on doors to ensure citizens are registered.

Convincing voters to actually show up and vote on Election Day is one of the hardest tasks that the parties face as it involves getting individuals to go to the polls, stand in line, and vote for the party's candidates. If they are voting by mail— one in three Americans now vote by absentee ballots or mail voting—voters still have to request the ballot, fill it out, and return it. Voter mobilization, once an art, has now become a science. Research has shown that face-to-face, in-person contacts are much more effective than mailings, robocalls, or TV advertising in mobilizing voters. Campaigns now organize large-scale voter-mobilization drives and field offices with hundreds of thousands of party workers and volunteers contacting millions of voters. In recent years, parties have developed extensive databases of over 240 million potential adult voters. Using vast computerized databases, data mining, social media, and other new techniques such as micro-targeting, modern political campaigns can predict who you will vote for and are extremely effective at turning out the voters who are most likely to vote for their candidates. *Micro-targeting* means tailoring campaign messages to individuals in small, homogenous groups (e.g., suburban housewives) and emphasizing specific issues, rather than a one-size-fits-all campaign message. This technique enables political parties to target candidates' strategies and messages to these very specific groups. Turnout is

People are more likely to turn out to vote if someone asks them face-to-face. Direct mail and impersonal phone calls are less likely to have an effect on turnout.

everything: after all, it doesn't matter which party has more support if that party's voters stay home on Election Day.

Parties Organize Power in Congress

Congress depends more on the party system than is generally recognized. For one thing, power in Congress is organized along party lines. The speakership of the House is essentially a party office because the Speaker is chosen by the **majority party**—that is, the party that holds the majority of seats in the House or Senate. (The other party is known as the **minority party**, meaning that it holds the minority of legislative seats in either the House or the Senate.) When the majority party presents a nominee to the entire House, its choice is then ratified in a straight vote along party lines.

The committee system of both houses of Congress is also a product of the two-party system. For example, each party is assigned a quota of members for each committee, depending on the percentage of total seats held by the party (see Chapter 9). The majority party makes sure that it has a majority of its members on each committee. Each party has a "committee on committees" to assign individual members to each committee and determine advancement up the committee seniority ladder toward serving as committee chair. Since the late nineteenth century, most advancements have been automatic—based on the length of continual service on the committee. This seniority system has existed only because of the support of the two parties, however; and either party can deviate from it—that is, pick someone with less seniority to chair a committee—by a simple vote.

Presidents Need Political Parties

Strong presidents with broad popular support can depend on party ties to get their legislation enacted in Congress. Yet there has been a trade-off in using the party machinery to support the president's legislative agenda and building it to support the party in congressional elections. Since the Eisenhower presidency, Republicans have paid much more attention to party building than have Democrats.[4] Given their party's minority status in the electorate for much of the past 50 years, Republican presidents have sought to enhance the party's capabilities to mobilize voters and win elections. George W. Bush's adviser Karl Rove hoped to build a strong party apparatus that would ensure a permanent Republican majority. Democratic presidents have put much less energy into building the party apparatus, focusing instead on their legislative agenda and their own re-election. It was only after their 2004 election defeat that Democrats began to pour their energies into building a stronger party when the Democratic National Committee (DNC) invested heavily in new technology and in creating party-mobilizing capabilities in states across the country, not just the traditionally "blue" states that have reliably voted Democratic.

The Obama campaign was able to use the party as a springboard for its own mobilizing organization, Obama for America. With detailed information about Democratic Party activists, Obama for America's database became an important political resource for mobilizing Democrats and for legislative candidates. After Obama took office, the organization was renamed Organizing for America (OFA) and became an independent project of the DNC. The president used OFA to mobilize grassroots support for his legislative agenda. Separate from the DNC, OFA provides training for volunteers to learn how to become organizers, and it has established offices in nearly every state.

● America Is One of the Few Nations with a Two-Party System

Describe the American party system and how it has changed over time

In his 1796 Farewell Address, President George Washington warned his countrymen to shun partisan politics. Nonetheless, a **two-party system**—a political system in which only two parties have a realistic opportunity to compete effectively for control of the government—emerged early in the history of the new Republic. Beginning with the Federalists and the Jeffersonian Republicans in the 1790s, two major parties have dominated national politics, although which particular two parties they have been has changed with the times and issues.

However, the term *party system* refers to more than just the number of parties competing for power or the set of parties that are important at any given time. It also includes the organization of the parties, the balance of power between and within party coalitions, the parties' social and institutional bases, and the issues and policies around which party competition is organized. Seen from this broader perspective, the character of a nation's party system can change even if the number of parties remains the same and even when the same two parties seem to be competing for power. Today's American party system is very different from the country's party system of 70 years ago, but the Democrats and Republicans continue to be the two major competing forces. Over the course of American history, changes in political forces and alignments have produced six distinctive party systems (see Figure 7.1).

The First Party System: Federalists and Jeffersonian Republicans The first party system emerged in the 1790s and pitted the Federalists, who favored a strong national government, against the Jeffersonian Republicans, or Antifederalists, who favored a weak national government and strong states. The Federalists were the establishment party at the time, and the Antifederalists were the outsiders. The Federalists represented New England merchants and supported a program of protective tariffs to encourage manufacturing, forgiving states' Revolutionary War debts, the creation of a national bank, and commercial ties with Britain. The Jeffersonians, led by southern agricultural interests, opposed these policies and instead favored free trade, the promotion of agricultural over commercial interests, and friendship with France. Over the years, the Federalists gradually weakened and disappeared altogether after the pro-British sympathies of some Federalist leaders during the War of 1812 led to charges of treason against the party.

From the collapse of the Federalists until the 1830s, America had only one political party, the Jeffersonian Republicans, who gradually came to be known as the Democrats. This period of one-party politics had an absence of party

FIGURE 7.1 **How the Party System Evolved**

During the nineteenth century, the Democrats and the Republicans emerged as the two dominant parties in American politics. As the American party system evolved, many third parties emerged, but few of them remained in existence for very long.

*Or in some cases, fourth parties; most of these parties lasted through only one term.
**The Anti-Masonics had the distinction of being not only the first third party but also the first party to hold a national nominating convention and the first to announce a party platform.

Year	Major Parties	Third Parties* and Independents
1788	Federalists	
1790	Jeffersonian	
1804	Republicans	
1808	(Democratic-	
1812	Republicans)	
1816		
1820		
1824	National	
1828	Democrats Republicans	
1832		Anti-Masonic**
1836	Whigs	
1840		Liberty
1844		
1848		Free Soil
1852		
1856	Republicans	American
1860		Constitutional
1864		Union
1868		
1872		
1876		
1880		Greenback Labor
1884	Prohibition	
1888		Union Labor
1892	Populist	
1896		
1900		
1904	Socialist	
1908		Theodore
1912		Roosevelt's
1916		Progressive
1920		(Bull Moose)
1924		Progressive
1928		Party
1932		
1936		
1940		
1944		
1948		States' Rights
1952		(Dixiecrats)
1956		
1960		Wallace's
1964		American
1968		Independent
1972		
1976		Anderson's
1980		National Unity
1984		Perot's
1988		United We Stand
1992		America
1996		Reform Party
2000		Green Party
2004		Nader's
2008		Independent Party
2012		
2016		

competition. Throughout this period, however, there was intense factional conflict within the Democratic Party, particularly between the supporters and opponents of General Andrew Jackson, America's great military hero of the War of 1812. Jackson was the first populist president with a wide base of mass support; he sought to give rank-and-file members more say in party politics. Jackson's opponents denied him the presidency in 1824, but Jackson won election in 1828 and again in 1832. Jackson's base of support was in the South and the West, and he espoused a program of free trade and other policies that appealed to those regions. During the 1830s, groups opposing Jackson united to form a new political force, the Whig Party, thus giving rise to the second American party system.

The Second Party System: Democrats and Whigs Both the Democrats and the Whigs built party organizations throughout the nation, and both sought to enlarge their bases of support by expanding the right to vote. They increased the number of eligible voters—though only white males—through the elimination of property restrictions and other barriers to voting. Support for the new Whig Party was stronger in the Northeast than in the South and West and among merchants than among small farmers. Hence, in some measure, the Whigs were the successors of the Federalists. Yet conflict between the two parties revolved more around personalities than policies. The Whigs were a diverse group united more by opposition to the Democrats than by agreement on programs. In 1840 the Whigs won their first presidential election by nominating a military hero, General William Henry Harrison. The Whig campaign carefully avoided issues—since the party could agree on almost none—and emphasized the personal qualities and heroism of the candidate. The Whigs also invested heavily in campaign rallies and entertainment to win over voters. The 1840 campaign came to be called the "hard cider" campaign because of the practice of using food and especially drink to win votes.

During the late 1840s and early 1850s, conflicts over slavery produced sharp divisions within both the Whig and the Democratic parties, despite the efforts of party leaders to develop compromises. By 1856 the Whig Party had all but disintegrated under the strain, and many Whig politicians and voters, along with antislavery Democrats, joined the new Republican Party, which pledged to ban slavery from the western territories. In 1860 the Republicans nominated Abraham Lincoln for the presidency. Lincoln's victory strengthened southern calls for secession from the Union and, soon thereafter, for all-out civil war.

The Civil War and Post–Civil War Party System: Republicans and Democrats During the course of the war, President Lincoln depended heavily on Republican governors and state legislatures to raise troops, provide funding, and maintain popular support for a long and bloody military conflict. The secession of the South had stripped the Democratic Party of many of its leaders and supporters, but the Democrats remained politically competitive throughout the war and nearly won the 1864 presidential election against Republican Lincoln because of northern war weariness. With the defeat of the Confederacy in 1865, some congressional Republicans sought to convert the South into a Republican bastion through a program of Reconstruction that granted the vote to newly freed slaves. This Reconstruction program collapsed in the 1870s as a result of disagreement within

Following the Civil War, the Republican Party remained dominant in the North. This poster supporting Republican Benjamin Harrison in the 1888 election promises protective tariffs and other policies that appealed to the industrial states in the North.

the Republican Party in Congress and violent resistance by southern whites. With the end of Reconstruction, the former Confederate states regained full membership in the Union and full control of their internal affairs. Throughout the South, African Americans were deprived of hard-won political rights, including the right to vote, despite post–Civil War constitutional guarantees to the contrary. The post–Civil War South was solidly Democratic in its political affiliation because of its resentment of Lincoln's Republican Party, and with a firm southern base, the national Democratic Party was able to confront the Republicans on a more or less equal basis. From the end of the Civil War to the 1890s, the Republican Party remained the party of the North, with strong business and middle-class support, while the Democrats were the party of the South, with support also from northern working-class and immigrant groups.

The System of 1896: Republicans and Democrats During the 1890s profound and rapid social and economic changes led to the emergence of a variety of protest parties, including the Populist Party, which appealed mainly to small farmers, western mining interests, and urban workers. In the 1892 presidential election, the Populist Party carried four states and elected governors in eight. In 1896 the Populist Party effectively merged with the Democrats, who nominated William Jennings Bryan, a Democratic senator with pronounced Populist sympathies, for the presidency. The Republicans nominated the conservative senator William McKinley. In the ensuing campaign, northern and midwestern businesses made an all-out effort to defeat what they saw as a radical threat from the Populist–Democratic alliance. By the time the dust settled, the Republicans had won a resounding victory and confined the Democrats to their smaller bases of support in the South and far West. For the next 36 years, the Republican Party was the nation's majority party, carrying seven of nine presidential elections and controlling both houses of Congress in 15 of 18 contests. The Republican Party of this era was the party of American business, advocating low taxes, high tariffs on imports, and a minimum of government regulation. The Democrats were far too weak to offer much opposition.

The New Deal Party System: Reversal of Fortune Soon after the Republican presidential candidate Herbert Hoover won the 1928 presidential election, the nation's economy collapsed. The Great Depression, which produced unprecedented economic hardship, stemmed from many causes; but from the perspective of millions of Americans, the Republican Party did not do enough to promote economic recovery. In 1932, Americans elected Franklin Delano Roosevelt (FDR) and a solidly Democratic Congress. FDR developed a program for economic recovery that he dubbed the "New Deal," under which the size and reach of America's national government increased substantially. The federal government took responsibility for economic management and social welfare to an extent that was unprecedented in American history. FDR designed many of his programs specifically to expand the political base of the Democratic Party. He rebuilt and revitalized the party around a nucleus of unionized workers, upper-middle-class intellectuals and professionals, southern farmers, Jews, Catholics, and African Americans—the so-called New Deal coalition that made the Democrats the nation's majority party for the next 36 years. Groping for a response to the New Deal, Republicans often wound up supporting popular New Deal programs such as Social Security in what was sometimes derided as "me-too" Republicanism. Even the relatively conservative administration of Dwight D. Eisenhower in the 1950s left the principal New Deal programs intact.

The New Deal coalition was severely strained during the 1960s by conflicts over civil rights and the Vietnam War. The struggle over civil rights divided northern Democrats who supported the civil rights cause from white southern Democrats who defended the system of racial segregation. The struggle over the Vietnam War further divided the Democrats, with upper-income liberal Democrats strongly opposing the Johnson administration's decision to greatly expand the numbers of U.S. troops fighting in Southeast Asia. These schisms provided an opportunity for the Republicans' "Grand Old Party," or GOP, which returned to power in 1968 under the leadership of Richard Nixon.

The Contemporary American Party System Although the number of Americans identifying as Democrats remained higher than those identifying as Republicans in the 1960s and '70s, the Republican Party widened its appeal in the second half of the twentieth century (see Figure 7.2). In 1964, for example, the conservative Republican presidential candidate Barry Goldwater argued in favor of substantially reduced levels of taxation and spending, less government regulation of the economy, and the elimination of many federal social programs. Though Goldwater was defeated by Lyndon Johnson, the ideas he espoused continued to be major themes for the Republican Party. It took Richard Nixon's "southern strategy" to give the GOP the votes it needed to end Democratic dominance of national politics. Nixon appealed to disaffected white southerners, and with the help of the independent candidate and former Alabama governor George Wallace, he sparked the shift of voters that gave the Republican Party a strong position in all the states of the former Confederacy. During the 1980s, under the leadership of President Ronald Reagan, Republicans added two important groups to their coalition. The first were religious conservatives, who were

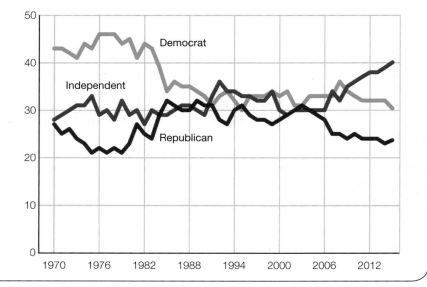

FIGURE 7.2 Trends in Party Identification, 1939–2015

Over time, the Democrats have lost strength as more Americans identified themselves as Republicans and independents. Since 2004, however, the number of Democrats has held steady and the number of Republicans has declined, while the number of Americans identifying as independent of either party has increased to an all-time high. Why do you think this is?

SOURCE: Pew Research Center, "Party Identification," www.pewresearch.org/data-trend/political-attitudes/party-identification/ (accessed 10/18/16).

PERCENTAGE IDENTIFYING
THEMSELVES AS . . .

offended by Democratic support for abortion and gay rights as well as perceived Democratic disdain for traditional cultural and religious values. The second were working-class whites, who were drawn to Reagan's tough approach to foreign policy and his positions against affirmative action. Many Republicans consider Reagan's tenure in office as a "golden era" that saw deregulation of many industries, reduced government intervention in the economy, and strong economic growth.

While Republicans built a political base around economic and social conservatives and white southerners, the Democratic Party maintained its support among a majority of unionized workers and upper-middle-class intellectuals and professionals. Democrats also appealed strongly to racial minorities. The 1965 Voting Rights Act had greatly increased black voter participation in the South and helped the Democratic Party retain some House and Senate seats in southern states. The Democrats appealed strongly to Americans concerned with inequality, abortion rights, gay rights, women's rights, the environment, and other progressive social causes.

In 2008, Democrats won control of Congress as well as the presidency for the first time since 1995. However, intense party conflict continued to characterize American politics. Republicans won control of the House of Representatives in 2010 and the Senate in 2012, even though Obama was re-elected to the presidency that year. In 2016, Republican Donald Trump was elected to the presidency in a tight race, and Republicans retained control of both chambers of Congress.

Electoral Realignments Define Party Systems in American History

Transitions between party systems in American history are sometimes called **electoral realignments**, the points in history when a new party replaces the ruling party, becoming in turn the dominant political force. During these periods, the coalitions that support the parties and the balance of power between the parties are redefined. In historical terms, realignments occur when new issues, combined with economic or political crises, mobilize new voters and persuade large numbers of voters to permanently shift their support from one party to another.

There is general agreement that five realignments have occurred since the Founding. The first took place around 1790–1800, when the Jeffersonian Republicans defeated the Federalists and became dominant. The second realignment occurred in about 1828, when the Jacksonian Democrats took control of the White House and the Congress. In the third period of realignment, centered on the 1860 election, the newly founded Republican Party, led by Abraham Lincoln, won power and in the process destroyed the Whig Party. Many northern voters who had supported the Whigs or the Democrats on the basis of their economic policies shifted their support to the Republicans as slavery replaced tariffs and economic concerns as the central issue on the nation's political agenda. Many southern Whigs shifted their support to the Democrats.

In the 1890s this alignment was at least partially supplanted by a party re-alignment based on economic and cultural factors, bringing about the fourth electoral realignment. In the election of 1896, the Republican candidate, William McKinley, emphasizing business, industry, and urban interests, defeated the Democrat, William Jennings Bryan, who spoke for sectional interests, farmers, and miners. Republican dominance lasted until the fifth realignment, during the period 1932–36, when the Democrats, led by Franklin Delano Roosevelt, took control of the White House and Congress. Despite sporadic interruptions, the Democrats maintained control of both through the 1960s. Since that time, American party politics has been characterized primarily by party polarization and by **divided government**, wherein the presidency is controlled by one party while the other party controls one or both houses of Congress.

Major partisan realignments are rare in the United States, occurring on average about once every 50 years. There are frequent false alarms, when pundits describe elections as realignments and they turn out not to be. When realignments do occur, it is often the result of new issues or societal problems, coupled with economic or political crises, that weaken the established political elite and allow new groups of politicians to create coalitions capable of capturing the reins of governmental power. In the 2016 presidential election, significant factions of the Republican Party were in disagreement over Donald Trump's candidacy, leading some observers to question whether the election was the beginning of a new party realignment. Many high-profile Republican politicians refused to support Trump, and some withdrew their support during the course of the campaign.

American Third Parties Sometimes Change the Major Parties and Election Outcomes

Although the United States has a two party–dominant system, the country has always had more than two parties. Typically, **third parties** in the United States (parties that organize to compete against the two major American political parties) have represented social and economic interests that, for one reason or another, were not given voice by the two major parties.[5] Such parties often provide new ideas and even party realignment. The Populists, a party centered in the rural areas of the West and Midwest, and the Progressives, spokespeople for the urban middle classes in the late nineteenth and early twentieth centuries, are the most important examples in the past 100 years. More recently, Ross Perot, who ran in 1992 for president as an independent and in 1996 as the Reform Party's nominee, won the votes of almost one in five Americans in 1992. In the extremely close 2000 presidential election, third-party candidate Ralph Nader won just 3 percent of the popular vote; but that was enough to swing the election to Republican George W. Bush. Table 7.1 lists the top presidential candidates in 2016. Third party candidates fared better in 2016 than in the last three presidential elections, leading some observers to suggest that third parties were one reason Clinton lost key battleground states and thus the election.

Although the Republican Party was the only American third party ever to make itself permanent (by replacing the Whigs), some third parties have enjoyed influence far beyond their electoral size. This was because large parts of their programs were adopted by one or both of the major parties, who sought to appeal to the voters mobilized by the new party to expand their own electoral strength. The Democratic Party, for example, became a great deal more liberal when it adopted most of the Progressive program early in the twentieth century. Many Socialists felt that FDR's New Deal had adopted most of their party's program, including old-age

TABLE 7.1

Parties and Candidates in 2016

CANDIDATE	PARTY	VOTE TOTAL*	PERCENTAGE OF VOTES
Hillary Clinton	Democratic	65,147,421	48%
Donald Trump	Republican	62,634,907	46%
Gary Johnson	Libertarian	4,454,855	3%
Jill Stein	Green	1,426,922	1%
Others candidates		1,047,140	0.8%

*Preliminary counts as of December 1, 2016.
SOURCE: U.S. Election Atlas, "2016 Presidential General Election Results," www.uselectionatlas.org/RESULTS
/national.php?year=2016&minper=0&f=0&off=0&elect=0 (accessed 12/1/16).

pensions, unemployment compensation, an agricultural marketing program, and laws guaranteeing workers the right to organize into unions.

Although it is not technically a political party, the rise of the Tea Party movement, an extremely conservative faction of the Republican Party, contributed to party polarization and had a considerable impact on the Republican Party primaries in 2010. In that midterm election, Tea Party candidates defeated several incumbents and candidates endorsed by Republican Party leaders. Some high-profile Tea Party candidates, including Senator Rand Paul (R-Ky.), then went on to win office in the 2010 midterm elections. On the whole, the Tea Party succeeded in electing about 32 percent of its candidates—a strong showing for a newly organized group, whose electoral influence was felt again in the 2014 and 2016 elections.[6]

Some proponents of election reform argue that two major parties are not sufficient to represent the varied interests of America's 320 million people and that more political parties would improve representation. Forms of **proportional representation**, multimember districts (more than one candidate elected from each district), or instant runoff voting would increase the probability of third-party representation in America. (Proportional representation is found in many other countries.) Yet state ballot-access laws are often a major impediment for third parties, imposing barriers such as registration fees or petition requirements in which a certain number of voters must sign a petition for a third-party or independent candidate to gain ballot access. States with lower access hurdles, such as Minnesota, have more third-party candidates. Supporters of the current two-party

The Tea Party movement emerged after the election of Barack Obama in 2008. During the 2010 midterm elections, Tea Party activists around the country rallied to "reclaim the Capitol" and succeeded in electing a number of their candidates to office, which further increased party polarization in Congress.

system contend that it creates stability in governing and prevents the need for coalition government, where multiple small parties work together to form a majority to govern.

Group Affiliations Are Based on Voters' Psychological Ties to One of the Parties

One reason parties are so important is that many voters develop **party identification** (an individual voter's psychological ties to one party or another) with one of the political parties. Party identification has been compared to wearing blue- or red-tinted glasses; it colors voters' understanding of politics in general and is the most important cue as to how to vote in elections. That is, most Republicans vote for Republican Party candidates, and most Democrats vote for Democratic Party candidates. Although it is an emotional tie, party identification also has a rational component. Voters generally form attachments to parties that reflect their views and interests. Once those attachments are formed, however, they are likely to persist and even to be handed down to children, unless some very strong factors convince individuals that their party is no longer an appropriate object of their affections. Figure 7.3 indicates the relationship between party identification and a number of social characteristics.

● Political Participation Takes Both Traditional and Digital Forms

Identify the most common forms of political participation

Political participation refers to a wide range of activities designed to influence government, politics, and policy. These activities include traditional forms of participation, such as voting and volunteering, as well as newer online forms of participation.

Voting Is the Most Important Form of Traditional Participation

Elections are the hallmark of political participation in a democracy. For most citizens today, voting is the most common form of participation in politics. In addition to voting, citizens can give money to politicians or political organizations, volunteer in campaigns, contact political officials, sign petitions, attend public meetings, join organizations, display campaign signs and pins, write letters to the editor, publish articles, attend rallies, or lobby their representatives in Congress. They can also join interest groups (see Chapter 8). These other forms of political action generally require more time, effort, or money than voting. In a survey of participation in the 2012 election, just 15 percent of respondents said they wore a campaign button or put a sticker on their car, 12 percent of those surveyed reported giving money to a candidate's campaign during the election, while only 3 percent worked for a party or a candidate.[7]

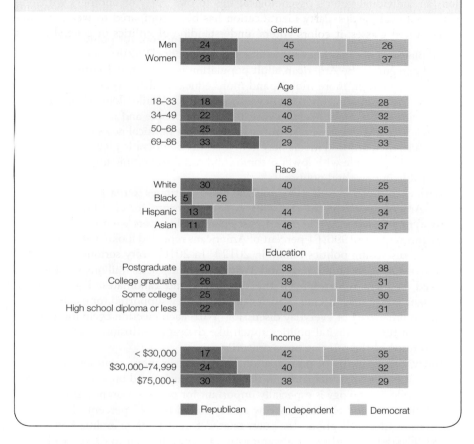

FIGURE 7.3 Who Identifies with Which Party?

Party identification varies by income, race, and gender. For example, as these statistics from 2015 show, Americans with higher incomes are more supportive of the Republican Party than are Americans with lower incomes. Women are significantly more likely than men to identify with the Democratic Party, whereas more men identify as independents.

NOTE: Percentages do not add to 100 because the category "Other/Don't know" is omitted.
SOURCE: Pew Research Center, "A Deep Dive into Party Affiliation," April 7, 2015, http://www.people-press.org /2015/04/07/a-deep-dive-into-party-affiliation/ (accessed 2/27/16).

Gender
	Republican	Independent	Democrat
Men	24	45	26
Women	23	35	37

Age
	Republican	Independent	Democrat
18–33	18	48	28
34–49	22	40	32
50–68	25	35	35
69–86	33	29	33

Race
	Republican	Independent	Democrat
White	30	40	25
Black	5	26	64
Hispanic	13	44	34
Asian	11	46	37

Education
	Republican	Independent	Democrat
Postgraduate	20	38	38
College graduate	26	39	31
Some college	25	40	30
High school diploma or less	22	40	31

Income
	Republican	Independent	Democrat
< $30,000	17	42	35
$30,000–74,999	24	40	32
$75,000+	30	38	29

Digital Political Participation Is Surging

Digital political participation is rapidly changing the way Americans experience politics. While traditional forms of participation remain important, the Internet gives citizens greater access to political information about candidates and campaigns and, at least potentially, a greater role in politics than ever before. Many forms of online participation build on traditional forms of participation, but the Internet makes many of these activities easier and gives them greater potential as community-building tools. Online participation in elections includes discussing issues or mobilizing supporters through email and social media, posting comments on blogs and online news stories, contributing money to candidates, visiting candidate and political party websites, creating and viewing online campaign ads, campaigning on social networking sites, and organizing face-to-face neighborhood meetings on sites such as Meetup.com.

Recent survey data illustrate how widespread digital politics has become. Today, 62 percent of Americans get news on social media.[8] One in three social media users have encouraged others to vote, and roughly the same percentage have shared their own thoughts or comments on politics or government using social media. About the same percentage of Democrats, Republicans, and independents use social media for politics.[9]

Twitter in particular has become a key networking tool for politics and a preferred platform of candidates and political organizations. Twitter users represented just 19 percent of the American adult population in 2016, but Twitter news consumers are younger, more mobile, and more educated than average Americans.[10] Twitter's forte is sharing breaking news about politics. While older and more affluent individuals are more likely to vote, it is young people and individuals making less than $75,000 a year who are more likely to post political news on Twitter and other social media. Social media may help level the democratic playing field, allowing the young, people with lower incomes, and racial and ethnic minorities to play a larger role in news and politics.[11]

With each successive election, political news continues to reach a greater number of Americans as the Internet creates new platforms for communication and political mobilization. While only 4 percent of likely voters went online for election information in 1996, 61 percent of Americans reported looking at information online or discussing politics online in 2012.[12] In 2016, every serious presidential candidate had a Facebook page and Twitter account, with millions of fans who received frequent updates from the campaigns and candidates. These fans, in turn, signaled to their "friends" which candidates they supported for elected office, making politics part of everyday discussion. With each election cycle more of the population turns to digital politics, much like the rapid diffusion of literacy with the invention of the printing press centuries ago.[13]

Today, online forms of participation have become more common than most traditional forms of participation in that they are performed on a daily or weekly basis. Mobile technology is especially important for organization necessary in protests, campaigns, and elections. A Pew survey found that 27 percent of registered voters used their cell phone for news related to elections or political events in 2012.[14] Candidates and political campaigns continue to turn to digital politics to reach their audience. If these trends are sustained, they may result in greater overall levels of political interest and activity.

An important question is whether online political participation influences offline participation, especially voting. Political participation requires that people be motivated and have an interest in the outcome of the election. They must have the knowledge or capacity to understand how to participate, and they must be mobilized.[15] Because digital technology encourages information-gathering and interaction between users by combining features of traditional media content with interpersonal communication for discussion and mobilization, the Internet has the potential to promote interest in politics and increase participation.

Voter Turnout in America Is Low

Today, voting rights are granted to all American citizens aged 18 and older, although some states revoke this right from those who have committed a felony or are mentally incompetent. Despite granting the right to vote, or **suffrage**, to women, racial minorities, and young adults, however, the percentage of eligible individuals who actually vote in America, or **turnout**, is low. Only 6 in 10 eligible Americans vote in presidential elections, and turnout for midterm elections (elections that fall between presidential elections) is typically lower, about one-third of eligible voters; for local elections, turnout is even lower[16] (see Figure 7.4). Turnout in state and local races that do not coincide with national contests is typically much lower. In most European countries

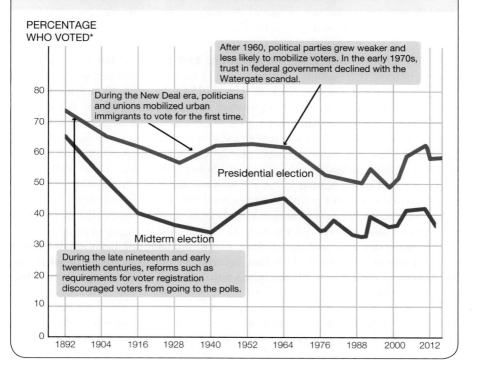

FIGURE 7.4 Voter Turnout in Presidential and Midterm Elections, 1892–2016

Since the 1890s, participation in elections has declined substantially. One pattern is consistent across time: more Americans tend to vote in presidential election years than in years when only congressional and local elections are held. What are some of the reasons that participation rose and fell during the last century?

*Percentage of voting-eligible population
SOURCES: Erik Austin and Jerome Clubb, *Political Facts of the United States since 1789* (New York: Columbia University Press, 1986); United States Election Project, www.electproject.org (accessed 11/14/16).

PERCENTAGE WHO VOTED*

After 1960, political parties grew weaker and less likely to mobilize voters. In the early 1970s, trust in federal government declined with the Watergate scandal.

During the New Deal era, politicians and unions mobilized urban immigrants to vote for the first time.

Presidential election

Midterm election

During the late nineteenth and early twentieth centuries, reforms such as requirements for voter registration discouraged voters from going to the polls.

and other Western democracies, by contrast, national voter turnout is usually between 70 and 90 percent.[17]

Why Do People Vote?

Three factors organize our understanding of voting in elections: (1) a person's social and demographic background and attitudes about politics, (2) the political environment in which elections take place and whether an election is contested among at least two political candidates, and (3) the state electoral laws that shape the political process.

Social Background Americans with higher levels of education, more income, and higher-level occupations—collectively, what social scientists call higher **socioeconomic status**—participate much more in politics than do those with less education and less income.[18] Education level is the single most important factor in predicting whether an individual will vote or engage in most other kinds of participation. Income is an important factor (not surprisingly) when it comes to people making campaign contributions. Those with money, time, and capacity to participate effectively in the political system are more likely to do so.[19] Other individual characteristics also affect participation. For example, African Americans, Asian Americans, and Latinos are less likely to participate than are whites, although when differences in education and income are taken into account, African Americans participate at similar levels to whites.[20] Finally, young people are far less likely to participate in politics than are older people. Individuals with strong partisan ties to one of the major political parties are more likely to vote than nonpartisans or independents.

The Political Environment, Mobilization, and Competition Political environments have increasingly proven to be significant. Whether or not people have resources, feel engaged, and are recruited to participate in politics depends very much on their social setting—what their parents are like, whom they know, what associations they belong to. A critical aspect of political environments is whether people are mobilized—by parties, candidates, campaigns, interest groups, and social movements. A recent comprehensive study of the decline in political participation in the United States found that half of the drop-off could be accounted for by reduced **mobilization** efforts—the process by which large numbers of people are organized for a political activity.[21]

An additional factor is whether elections are competitive—that is, whether there are at least two candidates actively contesting a position in government.[22] Competitive elections, and the campaign spending and mobilization efforts that go along with them, directly affect turnout rates.[23] Conversely, limited exposure to competitive elections may be one reason for the lower levels of turnout recorded since the 1960s.

State Electoral Laws State electoral laws, which vary widely from state to state, create formal barriers to voting that can reduce participation. In most other democratic nations, where voting rates are higher, citizens are automatically registered to vote; but the United States generally requires a two-step process: registering to vote and then voting. (Five states have recently adopted automatic voter registration, whereby eligible residents are automatically registered to vote.) Eleven states and Washington, D.C., allow voters to register and cast a ballot on the same day, but most states require registration in advance of Election Day. Registration requirements particularly reduce voting by the young, those with low education, and those with low incomes because registration requires higher political involvement, planning, and effort

Convenience voting, such as early voting and voting by mail, removes the need to stand in a potentially long line to cast a vote and may result in increased voter turnout.

than does the act of voting itself. Those with relatively little education may become interested in politics once the issues of a particular campaign become salient, but by then it may be too late for them to register, especially if they live in states that require registration up to a month before the election. And because young people tend to change residences more often than older people, registration requirements place a greater burden on them. (Information on registering to vote in your state is provided in the back of the book.)

In addition to registration, other election regulations have an impact on turnout. For example, in most other nations elections are held on weekends, when most people are not working, or Election Day is treated as a holiday. The United States holds elections during the work week. Many states maintain residency requirements that result in citizens' losing their registration if they move their residences even short distances. Most states purge their voter-registration rolls of voters who fail to vote for a given period of time. Americans hold many different elections, often at staggered times throughout the year, such as primary elections and elections for local offices and school budget votes, rather than consolidating elections at a single time. A relatively recent barrier is a requirement that voters provide proof of identity. As of the 2016 election, 32 states require all voters to show some form of ID before voting. Seven of these states require a photo ID, while another nine request photo ID but may count the vote with nonphoto ID under some circumstances. In the remaining states, nonphoto forms of ID are acceptable.[24] Voter ID laws in the states may disproportionately reduce voter turnout of certain groups: racial minorities, the elderly, and the poor.[25]

Some states have taken steps to make voting easier, such as same-day and automatic registration discussed above. Additionally, some western states use an all-mail voting system, thus eliminating polling places all together. Many states now allow early voting, which allows registered voters to cast a ballot at their regular polling place up to 40 days before the election.

AMERICA
Side by Side

Voter Turnout in Comparison

Over the past 20 years, voter turnout in U.S. national elections has hovered around 45 percent of the voting-age population. While the number is significantly higher in presidential elections than in midterm elections, voting rates in the United States still lag behind those in many other democratic countries. Australia, for instance, had almost 80 percent of their voting-age population (roughly 93 percent of registered voters) participate in the 2013 parliamentary election.

So why does voter turnout vary so much from country to country? Part of the explanation rests in how we calculate who is eligible to vote. In the United States, noncitizens and ex-felons are denied voting rights. If we exclude those populations when calculating voter percentages, U.S. turnout would be several percentage points higher.[a]

Another explanation relates to the rules governing elections. In many democracies, citizens are automatically registered to vote when they reach a certain age; in contrast, U.S. citizens generally have to register themselves, reregister if they move, and, in many states, register a certain number of days before the election. Many countries send their ballots through the mail, hold their elections on a Sunday, or declare their election day a national holiday. Voting is also compulsory in many countries. Australia, for instance, charges a $20 fine (about $17 U.S.) unless a citizen can provide a good excuse for why she did not vote.[b] These factors help explain why turnout is lower in the United States than in many other countries.

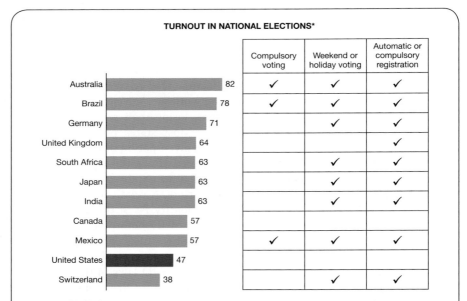

TURNOUT IN NATIONAL ELECTIONS*

	Turnout	Compulsory voting	Weekend or holiday voting	Automatic or compulsory registration
Australia	82	✓	✓	✓
Brazil	78	✓	✓	✓
Germany	71		✓	✓
United Kingdom	64			✓
South Africa	63		✓	✓
Japan	63		✓	✓
India	63		✓	✓
Canada	57			
Mexico	57	✓	✓	✓
United States	47			
Switzerland	38		✓	✓

*Average 1990–2016.
SOURCES: International Institute for Democracy and Electoral Assistance (IDEA) Voter turnout database, www.idea.int/vt/viewdata.cfm and the ACE Electoral Knowledge Network, www.aceproject.org/epic-en/CDMap?question=VR008&f= (accessed 3/27/16).

[a]Michael P. McDonald, "National General Election VEP Turnout Rates, 1789–Present," United States Election Project, June 11, 2014, www.electproject.org/national-1789-present (accessed 6/24/16).
[b]Juliet Lapidos, "Doing Democracy Right," Slate, October 17, 2008, www.slate.com/articles/news_and_politics/how_they_do_it/2008/10/doing_democracy_right.html (accessed 6/24/16).

Voters Decide Based on Party, Issues, and Candidate

Examine the factors that influence voters' decisions

Three key factors influence voters' decisions at the polls: party loyalty, issue and policy concerns, and candidate characteristics. The prominence of these three bases for electoral choice varies from contest to contest and voter to voter.

Party Loyalty Is Important

Most voters feel a certain sense of identification or kinship with the Democratic Party or the Republican Party. This sense of identification is often handed down from parents to children and reinforced by social and cultural ties. Partisan identification predisposes voters in favor of their party's candidates and oppose those of the other party (see Figure 7.5). At the level of the presidential contest, issues and candidate personalities may become very important, although even here many Americans support presidential candidates primarily because of party loyalty. But partisanship is more likely to be a factor in the less visible races, where issues and the candidates are not as well known. State legislative races, for example, are often decided by voters' party ties. Once formed, voters' partisan loyalties seldom change. Voters tend to keep

---

FIGURE 7.5 The Effect of Party Identification on the Vote, 2016

In 2016 about 90 percent of Democrats and Republicans supported their party's presidential candidate. Should candidates devote their resources to converting voters who identify with the opposition or to winning more support among independents? What factors might make it difficult for candidates to simultaneously pursue both courses of action?

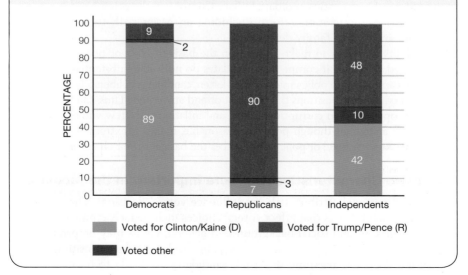

Voted for Clinton/Kaine (D)   Voted for Trump/Pence (R)

Voted other

---

their party affiliations unless some crisis causes them to reexamine the bases for their loyalty and decide to support a different party, such as happened at the beginning of the New Deal era, between 1932 and 1936, when millions of former Republicans transferred their allegiance to FDR and the Democrats.

After the 1960s, many analysts expressed concern that American parties had become too weak to play their role in converting popular political participation into effective government. These scholars noted such trends as a decline in partisan attachment within the electorate, a growth in the number of voters identifying as independents, and a rise in so-called split-ticket voting. This overall trend, sometimes termed "dealignment," was seen as a product of growing social diversity and educational attainment, which made voters less reliant on parties to guide their political decision making. The growth of the mass media, particularly television, also seemed to reduce the role of parties in elections as television tends to focus on the personalities of individual candidates rather than the "institution" of the party. Today, party loyalties in America continue to be in a state of flux. On the one hand, the percentage of voters who declare no party loyalty remains at an all-time high.[26] On the other hand, party identification among a large number of the most active voters has grown stronger.[27]

Issues Can Shape an Election

Issues and policy preferences are a second factor influencing voters' choices at the polls. Voters may cast their ballots for the candidate whose position on economic issues they believe to be closest to their own or the candidate who has what they believe to be the best record on foreign policy. Issues are more important in some races than in others. If candidates actually do "take issue" with one another—that is, articulate and publicize very different positions on important public questions—voters are more likely to be able to identify and act on whatever policy preferences they may have.

In 2016, for example, Donald Trump made immigration a key issue of the presidential campaign. His calls for harsh restrictions included building a wall along the U.S.-Mexico border and placing a temporary ban on Muslims immigrating to the United States. Democratic candidate Hillary Clinton, on the other hand, supported comprehensive immigration reform, including an easier path to full and equal citizenship and ending family detention.

The ability of voters to make choices on the basis of issue or policy preferences is diminished, however, if competing candidates do not differ substantially or do not focus their campaigns on policy matters. Very often, candidates deliberately take the safe course and emphasize positions that will not offend any voters. Thus, candidates often stress their opposition to corruption, crime, and inflation since few voters favor these things. Such a strategy, though perfectly reasonable, makes it extremely difficult for voters to make their issue or policy preferences the basis for their choice at the polls.

Candidate Characteristics Are More Important in the Media Age

Candidates' personal attributes always influence voters' decisions. The important candidate characteristics that affect voters' choices include race, ethnicity, religion, gender, geography, and social background. In general, voters may be proud to see someone of their ethnic, religious, or geographic background in a position of leadership, and they may presume that such candidates are likely to have views and perspectives close to their own. This is why, for many years, politicians sought to "balance the ticket," making certain that their party's ticket included members of as many important groups as possible.

Just as candidates' personal characteristics may attract some voters, they may repel others. Many voters are prejudiced against candidates of certain ethnic, racial, or religious groups. And for many years voters were reluctant to support the candidacies of women, although this appears to be changing. Indeed, that the 2008 Democratic candidate was a black man, the 2012 Republican presidential candidate a Mormon, and the 2016 Democratic candidate a woman indicates the increasing diversity of candidates for public office.

Voters also pay attention to candidates' personality characteristics, such as "decisiveness," "honesty," and "vigor." In recent years integrity has become a key election issue. In the 2016 presidential election, many Americans questioned the trustworthiness of both Hillary Clinton and Donald Trump. Nonetheless, Trump supporters saw their candidate as unafraid to speak his mind. Clinton supporters, on the other hand, admired her ambition, toughness, and discipline.

● The Electoral Process Has Many Levels and Rules

Explain the major rules, levels, and types of elections in the United States

Three types of elections are held in the United States: primary elections, general elections, and initiative and referendum elections; the last are where proposed laws are placed on the ballot for a popular vote.

Primary elections are elections within a political party to select each party's candidates for the general election. In the case of local and statewide offices, the winners of primary elections face one another as their parties' nominees in the general election. At the presidential level, however, primary elections are indirect because they are used to select state delegates to the national conventions, at which the major party presidential candidates are chosen. The United States is one of the few nations in the world to use primary elections. In most countries, nominations are controlled by party officials, as they once were here. The primary system was introduced at the turn of the twentieth century by Progressive reformers who hoped to weaken the power of party leaders by taking candidate nominations out of their hands.

Under the laws of most states, only registered members of a political party may vote in a primary election to select that party's candidates. This is called a **closed primary**. Other states allow all registered voters to choose on the day of the primary in which party's primary they will participate. This is called an **open primary**. In nominating presidential candidates, though most states hold primary elections, about one-third use **caucuses** instead, which are essentially party business meetings held to select candidates.

The primary is followed by the **general election**, a regularly scheduled election involving most districts in the nation or state, in which voters decide who wins office; in the United States, general elections for national office and most state and local offices are held on the first Tuesday following the first Monday in November in even-numbered years (every four years for presidential elections).

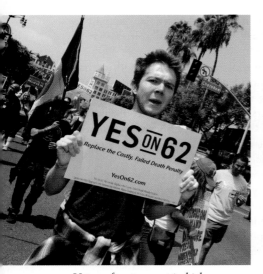

Voters often turn out in higher numbers when there are controversial initiatives on the ballot. In 2016, Californians voted on a total of 18 ballot measures, including whether or not to repeal the death penalty.

Beyond presidential and congressional elections, 24 states also provide for the initiative process. **Ballot initiatives** are proposed laws or policy changes placed on the ballot by citizens or interest groups for a popular vote. If a ballot measure receives majority support, it becomes law. In recent years voters in several states have voted to raise taxes on the wealthy, prohibit social services for illegal immigrants, end affirmative action, provide universal health care, create nonpartisan redistricting, protect open space and the environment, and prevent offshore drilling. At the turn of the twentieth century, ballot initiatives were used to grant women suffrage (the right to vote), prevent child labor, limit the workday to eight hours, adopt progressive taxes, and allow voters to elect U.S. senators directly (rather than having them chosen by state legislatures).

All 50 states have the legislative **referendum**, the practice of referring proposed laws passed by a legislature to the vote of the electorate for approval or rejection. Ballot initiative campaigns often involve high spending by proponents and opponents and mass media campaigns that can rival those of congressional and presidential candidates within a state. The general referendum and initiative are called direct democracy because they allow voters to govern directly without intervention by government officials or the political parties. The validity of ballot measure results, however, is subject to judicial action. If a court finds that an initiative violates the state or national constitution, it can overturn the result. This happened in the case of a 1995 California initiative curtailing social services to undocumented aliens and again in 2012 when the federal courts overturned California's Proposition 8 banning same-sex marriage.[28] Hundreds of initiatives and referenda appear on state election ballots every two years.

Eighteen states also have legal provisions for **recall** elections, which allow voters to remove governors and other state officials from office prior to the expiration of their terms. Generally, a recall effort begins with a petition campaign. In California, for example, if 12 percent of those who voted in the last general election sign petitions demanding a special recall election, one must be held. In 2003, many California voters blamed Governor Gray Davis for the state's $38 billion budget deficit, and he was turned out of office in a recall election. Federal officials, such as the president and members of Congress, are not subject to recall.

The Electoral College Still Organizes Presidential Elections

In the early history of popular voting, nations often made use of indirect elections. In these elections, voters would choose the members of an intermediate body. These members would, in turn, select public officials. The assumption underlying such processes was that ordinary citizens were not really qualified to choose their leaders and could not be trusted to do so directly. The last vestige of this procedure in America is the **electoral college**, the group of electors who formally select the president and vice president of the United States.

When Americans go to the polls on Election Day, they are technically not voting directly for presidential candidates, even though they mark ballots as such; they are instead choosing among slates of electors selected by each state's party and pledged, if elected, to support that party's presidential candidate. Electors are allocated to each state based on the size of the state's congressional delegation (senators and House members); larger-population states thus have more votes in the electoral college. North Dakota, for example, has 3 votes in the electoral college (based on its 2 senators plus 1 representative), while California has 55 (2 senators plus 53 representatives).

The presidential candidate who receives a majority of the electoral college's 538 votes (a majority is 270) becomes president—not necessarily the candidate with the most votes from the people. This is in part because the electoral college and most elections in the United States are governed by plurality, or winner-take-all, rules. With only two exceptions, each state awards *all* of its electors to the candidate who receives the most votes in the state.[29] Thus, Trump received all 29 of Florida's electoral votes, though he won only 49 percent of the votes in the state.

Only four times in the nation's history has the winner in the electoral college not won the popular vote. Since electoral votes are won on a state-by-state basis, it is mathematically possible for a candidate who receives a nationwide popular plurality to fail to carry states whose electoral votes would add up to a majority. Thus, in 1876, Rutherford B. Hayes was the winner in the electoral college despite receiving fewer popular votes than his rival, Samuel Tilden. In 1888, Grover Cleveland received more popular votes than Benjamin Harrison but fewer electoral votes, so Harrison was elected. In 2000 a lengthy legal battle over recounting votes in Florida ultimately ended with the Supreme Court's decision in *Bush v. Gore* that handed George W. Bush the presidency.[30] But while Bush had won a majority in the electoral college, Democratic candidate Al Gore had won more votes nationwide. Again in 2016, Donald Trump won in the electoral college, but Hillary Clinton won around 2.5 million more votes (based on preliminary tallies). These controversial elections generated new calls for electoral reform.

● The 2016 Elections

Analyze the strategies, issues, and outcomes of the 2016 elections

In 2016, Democrat Hillary Clinton ran against Republican Donald Trump in a dramatic presidential race. Despite media predictions that favored the Democrats, Trump won a surprise victory with a majority of votes in the electoral college, and the Republicans also retained control of both houses of Congress. In this section, we analyze how the 2016 race unfolded and the major factors that contributed to the results.

The 2016 Primaries Reflected Divisions within Both Parties

In 2016, each party's nomination was sharply contested by candidates representing different factions within the two parties and by "outsider" populist candidates, as we saw in the introduction to this chapter. On the Democratic side, Hillary Clinton faced a serious challenge from Vermont senator Bernie Sanders. Clinton's experience, control of the party machinery, support in minority communities, and fund-raising prowess initially seemed to make her nomination a foregone conclusion. The primary, however, was close enough to extend well into the spring, and Clinton did not secure enough delegates to ensure the nomination until just six weeks before the national convention in July. Ultimately, Sanders won 43 percent of the Democratic primary vote and carried 23 states compared to Clinton's 34.

On the Republican side, the conflict over the 2016 presidential nomination laid bare even deeper divisions within the party. Seventeen candidates competed in the Republican primaries, from "establishment" candidates such as Jeb Bush and Marco Rubio to libertarian Rand Paul and social conservatives such as Ted Cruz. As the Republican race got under way, real-estate mogul and reality-TV star Donald Trump was not taken seriously as a presidential candidate by most pundits and party leaders. During the Republican primaries, however, Trump campaigned cleverly, making use of social media, especially Twitter. Throughout the course of his campaign, Trump commanded headlines with controversial and incendiary comments, including his assertions that he would build a wall along the U.S.–Mexican border and place a temporary ban on Muslim immigration to the United States.

Trump was the plurality winner with roughly 40 percent of the popular vote in the primaries. Trump won more votes (over 13 million) in the presidential primaries than any Republican candidate in history, but he also received more votes *against* him than any candidate in history, with 16 million votes cast for other Republican candidates.

The General Election Was Bitterly Fought

With their parties' nominations in hand, Clinton and Trump faced one another in the general election. Clinton seemed to possess several critical advantages. Based on voting patterns in recent elections, significantly more states were considered either safely Democratic or favorable to the Democrats than to the Republicans. Moreover, Democratic candidates usually get support from the most dynamic and rapidly growing segments of the electorate—namely, minority voters and

Donald Trump's campaign rhetoric, including a promise to build a wall at the U.S.–Mexican border, helped energize supporters and generate media coverage.

immigrants—along with women and young people. Clinton also entered the race with an enormous fund-raising edge over Trump.

The Trump campaign was confident that it would be able to overcome the Democrats' advantages. First, Trump believed that his appeal to blue-collar white voters would make him competitive in Democratic strongholds in Midwestern states. Second, Trump calculated that he would increase Republican support among white voters sufficiently to offset the Democratic edge among nonwhite voters. Third, Trump hoped that his provocative style would continue to encourage extensive free media coverage, offsetting Clinton's fund-raising advantage and ability to spend on paid campaign ads.

Both campaigns calculated that the opposing candidate was quite vulnerable to personal attacks, and the race was characterized by intense personal attacks, scandal, and mudslinging. Leading up to the presidential election, Republicans opened fire in 2015 by launching a congressional investigation of Hillary Clinton's role in the deaths of U.S. embassy officials in Benghazi, Libya, and another investigation of Clinton's use of a private email server to handle official State Department correspondence during her tenure as secretary of state. Democrats charged that the primary purpose of these investigations was to damage Clinton's reputation as it was presumed that she would be the 2016 Democratic presidential nominee. While neither investigation led to formal charges against Clinton, both served to convince many Americans that the former secretary of state was dishonest and untrustworthy. During the course of the race, WikiLeaks made available a large quantity of hacked Clinton emails, which also painted an unflattering portrait of Clinton and her inner circle.

For their part, Democratic opposition researchers focused on Trump's many controversial remarks—such as his comments about women and statements blaming illegal immigrants for drugs, rape, and other crime—labeling them as offensive and Trump as xenophobic, racist, and sexist. On October 7, 2016, with one month before the November election, the *Washington Post* released a video from 2005 that showed Trump making lewd comments about women and bragging about how his celebrity status gave him license to touch women inappropriately—comments that many people felt condoned sexual assault. The release of the tape was followed by allegations from more than a dozen women who reported having experienced unwanted sexual advances by Trump or who accused the candidate of sexual assault.

Another issue was Trump's failure to release his tax returns, unprecedented among major-party presidential candidates during the last four decades. Investigative journalism revealed a 1995 tax return showing that Trump claimed $916 million in losses, which enabled him to avoid paying federal income taxes.[31]

In October 2016, a video from 2005 was released in which Donald Trump was heard boasting that his fame gave him license to touch women inappropriately. After the video was released, multiple women—including Karena Virginia, pictured here—came forward to accuse Trump of sexual assault or unwanted sexual contact.

Following these revelations, by mid-October most polls showed Clinton with a strong lead over Trump. As Election Day approached, most analysts gave Clinton a 70 to 80 percent chance of winning. Based on Clinton's apparently comfortable lead, the Democrats also hoped to take the Senate back from the Republicans.

White Working-Class Voters Were Key to Trump's Victory

In the end, the 2016 presidential election was a historic upset in which the national media and the polling forecasts got it wrong. (See Chapter 5 for a discussion of polling errors in 2016.) Trump prevailed in the electoral college, winning states for a total of 306 votes to Clinton's 232 votes (see Figure 7.6), but Clinton won the popular vote by around 2 percent, or 2.5 million votes (based on preliminary tallies).

Trump's popularity among working-class white Americans was crucial to his winning coalition. This demographic group had the most negative views of the economy and was generally opposed to the trade policies favored by the Democrats and mainstream conservatives. Many voters looked to Trump to bring back factory jobs that had moved overseas and saw Clinton as representing Wall Street, government, and—as one Trump ad put it—"more of the same." According to exit polls, Trump won 67 percent of the votes among whites without a college degree compared

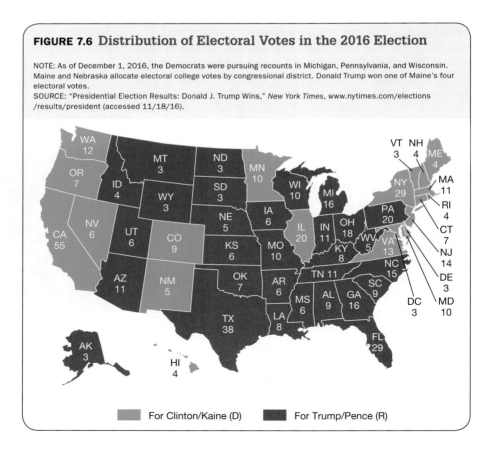

FIGURE 7.6 Distribution of Electoral Votes in the 2016 Election

NOTE: As of December 1, 2016, the Democrats were pursuing recounts in Michigan, Pennsylvania, and Wisconsin. Maine and Nebraska allocate electoral college votes by congressional district. Donald Trump won one of Maine's four electoral votes.
SOURCE: "Presidential Election Results: Donald J. Trump Wins," *New York Times*, www.nytimes.com/elections /results/president (accessed 11/18/16).

For Clinton/Kaine (D)   For Trump/Pence (R)

to just 28 percent for Clinton—a 14 percentage point gain for Trump compared with the Republican vote from this group in 2012. This support enabled Trump to build a winning coalition that also included traditional Republican partisans.

Among those who felt the country was generally going in the right direction, Hillary Clinton won 90 percent support. Clinton also received a majority of votes from women, African Americans, Latinos, Asian Americans, and younger college-educated voters. While less media coverage was devoted to policy issues in 2016 than in previous elections, the issues mattered. Clinton won more votes from individuals who felt foreign policy or the economy was the most important issue. Trump won more votes from those who felt immigration or terrorism was most important. Among voters saying their preferred candidate could bring needed change, 83 percent favored Trump. Among voters who said their preferred candidate had the right experience, 90 percent favored Clinton. In the end, a desire for change edged out the importance of experience.

The 2016 Election Raised Important Questions About the Future

As the long and bitterly fought 2016 election drew to a close, President-elect Trump, President Obama, Hillary Clinton, and a host of commentators and pundits declared that it was time to bring the nation back together. It seemed more likely, however, that competing political forces would lick their wounds and move their battles from the electoral arena to the nation's capital. With the House and Senate in Republican hands, Democrats would be hard-pressed to block Trump's agenda. Democratic congressional leaders, nevertheless, prepared to wage pitched and possibly prolonged battles over several major issues.

The events of 2016 also raised major questions about the future of America's political parties and the viability of America's electoral processes. Donald Trump's candidacy upended the Republican Party. Following the divisive primary fight and Trump's many controversial remarks, a number of well known and powerful Republicans had distanced themselves from him. Most observers thought his unprecedented rejection by party elders would doom the Trump ticket. Trump, however, mobilized millions of blue-collar voters from traditionally Democratic constituencies to win the election. The question for Republicans was whether established GOP leaders would be able to reconcile themselves to the new GOP and work with Trump to permanently tie his followers to the Republican coalition.

For the Democrats, Hillary Clinton's defeat prompted leaders of the party's left-liberal wing to assert that the Democratic Party needed to embrace a more progressive platform to recapture the White House. More moderate Democrats answered that Clinton was defeated because of her particular shortcomings, not her policy platform, and that a shift to the political left would wreck, rather than strengthen, the party.

Republicans and Democrats both were left to grapple with questions about the structure of America's electoral system. Should the parties reconsider their nominating rules? The GOP's open and fluid rules allowed the nomination to be captured by an outsider; the Democrats' more closed rules gave the nomination

Two groups that were crucial to Trump's success were men and white working-class voters. White working-class voters in particular were unhappy with the economy and turned to Trump to bring factory jobs back to the United States. Here, Trump supporters celebrate his victory on election night.

to a candidate with more support among party elites than voters. Moreover, was it finally time to reconsider the electoral college which produced a Trump victory even though Clinton won more popular votes? More generally, the lack of civil discourse during the campaign and the diminished faith in political institutions (including elections) raised questions about many aspects of American democracy.

As we saw in Chapter 1, the public's trust in government has been relatively low in recent decades, and the 2016 election may have not only reflected this trend but also contributed to it. Some observers worried that Trump's repeated claims of election fraud and rigged elections would cast doubt the ability of the government to hold free and fair elections. While Trump had raised eyebrows before the election by saying he might not accept the validity of the results, anti-Trump protesters after the election refuted the legitimacy of the outcome, chanting, "Not my president," and pointing to the fact that Clinton had won more popular votes. Trump's intense criticism of the national media throughout the campaign also challenged the important role of the media in informing the public. After the election, some Democrats added to this criticism by blaming the media for Clinton's defeat. Moreover, the high reliance on social media for news in 2016 may have affected the election. A study after the election showed that fake news stories, which are often circulated via Facebook and other social media, were more likely to go viral than authentic news stories.[32] The blurring of fact and fiction on social media made it difficult for the public to know what information to trust when it came to politics and government.

The 2016 election is now history, but the ways in which these trends and developments will shape the American political system in the future are yet to be seen.

● Money Is the Mother's Milk of Politics

Describe how candidates raise the money they need to run

Modern national political campaigns are fueled by enormous amounts of money. The 2016 election shattered previous records for campaign spending. Combined spending by candidates, parties, and interest groups on the congressional and presidential races was $6.9 billion in 2016 compared with $6.2 billion in 2012 and $5.3 billion in 2008. Of the $6.9 billion, $4.3 billion was spent on congressional races and S2.6 billion on the presidential race.

Campaign Funds Come from Direct Appeals, the Rich, PACs, and Parties

According to the Center for Responsive Politics, the $6.9 billion spent in 2016 included money from leadership PACs, super PACs, and 501(c)(4) "dark money" groups (who can shield donor identities). The two presidential candidates raised $1.3 billion combined, including about $500 million by Hillary Clinton's campaign, and $190 million from outside groups supporting her. Donald Trump raised only about $250 million with another $59 million from outside groups.[33]

Individual Donors Politicians devote a great deal of time to asking people for money. Money is solicited via direct mail, through the Internet, over the phone, and in numerous face-to-face meetings. Under federal law, individuals may donate as much as $2,700 per candidate per election, $5,000 per PAC per calendar year, $33,400 per national party committee per calendar year, and $10,000 to state and local committees per calendar year. There is no limit on the number of candidates that an individual can give to, however.[34]

Political Action Committees PACs are organizations established by corporations, labor unions, or interest groups to channel the contributions of their members and employees into political campaigns. Under the terms of the 1971 Federal Election Campaign Act, which governs campaign finance in the United States, PACs are permitted to make larger contributions to any given candidate than individuals are allowed to make. Moreover, allied or related PACs often coordinate their campaign contributions, greatly increasing the amount of money a candidate actually receives from the same interest group. More than 4,600 PACs are registered with the Federal Election Commission, which oversees campaign finance practices in the United States. Nearly two-thirds of all PACs represent corporations, trade associations, and other business and professional groups. Alliances of bankers, lawyers, doctors, and merchants all sponsor PACs.

Independent Spending—527, 501(c)(4), and Super PAC Committees
Committees known as **527s** and **501(c)(4)s** are independent groups that are not covered by the campaign-spending restrictions imposed in 2002 by the Bipartisan Campaign Reform Act. These groups, named for the sections of the tax code under which they are organized, can raise and spend unlimited amounts on political advocacy so long as their efforts are not coordinated with those of any candidate's campaign. A 527 is a group established specifically for the purpose of political advocacy and is required to report to the IRS. A 501(c)(4) is a nonprofit group that also engages in advocacy but may not spend more than half its revenues for political purposes. Unlike a 527, a 501(c)(4) is not required to disclose where it gets its funds or exactly what it does with them. As a result, its funding has earned the name "dark money" and has raised growing concern that the lack of transparency in campaign funding threatens fair elections. Wealthy and corporate donors now commonly route campaign contributions through 501(c)(4)s to avoid the legal limits on contributions through other channels. A new form of independent group, the independent expenditure committee, or "Super PAC," came about after the Supreme Court's 2010 decision in *Citizens United v. Federal Election Commission* that the government could not restrict independent expenditures by corporations or unions to political campaigns. Following that decision, *SpeechNow v. FEC* permitted individuals and organizations to form committees that could raise unlimited amounts of money to run advertising for and against candidates so long as their efforts were not coordinated with those of the candidates.[35]

In 2014 the Supreme Court removed additional limits on individuals' campaign contributions in its decision in *McCutcheon et al. v. Federal Election Commission*.[36] Outside spending via 527s, 501c(4)s, and Super PACs played an unprecedented role in the 2012 and 2016 presidential races as groups ran extensive television ads. Super PACs on both sides relied on very large contributions. In 2016, Super PACs supporting candidates' campaigns spent a total of $594 million. A growing concern is that elections in the United States can be bought with big money from corporations and wealthy donors, who will then hold significant influence when that candidate is elected. Political corruption and undue influence from Wall Street were recurrent themes among 2016 presidential candidates.

Public Funding The Federal Election Campaign Act also provides for public funding of presidential campaigns. As they seek a major-party presidential nomination, candidates become eligible for public funds by raising at least $5,000 in individual contributions of $250 or less in each of 20 states. Candidates who reach this threshold may apply for federal funds to match, on a dollar-for-dollar basis, all individual contributions of $250 or less that they receive. In 2016 candidates who accepted matching funds could spend no more than $48.7 million, including matching funds, in their presidential primary campaigns. The funds are drawn from the Presidential Election Campaign Fund. Taxpayers can contribute $3 to this fund, at no additional cost to themselves, by checking a box on the first page of their federal income tax returns. Major-party presidential candidates receive a lump sum (about $96 million in 2016, although neither Clinton nor Trump accepted this money in 2016) during the summer prior to the general election. They must meet all their general expenses from this money. Third-party candidates are eligible for public funding only if they received at least 5 percent of the vote in the previous presidential race. This stipulation effectively blocks preelection funding for third-party or independent candidates, although a third party that wins more than 5 percent of the vote can receive public funding after the election.

Under current law, no candidate is required to accept public funding for either the nominating races or the general presidential election. Candidates who do not accept public funding are not bound by any expenditure limits. In 2008, John McCain accepted public funding for the general election campaign, receiving $84 million, but Barack Obama declined, choosing to rely on his own fund-raising prowess. Obama ultimately outspent McCain by a wide margin. The 2008 race was the last time that major-party presidential candidates limited their own fund-raising in favor of public funding. Neither major party candidate accepted public funding in 2012 or 2016.

The Candidates Themselves On the basis of the Supreme Court's 1976 decision in *Buckley v. Valeo*, the right of individuals to spend their *own* money to campaign for office is a constitutionally protected matter of free speech and is not subject to limitation.[37] Thus, extremely wealthy candidates often contribute millions of dollars to their own campaigns. Donald Trump, for example, spent millions of his own money on his 2016 campaign, as did Ross Perot in 1992 and 1996. The only exception to the *Buckley* rule concerns presidential candidates

In 2014, Shaun McCutcheon successfully challenged the federal limit on the amount of money any one individual can donate to political campaigns and candidates. Many people worry that recent Supreme Court decisions overturning campaign spending reinforce the influence of the very affluent in American politics at the expense of everyone else.

who accept federal funding for their general-election campaigns. Such individuals are limited to $50,000 in personal spending.

Political Parties, Elections,

and Your Future

While party leaders exercise great control over party platforms, the party message, candidate funding, who holds elected office, and who wins the nomination for president, many aspects of party politics have been turned upside down with the digital revolution in communication and by "outsider" candidates running for president who have exploited digital platforms to advance their campaigns. Four resources that political parties use to contest and win elections (time, money, expertise, and organization) have all been altered by the Internet. New media are decentralizing party power as citizens can volunteer and give money to the party of their choice without ever being contacted by a party official. Online fund-raising allows millions of donors to give small contributions to parties, and new media allow the party to spread its message far and wide online. This is beneficial for parties because more people are involved, but there are more divergent opinions that must be recognized and appeased. At the same time, huge contributions from a handful of very wealthy individuals have increased. Will the ability of the mass public to make their desires known to party leaders mean that party leaders pay more attention to these preferences? Is the two-party system the optimal system for American politics, or should electoral reforms encourage more parties to form and, hence, provide more choice for voters?

The important role played by private funds in American elections affects the balance of power among contending economic groups. Politicians need large amounts of money to campaign successfully for major offices. This fact inevitably ties their interests to the interests of the groups and forces that can provide this money: the affluent. In a nation as large and diverse as the United States, to be sure, campaign contributors represent many different groups and, often, clashing interests. The fact remains, however, that those with more money will be able to give more and speak with a louder voice. Since 2000, a series of highly competitive presidential elections has spurred political campaigns to pay more attention to drawing greater numbers of voters from a variety of backgrounds into the political process; even so, many Americans still do not participate in politics. The "**Who Participates?**" feature shows who turned out to vote in the 2012 election.

Who Voted in 2012?

Age

45%	59%	67%	72%
18–29	30–44	45–64	65+

Income

55%	70%	78%
<$50,000	$50,000–$99,999	$100,000+

Race

64%	48%	66%	47%
White	Hispanic	African American	Asian

Sex

59%	63%
Men	Women

Education*

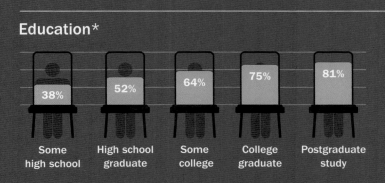

38%	52%	64%	75%	81%
Some high school	High school graduate	Some college	College graduate	Postgraduate study

*Highest level attained

SOURCE: U.S. Census Bureau, Current Population Survey, November 2012, http://www.census.gov/hhes/www/socdemo/voting/publications/p20/2012/tables.html?cssp=SERP (accessed 12/5/15).

WHAT YOU CAN DO ➡

WHAT YOU CAN DO

Vote

✓ Register to vote. See page 24.

✓ Find out what's on the ballot in upcoming elections in your state and district by entering your address at **www.vote411.org** (a website from the League of Women Voters).

✓ Cast your vote on Election Day. Consider encouraging others to vote too. Research shows that people are more likely to turn out to vote if a friend or family member asks them to.

chapterstudyguide

Practice Quiz

1. A political party is different from an interest group in that a political party *(p. 205)*
   a) seeks to control the government by nominating candidates and electing its members to office.
   b) is constitutionally exempt from taxation.
   c) is entirely nonprofit.
   d) has a much larger membership.
   e) has a much smaller membership.

2. Which party pledged to ban slavery from the western territories in the 1850s? *(p. 211)*
   a) American Independent
   b) Prohibition

   c) Republican
   d) Democratic
   e) Whig

3. The so-called New Deal coalition was severely strained *(p. 213)*
   a) during the 1860s by conflicts over slavery and southern secession.
   b) during the 1890s by conflicts over the gold standard.
   c) during the 1930s by conflicts over the Great Depression and America's involvement in World War II.
   d) during the 1960s by conflicts over civil rights and the Vietnam War.
   e) during the 1990s by conflicts over abortion and affirmative action.

4. The periodic episodes in American history in which an "old" dominant political party is replaced by a "new" dominant political party are called *(p. 215)*
   a) constitutional revolutions.
   b) divided governments.
   c) unified governments.
   d) dealignments.
   e) electoral realignments.

5. Third parties have influenced national politics mainly by *(pp. 216–17)*
   a) electing their candidates to the presidency.
   b) electing their candidates to Congress.
   c) supporting the major parties' platforms.
   d) promoting specific issues and taking votes from one of the two major parties.
   e) preventing realignments.

6. Which of the following is *not* a form of traditional political participation? *(p. 218)*
   a) volunteering in a campaign
   b) attending an abortion rights rally
   c) displaying a campaign sign
   d) voting in an election
   e) visiting the Democratic Party's website

7. Which of the following factors is *not* currently an obstacle to voting in the United States? *(p. 223)*
   a) registration requirements
   b) that elections occur on weekdays
   c) the restriction of voting rights for people who have committed a felony
   d) literacy tests
   e) voter identification laws

8. If a state has 10 members in the U.S. House of Representatives, how many votes in the electoral college does that state have? *(p. 229)*
   a) 2
   b) 10
   c) 12
   d) 20
   e) The number of votes cannot be determined from this information.

9. The main difference between a 527 committee and a 501c(4) committee is that *(p. 236)*
   a) a 527 is not legally required to disclose where it gets its money, while a 501c(4) is legally required to do so.
   b) a 501c(4) is not legally required to disclose where it gets its money, while a 527 is legally required to do so.
   c) a 527 can only contribute to one campaign, while a 501c(4) can contribute to many.
   d) a 501c(4) can only contribute to one campaign, while a 527 can contribute to many.
   e) a 527 can legally coordinate its spending with a candidate's campaign, while a 501c(4) cannot.

10. In the 2016 presidential election, public funding *(pp. 236–37)*
    a) was accepted by both major-party candidates.
    b) was accepted by Hillary Clinton only.
    c) was accepted by Donald Trump only.
    d) was declined by both major-party candidates.
    e) was not available.

11. In *Buckley v. Valeo*, the Supreme Court ruled that *(pp. 237–38)*
    a) PAC donations to campaigns are constitutionally protected.
    b) candidates cannot spend any of their own money to run for office.
    c) the right of individuals to spend their own money to campaign is constitutionally protected.
    d) there is no limit to the number of candidates that an individual can contribute money to.
    e) the Bipartisan Campaign Reform Act is unconstitutional.

Key Terms

ballot initiative *(p. 228)* a proposed law or policy change that is placed on the ballot by citizens or interest groups for a popular vote

caucus (political) *(p. 227)* a normally closed political party business meeting of citizens to select candidates, elect officers, plan strategy, or make decisions regarding legislative matters

closed primary *(p. 227)* a primary election in which voters can participate in the nomination of candidates but only of the party in which they are enrolled for a period of time prior to primary day

divided government *(p. 216)* the condition in American government wherein the presidency is controlled by one party while the opposing party controls one or both houses of Congress

electoral college *(p. 229)* the electors from each state who meet after the popular election to cast ballots for president and vice president

electoral realignment *(p. 215)* the point in history when a new party supplants the ruling party, becoming in turn the dominant political force; in the United States, this has tended to occur roughly every 30 years

501(c)(4)s *(p. 236)* politically active nonprofits; under federal law, these nonprofits can spend unlimited amounts on political campaigns and not disclose their donors as long as their activities are not coordinated with the candidate campaigns and political activities are not their primary purpose

527 committees *(p. 236)* nonprofit independent groups that receive and disburse funds to influence the nomination, election, or defeat of candidates; named after Section 527 of the Internal Revenue Code, which defines and provides tax-exempt status for nonprofit advocacy groups

general election *(p. 227)* a regularly scheduled election involving most districts in the nation or state, in which voters decide who wins office; in the United States, general elections for national office and most state and local offices are held on the first Tuesday following the first Monday in November in even-numbered years (every four years for presidential elections)

incumbent *(p. 206)* a candidate running for re-election to a position that he or she already holds

majority party *(p. 208)* the party that holds the majority of legislative seats in either the House or the Senate

minority party *(p. 208)* the party that holds the minority of legislative seats in either the House or the Senate

mobilization *(p. 222)* the process by which large numbers of people are organized for a political activity

nomination *(p. 206)* the process by which political parties select their candidates for election to public office

open primary *(p. 227)* a primary election in which the voter can wait until the day of the primary to choose which party to enroll in to select candidates for the general election

party identification *(p. 218)* an individual voter's psychological ties to one party or another

political action committee (PAC) *(p. 205)* a private group that raises and distributes funds for use in election campaigns

political parties *(p. 205)* organized groups that attempt to influence the government by electing their members to important government offices

primary elections *(p. 227)* elections within a political party to select the party's candidate for the general election

proportional representation *(p. 217)* a multiple-member district system that allows each political party representation in proportion to its percentage of the total vote

recall *(p. 228)* a procedure to allow voters to remove state officials from office before their terms expire by circulating petitions to call a vote

referendum *(p. 228)* the practice of referring a measure proposed or passed by a legislature to the vote of the electorate for approval or rejection

socioeconomic status *(p. 222)* status in society based on level of education, income, and occupational prestige

suffrage *(p. 221)* the right to vote; also called *franchise*

third parties *(p. 216)* parties that organize to compete against the two major American political parties

turnout *(p. 221)* the percentage of eligible individuals who actually vote

two-party system *(p. 209)* a political system in which only two parties have a realistic opportunity to compete effectively for control of the government

For Further Reading

Aldrich, John W. *Why Parties? The Origin and Transformation of Political Parties in America.* Chicago: University of Chicago Press, 1995.

Cohen, Marty, David Karol, Hans Noel, and John Zaller. *The Party Decides: Presidential Nominations before and after Reform.* Chicago: University of Chicago Press, 2008.

Crotty, William J., ed. *Winning the Presidency 2012.* Boulder, CO: Paradigm Publishers, 2013.

Ginsberg, Benjamin, and Martin Shefter. *Politics by Other Means: Institutional Conflict and the Declining Significance of Elections in America.* New York: W. W. Norton, 1999.

Maisel, L. Sandy. *Political Parties and Elections: A Very Short Introduction.* New York: Oxford University Press, 2007.

Maisel, L. Sandy, and Mark D. Brewer. *Parties and Elections in America.* 6th ed. Lanham, MD: Rowman & Littlefield, 2011.

McCarty, Nolan, Keith Poole, and Howard Rosenthal. *Polarized America: The Dance of Ideology and Unequal Riches.* Cambridge, MA: MIT Press, 2006.

Milkis, Sidney. *The President and the Parties: The Transformation of the American Party System since the New Deal.* New York: Oxford University Press, 1993.

Patterson, Thomas E. *The Vanishing Voter: Public Involvement in an Age of Uncertainty.* New York: Vintage Books, 2003.

Wayne, Stephen. *Is This Any Way to Run a Democratic Election?* 5th ed. Washington, DC: CQ Press, 2013.

West, Darrell. *The Next Wave.* Washington, DC: Brookings Institution Press, 2011.

The use of "fracking" to recover gas has brought environmental groups into conflict with the energy industry. Both sides have tried to influence government regulations related to fracking.

Interest Groups

8

WHAT GOVERNMENT DOES AND WHY IT MATTERS For the past several years, environmental groups and the nation's energy industry have been locked in a struggle over the issue of hydraulic fracturing, or "fracking." This is a method for recovering natural gas trapped in shale formations by pumping millions of gallons of water deep beneath the earth's surface. The energy industry, which stands to make enormous profits from extracting this gas, asserts that fracking is the key to achieving American energy independence. Environmental groups, on the other hand, argue that fracking produces greenhouse gas emissions, undermines air quality, increases the risk of earthquakes and tremors, and contaminates drinking water, while discouraging investment in cleaner, renewable forms of energy.

Despite these environmental concerns, large sections of the United States, including land in Pennsylvania, Texas, and Ohio, among other states, are being fracked for their natural gas. Environmental groups appear to be losing the battle. Why? First, fracking produces revenues and jobs. The second reason, though, is political. The energy industry, organized in groups such as the Natural Gas Alliance, the Independent Petroleum Association of America, and the American Gas Association, has deployed an army of nearly 800 lobbyists, including former members of Congress and other former high-ranking government officials, to promote their cause on Capitol Hill in Washington, D.C., and in the state capitals. The industry has also spent tens of millions of dollars on advertising and campaign contributions—filling the coffers of Democrats and Republicans alike.

The case of fracking exemplifies the power of interest groups in action. Tens of thousands of organized groups have formed in the United States, ranging from civic associations to huge nationwide groups such as the National Rifle Association, whose chief cause is opposition to restrictions on gun ownership, and Common Cause, a public interest group that advocates a variety of liberal political reforms. Despite the array of interest groups in American politics, however, not all interests are represented equally and the results of competition among various interests are not always consistent with the common good.

The preceding chapter, on political parties, participation, and elections, examined another way in which citizens can influence the government. Yet the interest group process, as we will see, is both more selective and more dynamic: selective because society's "elites" (those with more money, education, and other resources) are better able to exploit the interest group process to their advantage; dynamic because of the explosive growth in the sheer number and diversity of interest groups that have proliferated in the last four decades. In this chapter, we will examine the nature and consequences of interest group politics in the United States.

chaptergoals

- Describe the major types of interest groups and whom they represent (pp. 247–51)
- Describe how groups organize (pp. 251–55)
- Analyze why the number of interest and advocacy groups has grown in recent decades (pp. 255–56)
- Explain how interest groups try to influence government (pp. 256–65)

Interest Groups Form to Advocate for Different Interests

Describe the major types of interest groups and whom they represent

The framers of the U.S. Constitution feared the power that could be wielded by organized interests. Yet they believed that interest groups thrived because of liberty— the freedom that all Americans have to organize and express their views. If the government were given the power to regulate, restrict, or forbid efforts by organized interests to impose themselves in the political process, it would in effect have the power to suppress liberty. The solution to this dilemma was presented by James Madison in the *Federalist Papers*, no. 10:

> Take in a greater variety of parties and interests [and] you make it less probable that a majority of the whole will have a common motive to invade the rights of other citizens. . . . [Hence the advantage] enjoyed by a large over a small republic.[1]

According to the Madisonian theory, a good government encourages multitudes of interests so that no single interest can ever dominate the others. The basic assumption is that many competing interests will regulate one another, producing a kind of balance.[2] Today, this Madisonian principle of regulation is called **pluralism**. According to pluralist theory, all interests are and should be free to compete for influence in the United States. While an interest group may lose on one issue, it may win on the next; and overall the majority of society will be represented in government. Moreover, according to the theory of pluralism, the outcome of this competition is compromise and moderation since no group is likely to be able to achieve any of its goals without accommodating itself to some of the views of its many competitors.[3] Another assumption of pluralism is that all groups have equal access to the political process and that achieving an outcome favorable to a particular group depends only upon that group's strength and resources, not upon biases inherent in the political system. But, as we shall see, group politics has worked and continues to work more to the advantage of some types of interests than others.

Pluralism is a dominant view in political science, but critics point out that not all interests are equally represented in the competition for political influence. Some interests speak with loud voices, while others can barely make themselves heard. Pluralism does not guarantee political equality. Indeed, important research indicates that through group politics economic elites have considerably more influence than mass-based forces in the American political process.

An **interest group** is a group of individuals who organize to influence the government's programs and policies. This definition includes membership organizations composed of average citizens but also businesses, corporations, unions, universities, and other institutions that restrict membership to particular occupational groups or other categories of persons. Individuals form groups in order to increase the chance that their views will be heard and their interests treated favorably by the government.

Interest groups are sometimes referred to as "lobbies." They are also sometimes confused with **political action committees (PACs)**, which are private groups that raise and distribute funds for use in election campaigns. Thus, the purpose of PACs is to influence elections rather than to influence the elected. Another distinction is that interest groups are also different from political parties: interest groups tend to focus on the *policies* of government; parties tend to concern themselves with the *personnel* of government.

What Interests Are Represented?

Economic Groups Interest groups come in as many shapes and sizes as the interests they represent. The most obvious are groups with a direct economic interest in government policy. Businesses and corporations make up over 31 percent of those with lobbying offices in Washington, with trade associations comprising another 23 percent and labor unions just 2 percent of groups registered to lobby.[4] Trade associations are generally supported by groups of producers or manufacturers in a particular economic sector, such as the National Association of Manufacturers and the American Farm Bureau Federation. In addition, specific companies, such as Apple, Microsoft, Exxon, Dow Chemical, and General Motors, lobby on certain issues that are of particular concern to them.

Labor Groups Labor organizations are also active in lobbying government. The American Federation of Labor and Congress of Industrial Organizations (AFL-CIO), the United Mine Workers, and the Teamsters are all groups that lobby on behalf of organized labor. Other groups have organized to further the interests of public employees. According to one study, however, labor unions represent just 2 percent of the total number of registered lobby groups in Washington.[5] The America Side by Side on page 249 compares union membership in the United States with other advanced democracies. Despite being out-lobbied, labor unions continue to exercise influence in Washington. Union members vote, and organized labor can have a significant impact upon elections. Few members of Congress can ignore labor's power at the polls.

Although public school teachers are a minority of the total population, they are an influential interest group in many states because they are highly informed and act as a group in support of issues related to their profession, including teachers' salaries.

Professional Associations Professional lobbies such as the American Bar Association and the American Medical Association have been particularly successful at furthering their members' interests in Congress and state legislatures. Financial institutions, represented by organizations such as the American Bankers Association and the National Savings and Loan League, although often less visible than other lobbies, also play an important role in shaping legislative policy. These groups comprise 13 percent of all lobby groups in Washington.

Labor Union Membership in Global Decline

Labor union membership in the United States is lower than in most other advanced democracies. This difference is due, in part, to each country's economic history, as strong agricultural economies tend to have less unionization than industrial economies. Another reason is that class consciousness was historically much higher in Europe. European school systems funnel their students early into class-based categories, having distinct paths for vocational training and higher learning. Social interactions also reinforce class divisions, as accents, titles, and lifestyles are strong cues of class belonging.[a]

Many of Europe's socialist parties, such as the United Kingdom's Labour Party, were originally formed by union leaders and often maintain strong union ties. Europe's working class, therefore, has much higher economic, political, and social incentives to belong to a labor union than does the American working class.

Despite these differences, there has been one common pattern across advanced democracies in recent years: a decline in union membership. Part of this change is due to the significant economic restructuring of modern economies. In today's advanced economies, most of the labor force tends to be employed in the service sector or in hi-tech industries rather than in manufacturing. While some unions have formed to represent these groups, unions have been less successful in recruiting members or organizing politically than those representing manufacturing workers.

Given that labor unions have historically been a major force for mobilizing the working class and transmitting their policy interests to politicians, their decline raises an important representation question: In the absence of labor unions, who will represent the working class in policy debates?

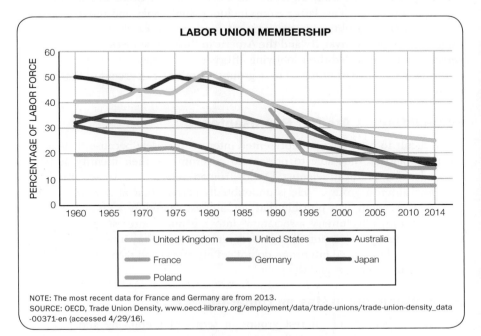

LABOR UNION MEMBERSHIP

NOTE: The most recent data for France and Germany are from 2013.
SOURCE: OECD, Trade Union Density, www.oecd-ilibrary.org/employment/data/trade-unions/trade-union-density_data-00371-en (accessed 4/29/16).

[a] Markus M. L. Crepaz and Jürg Steiner, *European Democracies*, 6th ed. (New York: Pearson, 2013).

Citizen Groups (or Public Interest Groups) Recent years have witnessed the growth of a powerful "public interest" lobby, purporting to represent the general good rather than its own economic interests. **Citizen groups** have been most visible in the consumer protection and environmental policy areas, although public interest groups cover a broad range of issues. The Natural Resources Defense Council, the Sierra Club, and Common Cause are all examples of citizen groups. Citizen groups comprise 20 percent of groups with lobbying offices in Washington. Claims to represent only the public interest should be viewed with caution, however: it is not uncommon to find decidedly private interests hiding behind the term *public interest*. For example, the benign-sounding Partnership to Protect Consumer Credit is a coalition of credit card companies fighting for less federal regulation of credit abuses.[6]

Ideological Groups Closely related to and overlapping public interest groups are ideological groups, organized in support of a particular political or philosophical perspective. The National Right to Life Committee and the Christian Coalition focus on conservative social goals, such as opposition to abortion and same-sex marriage. The National Taxpayers Union campaigns to reduce the size of the federal government. Liberal-leaning groups, including EMILY's List and MoveOn.org, support causes such as women's representation and increasing the minimum wage.

Public-Sector Groups The perceived need for representation on Capitol Hill has generated a public-sector lobby in the past several years, including the National League of Cities, the National Conference on State Legislatures, and the "research" lobby. This latter group includes think tanks and universities that have an interest in obtaining government funds for research and support—for example, Harvard University and the American Enterprise Institute. Indeed, universities have expanded their lobbying efforts even as they have reduced faculty positions and course offerings.[7] These groups represent 11 percent of Washington lobby groups.

Some Interests Are Not Represented

It is difficult to categorize unrepresented interests precisely because they are not organized and are not able to present to governments their identity and their demands. The political scientist David Truman referred to these interests as "potential interest groups."[8] He is undoubtedly correct that at any time, as long as there is freedom, it is possible that any interest shared by a lot of people can develop through "voluntary association" into a genuine interest group that can demand some representation. But the fact remains that many interests—including some very widely shared interests—do not get organized and recognized. Two such groups are the homeless and the poor.[9]

Group Membership Has an Upper-Class Bias

Despite the benefits of interest groups in terms of mobilizing and educating the public and the arguments in favor of pluralism, there are concerns about the influence of special interests in the United States. One long-standing critic is E. E. Schattschneider, who argued in a famous quote that "the flaw in the pluralist heaven is that the heavenly chorus sings with a strong upper-class accent."[10] Critics contend that pressure politics, or interest group politics, is heavily skewed in favor of corporate, business, and upper-class groups, leaving those with lower socioeconomic status less able to participate in and influence politics.

This is because people with higher incomes, more education, and management or professional occupations are much more likely to become members of groups than those who occupy the lower rungs on the socioeconomic ladder.[11] Well-educated, upper-income business- and professional people are more likely to have the time, money, information, and skills that are needed to play a role in a group or association. Moreover, for business- and professional people, group membership may provide personal contacts and access to information that can help advance their careers. At the same time, of course, corporations and businesses usually have ample resources to form or participate in groups that seek to advance their interests.

The result of this elitist tendency is that interest group politics in the United States has a very pronounced class bias. Certainly, there are many interest groups and political associations that have a working- or lower-class membership (labor organizations or welfare rights organizations, for example), but the great majority of interest group members are drawn from the middle and upper-middle classes. Even when interest groups take opposing positions on issues and policies, the conflicting positions they espouse usually reflect divisions among upper-income strata rather than conflicts between the upper and lower classes.

● The Organizational Components of Groups Include Money, Offices, and Members

Describe how groups organize

Although interest groups are many and varied, most share certain key organizational components. These include leadership, money, an agency or office, and members.

First, leadership and decision-making structure is vital for group organization. For some groups, this structure is very simple. For others, it can be quite elaborate and involve hundreds of local chapters that are melded into a national apparatus. Interest group leadership is, in some respects, analogous to business leadership. Political entrepreneurs initially organize and lead groups. Later, these leaders are replaced by a paid professional staff. In the 1960s, for example, Ralph Nader led a loosely organized band of consumer advocates (Nader's Raiders) in a crusade for product safety that resulted in the enactment of numerous regulations, such as the requirement that all new cars be equipped with seat belts and other safety devices. Today, Nader's ragtag band of raiders is a well-organized and well-financed phalanx of interlocking groups led by professional staff.

New **netroots** or online advocacy groups often have a streamlined staff structure with little bureaucracy. However, entrepreneurship may be even more important in the world of organizing online. As computer scientist Clay Shirky explains in *Here Comes Everybody*, the Internet has given rise to a proliferation of online organizations without formal organizing structures.[12] Examples include Wikipedia, whose content is provided by volunteers from around the world. But the real impact of the digital media revolution is not politics without groups but the advent of new forms of organization. Leadership remains a priority for online organizations: entrepreneurship and leadership are important for all interest groups but especially so for those with little staff and formal organization as the leader holds the organization together.

Second, every interest group must build a financial structure capable of sustaining an organization and funding the group's activities, although the costs of maintaining an online organization are lower. Most interest groups rely on membership dues and voluntary contributions from sympathizers. Many also sell services or benefits to members, such as insurance and vacation tours.

Third, most groups establish an agency that carries out the group's tasks, which may be a research organization, a public-relations office, or a lobbying office in Washington or a state capital.

Finally, all interest groups must attract and keep members. Somehow, groups must persuade individuals to invest the money, time, energy, or effort required to take part in the group's activities. Members play a larger role in some groups than in others. In **membership associations**, group members play a substantial role, serving on committees and engaging in group projects. In the case of labor unions, members pay dues and may march on picket lines; and in the case of political or ideological groups, members may participate in demonstrations and protests. In another set of groups, **staff organizations**, a professional staff conducts most of the group's activities. Members are called upon only to pay dues and make other contributions. Among well-known public interest groups, some, such as the National Organization for Women (NOW), are membership groups, whereas others, such as Defenders of Wildlife and the Children's Defense Fund, are staff organizations.

The "Free-Rider" Problem Whether they need individuals to volunteer or merely to write checks, interest groups need to recruit and retain members. Yet many groups find this task difficult, even when it comes to recruiting members who agree strongly with the group's goals. Why? As economist Mancur Olson explains, the benefits of a group's success are often broadly available and cannot be denied to nonmembers.[13] Such benefits are called **collective goods**. Following Olson's own example, suppose a number of private property owners live near a mosquito-infested swamp. Each owner wants this swamp cleared. But if only a few of the owners were to clear the swamp, their actions would benefit all the other owners as well, without any effort on the part of those other owners. Each of the inactive owners would be a **free rider** on the efforts of the ones who cleared the swamp; they would enjoy the benefits of collective goods but without having participated in acquiring them. Thus, there is a disincentive for any of the owners to undertake the job alone.

Since the number of concerned owners is small in this particular case, they might eventually be able to organize themselves to share the costs as well as enjoy the benefits of clearing the swamp. But suppose the number of interested people increases. Suppose the common concern is not the neighborhood swamp but polluted air or groundwater involving thousands of residents in a region or millions of residents in a whole nation. National defense is the most obvious collective good whose benefits are shared by all residents, regardless of the taxes they pay or the support they provide. As the size of the group increases, the free-rider problem becomes greater. Individuals do not have much incentive to become active members and supporters of a group if they are already benefiting from the group's activities.

Why Join Groups? To overcome the free-rider problem, interest groups offer numerous incentives to join. Most important, they make "selective benefits" available only to group members. These benefits can be information-related, material, solidary, or purposive. Table 8.1 gives some examples of the range of benefits in each of these categories.

Informational benefits are the most widespread and important category of selective benefits offered to group members. Information is provided through conferences, training programs, online communications, newsletters, and other periodicals sent automatically to those who have paid membership dues.

Material benefits include anything that can be measured monetarily, such as special goods, services, and even money, provided to members of groups to entice others to join. These benefits often include discount purchasing, shared advertising, and, perhaps most valuable of all, health and retirement insurance.

TABLE 8.1

Selective Benefits of Interest Group Membership

CATEGORY	BENEFITS
Informational benefits	Conferences
	Professional contacts
	Training programs
	Publications
	Coordination among organizations
	Research
	Legal help
	Professional codes
	Collective bargaining
Material benefits	Travel packages
	Insurance
	Discounts on consumer goods
Solidary benefits	Friendship
	Networking opportunities
Purposive benefits	Advocacy
	Representation before government
	Participation in public affairs

SOURCE: Adapted from Jack Walker, Jr., *Mobilizing Interest Groups in America: Patrons, Professions, and Social Movements* (Ann Arbor: University of Michigan Press, 1991), 86.

Another option identified in Table 8.1 is that of **solidary benefits**. These are selective benefits of group membership that include friendship, networking, and consciousness-raising, which provide the satisfaction of working toward a common goal with like-minded individuals, a phenomenon often important for netroots groups. One example of the latter are the claims of many women's organizations that active participation conveys to each female member of the organization an enhanced sense of her own value and a stronger ability to advance individual as well as collective rights. Members of associations based on ethnicity, race, or religion also derive solidary benefits from interacting with individuals they perceive as sharing their own backgrounds, values, and perspectives.

A fourth type of benefit involves the appeal of the purpose of an interest group. These **purposive benefits** emphasize the purpose and accomplishments of the group. For example, people join religious, consumer, environmental, or other civic groups to pursue goals important to them.

Many of the most successful interest groups of the past 20 years have been citizen groups or public interest groups, whose members are brought together largely around shared ideological goals, including government reform, election and campaign reform, civil rights, economic equality, "family values," and even opposition to government itself.

AARP and the Benefits of Membership One group that has been extremely successful in recruiting members and mobilizing them for political action is AARP (formerly called the American Association of Retired Persons). AARP was founded in 1958 as a result of the efforts of a retired California high school principal, Ethel Percy Andrus, to find affordable health insurance for herself and the thousands of members of the National Retired Teachers Association.

Today, AARP is a large and powerful organization with 38 million members and an annual income of $900 million. In addition, the organization receives $90 million in federal grants. Its national headquarters in Washington, D.C., staffed by nearly 3,000 full-time employees, is so large that it has its own zip code. Its monthly periodical, *AARP: The Magazine*, has a circulation larger than that of America's leading newsmagazines.

How did this large organization overcome the free-rider problem and recruit 38 million older people as members? First, no other organization has ever provided more successfully the selective benefits necessary to overcome the free-rider problem. It helps that AARP began as an organization to provide affordable health insurance for aging members rather than as an organization to influence public policy. But that fact only strengthens the argument that members need short-term individual benefits if they are to invest effort in a longer-term and less concrete set of benefits. As AARP evolved into a political interest group, its leadership added more selective benefits for members. They provided guidance against consumer fraud, offered low-interest credit cards, evaluated and endorsed products that were deemed of best value to members, and provided auto insurance and a discounted mail-order pharmacy.

The Internet Has Changed the Way Interest Groups Foster Participation

Digital media and social media have created a new kind of interest group politics in America that has revolutionized political advocacy. New netroots political associations, such as the liberal-leaning MoveOn.org, have arisen in recent years to play an increasingly important role in citizen participation in politics. Similar conservative groups include Freedomworks and Americans for Prosperity. These grassroots online activist organizations have redefined membership and fund-raising practices via innovative methods for communicating with their members, measuring the opinions of their members, and moving their members into action.

Traditional interest groups are expensive to organize (which is one reason group membership has an upper-class bias), and they rely on professional advocates and direct mail. They are also slow to change. By contrast, netroots associations are relatively inexpensive to organize and quick to adapt to an ever-changing world of politics. Netroots have lower costs than traditional interest groups because they have fewer staff who often work from virtual offices. This less expensive staff structure engages in different work routines that prioritize communication with members through email, Twitter, and other digital platforms rather than mailing expensive glossy newsletters or engaging in direct lobbying of members of Congress. Netroots associations employ novel grassroots strategies to pressure elected officials, including using online media to organize citizens to attend rallies and fund-raising events, start letter-writing campaigns, and organize boycotts and protests. These tactics have spread across the political advocacy system to more traditional interest groups.

The Number of Groups Has Increased in Recent Decades

Analyze why the number of interest and advocacy groups has grown in recent decades

Over the past several decades, there has been an enormous increase both in the number of interest groups seeking to play a role in the American political process and in the extent of their influence over that process. This explosion of interest group activity has two basic origins: first, the expansion of the role of government during this period and, second, the coming-of-age of a new dynamic set of political forces in the United States—forces that have relied heavily on public interest groups to advance their causes.

The Expansion of Government Has Spurred the Growth of Groups

Modern governments' extensive economic and social programs have powerful politicizing effects, often sparking the organization of new groups and interests. In other words, interest groups often form as the result of, or in response to, government actions, rather than groups pressing the government to take on new responsibilities. Even when national policies are enacted because of interest group pressure, government involvement in any area can be a powerful stimulus for political organization and action by those whose interests are affected. For example, during the 1970s, expanded federal regulation of the automobile, oil, gas, education, and health care industries impelled each of these interests to increase substantially its efforts to influence the government's behavior. These efforts, in turn, spurred the organization of other groups either to support or to oppose the activities of the first.[14] Similarly, federal social programs have sparked political organization and action by affected groups. For example, federal programs and court decisions in such areas as abortion, school prayer, and same-sex marriage helped spur the rise of fundamentalist religious groups. Thus, the expansion of government in recent decades has also stimulated increased group activity and organization.

Public Interest Groups Grew in the 1960s and '70s

The second factor accounting for the explosion of interest group activity was the emergence of a new set of forces in American politics that can collectively be called the "New Politics" movement.

The **New Politics movement** is made up of upper-middle-class professionals and intellectuals for whom the civil rights and anti–Vietnam War movements of the 1960s were formative experiences. The crusade against racial discrimination and the Vietnam War led these young men and women to see themselves as a political force, focusing their attention on such issues as environmental protection, women's rights, and nuclear disarmament.

Members of the New Politics movement founded or bolstered public interest groups such as Common Cause, the Sierra Club, the Environmental Defense Fund, Physicians for Social Responsibility, NOW, and the various organizations formed by consumer activist Ralph Nader. Through these groups, New Politics forces were able to influence the media, Congress, and the courts and enjoyed a remarkable degree of success, playing a major role in gaining the passage of environmental, consumer, and occupational health and safety legislation. Technology has also played a role in advancing the New Politics agenda. In the 1970s and '80s, computerized direct-mail campaigns allowed public interest groups to reach hundreds of thousands of potential sympathizers and contributors. Today, the Internet and digital platforms including social media, Twitter, and blogs serve the same function even more efficiently and at lower cost.

● Interest Groups Use Different Strategies to Gain Influence

Explain how interest groups try to influence government

As we have seen, interest groups work to improve the likelihood that their interests will be heard and treated favorably by the government. The quest for political influence or power takes many forms, but among the most frequently used strategies or "tactics of influence" (see Figure 8.1) are lobbying, gaining access to key decision makers, using the courts, mobilizing public opinion, and using electoral politics.

Many groups employ a mix of strategies. For example, environmental groups such as the Sierra Club lobby members of Congress and key congressional staff

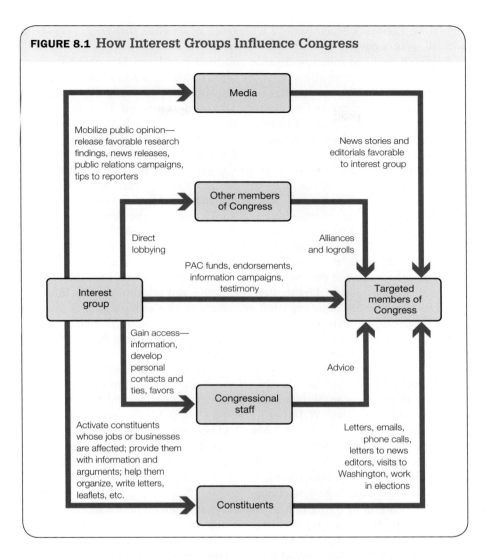

FIGURE 8.1 How Interest Groups Influence Congress

Media

Mobilize public opinion—
release favorable research
findings, news releases,
public relations campaigns,
tips to reporters

News stories and
editorials favorable
to interest group

Other members
of Congress

Direct
lobbying

Alliances
and logrolls

PAC funds, endorsements,
information campaigns,
testimony

Interest
group

Targeted
members of
Congress

Gain access—
information,
develop
personal
contacts and
ties, favors

Advice

Congressional
staff

Activate constituents
whose jobs or businesses
are affected; provide them
with information and
arguments; help them
organize, write letters,
leaflets, etc.

Letters, emails,
phone calls,
letters to news
editors, visits to
Washington, work
in elections

Constituents

members, participate in bureaucratic rule making by offering comments and suggestions to agencies on new environmental rules, and bring lawsuits under various environmental acts such as the Endangered Species Act, which authorizes groups and citizens to come to court if they believe the act is being violated. At the same time, the Sierra Club attempts to influence public opinion through media campaigns and electoral politics by supporting candidates who they believe share their environmental views and by opposing candidates they view as foes of environmentalism.

Direct Lobbying Combines Education, Persuasion, and Pressure

Lobbying is a strategy by which organized interests seek to influence the passage of legislation or other public policy by exerting direct pressure on members of the legislature. Lobbying encompasses a wide range of activities that groups engage in with all sorts of government officials and the public as a whole.

Lobbyists first and foremost provide information to lawmakers about their interests and the legislation at hand.[15] They often testify on behalf of their clients at congressional committee and agency hearings. Lobbyists talk to reporters, place ads in newspapers, and organize letter-writing and email campaigns. They also play an important role in fund-raising, helping to direct clients' contributions to members of Congress and presidential candidates.

Traditionally, the term *lobbyist* referred mainly to individuals who sought to influence the passage of legislation in the Congress. The First Amendment to the Constitution provides for the right to "petition the Government for a redress of grievances." But as early as the 1870s, *lobbying* became the common term for "petitioning." And since petitioning cannot take place on the floor of the House or Senate, petitioners must confront members of Congress in the lobbies of the legislative chamber—hence the term *lobbying*. Although interest groups do not necessarily buy votes, they do buy time, expertise, and influence. Studies have found that those interest groups providing the most money to representatives are more likely to be consulted by that representative and asked to provide information and expertise in discussing a bill pertaining to that group's area of interest. This, in essence, gives interest groups a voice in shaping how legislation is written, and while it cannot ensure votes for laws preferred by the group, it is an effective means for organized interests to influence policy.

Important interests that don't lobby soon learn their lesson. In 1999 members of Congress advised Wal-Mart that its efforts to win approval to operate savings and loans in its stores were doomed to failure if the retailer did not greatly increase its lobbying efforts. Wal-Mart learned its lesson, hired more lobbyists, and got what it wanted.[16] By 2005, Wal-Mart had become a seasoned political player, creating a "war room" in its Arkansas headquarters. Staffed by a phalanx of veteran political operatives from both parties, the war room is the nerve center of the giant retailer's lobbying and public-relations efforts.[17] Today, Wal-Mart spends more than $5 million a year on its lobbying efforts.[18]

The influence of lobbyists, in many instances, is based on personal relationships and the behind-the-scenes services they are able to perform for lawmakers. Many of Washington's top lobbyists have close ties to important members of Congress or are themselves former members of Congress, thus virtually guaranteeing that their clients will have direct access to congressional leaders.

Cultivating Access Means Getting the Attention of Decision Makers

In many areas, interest groups, government agencies, and congressional committees routinely work together for mutual benefit. The interest group provides campaign contributions for members of Congress, and it lobbies for larger budgets for the agency. The agency, in turn, provides government contracts for the interest group and constituency services for friendly members of Congress. The congressional committee or subcommittee, meanwhile, supports the agency's budgetary requests and the programs the interest group favors. This so-called **iron triangle** has one angle in an executive branch program, another angle in a Senate or House legislative committee or subcommittee, and a third angle in some highly stable and well-organized interest group. The angles in the triangular relationship are mutually supporting, especially if a committee member has seniority in Congress. Figure 8.2 illustrates one of the most important iron triangles in recent American political history: that of the defense industry. Iron triangles explain how interest groups have influence over both Congress and the government agency directly regulating their interests in many policy areas.

A number of important policy domains, such as the environmental and welfare arenas, are controlled not by highly structured iron triangles but by a jumble of issue networks. These networks consist of like-minded politicians, consultants, public officials, political activists, and interest groups having some concern with the issue in question. Activists and interest groups recognized as being involved in the area (the "stakeholders") are customarily invited to testify before congressional committees or give their views to government agencies considering action in their domain.

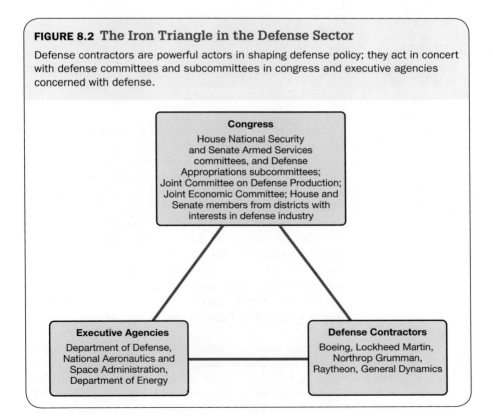

FIGURE 8.2 The Iron Triangle in the Defense Sector

Defense contractors are powerful actors in shaping defense policy; they act in concert with defense committees and subcommittees in congress and executive agencies concerned with defense.

Congress
House National Security and Senate Armed Services committees, and Defense Appropriations subcommittees; Joint Committee on Defense Production; Joint Economic Committee; House and Senate members from districts with interests in defense industry

Executive Agencies
Department of Defense, National Aeronautics and Space Administration, Department of Energy

Defense Contractors
Boeing, Lockheed Martin, Northrop Grumman, Raytheon, General Dynamics

Regulating Lobbying Lobbyists' extensive access to members of Congress has led to repeated calls for reform. In 2007, congressional Democrats secured the enactment of a new package of ethics rules designed to bring an end to lobbying abuses. The new rules prohibited lobbyists from paying for most meals, trips, parties, and gifts for members of Congress. Lobbyists were also required to disclose the amounts and sources of small campaign contributions they collected from clients and "bundled" into large contributions. And interest groups were required to disclose the funds they used to rally voters to support or oppose legislative proposals. According to the *Washington Post*, however, within a few weeks lobbyists had learned how to circumvent many of the new rules, and lobbying firms were as busy as ever.[19]

Using the Courts (Litigation) Can Be Highly Effective

Interest groups sometimes turn to litigation when they lack access or when they feel they have insufficient influence to change a law or policy. Interest groups can use the courts to affect public policy in at least three ways: (1) by bringing suit directly on behalf of the group itself, (2) by financing suits brought by individuals, and (3) by filing a companion brief as an amicus curiae (literally "friend of the court") to an existing court case.

Among the best-known illustrations of using the courts as a strategy for political influence is found in the history of the National Association for the Advancement of Colored People (NAACP). The most important of such court cases was *Brown v. Board of Education of Topeka, Kansas* (1954), in which the U.S. Supreme Court held that legal segregation of the schools was unconstitutional.[20] Later, extensive litigation spearheaded the women's rights movement of the 1960s and the rights of gays and lesbians since the 1990s.

The 1973 Supreme Court case of *Roe v. Wade*, which took away a state's power to ban abortions, sparked a controversy that brought conservatives to the fore on a national level.[21] Since 1973, conservative groups have made extensive and successful use of the courts to whittle away at the scope of the privacy doctrine upon which the ruling in *Roe v. Wade* was based. They won rulings, for example, that prohibit the use of federal funds to pay for voluntary abortions. In 1989, right-to-life groups were able to use the case of *Webster v. Reproductive Health Services* to restore the right of states to place restrictions on abortion, thus partly undermining the *Roe v. Wade* decision (see Chapter 4).[22] The *Webster* case brought more than 300 interest groups on both sides of the abortion issue to the Supreme Court's door. The movement to extend rights for gays and lesbians also found success in the courts. In 2015, in the case of *Obergefell v. Hodges*, the Supreme Court declared that the Fourteenth Amendment prohibited states from refusing to issue marriage licenses to same-sex couples.[23]

Litigation involving large businesses is voluminous in such areas as taxation, antitrust, interstate transportation, and product quality and standardization. Often a business is brought to litigation against its will by virtue of initiatives taken against it by other businesses or by government agencies. But many individual businesses bring suit themselves in order to influence government policy.

Mobilizing Public Opinion Brings Wider Attention to an Issue

Going public is a strategy that attempts to mobilize the widest and most favorable climate of opinion and a favored strategy of citizen groups and netroots or online activist groups. Many groups consider it imperative to maintain political pressure at all times. Citizen groups and online netroots organizations rely heavily on mobilizing their members via social media, Twitter campaigns, and targeted email messages on short notice. On any given day a new viral media story may become headline news, and in most cases an interest group is behind the story. Such groups span the ideological spectrum from liberal to conservative and can wield significant pressure on elected officials to act.

Institutional Advertising One of the best-known ways of going public is the use of **institutional advertising**—advertising designed to create a positive image of an organization. A casual scanning of important mass-circulation magazines, newspapers, and television provides numerous examples of expensive and well-designed ads by the major oil and gas companies, automobile and steel companies, other large corporations, and trade associations. The ads show how much these organizations are doing for the country, for the protection of the environment, or for the defense of the American way of life. The ads' purpose is to create and maintain a strongly positive public image in the hope of drawing on these favorable feelings as needed for specific political campaigns later on.

Protests and Demonstrations Many groups resort to going public because they lack the resources, the contacts, or the experience to use other political strategies. The sponsorship of boycotts, sit-ins, mass rallies, and marches by Martin Luther King, Jr.'s, Southern Christian Leadership Conference and related organizations in the 1950s and '60s is one of the most significant and successful cases of going public to create a more favorable climate of opinion by calling attention to abuses. The success of these events inspired similar efforts by women's groups. The 2010 GOP takeover of the House of Representatives began with the spontaneous self-organization of the Tea Party movement in 2009 as an angry response to the Obama administration's health care initiatives. In 2011 the Occupy Wall Street movement sparked demonstrations across America and around the world by those who were outraged by economic inequality. In 2014 the Black Lives Matter movement gained momentum after the shooting of a black teenager by a white police officer in Ferguson, Missouri. Police force against young black men in such cities as Baltimore, Chicago, New York, and many others led to major demonstrations under the banner of the movement. Around the same time, minority students on a number of college campuses launched protests demanding that colleges create environments that recognized the value of racial and gender diversity.

Grassroots Mobilization Another form of going public is **grassroots mobilization**. In such a campaign, a lobby group mobilizes its members throughout the country to contact government officials in support of the group's position.

Seeking to reform the criminal justice system and call attention to continued racism in the United States, the Black Lives Matter movement formed in 2012 and earned national attention following a series of high-profile shootings of African Americans by white police officers.

Among the most effective users of the grassroots lobby effort in contemporary American politics is the religious right. Networks of evangelical churches have the capacity to generate hundreds of thousands of letters and phone calls to Congress and the White House. For example, in 2007 a grassroots firm called Grassfire.org led the drive to kill the immigration reform bill supported by President Bush and a number of congressional Democrats that would have legalized the status of many illegal immigrants. Grassfire.org used the Internet and talk radio programs to generate a campaign that yielded 700,000 signatures on petitions opposing the bill. The petitions, along with tens of thousands of phone calls, letters, and emails generated by Grassfire.org and other groups, led to the bill's defeat in the U.S. Senate.[24]

One increasingly common way that corporations and interest groups have sought to help themselves politically is by adopting aliases in their advertising efforts. For example, the Save Our Species Alliance is an industry group seeking to weaken the Endangered Species Act, and Citizens for Asbestos Reform seeks to limit the ability of individuals harmed by asbestos from obtaining help in the courts. Both Americans for Balanced Energy Choices and the Coalition for Clean, Affordable, Reliable Energy sponsor ads promoting the virtues of coal as an energy source. As is often the case, the names chosen imply that these organizations are citizen-based, grassroots groups instead of front groups for large corporations. Attempts to require lobby groups to disclose their actual identities have been attacked by industry as a threat to free speech.

A notorious online grassroots organization is called Anonymous. Anonymous is a loosely associated network of activists and hackers that specializes in online protests. Some consider the group to be outside of the law as dozens of people have been arrested for involvement in Anonymous cyber attacks in countries around the world. Others consider them freedom fighters or digital Robin Hoods. The group's website describes it as "an internet gathering" with a decentralized organizational structure that operates on ideas rather than directives. The group became known for a series of well-publicized hacks and distributed denial-of-service attacks on government, religious organizations, and corporate websites. The organization helped promote the global Occupy Wall Street movement and the Arab Spring democratic protests in the Middle East; recently, it has been active in promoting the rights of gays and lesbians.

Groups Often Use Electoral Politics

In addition to the techniques already discussed, interest groups seek to use the electoral process to elect sympathetic legislators in the first place and to ensure that those who are elected will owe them a debt of gratitude for their support. While groups invest far more resources in lobbying than in electoral politics, financial support and campaign activism can be important tools for organized interests.

Political Action Committees By far the most common electoral strategy employed by interest groups is that of giving financial support to political parties or to candidates running for office. But such support can easily cross the threshold into outright bribery. Therefore, Congress has occasionally attempted to regulate this strategy. Its most recent effort was the Federal Election Campaign Act of 1971 (amended in 1974). This act limits campaign contributions and requires that each candidate or campaign committee itemize the full name and address, occupation, and principal business of each person who contributes more than $200. These provisions have been effective up to a point, resulting in numerous indictments, resignations, and criminal convictions in the aftermath of the 1972 Watergate scandal.

Reaction to Watergate produced further legislation on campaign finance in 1974 and 1976, but the effect has been to restrict individual rather than interest group campaign activity. Individuals may now contribute no more than $2,700 to any candidate for federal office in any primary or general election. A PAC, however, can contribute $5,000, provided it contributes to at least five different federal candidates each year. Beyond this, the laws permit corporations, unions, and other interest groups to form PACs and to pay the costs of soliciting funds from private citizens for the PACs. In other words, PACs operate in the electoral arena to represent the interests with which they are affiliated.

The flurry of reform legislation of the early and mid-1970s attempted to reduce the influence that special interests had over elections, but the effect has been almost the exact opposite. Electoral spending by interest groups has been increasing steadily. The number of PACs has also increased significantly—from 480 in 1972 to more than 5,000 in 2014. Opportunities for legally influencing campaigns are now widespread.

Given the enormous costs of television commercials, polls, computers, and other elements of the new political technology, most politicians are eager to receive PAC contributions and are at least willing to give a friendly hearing to the needs and interests of contributors. It is probably not the case that most politicians simply sell their votes to the interests that fund their campaigns. But there is considerable evidence to support the contention that interest groups' campaign contributions do influence the overall pattern of political behavior in Congress and in the state legislatures.

Concern about PACs grew through the 1980s and '90s, creating a constant drumbeat for reform of federal election laws. This resulted in the enactment of the McCain-Feingold bill, which became the Bipartisan Campaign Reform Act of 2002. When it was originally proposed, the bill was aimed at reducing or eliminating PACs. But in a stunning about-face, when campaign finance reform was adopted, it did not restrict PACs in any significant way. Rather, it eliminated unrestricted "soft money" donations to the national political parties.

Favorable court rulings in 2010, including the Supreme Court's *Citizens United* case, struck down limits on corporate political spending, which gave rise to so-called Super PACs.[25] These organizations may not contribute money directly to (or coordinate their activities with) campaigns but may spend unlimited amounts of money on behalf of parties or campaigns they support. These Super PACs are often headed by former party officials. In 2016, Super PACs spent more than $1.1 billion on House and Senate races.[26] The unlimited money raised and spent by independent political committees makes the formal regulations on PACs and individual contributions almost irrelevant. Spending is far higher in U.S. elections than in those of any other country in the world.

The Initiative Another political tactic sometimes used by interest groups is sponsorship of ballot initiatives at the state level. The initiative, a device adopted by a number of states around 1900, allows proposed laws to be placed on the general-election ballot and submitted directly to the state's voters, by-passing the state legislature and governor. The initiative was originally promoted by late nineteenth-century Populists and Progressives as a mechanism that would allow the people to govern directly—an antidote to interest group influence in the legislative process.

Ironically, studies have suggested that many initiative campaigns today are actually sponsored by interest groups seeking to circumvent legislative opposition to their goals. In recent years, for example, initiative campaigns have been sponsored by the insurance industry, trial lawyer associations, and tobacco companies.[27] Liberal activists have developed their own issue campaigns to promote issues such as increasing the minimum wage, promoting clean energy, strengthening environmental protection laws, and the decriminalization of marijuana.

Groups, Interests,
and Your Future

There is considerable competition among organized groups in the United States. Although the weak and poor do occasionally become organized to assert their rights, interest group politics is generally a form of political competition best suited to the wealthy and powerful, suggesting that, in the realm of group politics, liberty seems inconsistent with equality.

Moreover, although groups sometimes organize to promote broad public concerns, interest groups more often represent relatively narrow, selfish interests. Small, self-interested groups can be organized much more easily than large, more diffuse collectives. For one thing, the members of a relatively small group (say, bankers or hunting enthusiasts) are usually able to recognize their shared interests and the need to pursue them in the political arena. Members of large and more diffuse groups (say, consumers or potential victims of firearms) often find it difficult to recognize their shared interests or the need to engage in collective action to achieve them.[28] This is why causes presented as public interests by their proponents often turn out, upon examination, to be private interests wrapped in a public mantle. Thus, the elitist quality of group politics often appears to be inconsistent with democracy.

As this chapter has shown, major changes to political or social institutions can have a significant impact on the number and identity of interest groups. One of the major social trends of our time is demographic change. Notable, the baby boomers, a large generation of Americans born in the period after World War II, are now reaching retirement and old age. Elderly Americans are highly organized and represented by interest groups, such as AARP, that lobby government for benefits, including health care subsidies to keep the cost of their medical care low. Because resources are limited, however, benefits to elderly Americans may come at the expense of social goals that may be more important to other generations. Today's college students are part of the millennial generation, born 1980–2001, who are more numerous than baby boomers. Young people are most affected by the cost of a college education and the job opportunities that exist when they graduate, rather than health care, since the young tend to be relatively healthy but need education and experience. Yet it is difficult to organize college students and the millennial generation on a national or statewide scale to lobby government to spend more on higher education or job opportunities. Why are young people's interests poorly represented and those of elderly people better represented? Could new organizational routines from netroots help young people organize?

Interest groups sometimes seem to have a greater impact than voters on the government's policies and programs, especially through lobbying and financial contributions to political candidates. (The "**Who Participates?**" feature on the facing page shows how much major grounds spend on lobbying activities). Yet, before we decide that we should do away with interest groups, we should think carefully: If there were no organized interests, would the government pay more attention to ordinary voters? Would young people be better or worse off if there were no interest groups in the United States? Or would the government simply pay less attention to everyone? In his work Democracy in America, Alexis de Tocqueville argued that the proliferation of groups promoted democracy by encouraging governmental responsiveness. Does group politics foster democracy or impede democracy? It does both.

How Much Do Major Groups Spend?

Lobbying Expenditures, 2011–15 (By selected major groups)

	2011	2012	2013	2014	2015	
U.S. Chamber of Commerce	$66 million	$136 million	$74 million	$124 million	$64 million	
American Medical Association	$21 million	$16 million	$18 million	$19 million	$23 million	
General Electric	$26 million	$18 million	$16 million	$15 million	$16 million	
AARP	$15 million	$9 million	$9 million	$8 million	$5 million	
National Rifle Association	$2 million	$2 million	$3 million	$3 million	$2 million	
Human Rights Campaign	$1 million	$1 million	$1 million	$1 million	$1 million	

SOURCE: Open Secrets, Center for Responsive Politics, www.opensecrets.org/lobby (accessed 11/13/15)

WHAT YOU CAN DO ➡

WHAT YOU CAN DO

Get Involved with Interest Groups and Lobbying

 Find an interest group that appeals to you at **votesmart.org/interest-groups**, then follow that group on Facebook or Twitter.

 Find out which groups give the most money to your representatives in Congress by clicking "Congress" at **www.opensecrets.org/politicians**. You can look up your representatives by zip code.

☑ Contact your Center for Campus Life to find out if groups you're interested in have chapters on your campus. Many groups will gladly help students start campus chapters.

chapterstudyguide

Practice Quiz

1. The theory that competition among organized interests will produce balance, with all the interests regulating one another is called *(p. 247)*
   a) pluralism.
   b) elite power politics.
   c) democracy.
   d) socialism.
   e) libertarianism.

2. Groups that claim to serve the general good, rather than their own particular interests, are referred to as *(p. 250)*
   a) membership associations.
   b) citizen groups.
   c) professional associations.

   d) ideological groups.
   e) public-sector groups.

3. To overcome the free-rider problem, groups *(p. 253)*
   a) lobby.
   b) litigate.
   c) provide selective benefits.
   d) provide collective goods.
   e) go public.

4. Discount purchasing and health insurance are examples of *(p. 253)*
   a) purposive benefits.
   b) informational benefits.
   c) solidary benefits.
   d) material benefits.
   e) member dues.

5. Friendship and networking are examples of *(p. 254)*
   a) purposive benefits.
   b) informational benefits.
   c) solidary benefits.
   d) material benefits.
   e) member dues.

6. Which of the following is an important reason for the enormous increase in the number of groups seeking to influence the American political system? *(pp. 255–56)*
   a) the decrease in the size and activity of government during the last few decades
   b) the increase in the size and activity of government during the last few decades
   c) the increase in the amount of soft money in election campaigns in recent decades
   d) the increase in legal protection provided to interest groups as a result of the Supreme Court's evolving interpretation of the First Amendment
   e) the increase in the number of people identifying themselves as an independent in recent decades

7. Which types of interest groups are most often associated with the New Politics movement? *(p. 256)*
   a) political action committees
   b) professional associations
   c) government groups
   d) labor groups
   e) public interest groups

8. Which of the following is *not* an activity in which interest groups frequently engage? *(pp. 256–65)*
   a) starting their own political party
   b) litigation
   c) sponsoring ballot initiatives at the state level
   d) lobbying
   e) contributing to campaigns

9. A loose network of elected leaders, public officials, activists, and interest groups drawn together by a public policy issue is referred to as *(p. 259)*
   a) an issue network.
   b) a public interest group.
   c) a political action committee.

d) pluralism.
e) an iron triangle.

10. Which of the following best describes the federal government's rules regarding lobbying? *(p. 260)*
   a) Federal rules allow lobbying but only on issues related to taxation.
   b) Federal rules allow lobbying but only if the lobbyists receive no monetary compensation for their lobbying.
   c) Federal rules strictly prohibit any form of lobbying.
   d) Federal rules require all lobbyists to disclose the amounts and sources of small campaign contributions they collect from clients and "bundle" into large contributions
   e) There are no rules regulating lobbying because the federal government has never passed any legislation on the legality of the activity.

11. Which of the following is a way that interest groups use the courts to influence public policy? *(p. 260)*
   a) supplying judges with solidary benefits
   b) joining an issue network
   c) creating an iron triangle
   d) forming a political action committee
   e) filing amicus briefs

12. Which of the following are examples of the "going public" strategy? *(pp. 261–63)*
   a) free riding, pluralism, and issue networking
   b) donating money to political parties, endorsing candidates, and sponsoring ballot initiatives
   c) institutional advertising, grassroots advertising, and protests and demonstrations
   d) providing informational benefits, providing solidary benefits, and providing material benefits
   e) filing an amicus brief, bringing a lawsuit, and financing those who are filing a lawsuit

Key Terms

citizen groups *(p. 250)* groups that claim they serve the general good rather than only their own particular interest

collective goods *(p. 252)* benefits, sought by groups, that are broadly available and cannot be denied to nonmembers

free riders *(p. 252)* those who enjoy the benefits of collective goods but did not participate in acquiring them

grassroots mobilization *(p. 261)* a lobbying campaign in which a group mobilizes its membership to contact government officials in support of the group's position

informational benefits *(p. 253)* special newsletters, periodicals, training programs, conferences, and other information provided to members of groups to entice others to join

institutional advertising *(p. 261)* advertising designed to create a positive image of an organization

interest group *(p. 247)* individuals who organize to influence the government's programs and policies

iron triangle *(p. 259)* the stable, cooperative relationships that often develop among a congressional committee, an administrative agency, and one or more supportive interest groups; not all of these relationships are triangular, but the iron triangle is the most typical

lobbying *(p. 257)* a strategy by which organized interests seek to influence the passage of legislation or other public policy by exerting direct pressure on members of the legislature

material benefits *(p. 253)* special goods, services, or money provided to members of groups to entice others to join

membership association *(p. 252)* an organized group in which members actually play a substantial role, sitting on committees and engaging in group projects

netroots *(p. 251)* grassroots online activist organizations that have redefined membership and fund-raising practices and streamlined staff structure

New Politics movement *(p. 256)* a political movement that began in the 1960s and '70s, made up of professionals and intellectuals for whom the civil rights and antiwar movements were formative experiences; the New Politics movement strengthened public interest groups

pluralism *(p. 247)* the theory that all interests are and should be free to compete for influence in the government; the outcome of this competition is compromise and moderation

political action committee (PAC) *(p. 248)* a private group that raises and distributes funds for use in election campaigns

purposive benefits *(p. 254)* selective benefits of group membership that emphasize the purpose and accomplishments of the group

solidary benefits *(p. 254)* selective benefits of group membership that emphasize friendship, networking, and consciousness-raising

staff organization *(p. 252)* type of membership group in which a professional staff conducts most of the group's activities

For Further Reading

Ainsworth, Scott. *Analyzing Interest Groups*. New York: W. W. Norton, 2002.

Baumgartner, Frank, Jeffrey M. Berry, Beth L. Leech, David C. Kimball, and Marie Hojnacki. *Lobbying and Policy Change: Who Wins, Who Loses, and Why*. Chicago: University of Chicago Press, 2009.

Berry, Jeffrey M., and Clyde Wilcox. *Interest Group Society*. 5th ed. New York: Routledge, 2008.

Cigler, Allan J., and Burdett A. Loomis, eds. *Interest Group Politics*. 9th ed. Washington, DC: CQ Press, 2015.

Drutman, Lee. *The Business of America Is Lobbying: How Corporations Became Politicized and Politics Became More Corporate*. New York: Oxford University Press, 2015.

Goldstein, Kenneth. *Interest Groups, Lobbying, and Participation in America*. New York: Cambridge University Press, 2008.

Herrnson, Paul, and Christopher Deering. *Interest Groups Unleashed*. Washington, DC: CQ Press, 2012.

Karpf, David. *The MoveOn Effect: The Unexpected Transformation of American Political Advocacy*. New York: Oxford University Press, 2012.

Lowi, Theodore J. *The End of Liberalism*. New York: W. W. Norton, 1979.

Olson, Mancur, Jr. *The Logic of Collective Action: Public Goods and the Theory of Groups*. Cambridge, MA: Harvard University Press, 1971.

Spitzer, Robert J. *The Politics of Gun Control*. 6th ed. Boulder, CO: Paradigm Publishers, 2015.

Strolovitch, Dara. *Affirmative Advocacy: Race, Class, and Gender in Interest Group Politics*. Chicago: University of Chicago Press, 2007.

In addition to its lawmaking powers, Congress plays a critical role in American democracy as a representative institution. The members of Congress—100 senators and 435 representatives—represent the voices of the people across America. Yet some observers worry that Congress does not represent all voices equally.

Congress

9

WHAT GOVERNMENT DOES AND WHY IT MATTERS In October 2015, Congress confronted two big deadlines. It had to approve a budget by the end of the month to avoid a government shutdown. It also had to raise the debt limit to keep the government from defaulting on its debt. Failure to act on either would have serious consequences, as members of Congress knew well. Partisan stalemate on the budget had caused a government shutdown in 2013 that laid off workers, shuttered government facilities, and ultimately cost the economy billions of dollars.[1] Failure to raise the debt ceiling in 2015 threatened even more dire financial consequences by risking the credit rating of the American government in international markets. With the clock ticking down, Congress showed no signs of reaching a decision. Yet, just when it seemed that agreement would not be possible, congressional leaders and the president, meeting in secret over a long weekend, managed to strike a deal. With a two-year budget framework in place and a suspension of the debt ceiling until 2017, the federal government was back in business.

But on other important issues, the 114th Congress was unable to reach agreement. Judicial appointments proved particularly divisive. Supreme Court Justice Antonin Scalia's sudden death in February 2016 had left the nation's highest court with only eight members. Although President Obama nominated a highly experienced replacement, the Senate refused to hold confirmation hearings until after Obama left office. Left with only eight members for most of 2016, the Court's deliberations ended in ties on several important decisions. Even more significant was the mounting number of vacancies in the district courts as Congress failed to approve appointees. By fall 2016, 12 percent of district court judgeships remained unfilled, a significantly higher rate than in earlier decades. Without enough judges, lower courts proved unable to manage growing caseloads, leaving cases undecided for prolonged periods.[2] Once Republican Donald Trump was elected to the presidency, however, Senate leaders signaled their willingness to swiftly consider the new president's judicial nominees.

Congress has vast authority over most aspects of American life. In addition to federal judicial appointments, laws related to federal spending, taxing, and regulation pass through Congress. While the debates over these laws may seem hard to follow because they are often complex and technical or because heated, partisan struggles distract from the substance of the issue, it is important for the American people to learn about what Congress is doing. As the example of near government shutdown indicates, actions taken—or not taken—in Congress affect Americans' everyday lives. With its power to spend and tax, Congress also affects the choices that people face and the opportunities they can expect in life. In this chapter, we will see how Congress operates and how forces like interest groups and political parties shape its actions.

chaptergoals

- Describe who serves in Congress and how they represent their constituents (pp. 275–86)
- Explain how party leadership, the committee system, and the staff system help structure congressional business (pp. 286–89)
- Outline the steps in the process of passing a law (pp. 291–95)
- Analyze the factors that influence which laws Congress passes (pp. 295–301)
- Describe Congress's influence over other branches of government (pp. 301–3)

Congress Represents the American People

Describe who serves in Congress and how they represent their constituents

Congress is the most important representative institution in American government. Each member's primary responsibility in theory is to the district, to the **constituency** (the residents in the area from which an official is elected), not to the congressional leadership, a party, or even Congress itself. Yet the task of representation is not a simple one. Views about what constitutes fair and effective representation differ, and constituents can make very different kinds of demands on their representatives. Members of Congress must consider these diverse views and demands as they represent their districts.

The House and Senate Offer Differences in Representation

The framers of the Constitution provided for a **bicameral** legislature—that is, a legislative body consisting of two chambers or houses. The 435 members of the House are elected from districts apportioned according to population; the 100 members of the Senate are elected in a statewide vote, with two senators from each. Senators have much longer terms in office and usually represent much larger and more diverse constituencies than do their counterparts in the House (see Table 9.1).

Both formal and informal factors contribute to differences between the two chambers of Congress. Differences in the length of terms and requirements for holding office specified by the Constitution in turn generate differences in how members of each body develop their constituencies and exercise their powers of office. The small size and relative homogeneity of their constituencies and the frequency with which they must seek re-election—every two years—make House members more attuned to the legislative needs of local interest groups. The result is that members of the House most effectively and frequently serve as the agents of well-organized local interests with specific legislative agendas—for instance,

---

TABLE 9.1

Differences between the House and the Senate

	HOUSE	SENATE
Minimum age of member	25 years	30 years
U.S. citizenship	At least 7 years	At least 9 years
Length of term	2 years	6 years
Number representing each state	1–53 per state (depends on population)	2 per state
Constituency	Local	Local and statewide

used-car dealers seeking relief from regulation, labor unions seeking more favorable legislation, or farmers looking for higher subsidies. Because House members seek re-election every two years, they are interested in doing what their constituents want right *now*.

Senators, on the other hand, serve larger and more heterogeneous constituencies. As a result, they are somewhat better able than members of the House to serve as the agents for groups and interests organized on a statewide or national basis. Moreover, with longer terms in office (six years), senators have the luxury of considering "new ideas" or seeking to bring together new coalitions of interests rather than simply serving existing ones.

Representation Can Be Sociological or Agency

We have become so accustomed to the idea of representative government that we tend to forget what a peculiar concept representation really is. A representative claims to act or speak for some other person or group. But how can one person be trusted to speak for another? How do we know that those who call themselves our representatives are actually speaking on our behalf rather than simply pursuing their own interests?

There are two circumstances under which one person reasonably might be trusted to speak for another. The first of these occurs if the two individuals are so similar in background, character, interests, and perspectives that anything said by one would very likely reflect the views of the other as well. This principle is at the heart of what is sometimes called **sociological representation**—a type of representation in which representatives have the same racial, gender, ethnic, religious, or educational backgrounds as their constituents. The assumption is that sociological similarity helps promote good representation; thus, the composition of a properly constituted representative assembly should mirror the composition of society.

The second circumstance under which one person might be trusted to speak for another occurs if the two are formally bound together so that the representative is in some way accountable to those she purports to represent. If representatives can somehow be punished or held to account for failing to represent their constituents properly, then they have an incentive to provide good representation even if their own personal backgrounds, views, and interests differ from those of the people they represent. This principle is called **agency representation**—the sort of representation that takes place when constituents have the power to hire and fire their representatives.

Both sociological and agency representation play a role in the relationship between members of Congress and their constituencies.

The Social Composition of the U.S. Congress The extent to which the U.S. Congress is representative of the American people in a sociological sense can be seen by examining the distribution of important social characteristics in the House and Senate today.

African Americans, women, Latinos, and Asian Americans have increased their congressional representation in the past two decades (see Figure 9.1); but for most of American history, these groups had no representatives in Congress. Even now,

FIGURE 9.1 Women, African Americans, and Latinos in the U.S. Congress, 1971–2016

Congress has become much more socially diverse since the 1970s. How closely does the number of female, African American, and Latino representatives reflect their proportion of the total U.S. population?

SOURCES: Harold W. Stanley and Richard G. Niemi, eds., *Vital Statistics on American Politics 2003–2004* (Washington, DC: CQ Press, 2003), 207, Table 5–2; Jennifer E. Manning, *Membership of the 113th Congress: A Profile*, Congressional Research Service 7-5700, January 13, 2014, www.fas.org/sgp/crs/misc/R42964.pdf (accessed 2/24/14); Jennifer E. Manning, *Membership of the 114th Congress: A Profile*, Congressional Research Service, 7-5700 September 17, 2015, www.fas.org/sgp/crs/misc/R43869.pdf; R. Eric Petersen, *Representatives and Senators: Trends in Member Characteristics since 1945*, Congressional Research Service 7-5700, February 17, 2012, www.fas.org/sgp/crs/misc/R42365.pdf (accessed 9/28/15).

their representation in Congress is not comparable to the proportions in the general population. As the United States has become a more diverse nation, Congress has lagged behind in sociological representation. Similarly, the number of women in Congress continues to trail far behind their proportion of the population. In 2006, California Democrat Nancy Pelosi became the first female Speaker of the House of Representatives. She held that position through 2010. Following the 2016 elections, the 115th Congress (2017–18) included 82 women in the House of Representatives and 21 women in the Senate, an all-time high. Since

To more effectively promote a legislative agenda addressing issues that disproportionately affect racial and ethnic minority groups, members of Congress from those groups have formed caucuses. Here, members of the Congressional Black Caucus announce their endorsement of 2016 Democratic presidential candidate Hillary Clinton.

many important contemporary issues do cut along racial and gender lines, a considerable clamor for reform in the representative process is likely to continue until these groups are fully represented.

The occupational backgrounds of members of Congress have always been a matter of interest because many issues cut along economic lines that are relevant to occupations and industries. The legal profession is the dominant career of most members of Congress prior to their election, and public service or politics is also a significant background. In addition, many members of Congress have important ties to business and industry.[3]

Is Congress still able to legislate fairly or take account of a diversity of views and interests if it is not a sociologically representative assembly? The task is certainly much more difficult. Yet there is reason to believe it can. Representatives can serve as the agents of their constituents, even if they do not precisely mirror their sociological attributes.

Representatives as Agents A good deal of evidence indicates that whether or not members of Congress share their constituents' sociological characteristics, they do work very hard to speak for their constituents' views and serve their constituents' interests in the governmental process. The idea of representative as agent is similar to the relationship of lawyer and client. True, the relationship between the House member and an average of 710,767 "clients" in the district, or the senator and millions of "clients" in the state, is very different from that of the lawyer and client. But the criteria of performance are comparable. One expects at the very least that each representative will constantly be seeking to discover the interests of the constituency and will take those interests into account.[4] Whether members of Congress always represent the interests of their constituents is another matter, as we will see later in this chapter.

There is constant communication between constituents and congressional offices, and the volume of email from constituents and advocacy groups has grown so large so quickly that congressional offices have struggled to find effective ways to respond in a timely manner.[5] At the same time, members of Congress have found new ways to communicate with constituents. They have created websites describing their achievements, established a presence on social networking sites, and issued e-newsletters that alert constituents to current issues. Many have also set up blogs and Twitter accounts to establish a more informal style of communication with constituents.

The seriousness with which members of the House behave as representatives can be seen in the amount of time spent on behalf of their constituents. Well over one-quarter of their time and nearly two-thirds of the time of their staff members is devoted to constituency service (called "casework"). This service is not merely a matter of writing and mailing letters. It includes talking to constituents, providing them with minor services, presenting special bills for them, attempting to influence decisions by regulatory commissions on their behalf, helping them apply for federal benefits such as Social Security and Small Business Administration loans, and assisting them with immigration cases.[6] For example, during his fight for re-election in 2014, Senate Minority Leader Mitch McConnell (R-Ky.) ran a campaign ad featuring Noelle Hunter, a Kentucky resident whose ex-husband abducted their daughter and took her to Africa. According to Hunter, McConnell "took up my cause personally" and worked with the State Department to bring her daughter back home.[7]

In many districts there are two or three issues that are top priorities for constituents and, therefore, for the representatives. For example, representatives from districts that grow wheat, cotton, or tobacco will likely give legislation on these subjects great attention. In oil-rich states such as Oklahoma, Texas, and California, senators and members of the House are likely to be leading advocates of oil interests. For one thing, representatives are probably fearful of voting against their district interests; for another, the districts are unlikely to have elected representatives who would *want* to vote against them. On the other hand, on many issues, constituents do not have very strong views, so representatives are free to act as they think best. Foreign policy issues often fall into this category.

The influence of constituencies is so pervasive that both parties generally agree that nothing should be done, with regard to constituencies, that would endanger the re-election chances of any member. Party leaders obey this rule fairly consistently by not asking any member to vote in a way that might conflict with a district interest.

The Electoral Connection Hinges on Incumbency

The sociological composition of Congress and the activities of representatives once they are in office are very much influenced by electoral considerations. Two factors related to the U.S. electoral system affect who gets elected and what they do once in office. The first factor is that of incumbency advantage. The second is the way congressional district lines are drawn, which can greatly affect the outcome of an election. Let us examine more closely the impact that these considerations have on representation.

Incumbency—holding a political office for which one is running—plays a very important role in the American electoral system and in the kind of representation citizens get in Washington. Once in office, members have access to an array of tools that they can use to stack the deck in favor of their re-election. The most important of these is constituency service—taking care of the problems and requests of individual voters. Congressional offices will intervene on behalf of constituents when they have problems with federal programs or agencies, in such areas as Social Security benefits, veterans' benefits, and passports. When congressional offices contact federal agencies dealing with such matters, the offices usually respond with extra speed, knowing that members of Congress can embarrass or penalize an agency that doesn't do its job properly. Through such services and through regular e-newsletters, the incumbent seeks to establish a "personal" relationship with the constituents. The success of this strategy is evident in the high rates of re-election for congressional incumbents, which are as high as 98 percent for House members and 90 percent for members of the Senate in recent years (see Figure 9.2). It is also evident in what is called "sophomore surge"—the tendency for incumbent candidates to win a higher percentage of the vote when seeking future terms in office.

FIGURE 9.2 The Power of Incumbency

Members of Congress who run for re-election have a very good chance of winning. Has the incumbency advantage generally been greater in the House or in the Senate? What are the consequences of the incumbency advantage for who serves in Congress?

SOURCE: Norman J. Ornstein et al., eds., *Vital Statistics on Congress, 1999–2000* (Washington, DC: AEI Press, 2000), 57–58; and authors' update.

Voter dissatisfaction with the progress of the Iraq War caused incumbents to lose ground in 2006, although the overwhelming majority of congressional members were re-elected.

Increased political competition in the post-Watergate era created a large turnover in the Senate between 1974 and 1980.

PERCENTAGE RE-ELECTED

House

Senate

Incumbency re-election dipped some in 2010. Democrats were particularly vulnerable because their party controlled the presidency and both houses of Congress in a year when economic woes contributed to strong anti-incumbent sentiment. As a result, 54 incumbent Democratic members of the House and 2 incumbent Democratic senators lost their seats in 2010, and the Republicans regained control of the House. Incumbents have fared better in recent elections. In 2016, Trump's surprise victory in the presidential race benefited Republican incumbents, who appeared to be in danger of losing their seats.

Incumbency can also help a candidate by scaring off potential challengers. In many races, potential candidates may decide not to run because they fear that the incumbent simply has too much money or is too well liked or too well known. Potentially strong challengers may also decide that a district's partisan leanings are too unfavorable. The efforts of incumbents to raise funds to ward off potential challengers start early. Connecticut Democratic House member Joe Courtney won his seat in 2006 by a very small margin, with only 91 more votes than his opponent. He began fund-raising for the 2008 election even before he was sworn in for his first term. In addition, the Democratic Congressional Campaign Committee placed him on its "Frontline" team, a group of the 29 most vulnerable Democrats—these representatives were given high-profile speaking assignments and important committee appointments to elevate their profiles. In 2008, Courtney was re-elected by a 2-to-1 margin over his opponent and was easily re-elected in the four following elections as well.

The advantage of incumbency thus tends to preserve the status quo in Congress. This fact has implications for the social composition of Congress. For example, incumbency advantage makes it harder for women to increase their numbers in Congress because most incumbents are men. Women who run for open seats (that is, seats for which there are no incumbents) are just as likely to win as male candidates.[8] Supporters of **term limits** (legally prescribed limits on the number of terms an elected official can serve) argue that such limits are the only way to get new faces into Congress.

Apportionment and Redistricting Another major factor that affects who wins a seat in Congress is the way congressional districts are drawn. Every 10 years, state legislatures must redraw election districts and redistribute legislative representatives to reflect population changes or in response to legal challenges to existing districts. Because the number of congressional seats has been fixed at 435 since 1929, redistricting is a zero-sum process; for one state to gain a seat, another must lose one. The process of allocating congressional seats among the 50 states is called **apportionment**. Over the past several decades, the shift of the American population to the South and the West has greatly increased the size of the congressional delegations from those regions. This trend continued after the 2010 census (see Figure 9.3). Texas emerged as the biggest winner, with a gain of four seats, while Florida added two seats and Arizona, Georgia, Nevada, South Carolina, Utah, and Washington all added one seat.[9] Latino voters are nearly three times as prevalent in states that gained seats than in states that lost seats, suggesting that the growth of the Latino population is a major factor in the American political landscape.[10]

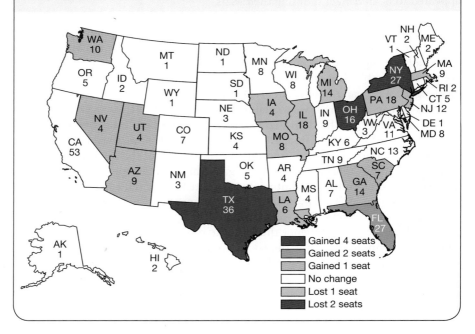

FIGURE 9.3 Results of Congressional Reapportionment, 2010

States in the West and parts of the South were the big winners in the reapportionment of House seats following the 2010 census. The old manufacturing states in the Midwest and Mid-Atlantic regions were the biggest losers. Which states have the greatest number of House seats?

SOURCE: U.S. Census Bureau, 2010 Apportionment of the U.S. House of Representatives Map, www.census.gov /library/visualizations/2010/dec/2010-map.html (accessed 8/15/16).

Legend:
- Gained 4 seats
- Gained 2 seats
- Gained 1 seat
- No change
- Lost 1 seat
- Lost 2 seats

States that gain or lose seats must then redraw their Congressional district borders. This is a highly political process: districts are shaped to create an advantage for the party with a majority in the state legislature, which controls the **redistricting** process. In this complex process, those charged with drawing districts use sophisticated computer technologies to come up with the most favorable district boundaries. Redistricting can create open seats and pit incumbents of the same party against one another, ensuring that one of them will lose. Redistricting can also give an advantage to one party by clustering voters with certain ideological or sociological characteristics in a single district or by diluting the influence of voter blocs by separating those voters into two or more districts. The manipulation of electoral districts to serve the interests of a particular group is known as **gerrymandering**.

Since the passage of the 1982 amendments to the 1964 Civil Rights Act, race has become a major (and controversial) consideration in drawing voting districts. These amendments, which encouraged the creation of districts in which members of racial minorities have decisive majorities, have greatly increased the number of minority representatives in Congress. After the 1990 redistricting cycle, the number of predominantly minority districts doubled, rising from 26 to 52. Among the

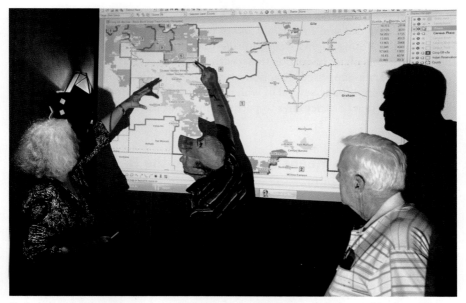

Redrawing legislative districts is a difficult task because it has implications for who will be elected. Here, the attorney for Arizona's Independent Redistricting Commission discusses a possible layout with a city council member from Casa Grande. Arizona gained one congressional seat following the 2010 census.

most fervent supporters of the new minority districts were white Republicans, who used the opportunity to create more districts dominated by white Republican voters. These developments raise thorny questions about representation. Some analysts argue that the system may grant minorities greater sociological representation, but it has made it more difficult for them to win substantive policy goals. This was a common argument after the sweeping Republican victories in the 1994 congressional elections. Others dispute this argument, noting that the strong surge of Republican voters was a more significant factor in those elections than any Democratic losses due to racial redistricting.[11]

In the case of *Miller v. Johnson* (1995), the Supreme Court limited racial redistricting by ruling that race could not be the predominant factor in creating electoral districts.[12] The distinction between race being a "predominant" factor and its being one factor among many is hazy. As a result, concerns about redistricting and representation persist.[13] Questions about minority representation emerged in 2011 in Texas, which gained four seats as a result of reapportionment. The Republican legislature drew a map that advantaged Republicans in three of those districts. But the plan drew a legal challenge on the grounds that it underrepresented Hispanic voters, who accounted for most of the state's population growth. Although federal judges drew a map more favorable to minorities (and Democrats), the Supreme Court ruled that the state did not have to use the map drawn by judges. The state ultimately agreed to a map that added two Latino-dominated districts. However, federal courts ruled that this map also weakened Latino and African American political power by creating too few minority districts.

The future of race in redistricting became more uncertain after the 2013 Supreme Court decision in *Shelby County v. Holder*. That decision invalidated a section of the Voting Rights Act requiring that the Justice Department approve the redistricting plans of jurisdictions with a history of racial discrimination.[14] Many Democrats expressed disappointment with the decision, fearing that the previously covered states, several of which are controlled by Republican majorities, might try to redraw district lines to partisan ends and further bias districts toward Republicans.[15]

Direct Patronage Means Bringing Home the Bacon

Members of Congress have numerous opportunities to provide direct benefits, or **patronage**, for their constituents. Patronage resources are available to higher officials and include making partisan appointments to offices and conferring grants, licenses, or special favors to supporters. The most important such opportunity for direct patronage is in so-called **pork-barrel legislation (or pork)**—appropriations made by legislative bodies for local projects that are often not needed but that are created to help local representatives win re-election in their home districts. This type of legislation specifies a project to be funded and the location of the project within a particular district. Many observers of Congress argue that pork-barrel bills are the only ones that some members are serious about moving toward actual passage because they are seen as so important to members' re-election bids.

A common form of pork-barreling is the "earmark," the practice through which members of Congress insert into bills language that provides special benefits for their own constituents. Highway bills are a favorite vehicle for congressional pork-barrel spending. The 2005 highway bill was full of such items, containing more than 6,000 projects earmarked for specific congressional districts. These measures often have little to do with transportation needs, instead serving as evidence for constituents that congressional members can bring federal dollars back home. Perhaps the most extravagant item in the 2005 bill—and the one least needed for transportation—was a bridge in Alaska designed to connect a barely populated island to the town of Ketchikan, whose population is just short of 8,000. At a cost of $2 billion, the bridge would have replaced an existing five-minute ferry ride. After Hurricane Katrina, "the bridge to nowhere" became a symbol of wasteful congressional spending. Sensitive to this criticism, Congress removed the earmarks for the bridge from the final legislation. In 2007, the state quietly dropped the project.

When Democrats took over Congress in 2007, they vowed to limit the use of earmarks, which had grown from 1,439 per year in 1995 to 15,268 in 2006. More troubling, earmarks were connected to congressional scandals. For example, Republican House member Randy "Duke" Cunningham (R-Calif.) was sent to jail in 2005 for accepting bribes by companies hoping to receive earmarks in return.[16] The House passed a new rule requiring that those representatives supporting each earmark identify themselves and guarantee that they have no personal financial stake in the requested project. A new ethics law applies similar provisions to the Senate. The new requirements appear to have had some impact: the 2007 military bill, for example, cut in half the earmark spending contained in the military bill passed in 2006. But in the midst of the sharp economic downturn in 2009, Congress passed a bill designed to stimulate the economy that contained more than 8,000 earmarks. In many cases, Republicans and some Democrats who voted against the bill were later happy to take credit from their constituents for the earmarks they had placed in it. In his 2010 State of the Union address, President Obama called for Congress to publish a list of all earmark requests on a single website. Congress not only failed to enact such legislation, in 2010 it set a new record by passing 11,320 earmarks, worth $32 billion. But in 2011, the House and the Senate agreed to a two-year moratorium on earmarks in spending bills and renewed the ban for the 113th and 114th Congresses.[17] Despite the moratorium, few members of Congress supported making the moratorium permanent.[18] Some analysts claim that the lack of earmarks contributes to congressional gridlock. They argue that earmarks provide congressional leaders with incentives to promote compromise among members. Supporters of this position contend that earmarks are not inherently an abuse of power and note that they often support legitimate district projects, such as transportation and parks.[19]

There are a few other types of direct patronage (see Figure 9.4). One important form of constituency service is intervention with federal administrative agencies on behalf of constituents. Members of the House and Senate and their staffs spend a great deal of time on the telephone and in administrative offices seeking to secure favorable treatment for constituents and supporters. For example, members

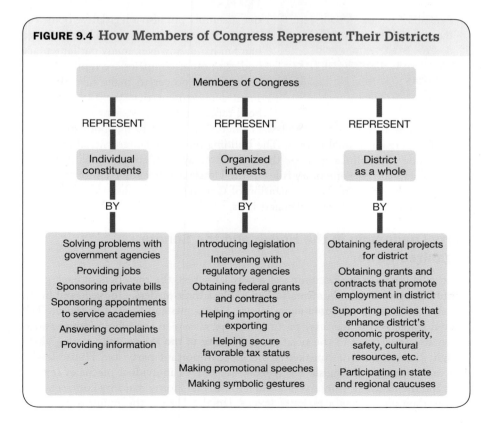

FIGURE 9.4 How Members of Congress Represent Their Districts

Members of Congress

REPRESENT — Individual constituents — BY
- Solving problems with government agencies
- Providing jobs
- Sponsoring private bills
- Sponsoring appointments to service academies
- Answering complaints
- Providing information

REPRESENT — Organized interests — BY
- Introducing legislation
- Intervening with regulatory agencies
- Obtaining federal grants and contracts
- Helping importing or exporting
- Helping secure favorable tax status
- Making promotional speeches
- Making symbolic gestures

REPRESENT — District as a whole — BY
- Obtaining federal projects for district
- Obtaining grants and contracts that promote employment in district
- Supporting policies that enhance district's economic prosperity, safety, cultural resources, etc.
- Participating in state and regional caucuses

of Congress can assist senior citizens who are having Social Security or Medicare benefit eligibility problems. A small but related form of patronage is securing an appointment to one of the military academies for the child of a constituent. Traditionally, these appointments are allocated one to a district.

A different form of patronage is the **private bill**—a bill in Congress to provide a specific person with some kind of relief, such as a special exemption from immigration quotas. It is distinguished from a public bill, which is supposed to deal with general rules and categories of behavior, people, and institutions. As many as 75 percent of all private bills introduced (and one-third of those that pass) are concerned with obtaining citizenship for foreign nationals who cannot get permanent visas to the United States because the immigration quota for their country is filled or because of something unusual about their particular situation.[20] For example, in 2012 a private bill granted a Nigerian immigrant—who was living in Michigan on an expired visa after coming to the United States as a teenager to undergo treatment for life-threatening facial tumors—a green card that would allow him to attend an Ohio medical school.[21]

● The Organization of Congress Is Shaped by Party

> **Explain how party leadership, the committee system, and the staff system help structure congressional business**

The U.S. Congress is not only a representative assembly but also a legislative body. For Americans, representation and legislation go hand in hand; however, many parliamentary bodies in other countries are representative without the power to make laws. It is no small achievement that the U.S. Congress both represents *and* governs.

To exercise its power to make laws, Congress must first bring about something close to an organizational miracle. The building blocks of congressional organization include the political parties, the committee system, congressional staff, the caucuses, and the parliamentary rules of the House and Senate. Each of these factors plays a key role in the organization of Congress and in the process through which Congress formulates and enacts laws.

Party Leadership in the House and the Senate Organizes Power

Every two years, at the beginning of a new Congress, the members of each party in the House of Representatives gather to elect their leaders. House Republicans call their gathering the **conference**. House Democrats call theirs the *caucus*. The elected leader of the majority party is later proposed to the whole House and is automatically elected to the position of **Speaker of the House**, with voting along straight party lines. The Speaker is the most important party and House leader and can influence the legislative agenda, the fate of individual pieces of legislation, and members' positions within the House. The House majority conference or caucus then also elects a **majority leader**. (In the House, the majority leader is subordinate in the party hierarchy to the Speaker of the House.) The minority party goes through the same process and selects the **minority leader**. Both parties also elect assistants to their party leaders, called **whips**, who are responsible for coordinating the party's legislative strategy, building support for key issues, and counting votes.

Next in line of importance for each party after the Speaker and majority or minority leader is what Democrats call the Steering and Policy Committee—Republicans have a separate Steering Committee and a separate Policy Committee—whose tasks are to assign new legislators to committees and to deal with the requests of incumbent members for transfers from one committee to another.

Generally, members of Congress seek assignments that will allow them to influence decisions of special importance to their districts. Representatives from farm districts, for example, may request seats on the Agriculture Committee.[22] Seats on powerful committees such as Ways and Means, which is responsible for tax legislation, and Appropriations are especially popular.

Within the Senate, the majority party usually designates a member of the majority party with the greatest seniority to serve as president pro tempore, a position of primarily ceremonial leadership. Real power is in the hands of the majority leader and minority leader, each elected by party conference. Together they control the Senate's calendar, or agenda for legislation. Each party also elects a Policy Committee, which advises the leadership on legislative priorities.

The Committee System Is the Core of Congress

The committee system is central to the operation of Congress. At each stage of the legislative process, Congress relies on committees and subcommittees to do the hard work of sorting through alternatives and writing legislation. There are several different kinds of congressional committees; these include standing committees, select committees, joint committees, and conference committees.

Standing committees are the most important arenas of congressional policy making. These permanent committees remain in existence from one session of Congress to the next; they have the power to propose and write legislation. The jurisdiction of each standing committee covers a particular subject matter, such as finance or agriculture, which in most cases parallels the major departments or agencies in the executive branch. Among the most important standing committees are those in charge of finances. The House Ways and Means Committee and the Senate Finance Committee are powerful because of their jurisdiction over taxes, trade, and expensive entitlement programs such as

After divisions within the Republican Party caused Speaker of the House John Boehner to resign in 2015, Paul Ryan took over the role and attempted to keep his party unified.

Social Security and Medicare. The Senate and House Appropriations committees also play important ongoing roles because they decide how much funding various programs will actually receive; they also determine exactly how the money will be spent. A seat on the Appropriations Committee allows a member the opportunity to direct funds to a favored program—perhaps one in his home district.

Except for the House Rules Committee, all standing committees receive proposals for legislation and process them into official bills. The House Rules Committee decides the order in which bills come up for a vote on the House floor and determines the specific rules that govern the length of debate and opportunity for amendments. The Senate, which has less formal organization and fewer rules, does not have a rules committee.

Select committees are usually temporary and normally do not have the power to present legislation to the full Congress but rather are set up to highlight or investigate a particular issue or address an issue not within the jurisdiction of existing committees. (The House and Senate Select Intelligence committees are permanent, however, and do have the power to report legislation, which means they can send legislation to the full House or Senate for consideration.) These committees may hold hearings and serve as focal points for the issues they are charged with considering. Congressional leaders form select committees when they want to take up issues that fall between the jurisdictions of existing committees, to highlight an issue, or to investigate a particular problem. Examples of select committees investigating political scandals include the Senate Watergate Committee of 1973, the committees set up in 1987 to investigate the Iran–Contra affair, and the House Select Committee on Benghazi, established to investigate the 2012 attack on the U.S. Embassy in Benghazi, Libya. Select committees set up to highlight ongoing issues have included the House Select Committee on Hunger, established in 1984, and the House Select Committee on Energy Independence and Global Warming, created in 2007 but abolished in 2011, when Republicans assumed control of the House.

Joint committees are formed of members of both the Senate and the House. There are four such committees: economic, taxation, library, and printing. These joint committees are permanent, but they do not have the power to report legislation. The Joint Economic Committee and the Joint Taxation Committee have often played important roles in collecting information and holding hearings on economic and financial issues. In 2011, Congress created the Joint Select Committee on Deficit Reduction and, in an unusual move, gave the committee the power to write and report legislation. Informally known as "the super-committee," it was charged with coming up with $1.2 trillion in debt reduction. Formed after a contentious debate about raising the debt limit (usually a routine matter) the super-committee proved unable to come to an agreement and disbanded less than four months after it was created.

Finally, **conference committees** are temporary joint committees whose members are appointed by the Speaker of the House and the presiding officer of the Senate. These committees are charged with working out a compromise on legislation that has been passed by the House and the Senate but in different versions. Conference committees play an extremely important role in determining what laws are actually passed because they must reconcile any differences in the legislation passed by the House and Senate.

When control of Congress is divided between two parties, each is guaranteed significant representation in conference committees. When a single party controls both houses, the majority party is not obligated to offer such representation to the minority party. In 2003, Democrats complained that Republicans took this power to the extreme by excluding them and adding new provisions to legislation at the conference committee stage. Democrats even prevented several conference committees from convening to protest their near exclusion from conference committees on major energy, health care, and transportation laws. After the Democrats returned to power in 2007, they largely bypassed the conference committees; when their early efforts to reach compromises in the conference were derailed by partisan differences, the Democrats began making closed-door agreements between top leaders in the House and the Senate. Although the process facilitated compromises across the two chambers, it meant that important changes to bills were made in private, without the transparency that would have been part of the conference committee process. After 2010, Congress continued to avoid conference committees. Instead, the Republican House and Democratic Senate exchanged amendments as they sought to reach agreement on the final version of a bill, a practice known informally as "ping pong."[23]

Within each committee, hierarchy is based on seniority. **Seniority** is the ranking given to an individual on the basis of length of continuous service on a committee in Congress. In general, each committee is chaired by the most senior member of the majority party. But the principle of seniority is not absolute. Both Democrats and Republicans have violated it on occasion. In 1995, when the Republicans won control of the House, then-Speaker Newt Gingrich instituted a new practice of frequent seniority violations, often selecting committee chairs based on loyalty or fund-raising abilities, a practice that subsequent Republican leaders have maintained. In 2007, the Democrats returned to the seniority principle to select committee chairs but altered traditional practices in other ways by offering freshman Democrats choice committee assignments to increase their chances of re-election.[24]

The Staff System Is the Power behind the Power

The congressional institution second in importance only to the committee system is the staff system. Every member of Congress employs a large number of staff members, whose tasks include handling constituent requests and, to a large and growing extent, dealing with legislative details and the activities of administrative agencies. Increasingly, staffers bear the primary responsibility for formulating and drafting proposals, organizing hearings, dealing with administrative agencies, and negotiating with lobbyists. Indeed, legislators typically deal with one another through staff rather than through direct, personal contact. Today, staffers develop policy ideas, draft legislation, and have a good deal of influence over the legislative process.

Representatives and senators together employ about 11,500 staffers in their Washington and home offices. In addition, Congress employs more than 2,000 committee staffers. These individuals make up the permanent staff, who stay attached to every House and Senate committee regardless of turnover in Congress and who are responsible for organizing and administering the committee's work, including researching, scheduling, organizing hearings, and drafting legislation. Committee staffers also play key roles in the legislative process.

AMERICA
Side *by* Side

Legislatures in Comparison

While in most democracies the executive takes the lead role in initiating and directing the legislative process (with the parliament limited to amending or vetoing legislation), the U.S. Constitution gives this power to Congress. Reflecting this greater power, the budget of the U.S. Congress is the highest in the world, as is the number of staff members working for it.

The membership of the U.S. Congress also *looks* different than those of most other legislative bodies; its members tend to be older, and there are fewer women, than the global democracy average. While countries like Finland are nearing gender equality in their representation, women make up less than one-fifth of the U.S. Congress. Many countries have set compulsory or voluntary gender quotas for their list of candidates running for election, or have reserved a percentage of seats for women in their parliament. The United States has no such quotas. However, it is unclear whether quotas lead to more women in parliament, or whether the societies that value women's representation (and therefore already elect more women) choose to create gender quotas.

Another difference is that the U.S. Congress has more "professional politicians"—representatives who have only had political careers. While some analysts have argued that professional politicians are more "out of touch" with life outside of politics, others point out that professional politicians are more knowledgeable and effective at navigating the political system, and thus better able to represent their constituents' interests.

	United States (114th Congress)	Democracy Average*	Finland
Structure of Legislature			
Bicameral or unicameral?	Bicameral	Unicameral more common	Unicameral
Number of representatives	535	214	200
Citizens per representative	588,100	70,100	26,600
Budget (in U.S. dollars)	$5.1 billion	$264.8 million	$145.3 million
Cost per inhabitant	$16.27	$22.30	$27.29
Average number of staff per member	29.7	3.3	2.36
Membership Demographics			
"Professional politicians"	62%	13.3%	18%
Average age	57 (House) 61 (Senate)	54	52
Women	19.4% (House) 20% (Senate)	21.8% (Lower House) 26.7% (Upper House)	41.5%

*Of the 129 parliaments who provided voluntary data to *2012 Global Parliamentary Report,* only 86 were rated as "free" that year according to Freedom House. These 86 were selected to represent the democracy average.

SOURCES: Jennifer E. Manning, "Membership of the 114th Congress: A Profile," October 13, 2015, www.senate.gov /CRSReports/crs-publish.cfm?pid=%260BL*RLC2%0A (accessed 11/30/15); IPU and UNDP, *Global Parliamentary Report,* 2012; www.ipu.org/gpr-e/downloads/index.htm (accessed 4/29/16); and IPU Parline Database, "Women in National Parliaments," 2015, www.ipu.org/wmn-e/classif.htm (accessed 4/30/16).

Rules of Lawmaking Explain How a Bill Becomes a Law

Outline the steps in the process of passing a law

The institutional structure of Congress is one key factor that helps shape the legislative process. A second and equally important set of factors is the rules of congressional procedure. These rules govern everything from the introduction of a **bill** (a proposed law that has been sponsored by a member of Congress and submitted to the clerk of the House or Senate) through its submission to the president for signing (see Figure 9.5). Not only do these regulations influence the fate of each and every bill but they also help determine the distribution of power in the Congress.

The First Step Is Committee Deliberation

Even if a member of Congress, the White House, or a federal agency has spent months developing and drafting a piece of legislation, it does not become a bill until it is submitted officially by a senator or representative to the clerk of the House or Senate and referred to the appropriate committee for deliberation. Bills can originate in the House or the Senate, but only the House can introduce "money bills": those that spend or raise revenues. The framers inserted this provision in the Constitution because they believed that the chamber closest to the people should exercise greater authority over taxing and spending. No floor action on any bill can take place until the committee with jurisdiction over it has taken all the time it needs to deliberate. During the course of its deliberations, the committee typically refers the bill to one of its subcommittees, which may hold hearings, listen to expert testimony, and amend the proposed legislation before referring the bill to the full committee for consideration. The full committee may accept the recommendation of the subcommittee or hold its own hearings and prepare its own amendments. Or, even more frequently, the committee and subcommittee may do little or nothing with a bill that has been submitted to them. Many bills are simply allowed to "die in committee" without serious consideration given to them. In a typical congressional session, 80-90 percent of the roughly 10,000 bills introduced die in committee—an indication of the power of the congressional committee system.

The relative handful of bills that are reported out of committee must, in the House, pass one additional hurdle within the committee system: the Rules Committee, which determines the rules that will govern action on the bill on the House floor. In particular, the Rules Committee allots the time for debate and decides to what extent amendments to the bill can be proposed from the floor. In recent years, the Rules Committee has become less powerful because the House leadership exercises so much influence over its decisions.

Debate Is Less Restricted in the Senate Than in the House

In the House, virtually all the time allotted for debate on a given bill is controlled by the bill's sponsor and by its leading opponent. In almost every case, these two people are the committee chair and the ranking minority member of the

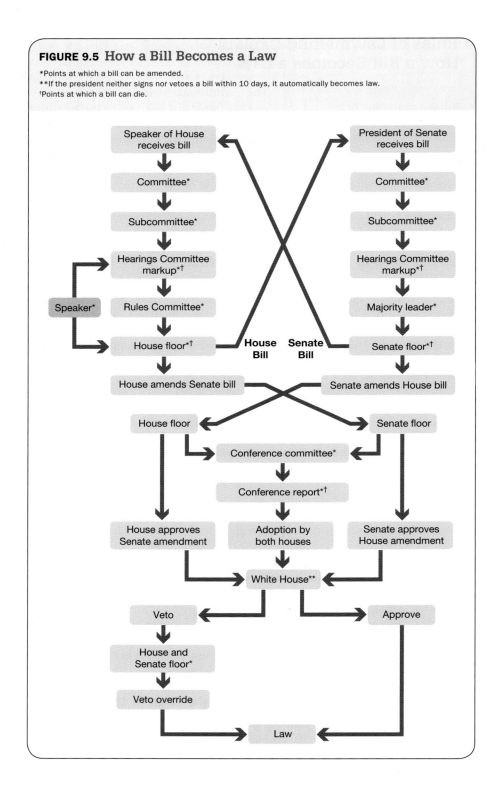

FIGURE 9.5 How a Bill Becomes a Law

*Points at which a bill can be amended.
**If the president neither signs nor vetoes a bill within 10 days, it automatically becomes law.
†Points at which a bill can die.

Speaker of House receives bill → Committee* → Subcommittee* → Hearings Committee markup*† → Rules Committee* → House floor*† → House amends Senate bill

Speaker*

President of Senate receives bill → Committee* → Subcommittee* → Hearings Committee markup*† → Majority leader* → Senate floor*† → Senate amends House bill

House Bill   Senate Bill

House floor   Senate floor

Conference committee* → Conference report*†

House approves Senate amendment   Adoption by both houses   Senate approves House amendment

White House**

Veto   Approve

House and Senate floor*

Veto override

Law

committee that processed the bill—or those they designate. These two participants are, by rule and tradition, granted the power to allocate most of the debate time in small amounts to members who are seeking to speak for or against the measure. Preference in the allocation of time goes to the members of the committee whose jurisdiction covers the bill.

The Filibuster In the Senate, the leadership has much less control over floor debate. Indeed, the Senate is unique among the world's legislative bodies for its commitment to unlimited debate. Once given the floor, a senator may speak as long as she wishes. On a number of memorable occasions, senators have used the right to talk without interruption for as long as they want to prevent action on legislation they opposed. Through this tactic, called the **filibuster**, members of the Senate can prevent action on legislation they oppose by continuously holding the floor and speaking until the majority backs down (or the filibustering senator gives up). Once given the floor, senators have unlimited time to speak. A vote of three-fifths of the Senate, or 60 votes, is required to end a filibuster. This procedure to end a filibuster is called **cloture.** For much of American history, senators only rarely used the filibuster, though during the 1950s and '60s, opponents of civil rights legislation often used filibusters to block its passage. In the last 20 years, the filibuster has become so common that observers routinely note that it takes 60 votes to get anything passed in the Senate. The 113th Congress (2013–14) set a new record, with 218 cloture votes (the vote to end a filibuster).[25]

In 2013 the Democratic Senate leader Harry Reid (Nev.) mobilized his party to alter the filibuster rules for the first time in many decades. Frustrated by the repeated failure of the Senate to vote on many of President Obama's nominees to fill positions in the executive branch, as well as judgeships to important federal courts, Reid invoked what senators had come to call "the nuclear option," a change to the filibuster rules in the middle of the session by simple majority vote. Under the new rules, nominees for executive branch appointments and federal court nominees—except the Supreme Court—cannot be filibustered, meaning that they can be approved by a simple majority vote. (Filibusters of legislation were still allowed.) Not surprisingly, the two parties had different views on the decision. Reid defended it as necessary, due to what he called "unbelievable, unprecedented obstruction." Republicans denounced the new rule, stating, in the words of Pat Roberts (R-Kans.), "We have weakened this body permanently."[26] After they assumed leadership of the Senate in 2015, Republicans retained Reid's filibuster rules for some executive branch nominees but have retained the filibuster for legislation despite calls from some Republicans to eliminate the filibuster altogether.[27]

Voting Once debate is concluded on the floor of the House and the Senate, the leaders schedule it for a vote on the floor of each chamber. By this time, congressional leaders know what the vote will be; leaders do not bring legislation to the floor unless they are fairly certain it is going to pass. As a consequence, it is unusual for the leadership to lose a bill on the floor. On rare occasions, the last moments of the floor vote can be very dramatic as each party's leadership puts its whip organization into action to make sure that wavering members vote with the party. In 2015 the House of Representatives failed to pass a spending bill to fund the Department of Homeland Security, hours before the agency was to run out of money and begin to shut down. Despite having a majority in the chamber and an early vote that suggested that the bill would pass easily, House GOP leaders failed to prevent the most conservative members of the party from suddenly abandoning the bill over objections that it left out provisions to block President Obama's executive actions on immigration. As midnight approached, the House agreed on a one-week extension to keep the department open.[28] Leaders later secured sufficient support to enact longer term funding for Homeland Security.

Conference Committees Reconcile House and Senate Versions of Legislation

Getting a bill out of committee and through both houses of Congress is no guarantee that it will be enacted into law. Before a bill can be sent to the president, both houses must pass it in the identical form. Frequently, bills that began with similar provisions in both chambers emerge with little resemblance to each other. Alternatively, a bill may be passed by one chamber but undergo substantial revision in the other chamber. In such a case, a conference committee composed of the senior members of the committees or subcommittees that initiated the bill may be convened to iron out differences between the two pieces of legislation.

When a bill comes out of conference, it faces one more hurdle. Before it can be sent to the president for signing, the House–Senate conference committee's version of the bill must be approved on the floor of each chamber. Usually such approval is given quickly. Occasionally, however, a bill's opponents use this round of approval as one last opportunity to defeat a piece of legislation. In recent years, as we have seen, polarization in Congress has led to much less reliance on conference committees. Instead, leaders exchange amendments in hopes of reaching agreement.

The President's Veto Controls the Flow of Legislation

Once adopted by the House and Senate, a bill goes to the president, who may choose to sign it into law or **veto** it. If the president neither signs nor vetoes it within 10 days and Congress is in session, the bill automatically becomes law. The veto is the president's constitutional power to reject a piece of legislation. To veto a bill, the president returns it unsigned within 10 days to the house of Congress in which it originated. If Congress adjourns during the 10-day period, such that congressional adjournment prevents the president from returning the bill to Congress, the bill is also considered to be vetoed. This latter method is known as the **pocket veto**. Unlike a regular or return veto, a pocket-vetoed bill cannot be overridden; the bill simply dies. The possibility of a presidential veto affects how willing members of Congress are to push for different pieces of legislation at different times. If they think a proposal is likely to be vetoed, they might shelve it for a later time or alter it to suit the president's preferences.

A presidential veto may be overridden by a two-thirds vote in both the House and the Senate. Successful overrides are rare but are a blow to the president.

Several Factors Influence How Congress Decides

Analyze the factors that influence which laws Congress passes

What determines the kinds of legislation that Congress ultimately produces? According to the simplest theories of representation, members of Congress respond to the views of their constituents. In fact, creating a legislative agenda, drawing up a list of possible measures, and deciding among them is a complex process in which a variety of influences from inside and outside government play important roles. External influences include a legislator's constituency and various interest groups. Influences from inside government include party leadership, congressional colleagues, and the president. Let us examine each of these influences individually and then consider how they interact to produce congressional policy decisions.

Constituents Matter

Because members of Congress, for the most part, want to be re-elected, we would expect the views of their constituents to be a primary influence on the decisions those legislators make. Yet most constituents pay little attention to politics and often do not even know what policies their representatives support. Nonetheless, members of Congress spend a lot of time worrying about what their constituents think because these representatives realize that the choices they make may be scrutinized in a future election and used as ammunition by an opposing candidate. Because of this possibility, members of Congress do try to anticipate their constituents' policy views.[29]

Interest Groups Influence Constituents and Congress

Interest groups are another important external influence on congressional policies. Members of Congress pay close attention to interest groups for a number of reasons: interest groups can mobilize constituents, serve as watchdogs on congressional action, and supply candidates with money. When members of Congress are making voting decisions, those interest groups that have some connection to constituents or that can mobilize followers in particular members' districts are most likely to be influential.

Interest groups also have substantial influence in setting the legislative agenda and helping craft specific language in legislation. Today, sophisticated lobbyists win influence by providing information about policies, as well as campaign contributions, to busy members of Congress. The $1.1 trillion end-of-year spending bill passed at the end of 2014 included an amendment exempting many financial transactions from federal regulation under the Dodd-Frank Act. The amendment language was taken from a bill originally written by Citigroup lobbyists, with

Representatives spend a lot of time meeting with constituents in their districts to explain how they have helped their district and learn what issues their constituents care about. Such meetings are often informal events at local restaurants or fairs.

70 of 85 lines of the bill directly copying Citigroup's language.[30] In recent years, interest groups have also begun to build broader coalitions and comprehensive campaigns around particular policy issues. These coalitions do not rise from the grass roots but instead are put together by Washington lobbyists who launch comprehensive lobbying campaigns that combine simulated grassroots activity with information and campaign funding for members of Congress.

Concerns that special interests exert too much influence led Congress to enact new ethics legislation in 2007. The law set new restrictions on the gifts lobbyists can bestow on lawmakers and limited privately funded travel. The law also prohibited members of Congress from lobbying for two years after they retired (it had been one year) and required lawmakers to identify the earmarks they inserted in legislation. Further, it aimed to shine light on the practice of "bundling," in which lobbyists assemble money from a number of clients to make a single political donation. Now lobbyists are required to disclose the names of the individual contributors to these political donations. Although the new law provides additional transparency, it does not fundamentally alter the fact that wealthy interest groups continue to exercise tremendous influence in Congress.

Moreover, the large sums of cash raised by Super political action committees (PACs)—discussed in Chapter 7—have introduced a whole new set of questions about the role of special interests in politics, especially because donors to Super PACs can remain anonymous. Although they cannot openly coordinate with candidates, Super PACs can endorse candidates by name and are often run by people close to the candidates they support. In 2016, Super PACs poured unprecedented sums of money into the race for president, but they also targeted key congressional contests in an effort to affect the balance of power between the parties in Congress.

Party Leaders Rely on Party Discipline

In both the House and the Senate, party leaders have a good deal of influence over the behavior of their party members. This influence, sometimes called "party discipline," was once so powerful that it dominated the lawmaking process. In the 1800s party leaders could often command the allegiance of more than 90 percent of their members. A vote in which half or more of the members of one party take one position while at least half of the members of the other party take the opposing position is called a **party unity vote**. At the beginning of the twentieth century, nearly half of all **roll-call votes** (votes in which each legislator's yes-or-no vote is recorded as the clerk calls the names of the members alphabetically) in the House of Representatives were party votes. While party voting is rarer today than a century ago, in the last decade it has been fairly common to find at least a majority of the Democrats opposing a majority of the Republicans on any given issue.

Typically, party unity is greater in the House than in the Senate. House rules give more power to the majority party leaders, which gives them more influence over House members. In the Senate, however, the leadership has few controls over its members. Former Senate majority leader Tom Daschle once observed that a Senate leader seeking to influence other senators has as incentives "a bushel full of carrots and a few twigs."[31]

Party unity has been on the rise in recent years because the divisions between the parties have deepened on many high-profile issues such as abortion, affirmative action, the minimum wage, and school vouchers (see Figure 9.6) and because the majority–minority party difference has been small. In 2015, House Democrats voted with the majority 92 percent of the time, matching the all-time high previously reached in 2007 and 2008. Senate Democrats voted with their caucus 91 percent of the time, three points below the record set in 2013. Republicans were also very united. In 2015, House Republicans voted

FIGURE 9.6 Party Unity Votes by Chamber

Party unity votes are roll-call votes in which a majority of one party lines up against a majority of the other party. Party unity votes increase when the parties are polarized and when the party leadership can enforce discipline. Why did the percentage of party unity votes decline in the 1970s? Why has it risen in recent years?

SOURCES: "CQ Roll Call's Vote Studies—2013 in Review," http://media.cq.com/votestudies (accessed 6/9/14); Eliza Newlin Carney, "Standing Together against Any Action," *CQ Weekly* (March 16, 2015); and "2015 Vote Studies: Party Unity Remained Strong," *CQ Weekly* (February 8, 2016).

PERCENTAGE OF ALL VOTES

Party unity votes have increased as partisan polarization in Congress has increased.

Senate

House

During the 1970s, weaker party leadership was one reason that relatively few votes pitted the parties against one another.

with their party 92 percent of the time, matching the record high set in 2013; Senate Republicans voted with their party 89 percent of the time, the highest level seen since 2010.[32]

Although party organization has weakened since the turn of the twentieth century, today's party leaders still have resources to reward loyal members who vote with the party: (1) leadership PACs, (2) committee assignments, (3) access to the floor, (4) the whip system, (5) logrolling, and (6) the presidency.

Leadership PACs Leaders have increased their influence over members in recent years with aggressive use of leadership PACs. Leadership PACs are organizations that members of Congress use to raise funds that they then distribute to other members of their party running for election. Republican congressional leaders pioneered the aggressive use of leadership PACs to win their congressional majority in 1995, and the practice has spread widely since that time. Money from leadership PACs can be directed to the most vulnerable candidates or to candidates who are having trouble raising money. They can also be used to influence primary elections. For example, Kirsten Gillibrand, the junior Democratic senator from New York, has used her leadership PAC to promote Democratic women candidates running for Congress. In 2016 the PAC, which she named Off the Sidelines, supplied funds to 61 candidates running for seats in the House and 10 for the Senate, all of them women.[33]

Committee Assignments Party leaders can create debts among members by helping them get favorable committee assignments. These assignments are made early in the congressional careers of most members and cannot be taken from them if they later go against party discipline. Nevertheless, if the leadership goes out of its way to get the right assignment for a member, this effort is likely to create a bond of obligation that can be called upon without any other payments or favors. This is one reason the Republican leadership gave freshmen favorable assignments when the Republicans took over Congress in 1995. When the Democrats won control of Congress in 2007, House Speaker Nancy Pelosi gave desirable and prestigious committee assignments to Democratic House members who faced competitive re-election races, to assist them in their home districts and increase their loyalty.

Access to the Floor The most important everyday resource available to the parties is control over access to the floor. With thousands of bills awaiting passage and most members clamoring for access in order to influence a bill or to publicize themselves, floor time is precious. In the Senate, the leadership allows ranking committee members to influence the allocation of floor time—who will speak for how long. In the House, the Speaker, as head of the majority party (in consultation with the minority leader), allocates large blocks of floor time. Thus, floor time is allocated in both houses of Congress by the majority and minority leaders. More important, the Speaker of the House and the majority leader in the Senate possess the power of recognition—that is, they decide who may and may not speak on the floor. This authority is quite formidable and can be used to stymie a piece of legislation completely or to frustrate a member's attempts to speak on a particular issue. Because the power is significant, members of Congress usually attempt to stay on good terms with the Speaker and the majority leader in order to ensure that they will continue to be recognized.

The Whip System Some influence accrues to party leaders through the whip system, which is primarily a communications network in each house of Congress for conveying the leaders' wishes and plans to the members. Between 12 and 20 assistant and regional whips are selected to operate at the direction of the majority or minority leader and the whip. They take polls of all the members to learn their intentions on specific bills, enabling the leaders to know whether they have enough support to allow a vote as well as whether the vote is so close that they need to put pressure on undecided members. In those instances, the Speaker or a lieutenant will go to a few party members who have indicated they will switch if their vote is essential—an expedient that the leaders try to limit to a few times per session.

The whip system helps maintain party unity in both houses of Congress, but it is particularly critical in the House of Representatives because of the large number of legislators whose positions and votes must be accounted for. The majority and minority whips and their assistants must be adept at inducing compromise among legislators who hold widely differing viewpoints.

When Republicans retook control of the House in 2010, the whip operation faced significant challenges from the unusually large number of freshman members of Congress elected in 2010, many of whom identified with the conservative Tea Party movement. Of the 87 newly elected freshmen, 40 percent had never held elected office before, calling themselves "citizen politicians." Since 2010, the whip operation has been faced with significant challenges from conservative members. In 2015, a small group of conservative Republicans, organized into the House Freedom Caucus, regularly disputed the positions of the party leadership. Frustrated with the lack of discipline, House Majority Whip Steve Scalise (R-La.) expelled several members from his whip team for failing to support party positions.[34] Indeed, conflict with these rebellious Republicans prompted Speaker John Boehner to make the stunning announcement in September 2015 of his retirement from the speakership and from the House.

Logrolling A legislative practice wherein agreements are made between legislators in voting for or against a bill is called **logrolling**. Unlike with bargaining, legislators who are logrolling have nothing in common but their desire to exchange support. The agreement states, in effect, "You support me on bill X, and I'll support you on bill Y." Since party leaders are the center of the communications networks in the two chambers, they can help members create large logrolling coalitions. Hundreds of logrolling deals are made each year, and although there are no official record-keeping books, it would be a poor party leader whose whips did not know who owed what to whom.

The Presidency Of all the influences that maintain the clarity of party lines in Congress, the influence of the presidency is probably the most important. Indeed, the office is a touchstone of party discipline in Congress. Since the late 1940s, under President Harry Truman, presidents each year have identified a number of bills to be considered part of their administration's program. By the mid-1950s, both parties in Congress began to look to the president for these proposals, which became the most significant part of Congress's agenda. The president's support is an important criterion for party loyalty, and party leaders are able to use it to rally some members. Party polarization limited President Obama's agenda-setting powers for the majority of his presidency, which saw a Republican-controlled House for his last six years and a Republican-controlled Senate for his last two. Instead, his proposals became targets for congressional opponents.

Partisanship Has Thwarted the Ability of Congress to Decide

Recent congresses have been notable for their inability to pass laws. The 113th Congress (2013–14) and the 112th Congress (2012–13) were the two least productive congresses in modern history. In November 2013, Congress received the lowest levels of approval ever recorded in public opinion polls. Just 9 percent approved of the job Congress was doing, while 86 percent expressed disapproval.[35] That reputation had improved little by 2015, when 14 percent of Americans stated that they approved of the job that Congress was doing.[36]

Indeed, many high-profile bills ended in failure throughout 2012 and 2013. In 2013, for example, House Republicans refused to pass a bill funding government operations or extending the debt ceiling unless the spending bill included language delaying implementation of the Affordable Care Act (ACA).[37] As a consequence, the federal government shut down for the first time in almost two decades. Ultimately as public ire rose over the continued shutdown, the House voted to pass a Senate bill—which contained virtually no concessions to the GOP—to reopen the government and extend the debt limit, just hours before the United States was set to cross the debt-ceiling deadline.[38] Democrats and Republicans succeeded in averting a second showdown over the debt ceiling when both sides agreed on a budget deal in late 2013.

In 2015 the most conservative factions of the Republican Party in Congress, frustrated that Speaker of the House John Boehner hadn't been more effective against the Obama administration, pressured him to resign.

As noted earlier, in 2015 bitter political disagreements among House Republicans prompted the resignation of House Speaker John Boehner. A small group of conservative Republicans—associated with the Tea Party movement and later organized as the Freedom Caucus—announced their intention to block any budget bill that included funding for Planned Parenthood, an organization that provides a variety of health services to women, including abortion. Yet it was apparent that the Senate would not approve a bill that failed to fund Planned Parenthood and that

President Obama would veto such a bill. Even so, House conservatives refused to back down. Without congressional approval on a short-term budget, the federal government once again faced the prospect of a shut down. Weary of tangling with members of his own party, Boehner stunned the political world by announcing his resignation as House Speaker. His decision allowed conservatives to claim a victory and led them to approve the short-term spending bill to keep the government open. But the divisions that led to Boehner's resignation promised to create more challenges to congressional efforts to enact legislation. When Paul Ryan (R-Wisc.) became Speaker in October 2015, many were hopeful that congressional stalemate would be a thing of the past. Ryan enjoyed support from all wings of the Republican Party. Although the new Speaker avoided the open confrontation with the Freedom Caucus, he, too, faced governing challenges, as conservative members of his own party defeated key legislation.[39]

Congressional Polarization Congress's inability to decide reflects the deep ideological differences that separate the two parties. Efforts to measure the ideological distance between the two parties show that since the mid-1970s Republicans and Democrats have been diverging sharply and are now more polarized than at any time in the last century. Democrats have become more liberal and Republicans have become more conservative on issues related to the economy and the role of government.[40] The Republican Party has experienced the greatest ideological shift, becoming sharply more conservative. Moreover, because congressional districts are increasingly homogeneous in their ideology—in part due to gerrymandering but mainly because of natural clustering of the population—most members of Congress are in safe seats. Their constituents will not punish them for failing to compromise. Additionally, active mobilization by organizations on the right, such as the Club for Growth, means that Republican members of Congress who support compromises might be punished. These outside organizations have financed alternative candidates to challenge members who vote against the organizations' positions. Partisan polarization also affected the effort to fill the Supreme Court seat left vacant by Justice Antonin Scalia's death, as we saw in the introduction to this chapter. When President Obama nominated Merrick Garland, a well-respected moderate judge, many Republicans, who had called on Obama to let the next president fill the vacancy, vowed never to meet with the nominee. The Senate Judiciary committee declined to schedule hearings, hoping that there would be a Republican president in 2016 who would have the opportunity to fill the vacancy with a conservative judge.

● Much Congressional Energy Goes to Tasks Other Than Lawmaking

Describe Congress's influence over other branches of government

In addition to the power to make the law, Congress has at its disposal an array of other instruments through which to influence the process of government. The Constitution gives the Senate the power to approve treaties and appointments. And Congress has a number of other powers through which it can share with the other branches the capacity to administer the laws.

Congress Oversees How Legislation Is Implemented

Oversight refers to the effort by Congress, through hearings, investigations, and other techniques, to exercise control over the activities of executive agencies. Oversight is carried out by committees or subcommittees of the Senate or the House, which conduct hearings and investigations to analyze and evaluate bureaucratic agencies and the effectiveness of their programs. Their purpose may be to locate inefficiencies or abuses of power, to explore the relationship between what an agency does and what a law intends, or to change or abolish a program. Most programs and agencies are subject to some oversight every year during the course of hearings on **appropriations**—that is, the amounts of money approved by Congress in statutes (bills) that each unit or agency of government can spend.

Committees or subcommittees have the power to subpoena witnesses, administer oaths, cross-examine, compel testimony, and bring criminal charges for contempt (refusing to cooperate) and perjury (lying). Hearings and investigations resemble each other in many ways, but they differ on one fundamental point. A hearing is usually held on a specific bill, and the questions asked there are usually intended to build a record with regard to that bill. In an investigation, the committee or subcommittee does not begin with a particular bill but examines a broad area or problem and then concludes its investigation with one or more proposed bills.

Oversight hearings can serve as political tools. The Select Committee on Benghazi, formed in 2014 to investigate the deaths of four American diplomats in Libya, became enmeshed in partisan contention after Hillary Clinton—secretary of state during the attacks—announced that she would run for president. In 2015, as revelations emerged that Clinton had used a private email server during her tenure as secretary of state, the committee began to investigate whether appropriate procedures had been followed and whether national security was compromised.[41] When the FBI undertook an investigation into the matter in 2016, FBI Director James Comey recommended no criminal charges against Clinton but also questioned her judgment and called her actions "extremely careless."[42] The next day, Attorney General Loretta Lynch accepted the FBI's findings, affirming that the Justice Department would not seek criminal charges.

Special Senate Powers Include Advice and Consent

The Constitution has given the Senate a special power, one that is not based on lawmaking. The president has the power to make treaties and to appoint top executive officers, ambassadors, and federal judges—but only "with the Advice and Consent of the Senate" (Article II, Section 2). For treaties, two-thirds of senators present must concur; for appointments, a simple majority is required.

The power to approve or reject presidential requests includes the power to set conditions. The Senate only occasionally exercises its power to reject treaties and appointments, and usually that is when opposite parties control the Senate and the White House.

Impeachment Is the Power to Remove Top Officials

The Constitution also grants Congress the power of **impeachment** over the president, vice president, top executive branch officials, and judicial officials. To impeach means the House of Representatives charges a government official (president or otherwise) with "Treason, Bribery, or other high Crimes and Misdemeanors" and brings that person before Congress to determine guilt. Impeachment is thus like a criminal indictment in which the House of Representatives acts like a grand jury, voting (by simple majority) on whether the accused ought to be impeached. If a majority of the House votes to impeach, an impeachment trial is conducted in and by the Senate, which acts like a trial jury by voting whether to convict and remove the person from office (this vote requires a two-thirds majority of the Senate).

Controversy over Congress's impeachment power has arisen over the grounds for impeachment, especially the meaning of "high Crimes and Misdemeanors." A strict reading of the Constitution suggests that the only impeachable offense is an actual crime. But a more common working definition is that "an impeachable offense is whatever the majority of the House of Representatives considers it to be at a given moment in history."[43] In other words, impeachment, especially impeachment of a president, is a political decision.

The political nature of impeachment was very clear in the two instances of presidential impeachment that have occurred in American history. In 1867, President Andrew Johnson, a southern Democrat who had battled a congressional Republican majority over Reconstruction, was impeached by the House but saved from conviction by one vote in the Senate. On December 19, 1998, the House of Representatives approved two articles of impeachment against President Bill Clinton, accusing him of lying under oath and obstructing justice during the investigation of his affair with White House intern Monica Lewinsky. The vote was highly partisan, with only five Democrats voting for impeachment on each charge. In the Senate, where a two-thirds majority was needed to convict the president, only 45 senators voted to convict on the first count of lying and 50 voted to convict on the second charge of obstructing justice. As in the House, the vote for impeachment was highly partisan, with all Democrats and only five Republicans supporting the president's ultimate acquittal.

Congress
and Your Future

When Congress is ineffective, American democracy suffers. As we have seen in this chapter, prolonged stalemates in Congress have led to a reduction in America's credit rating and a costly government shutdown. Moreover, Americans have lost confidence in Congress as it has lurched from crisis to crisis. Is it time for some major changes to make Congress work better? Disillusionment with congressional gridlock has led some to say that the United States should become a parliamentary system, where the winning party can enact the legislation it promised in its party platform. Such a system is more accountable to voters and less prone to stalemate.

But Americans would have to jettison the presidency and become a unicameral body to operate as a true parliamentary system, like that of Britain.

Short of such major institutional transformations, are there changes that would make Congress work better? One measure that might lead to more bipartisan agreement—the appointment of citizen commissions to reapportion congressional district lines—has been adopted in some states. If this practice became more widespread, it is possible that it would lead to election of more moderate candidates, making it easier to compromise in Congress. Changes in the way Congress conducts its business could also promote more bipartisan decision making. For example, former House Speaker John Boehner decided that he would only bring legislation to the floor if a majority of Republicans supported it. Boehner's successor, Paul Ryan, also vowed to follow the same practice. The "Hastert rule," as this practice is called, after former speaker Dennis Hastert, is not a formal rule of Congress but a norm that Boehner decided to implement. It is a practice that could easily be abandoned, allowing bipartisan majorities to enact legislation. Another significant change—eliminating the filibuster in the Senate—would heighten partisan differences but ease gridlock. As we have seen, the Senate voted to eliminate the filibuster for executive branch appointments and judicial candidates (except for the Supreme Court) in 2013. Abandoning the filibuster altogether would allow legislation to move more smoothly through the Senate. Will any of these changes—or other measures—be adopted? Each carries risks to political parties and to politicians. Yet, gridlock also carries political risks as the public grows frustrated with congressional inaction on important policy areas. How politicians weigh these different choices will shape how—and whether—Congress fills its central position in American democracy.

Gridlock and bitter disagreements in Congress turn some Americans off to politics. However, as the core representative institution of government, Congress is supposed to represent all Americans. As the **"Who Participates?"** feature on the facing page shows, the electorate that turns out to vote for Congress is on average older, whiter, and more affluent than the average American.

Who Elects Congress?

2014 Voters as Compared with U.S. Population

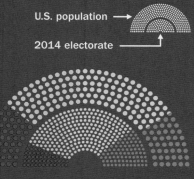

U.S. population →

2014 electorate →

Gender

	U.S. pop.	Electorate
Women	51%	51%
Men	49%	49%

Age

	U.S. pop.	Electorate
18–29	22%	13%
30–44	25%	22%
45–64	34%	43%
65+	19%	22%

Race

	U.S. pop.	Electorate
White	62%	75%
Black	13%	12%
Latino	17%	8%
Asian	5%	3%
Other	3%	3%

Income

	U.S. pop.	Electorate
Under $30k	52%	16%
$30–$50k	20%	20%
$50–$100k	20%	34%
$100–$200k	6%	23%
Over $200k	2%	7%

SOURCES: CNN House Exit Polls, www.cnn.com/election/2014/results
/race/house#exit-polls (accessed 9/29/15); Wage Statistics for 2014,
www.ssa.gov/cgi-bin/netcomp.cgi?year=2014 (accessed 10/22/15);
U.S. Census Bureau 2014 American Community Survey, www.census
.gov/programs-surveys/acs/data.html (accessed 10/22/15).

WHAT YOU CAN DO →

WHAT YOU CAN DO

Know Your Members of Congress

☑ Vote in the next congressional election. If you haven't registered, see page 24 for instructions on how to do so.

☑ Discover what bills are currently under consideration in Congress by visiting **www.congress.gov**.

☑ Contact your member of Congress to state your opinion. Go to **www.house.gov** and enter your ZIP code to find your representative. Go to **www.senate.gov** and find your state in the drop-down menu to find your two U.S. senators.

chapterstudyguide

Practice Quiz

1. Which of the following is a way in which the House and the Senate are different? *(pp. 275–76)*
   a) Senators are more interested in doing what their constituents want right now, while members of the House have more time to consider "new ideas" and bring together new coalitions of interests.
   b) Members of the House are more interested in doing what their constituents want right now, while senators have more time to consider "new ideas" and to bring together new coalitions of interests.
   c) Senators serve smaller and more homogenous constituencies than members of the House.

   d) Senators are often more attuned to the legislative needs of local interest groups than members of the House.
   e) There are no important differences between the House and the Senate.

2. Which type of representation is described when constituents have the power to hire and fire their representative? *(p. 276)*
   a) agency representation
   b) sociological representation
   c) philosophical representation
   d) ideological representation
   e) economic representation

3. Which of the following statements best describes the social composition of the U.S. Congress? *(pp. 276–78)*
   a) The majority of representatives do not have university degrees.
   b) Men and women are equally represented in Congress.
   c) Most members of Congress do not affiliate with any specific religion.
   d) The legal profession is the dominant career of most members of Congress prior to their election.
   e) The number of African American, Latino, and Asian American representatives has decreased over the last 20 years.

4. Which of the following is an advantage that incumbents have in winning re-election? *(pp. 280–81)*
   a) Challengers are not legally allowed to spend more money campaigning than incumbents.
   b) Incumbents can provide constituency services during their tenure in office.
   c) Term limits for incumbents mean they always know when an election will be their last.
   d) The Supreme Court has ruled that a district cannot be redrawn while an incumbent remains in office.
   e) Incumbents have no advantage over challengers in winning office.

5. The Supreme Court has ruled that
   a) congressional districts cannot be drawn in a way to favor the incumbent candidate. *(p. 283)*
   b) race can be the predominant factor in drawing congressional districts.
   c) race cannot be the predominant factor in drawing congressional districts.
   d) states can forgo the redistricting process if they lose more than 10 percent of their population between censuses.
   e) the use of computer technologies to draw congressional districts is unconstitutional.

6. An "earmark" is *(p. 284)*
   a) a rule in the House of Representatives that limits who can be heard during legislative debates.
   b) a congressional district drawn to advantage candidates from a certain racial or ethnic group.
   c) a law that grants some special privilege or exemption to a single individual.
   d) language inserted into a bill by a member of Congress that provides special benefits for the member of Congress's constituents.
   e) a weekly, informal meeting between members of Congress and their constituents.

7. Which of the following types of committees includes members of both the House and the Senate on the same committee? *(pp. 287–88)*
   a) standing committee
   b) conference committee
   c) select committee
   d) All committees include both House members and senators.
   e) No committees include both House members and senators.

8. Which of the following is a technique that can be used to block action on legislation in the Senate? *(p. 293)*
   a) filibuster
   b) conference committee
   c) roll-call voting
   d) cloture
   e) logrolling

9. Members of Congress take their constituents' views into account because *(pp. 295–96)*
   a) the Supreme Court can invalidate laws passed without majority support in the public.
   b) interest groups are forbidden from lobbying during legislative votes.
   c) most constituents pay close attention to what's going on in Congress at all times.
   d) they worry that their voting record will be scrutinized at election time.
   e) they can be impeached if they go against their constituents' policy preferences.

10. Which of the following is *not* a resource that party leaders in Congress use to create party discipline? *(pp. 298–300)*
    a) leadership PACs
    b) committee assignments
    c) access to the floor
    d) the whip system
    e) party unity votes

11. An agreement between members of Congress to trade support for each other's bills is known as *(p. 299)*
    a) oversight.
    b) filibuster.
    c) logrolling.
    d) patronage.
    e) cloture.

12. Congressional polarization *(p. 301)*
    a) has decreased since the mid-1970s.
    b) has increased since the mid-1970s.
    c) has remained the same since the mid-1970s.
    d) has been driven entirely by Democrats becoming more liberal since the mid-1970s.
    e) has not been measured since the mid-1970s.

13. When Congress conducts an investigation to explore the relationship between what a law intended and what an executive agency has done, it is engaged in *(p. 302)*
    a) oversight.
    b) advice and consent.
    c) appropriations.
    d) executive agreement.
    e) direct patronage.

14. Which of the following statements about impeachment is *not* true? *(p. 303)*
    a) The president is the only official who can be impeached by Congress.
    b) Impeachment means to charge a government official with "Treason, Bribery, or other high Crimes and Misdemeanors."
    c) The House of Representatives decides by simple majority vote whether the accused ought to be impeached.
    d) The Senate decides whether to convict and remove the person from office.
    e) There have only been two instances of presidential impeachment in American history.

Key Terms

agency representation *(p. 276)* a type of representation in which a representative is held accountable to a constituency if he or she fails to represent that constituency properly; this is incentive for the representative to provide good representation when his or her personal backgrounds, views, and interests differ from those of his or her constituency

apportionment *(p. 281)* the process, occurring after every decennial census, that allocates congressional seats among the 50 states

appropriations *(p. 302)* the amounts of money approved by Congress in statutes (bills) that each unit or agency of government can spend

bicameral *(p. 275)* having a legislative assembly composed of two chambers or houses; distinguished from *unicameral*

bill *(p. 291)* a proposed law that has been sponsored by a member of Congress and submitted to the clerk of the House or Senate

cloture *(p. 293)* a rule or process in a legislative body aimed at ending debate on a given bill; in the U.S. Senate, 60 senators (three-fifths) must agree in order to impose a time limit and end debate

conference *(p. 286)* a gathering of House Republicans every two years to elect their House leaders; Democrats call their gathering the *caucus*

conference committees *(p. 288)* joint committees created to work out a compromise cn House and Senate versions of a piece of legislation

constituency *(p. 275)* the residents in the area from which an official is elected

filibuster *(p. 293)* a tactic used by members of the Senate to prevent action on legislation they oppose by continuously holding the floor and speaking until the majority backs down; once given the floor, senators have unlimited time to speak, and it requires a vote of three-fifths of the Senate to end a filibuster

gerrymandering *(p. 282)* the apportionment of voters in districts in such a way as to give unfair advantage to one racial or ethnic group or political party

impeachment *(p. 303)* the formal charge by the House of Representatives that a government official has committed "Treason, Bribery, or other high Crimes and Misdemeanors"

incumbency *(p. 280)* holding the political office for which one is running

joint committees *(p. 288)* legislative committees formed of members of both the House and Senate

logrolling *(p. 299)* a legislative practice whereby agreements are made between legislators in voting for or against a bill; vote trading

majority leader *(p. 286)* the elected leader of the majority party in the House of Representatives or in the Senate; in the House, the majority leader is subordinate in the party hierarchy to the Speaker of the House

minority leader *(p. 287)* the elected leader of the minority party in the House or Senate

oversight *(p. 302)* the effort by Congress, through hearings, investigations, and other techniques, to exercise control over the activities of executive agencies

party unity vote *(p. 296)* a roll-call vote in the House or Senate in which at least 50 percent of the members of one party take a particular position and are opposed by at least 50 percent of the members of the other party

patronage *(p. 284)* the resources available to higher officials, usually opportunities to make partisan appointments to offices and to confer grants, licenses, or special favors to supporters

pocket veto *(p. 294)* a presidential veto that is automatically triggered if the president does not act on a given piece of legislation passed during the final 10 days of a legislative session

pork-barrel legislation (or pork) *(p. 284)* appropriations made by legislative bodies for local projects that are often not needed but that are created so that local representatives can win re-election in their home districts

private bill *(p. 286)* a proposal in Congress to provide a specific person with some kind of relief, such as a special exemption from immigration quotas

redistricting *(p. 282)* the process of redrawing election districts and redistributing legislative representatives; this happens every 10 years to reflect shifts in population or in response to legal challenges to existing districts

roll-call vote *(p. 296)* a vote in which each legislator's yes-or-no vote is recorded as the clerk calls the names of the members alphabetically

select committees *(p. 288)* (usually) temporary legislative committees set up to highlight or investigate a particular issue or address an issue not within the jurisdiction of existing committees

seniority *(p. 289)* the ranking given to an individual on the basis of length of continuous service on a committee in Congress

sociological representation *(p. 276)* a type of representation in which representatives have the same racial, gender, ethnic, religious, or educational backgrounds as their constituents. It is based on the principle that if two individuals are similar in background, character, interests, and perspectives, then one can correctly represent the other's views

Speaker of the House *(p. 286)* the chief presiding officer of the House of Representatives; the Speaker is the most important party and House leader and can influence the legislative agenda, the fate of individual pieces of legislation, and members' positions within the House

standing committee *(p. 287)* a permanent committee with the power to propose and write legislation that covers a particular subject, such as finance or agriculture

term limits *(p. 281)* legally prescribed limits on the number of terms an elected official can serve

veto *(p. 294)* the president's constitutional power to prevent a bill from becoming a law; a presidential veto may be overridden by a two-thirds vote of each house of Congress

whip *(p. 287)* a party member in the House or Senate responsible for coordinating the party's legislative strategy, building support for key issues, and counting votes

For Further Reading

Dodd, Lawrence, and Bruce I. Oppenheimer, eds. *Congress Reconsidered*. 10th ed. Washington, DC: CQ Press, 2012.

Dodson, Debra L. *The Impact of Women in Congress*. New York: Oxford University Press, 2006.

Fenno, Richard F. *Homestyle: House Members in Their Districts*. Boston: Little, Brown, 1978.

Fiorina, Morris. *Congress: Keystone of the Washington Establishment*. 2nd ed. New Haven, CT: Yale University Press, 1989.

Fisher, Louis. *On Appreciating Congress*. Boulder, CO: Paradigm Publishers, 2010.

Koger, Gregory. *Filibustering: A Political History of Obstruction in the House and Senate*. Chicago: University of Chicago Press, 2010.

Mann, Thomas E., and Norman J. Ornstein. *It's Even Worse Than It Looks: How the American Constitutional System Collided with the New Politics of Extremism*. New York: Basic Books, 2012.

Mayhew, David R. *Congress: The Electoral Connection*. New Haven, CT: Yale University Press, 1974.

Palmer, Barbara, and Denise Simon. *Breaking the Political Glass Ceiling: Women and Congressional Elections*. 2nd ed. New York: Routledge, 2008.

Sinclair, Barbara. *Unorthodox Lawmaking*. 4th ed. Washington, DC: CQ Press, 2012.

Smith, Steven S., and Christopher Deering. *Committees in Congress*. 3rd ed. Washington, DC: CQ Press, 1997.

Spitzer, Robert J. *President and Congress*. New York: McGraw-Hill, 1993.

Tate, Katherine. *Concordance: Black Lawmaking in the U.S. Congress from Carter to Obama*. Ann Arbor: University of Michigan Press, 2014.

When Donald Trump succeeded Barack Obama as president in 2017, he inherited numerous challenges, but also a presidency more powerful than the institution imagined by the Founders.

10

The Presidency

WHAT GOVERNMENT DOES AND WHY IT MATTERS By 2016, President Barack Obama could look back over his two terms in office and reasonably claim that he had achieved a number of the goals he had set for himself. Under the president's leadership, the nation's health care system had been significantly redesigned so that, beginning in 2014, health insurance was offered to 32 million previously uninsured Americans. With the president's signature in 2010, the Dodd-Frank Wall Street Reform and Consumer Protection Act imposed a major set of new regulations on the financial services sector, whose practices had been blamed for the "great recession" of 2008. The president ended the war in Iraq and brought most American troops home from Afghanistan. Terrorist mastermind Osama bin Laden was killed by U.S. special operations troops. And, in pitched battles with congressional Republicans, the president forced Congress to end the 2013 government shutdown, to agree to an increase in the national debt limit, to accept several of his most controversial judicial and executive branch nominees, and, in 2015, to enact a controversial nuclear weapons agreement with Iran.

Obama's successes reflect the considerable power of the contemporary presidency. But President Obama also suffered a number of significant setbacks and faced new questions about the propriety of the president's use of power. Despite throwing his full political weight behind popular new gun control legislation, Congress failed to act. His efforts to bring about immigration reform and increase the federal minimum wage were blunted. Some of the president's actions, such as the Iran agreement, which ended economic sanctions against Iran in exchange for an Iranian promise to slow the development of nuclear weapons, were criticized as an example of presidential overreach and a failure to fully consult Congress in matters of foreign policy. Even the president's health care triumph was dampened by the errors, mismanagement, and confusion surrounding the rollout of the program in 2014. Thus, despite Obama's efforts and notable policy successes, the president and the nation continued to confront major problems, including budget deficits, unemployment, failing schools, and challenges abroad, which would need to be addressed by the new president and new Congress elected in 2016.

President Obama's record of successes and failures is a reflection of the strengths and limits of the institution. Obama inherited a presidency considerably more powerful than the institution imagined by the framers of the U.S. Constitution. In this chapter, we will examine the foundations, powers, and limits of the presidency. Ironically, national emergencies present some of the biggest challenges to presidents but also have strengthened the office.

chaptergoals

- Outline the powers the Constitution gives the president (pp. 315–24)
- Identify the institutional resources presidents have to help them exercise their powers (pp. 324–28)
- Explain how modern presidents have become even more powerful (pp. 328–36)

● Presidential Power Is Rooted in the Constitution

Outline the powers the Constitution gives the president

The presidency was established by Article II of the Constitution, which begins by asserting "The executive power shall be vested in a President of the United States of America." The article goes on to describe the manner in which the president is to be chosen and defines the basic powers of the presidency. By vesting the executive power in a single president, the framers were emphatically rejecting proposals for various forms of collective leadership.

The presidential selection process defined by Article II resulted from a struggle between those delegates who wanted the president to be selected by, and thus responsible to, Congress and those who preferred that the president be elected directly by the people. Direct popular election would create a more independent and more powerful presidency. With the adoption of a scheme of indirect election through an electoral college, in which the electors would be selected by the state legislatures (and elections failing to produce an electoral college majority would be resolved in the House of Representatives), the framers hoped to achieve a "republican" solution: a strong president responsible to state and national legislators rather than directly to the electorate. This indirect method of electing the president probably did dampen the power of most presidents in the nineteenth century. This conclusion is supported by the fact that, as we shall see later in this chapter, presidential power increased as the president developed a closer and more direct relationship with a mass electorate.

The framers' idea that electors would be chosen by the state legislatures gave way during the nineteenth century to various systems of popular selection of the electors. This made the presidency a more democratic institution and made the president more directly responsible to the American people than to the states. Today, in 48 of the 50 states, the candidate who wins a state's popular vote wins

The election of the American president does not formally conclude on Election Day in November. In December, electors from each state cast their votes for president. The state electoral votes are then counted in January in the House of Representatives, which announces the victor.

all of that state's electoral college votes. The presidential candidate with a majority of votes in the electoral college—not necessarily the candidate with the most votes from the people—becomes president. The number of electors assigned to each state is equal to its number of representatives in the House and Senate; thus, small states are overrepresented in the electoral college. As a result, the electoral college system can sometimes distort the outcomes of presidential races when the electoral college vote totals are compared with the nationwide popular vote.

While Section 1 of Article II explains how the president is to be chosen, Sections 2 and 3 outline the powers and duties of the president. These two sections identify two sources of presidential power. Some presidential powers are specifically established by the language of the Constitution. For example, the Constitution authorizes the president to make treaties, grant pardons, and nominate judges and other public officials. These specifically defined powers granted to the president in the Constitution are called the **expressed powers** of the office and cannot be revoked by the Congress or any other agency without an amendment to the Constitution. Other expressed powers include the power to receive ambassadors and command of the military forces of the United States.

In addition to the president's expressed powers, Article II declares that the president "shall take Care that the Laws be faithfully executed." Since the laws are enacted by Congress, this language implies that Congress is to delegate to the president the power to implement or execute its will. Powers given to the president by Congress are called **delegated powers** (constitutional powers that are assigned to one governmental agency but that are exercised by another agency with the express permission of the first). In principle, Congress delegates to the president only the power the president needs to carry out congressional decisions. So, for example, if Congress determines that air quality should be improved, it might delegate to the executive branch the power to identify the best means of bringing about such an improvement and the power to implement the actual cleanup process. By delegating power to the executive branch, Congress substantially enhances the importance of the presidency. In most cases, Congress delegates power to executive agencies rather than to the president; but as we shall see, contemporary presidents have found ways to capture a good deal of this delegated power for themselves.

Expressed Powers Come Directly from the Words of the Constitution

The president's expressed powers, as defined by Sections 2 and 3 of Article II, fall into several categories:

1. *Military.* Article II, Section 2, provides for the power as "Commander in Chief of the Army and Navy of the United States, and of the Militia of the several States, when called into the actual Service of the United States."

2. *Judicial.* Article II, Section 2, also provides the power to "grant Reprieves and Pardons for Offenses against the United States, except in Cases of Impeachment."

3. *Diplomatic.* Article II, Section 2, also provides the power "by and with the Advice and Consent of the Senate, to make Treaties." Article II, Section 3, provides the power to "receive Ambassadors and other public Ministers."

4. *Executive.* Article II, Section 3, authorizes the president to see to it that all the laws are faithfully executed; Section 2 gives the chief executive the power to appoint, remove, and supervise all executive officers and to appoint all federal judges.

5. *Legislative.* Article I, Section 7, and Article II, Section 3, give the president the power to participate authoritatively in the legislative process.

Military The president's military powers are among the most important exercised by the chief executive. The position of **commander in chief** (the role of the president as commander of the national military and the state National Guard units when called into service) makes the president the highest military authority in the United States. Within the executive branch, the president directs the secretary of defense, who heads the vast Defense Department, encompassing all the military branches of service. The president also directs the nation's intelligence network, which includes not only the Central Intelligence Agency (CIA) but also the National Security Council (NSC), the National Security Agency (NSA), the Federal Bureau of Investigation (FBI), and a host of less well-known but very powerful international and domestic security agencies.

Military Sources of Domestic Power The president's military powers extend into the domestic sphere. Article IV, Section 4, provides that the "United States shall [protect] every State . . . against Invasion . . . and . . . domestic Violence," and Congress has made this an explicit presidential power through statutes directing the president as commander in chief to discharge these obligations.[1] The Constitution restrains the president's use of domestic force by providing that a state legislature (or governor, when the legislature is not in session) must request federal troops before the president can send them into the state to provide public order. Yet this proviso is not absolute. First, presidents are not obligated to deploy national troops merely because the state legislature or governor makes such a request. More important, the president may deploy troops in a state or city without a specific request from the state legislature or governor if the president considers it necessary to maintain an essential national service during an emergency, enforce a federal judicial order, or protect federally guaranteed civil rights.

One historic example of the unilateral use of presidential emergency power, even when the state didn't request it, was the decision by President Dwight Eisenhower in 1957 to send troops into Little Rock, Arkansas, against the wishes of the state of Arkansas, to enforce court orders to integrate Little Rock's Central High School. The governor of Arkansas, Orval Faubus, had actually posted the Arkansas National Guard at the entrance of Central High School to prevent the court-ordered admission of nine black students. After an effort to negotiate with Governor Faubus failed, President Eisenhower reluctantly sent 1,000 paratroopers to Little Rock, who stood watch while the black students took their places in the all-white classrooms.

Military emergencies have typically also led to expansion of the domestic powers of the executive branch. This was true during the First and Second World Wars and in the wake of the war on terrorism. Within a month of the

September 11 attacks, the White House had drafted and Congress had enacted the USA PATRIOT Act, expanding the power of government agencies to engage in domestic surveillance activities, including electronic surveillance, and restricting judicial review of such efforts. The act also gave the attorney general greater authority to detain and deport aliens suspected of having terrorist affiliations. The following year, Congress created the Department of Homeland Security, combining offices from 22 federal agencies into one huge new cabinet department responsible for protecting the nation from attack and responding to other emergencies. The White House drafted the actual reorganization plan, but Congress weighed in to make certain that the new agency's workers had civil service and union protections.

Judicial The presidential power to grant reprieves, pardons, and amnesty involves the power of life and death over all individuals who may be a threat to the security of the United States. Presidents may use this power on behalf of a particular individual, as did Gerald Ford when he pardoned Richard Nixon in 1974 "for all offenses against the United States which he . . . has committed or may have committed." Or they may use it on a large scale, as did President Andrew Johnson in 1868 when he gave full amnesty to all southerners who had participated in the "Late Rebellion," and President Jimmy Carter in 1977 when he declared an amnesty for all the draft evaders of the Vietnam War. President Bill Clinton created great controversy with a large number of last-minute pardons issued in the final days of his presidency in 2000. President George W. Bush, on the other hand, issued fewer pardons than any president in modern times.[2]

As the head of state, the president is America's chief representative in dealings with other countries. Here, President Obama meets with Cuban president Raúl Castro after restoring diplomatic relations with Cuba more than 50 years after Dwight D. Eisenhower had severed ties with the country.

Diplomatic The president is America's "head of state"—its chief representative in dealings with other nations. As head of state, the president has the power to make treaties for the United States (with the advice and consent of the Senate) as well as the power to "recognize" other countries. Diplomatic recognition means that the United States acknowledges a government's legitimacy and territorial claims. In 2015, President Obama restored American diplomatic ties with Cuba, which had been severed by President Eisenhower in 1961 after the United States' relations with the Castro regime deteriorated. The recognition power gives the president the almost unconditional authority to review the claims of any new ruling groups in order to determine if they indeed control the territory and population of their country so that they can commit it to treaties and other agreements.

In recent years, presidents have expanded the practice of using executive agreements instead of treaties to establish relations with other countries.[3] An **executive agreement** is exactly like a treaty because it is a contract between two countries that has the force of a treaty, but it does not require the Senate's "advice and consent." (Senate treaty approval requires a two-thirds vote.) Ordinarily, executive agreements are used to carry out commitments already made in treaties or laws or to arrange for matters well below the level of policy. But when presidents have found it expedient to use an executive agreement in place of a treaty, Congress has typically acquiesced.

Executive Power The most important basis of the president's power as chief executive is to be found in Article II, Section 3, which stipulates that the president must see that all the laws are faithfully executed, and Section 2, which provides that the president will appoint and supervise all executive officers and appoint all federal judges (with Senate approval; after some early controversy, presidents' sole power to remove executive branch officials was accepted). The power to appoint the principal executive officers and to require each of them to report to the president on subjects relating to the duties of their departments makes the president the true chief executive officer (CEO) of the nation. In this manner, the Constitution focuses executive power and legal responsibility on the president. The president is subject to some limitations because the appointment of all such officers, including ambassadors, ministers, and federal judges, is subject to majority approval by the Senate. But these appointments are at the discretion of the president, and these appointees are generally loyal to the president.

Legislative Power The president plays a role not only in the administration of government but also in the legislative process. Two constitutional provisions are the primary sources of the president's power in the legislative arena. The first of these is the provision in Article II, Section 3, that the president "shall from time to time give to the Congress Information of the State of the Union, and recommend to their Consideration such Measures as he shall judge necessary and expedient."

Delivering a State of the Union address may at first appear to be little more than the president's obligation to make recommendations for Congress's consideration. But as political and social conditions began to favor an increasingly prominent presidential role, each president, especially since Franklin Delano Roosevelt, began to rely on this provision in order to become the primary initiator of proposals for congressional action and the principal source for public awareness of national issues. Few today doubt that the president and the executive branch together are the primary source for many important congressional actions.[4]

The second of the president's legislative powers is the veto power assigned by Article I, Section 7.[5] The **veto** power is the president's constitutional power to prevent a bill from becoming a law (see Figure 10.1). It makes the president the single most important legislative leader.[6] No bill vetoed by the president can become law unless both the House and the Senate override the veto by a

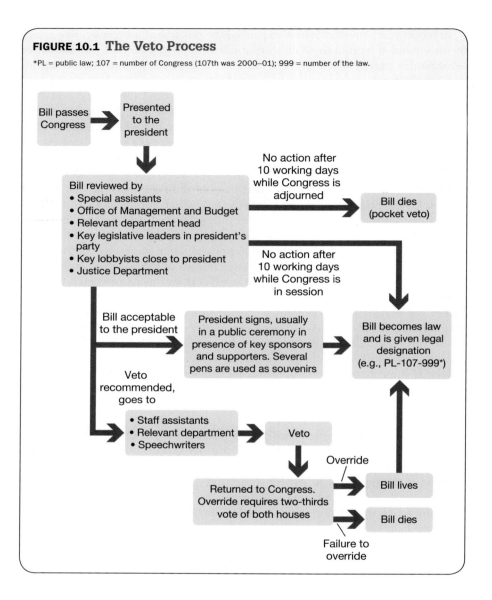

FIGURE 10.1 The Veto Process

*PL = public law; 107 = number of Congress (107th was 2000–01); 999 = number of the law.

Bill passes Congress → Presented to the president

Bill reviewed by
• Special assistants
• Office of Management and Budget
• Relevant department head
• Key legislative leaders in president's party
• Key lobbyists close to president
• Justice Department

No action after 10 working days while Congress is adjourned → Bill dies (pocket veto)

No action after 10 working days while Congress is in session

Bill acceptable to the president → President signs, usually in a public ceremony in presence of key sponsors and supporters. Several pens are used as souvenirs → Bill becomes law and is given legal designation (e.g., PL-107-999*)

Veto recommended, goes to
• Staff assistants
• Relevant department
• Speechwriters → Veto

Veto → Returned to Congress. Override requires two-thirds vote of both houses

Override → Bill lives

Failure to override → Bill dies

two-thirds vote. In the case of a **pocket veto**, Congress does not have the option of overriding the veto but must reintroduce the bill in the new Congress. A pocket veto is a presidential veto that is automatically triggered if the president does not act on a given piece of legislation passed during the final 10 days of a legislative session. Usually, if a president does not sign a bill within 10 days, it automatically becomes law. But this is true only while Congress is in session. If a president chooses not to sign a bill presented within the last 10 days of a legislative session and Congress is out of session when the 10-day limit expires such that returning the bill to Congress is not possible, the bill is vetoed and dies.

Use of the veto varies according to the political situation each president confronts. President George W. Bush vetoed only 12 bills in his eight-year presidency, the lowest per-year average of any president since the nineteenth century. Eleven of those vetoes came during his last two years in office, when the Democratic Party controlled both houses of Congress. Similarly, 10 of President Obama's 12 vetoes occurred during his last two years in office, when Republicans held the majority in both Houses. The veto power is effective: more than 90 percent of all vetoes in history have been upheld.

Although not explicitly stated, the Constitution implies that the president has the power of **legislative initiative**—the president's implied power to bring a legislative agenda before Congress. To "initiate" means to originate, and in government that can mean power. "Initiative" obviously suggests the ability to formulate proposals for important policies, and the president, as an individual with a great deal of staff assistance, is able to initiate decisive action more frequently than Congress, with its large assemblies that have to deliberate and debate before taking action. With some important exceptions, Congress depends on the president to set the agenda of public policy. For example, during the weeks following September 11, 2001, George W. Bush took many presidential initiatives to Congress, and each was given nearly unanimous support. President Obama made health care his chief domestic priority and engaged in sharp battles with congressional Republicans to win enactment of the Affordable Care Act in 2010 (known as "Obamacare").

The president's initiative does not end with congressional policy making and the making of laws in the ordinary sense of the term. The president has still another legislative role (in all but name) within the executive branch. This is the president's power to issue **executive orders** (sometimes in the form of presidential memoranda to the executive branch). The executive order is a rule or regulation issued by the president that has the effect and formal status of legislation, except that it is limited to the executive branch. It is first and foremost a normal tool of management, a power possessed by virtually any CEO to make "company policy": rules setting procedures, etiquette, chains of command, functional responsibilities, and so on. But evolving out of this normal management practice is a recognized presidential power to promulgate rules governing the executive branch that have the force of law. Most of the executive orders of the president provide for the reorganization of structures and procedures or otherwise direct the affairs of the executive branch. For example, President Obama signed an executive order in January 2016 aimed at reducing gun violence, including plans to extend background checks and improve mental health services. Executive orders can also establish new agencies, as with President Nixon's order in 1970–71 establishing the Environmental Protection Agency.

Delegated Powers Come from Congress

Many of the powers exercised by the president and the executive branch are not found in the Constitution but are the products of congressional statutes (laws) and resolutions. Over the past century, Congress has voluntarily delegated a great deal of its own legislative authority to the executive branch. This delegation of

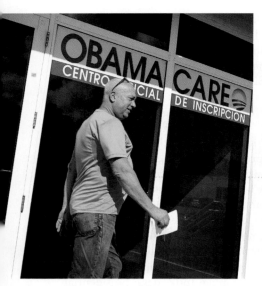

power has been an almost inescapable consequence of the expansion of government activity in the United States since the New Deal. Given the vast range of the federal government's responsibilities, Congress cannot execute and administer all the programs it creates and the laws it enacts. Inevitably, Congress must turn to the hundreds of departments and agencies in the executive branch or, when necessary, create new agencies to implement its goals. Thus, for example, in 2002, when Congress sought to protect America from terrorist attacks, it established the Department of Homeland Security with broad powers in the realms of law enforcement, public health, and immigration.

The influence of the president and the executive branch is widespread as the executive is responsible for the implementation of many laws that Congress passes. The executive branch orchestrated the health insurance enrollment process for millions of Americans under the Affordable Care Act.

Modern Presidents Have Claimed Inherent Powers

Presidents have claimed a third source of power beyond expressed and delegated powers. These are powers not specified in the Constitution or the law but "powers over and beyond those expressly granted in the Constitution or reasonably to be implied from express grants."[7] These powers are referred to as the **inherent powers** of the presidency and have been asserted by recent presidents in times of war or national emergency. Yet not all powerful presidents claimed inherent powers.

For example, after the outbreak of the Civil War in 1861, President Abraham Lincoln issued a series of executive orders for which he had no clear legal basis. Without Congress in session, Lincoln combined the state militias into a 90-day national volunteer force, called for 40,000 new volunteers, enlarged the regular army and navy, diverted $2 million in unspent appropriations to military needs, instituted censorship of the U.S. mail, ordered a blockade of southern ports, suspended the writ of habeas corpus in the border states, and ordered the arrest by military police of individuals whom he deemed to be guilty of engaging in or even just contemplating treasonous actions.[8] Lincoln asserted that these extraordinary measures were necessary to confront this crisis. When Congress convened in July, he reported his actions to it, saying that they could only be legal if Congress passed a law making them so, which it did. Even though Lincoln never claimed inherent powers, his example was used by later presidents as justification, including George W. Bush in the wake of the September 11 terror attacks.[9]

When North Korean forces invaded South Korea in June 1950, Congress was actually prepared to declare war, but President Harry S. Truman decided not to

Executive Branches in Comparison

All democracies have an executive branch, but the specific form it takes varies. In presidential systems, such as the United States, the position of the *head of state* (the symbolic leader of a country) and the *head of government* (the leader in charge of the day-to-day running of the government) is combined into one position—the president. In parliamentary systems, these roles are often held by different people, with the head of government being the more powerful position. For example, in Germany, the head of government is the prime minister (called the chancellor), while the head of state is the president, who plays a largely ceremonial role similar to the United Kingdom's queen.

Most democracies use parliamentary executive systems, though presidential systems are common in the Americas, in part due to the historical influence of the United States. A small but growing group of countries use a hybrid "semi-presidential" system. France, for instance, divides the executive between a powerful head of state (the president) and the head of government (the prime minister), who have different but (theoretically) equal powers.

	Presidential	Parliamentary
Examples	United States, Mexico, Brazil	United Kingdom, India, Germany, Japan
Executive title	President	Prime Minister, Chancellor, etc.
Is the executive the...		
Head of state?	Yes	No
Head of government?	Yes	Yes
Executive elected by...	voters*	parliament
Term in office	Fixed by law	Subject to support of the parliament
Separation of powers	Yes	No; the PM is a member of the parliament
Executive role in legislating	Veto power	Initiates most bills

*In the United States, the president is elected by the Electoral College, not by the voters directly. Other presidential systems have the voters directly elect the president.

ask for congressional action. Instead, Truman asserted the principle that the president and not Congress could decide when and where to deploy America's military might. Truman dispatched American forces to Korea without a congressional declaration, and in the face of the emergency, Congress felt it had to acquiesce and approved money to finance the conflict. This became the pattern for future congressional-executive relations in the military realm: the wars in Vietnam, Bosnia, Afghanistan, and Iraq, as well as a host of lesser conflicts, were all fought without formal declarations of war.

In 1973, Congress responded during the Vietnam War to presidential unilateralism by passing the **War Powers Resolution** over President Richard Nixon's veto. This law states that the president can send troops into action abroad only by authorization of Congress or if American troops are already under attack or serious threat. It reasserted the principle of congressional war power, required the president to inform Congress of any planned military campaign, and stipulated that forces must be withdrawn within 60 days unless Congress acts to extend military action. Presidents, however, have often ignored the War Powers Resolution, claiming inherent executive power to defend the nation.

President George W. Bush responded to the 2001 attacks by Islamist terrorists by organizing a major military campaign to overthrow the Taliban regime in Afghanistan, which had sheltered the terrorists. In 2003, Bush ordered the invasion of Iraq, which he accused of posing a threat to the United States. In both instances, Congress passed resolutions approving the president's actions beforehand, but the president was careful to assert that he did not need congressional authorization. President Obama, for his part, made frequent use of special operations forces and unmanned aerial vehicles (or drones) to conduct military operations, and Congress was not consulted. Thus, in 2015, members of Congress and other Americans learned of drone strikes against leaders of the terrorist group the Islamic State of Iraq and Syria (ISIS) only as the strikes were being reported by the media.

● Institutional Resources of Presidential Power Are Numerous

Identify the institutional resources presidents have to help them exercise their powers

Constitutional sources of power are not the only resources available to the president. Presidents have at their disposal a variety of other formal and informal resources that have important implications for their ability to govern (see Figure 10.2). Indeed, without these other resources, presidents would lack the ability—the tools of management and public mobilization—to make much use of the power and responsibility given to them by Congress. Let us first consider the president's formal institutional resources and then, in the section following, turn to the more informal political resources that affect a president's capacity to govern, in particular the president's base of popular support.

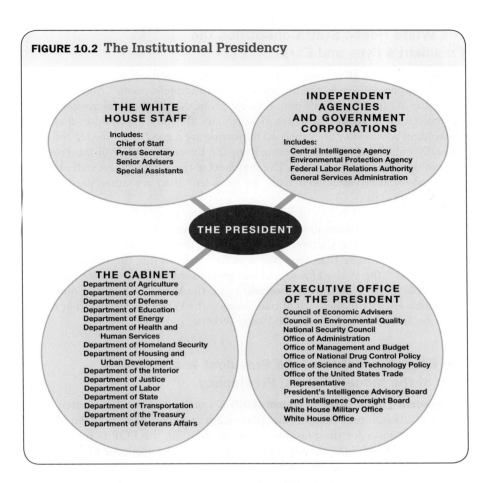

FIGURE 10.2 The Institutional Presidency

THE WHITE HOUSE STAFF

Includes:
- Chief of Staff
- Press Secretary
- Senior Advisers
- Special Assistants

INDEPENDENT AGENCIES AND GOVERNMENT CORPORATIONS

Includes:
- Central Intelligence Agency
- Environmental Protection Agency
- Federal Labor Relations Authority
- General Services Administration

THE PRESIDENT

THE CABINET

Department of Agriculture
Department of Commerce
Department of Defense
Department of Education
Department of Energy
Department of Health and
    Human Services
Department of Homeland Security
Department of Housing and
    Urban Development
Department of the Interior
Department of Justice
Department of Labor
Department of State
Department of Transportation
Department of the Treasury
Department of Veterans Affairs

EXECUTIVE OFFICE OF THE PRESIDENT

Council of Economic Advisers
Council on Environmental Quality
National Security Council
Office of Administration
Office of Management and Budget
Office of National Drug Control Policy
Office of Science and Technology Policy
Office of the United States Trade
    Representative
President's Intelligence Advisory Board
    and Intelligence Oversight Board
White House Military Office
White House Office

The Cabinet Is Often Distant from the President

In the American system of government, the **Cabinet** is the traditional but informal designation for the heads (secretaries, or chief administrators) of all the major federal government departments. Cabinet secretaries are appointed by the president with the consent of the Senate. The Cabinet has no constitutional status. Unlike in Great Britain and many other parliamentary countries, where the cabinet *is* the government, the American Cabinet meets but makes no decisions as a group. The Senate must approve each appointment, but Cabinet members are responsible to the president, not to the Senate or to Congress at large. Since Cabinet appointees generally have not shared political careers with the president or one another and since they may meet literally for the first time only after their selection, the formation of an effective governing group out of this diverse collection of appointments is highly unlikely.

The White House Staff Constitutes the President's Eyes and Ears

The **White House staff** is composed mainly of analysts and advisers who are closest to, and most responsive to, the president's needs and preferences.[10] Although many of the top White House staff members are given the title "special assistant" for a particular task or sector, the types of judgments they are expected to make and the kinds of advice they are supposed to provide are a good deal broader and more generally political than those coming from the Executive Office of the President or from the cabinet departments. The members of the White House staff also tend to be more closely associated with the president than are other presidentially appointed officials.

From an informal group of fewer than a dozen people (popularly called the **Kitchen Cabinet**—advisers to whom the president turns for counsel and guidance; members of the official Cabinet may or may not also be members of the Kitchen Cabinet) and no more than four dozen at its height during the Roosevelt presidency in 1937, the White House staff has grown substantially.[11] Nixon employed 550 people in 1972. In Obama's second term, the White House staff numbered approximately 450. In the spirit of transparency, the White House lists their names, positions, and salaries on the White House website.

The Executive Office of the President Is a Visible Sign of the Modern Strong Presidency

The **Executive Office of the President (EOP)** is a major part of what is often called the "institutional presidency"—the permanent agencies that perform defined management tasks for the president. Created in 1939, the EOP is composed of between 1,500 and 2,000 highly specialized people who work for EOP agencies. The most important and largest EOP agency is the Office of Management and Budget (OMB). Its roles in preparing the national budget, designing the president's program, reporting on agency activities, and overseeing regulatory proposals make OMB personnel part of virtually every conceivable presidential responsibility. The status and power of the OMB have grown in importance with each successive president. The process of budgeting at one time was a "bottom-up" procedure, with expenditure and program requests passing from the lowest bureaus through the departments to "clearance" in the OMB and hence to Congress, where each agency could be called in to reveal what its "original request" was before the OMB revised it. Now the budgeting process is "top-down": the OMB sets priorities for agencies as well as for Congress.

The staff of the Council of Economic Advisers (CEA) constantly analyzes the economy and economic trends and attempts to give the president the ability to anticipate events rather than waiting for and reacting to them. The Council on Environmental Quality was designed to do for environmental issues what the CEA does for economic issues. The NSC is composed of designated cabinet officials and others spanning military, diplomatic, and intelligence areas who meet regularly with the president to give advice on national security matters. Other EOP agencies perform more specialized tasks.

The Vice Presidency Has Become More Important since the 1970s

The vice presidency is a constitutional anomaly even though the Constitution created the office along with the presidency. The vice president exists for two purposes only: to succeed the president in case of death, resignation, or incapacity and to preside over the Senate, casting a tie-breaking vote when necessary.[12]

The main value of the vice president as a political resource for the president is electoral. Traditionally, presidential candidates choose running mates who can win the support of at least one state (preferably a large one) not otherwise likely to support the ticket. It is very doubtful that John Kennedy would have won in 1960 without his vice-presidential candidate, Texan Lyndon Johnson, and the contribution Johnson made to winning his home state. Another rule holds that the vice-presidential nominee should provide some regional balance and, wherever possible, some balance among various ideological or ethnic subsections of the party. In 2016, Donald Trump chose Governor Mike Pence of Indiana as his running mate for a number of reasons. First, Indiana is a state Trump had to carry to win the election. Second, Pence, a former host of conservative radio and television talk shows, was well known among conservatives. His radio and television background also meant that Pence was an experienced public speaker. Third, Pence served in Congress for 12 years. He worked to reassure skeptical party leaders that Trump was a qualified candidate. Fourth and most important, Pence is a devout Christian who is very well regarded by social conservatives.

As the institutional presidency has grown in size and complexity, most presidents of the past 25 years have sought to use their vice presidents as a management resource after the election. President George W. Bush granted unprecedented power and responsibility to his vice president, Dick Cheney, who helped shape the "war on terror." In the Obama White House, Vice President Joe Biden was said to be regarded as the "skeptic-in-chief."[13] Biden's role was to question and criticize policy recommendations made to the president until, of course, the president made a decision, at which point the vice president fell loyally in step.

The First Spouse Has Become Important to Policy

The president serves as both chief executive and chief of state—the equivalent of Great Britain's prime minister and monarch rolled into one, simultaneously leading the government and representing the nation at official ceremonies and functions.

Because they are generally associated with the head-of-state aspect of America's presidency, presidential spouses are usually not subject to the same degree of media scrutiny or partisan attack as the president. Traditionally, most first ladies have limited their activities to the ceremonial portion of the presidency. First ladies greet foreign dignitaries, visit other countries, and attend important national ceremonies.

Some first spouses, however, have had considerable influence over policy. Franklin Roosevelt's wife, Eleanor, was widely popular but also widely criticized for her active role in many elements of her husband's presidency. During the 1992 campaign, Bill Clinton often implied that his wife would be active in the administration; he joked that voters would get "two for the price of one." After the election, Hillary Clinton took a leading role in many policy areas, most notably

Mike Pence is devoutly Christian and socially conservative. He helped improve Donald Trump's electoral appeal among social conservatives and establishment Republicans.

heading the administration's health care reform effort. She also became the first first lady to win public office on her own, winning a seat in the U.S. Senate from New York in 2000. She also ran for the presidency in 2008 and 2016, having served as Barack Obama's secretary of state from 2009 to 2013. Melania Trump is the first foreign-born first lady in almost 200 years. With no political or public affairs experience, Mrs. Trump said that she would be a traditional first lady. Given the current expectation that the first spouse should assume some public responsibility, however, Mrs. Trump seems likely to take on some visible role in the Trump administration.

● Party, Popular Mobilization, and Administration Make Presidents Stronger

Explain how modern presidents have become even more powerful

During the nineteenth century, Congress was America's dominant institution of government, and members of Congress sometimes treated the president with disdain. Today, however, no one would assert that the presidency is unimportant. Presidents seek to dominate the policy-making process and claim the inherent power to lead the nation in time of war. The expansion of presidential power over the course of the past century has come about not by accident but as the result of an ongoing effort by successive presidents to enlarge the powers of the office.

Generally, presidents can expand their power in two ways: through popular mobilization and through the administration. First, presidents may use popular appeals to create a mass base of support that will allow them to dominate their political foes, a tactic called "going public."[14] Second, presidents may seek to bolster their control of established executive agencies or to create new administrative institutions and procedures that will reduce their dependence on Congress and give them a more independent governing and policy-making capability. Perhaps the most obvious example of this is the use of executive orders to achieve policy goals in lieu of seeking to persuade Congress to enact legislation.

Presidents do have a third possible tool: their political party. Each president has relied on his own party to implement his legislative agenda. In 2015, for example, President Obama relied on congressional Democrats to prevent rejection of his agreement with Iran to limit its nuclear program in the face of virtually unanimous Republican opposition. However, the president does not control his party; party members have considerable autonomy. Moreover, in America's system of separated powers, the president's party may be in the minority in Congress and unable to do much for the chief executive's programs. Consequently, although their party is valuable to chief executives, it has not been a fully reliable presidential tool. As a result, contemporary presidents are more likely to use the two other methods, popular mobilization and executive administration, to achieve their political goals.

Going Public Means Trying to Whip Up the People

During the nineteenth century, it was considered inappropriate for presidents to engage in personal campaigning on their own behalf or in support of programs and policies. When Andrew Johnson broke this unwritten rule and made a series of speeches vehemently seeking public support for his Reconstruction program, even some of Johnson's most ardent supporters were shocked at what they saw as his lack of decorum and dignity. The president's opponents cited his "inflammatory" speeches in one of the articles of impeachment drafted by the Congress pursuant to the first impeachment trial of a president in history.[15]

In the twentieth century, though, popular mobilization became a favored weapon in the political arsenals of most presidents. Among modern presidents, the one who used public appeals most effectively was Franklin Delano Roosevelt (FDR). FDR was "firmly persuaded of the need to form a direct link between the executive office and the public."[16] He developed a number of tactics aimed at forging such a link. He made important use of the new electronic medium, the radio, to reach millions of Americans. In his famous "fireside chats," the president, or at least his voice, came into every living room in the country to discuss programs and policies and generally to assure Americans that he was aware of their difficulties and working diligently toward solutions.

President Franklin Delano Roosevelt's direct appeals to the American people allowed him to "reach over the heads" of congressional opponents and force them to follow his lead because their constituents demanded it.

FDR was also an innovator in the realm of what is now called press relations. When he entered the White House, FDR faced a mainly hostile press typically controlled by conservative members of the business establishment. As the president wrote, "All the fat-cat newspapers—85 percent of the whole—have been utterly opposed to everything the Administration is seeking."[17] FDR hoped to use the press to mold public opinion, but to do so he needed to circumvent the editors and publishers who were generally unsympathetic to his goals. To this end, he worked to cultivate the reporters who covered the White House. FDR made himself available for biweekly press conferences, where he offered candid answers to reporters' questions and made certain to make important policy announcements that would provide the reporters with significant stories for their papers.[18]

Every president since FDR has sought to craft a public-relations strategy that would emphasize the incumbent's strengths and maximize his popular appeal. For John F. Kennedy, handsome and quick-witted, the televised press conference was an excellent public-relations vehicle. Both Bill Clinton and Barack Obama made extensive use of televised town meetings—carefully staged events that gave the presidents an opportunity to appear to consult with rank-and-file citizens about goals and policies without having to face pointed questions preferred by reporters. President Obama was a talented and effective speaker who often relied on his own speaking abilities rather than material crafted by the Communications Office.

Going Public Online President Obama was also the first to make full use of another communication medium—the Internet. Drawing on the interactive tools of the Web, Obama's 2008 and 2012 campaigns changed the way politicians organize supporters, advertise to voters, defend against attacks, and communicate with their constituents.[19] Donald Trump's and Hillary Clinton's presidential campaigns in 2016 followed his example. Trump and Clinton made particular use of Twitter to communicate with millions of voters, bypassing traditional media.

The Internet has changed not only the way modern presidents campaign but also how they govern. The Whitehouse.gov website keeps the president's constituents abreast of his policy agenda with a weekly streaming video address by the president, press briefings, speeches and remarks, a daily blog, photos of the president, the White House schedule, and other information. Virtually everything the president does is recorded online. YouTube aired Obama's press conferences and public appearances on a daily basis. Every presidential address is now streamed live online.

Circumventing television and other traditional media, the Internet allows the president to reach citizens directly. In 2014, Obama broke new media ground again, appearing on the comic website Funny or Die's program *Between Two Ferns*, where he was interviewed by comic actor Zach Galifianakis. Obama's purpose was to reach out to uninsured young people to prod them to sign up for medical insurance. Obama's Facebook page offered another way to reach his constituents and the causes they care about, and as of July 2016, Obama's Twitter page had 76 million followers. These new media forums facilitate direct communication between the president and the people, creating a virtual network of constituents. Like FDR in the 1930s and '40s and Kennedy in the 1960s, Obama may have changed how future presidents govern.

The Limits of Going Public Some presidents have been able to make effective use of popular appeals to overcome congressional opposition. Popular support, though, has not been a firm foundation for presidential power. The public is notoriously fickle. President George W. Bush maintained an approval rating of over 70 percent for more than a year following the September 11, 2001, terrorist attacks. By the end of 2005, however, Bush's approval rating had dropped to 39 percent as a result of the growing unpopularity of the Iraq War, the administration's inept handling of hurricane relief, and several White House scandals, including the conviction of Vice President Cheney's chief of staff on charges of lying to a federal grand jury. Between the time President Obama took office in 2009 and May 2016, his public approval ranged from a high of 76 percent in January 2009 to a low of 36 percent in the fall of 2014.[20] Such declines in popular approval during a president's term in office are nearly inevitable and follow a predictable pattern.[21] Presidents generate popular support by promising to undertake important programs that will contribute directly to the well-being of large numbers of Americans. Almost without exception, presidential performance falls short of promises and popular expectations, leading to a decline in public support and the ensuing weakening of presidential influence.[22] It is a rare American president, such as Bill Clinton, who exits the White House more popular than when he went in.

The Administrative Strategy Increases Presidential Control

Contemporary presidents have increased the administrative capabilities of their office in four ways. First, they have enhanced the reach and power of the EOP. Second, they have sought to increase White House control over the federal bureaucracy. Third, they have expanded the role of executive orders. Fourth, they have made frequent use of signing statements and other instruments of direct presidential governance. Taken together, these four components of what might be called the White House "administrative strategy" have given presidents a capacity to achieve their programmatic and policy goals even when they are unable to secure congressional approval. Indeed, some recent presidents have been able to accomplish a great deal with remarkably little congressional, partisan, or even public support.

The Executive Office of the President The EOP has grown from six administrative assistants in 1939 to today's several hundred employees working directly for the president in the White House office along with some 2,500 individuals staffing the divisions of the Executive Office.[23] The creation and growth of the White House staff give the president an enormously enhanced capacity to gather information, plan programs and strategies, communicate with constituencies, and exercise supervision over the executive branch. The staff multiplies the president's eyes, ears, and arms, becoming a critical instrument of presidential power.[24]

In particular, the OMB serves as a potential instrument of presidential control over federal spending and hence a mechanism through which the White House has greatly expanded its power. In addition to its power over the federal budget process (discussed earlier), the OMB has the capacity to analyze and approve all legislative proposals, not only budgetary requests, emanating from all federal agencies before they are submitted to Congress. This procedure, now a matter of routine, greatly enhances the president's control over the entire executive branch. All legislation originating in the White House and all executive orders also go through the OMB.[25] Thus, through one White House agency, the president has the means to exert major influence over the flow of money and the shape and content of national legislation.

Regulatory Review A second tactic that presidents have used to increase their power and reach is the process of regulatory review, through which they have sought to seize control of rule making by the agencies of the executive branch (see also Chapter 11). Whenever Congress enacts a statute, the statute's actual implementation requires the promulgation of hundreds of rules by the agency charged with administering the law and giving effect to the will of Congress. Some congressional statutes are quite detailed and leave agencies with relatively little discretion. Typically, however, Congress enacts a relatively broad statement of legislative intent and delegates to the appropriate administrative agency the power to fill in many important details.[26] In other words, Congress typically says to an administrative agency, "Here is the problem: deal with it."[27]

The discretion Congress delegates to administrative agencies has provided recent presidents with an important avenue for expanding their own power. During his administration, President Clinton issued 107 directives to administrators ordering them to propose specific rules and regulations. In some instances, the language of the rule to be proposed was drafted by the White House staff; in other cases, the president asserted a priority but left it to the agency to draft the precise language of the proposal. President George W. Bush continued the Clinton-era practice of issuing presidential directives to agencies to spur them to issue new rules and regulations. Obama's first regulatory director, Cass Sunstein, not only issued a number of major regulatory directives to federal agencies but also launched a "look back" program. Under this program, the administration sought to eliminate several hundred existing rules it deemed obsolete.[28] In 2015, Obama sought new regulations governing power plant emissions, overtime pay for workers, the educational practices of career (for-profit) colleges, and a host of other matters.

Governing by Decree: Executive Orders Another mechanism through which contemporary presidents have sought to enhance their power to govern unilaterally is the use of executive orders and other forms of presidential decrees, including executive agreements, memoranda, national security findings and directives, proclamations, reorganization plans, signing statements, and a host of other tools.[29] Executive orders have a long history in the United States and have been the vehicles for a number of important government policies, including the purchase of Louisiana, the annexation of Texas, the emancipation of the slaves, the internment of people of Japanese descent, the desegregation of the military, the initiation of affirmative action, and the creation of important federal agencies, among them the Environmental Protection Agency, the Food and Drug Administration, and the Peace Corps.[30]

Presidents may not use executive orders to issue whatever commands they please. The use of such decrees is bound by law. If a president issues an executive order, proclamation, directive, or the like, in principle he does so pursuant to the powers granted to him by the Constitution or delegated to him by Congress, usually through a statute. When presidents issue such orders, they generally state the constitutional or statutory basis for their actions. For example, when President

Truman ordered the desegregation of the armed services, he did so pursuant to his constitutional powers as commander in chief. Where an executive order has no statutory or constitutional basis, the courts have held it to be void.[31]

President George W. Bush did not hesitate to use executive orders, issuing nearly 300 during his two terms. During his first months in office, Bush issued orders prohibiting the use of federal funds to support international family planning groups that provided abortion counseling services and limiting the use of embryonic stem cells in federally funded research projects. Throughout his administration, Bush made very aggressive use of executive orders in response to the threat of terrorism. In November 2001, for example, he issued a directive authorizing the creation of military tribunals to try noncitizens accused of involvement in acts of terrorism against the United States. In the first seven years of his presidency, Barack Obama issued 242 executive orders and 219 presidential memoranda, using some of them to reverse executive orders of his predecessor (just as Bush reversed some of those of the Clinton years). Obama's executive orders authorized stem cell research, restored funding for international family planning organizations, opened access to presidential papers, enhanced federal gun regulations, and barred improper interrogation methods of detainees captured by the United States.[32] In 2014, Obama issued executive orders that would protect some 4 million undocumented immigrants from the threat of deportation. These orders provoked an outcry form congressional Republicans, and in 2016, the eight-member Supreme Court (in the wake of Justice Antonin Scalia's death) divided 4–4 on the case.[33] The tie left intact a lower court ruling blocking the order within its own jurisdiction but not invalidating the order itself.

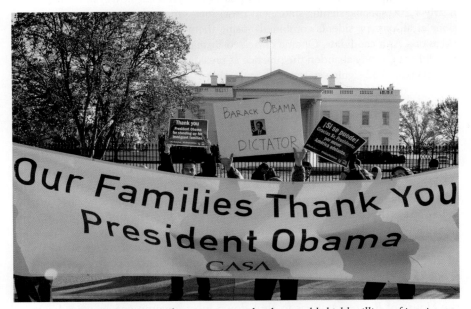

In 2014, President Obama issued an executive order that would shield millions of immigrants from deportation. In 2016 the validity of Obama's order was called into question when the Supreme Court split 4–4 over a lower court decision against the president.

Signing Statements To negate congressional actions to which they object, recent presidents have made frequent and calculated use of presidential **signing statements**.[34] The signing statement is an announcement made by the president at the time of signing a congressional enactment into law, often presenting the president's interpretation of the law in addition to the usually innocuous remarks about the many benefits the law will bring the nation. Occasionally presidents have used signing statements to point to sections of the law they deem improper or even unconstitutional and to instruct executive branch agencies how to execute the law.[35] In 2013, for example, President Obama signed a bill containing a provision requiring the president to notify Congress before transferring any prisoner from Guantánamo Bay. In his signing statement, Obama declared that the provision was unconstitutional; and in 2014 he failed to notify Congress when he exchanged five Guantánamo prisoners for an American being held in Afghanistan.

Presidents have made signing statements throughout American history, though many were not recorded and did not become part of the official legislative record. Ronald Reagan's attorney general, Edwin Meese, is generally credited with transforming the signing statement into a significant tool of presidential direct action.[36]

With the way paved, Reagan and his successors proceeded to use detailed and artfully designed signing statements (prepared by the Department of Justice) to attempt to reinterpret congressional enactments. For example, when signing the Safe Drinking Water Act Amendments of 1986, Reagan issued a statement that interpreted sections of the act to allow discretionary enforcement when the Congress seemed to call for mandatory enforcement.[37] Reagan hoped the courts would accept his version of the statute when examining subsequent enforcement decisions. In other cases, Reagan used his signing statements to attempt to nullify portions of statutes. George W. Bush issued 161 signing statements. Within these 161 statements, however, Bush inserted nearly 1,200 specific signing statement provisions—more than twice as many provisions as all past presidents combined—using them to rewrite the law on numerous occasions. As a candidate, Obama criticized Bush's prolific use of signing statements but did not entirely abandon the practice as president. In his first seven years in office, Obama issued 32 signing statements containing 102 specific provisions.[38]

Presidential Power Has Limits

Though the "administrative strategy" has provided presidents with a host of new powers, presidents are not dictators or kings. The president is limited in the implementation of his legislative agenda by the party in control of the House and Senate. As Figure 10.3 shows, presidential success on congressional votes is much higher when his party is in the majority in Congress. In periods of divided government, when one or both houses of Congress are controlled by the opposition party, the president has much more difficulty implementing his agenda.

The president's power is also limited by the congressional power of the purse. In 2011 and again in 2013, Congress demonstrated that its control over federal spending and borrowing papers could force the president to pay attention to the legislative branch. In the budget battle of 2013, Republicans used their control of the House of Representatives to shut down most government agencies for more than two weeks until a budgetary compromise was reached.

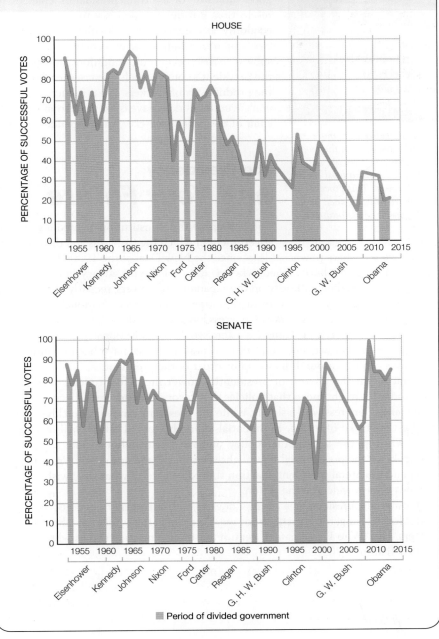

FIGURE 10.3 Presidential Success on Congressional Votes, 1953–2013*

Presidents have more success in Congress when their party is in the majority. Can you identify the periods when presidents had majority support in Congress and when they did not?

*Percentages based on votes on which presidents took a position.
SOURCE: Congressional Quarterly, http://media.cq.com/votestudies (accessed 3/17/14).

HOUSE

SENATE

■ Period of divided government

Because of the Federal Government SHUTDOWN, All National Parks Are CLOSED.

While presidents are more powerful today than they were 200 years ago, they are still subject to constitutional checks and balances. This process can lead to frustration, such as the 2013 government shutdown.

Another area in which the president has limited influence is the overall state of the national economy. The public frequently blames or rewards the president for economic performance; the Consumer Confidence Index, a measure of how optimistic consumers are about the future of the economy, is a very good indicator of a sitting president's chances for re-election. But the president's actual impact on the economy is limited. Unemployment and inflation, two important indicators of economic health, are subject to macroeconomic conditions largely outside the president's control, such as consumer demand or the productivity of workers. What influence the federal government does have is exercised mainly by the chair of the Federal Reserve, an independent agency.

The Presidency
and Your Future

The framers of the Constitution created a system of government in which the Congress and the executive branch were to share power. At least since the New Deal of the 1930s, however, the powers of Congress have waned, whereas those of the presidency have expanded. Louis Fisher, a leading authority on the separation of powers, recently observed that in what are arguably the two most important policy arenas, national defense and the federal budget, the powers of Congress have been in decline for at least the past 50 years.[39] The last time Congress exercised its constitutional power to declare war was 1942, and yet, since that time, American forces have been committed to numerous conflicts around the world by order of the president.

What might the growth of presidential power mean for students reading this book today? It might mean that policies they favor can more easily become the law of the land. Congress works slowly, while the president can work quickly—making law by the stroke of a pen. Presidential strength works both ways, however: for those who oppose a particular policy or have qualms about some aspect of it, the stroke of the presidential pen might seem hasty and autocratic. Proponents of quick and unilateral presidential action should be careful what they wish for. They may not always welcome the action.

A powerful presidency, a weak Congress, and a partially apathetic electorate make for a dangerous mix. Who we vote into the office of the president matters. The "**Who Participates?**" feature on the facing page shows who voted for Donald Trump in 2016.

Who Voted for Donald Trump in 2016?

Age

37% 55%	42% 50%	53% 44%	53% 45%
18–29	30–44	45–64	65+

Race

58% 37%	8% 88%	29% 65%
White	African American	Hispanic

29% 65%	37% 56%
Asian American	Other

Income

41% 52%	50% 46%	48% 47%
<$50,000	$50,000–$99,999	$100,000+

Sex

53% 41%	42% 54%
Men	Women

●	Trump
●	Clinton
●	Other candidates

SOURCE: "2016 Election Exit Polls," *Washington Post*, November 10, 2016, www.washingtonpost.com/graphics/politics/2016-election/exit-polls/ (accessed 11/10/16).

WHAT YOU CAN DO ➡

WHAT YOU CAN DO

Contact the White House

 After he or she is elected, the president is expected to represent all Americans. Ask a question or share your view on a policy with the president and White House staff via **www.whitehouse.gov/contact**.

 Create a petition at **http://petitions.whitehouse.gov** regarding an issue you care about, and try to get as many signatures as possible.

☑ Watch a few recent presidential speeches, including this year's State of the Union address, on YouTube. Share your views with your fellow students, friends, and family.

chapter**study**guide

Practice Quiz

1. Which article of the Constitution describes the basic powers of the presidency and the means of selecting presidents? *(p. 315)*
   a) Article I
   b) Article II
   c) Article III
   d) Article IV
   e) Article V

2. The Founders chose to select the president through an indirect election in order to *(p. 315)*
   a) increase the strength and influence of political parties.
   b) build an imperial presidency that would overwhelm the power of Congress.

   c) force the president to be responsive to the will of the people.
   d) make the president responsible to state and national legislators.
   e) create a more independent chief executive.

3. Which of the following military and war powers does the Constitution *not* assign to the president? *(pp. 317–18)*
   a) command of the army and navy of the United States
   b) the power to declare war
   c) command of the state militias
   d) the power to make treaties
   e) The Constitution assigns all of the powers above to the president.

4. Executive agreements are exactly like treaties except that *(p. 319)*
   a) executive agreements involve only domestic, not international, affairs.
   b) the Constitution explicitly mentions the president's ability to make executive agreements.
   c) executive agreements do not require the Senate's "advice and consent."
   d) executive agreements are ordinarily used to carry out commitments not already made in treaties or laws.
   e) executive agreements require a two-thirds approval vote in the Senate.

5. What are the requirements for overriding a presidential veto? *(pp. 319–20)*
   a) 50 percent plus one vote in both houses of Congress
   b) two-thirds vote in both houses of Congress
   c) two-thirds vote in the Senate only
   d) three-fourths vote in both houses of Congress
   e) A presidential veto cannot be overridden by Congress.

6. When the president issues a rule or regulation that reorganizes or otherwise directs the affairs of the executive branch, it is called *(p. 321)*
   a) an executive agreement.
   b) an executive order.
   c) an executive mandate.
   d) administrative oversight.
   e) legislative initiative.

7. The War Powers Resolution of 1973 was an act passed by Congress that *(p. 324)*
   a) required the CIA to collect intelligence on all Americans born in a foreign country.
   b) outlawed presidential use of executive agreements.
   c) created the National Security Council.
   d) granted the president the authority to declare war.
   e) stipulated that military forces must be withdrawn within 60 days in the absence of a specific congressional authorization for their continued deployment.

8. Approximately how many people work for agencies within the Executive Office of the President? *(p. 326)*
   a) 25 to 50
   b) 500 to 750
   c) 1,500 to 2,000
   d) 4,500 to 5,000
   e) over 10,000

9. The Office of Management and Budget is part of *(p. 326)*
   a) the Executive Office of the President.
   b) the White House staff.
   c) the Cabinet.
   d) the Council of Economic Advisers.
   e) the Kitchen Cabinet

10. Which of the following statements about vice presidents is not true? *(p. 327)*
    a) The vice president succeeds the president in case of death, resignation, or incapacitation.
    b) The vice president casts the tie-breaking vote in the Senate when necessary.
    c) The vice president also serves as an honorary member of the Supreme Court.
    d) Modern presidents often use their vice presidents as a management resource.
    e) Presidential candidates typically select a vice-presidential candidate who is likely to bring the support of a state that would not otherwise support the ticket.

11. What are two ways that presidents can expand their power? *(pp. 328–29)*
    a) avoiding popular appeals and loosening their control of executive agencies
    b) using popular appeals and bolstering their control of executive agencies
    c) using popular appeals and loosening their control of executive agencies
    d) avoiding popular appeals and bolstering their control of executive agencies
    e) weakening national partisan institutions and bolstering their control of executive agencies

12. When the president makes an announcement about his interpretation of a congressional enactment that he is signing into law, it is called *(p. 334)*
    a) a signing statement.
    b) a line-item veto.
    c) an executive order.
    d) legislative initiative.
    e) executive privilege.

Key Terms

Cabinet *(p. 325)* the secretaries, or chief administrators, of the major departments of the federal government; Cabinet secretaries are appointed by the president with the consent of the Senate

commander in chief *(p. 317)* the role of the president as commander of the national military and the state National Guard units (when called into service)

delegated powers *(p. 316)* constitutional powers that are assigned to one governmental agency but that are exercised by another agency with the express permission of the first

executive agreement *(p. 319)* an agreement, made between the president and another country, that has the force of a treaty but does not require the Senate's "advice and consent"

Executive Office of the President (EOP) *(p. 326)* the permanent agencies that perform defined management tasks for the president; created in 1939, the EOP includes the OMB, the CEA, the NSC, and other agencies

executive order *(p. 321)* a rule or regulation issued by the president that has the effect and formal status of legislation

expressed powers *(p. 316)* specific powers granted by the Constitution to Congress (Article I, Section 8) and to the president (Article II)

inherent powers *(p. 322)* powers claimed by a president that are not expressed in the Constitution but are inferred from it

Kitchen Cabinet *(p. 326)* an informal group of advisers to whom the president turns for counsel and guidance; members of the official Cabinet may or may not also be members of the Kitchen Cabinet

legislative initiative *(p. 321)* the president's implied power to bring a legislative agenda before Congress

pocket veto *(p. 320)* a presidential veto that is automatically triggered if the president does not act on a given piece of legislation passed during the final 10 days of a legislative session

signing statements *(p. 334)* announcements made by the president when signing bills into law, often presenting the president's interpretation of the law

veto *(p. 319)* the president's constitutional power to prevent a bill from becoming a law; a presidential veto may be overridden by a two-thirds vote of each house of Congress

War Powers Resolution *(p. 324)* a resolution of Congress that the president can send troops into action abroad only by authorization of Congress or if American troops are already under attack or serious threat

White House staff *(p. 326)* analysts and advisers to the president, each of whom is often given the title "special assistant"

For Further Reading

Crenson, Matthew, and Benjamin Ginsberg. *Presidential Power: Unchecked and Unbalanced*. New York: W. W. Norton, 2007.

Crouch, Jeffrey P. *The Presidential Pardon Power*. Lawrence: University Press of Kansas, 2009.

Dodds, Graham. *Take Up Your Pen: Unilateral Presidential Directives in American Politics*. Philadelphia: University of Pennsylvania Press, 2013.

Edwards, George. *Why the Electoral College Is Bad for America*. New Haven, CT: Yale University Press, 2004.

Fisher, Louis. *Constitutional Conflicts between President and Congress*. 6th ed. Lawrence: University Press of Kansas, 2014.

Fisher, Louis. *The Law of the Executive Branch*. New York: Oxford University Press, 2014.

Genovese, Michael, and Robert J. Spitzer. *The Presidency and the Constitution*. New York: Palgrave/Macmillan, 2005.

Han, Lori Cox, and Diane Heith. *Presidents and the American Presidency*. New York: Oxford University Press, 2013.

Kernell, Samuel. *Going Public: New Strategies of Presidential Leadership*. 4th ed. Washington, DC: CQ Press, 2006.

Neustadt, Richard E. *Presidential Power: The Politics of Leadership from Roosevelt to Reagan*. Rev. ed. New York: Free Press, 1990.

Spitzer, Robert J. *The Presidential Veto: Touchstone of the American Presidency*. Albany: State University of New York Press, 1988.

Government bureaucracies affect ordinary Americans in countless ways. For example, the Environmental Protection Agency (EPA) proposes and enforces regulations that protect Americans' health and the environment. Here, an EPA worker vacuums a gasoline-like substance that contains the cancer-causing chemical benzene from the South Platte River, north of Denver, Colorado.

11

Bureaucracy

WHAT GOVERNMENT DOES AND WHY IT MATTERS Americans depend on government bureaucracies to accomplish the most spectacular achievements as well as the most mundane. Yet they often do not realize that public bureaucracies are essential for providing the services they use every day and rely on in emergencies. On a typical day, a college student might check the weather forecast, drive on an interstate highway, mail the rent check, drink from a public water fountain, check the calories on the side of a yogurt container, attend a class, go online, and meet a relative at the airport. Each of these activities is possible because of the work of a government bureaucracy: the U.S. Weather Service, the U.S. Department of Transportation, the U.S. Postal Service, the Environmental Protection Agency, the Food and Drug Administration (FDA), the student loan programs of the U.S. Department of Education, the Advanced Research Projects Agency (which developed the Internet in the 1960s), and the Federal Aviation Administration. Without the ongoing work of these agencies, many of these common activities would be impossible, unreliable, or more expensive. Even though bureaucracies provide essential services that all Americans rely on, they are often disparaged by politicians and the general public alike.

In emergencies, the national perspective on bureaucracy and, indeed, on "big government" shifts. After the September 11, 2011, terrorist attacks, all eyes turned to Washington. The federal government responded by strengthening and reorganizing the bureaucracy to undertake a whole new set of responsibilities designed to keep America safe. In the biggest government reorganization in over half a century, Congress created the Department of Homeland Security in 2002. The massive new department merged 22 existing agencies into a single department employing nearly 170,000 workers. Although the Bush administration presided over the creation of the Department of Homeland Security, Bush, like his Republican predecessors Ronald Reagan and George H. W. Bush, sought to roll back the regulatory role of the government.

In Chapters 9 and 10, we examined the two branches of government that exercise ultimate responsibility over the bureaucracy: Congress and the presidency. The numerous departments, agencies, offices, and bureaus that make up the bureaucracy exist because Congress created them by legal enactment. Congress oversees the activities of agencies, controls their funding, and can even reorganize or dismantle them. The president, as chief executive, can appoint top agency officials (with Senate approval), issue rules to govern agency behavior, control agency funding requests, and apply various other political pressures to compel agencies to respond to presidential priorities. Yet despite these many controls, members of Congress and presidents often express frustration at what they claim are the severe limits on the powers they can exercise to control the bureaucracy. These tensions suggest a separation-of-powers approach to studying the relationships among these three parts of the government.

chaptergoals

- Define bureaucracy, and describe the basic features of the executive branch (pp. 345–51)

- Describe the major goals we expect federal agencies to promote (pp. 351–58)

- Explain why it is often difficult to control the bureaucracy (pp. 359–63)

Bureaucracy Exists to Improve Efficiency

> **Define bureaucracy, and describe the basic features of the executive branch**

Bureaucracy is simply a form of organization. *Bureau*, a French word, can mean either "office" or "desk." *Cracy* is the Greek word for "rule" or "form of rule." Putting *bureau* and *cracy* together produces a very interesting definition: rule by offices and desks. In fact, **bureaucracy** is the complex structure of offices, tasks, rules, and principles of organization that are employed by all large-scale institutions to coordinate effectively the work of their personnel. Each member of an organization has an office, meaning a place as well as a set of responsibilities. That is, each "office" is made up of a set of tasks that are specialized to the needs of the organization, and the person holding that office (or position) performs those specialized tasks. Specialization and repetition are essential to the efficiency of any organization. Therefore, when an organization is inefficient, it is almost certainly because it is not bureaucratized enough!

Bureaucracies not only perform specialized tasks that require routine action but also undertake politically controversial tasks that require them to exercise a great deal of discretion and professional judgment. In many areas of policy, Congress writes laws that are very broad, and it is up to the bureaucracy to define what the laws will mean in practice. The decisions that bureaucrats make, often based on professional judgments, can themselves become politically contentious.

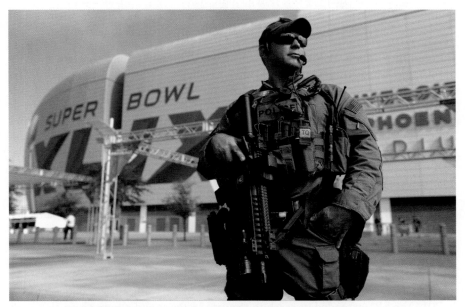

The Department of Homeland Security (DHS) is tasked with the broad goal of keeping America safe. Its 240,000 employees work in jobs as diverse as aviation security, emergency response, and chemical facility inspection. The DHS also provided security for the 2015 Super Bowl, an event attended by approximately 70,000 people.

Both routine and exceptional tasks require the organization, specialization, and expertise found in bureaucracies. To provide these services, government bureaucracies employ specialists such as meteorologists, doctors, and scientists. To do their job effectively, these specialists require resources and tools (ranging from paper to complex computer software); they have to coordinate their work with others (e.g., traffic engineers must communicate with construction engineers); and there must be effective outreach to the public (e.g., doctors must be made aware of health warnings). Bureaucracy is a means of coordinating the many different parts that must work together to provide useful services.

Bureaucrats Fulfill Important Roles

Congress is responsible for making the laws, but in most cases legislation only sets the broad parameters for government action. Bureaucracies are responsible for filling in the blanks by determining how the laws should be implemented. This requires bureaucracies to draw up much more detailed rules that guide the process of **implementation** (the efforts of departments and agencies to translate laws into specific bureaucratic rules and actions) and to play a key role in enforcing the laws. Congress needs the bureaucracy to engage in rule making and implementation for several reasons. One is that bureaucracies employ people who have much more specialized expertise in specific policy areas than do members of Congress. Decisions about how to achieve many policy goals—from managing the national parks to regulating air quality to ensuring a sound economy—rest on the judgment of specialized experts. A second reason that Congress needs bureaucracy is that because updating legislation can take many years, bureaucratic flexibility can ensure that laws are a dministered in ways that take new conditions into account. Finally, members of Congress often prefer to delegate politically difficult decisions to bureaucrats.

Bureaucrats Make Rules One of the most important things that government agencies do is issue rules that provide more detailed and specific indications of what a given congressional policy will actually mean. For example, the Clean Air Act empowers the Environmental Protection Agency (EPA) to assess whether current or projected levels of air pollutants pose a threat to public health, to identify whether motor vehicle emissions are contributing to such pollution, and to create rules designed to regulate these emissions. Under the George W. Bush administration, the EPA claimed it did not have the authority to regulate a specific group of pollutants commonly referred to as "greenhouse gases" (for example, carbon dioxide). In 2007 the Supreme Court ruled that the EPA did have that authority and had to provide a justification for not regulating such emissions.[1] In the first year of the Obama administration, the agency ruled that greenhouse gases did pose a threat to public health and that the emissions from motor vehicles contributed to greenhouse gas pollution.[2] The agency then imposed new emission standards for automobiles, which would raise the average per-vehicle fuel economy for new vehicles to 35.5 miles per gallon starting in 2016, a standard later boosted to 54.4 miles per gallon by 2025.[3] In 2014 the EPA extended its reach to regulate factories and power plants that emit greenhouse gases. Especially controversial was a set of regulations that requires power plants to reduce greenhouse gas emissions by 32 percent by 2030. When the rule—called the Clean Power Plan—was announced, 24 states along with firms in the energy industry filed lawsuits challenging it. In 2016 the Supreme Court temporarily blocked implementation of the Clean Power Plan while it is being challenged in court. Litigation was expected to last for years in what one observer predicted would be "the superbowl of climate politics."[4]

Once a new law is passed, the agency studies the legislation and proposes a set of rules to guide implementation. These proposed rules are then open to comment by anyone who wishes to weigh in. Representatives for the regulated industries and advocates of all sorts commonly submit comments. But anyone who wants to can go to www.regulations.gov to read proposed rules, enter comments, and view the comments of others. Once rules are approved, they are published in the *Federal Register* and have the force of law.

Bureaucrats Enforce Laws In addition to rule making, bureaucracies play an essential role in enforcing the laws. In doing so, bureaucracies exercise considerable power over private actors. In 2015, the EPA charged Volkswagen with cheating on emissions tests of its diesel vehicles. For over seven years, the company had installed software that showed emissions at legal levels during testing conditions but, once the cars were on the road, showed that emissions were actually 10 to 40 percent higher. After the EPA threatened to bar the company from selling some of its 2016 cars in the United States, Volkswagen admitted that it had cheated. The financial repercussions for the company will be long-lasting. In 2016 the company agreed to a $15.8 billion dollar settlement that required it to buy back the faulty vehicles and compensate owners. As part of the settlement, Volkswagen also agreed to fund several clean air programs. Even with these payments, Volkswagen faced additional lawsuits from states and investors.[5]

The Merit System: How to Become a Bureaucrat Public bureaucrats are rewarded with greater job security than employees of most private organizations. More than a century ago, the federal government attempted to imitate business by passing the Pendleton Civil Service Act of 1883, which was followed by almost universal adoption of equivalent laws in state and local governments. These laws required that appointees to public office be qualified, as measured by competitive examinations, for the job to which they were appointed. This policy came to be called the **merit system**; its purpose was to put an end to political appointments under the "spoils system," when government jobs were given out based on political connections rather than merit. Under the old spoils system, presidents filled up to 200,000 federal jobs with political friends and supporters. In 1881, President James A. Garfield wrote, "My day is frittered away with the personal seeking of people when it ought to be given to the great problems which concern the whole country."[6] Ironically, the final push to enact civil service reform occurred when a frustrated office seeker shot and killed President Garfield in 1881. At the higher levels of government agencies, including such posts as cabinet secretaries and assistant secretaries, many jobs are filled with political appointees and are not part of the merit system.

As a further safeguard against political interference (and to compensate for the lower-than-average pay given to public employees), merit system employees—genuine civil servants—were given legal protection against being fired without a show of cause. Reasonable people may disagree about the value of such security and how far it should extend in the civil service, but the justifiable objective of this job protection (cleansing bureaucracy of political interference while upgrading performance) cannot be disputed.

The Size of the Federal Service Has Actually Declined

For decades, politicians from both parties have asserted that the federal government is too big. Ronald Reagan led the way with his 1981 statement that government was the problem, not the solution. Fifteen years later, President Bill Clinton abandoned the traditional Democratic defense of government, declaring that "the era of big government is over." President George W. Bush voiced similar sentiments when he accepted his party's nomination for president in 2000, proclaiming, "Big government is not the answer!" President Obama struck a different tone. Addressing Congress on the topic of health care reform, he noted that while Americans had a "healthy skepticism of government," they also believed that "hard work and responsibility should be rewarded by some measure of security and fair play," noting "that sometimes government has to step in to help deliver that promise."[7] Despite fears of bureaucratic growth getting out of hand, however, the federal service has hardly grown at all since 1980; it reached its peak postwar level in 1968 with 3.0 million civilian employees plus 3.6 million military personnel (a figure swollen by the war in Vietnam). The number of civilian federal employees has since fallen to fewer than 2.7 million in 2014; the number of military personnel totals 1.5 million.[8]

The growth of the federal service in the second half of the twentieth century and the beginning of the twenty-first is even less imposing when placed in the context of the total workforce and when compared with the size of state and local public employment. Figure 11.1 indicates that since 1950 the ratio of federal employment

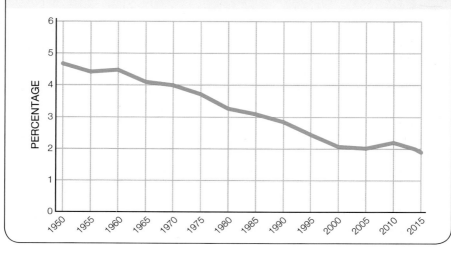

FIGURE 11.1 Employees in the Federal Service as a Percentage of the National Workforce, 1950–2015

Since 1950, the ratio of federal employment to the total workforce has gradually declined. Today, federal employees make up less than 2 percent of the total workforce in the United States. Even at its height, federal employees made up less than 6 percent. What do these numbers suggest about the size of the federal government today?

NOTE: Employment numbers are for December of each year.
SOURCE: Bureau of Labor Statistics, Current Employment Statistics, "Table B-1. Employees on Nonfarm Payrolls By Industry Sector and Selected Industry Detail," www.bls.gov/webapps/legacy/cesbtab1.htm (accessed 7/9/16).

to the total workforce has in fact *declined* slightly. Meanwhile, state and local employment has grown: in 1950, there were 4.3 million state and local civil service employees (about 6.5 percent of the country's workforce). In 2015 there were roughly 19.3 million state and local employees (nearly 15 percent of the nation's employed workforce).[9] Federal employment, in contrast, exceeded 6 percent of the workforce only during World War II, and almost all of that temporary growth was military.

Another useful comparison is illustrated in Figure 11.2. Although the dollar increase in federal spending shown by the bars looks impressive, the trend line indicating the relation of federal spending to the gross domestic product (GDP) remained close to what it had been in 1960. This changed in 2009, when the recession pushed spending up dramatically as the federal government sought to stimulate the economy and spending rose on other recession-related programs, such as unemployment insurance. After 2009 the budget also reflected the costs of the wars in Iraq and Afghanistan, which had not been included in the Bush administration's budgets.

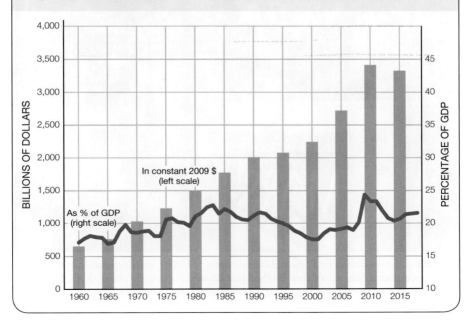

FIGURE 11.2 Annual Federal Outlays, 1960–2018*

As the bars in the figure indicate, when measured in dollars, federal government spending has gone up over time, from $423 billion in 1950 to over $3 trillion in 2015. (The amounts here are measured in constant 2009 dollars, which means the numbers have been adjusted for inflation.) But as the red line shows, federal spending as a percent of gross domestic product (GDP) has moved up and down just slightly over time. Thus, while government spending has grown, it has basically kept pace with the growing size of the U.S. economy.

*Data for 2016–18 are estimated.
SOURCE: Office of Management and Budget, "Table 1.3—Summary of Receipts, Outlays, and Surpluses or Deficits (−) in Current Dollars, Constant (FY 2009) Dollars, and as Percentages of GDP: 1940–2021." www.whitehouse.gov/omb /budget/historicals (accessed 7/9/16).

In sum, the national government is indeed "very large," but it has not been growing any faster than the economy or society. The same is roughly true of the growth pattern of state and local public personnel. Bureaucracy keeps pace with society, despite people's seeming dislike of it, because the air traffic control towers, the prisons, the Social Security system, and other essential elements of modern-day society cannot operate without bureaucracy.

The Executive Branch Is Organized Hierarchically

Cabinet departments, agencies, and bureaus are the operating parts of the bureaucratic whole. A **department** is the largest subunit of the executive branch. At the top is the head of the department, who in the United States is called the "secretary" of the department.[10] Below the secretary and the deputy secretary are the "undersecretaries," who have management responsibilities for one or more operating agencies. Those operating agencies are the most directly responsible for shaping the department's actual programs and are called the "bureau level." Each bureau-level agency usually operates under the statute adopted by Congress that set up the agency and gave it its authority and jurisdiction. The names of these bureau-level agencies are often quite well known to the public—the Forest Service and the Agricultural Research Service, for example. These are the so-called line agencies, or agencies that deal directly with the public. Each bureau or agency is subdivided into still other units, known as "divisions," "offices," or "units." All are parts of the bureaucratic hierarchy.

The National Aeronautics and Space Administration (NASA), an independent agency of the federal government, was established by President Eisenhower in 1958. Here, NASA public affairs officer Dwayne Brown announces the presence of water on Mars.

Not all government agencies are part of cabinet departments. Some **indepen-dent agencies** are set up by Congress outside the departmental structure alto-gether, even though the president appoints and directs the heads of these agencies. Independent agencies usually have broad powers to provide public services that are either too expensive or too important to be left to private initiatives. Some examples of independent agencies are the National Aeronautics and Space Administration (NASA), the Central Intelligence Agency (CIA), and the EPA. **Government corporations** are a third type of government agency but are more like private businesses in performing and charging for a market service, such as trans-porting railroad passengers (Amtrak).

Yet a fourth type of agency is the independent regulatory commission, given broad discretion to make rules. The first regulatory agencies established by Congress, beginning with the Interstate Commerce Commission in 1887, were set up as independent regulatory commissions because Congress recognized that regulatory agencies are "mini-legislatures," whose rules are exactly the same as legislation but require the kind of expertise and full-time attention that is be-yond the capacity of Congress. Until the 1960s, most of the regulatory agencies that were set up by Congress, such as the Federal Trade Commission (1914) and the Federal Communications Commission (FCC; 1934), were independent regulatory commissions. But beginning in the late 1960s and the early 1970s, all new regulatory programs, with two or three exceptions (such as the Federal Elec-tion Commission), were placed within existing departments and made directly responsible to the president. The first new major regulatory agency established in decades was approved by Congress in 2010, the Consumer Financial Protection Bureau. It was created to protect consumers by carrying out federal consumer financial protection laws. It functions as an independent unit within the U.S. Federal Reserve.

● Federal Bureaucracies Promote Welfare and Security

Describe the major goals we expect federal agencies to promote

The different agencies of the executive branch can be classified into three main groups based on the services they provide to the American public. The first category of agencies provides services and products that seek to promote the public welfare. The second group provides services that help maintain a strong economy. The third group works to promote national security. Let us look more closely at what each set of agencies offers to the public.

Federal Bureaucracies Promote the Public Welfare

One of the most important activities of the federal bureaucracy is to promote the public welfare. Americans often think of government welfare as a single program that goes only to the very poor, but a number of federal agencies provide services, build infrastructure, and enact regulations designed to enhance the well-being of the vast majority of citizens. Departments that have important responsibilities for promoting the public welfare in this sense include the Department of Housing and Urban Development, the Department of Health and Human Services, the Department of Veterans' Affairs, the Department of the Interior, the Department of Education, and the Department of Labor. Ensuring the public welfare is also the main activity of agencies in other departments, such as the Department of Agriculture's Food and Nutrition Service, which administers the federal school lunch program and the Supplemental Nutrition Assistance Program (SNAP; formerly known as "food stamps"). In addition, a variety of independent regulatory agencies enforce regulations to safeguard the public health and welfare.

Federal bureaucracies promote the public welfare with a diverse set of services, products, and regulations. The Department of Health and Human Services, for example, oversees the National Institutes of Health (NIH), which is responsible for cutting-edge biomedical research, and the two major health programs provided by the federal government: Medicaid, which provides health care for low-income families and for many elderly and disabled people, and Medicare, which is the health insurance available to most elderly people in the United States.

A different notion of the public welfare, but one highly valued by most Americans, is provided by the National Park Service, under the Department of the Interior. Created in 1916, the National Park Service is responsible for the care and upkeep of national parks. Since the nineteenth century, Americans have seen protection of the natural environment as an important public goal and have looked to federal agencies to implement laws and administer programs that preserve natural areas and keep them open to the public.

The federal bureaucracy also promotes public welfare through the watchdog activities of many **regulatory agencies**—departments, bureaus, or independent agencies whose primary mission is to impose limits, restrictions, or other obligations on the conduct of individuals or companies in the private sector. These include the FDA within the Department of Health and Human Services, the Occupational Safety and Health Administration (OSHA) in the Department of Labor, and independent regulatory commissions, such as the FCC and the EPA. An agency or commission is regulatory if Congress delegates to it relatively broad powers over a sector of the economy or a type of commercial activity and authorizes it to make rules within that jurisdiction. Rules made by regulatory agencies have the force of law.

Often working behind the scenes, these agencies seek to promote the welfare of all Americans. The EPA, for example, works to protect public health by ensuring the provision of clean and safe drinking water. Just as the agency sets standards to limit emissions from automobiles to protect the public from air pollutants, as we saw earlier, the EPA also sets national water quality standards to protect against contaminants that may pose health risks. The safety standards apply to the more than 170,000 public water systems around the country that support our access to safe drinking water and are implemented by states, local governments, and water suppliers—all of which are overseen by the EPA to ensure compliance.[11] Unsafe

AMERICA Side by Side

Bureaucracy in Comparison

As one of the world's largest and most populous countries, the United States has a vast bureaucracy to run government programs and services. However, as a percentage of the labor force, the number of government employees in the United States is not especially high. As the first graph below shows, the size of government bureaucracies, relative to each country's work force, varies widely. For example, the Norwegian government employs almost 35 percent of the labor force, whereas only around 8 percent of Japanese workers work for the government.

We can also see differences in whether most government employees work at the national level or the subnational level in each country. In the United States, most government employees work at the state or local level, rather than the national level. In other countries like Turkey, most bureaucrats work for the national government. What do you think accounts for these differences? How does federalism influence American bureaucracy, and what differences do we see in countries like Norway that do not have federalist systems?

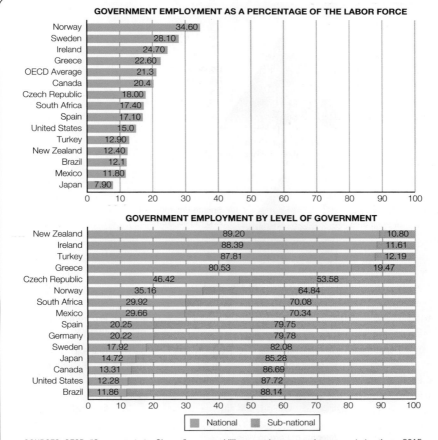

GOVERNMENT EMPLOYMENT AS A PERCENTAGE OF THE LABOR FORCE

Country	Percentage
Norway	34.60
Sweden	28.10
Ireland	24.70
Greece	22.60
OECD Average	21.3
Canada	20.4
Czech Republic	18.00
South Africa	17.40
Spain	17.10
United States	15.0
Turkey	12.90
New Zealand	12.40
Brazil	12.1
Mexico	11.80
Japan	7.90

GOVERNMENT EMPLOYMENT BY LEVEL OF GOVERNMENT

Country	National	Sub-national
New Zealand	89.20	10.80
Ireland	88.39	11.61
Turkey	87.81	12.19
Greece	80.53	19.47
Czech Republic	46.42	53.58
Norway	35.16	64.84
South Africa	29.92	70.08
Mexico	29.66	70.34
Spain	20.25	79.75
Germany	20.22	79.78
Sweden	17.92	82.08
Japan	14.72	85.28
Canada	13.31	86.69
United States	12.28	87.72
Brazil	11.86	88.14

National   Sub-national

SOURCES: OECD, "Government at a Glance," www.oecd-ilibrary.org/governance/government-at-a-glance-2015 _gov_glance-2015-en (accessed 11/18/15), and U.S. data from the U.S. Bureau of Labor Statistics, "Industry Employment and Output Projections to 2022," www.bls.gov/opub/mlr/2013/article/industry-employment-and -output-projections-to-2022-1.htm (accessed 11/18/15).

drinking water may seem like a concern of less-developed countries, but in 2016, drinking water in Flint, Michigan, was found to have high levels of lead content, potentially harming children's brain development for life. The state and Michigan and the EPA both failed to act quickly to remedy the problem, although complaints about the water had emerged two years earlier.

As we saw in Chapters 8 and 9, government agencies often develop close ties to the groups in society that they are supposed to regulate. This close political connection is known as an **iron triangle**: the stable, cooperative relationships that often develop among a congressional committee, an administrative agency, and one or more interest groups (see Figure 11.3). These relationships may push policies in a direction favorable to particular interests but inimical to the public interest.

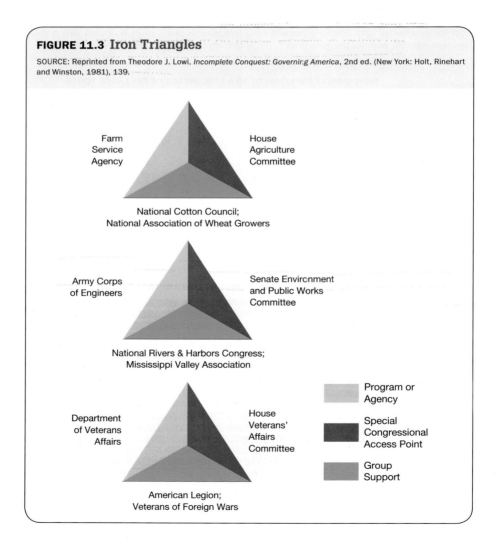

FIGURE 11.3 Iron Triangles

SOURCE: Reprinted from Theodore J. Lowi, *Incomplete Conquest: Governing America*, 2nd ed. (New York: Holt, Rinehart and Winston, 1981), 139.

Farm Service Agency

House Agriculture Committee

National Cotton Council; National Association of Wheat Growers

Army Corps of Engineers

Senate Environment and Public Works Committee

National Rivers & Harbors Congress; Mississippi Valley Association

Department of Veterans Affairs

House Veterans' Affairs Committee

American Legion; Veterans of Foreign Wars

Program or Agency

Special Congressional Access Point

Group Support

Federal Agencies Provide for National Security

One of the remarkable features of American federalism is that the most vital agencies for providing security for the American people (namely, the police) are located in state and local governments. But some agencies vital to maintaining national security are located in the national government, and they can be grouped into two categories: (1) agencies to confront threats to internal national security and (2) agencies to defend American security from external threats. The departments of greatest influence in these two areas are Homeland Security, Justice, Defense, and State.

Agencies for Internal Security The task of maintaining domestic security changed dramatically after the terrorist attacks of September 11, 2001. The creation of the Department of Homeland Security (DHS) in 2002 signaled the high priority that domestic security would now have. The orientation of domestic agencies also shifted as agencies geared up to prevent terrorism, a task that differed greatly from their former charge of investigating crime. With this shift in responsibility came broad new powers, many of them controversial—including the power to detain terrorist suspects and to engage in extensive domestic intelligence-gathering about possible terrorists. Since its creation, the DHS has also assumed a large role in domestic security, bringing under its umbrella such responsibilities as border safety and security (including immigration and customs); emergency preparedness; science-related concerns pertaining in particular to chemical, biological, and nuclear threats; and information and intelligence analysis and assessment.

Growing pains were evident in the DHS's first years. Different bureaucratic cultures, now part of a single operation, quickly became embroiled in turf battles with one another and with the Federal Bureau of Investigation (FBI, which remained in the Justice Department) as the two departments attempted to sort out their respective responsibilities. These early problems signaled deeper challenges that the DHS has continued to face. The DHS has struggled to establish itself as a strong, institutionally coherent presence capable of coordinating government action. Part of the problem is that the DHS portfolio of responsibilities is both large and vague. In addition, the agency failed to establish strong links with state and local agencies whose activities remain critical to its on-the-ground capabilities.

Agencies for External National Security Two departments occupy center stage in maintaining national security: the Departments of State and Defense.

The State Department's primary mission is diplomacy. As the most visible public representative of American diplomacy, the secretary of state works to promote American perspectives and interests in the world. For example, in 2015, Secretary of State John Kerry convened a meeting with leaders from Europe and the Middle East—including Iran—to try to find a diplomatic solution to the civil war in Syria. Concern about the flow of refugees in Europe, the increased role of Russia in the war, and the growing power of Islamic State of Iraq and Syria (ISIS) in Syria all led the secretary to step up his efforts to negotiate an end to the war, including the controversial step of including Iran in the talks.[12] Although diplomacy is the primary task of the State Department, diplomatic missions are only one of its organizational dimensions. As of 2016, the State Department also included 35 bureau-level units, each under the direction of an undersecretary.

These bureaus support the responsibilities of the elite foreign service officers, who staff U.S. embassies around the world and who hold almost all of the most powerful positions in the department below the rank of ambassador.[13] The ambassadorial positions, especially the plum positions in the major capitals of the world, are filled by presidential appointees, many of whom get their positions by having been important donors to victorious political campaigns.

Despite the importance of the State Department in foreign affairs, fewer than 20 percent of all U.S. government employees working abroad are directly under its authority. By far the largest number of career government professionals working abroad are under the authority of the Defense Department. In 2002, the Defense Department created the U.S. Northern Command, a regional command charged with ensuring homeland defense, directing military operations inside the nation's borders, and providing emergency backup to state and local governments, which are the first responders to any security disaster. The creation of a regional command within the United States was an unprecedented move, breaching a long-standing line between domestic law enforcement and foreign military operations.

As the creation of a military capacity within the United States suggests, addressing the threat of terrorism calls for greater coordination of internal and external security. In 2004 the National Commission on Terrorist Attacks upon the United States (the 9/11 Commission) issued a widely read report that called for a major reorganization of bureaucratic responsibilities for internal and external security. The report revealed that different departments of the American government had information that, if handled properly, might have prevented the attacks of September 11, 2001.

The 9/11 Commission's work prompted a major reorganization of the fragmented intelligence community. In 2005, a new office, the Director of National Intelligence, took over responsibility for coordinating the efforts of the 16 different agencies that gather intelligence. The Director of National Intelligence reports directly to the president each morning.

National Security and Democracy Of all the agencies in the federal bureaucracy, those charged with providing national security most often come into conflict with the norms and expectations of American democracy. Two issues in particular arise as these agencies work to ensure national security: (1) the trade-offs between respecting the personal rights of individuals and protecting the general public and (2) the need for secrecy in matters of national security versus the public's right to know what the government is doing.

Protecting national security often requires the government to conduct its activities in secret. Yet, as Americans have come to expect a more open government in the past three decades, many believe that federal agencies charged with national security keep too many secrets from the American public. The effort to make information related to national security more available began in 1966 with the passage of the Freedom of Information Act (FOIA). The information obtained often reveals unflattering or unsuccessful aspects of national security activities. One private organization, the National Security Archive, makes extensive use of FOIA to obtain information about the activities of national security agencies.

The website's "The Torture Archive," for example, is a searchable database of documents related to the detention of individuals in the war on terrorism and the authorized use of torture by the American government.

The tension between secrecy and democracy has sharpened dramatically with the threat of terrorism. The FOIA has been curtailed, and the range of information deemed sensitive has greatly expanded. President George W. Bush defended the new secrecy, declaring, "We're an open society, but we're at war. Foreign terrorists and agents must never again be allowed to use our freedoms against us." Although most Americans agreed that enhanced secrecy was needed to ensure domestic security, concerns about excessive secrecy mounted. Some analysts worried that secrecy would prevent Congress from carrying out its basic oversight responsibilities and that much of the secrecy had nothing to do with national security. The day after President Obama's election, he implemented the Open Government Directive. He also instructed federal agencies that they should administer the FOIA liberally: when in doubt, err on the side of openness. And in the most substantive change, Obama issued an executive order designed to promote more rapid declassification of secret documents. However, the Obama administration also continued some of the secrecy practices initiated in the Bush years. Most notably, it invoked the state secrets privilege to prevent lawsuits related to warrantless wiretapping and torture from going to trial.[14]

Massive leaks of sensitive national security documents by national security contractor Edward Snowden in 2013 exposed the extent, and potential illegality, of the National Security Agency's (NSA's) global surveillance operations. They showed that the NSA was collecting private data on millions of Americans and foreign nationals, including the tracking of phone calls, email messages, web browser histories, and personal contacts. The revelations prompted outrage at home and abroad.[15] President Obama responded by appointing an independent panel of intelligence experts to assess the NSA's activities, which determined that its massive data collection "made only a modest contribution to the nation's security." They recommended, among dozens of other reforms, that the government stop the collection program and relinquish the files to a third party. Even after these reforms more Americans disapproved than approved of the government's role in collecting Internet and telephone data.[16] Congress responded to such concerns in 2015 when it barred bulk collection of telephone data and instituted other limits on government surveillance in the USA Freedom Act.

Federal Bureaucracies Help to Maintain a Strong National Economy

In our capitalist economic system, the government does not directly run the economy. Yet many federal government activities are critical to maintaining a strong economy. Foremost among these are the agencies that are responsible for fiscal and monetary policy. Other agencies, such as the Internal Revenue Service (IRS), collect private resources into federal funds for public purposes. Tax policy may also strengthen the economy through decisions about whom to tax, how much, and when. Finally, the federal government, through such agencies as the Department of Transportation, the Commerce Department, and the Energy Department, may directly provide services or goods that bolster the economy.

Fiscal and Monetary Agencies **Fiscal policy**—the government's use of taxing, monetary, and spending powers to manipulate the economy—can refer to any government policy having to do with public finance. However, Americans often reserve the word *fiscal* for taxing and spending policies and use the term *monetary* for policies having to do with banks, credit, and currency.

While the responsibility for making fiscal policy lies with Congress, the administration of fiscal policy occurs primarily in the Treasury Department. In addition to collecting income, corporate, and other taxes, the Treasury manages the national debt—over $19 trillion in 2016.[17] The Treasury Department is also responsible for printing the U.S. currency, but currency represents only a tiny proportion of the entire money economy. Most of the trillions of dollars used in the transactions of the private and public sectors of the U.S. economy exist in computerized accounts rather than actual currency.

A key monetary agency is the **Federal Reserve System**, a system of 12 Federal Reserve banks, headed by the Federal Reserve Board, that facilitates exchanges of cash, checks, and credit; regulates member banks; and uses monetary policies to fight inflation and deflation. The Federal Reserve System (called the Fed) has authority over the interest rates and lending activities of the nation's most important banks. Congress established the Fed in 1913 as a clearinghouse responsible for adjusting the supply of money and credit to the needs of commerce and industry in different regions of the country. The Fed is also responsible for ensuring that banks do not overextend themselves, a policy that guards against bank failures during a sudden economic scare, such as occurred in 1929 and again in 2008. The Treasury and the Federal Reserve took center stage in 2008 when a string of bank failures threatened economic catastrophe. These agencies designed a $700 billion bailout package and persuaded Congress that a rapid response was needed to avert a worldwide depression. Although the Treasury and the Federal Reserve sprang into action when economic calamity loomed, critics charged that the crisis could have been prevented if these agencies had exercised more regulatory oversight over the financial sector during the previous decade. In 2010, Congress and the president created the Financial Stability Oversight Council to identify system-wide risks to the financial sector. The financial industry has kept a close eye on these developments, aiming to limit the regulatory reach of the new council.[18]

Revenue Agencies **Revenue agencies** are responsible for collecting taxes. Examples include the Bureau of Alcohol, Tobacco, Firearms and Explosives, for collection of taxes on the sales of those particular products, and federal customs agents (part of the DHS), who oversee the collection of taxes on imports at every U.S. seaport and international airport. But far and away the most important of the revenue agencies is the IRS, which collects income taxes.

The IRS is the government agency that Americans love to hate. Taxpayers complain about the IRS's needless complexity, its lack of sensitivity and responsiveness to individual taxpayers, and its overall lack of efficiency. Such complaints led Congress to pass the IRS Restructuring and Reform Act of 1998, which instituted a number of new protections for taxpayers.

Several Forces Control Bureaucracy

By their very nature, bureaucracies pose challenges to democratic governance. Although they provide the expertise needed to implement the public will, they can also become entrenched organizations that serve their own interests. The task is neither to retreat from bureaucracy nor to attack it but to take advantage of its strengths while making it more accountable to the demands of democratic politics and representative government.

We return to James Madison's observation: "You must first enable the government to control the governed; and in the next place oblige it to control itself."[19] Today, the problem is the same, only now the process has a name: administrative accountability. Accountability implies that some higher authority will guide and judge the actions of the bureaucracy. The highest authority in a democracy is *demos* ("the people"), and the guidance for bureaucratic action is the popular will. But that ideal of accountability must be translated into practical terms by the president and the Congress.

The President as Chief Executive Can Direct Agencies

In 1937, President Franklin Roosevelt's Committee on Administrative Management officially addressed a plea that had been growing increasingly urgent: "The president needs help." The national government had grown rapidly during the preceding 25 years, but the structures and procedures necessary to manage the burgeoning executive branch had not yet been established. The response to the call for "help" for the president initially took the form of three management policies: (1) all communications and decisions that related to executive policy decisions must pass through the White House; (2) in order to cope with such a flow, the White House must have adequate staffs of specialists in research, analysis, legislative and legal writing, and public affairs; and (3) the White House must have additional staff to ensure that presidential decisions are made, communicated to Congress, and carried out by the appropriate agency.

Making the Managerial Presidency The story of the modern presidency can be told largely as a series of responses to the plea for managerial help. Indeed, each expansion of the national government into new policies and programs in the twentieth and twenty-first centuries has been accompanied by a parallel expansion of the president's management authority.[20]

President Jimmy Carter's interest in administrative reform and reorganization resulted in his reorganization of the civil service and will long be recognized as one of the most significant contributions of his presidency. The Civil Service Reform Act of 1978 was the first major revamping of the federal civil service since its creation in 1883. The 1978 act created the Merit Systems Protection Board to defend competitive merit recruitment and promotion from political encroachment. The separate Federal Labor Relations Authority was set up to administer

In recent decades there have been several attempts to "reinvent government." On David Letterman's show in 1993, Vice President Al Gore railed against the government's procurement requirements, which even specified the number of places into which a government ashtray may shatter.

collective bargaining and individual personnel grievances. The third new agency, the Office of Personnel Management, was created to manage recruiting, testing, training, and the retirement system. The Senior Executive Service—a top management rank for civil servants—was also created at this time to recognize and foster "public management" as a profession and to facilitate the movement of top, "supergrade" career officials across agencies and departments.[21]

Carter also tried to impose a stringent budgetary process on all executive agencies. Called "zero-base budgeting," it was a method of budgeting from the bottom up, wherein each agency was required to rejustify its entire mission rather than merely its increase for the next year. Zero-base budgeting did not succeed, but the effort was not lost on President Reagan. From Carter's "bottom-up" approach, Reagan went to a "top-down" approach, whereby the initial budgetary decisions would be made in the White House and the agencies would be required to abide by those decisions. This process converted the Office of Management and Budget (OMB) into an agency of policy determination and presidential management.[22] President George H. W. Bush took Reagan's centralization strategy even further in using the White House staff instead of cabinet secretaries for managing the executive branch.[23]

President Bill Clinton engaged in the most systematic effort to "change the way the government does business," a phrase he used often to describe the goal of his National Performance Review, one of the most important administrative reform efforts of the twentieth century. Clinton launched the National Performance Review to make the federal bureaucracy more efficient, accountable, and effective. The National Performance Review sought to prod federal agencies into adopting flexible, goal-driven practices. Clinton promised that the result would be a government that would "work better and cost less." Virtually all observers agreed that the National Performance Review made substantial progress. Its original goal was to save more than $100 billion over five years, in large part by cutting the federal workforce by 12 percent (more than 270,000 jobs) by the end of 1999. By the end of 2000, $136 billion in savings was achieved and the federal workforce had been cut by 426,200.[24]

Like his predecessors, George W. Bush pursued a strategy different from those of previous presidents, dismantling Clinton's National Performance Review and favoring **privatization**—the transfer of all or part of a program from the public sector to the private sector. Bush was the first president with a degree in business, and his management strategy followed a standard business school dictum: select skilled subordinates and delegate responsibility to them. Bush followed this model closely in his appointment of highly experienced officials to cabinet positions and in his selection of Dick Cheney for vice president. But critics contended that the Bush administration's distrust of the bureaucracy led it to exercise inappropriate political control.

After Obama took office, his administration sought to reinvigorate federal agencies, which reflected the Democrats' greater support for strong government institutions. Obama's approach to the managerial presidency featured a deep belief in the importance of scientific expertise in government service. The president's appointees to head key regulatory agencies, including the EPA, OSHA, and the FDA, reflected this conviction. Some of the new agency leaders were well-known academic experts.

Congress Promotes Responsible Bureaucracy

Congress is constitutionally essential to responsible bureaucracy because the key to bureaucratic responsibility is legislation. When a law is passed and its intent is clear, the accountability for implementation of that law is also clear. Then the president knows what to "faithfully execute," and the responsible agency understands what is expected of it. But when Congress enacts vague legislation, agencies must resort to their own interpretations. The president and the federal courts often step in to tell agencies what the legislation intended. And so do interest groups. Yet when everybody, from president to courts to interest groups, gets involved in the actual interpretation of legislative intent, to whom and to what is the agency accountable?

Congress's answer is **oversight**—the effort by Congress, through hearings, investigations, and other techniques, to exercise control over the activities of executive agencies. The more power Congress has delegated to the executive, the more it has sought to reinvolve itself in directing the interpretation of laws through committee and subcommittee oversight of each agency. The standing committee system in Congress is well suited for oversight, inasmuch as most of the congressional committees and subcommittees have jurisdictions roughly parallel to one or more departments and agencies, and members of Congress who sit on these committees can develop expertise equal to that of the bureaucrats.

The most visible indication of Congress's oversight efforts is the use of public hearings, before which bureaucrats and other witnesses are summoned to discuss and defend agency budgets and past decisions. In 2013 and 2014, for example, Congress held high-profile hearings on topics as diverse as the attack on the American mission in Benghazi, Libya; reform of the Postal Service; and security

The most visible aspect of congressional oversight is the use of public hearings. Following the 2012 attack on the U.S. embassy in Benghazi, Libya, Congress held multiple highly publicized—and highly politicized—hearings to investigate the matter, focusing on the activities of former secretary of state Hillary Clinton.

concerns about the Department of Health and Human Services' new Health-care.gov website. Oversight hearings can also become highly politicized. In 2015 the House Select Committee on Benghazi, which was the eighth committee to investigate the matter, called former secretary of state Hillary Clinton to appear for a second time. During the televised hearings Republican members of the committee aggressively questioned the former secretary for more than eight hours. Democrats charged that the hearing was designed to harm Clinton's presidential campaign.[25]

The data drawn from studies of congressional committee and subcommittee hearings and meetings show quite dramatically that Congress has tried through oversight to keep pace with the expansion of the executive branch. The annual number of oversight hearings has grown over time as the bureaucracy has expanded. Oversight hearings in both the Senate and the House increased dramatically in the 1970s, in the aftermath of the Watergate scandal. In recent years, oversight has become a topic of substantial political concern. After the Republicans took over Congress in 1995, they concentrated their oversight power on investigating scandal. When George W. Bush became president in 2001, congressional oversight virtually disappeared. After winning back Congress in 2006, the Democrats revived the oversight role, holding hearings on such issues as the use of government contractors in the Iraq and Afghanistan wars and the Troubled Asset Relief Program, which was instituted to help bail out the banks in 2008. When Republicans took control of the House in 2010, oversight hearings focused on the Democratic administration's programs, such as the Consumer Financial Protection Bureau; and in 2013 hearings focused on the troubled rollout of the Affordable Care Act.

In addition, Congress created three agencies whose obligations are to engage in constant research for Congress on problems taking place in or confronted by the executive branch. These are the Government Accountability Office, the

Congressional Research Service, and the Congressional Budget Office. Each of these agencies is designed to give Congress information independent of the information it can get directly from the executive branch through hearings and other communications.[26] Another source of information for oversight comes directly from citizens through the FOIA, which, as we have seen, gives ordinary citizens the right of access to agency files and agency data.

Can the Bureaucracy Be Reformed?

When citizens complain that government is too bureaucratic, what they often mean is that government bureaucracies seem inefficient and waste money. Do these frustrations mean that bureaucracy needs to be reformed? In a sense, bureaucracy is always in need of reform. Yet, reforms may be more difficult to implement in the public sector because the government is held to much higher standards of accountability than are private companies. The government has sought various ways to make the federal bureaucracy more efficient. The key strategies used to promote reform include termination, devolution, and privatization. In general, Democratic administrations have aimed to make the existing bureaucracy work more effectively, whereas Republican administrations have sought to sideline the bureaucracy, especially by contracting out government work to private companies.

The only *certain* way to reduce the size of the bureaucracy is to eliminate programs. But termination is extraordinarily difficult. Even in the 12 years of the Reagan and George H. W. Bush administrations, both of which proclaimed a strong commitment to the reduction of the national government, not a single national government agency or program was terminated. In the 1990s, Republicans did succeed in eliminating two small agencies.

The next most effective approach to genuinely reducing the size of the federal bureaucracy is **devolution**, downsizing the federal bureaucracy by delegating the implementation of programs to state and local governments. Often the central aim of devolution is to provide more efficient and flexible government services. Yet by its very nature, devolution entails variation across the states. Up to a point, variation can be considered one of the virtues of federalism. But in a democracy, it is inherently dangerous to have large variations in the provision of services and benefits.

Privatization simply means that a formerly public activity is picked up under contract by a private company or companies. But such programs are still very much government programs—paid for by government and supervised by government. Privatization downsizes the government only in that the workers providing the service are no longer counted as part of the government bureaucracy. When private contractors can perform a task as well as government can but for less money, taxpayers win. But private firms are not necessarily more efficient or less costly than government, especially when there is little competition among private firms and when public bureaucracies are not granted a fair chance to bid in the contracting competition. In addition, concerns about adequate government oversight and accountability of private contractors have escalated as the scale of contracting has dramatically increased. Congress and presidents have reacted to these concerns in several ways, but conducting adequate oversight of contractors remains a challenge.

Bureaucracy, Democracy,
and Your Future

Reconciling bureaucracy and democracy requires clear rules and laws, maximum openness in agency decisions, clear rationales for those decisions, and accessible means for questioning and appealing those decisions. One important way for Congress to ensure accountability of the bureaucracy is for it to spend more time clarifying its legislative intent. Bureaucrats are more responsive to clear legislative guidance than to anything else, and when Congress and the president are at odds about the interpretation of laws, bureaucrats can evade responsibility by playing off one branch against another. Moreover, clearer laws from Congress and clearer rules and decisions made by administrative agencies would reduce the need for courts to review those laws and decisions, which is expensive and time-consuming. Adequate congressional oversight is also important because a bureaucracy that is out of the public eye may wind up pursuing its own interests or narrowly focused private interests rather than those of the public. Even so, an administration whose every move is subject to intense public scrutiny may be hamstrung in its efforts to carry out the public interest. (The "**Who Participates?**" feature on the facing page shows the public's efforts to get information from the bureaucracy under the Freedom of Information Act.) Finding the right balance between bureaucratic autonomy and public scrutiny is a central task of creating an effective government; it requires both presidential and congressional vigilance to build an effective and responsive bureaucracy.

The emergence of "big data" is likely to change the way bureaucracies operate in the future. *Big data* refers to huge data sets that involve information on a wide range of topics including climate, traffic, health, and the NSA's massive database of phone calls and use of social media. Big data has the potential to improve government performance by linking sources of information that were previously unconnected. It also allows the government to analyze information that was stored as text or went uncollected. Advances in government's ability to implement programs in public health, food safety, and transportation are only the beginning of what big data promises. At the same time, however, big data poses a threat to individual privacy, as the revelations about the NSA's data suggest. As bureaucracies tap into the promise of big data to create more effective programs, a close public eye on the implications for the right to privacy will be needed. How might big data improve the government's delivery of services in the future? What additional safeguards might be needed to protect individuals' privacy?

Getting Information from the Bureaucracy

FOIA Requests Received

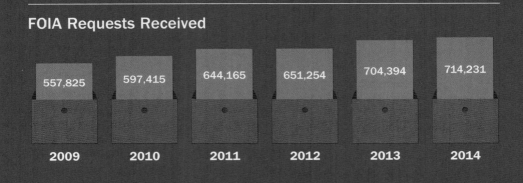

557,825	597,415	644,165	651,254	704,394	714,231
2009	2010	2011	2012	2013	2014

Backlogged FOIA Requests

77,377	69,526	83,490	71,790	95,564	159,741
2009	2010	2011	2012	2013	2014

Responses to FOIA Requests, 2014

9%
42%
49%

Released
- In full
- In part
- Denied

SOURCE: U.S. Department of Justice, "Summary of Annual FOIA Reports
for Fiscal Year 2014," www.justice.gov/sites/default/files/oip/pages
/attachments/2015/05/01/fy_2014_annual_report_summary.pdf
(accessed 4/12/16), pp. 2, 6, and 9.

WHAT YOU CAN DO ➡

WHAT YOU CAN DO

Ask Questions about Federal Agencies

 Learn more about the Freedom of Information Act (FOIA), including how to submit your own request, at **www.foia.gov/faq.html**. For a selection of records released under FOIA, go to **www.foia.state.gov/Search/Collections.aspx**.

 The Freedom of Information Act only applies to classified information. Federal agencies provide a vast amount of other government information as a standard part of their work. For a list of federal agencies and their websites, go to **www.usa.gov/federal-agencies**.

Ask a question about how federal agencies can help you. Most agencies have FAQ and contact pages on their websites.

chapterstudyguide

Practice Quiz

1. Which of the following statements about Congress and the bureaucracy is not true? *(pp. 345–46)*
   a) Bureaucracies employ people who have much more specialized expertise in specific policy areas than do members of Congress.
   b) Members of Congress often prefer to delegate politically difficult decision making to bureaucrats.
   c) While Congress is responsible for making laws, the bureaucracy is responsible for filling in the blanks by determining how the laws should be implemented.
   d) Congress banned rule making by the federal bureaucracy in 1995.
   e) Congress relies heavily on bureaucratic flexibility in implementing laws because updating legislation can take many years and bureaucrats can ensure that laws are administered in ways that take new conditions into account.

2. State and local laws similar to the Civil Service Act of 1883 require that appointees to public office *(p. 347)*
   a) pledge an oath of loyalty to the United States.
   b) be qualified for the job to which they are appointed.
   c) not belong to any political party.
   d) not be fired for any reason.
   e) serve terms of fewer than 4 years.

3. Which of the following best describes the size of the federal service? *(p. 348)*
   a) The size of the federal service has grown exponentially since 1980.
   b) The size of the federal service has changed very little since 1980.
   c) The size of the federal service reached its peak in 1955 and has been dramatically declining ever since.
   d) The federal service has employed at least 15 percent of the American workforce every year since 1950.
   e) The federal service was eliminated during the 1990s in order to hire more state government employees.

4. Which of the following is an example of a government corporation? *(p. 351)*
   a) National Aeronautics and Space Administration
   b) Amtrak
   c) Federal Bureau of Investigation
   d) Environmental Protection Agency
   e) Department of Justice

5. A stable relationship between a bureaucratic agency, a clientele group, and a legislative committee is called *(p. 354)*
   a) a standing committee.
   b) a conference committee.
   c) a cabinet.
   d) an issue network.
   e) an iron triangle.

6. The State Department's primary mission is *(p. 355)*
   a) gathering intelligence.
   b) unifying the nation's military departments.
   c) engaging in diplomacy.
   d) investigating terrorism.
   e) overseeing domestic security efforts.

7. Which of the following statements about the Freedom of Information Act (FOIA) is most accurate? *(pp. 356–57)*
   a) It was passed following the September 11, 2001, terrorist attacks.
   b) The National Security Archive is legally prohibited from using the FOIA to obtain information about the activities of national security agencies.
   c) The range of information deemed sensitive has been heavily reduced in response to the threat of terrorism.
   d) The range of information deemed sensitive has been greatly expanded in response to the threat of terrorism.
   e) President Obama instructed federal agencies that they should reject all FOIA requests made during his term in office.

8. Americans refer to government policy about banks, credit, and currency as *(p. 358)*
   a) monetary policy.
   b) deficit policy.
   c) fiscal policy.
   d) interstate commerce policy.
   e) regulatory policy.

9. Which of the following is an example of a revenue agency? *(p. 358)*
   a) the Office of Management and Budget
   b) the Treasury Department
   c) the Federal Reserve Board
   d) the Internal Revenue Service
   e) the Commerce Department

10. Which president instituted the bureaucratic reform of the National Performance Review? *(p. 360)*
    a) Richard Nixon
    b) Lyndon Johnson
    c) Jimmy Carter
    d) Bill Clinton
    e) George W. Bush

11. The concept of *oversight* refers to the effort made by *(pp. 361–62)*
    a) Congress to make executive agencies accountable for their actions.
    b) the president to make executive agencies accountable for their actions.
    c) the president to make Congress accountable for its actions.
    d) the courts to make executive agencies responsible for their actions.
    e) the states to make the executive branch accountable for its actions.

12. *Devolution* refers to *(p. 363)*
   a) the gradual decline in efficiency that always comes when government begins to implement a new program.
   b) moving all or part of a program from the public sector to the private sector.
   c) a policy of reducing or eliminating regulatory restraints on the conduct of individuals or private institutions.
   d) a policy to remove a program from one level of government by passing it down to a lower level of government.
   e) reducing the overall number of regulatory agencies in the federal bureaucracy.

Key Terms

bureaucracy *(p. 345)* the complex structure of offices, tasks, rules, and principles of organization that are employed by all large-scale institutions to coordinate effectively the work of their personnel

department *(p. 350)* the largest subunit of the executive branch; the secretaries of the 15 departments form the Cabinet

devolution *(p. 363)* a policy to remove a program from one level of government by delegating it or passing it down to a lower level of government, such as from the national government to the state and local governments

Federal Reserve System *(p. 358)* a system of 12 Federal Reserve banks that facilitates exchanges of cash, checks, and credit; regulates member banks; and uses monetary policies to fight inflation and deflation

fiscal policy *(p. 358)* the government's use of taxing, monetary, and spending powers to manipulate the economy

government corporation *(p. 351)* government agency that performs a service normally provided by the private sector

implementation *(p. 346)* the efforts of departments and agencies to translate laws into specific bureaucratic rules and actions

independent agency *(p. 351)* agency that is not part of a cabinet department

iron triangle *(p. 354)* the stable, cooperative relationships that often develop among a congressional committee, an administrative agency, and one or more supportive interest groups; not all of these relationships are triangular, but the iron triangle is the most typical

merit system *(p. 347)* a product of civil service reform, in which appointees to positions in public bureaucracies must objectively be deemed qualified for those positions

oversight *(p. 361)* the effort by Congress, through hearings, investigations, and other techniques, to exercise control over the activities of executive agencies

privatization *(p. 361)* the transfer of all or part of a program from the public sector to the private sector

regulatory agency *(p. 352)* a department, bureau, or independent agency whose primary mission is to impose limits, restrictions, or other obligations on the conduct of individuals or companies in the private sector

revenue agency *(p. 358)* an agency responsible for collecting taxes; examples include the Internal Revenue Service for income taxes, the U.S. Customs Service for tariffs and other taxes on imported goods, and the Bureau of Alcohol, Tobacco, Firearms and Explosives for collection of taxes on the sales of those particular products

For Further Reading

Arnold, Peri E. *Making the Managerial Presidency: Comprehensive Organization Planning*. Princeton, NJ: Princeton University Press, 1986.

Gormley, William, and Stephen Balla. *Bureaucracy and Democracy: Accountability and Performance*. 3rd ed. Washington, DC: CQ Press, 2012.

Kettl, Donald F. *System under Stress: The Challenge to 21st Century Governance*. 3rd ed. Los Angeles: Sage/CQ Press, 2014.

Kettl, Donald F. *The Politics of the Administrative Process*. 6th ed. Los Angeles: Sage/CQ Press, 2014.

Light, Paul C. *A Government Ill Executed: The Decline of the Federal Service and How to Reverse It*. Cambridge, MA: Harvard University Press, 2008.

Lowi, Theodore J. *The End of Liberalism*. New York: W. W. Norton, 1979.

Moffitt, Susan. *Making Public Policy: Participatory Bureaucracy in American Democracy*. New York: Cambridge University Press, 2014.

Verkuil, Paul. *Outsourcing Sovereignty: Why Privatization of Government Functions Threatens Democracy and What We Can Do about It*. New York: Cambridge University Press, 2007.

Weiner, Tom. *Legacy of Ashes: The History of the CIA*. New York: Doubleday, 2007.

Wildavsky, Aaron, and Naomi Caiden. *The New Politics of the Budgetary Process*. New York: Longman, 2003.

Wood, B. Dan. *Bureaucratic Dynamics: The Role of Bureaucracy in a Democracy*. Boulder, CO: Westview, 1994.

Although the Supreme Court is often viewed as the least political of the three branches, its rulings touch on major political issues that affect Americans in many ways. Here, demonstrators call on the other two branches of government to put partisanship aside and fill the Court vacancy left by the death of Justice Antonin Scalia.

12

The Federal Courts

WHAT GOVERNMENT DOES AND WHY IT MATTERS The Supreme Court sits at the top of the judicial branch of the U.S. government. Many Americans view the Supreme Court as aloof and apolitical because, unlike the president and members of Congress, the judges who sit on the Supreme Court are appointed, not elected. Thus, they do not need to campaign the way politicians do. But the issues the Supreme Court decides are often as political as those voted on in Congress, and the Supreme Court is often asked to hear questions that touch the lives of ordinary Americans, including students, in a very direct and meaningful way.

Since the 1980s, politically conservative justices appointed by Presidents Ronald Reagan, George H. W. Bush, and George W. Bush constituted a conservative majority on the Supreme Court. Though this majority did not prevail in each and every case, many of the most important cases over the past three decades were decided by 5–4 votes in favor of the conservatives.

In February 2016, Justice Antonin Scalia, who spoke for conservative and religious values on the Court, died unexpectedly. Scalia's death gave President Obama an opportunity to create a liberal majority on the Court for the first time in decades, and he quickly nominated Judge Merrick Garland as Scalia's replacement. Garland, a moderate liberal, was supported by most Republican senators when Bill Clinton appointed him to the Appeals Court in 1997. When it comes to the Supreme Court, however, the stakes are much higher. In an effort to prevent tipping the ideological balance of the Court toward the liberals, Senate Republicans decided not to act on the Garland nomination, hoping that a Republican president would be elected in 2016 and have the opportunity to nominate another conservative to the Court. While Republicans called on Obama to leave the appointment to his successor, Democrats called on Republicans to fill the vacancy, leaving the matter at a standstill for months. With only eight justices, the Court found itself evenly split on some important matters. For example, on a 4–4 vote the Court let stand a lower-court decision striking down President Obama's executive orders blocking the deportation of as many as 5 million undocumented immigrants.[1] During the 2016 presidential campaign, Donald Trump released a list of individuals whom he would consider for the Supreme Court. With Trump's election it seemed certain that the Court would regain its 5–4 conservative majority.

Unlike the two branches of government examined in Chapters 10 and 11, the courts are fundamentally undemocratic: as we have seen, their members are not elected (Supreme Court members serve for "lifetime during good behavior"), and they are therefore insulated from public pressures. That does not mean that politics has no effect on court decisions—far from it. In addition, both Congress and the president have a hand in making law; judges can affect the meaning of law only through interpretation. That power, however, is an important one, as examples in this chapter will demonstrate. The courts not only interpret the laws passed by Congress and the decisions of presidents when challenges arise but also interpret and apply fundamental rights.

chaptergoals

- Identify the general types of cases and types of courts in our legal system (pp. 373–77)

- Describe the different levels of federal courts and their functions (pp. 377–81)

- Explain how the Supreme Court exercises the power of judicial review (pp. 382–86)

- Describe the process the Supreme Court follows in the exercise of its power of judicial review (pp. 386–92)

- Consider the personal and political influences on judges and the courts (pp. 392–95)

The Legal System Settles Disputes

Identify the general types of cases and types of courts in our legal system

Originally, a "court" was the place where a sovereign ruled—where the king or queen governed. Settling disputes between citizens was part of governing. In modern democracies, courts and judges have taken over from monarchs the power to resolve disputes by hearing the facts on both sides, applying the relevant law or principle to the facts, and deciding which side possesses greater merit. But since judges are not monarchs, they must have a basis for their authority. That basis in the United States is the Constitution and the law.

Court Cases Proceed under Criminal and Civil Law

Court cases in the United States proceed under two broad categories of law: criminal law and civil law.

Cases of **criminal law** deal with disputes or actions involving criminal penalties. Criminal law regulates the conduct of individuals, defines crimes, and specifies punishment for acts defined as illegal. The government charges an individual with violating a statute (a law) that has been enacted to protect the public health, safety, morals, or welfare. In criminal cases, the government is always the **plaintiff** (the individual or organization that brings a complaint in court) and alleges that a criminal violation has been committed by a named **defendant** (the one against whom a complaint is brought in a criminal or civil case). Most criminal cases arise in state and municipal courts and involve matters ranging from traffic offenses to

In criminal cases, the government charges an individual with violating a statute protecting health, safety, morals, or welfare. Most such cases arise in state and municipal courts. Here, an Illinois county court hears testimony in a murder case.

robbery and murder. While the great bulk of criminal law is still a state matter, a large and growing body of federal criminal law deals with infringements from tax evasion and mail fraud to acts of terrorism and the sale of narcotics. Defendants found guilty of criminal violations may be fined or sent to prison.

Cases of **civil law** involve disputes among individuals or between individuals and the government that do not involve criminal penalties. Unlike criminal cases, the losers in civil cases cannot be fined or incarcerated, although they may be required to pay monetary damages for their actions. In a civil case, the one who brings a complaint is the plaintiff and the one against whom the complaint is brought is the defendant. The two most common types of civil cases involve contracts and torts. In a typical contract case, an individual or a corporation charges that it has suffered because of another's violation of a specific agreement between the two. For example, the Smith Manufacturing Corporation may charge that Jones Distributors failed to honor an agreement to deliver raw materials at a specified time, causing Smith to lose business. Smith asks the court to order Jones to compensate it for the damage it allegedly suffered. In a typical tort case, one individual charges that he has been injured by another's negligence or malfeasance. Medical malpractice suits are one example of tort cases. Another important area of civil law is administrative law, which involves disputes over the jurisdiction, procedures, or authority of administrative agencies. A plaintiff may assert, for example, that an agency did not follow proper procedures when issuing new rules and regulations. A court will then examine the agency's conduct in light of the Administrative Procedure Act, the legislation that governs agency rule making.

In deciding cases, courts apply statutes (laws) and legal **precedents** (prior cases whose principles are used by judges as the basis for their decisions in present cases). State and federal statutes, for example, often govern the conditions under which contracts are and are not legally binding. Jones Distributors might argue that it was not obliged to fulfill its contract with the Smith Manufacturing Corporation because actions by Smith, such as the failure to make promised payments, constituted fraud under state law. Attorneys for a physician being sued for malpractice, meanwhile, may search for prior instances in which courts ruled that actions similar to those of their client did not constitute negligence. Such precedents are applied under the doctrine of **stare decisis**, a Latin phrase meaning "let the decision stand." It is the doctrine that a previous decision by a court applies as a precedent in similar cases until that decision is overruled.

Types of Courts Include Trial, Appellate, and Supreme

In the United States, systems of courts have been established both by the federal government and by the governments of the individual states. Both systems have several levels, as shown in Figure 12.1. More than 97 percent of all court cases in the United States are heard in state courts. The overwhelming majority of criminal cases, for example, involve violations of state laws prohibiting such actions as murder, robbery, fraud, theft, and assault. If such a case is brought to trial, it will be heard in a state **trial court** (the first court to hear a criminal or civil case), in front of a judge and sometimes a jury, who will determine whether the defendant violated state law. If the defendant is convicted, she may appeal the conviction to

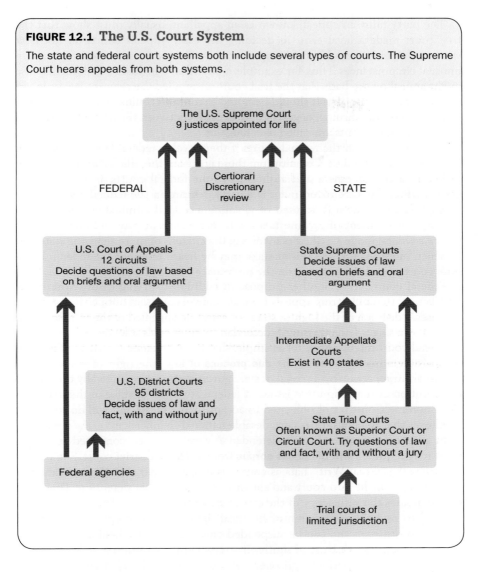

FIGURE 12.1 The U.S. Court System

The state and federal court systems both include several types of courts. The Supreme Court hears appeals from both systems.

The U.S. Supreme Court
9 justices appointed for life

FEDERAL

Certiorari Discretionary review

STATE

U.S. Court of Appeals
12 circuits
Decide questions of law based on briefs and oral argument

State Supreme Courts
Decide issues of law based on briefs and oral argument

Intermediate Appellate Courts
Exist in 40 states

U.S. District Courts
95 districts
Decide issues of law and fact, with and without jury

State Trial Courts
Often known as Superior Court or Circuit Court. Try questions of law and fact, with and without a jury

Federal agencies

Trial courts of limited jurisdiction

a higher court, such as a state **court of appeals** (a court that hears the appeals of trial court decisions) and from there to a state's **supreme court** (the highest court in a particular state or in the United States, which primarily serves an appellate function). The government is not entitled to appeal if the defendant is found not guilty in a criminal case.

Similarly, in civil cases, most litigation is brought in the courts established by the state in which the activity in question took place. For example, a patient bringing suit against a physician for malpractice would file the suit in the appropriate court in the state where the alleged malpractice occurred. The judge hearing the case would apply state law and state precedent to the matter at hand. In a civil case, such as malpractice, either side may appeal the verdict if it loses.

The party filing an appeal, known as an appellant, usually must show that the trial court made a legal error in deciding the case. Appeals courts do not hear witnesses or examine additional evidence and will only consider new facts under unusual circumstances. Thus, for example, a physician who loses a malpractice case might appeal on the basis that the trial court misapplied the relevant law or incorrectly instructed the jury. It should be noted that most criminal and civil cases are settled before trial through negotiated agreements between the parties. In criminal cases, these agreements are called **plea bargains**.

Cases are heard in the federal courts if they involve federal laws, treaties with other nations, or the U.S. Constitution; these areas are the official **jurisdiction** (the sphere of a court's power and authority) of the federal courts. In addition, any case in which the U.S. government is a party is heard in the federal courts. If, for example, an individual is accused of violating a federal criminal statute, such as evading the payment of income taxes, a federal prosecutor would bring charges before a federal judge. Civil cases involving the citizens of more than one state and in which more than $75,000 is at stake may be heard in either the federal or the state courts, usually depending on the preference of the plaintiff.

Federal courts serve another purpose in addition to trying cases within their jurisdiction: that of hearing appeals from state-level courts. In both civil and criminal cases, a decision of the highest state court can be appealed to the U.S. Supreme Court by raising a federal issue. A defendant who appeals a lower-court decision in federal court might assert, for example, that he was denied the right to counsel or was otherwise deprived of the **due process of law** (the right of every citizen against arbitrary action by national or state governments) guaranteed by the federal Constitution or that important issues of federal law were at stake in the case. The U.S. Supreme Court is not obligated to accept such appeals and will do so only if it believes that the matter has considerable national significance.

In addition, in criminal cases, defendants who have been convicted in a state court may request a **writ of habeas corpus** from a federal district court. Sometimes known as the "Great Writ," habeas corpus is a court order that the individual in custody be brought into court and shown the cause for her detention. The court then evaluates the sufficiency of the cause and may order the release of a prisoner deemed to be held in violation of his legal rights. Habeas corpus is guaranteed by the Constitution and can be suspended only in cases of rebellion or invasion. In 1867, Congress's distrust of southern courts led it to authorize federal district judges to issue such writs to prisoners who they believed had been deprived of constitutional rights in state court. Generally speaking, state defendants seeking a federal writ of habeas corpus must show that they have exhausted all available state remedies and must raise issues not previously raised in their state appeals. Federal courts of appeal and, ultimately, the U.S. Supreme Court have appellate jurisdiction for federal district court habeas decisions.

Although the federal courts hear only a small fraction of all the civil and criminal cases decided each year in the United States, their decisions are extremely important. It is in the federal courts that the Constitution and federal laws that govern all Americans are interpreted and their meaning and significance established. Moreover, it is in the federal courts that the powers and limitations of the increasingly powerful national government are tested. Finally, through their power to review the decisions of the state courts, it is ultimately the federal courts that dominate the American judicial system.

● The Federal Courts Hear a Small Percentage of All Cases

Describe the different levels of federal courts and their functions

During the year ending in March 2015, federal district courts (the lowest federal level) received 376,905 cases. Though large, this number is approximately 3 percent of the number of cases heard by state courts. The federal courts of appeal listened to 54,244 cases in 2015, and about 15 percent of the verdicts were appealed to the U.S. Supreme Court. Most of the roughly 9,000 cases filed with the Supreme Court yearly are dismissed without a ruling on their merits. The Court has broad latitude to decide what cases it will hear and generally listens to only those cases it deems raise the most important issues. In recent years, fewer than 80 cases per year have received full-dress Supreme Court review.[2]

The Lower Federal Courts Handle Most Cases

Most of the cases of original federal jurisdiction are handled by the federal district courts. **Original jurisdiction** is the authority to initially consider a case. It is distinguished from *appellate jurisdiction*, which is the authority to hear appeals from a lower court's decision. Courts of original jurisdiction are the courts that are responsible for discovering the facts in a controversy and creating the record on which a judgment is based. In courts that have appellate jurisdiction, judges receive cases after the factual record is established by the trial court. Ordinarily, new facts cannot be presented before appellate courts. Article III of the Constitution gives the Supreme Court original jurisdiction in a limited number of cases including (1) cases between the United States and one of the 50 states, (2) cases between two or more states, (3) cases involving foreign ambassadors or other ministers, and (4) cases brought by one state against citizens of another state or against a foreign country. Article III assigns original jurisdiction in all other federal cases to the lower courts that Congress was authorized to establish. Importantly, the Constitution gives the Supreme Court appellate jurisdiction in *all* federal cases. Almost all cases heard by the Supreme Court are under its appellate jurisdiction.

The 94 federal district courts are staffed by 678 federal district judges. District judges are assigned to district courts according to the workload; the busiest of these courts may have as many as 28 judges. Only one judge is assigned to each case, except where statutes provide for three-judge courts to deal with special issues. The routines and procedures of the federal district courts are essentially the same as those of the lower state courts, except that federal procedural requirements tend to be stricter. States, for example, do not have to provide a grand jury, a 12-member trial jury, or a unanimous jury verdict. Federal courts must follow all these procedures.

The Appellate Courts Hear 20 Percent of Lower-Court Cases

Roughly 20 percent of all lower-court and federal agency cases are accepted for review by the federal appeals courts and by the Supreme Court in its capacity as an appellate court. There are 13 U.S. Court of Appeals judicial districts, or circuits, with a total of 179 judges. Those districts consist of 11 that divide up the nation geographically plus one for the District of Columbia and one federal circuit that deals with patents, trademarks, international trade, and claims against the federal government (see Figure 12.2).

Except for cases selected for review by the Supreme Court, decisions made by the appeals courts are final. Because of this finality, certain safeguards have been built into the system. The most important is the provision of more than one judge for every appeals case. Each court of appeals has from 6 to 28 permanent judgeships, depending on the workload of the circuit. Although normally three judges hear appealed cases, in some instances a larger number of judges sit together en banc.

Another safeguard is provided by the assignment of a Supreme Court justice as the circuit justice for each of the circuits. Since the creation of the appeals court in 1891, the circuit justice's primary duty has been to review appeals arising in the circuit in order to expedite Supreme Court action. The most frequent and

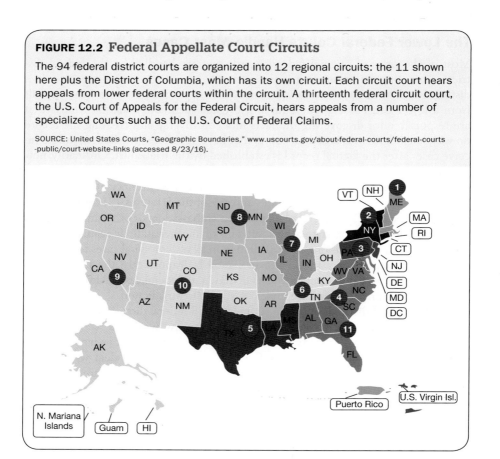

FIGURE 12.2 Federal Appellate Court Circuits

The 94 federal district courts are organized into 12 regional circuits: the 11 shown here plus the District of Columbia, which has its own circuit. Each circuit court hears appeals from lower federal courts within the circuit. A thirteenth federal circuit court, the U.S. Court of Appeals for the Federal Circuit, hears appeals from a number of specialized courts such as the U.S. Court of Federal Claims.

SOURCE: United States Courts, "Geographic Boundaries," www.uscourts.gov/about-federal-courts/federal-courts
-public/court-website-links (accessed 8/23/16).

best-known action of circuit justices is that of reviewing requests for stays of execution when the full Court is unable to do so—primarily during the summer, when the Court is in recess.

The Supreme Court Is the Court of Final Appeal

The Supreme Court is America's highest court. Article III of the Constitution vests "the judicial power of the United States" in the Supreme Court, and this court is supreme in fact as well as form. The Supreme Court is the only federal court established by the Constitution. The lower federal courts were created by Congress and can be restructured or, presumably, even abolished by the legislative branch. The Supreme Court is made up of a chief justice and eight associate justices (see Table 12.1). The **chief justice** presides over the Court's public sessions and conferences and is the first to speak and vote. Voting then proceeds from most to least senior. In the Court's actual deliberations and decisions, however, the chief justice has no more authority than the other justices. Each justice casts one vote. To some extent, the influence of the chief justice is a function of her own leadership ability. Some chief justices, such as the late Earl Warren, have been able to lead the Court in a new direction. In other instances, forceful associate justices, such as the late Felix Frankfurter, are the dominant figures on the Court.

The Constitution does not specify the number of justices who should sit on the Supreme Court; Congress has the authority to change the Court's size. In the early nineteenth century, there were six Supreme Court justices; later there were seven. Congress set the number of justices at nine in 1869, and the Court has remained that size ever since. In 1937, President Franklin Delano Roosevelt (FDR), infuriated by several Supreme Court decisions that struck down New Deal programs, asked Congress to enlarge the Court so that he could add a few

TABLE 12.1

Supreme Court Justices, 2016 (in Order of Seniority)

NAME	YEAR OF BIRTH	PRIOR EXPERIENCE	APPOINTED BY	YEAR OF APPOINTMENT
Anthony Kennedy	1936	Federal judge	Reagan	1988
Clarence Thomas	1948	Federal judge	G. H. W. Bush	1991
Ruth Bader Ginsburg	1933	Federal judge	Clinton	1993
Stephen Breyer	1938	Federal judge	Clinton	1994
John Roberts, Jr. (Chief Justice)	1955	Federal judge	G. W. Bush	2005
Samuel Alito	1950	Federal judge	G. W. Bush	2006
Sonia Sotomayor	1954	Federal judge	Obama	2009
Elena Kagan	1960	Solicitor general	Obama	2010
(vacant seat)*				

* As of November 2016.

sympathetic justices to the bench. Although Congress balked at Roosevelt's "court packing" plan, the Court gave in to FDR's pressure and began to take a more favorable view of his policy initiatives. The president, in turn, dropped his efforts to enlarge the Court. The Court's surrender to FDR came to be known as "the switch in time that saved nine."

Judges Are Appointed by the President and Approved by the Senate

Federal judges are nominated by the president and are generally selected from among the more prominent or politically active members of the legal profession. Many federal judges previously served as state court judges or state or local prosecutors. Before the president makes a formal nomination, however, the senators from the candidate's own state must indicate that they support the nominee. This is an informal but seldom violated practice called **senatorial courtesy.** If one or both senators from a prospective nominee's home state belong to the president's political party, the president will almost invariably consult them and secure their blessing for the nomination. Because the president's party in the Senate will rarely approve a nominee opposed by a home-state senator from its ranks, the president will usually not bother to present such a nomination to the Senate. Through this arrangement, senators are able to exercise veto power over appointments to the federal bench from their own states. If the state has no senator from the president's party, the governor or members of the state's House delegation may make suggestions. The practice of "courtesy" generally does not apply to Supreme Court appointments, only to district and circuit court nominations.

Federal appeals court nominations follow much the same pattern. Since appeals court judges preside over jurisdictions that include several states, however, senators do not have as strong a role in proposing potential candidates. Instead, potential appeals court candidates are generally suggested to the president by the Justice Department or by important members of the administration. The senators from the nominee's own state are still consulted, however, before the president formally acts.

There are no formal qualifications for service as a federal judge. In general, presidents endeavor to appoint judges who possess legal experience and good character and whose partisan and ideological views are similar to their own. Once the president has formally nominated an individual, the nominee must be considered by the Senate Judiciary Committee and confirmed by a majority vote in the full Senate. In recent years, the judicial appointments process has been affected by increasing partisan conflict. Senate Democrats have sought to prevent Republican presidents from appointing conservative judges, while Senate Republicans have worked to prevent Democratic presidents from appointing liberal judges. During the early months of the Obama administration, Republicans were able to slow the judicial appointment process through filibusters and other procedural maneuvers so that only 3 of the president's 23 nominations for federal judgeships were confirmed by the Senate.[3] Obama's allies urged the president to take a more aggressive stance or risk allowing Republicans to block what had been considered a key Democratic priority. In 2013, the Senate voted 52 to 48 to end the use of the filibuster against all executive branch and judicial nominees except those to the Supreme Court. As of August 2016, Obama had won the appointment of 329 new district court judges, 55 new appeals court judges, and 2 Supreme Court justices.[4]

If political factors play an important role in the selection of district and appellate court judges, they are decisive when it comes to Supreme Court appointments. Because the Court has so much influence over law and politics, virtually all presidents have made an effort to select justices who share their political views.

As of November 2016, four of the eight current justices were appointed by Republican presidents. Before the passing of Justice Antonin Scalia, the Court had a conservative majority for 45 years, most recently consisting of Chief Justice John Roberts and Justices Samuel Alito, Anthony Kennedy, Antonin Scalia, and Clarence Thomas. As we saw in this chapter's introduction, this majority propelled the Court in a more conservative direction in a variety of areas. In 2011 and 2012, however, Chief Justice Roberts joined the liberal bloc in two important cases. The first was the Court's decision to invalidate portions of an Arizona law designed to identify and apprehend illegal aliens.[5] The second was the Court's 5–4 decision to uphold the Affordable Care Act (ACA), President Obama's major legislative achievement. In 2015, Roberts again voted to uphold the ACA, writing the majority opinion.[6]

Supreme Court nominations have come to involve intense partisan struggle in recent decades. Typically, after the president has named a nominee, interest groups opposed to the nomination have mobilized opposition in the media, among the public, and in the Senate. When President George H. W. Bush proposed conservative judge Clarence Thomas for the Court, for example, liberal groups launched a campaign to discredit Thomas. After extensive research into his background, opponents of the nomination were able to produce evidence suggesting that Thomas had sexually harassed a former subordinate, Anita Hill. Thomas denied the charge. After contentious Senate Judiciary Committee hearings, highlighted by testimony from both Thomas and Hill, Thomas narrowly won confirmation.

Republicans severely criticized Obama's nomination of Sonia Sotomayor in 2009 and Elena Kagan in 2010, though both were ultimately confirmed by the Senate.[7] Because Sotomayor and Kagan replaced liberal justices, they did not affect the balance of power on the Court. In 2016, however, the death of conservative justice Antonin Scalia gave Obama an opportunity to replace Scalia with a more liberal jurist, and Obama named Judge Merrick Garland. Senate Republicans refused to take action on the nomination, preferring to wait and see whether a Republican might be elected to the presidency in 2016 and have the opportunity to nominate another conservative to the Court. With Donald Trump's election in 2016, this strategy seemed to have paid off.

After the death of conservative justice Antonin Scalia in 2016, Republican senators called on President Obama to leave the nomination of his replacement to the next president. Obama nominated Merrick Garland, a moderate Democrat, hoping to persuade the Senate to hold a hearing and a vote.

The Power of the Supreme Court Is Judicial Review

Explain how the Supreme Court exercises the power of judicial review

The term **judicial review** refers to the power of the judiciary to review and, if necessary, declare actions of the legislative and executive branches invalid or unconstitutional. It is sometimes also used to describe the scrutiny that appellate courts give to the actions of trial courts, but strictly speaking, this is improper usage. A higher court's examination of a lower court's decisions might be called "appellate review," but it is not judicial review.

Judicial Review Covers Acts of Congress

Because the Constitution does not give the Supreme Court the power of judicial review over congressional enactments, the Court's exercise of it seems like something of a usurpation. But judicial review was debated at the Constitutional Convention. Some delegates expected the courts to exercise this power, while many others were "departmentalists," believing that each branch of the new government would interpret the Constitution as it applied to its own actions, with the judiciary mainly ensuring that individuals did not suffer injustices. Ambiguity over the framers' intentions was settled in 1803 in the case of *Marbury v. Madison*.[8] The Court said,

> It is emphatically the province and duty of the Judicial Department [the judicial branch] to say what the law is. Those who apply the rule to particular cases must, of necessity, expound and interpret that rule. If two laws conflict with each other, the Courts must decide on the operation of each. . . . So, if a law [e.g., a statute or treaty] be in opposition to the Constitution, if both the law and the Constitution apply to a particular case, so that the Court must either decide that case conformably to the law, disregarding the Constitution, or conformably to the Constitution, disregarding the law, the Court must determine which of these conflicting rules governs the case. This is of the very essence of judicial duty.

The Court's legal power to review acts of Congress has not been seriously questioned since 1803 in part because the Supreme Court tends to give acts of Congress an interpretation that will make them constitutional. For example, in its 2012 decision upholding the constitutionality of the ACA, the Court agreed with the many legal scholars who had argued that Congress had no power under the Constitution's commerce clause to order Americans to purchase health insurance. But rather than invalidate the act, the Court declared that the law's requirement that all Americans purchase insurance was actually a tax and, thus, represented a constitutionally acceptable use of Congress's power to levy taxes.[9]

In more than two centuries, the Court has concluded that fewer than 160 acts of Congress directly violated the Constitution.[10] These cases are often highly controversial. For example, in 2007, 2010, and 2014, the high court struck down key portions of the Bipartisan Campaign Reform Act, through which Congress had

Judicial Review across the Globe

A strong, independent judiciary is a major component of most modern democracies today. In 1946 only about a quarter of democracies had a constitutional court that possessed the power of judicial review, whereby the court can review the constitutionality of an act; by 2006 almost 90 percent did.[a]

However, the type of judicial review varies greatly by county. The U.S. Supreme Court has *concrete* judicial review, meaning that the Court can only rule whether or not a law is constitutional if it receives a specific case challenging that law. In contrast, countries with *abstract* judicial review do not require a case to make such a ruling. France's Conseil Constitutionnel, for example, can rule on the constitutionality of a law before the law is even enacted, if it receives a request by an elected official, such as a member of parliament or local government, to review the bill. France was long known for being the only country to use solely abstract review, but in 2010, France's courts gained the power to respond to enacted legislation as well, meaning that the courts now have the power of both abstract and concrete judicial review.

Country	Constitutional Court	Concrete, Abstract, or Both?	What Can Be Reviewed
Brazil	Supreme Federal Court	Both	• National legislation • Lower court decisions • State and local laws
France	Conseil Constitutionnel	Both	• National legislation • Legislation pertaining to cases before other high courts
Germany	Federal Constitutional Court	Both	• National legislation • Actions of other national government institutions • State and local laws • Constitutional amendments • Election law violations
India	Supreme Court	Concrete	• National legislation • Actions of other national government institutions • State and local laws • Lower court decisions and appeals • Past judgments by the Supreme Court
Japan	Supreme Court	Concrete	• National legislation • Local laws • Administrative actions
South Africa	Constitutional Court	Both	• National legislation • Actions of other national government institutions • Local laws • Lower court decisions and appeals
United States	Supreme Court	Concrete	• National legislation • Actions of other national government institutions (e.g., executive orders) • State and local laws • Lower court decisions and appeals

[a]David S. Law and Mila Versteeg, "The Evolution and Ideology of Global Constitutionalism," *California Law Review*, 99, no. 5 (2010): 1163–1257.

sought to regulate spending in political campaigns.[11] The Court found that provisions of the act limiting political advertising violated the First Amendment. These cases are unusual in that the Court rarely overturns acts of Congress.

Judicial Review Applies to Presidential Actions

The federal courts also review presidential actions from time to time. In recent decades, the courts have, more often than not, upheld presidential power in such areas as foreign policy, war and emergency powers, legislative power, and administrative authority. But the Supreme Court ruled on three cases involving President George W. Bush's antiterrorism initiatives and claims of executive power and in two of the three cases placed some limits on presidential authority.

One important case was *Hamdi v. Rumsfeld*.[12] Yaser Esam Hamdi, apparently a Taliban soldier, was captured by American forces in Afghanistan and brought to the United States, where he was incarcerated at the Norfolk Naval Station. Hamdi was classified as an enemy combatant and denied civil rights, including the right to counsel, despite the fact that he had been born in the United States and was a U.S. citizen. In 2004 the Supreme Court ruled that Hamdi was entitled to a lawyer and "a fair opportunity to rebut the government's factual assertions." Thus, the Court imposed restrictions on the president's power, although it also affirmed the president's most important claim: the unilateral power to declare individuals, including U.S. citizens, "enemy combatants" who could be detained by the United States.

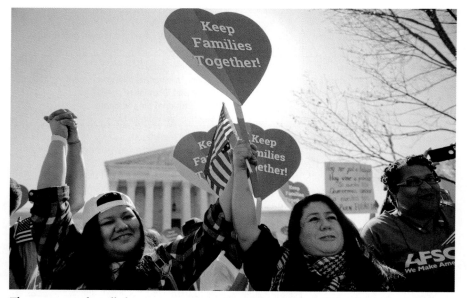

The courts may be called on to review the actions of the president. When President Obama passed an executive order that would protect millions of immigrants from deportation, opponents of the order challenged the legality of his actions. In 2016 the Court issued a 4–4 tie, calling into question Obama's plan.

In the 2006 case of *Hamdan v. Rumsfeld*,[13] Salim Hamdan, a Taliban fighter, was captured in Afghanistan and held at the Guantánamo Bay naval base. The Bush administration planned to try Hamdan before a military commission created by a 2002 presidential order. The Supreme Court ruled that this presidentially created commission violated federal law and U.S. treaty obligations. In response, Bush pressed Congress to rewrite the law, which it did, enacting the Military Commissions Act. This law gave the president legal authority for his actions. Section 7 of the law said that Guantánamo prisoners could not bring habeas corpus petitions to federal courts to seek their release. In the 2008 case of *Boumediene v. Bush*,[14] however, the Supreme Court struck down Section 7, saying that habeas corpus was a fundamental right.

Judicial Review Also Applies to State Actions

The logic of the **supremacy clause** of Article VI of the Constitution, which states that laws passed by the national government and all treaties "shall be the supreme Law of the Land" and superior to all laws adopted by any state or any subdivision, implies that the Court may review the constitutionality of state laws. Furthermore, in the Judiciary Act of 1789, Congress conferred on the Supreme Court the power to reverse state constitutions and laws whenever they are clearly in conflict with the U.S. Constitution, federal laws, or treaties.[15] This power gives the Supreme Court appellate jurisdiction over all of the millions of cases handled by U.S. courts each year.

The supremacy clause of the Constitution also provides that "the Judges in every State shall be bound thereby, any Thing in the Constitution or Laws of any State to the Contrary notwithstanding." Under this authority, the Supreme Court has frequently overturned state constitutional provisions or statutes and state court decisions it deems contrary to the federal Constitution or federal statutes.

The civil rights arena abounds with examples of state laws that were overturned because the statutes violated guarantees of due process and equal protection contained in the Constitution's Fourteenth Amendment. For example, in the 1954 case of *Brown v. Board of Education*, the Court overturned statutes from Kansas, South Carolina, Virginia, and Delaware that either required or permitted segregated public schools, on the basis that such statutes denied black schoolchildren equal protection of the law.[16] In 2003, the Court ruled that Texas's law criminalizing sodomy violated the right to liberty protected by the due process clause.[17]

Sometimes Court decisions are so broad and sweeping that they have the effect of changing the law, and legal practices, across the country. In the 1973 Supreme Court case of *Roe v. Wade*, for example, the Court ruled that a safe, legal abortion was a constitutionally protected right for women under most circumstances. This decision had the effect of striking down restrictive abortion laws in more than 40 states.

One realm in which the Court constantly monitors state conduct is that of law enforcement. As we saw in Chapter 4, the Supreme Court has developed

In 2012, the Supreme Court heard the case of Evan Miller, who was sentenced to life imprisonment without parole for a crime he allegedly committed when he was 14 years old. The Court ruled that a life-without-parole sentence for a 14-year-old violates the Eighth Amendment's prohibition against cruel and unusual punishment.

a number of principles regulating police conduct to ensure that the police do not violate constitutional liberties. These principles, however, must often be updated to keep pace with changes in technology. In the 2012 case of *United States v. Jones*, the Supreme Court found that police use of a Global Positioning System tracker—a device invented more than two centuries after the adoption of the Bill of Rights—constituted a "search" as defined by the Fourth Amendment. In the 2014 case of *Riley v. California*, the Court held that the police could not undertake a warrantless search of the digital contents of a cell phone—another device hardly imagined by the framers.[18] Recent Court decisions overturning state law have come in cases concerning criminal punishments. For example, in 2012 the Court struck down Alabama and Arkansas statutes that mandated a sentence of life in prison without possibility of parole for minors who were found guilty of homicide. The Court held that this statute violated the Eighth Amendment's prohibition of cruel and unusual punishment.[19]

Most Cases Reach the Supreme Court by Appeal

> **Describe the process the Supreme Court follows in the exercise of its power of judicial review**

Article III of the Constitution and Supreme Court decisions define judicial power as extending only to "cases and controversies." This means that the case before a court must be an actual controversy, not a hypothetical one, with two truly adversarial parties. The courts have interpreted this language to mean that they do not have the power to render advisory opinions to legislatures or agencies about the constitutionality of proposed laws or regulations. Furthermore, even after a law is enacted, the courts will generally refuse to consider its constitutionality until it is actually applied. Even with this provision, given that millions of disputes arise every year, the job of the Supreme Court would be impossible if it were not able to control the flow of cases and its own caseload. As noted earlier, cases that come first to the Supreme Court are very few in number.

Most cases reach the Supreme Court through the **writ of certiorari**, which is granted whenever four of the nine justices agree to review a decision of a lower court. (*Certiorari* comes from the Latin for "to make more certain.") The term *certiorari* is sometimes shortened to *cert*, and cases deemed to merit certiorari are referred to as "certworthy." An individual who loses in a lower federal court or state court and wants the Supreme Court to review the decision has 90 days to file a petition for a writ of certiorari with the clerk of the U.S. Supreme Court. Petitions for thousands of cases are filed with the Court every year.

Since 1972, most of the justices have participated in a "certiorari pool" in which their law clerks work together to evaluate the petitions. Each petition is reviewed by one clerk, who writes a memo for all the justices participating in the pool, summarizing the facts and issues and making a recommendation. Clerks for the other justices add their comments to the memo. After the justices have reviewed the memos, any one of them may place any case on the discuss list, which is circulated by the chief justice. If a case is not placed on the discuss list, it is automatically denied certiorari. Cases placed on the discuss list are considered and voted on during the justices' closed-door conference.

For certiorari to be granted, four justices must be convinced that the case satisfies Rule 10 of the Rules of the U.S. Supreme Court. Rule 10 states that certiorari is not a matter of right but is to be granted only when there are special and compelling reasons. These include conflicting decisions by two or more circuit courts, conflicts between circuit courts and state courts of last resort, conflicting decisions by two or more state courts of last resort, decisions by circuit courts on matters of federal law that should be settled by the Supreme Court, a circuit court decision on an important question that conflicts with Supreme Court decisions, cases that present important questions of civil rights or civil liberties, and cases in which the federal government is an appellant. It should be clear from this list that the Court will usually take action under only the most compelling circumstances. Ultimately, however, the question of which cases to accept can come down to the preferences and priorities of the justices.

As Figure 12.3 shows, the Court is inundated by appeals, and the number of appeals has skyrocketed over the years, even though the Court actually rules on less than 1 percent of these appeals.

The Solicitor General, Law Clerks, and Interest Groups Also Influence the Flow of Cases

In addition to the judges themselves, three other entities play an important role in shaping the flow of cases through the federal courts: the solicitor general, federal law clerks, and interest groups.

The Solicitor General If any single person has greater influence than individual judges over the federal courts, it is the **solicitor general** of the United States. The solicitor general is the third-ranking official in the Justice Department (below the attorney general and the deputy attorney general) but the top government lawyer in virtually all cases before the Supreme Court in which the government is a party. The solicitor general controls the flow of cases by screening them before any agency of the federal government can appeal them to the Supreme Court; indeed, the justices rely on the solicitor general to "screen out undeserving litigation and

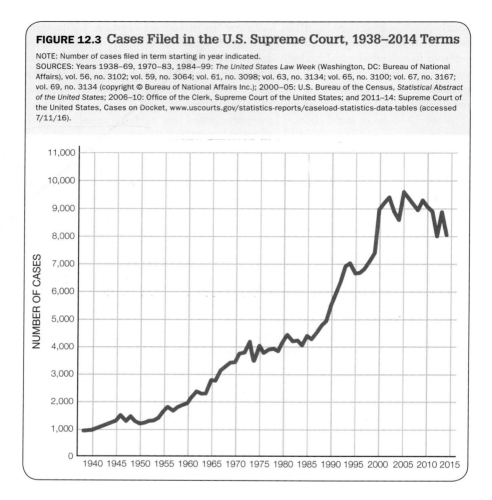

FIGURE 12.3 Cases Filed in the U.S. Supreme Court, 1938–2014 Terms

NOTE: Number of cases filed in term starting in year indicated.

SOURCES: Years 1938–69, 1970–83, 1984–99: *The United States Law Week* (Washington, DC: Bureau of National Affairs), vol. 56, no. 3102; vol. 59, no. 3064; vol. 61, no. 3098; vol. 63, no. 3134; vol. 65, no. 3100; vol. 67, no. 3167; vol. 69, no. 3134 (copyright © Bureau of National Affairs Inc.); 2000–05: U.S. Bureau of the Census, *Statistical Abstract of the United States*; 2006–10: Office of the Clerk, Supreme Court of the United States; and 2011–14: Supreme Court of the United States, Cases on Docket, www.uscourts.gov/statistics-reports/caseload-statistics-data-tables (accessed 7/11/16).

furnish them with an agenda to government cases that deserve serious consideration."[20] More than half of the Supreme Court's total workload consists of cases under the direct charge of the solicitor general. Typically, more requests for appeals are rejected than are accepted by the solicitor general. Without the solicitor general's support, requests directly from government agencies are seldom reviewed by the Court.

The solicitor general can enter a case even when the federal government is not a direct litigant, by writing an **amicus curiae** ("friend of the court") brief. A "friend of the court" is not a direct party to a case but seeks to assist the Supreme Court in reaching a decision by presenting additional briefs. Other interested parties may file amicus briefs as well.

In addition to exercising substantial control over the flow of cases, the solicitor general can shape the arguments used before the federal courts. Indeed, the Supreme Court tends to give special attention to the way the solicitor general characterizes the issues.

Law Clerks Every federal judge employs law clerks to research legal issues and assist with the preparation of opinions. Each Supreme Court justice is assigned four clerks. The clerks are almost always honors graduates from the nation's most prestigious law schools. A clerkship with a Supreme Court justice is a great honor and generally indicates that the fortunate individual is likely to reach the very top of the legal profession. The work of the Supreme Court clerks is a closely guarded secret, but some justices rely heavily on their clerks for advice in writing opinions and in deciding whether specific cases ought to be heard by the Court. In a recent book, a former law clerk to the late justice Harry Blackmun charged that Supreme Court justices yielded "excessive power to immature, ideologically driven clerks, who in turn use that power to manipulate their bosses."[21]

Lobbying for Access: Interests and the Court At the same time that the Court exercises discretion over which cases it will review, groups and forces in society often seek to persuade the justices to listen to their problems. Lawyers representing interest groups try to choose the proper client and the proper case so that the issues in question are most dramatically and appropriately portrayed. When possible, they also pick a district with a sympathetic judge in which to bring the case. Sometimes they wait for an appropriate political climate.

Group litigants have to plan carefully when to use and when to avoid publicity. They must also attempt to develop a proper record at the trial court level, one that includes some constitutional arguments and even, when possible, errors on the part of the trial court. One of the most effective strategies that litigants use in getting cases accepted for review by the appellate courts is to bring the same type of suit in more than one circuit (that is, to develop a "pattern of cases"), in the hope that inconsistent treatment by two different courts will improve the chance of a Supreme Court review.

The two most notable users of the "pattern of cases" strategy in recent years have been the National Association for the Advancement of Colored People (NAACP) and the American Civil Liberties Union (ACLU). For many years, the NAACP (and its Defense Fund—now a separate group) has worked through local chapters and with many individuals to encourage litigation on issues of racial discrimination and segregation. Sometimes it distributes petitions to be signed by parents and filed with local school boards and courts, deliberately sowing the seeds of future litigation. The NAACP and the ACLU often encourage private parties to bring suit and then join the suit as amici curiae.

The Supreme Court's Procedures Mean Cases May Take Months or Years

The Preparation The Supreme Court's decision to accept a case is the beginning of what can be a lengthy and complex process (see Figure 12.4). First, the attorneys on both sides must prepare **briefs**—written documents that may be several hundred pages long in which the attorneys explain, using case precedents, why the Court should rule in favor of their client. Briefs are filled with referrals to precedents specifically chosen to show that other courts have frequently ruled in

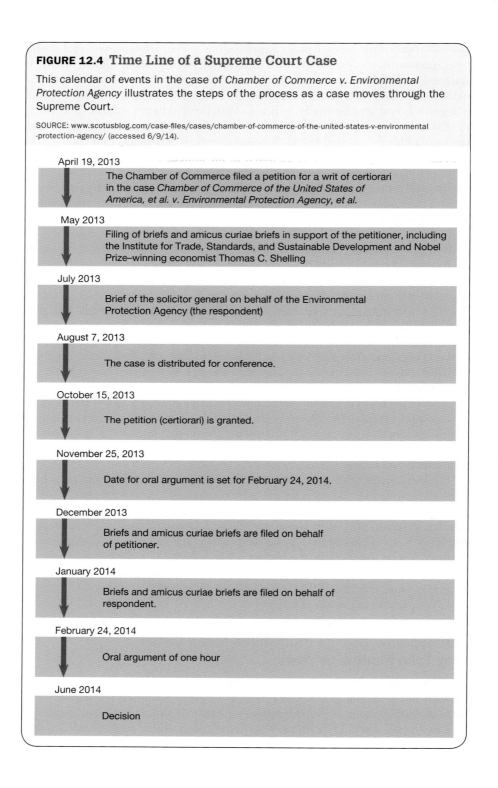

FIGURE 12.4 Time Line of a Supreme Court Case

This calendar of events in the case of *Chamber of Commerce v. Environmental Protection Agency* illustrates the steps of the process as a case moves through the Supreme Court.

SOURCE: www.scotusblog.com/case-files/cases/chamber-of-commerce-of-the-united-states-v-environmental-protection-agency/ (accessed 6/9/14).

April 19, 2013

The Chamber of Commerce filed a petition for a writ of certiorari in the case *Chamber of Commerce of the United States of America, et al. v. Environmental Protection Agency, et al.*

May 2013

Filing of briefs and amicus curiae briefs in support of the petitioner, including the Institute for Trade, Standards, and Sustainable Development and Nobel Prize–winning economist Thomas C. Shelling

July 2013

Brief of the solicitor general on behalf of the Environmental Protection Agency (the respondent)

August 7, 2013

The case is distributed for conference.

October 15, 2013

The petition (certiorari) is granted.

November 25, 2013

Date for oral argument is set for February 24, 2014.

December 2013

Briefs and amicus curiae briefs are filed on behalf of petitioner.

January 2014

Briefs and amicus curiae briefs are filed on behalf of respondent.

February 24, 2014

Oral argument of one hour

June 2014

Decision

the same way that the Supreme Court is being asked to rule. The attorneys for both sides muster the most compelling precedents they can in support of their arguments.

As the attorneys prepare their briefs, they often ask sympathetic interest groups for help. Groups are asked to file amicus curiae (friend of the court) briefs that support the claims of one or the other litigant. In a case involving separation of church and state, for example, liberal groups such as the ACLU and Citizens for the American Way are likely to be asked to file amicus briefs in support of strict separation, whereas conservative religious groups are likely to file amicus briefs advocating increased public support for religious ideas. Often, dozens of briefs will be filed on each side of a major case. Amicus filings are a primary method used by interest groups to lobby the Court.

Oral Argument The next stage of a case is **oral argument**, in which attorneys for both sides appear before the Court to present their positions and answer questions posed by justices. Each attorney has only a half hour to present the case, and this time includes interruptions for questions. Certain members of the Court, such as the late Justice Scalia, are known to interrupt attorneys dozens of times. Others, such as Justice Thomas, seldom ask questions. For an attorney, the opportunity to argue a case before the Supreme Court is a singular honor and a mark of professional distinction. It can also be a harrowing experience as justices interrupt a carefully prepared presentation to ask pointed questions. Oral argument can be very important to the outcome of a case. It allows justices to better understand the heart of the case and to raise questions that might not have been addressed in the opposing side's briefs. It is not uncommon for justices to go beyond the strictly legal issues and ask opposing counsel to discuss the implications of the case for the Court and the nation at large.

The Conference Following oral argument, the Court discusses the case in its Wednesday or Friday conference, a strictly private meeting that no outsiders are permitted to attend. The chief justice presides over the conference and speaks first; the other justices follow in order of seniority. The justices discuss the case and eventually reach a decision on the basis of a majority vote. If the Court is divided, a number of votes may be taken before a final decision is reached. As the case is discussed, justices may try to influence or change one another's opinions. At times, this may result in compromise decisions.

Opinion Writing After a decision has been reached, one of the members of the majority is assigned to write the **opinion**—the written explanation of the Supreme Court's decision in a particular case. This assignment is made by the chief justice or by the most senior justice in the majority if the chief justice is on the losing side. The assignment of the opinion can make a significant difference to the interpretation of a decision. Lawyers and judges in the lower courts will examine the opinion carefully to ascertain the Supreme Court's intent. Differences in wording and emphasis can have important implications for future litigation. Once the majority opinion is drafted, it is circulated to the other justices. Some members of the majority may decide that they do not agree with all the language of the opinion and therefore write "concurring" opinions that support the decision but offer a different rationale or emphasis. In assigning an opinion, serious thought must be given to the impression the case will make on lawyers and the public and to the probability that one justice's opinion will be more widely accepted than another's.

One of the more dramatic instances of this tactical consideration occurred in 1944, when Chief Justice Harlan F. Stone chose Justice Felix Frankfurter to write the opinion in the "white primary" case *Smith v. Allwright*. The chief justice believed that this sensitive case, which overturned the southern practice of prohibiting black participation in nominating primaries, required the efforts of the most brilliant and scholarly jurist on the Court. But the day after Stone made the assignment, Justice Robert H. Jackson wrote a letter to Stone urging a change of assignment. In his letter, Jackson argued that Frankfurter, a foreign-born Jew from New England, would not win the South with his opinion, regardless of its brilliance. Stone accepted the advice and substituted Justice Stanley Reed, an American-born Protestant from Kentucky and a southern Democrat in good standing.[22]

Dissent Justices who disagree with the majority decision of the Court may choose to publicize their disagreement in the form of a **dissenting opinion** (a decision written by a justice in the minority in a particular case in which the justice wishes to express his reasoning in the case). Dissents can be used to express opposition to an outcome or to signal to defeated political forces in the nation that their position is supported by at least some members of the Court. Because there is no need to please a majority, dissenting opinions can be more eloquent and less guarded than majority opinions. The Supreme Court often produces 5–4 decisions, with dissenters writing long and detailed opinions that, they hope, will help them to persuade a swing justice to join their side on the next round of cases dealing with a similar topic. During the Court's 2006–07 term, Justice Ruth Bader Ginsburg was so unhappy about the majority's decisions in a number of cases that she began to read forceful dissents from the bench, a practice she has continued to underscore her disagreements with several recent decisions and point the way toward other possibilities.

● Supreme Court Decisions Are Influenced by Activism and Ideology

Consider the personal and political influences on judges and the courts

The Supreme Court explains its decisions in terms of law and precedent. But although law and precedent do have an effect on the Court's deliberations and eventual decisions, throughout its history, the Court has shaped and reshaped the law. In the late nineteenth and early twentieth centuries, for example, the Supreme Court held that the Constitution, law, and precedent permitted racial segregation in the

United States. Beginning in the late 1950s, however, the Court found that the Constitution prohibited segregation on the basis of race and ruled that racial categories in legislation were always suspect. By the 1970s and '80s the Court once again held that the Constitution permitted the use of racial categories—when such categories were needed to help members of minority groups achieve full participation in American society. In the 1990s the Court began to retreat from this position, too, indicating that governmental efforts to provide extra help to racial minorities could represent an unconstitutional infringement on the rights of the majority.

Institutional Interests The Supreme Court's justices are acutely aware of the Court's place in history, and they care about protecting the Court's power and reputation. This desire to protect the institutional integrity of the Court can sometimes influence judicial thinking. Chief Justice John Roberts seemed to have institutional concerns in mind when he surprised fellow conservatives by casting the deciding vote in favor of the constitutionality of the ACA in 2012. Roberts had been widely expected to oppose the president's health care reform effort. However, the Court's conservative majority had come under increasing political fire for its positions on such matters as campaign finance and affirmative action. Roberts, according to one commentator, saw himself as "uniquely entrusted with the custodianship of the court's legitimacy, reputation, and stature" and was determined to show that the Court stood above mere political ideology.[23] As we saw above, Roberts repeated his support of the ACA in 2015 in the case of *King v. Burwell*.

Activism and Restraint The judicial philosophy of judges plays an important role in their decision making. One element of judicial philosophy is the issue of activism versus restraint. Over the years, some justices have believed that courts should narrowly interpret the Constitution according to the stated intentions of its framers and defer to the views of Congress when interpreting federal statutes. Justice Frankfurter, for example, advocated judicial deference to legislative bodies and avoidance of the "political thicket" in which the Court would entangle itself by deciding questions that were essentially political rather than legal in character. Advocates of **judicial restraint** are sometimes called "strict constructionists" because they refuse to go beyond the clear words of the Constitution in interpreting the document's meaning.

The alternative to restraint is **judicial activism.** Activist judges, such as the former chief justice Earl Warren, believe that the Court should go beyond the words of the Constitution or a statute to consider the broader societal implications of its decisions. Activist judges sometimes strike out in new directions, promulgating new interpretations or inventing new legal and constitutional concepts when they believe these to be socially desirable. For example, Justice Harry Blackmun's opinion in *Roe v. Wade* was based on a constitutional right to privacy that is not found in the words of the Constitution but was, rather, from the Court's prior decision in *Griswold v. Connecticut*.[24] Blackmun and the other members of the majority in the *Roe* case argued that the right to privacy was implied by other constitutional provisions. In this instance of judicial activism, the Court knew the result it wanted to achieve and was not afraid to make the law conform to the desired outcome.

Activism and restraint are sometimes confused with liberalism and conservatism. For example, conservative politicians often castigate "liberal activist" judges and call for the appointment of conservative jurists who will refrain from reinterpreting the law. To be sure, some liberal jurists are activists and some conservatives have been advocates of restraint, but the reverse is also true—liberals can be restrained and conservatives activist. Indeed, the Rehnquist Court, dominated by conservatives, was among the most activist courts in American history, striking out in new directions in such areas as federalism and election law. The Roberts Court is continuing along the same route. As the examples of these conservative courts illustrate, a judge may be philosophically conservative and believe in strict construction of the Constitution but also be jurisprudentially activist and believe that the courts must play an active and energetic role in policy making, if necessary striking down acts of Congress to ensure that the intent of the framers is fulfilled.

Political Ideology and Partisanship The philosophy of activism versus restraint is sometimes a smokescreen for political ideology, and indeed, the liberal or conservative attitudes of justices play an important role in their decisions. A study by three political scientists found that in First Amendment free speech cases that came before the Supreme Court between 1953 and 2011,

In a historic decision in 2015, the Supreme Court declared same-sex marriage a fundamental right protected by the due process and equal protection clauses of the Fourteenth Amendment to the Constitution.

liberal justices were more likely to vote to support the free speech rights of liberals, and conservative justices were more likely to support the free speech rights of conservative speakers. This trend, however, was even stronger for conservative justices than liberal justices. For example, the late conservative justice Antonin Scalia voted in favor of conservative speakers 65 percent of the time but in favor of liberal speakers 21 percent. The study, commented one legal analyst, "shows how much justices' ideology influences the speech they are willing to protect."[25]

Historically, liberal judges have been activists, willing to use the law to achieve social and political change, whereas conservatives have been associated with judicial restraint. In recent years, however, some conservative justices who have long called for restraint have actually become activists in seeking to undo some of the work of liberal jurists over the past several decades.

From the 1950s to the '80s, the Supreme Court took an activist role in such areas as civil rights, civil liberties, abortion, voting rights, and police procedures. For example, the Supreme Court was more responsible than any other governmental institution for breaking down America's system of racial segregation. The Supreme Court virtually prohibited states from interfering with the right of a woman to seek an abortion and sharply curtailed state restrictions on voting rights. And it was the Supreme Court that placed restrictions on the behavior of local police and prosecutors in criminal cases. In a series of decisions between 1989 and 2008, however, the conservative justices appointed by Ronald Reagan, George H. W. Bush, and George W. Bush were able to swing the Court to a more conservative position on civil rights, affirmative action, abortion rights, property rights, criminal procedure, voting rights, desegregation, and the power of the national government.

The Federal Judiciary
and Your Future

In the original conception of the framers, the judiciary was to be the institution that would protect individual liberty from the government. As we saw in Chapter 2, the framers believed that in a democracy the great danger was what they termed "tyranny of the majority"—the possibility that a popular majority, "united or actuated by some common impulse or passion," would "trample on the rules of justice."[26] The framers hoped that the courts would protect liberty from the potential excesses of democracy. And for most of American history, this was precisely the role played by the federal courts. The courts' most important decisions were those that protected the freedoms—to speak, worship, publish, vote, and attend school—of groups and individuals whose political views, religious beliefs, or racial or ethnic backgrounds made them unpopular.

Today, Americans of all political persuasions seem to view the courts as useful instruments through which to pursue their political and policy goals. Conservatives want to ban abortion and help business maintain its profitability, whereas liberals want to promote school integration and help enhance the power of workers in the workplace. (The "**Who Participates?**" feature on the facing page looks at efforts to influence the Supreme Court through amicus briefs). These may all be noble goals, but they present a basic dilemma for students of American government. If the courts are simply one more set of policy-making institutions, then who is left to protect the liberty of individuals?

Students should realize that the decisions made by the Supreme Court today will have important consequences for their lives and futures. The Court's campaign finance decisions will have consequences for who will govern the nation you inherit. The Court's decisions on health care influence your access to health insurance, the type of care you receive, and its cost. The Court's decisions in the realm of equal protection do and will impact your life (in particular, gays and lesbians with respect to marriage) and career chances. The Court's decisions in the realm of immigration will affect who will and will not be able to call themselves Americans. The Supreme Court is not an abstract entity in far-off Washington. It reaches directly into your life.

Influencing the Supreme Court?

Average Amicus Briefs per Case

1 — 1960s
2 — 1970s
4 — 1980s
5 — 1990s
8 — 2000s
11 — 2010s

(through 2015)

Amicus Briefs for Selected Landmark Cases

6 — **Brown v. Board of Education, 1954** (racial segregation)

107 — **Grutter v. Bollinger, 2003** (affirmative action admissions policy)

136 — **National Federation of Independent Business v. Sebelius, 2012** (Affordable Care Act, individual mandate)

147 — **Obergefell v. Hodges, 2015** (marriage equality)

SOURCES: Anthony J. Franze and R. Reeves Anderson, "Record Breaking Term for Amicus Curiae in Supreme Court Reflects New Norm," *The National Law Journal*, August 19, 2015, www.nationallawjournal.com /supremecourtbrief/id=1202735095655/Record-Breaking-Term-for -Amicus-Curiae-in-Supreme-Court-Reflects-New-Norm (accessed 12/8/15); Thomas G. Hansford and Kristen Johnson, "The Supply of Amicus Curiae Briefs in the Market for Information at the U.S. Supreme Court," *Justice System Journal*, 35, no. 4 (2014): 362–82; plus authors' updates.

WHAT YOU CAN DO ➡

WHAT YOU CAN DO

Look Inside the Federal Courts

 Find which groups filed amicus briefs for U.S. Supreme Court cases at **www.scotusblog.com**, and read a few of the briefs.

 Click on the "Court Locator" tab at **www.uscourts.gov** to find which federal courts are near you and to view their calendar of oral arguments. Court dockets and some case files are available at **www.pacer.gov**.

 Watch videos of cases from the Cameras in Courts pilot project at **www.uscourts.gov/about-federal-courts/cameras-courts**.

chapterstudyguide

Practice Quiz

1. What is the name for the body of law that deals with disputes not involving criminal penalties? *(p. 374)*
   a) civil law
   b) privacy law
   c) plea bargains
   d) household law
   e) common law

2. The doctrine that previous court decisions should apply as precedents in similar cases is known as *(p. 374)*
   a) habeas corpus
   b) a writ of certiorari
   c) stare decisis
   d) rule of four
   e) senatorial courtesy

3. Where do most trials in the United States take place? *(p. 374)*
   a) state courts
   b) appellate courts
   c) federal courts
   d) federal circuit courts
   e) the Supreme Court

4. The term *writ of habeas corpus* refers to *(p. 374)*
   a) a short, unsigned decision by an appellate court that rejects a petition to review the decision of a lower court
   b) a criterion used by courts to screen cases that no longer require resolution.

c) a decision of at least four of the nine Supreme Court justices to review a decision of a lower court

d) a court order that an individual in custody be brought into court and shown the cause for his or her detention.

e) a brief filed by the solicitor general when the federal government is not a direct litigant in a Supreme Court case.

5. Which of the following is not included in the original jurisdiction of the Supreme Court? *(p. 377)*
   a) cases between the United States and one of the 50 states
   b) cases brought by one state against citizens of another state or against a foreign country
   c) cases involving challenges to the constitutionality of state laws
   d) cases between two or more states
   e) cases involving foreign ambassadors or other ministers

6. The size of the Supreme Court is determined by *(p. 379)*
   a) the president.
   b) the chief justice.
   c) the Department of Justice.
   d) Congress.
   e) the Constitution.

7. The Supreme Court's decision in *Marbury v. Madison* was important because *(p. 382)*
   a) it invalidated state laws prohibiting interracial marriage.
   b) it ruled that the recitation of prayers in public schools is unconstitutional under the establishment clause of the First Amendment.
   c) it established that arrested people have the right to remain silent, the right to be informed that anything they say can be held against them, and the right to counsel before and during police interrogation.
   d) it provided an expansive definition of *commerce* under the interstate commerce clause.
   e) it established the power of judicial review.

8. Which of the following play an important role in shaping the flow of cases heard by the Supreme Court? *(pp. 387–89)*
   a) the attorney general and the secretary of state
   b) the solicitor general and federal law clerks
   c) the president and Congress
   d) state legislatures
   e) the federal district and circuit courts

9. Which government official is responsible for arguing the federal government's position in cases before the Supreme Court? *(pp. 387–88)*
   a) the vice president
   b) the solicitor general
   c) the attorney general
   d) the chief justice
   e) the U.S. district attorney

10. Which of the following is a brief submitted to the Supreme Court by someone other than one of the parties in the case? *(p. 388)*
    a) amicus curiae
    b) habeas corpus
    c) writ of certiorari
    d) ex post brief
    e) de jure brief

11. A dissenting opinion is written by *(p. 392)*
    a) the chief justice of the Supreme Court.
    b) a Supreme Court justice who agrees with the majority's ultimate decision but wishes to offer a different rationale or emphasis.
    c) a Supreme Court justice who disagrees with the majority decision.
    d) the solicitor general.
    e) a Supreme Court justice assigned by the chief justice.

12. If a justice favors going beyond the words of the Constitution to consider the broader societal implications of the Supreme Court's decisions, he or she would be considered an advocate of which judicial philosophy? *(p. 393)*
    a) judicial restraint
    b) judicial activism
    c) stare decisis
    d) judicial liberalism
    e) judicial conservatism

Key Terms

amicus curiae *(p. 388)* literally, "friend of the court"; individuals or groups who are not parties to a lawsuit but who seek to assist the Supreme Court in reaching a decision by presenting additional briefs

briefs *(p. 389)* written documents in which attorneys explain, using case precedents, why the court should find in favor of their client

chief justice *(p. 379)* justice on the Supreme Court who presides over the Court's public sessions and whose official title is chief justice of the United States

civil law *(p. 374)* the branch of law that deals with disputes that do not involve criminal penalties

court of appeals *(p. 375)* a court that hears the appeals of trial court decisions

criminal law *(p. 373)* the branch of law that regulates the conduct of individuals, defines crimes, and specifies punishment for acts defined as illegal

defendant *(p. 373)* the one against whom a complaint is brought in a criminal or civil case

dissenting opinion *(p. 392)* a decision written by a justice in the minority in a particular case in which the justice wishes to express his or her reasoning in the case

due process of law *(p. 376)* the right of every citizen against arbitrary action by national or state governments

judicial activism *(p. 393)* judicial philosophy that posits that the Court should go beyond the words of the Constitution or a statute to consider the broader societal implications of its decisions

judicial restraint *(p. 393)* judicial philosophy whose adherents refuse to go beyond the clear words of the Constitution in interpreting the document's meaning

judicial review *(p. 382)* the power of the courts to review and, if necessary, declare actions of the legislative and executive branches invalid or unconstitutional; the Supreme Court asserted this power in *Marbury v. Madison*

jurisdiction *(p. 376)* the sphere of a court's power and authority

opinion *(p. 391)* the written explanation of the Supreme Court's decision in a particular case

oral argument *(p. 391)* the stage in Supreme Court procedure in which attorneys for both sides appear before the Court to present their positions and answer questions posed by justices

original jurisdiction *(p. 377)* the authority to initially consider a case; distinguished from *appellate jurisdiction*, which is the authority to hear appeals from a lower court's decision

plaintiff *(p. 373)* the individual or organization that brings a complaint in court

plea bargain *(p. 376)* a negotiated agreement in a criminal case in a which a defendant agrees to plead guilty in return for the state's agreement to reduce the severity of the criminal charge the defendant is facing

precedent *(p. 374)* prior case whose principles are used by judges as the basis for their decisions in present cases

senatorial courtesy *(p. 380)* the practice whereby the president, before formally nominating a person for a federal judgeship, seeks the indication that senators from the candidate's own state support the nomination

solicitor general *(p. 387)* the top government lawyer in all cases before the Supreme Court in which the government is a party

stare decisis *(p. 374)* literally, "let the decision stand"; the doctrine that a previous decision by a court applies as a precedent in similar cases until that decision is overruled

supremacy clause *(p. 385)* Article VI of the Constitution, which states that laws passed by the national government and all treaties "shall be the supreme Law of the Land" and superior to all laws adopted by any state or any subdivision

supreme court *(p. 375)* the highest court in a particular state or in the United States; this court primarily serves an appellate function

trial court *(p. 374)* the first court to hear a criminal or civil case

writ of certiorari *(p. 386)* a decision of at least four of the nine Supreme Court justices to review a decision of a lower court; *certiorari* is Latin, meaning "to make more certain"

writ of habeas corpus *(p. 376)* a court order that the individual in custody be brought into court and shown the cause for detention; habeas corpus is guaranteed by the Constitution and can be suspended only in cases of rebellion or invasion

For Further Reading

Baum, Lawrence. *The Supreme Court*. 12th ed. Washington, DC: CQ Press, 2015.

Breyer, Stephen. *The Court and the World: American Law and the New Global Realities*. New York: Knopf, 2015.

Epstein, Lee, and Thomas G. Walker. *Constitutional Law for a Changing America*. 8th ed. Washington, DC: CQ Press, 2013.

Fisher, Louis. *Constitutional Dialogues*. Princeton, NJ: Princeton University Press, 1988.

Greenberg, Jan Crawford. *Supreme Conflict: The Inside Story of the United States Supreme Court*. New York: Penguin, 2008.

Hall, Kermit L., James Ely, and Joel Grossman. *The Oxford Companion to the Supreme Court*. New York: Oxford University Press, 2005.

Hirshman, Linda. *Sisters in Law: How Sandra Day O'Conner and Ruth Bader Ginsburg Went to the Supreme Court and Changed the World*. New York: Harper, 2015.

Irons, Peter. *A People's History of the Supreme Court*. New York: Penguin, 2006.

Johnson, Timothy R. *Oral Arguments and Decision Making on the U.S. Supreme Court*. Albany, NY: SUNY Press, 2004.

O'Brien, David M. *Storm Center: The Supreme Court in American Politics*. 10th ed. New York: W. W. Norton, 2014.

Spitzer, Robert J., ed. *Politics and Constitutionalism*. Albany, NY: SUNY Press, 2000.

Spitzer, Robert J. *Saving the Constitution from Lawyers*. New York: Cambridge University Press, 2008.

Toobin, Jeffrey. *The Oath: The Obama White House and the Supreme Court*. New York: Anchor, 2013.

Health care is an area of social policy that has been controversial. Although most Americans support universal access to health care, they disagree about the best way to ensure high-quality health care. Americans were divided over President Obama's 2010 comprehensive health care reform initiative, the Affordable Care Act, which underwent two Supreme Court challenges.

13

Domestic Policy

WHAT GOVERNMENT DOES AND WHY IT MATTERS *Public policy* refers to the decisions, rules, and regulations produced by the government. This chapter gives much of its attention to one broad subcategory of public policy: social policy. Social policies are important because they promote a range of public goals found in most public policies. The first is to protect against the risks and insecurities that most people face over the course of their lives. These include illness, disability, temporary unemployment, and the reduced earning capability that comes with old age. Most spending on social welfare in the United States goes to programs that serve these purposes, such as Social Security and medical insurance for the elderly. These are widely regarded as successful and popular (though expensive) programs.

Comprehensive health care reform is more controversial. Most Americans support universal access to health care, but when it comes to specific proposals, they often express doubts. Democrats experienced the public's ambivalence about health care reform after they enacted major changes to the system in 2010. The Patient Protection and Affordable Care Act was complex legislation that many people found hard to understand. Some parts of it were clearly popular, such as the provisions allowing young people to remain on their parents' insurance until they reached the age of 26 and providing full coverage of many preventive health services for adults and children. Other features, such as the requirement that everyone purchase insurance—with federal assistance—were unpopular. Even after the law was fully implemented in 2014 and survived another Supreme Court challenge in 2015, the public was split, with 42 percent of Americans holding an unfavorable view of the law and 42 percent holding a favorable view. Nearly five years after its enactment, Americans could not agree about the role government should play in ensuring health care for all.[1]

In the last several chapters, we examined the parts of the government that make policy: Congress, the presidency, the bureaucracy, and the courts. This chapter and Chapter 14 examine policy that is produced by the government—namely, public policy. The chapters will divide the subject in half and focus on a few selected examples. This chapter will focus on domestic policy, meaning policies that shape what happens within our nation's borders. Chapter 14 will examine foreign policy, meaning policies that shape America's relations with the other nations of the world.

In this chapter, we will examine the different approaches to achieving policy goals. We will then examine one broad area of domestic public policy, social policy. We focus on social policy because much of the government's annual budget goes to social programs, because such spending is often controversial, and because this process illustrates how the government tries to accomplish its goals.

chaptergoals

- Explain how different kinds of public policies achieve their goals using different means (pp. 405–12)

- Trace the history of government programs designed to promote economic security (pp. 412–18)

- Describe how education, health, and housing policies try to advance equality of opportunity (pp. 418–26)

- Explain how contributory and noncontributory programs benefit different groups of Americans (pp. 426–31)

The Tools for Making Policy Are Techniques of Control

Explain how different kinds of public policies achieve their goals using different means

Most of this book has focused on how government gets things done. This chapter and Chapter 14 will focus on what the government produces, called **public policy.** *Public policy* can be defined simply as a law, a rule, a statute, or an edict that expresses the government's goals and provides for rewards and punishments to promote those goals' attainment. Public policy can include a law passed by Congress, a presidential directive, a Supreme Court ruling, or a rule issued by a bureaucratic agency.

In trying to achieve some purpose, public policy is inherently coercive, even when motivated by the best and most benign intentions. Note that the word *policy* shares a root with the word *police*. Both terms come from the Greek words *polis* and *politeia*, which refer to the political community and the sources of public authority. So it is important to remember that although the idea of coercion seems inherently negative, it is in fact a vital and necessary part of governing. (If overused or misused, however, coercion can obviously be harmful.)

Techniques of control are to policy makers what tools are to a carpenter. There are a limited number of techniques that the government can use, each with its own logic and limitations. An accumulation of experience helps us to understand when a certain technique is likely to work. Still, just as carpenters will have different ideas about the best tool for a job, so policy makers will disagree about which techniques work best and when. What we offer here is a workable elementary handbook of techniques that will be useful for analyzing policy.

Table 13.1 lists some important techniques of control available to policy makers. These techniques can be grouped into three categories: promotional, regulatory, and redistributive policies.

Promotional Policies Get People to Do Things by Giving Them Rewards

Promotional policies are the carrots of public policy. Their purpose is to encourage people to do something they might not otherwise do or to get people to do more of what they are already doing. Sometimes the purpose is merely to compensate people for something done in the past. Promotional techniques can be classified into at least two separate types: subsidies and contracting.

Subsidies **Subsidies** are simply government grants of cash or other valuable commodities, such as land, to individuals or an organization that are used to promote activities desired by the government, to reward political support, or to buy off political opposition. Subsidies were the dominant form of public policy of the national government and the state and local governments throughout the nineteenth century. They continue to be an important category of public policy at all levels of government.

TABLE 13.1

Techniques of Public Control

TYPE OF POLICY	TECHNIQUES	DEFINITIONS AND EXAMPLES
Promotional	Subsidies and grants of cash, land, etc.	"Patronage"—the promotion of private activity through what recipients consider "benefits" (example: in the nineteenth century the government encouraged westward settlement by granting land to those who went west)
	Contracts	Agreements with individuals or firms in the "private sector" to purchase goods or services
	Licenses	Unconditional permission to do something that is otherwise illegal (franchise, permit)
Regulatory	Criminal penalties	Heavy fines or imprisonment, loss of citizenship
	Civil penalties	Less onerous fines, probation, public exposure, restitution
	Administrative regulations	The setting of interest rates, maintenance of health and safety standards, and the investigation and publicizing of wrongdoing
	Subsidies and contracts	Can be considered regulatory when certain conditions are attached (example: the government refuses to award a contract to firms that show no evidence of affirmative action in hiring)
	Regulatory taxes	Taxes that keep down consumption or production (liquor, gas, cigarette taxes)
	Expropriation	"Eminent domain"—the power to take private property for public use
Redistributive	Taxes	Alteration of the redistribution of money by changing taxes or tax rules
	Budgeting and spending through subsidies and contracts	Deficit spending to pump money into the economy when it needs a boost; creation of a budget surplus by cutting spending or increasing taxes to discourage consumption in inflationary times
	Fiscal use of credit and interest (monetary techniques)	Change in interest rates to affect both demand for money and consumption (example: the Federal Reserve Board raises interest rates to slow economic growth and ward off inflation)

During the nineteenth century, subsidies in the form of land grants were given to farmers and to railroad companies to encourage western settlement. Substantial cash subsidies have traditionally been given to shipbuilders to help build the commercial fleet and to guarantee the use of their ships as military personnel carriers in time of war. Policies using the subsidy technique have continued to be plentiful in the modern era, even after the 1990s, when there was widespread public and official hostility toward subsidies. For example, in 2007, the annual value of corporate subsidies, not including agriculture, was estimated at $92 billion.[2]

Subsidies have always been a technique favored by politicians because they can be treated as benefits that can be spread widely in response to many demands that might otherwise produce profound political conflict. Subsidies can, in other words, be used to buy off the opposition. And once subsidies exist, the threat of their removal becomes a very significant technique of control.

Contracting Like any corporation, a government agency must purchase goods and services by contract. The law requires open bidding for a substantial proportion of these contracts because government contracts are extremely valuable to businesses in the private sector and because the opportunities and incentives for abuse are very great. Yet contracting is more than a method of buying goods and services. It is also an important technique of policy because government agencies are often authorized to use their **contracting power** (the power of government to set conditions on companies seeking to sell goods or services to government agencies) as a means of encouraging corporations to improve themselves, as a means of helping to build up whole sectors of the economy, and as a means of encouraging certain desirable goals or behavior, such as equal employment opportunity. For example, the infant airline industry of the 1930s was nurtured by the national government's lucrative contracts to carry airmail.

Military contracting has long been a major element in government spending. So tight was the connection between defense contractors and the federal government during the Cold War that as he was leaving office President Eisenhower warned the nation to beware of the powerful "military–industrial complex." After the Cold War, as military spending and production declined, major defense contractors began to look for alternative business activities to supplement the reduced demand for weapons. For example, Lockheed Martin, the nation's largest defense contractor, began to bid on contracts related to welfare reform. Since the terrorist attacks of 2001, however, the military budget has been awash in new funds, and military contractors are flooded with business. President George W. Bush increased the Pentagon budget by more than 7 percent a year, requesting so many weapons systems that one observer called the budget a "weapons smorgasbord."[3] Military contractors geared up to produce not only weapons for foreign warfare but also surveillance systems to enhance domestic security.

Regulatory Policies Are Rules Backed by Penalties

If promotional policies are the carrots of public policy, regulatory policies can be considered the sticks. Regulation is a technique of control in which the government adopts rules that impose restrictions on the conduct of private citizens. The conduct may be regulated because people feel it is harmful to others, or threatens to be, such as drunk driving or false advertising. Or the conduct may be regulated because people think it's immoral, whether it harms others or not, such as prostitution, gambling, or drinking. Because there are many forms of regulation, we have subdivided them here: (1) police regulation, through civil and criminal penalties; (2) administrative regulation; (3) regulatory taxation; and (4) expropriation.

Police Regulation "Police regulation" comes closest to the traditional exercise of police power—a power traditionally reserved to the states to regulate the health, safety, and morals of its citizens. After a person's arrest and conviction, these techniques are administered by courts and, where necessary, penal institutions. They are regulatory techniques.

Civil penalty usually refers to a fine or some other form of material restitution (such as public service) as a sanction for violating civil laws or common law principles or committing negligence. Civil penalties can range from a five-dollar fine for a parking violation to a more onerous penalty for late payment of income taxes to the much more onerous penalties for violating antitrust laws against unfair competition or environmental protection laws against pollution. *Criminal penalty* usually refers to imprisonment but can also involve heavy fines and the loss of certain civil rights and liberties, such as the right to vote.

Administrative Regulation Police regulation addresses conduct considered immoral. In order to eliminate such conduct, strict laws have been passed and severe sanctions enacted. But what about conduct that is not considered morally wrong but that may have harmful consequences? For example, there is nothing morally wrong with radio or television broadcasting. But government regulates broadcasting on a particular frequency or channel because there would be virtual chaos if everybody could broadcast on any frequency at any time.

This kind of conduct is thought of less as *policed* conduct and more as *regulated* conduct. When conduct is said to be regulated, the purpose is rarely to eliminate it but rather to influence it toward more appropriate channels, toward more appropriate locations, or toward certain qualified types of persons, all for the purpose of minimizing injuries or inconveniences. This type of regulation is sometimes called *administrative regulation* because the controls are given over to civilian agencies rather than to the police and the rules are made by regulatory agencies and commissions. Each regulatory agency has extensive powers to keep a sector of the economy under surveillance and to make rules dealing with the behavior of individual companies and people. But these administrative agencies have fewer powers of punishment than the police and the courts have, and the administrative agencies generally rely on the courts to issue orders enforcing the rules and decisions made by the agencies.

Table 13.1 lists subsidies and contracts as examples of both promotional and regulatory policies; although these techniques might normally be thought of as strictly promotional policies, they can also be used for administrative regulation. It all depends on whether the law sets serious conditions on eligibility for the subsidy or contract. To put it another way, the government can use the threat of losing a valuable subsidy or contract to improve compliance with the goals of regulation. For example, the threat of removal of the subsidies called "federal aid to education" has had a very significant influence on the willingness of schools to cooperate in the desegregation of their student bodies and faculties. For another example, social welfare subsidies (benefits) can be lowered to encourage or force people to take low-paying jobs, or they can be increased to calm political unrest when people are engaging in political protest.[4]

Regulatory Taxation In many instances, the primary purpose of a tax is not to raise revenue but to influence conduct, often to discourage or eliminate an activity altogether by making it too expensive for most people. Such taxes are called regulatory taxes. For example, since the end of Prohibition, although there has been no penalty for the production or sale of alcoholic beverages, the alcohol industry has not been free from regulation. First, all alcoholic beverages have to be licensed, allowing only those companies that are "bonded" to put their product on the market. Beyond that, federal and state taxes on alcohol are made disproportionately high, on the theory that, in addition to the revenue gained, less alcohol will be consumed. The same is true of cigarette taxes.

Expropriation Confiscation of property with or without compensation for a public use, or *expropriation*, is a widely used technique of control in the United States, especially in land-use regulation. Almost all public works, from highways to parks to government office buildings, involve the forceful taking of some private property in order to acquire sufficient land for the necessary construction.

We generally call the power to expropriate *eminent domain* (the right of government to take private property for public use), a power that is recognized as inherent in any government. The Fifth Amendment of the U.S. Constitution provides an important safeguard against abuse, saying that private property cannot be taken for public use "without just compensation." Thus, the government is not permitted to use that power except through a strict due process, and it must offer "fair market value" for the land sought.[5]

Forcing individuals to work for a public purpose is another form of expropriation. The draft of young men for the armed forces, court orders to strikers to return to work, and sentences for convicted felons to do community service are examples of the regular use of expropriation in the United States.

Redistributive Policies Affect Broad Classes of People

Redistributive policies (also called *macroeconomic policies*) are usually of two types, monetary and fiscal; but they have a common purpose: to control people by manipulating the entire economy rather than by regulating *people* directly. (*Macroeconomic* refers to the economy as a whole.) Whereas regulatory policies focus on individual conduct, redistributive policies seek to control conduct more indirectly by altering the conditions of conduct or manipulating the environment of conduct.

Monetary Policies **Monetary policies** allow government to regulate the economy through the manipulation of the supply of money and credit. America's most powerful institution in this area of monetary policy is the Federal Reserve Board (the Fed), the governing board of the **Federal Reserve System**, consisting of a chair and six other members, all appointed by the president with the consent of the Senate. The Fed can affect the total amount of credit available through the

At her confirmation hearing in 2013, chair of the Federal Reserve Janet Yellen discussed the role of the Fed in reducing unemployment and in keeping inflation at approximately 2 percent a year.

interest (called the federal funds rate) that member banks charge one another for loans. If the Fed significantly decreases the federal funds rate, it can give a boost to a sagging economy. During 2001 the Fed cut interest rates 11 times to combat the combined effects of recession and the terrorist attacks. In the steep recession that began in 2008, the Fed acted aggressively. By December 2008 it had cut rates nine times, from a high in September 2007 of 4.75 percent to a historically low zero percentage rate. Moreover, the Federal Reserve kept interest rates at or near that level well into 2015, in an attempt to encourage new lending and thus economic growth,[6] although these low rates also had the effect of discouraging people from saving money because the rate of return on savings accounts was so low. If the Fed raises the federal funds rate, it can put a brake on the economy because the higher discount rate also increases the general interest rates charged by leading private banks to their customers. The Federal Reserve is responsible for ensuring high employment as well as price stability, but it has been particularly important in fighting inflation. During the late 1970s and early '80s, with inflation at record-high levels, Federal Reserve chair Paul Volcker aggressively raised interest rates in order to dampen inflation. Although his actions provoked a sharp recession, they raised the stature of the Fed, demonstrating its ability to manage the economy.

Fiscal Policies **Fiscal policies** are the government's use of taxing, monetary, and spending powers to manipulate the economy. Personal and corporate income taxes, which raise most of the U.S. government's revenues, are the most prominent examples. While the direct purpose of an income tax is to raise revenue, each tax has a different impact on the economy; and government can plan for that impact. Although the primary purpose of the graduated income tax is, of course, to raise revenue, an important second objective is to collect revenue in such a way as to reduce the disparities of wealth between the lowest and the highest income brackets. We call this a policy of **redistribution**. Another policy objective of the income tax is the encouragement of the capitalist economy by rewarding investment. The tax laws allow individuals or companies to deduct from their taxable income any money they can justify as an investment or a "business expense"; this gives an incentive to individuals and companies to spend money to expand their production, their advertising, or their staff and reduces the income taxes that businesses have to pay.

Americans have long debated the appropriate levels of taxation on individual and corporate income. After passing major income tax cuts in 2001, President Bush proposed and Congress passed a sweeping new round of cuts in 2003. Bush's plan was intended to promote investment by reducing taxes on most stock dividends, to spur business activity by offering tax breaks to small businesses, and to stimulate the economy by reducing the tax rates for all taxpayers. In 2006, Congress extended the rate reductions on dividends and capital gains, a move that estimates showed would cost the treasury $70 billion over five years.

President Obama and the Democratic leadership proposed extending the tax cuts for everyone with annual incomes under $250,000; those making more would have their income taxes revert back to the rates in the 1990s. Republicans and some Democrats preferred to extend the tax cuts for everyone. At the end of 2010, Obama and Congress reached a deal to extend the Bush tax cuts for two years. In 2013, they were extended again and made permanent.

Spending Power as Fiscal Policy Perhaps the most important redistributive technique of all is the most familiar one: the "spending power," which is a combination of subsidies and contracts. Government can use these techniques to achieve policy goals far beyond buying goods and services and regulating individual conduct. This is why subsidies and contracts show up yet again in Table 13.1 as redistributive techniques.

Agricultural subsidies are one example of the national government's use of its purchasing power as a fiscal or redistributive technique. Since the 1930s the federal government has attempted to raise and to stabilize the prices of several important agricultural products, such as corn and wheat, by authorizing the Department of Agriculture to buy enormous amounts of these commodities if prices on the market fall below a fixed level.

Should the Government Intervene in the Economy?

All politicians want a healthy economy, but they often differ in their views about how to attain it. Addressing economic challenges and maintaining a strong economy are extremely important to political leaders. Until 1929, most Americans believed that government had little to do with actively managing the economy. The world was guided by the theory that the economy, if left to its own devices, would produce full employment and maximum production. This traditional view of the relationship between government and the economy crumbled in 1929 before the stark reality of the Great Depression of 1929–39. When President Franklin Delano Roosevelt took office in 1933, he energetically threw the federal government into the business of fighting the depression. One of the main ways that the federal government sought to keep the economy healthy was through decisions about taxing and spending in accordance with the ideas of the British economist John Maynard Keynes. Keynesians argue that by pumping money into the economy, particularly by running deficits during periods of recession, government can stimulate demand and create a cycle of increased production and jobs that will pull the economy out of recession.

In the 1980s, growing numbers of Republicans began to reject the idea that government could help ensure economic prosperity. Instead, they argued that freeing markets from government intervention would produce the best economic results. As Ronald Reagan put it in his first inaugural address, "Government is not the solution to our problem, government is the problem."[7] Many Democrats, on the other hand, continued to believe that government has an important role to play in promoting a strong economy. This fundamental disagreement between the parties over the appropriate role of government underlies the fierce contemporary political debates over the government's role in the economy.

Today, some of the most intense conflicts between Democrats and Republicans concern taxes. As Republicans embraced the idea that reducing the role of government in the economy would promote investment and spur economic growth, they made tax cuts their highest priority. Because no one really likes to pay taxes, Republican support for tax cuts creates a political dilemma for Democrats. How can they defend taxes? Polls show that most of the time—although not always—a majority of Americans think that their taxes are too high.[8] Aware of the political damage that might come from opposing tax cuts, many Democratic members of Congress have supported tax cuts. But because most Democrats favor higher levels of public spending than do Republicans, they ultimately need taxes to fund government programs. To resolve this political problem, Democrats have sought to increase taxes on the wealthy. One reliable finding in public opinion polls is that the majority of Americans agree that upper-income people are not paying their fair share of taxes.[9] Raising taxes on the wealthy involves boosting taxes on investment income, which accounts for a much greater share of the income for the wealthy.

Social Policy and the Welfare System Buttress Equality

Trace the history of government programs designed to promote economic security

For much of American history, local governments and private charities—not the federal government—were in charge of caring for the poor. During the 1930s, when this largely private system of charity collapsed in the face of widespread economic destitution, the federal government created the beginnings of an American welfare state. The idea of the welfare system was new; it meant that the national government would oversee programs designed to promote economic security for all Americans—not just for the poor. The American system of social welfare includes many different policies enacted over the years since the Great Depression. Because each program is governed by distinct rules, the kind and level of assistance available vary widely.

The History of the Government Welfare System Dates Only to the 1930s

There has always been a welfare system in America, but until 1935 it was almost entirely private, composed of an extensive system of voluntary philanthropy through churches and other religious groups, ethnic and fraternal societies, communities and neighborhoods, and philanthropically inclined rich individuals. Most often it was called *charity*, and although it was private and voluntary, it was thought of as a public obligation.

The traditional approach of charity crumbled in the face of the stark reality of the Great Depression. During the depression, misfortune became so widespread

During the depression, the government took a more active role in helping poor and struggling Americans. Here, people line up to receive free bread.

and private wealth shrank so drastically that private charity was out of the question and the distinction between deserving and undeserving became impossible to draw. Following the crash of 1929 around 20 percent of the workforce immediately became unemployed; this figure grew as the depression stretched into years. Moreover, few of the unemployed had any monetary resources or any family farm on which to fall back. Banks failed, wiping out the savings of millions who had been prudent enough or fortunate enough to have any savings at all. Thousands of businesses failed as well, throwing middle-class Americans onto the bread lines along with unemployed laborers, dispossessed farmers, and those who had never worked in any capacity whatsoever. The Great Depression proved to Americans that poverty could be a result of imperfections in the economic system as well as of individual irresponsibility. It also forced Americans to drastically alter their standards regarding who was deserving and who was not.

Once poverty and dependency were accepted as problems inherent in the economic system, a large-scale public policy approach was not far away. By the time President Franklin Delano Roosevelt took office in 1933, the question was not whether there was to be a public welfare system but how generous or restrictive that system would be.

The Social Security Act of 1935 Was the Foundation of the Welfare System

The modern welfare state in the United States began with the enactment of the Social Security Act of 1935. This act created two separate categories of welfare: contributory and noncontributory.

Contributory Programs The category of welfare programs that are financed by taxation or other mandatory contributions by their present or future recipients can justifiably be called "forced savings" because these programs force working

Americans to contribute a portion of their earnings to provide income and benefits during their retirement years. These **contributory programs** are what most people have in mind when they refer to **Social Security** or social insurance, a contributory welfare program into which working Americans contribute a percentage of their wages and from which they receive cash benefits after retirement. Under the original contributory program, old-age insurance, the employer and the employee were each required to pay an equal amount, which in 1937 was set at 1 percent of the first $3,000 of wages, to be deducted from the paycheck of each employee and matched by the same amount from the employer. This percentage has increased over the years; the contribution in 2016 was 7.65 percent subdivided as follows: 6.2 percent on the first $118,500 of income for Social Security benefits, plus 1.45 percent on all earnings for Medicare.[10] Starting in 2014, households earning over $250,000 a year paid an extra 0.9 percent in Medicare taxes as a result of a provision in the Affordable Care Act. In the short term, Social Security redistributes money from younger workers to older retirees: the taxes of current workers are paying for the benefits received by retirees, raising concerns that we have reached the point where more people are receiving benefits than are paying into the system. But Social Security also plays a vital role for young people by providing survivor benefits to those whose parents have died, retired, or become disabled. Surviving spouses also receive survivor benefits. Today, the average Social Security payment is $1,335 each month.[11]

The biggest single expansion in contributory programs since 1935 was the establishment in 1965 of **Medicare**, a form of national health insurance for the elderly and the disabled that provides substantial medical services to elderly persons who are already eligible to receive old-age, survivors', and disability insurance under the original Social Security system. In 2003, Congress added a prescription drug benefit to the package of health benefits for the elderly. Social Security benefits and costs are adjusted through **indexing** (a periodic process of adjusting of social benefits or wages to account for increases in the cost of living), whereby benefits paid out under contributory programs are modified annually by **cost-of-living adjustments (COLAs)**—changes made to the level of benefits of a government program based on the rate of inflation. Of course, Social Security taxes (contributions) also increased after almost every benefit increase.

Unemployment insurance is another contributory program that is funded by a combination of federal and state taxes. States set benefit levels and eligibility criteria for receiving unemployment insurance and tax employers to fund the program. In most states, benefits last for a maximum of 26 weeks. Such benefits are generally funded by federal taxes. Unemployment benefits are meant to help replace lost wages, but they do so at a low level: most workers receive only half of their wages. Moreover, because states impose criteria about how long people must work or how much they must earn to become eligible for unemployment insurance, only about half of workers who lose their jobs receive unemployment benefits.[12]

Noncontributory Programs Social programs that provide assistance to people based on demonstrated need rather than any contribution they have made—**noncontributory programs**—are also known as "public-assistance programs" or, more commonly, as "welfare." Until 1996, the most important noncontributory program was Aid to Families with Dependent Children (AFDC), which provided federal funds, administered by the states, for children living with parents or relatives who fell below state standards of need. It was founded in 1935 by the original Social Security Act. In 1996, Congress abolished AFDC and replaced it with the Temporary Assistance to Needy Families (TANF) block grant. Eligibility for public assistance is determined by **means testing**, a procedure that requires applicants to show a financial need for assistance. Between 1935 and 1965, the government created programs to provide housing assistance, school lunches, and food stamps to other needy Americans.

As with contributory programs, the noncontributory public-assistance programs made their most significant advances in the 1960s and '70s. The largest single category of expansion was the establishment in 1965 of **Medicaid**, a federally and state-funded, state-operated program that provides extended medical services to low-income Americans. Noncontributory programs underwent another major transformation in the 1970s in the level of benefits they provide. Besides being means-tested, noncontributory programs are state-based; grants-in-aid are provided by the federal government to the states as incentives to establish the programs, but states retain considerable leeway to establish eligibility criteria (see Chapter 3). Thus, from the beginning there were considerable disparities in benefits from state to state. The national government sought to rectify the disparities in levels of old-age benefits in 1974 by creating the Supplemental Security Income (SSI) program to augment benefits for the aged, the blind, and the disabled. SSI provides uniform minimum benefits across the entire nation and includes mandatory COLAs. States are allowed to be more generous if they wish, but no state is permitted to provide benefits below the minimum level set by the national government.

The TANF program is also administered by the states, and, as with the old-age benefits just discussed, benefit levels vary widely from state to state (see Figure 13.1). In 2015 the states' monthly TANF benefits for a family of three varied from $170 in Mississippi to $923 in Alaska.[13] Even the most generous TANF payments are well below the federal poverty line. In 2016 the poverty level for a family of three included those earning less than $20,160 a year or $1,680 a month.[14]

The number of people receiving AFDC benefits expanded in the 1970s, in part because new welfare programs had been established in the mid-1960s: Medicaid (discussed earlier) and the **Supplemental Nutrition Assistance Program (SNAP)**, which is still sometimes called by its old name, *food stamps*. SNAP is the largest antipoverty program, which provides recipients with a debit card for food at most grocery stores. Collectively, these programs provide what are called **in-kind benefits**—noncash goods and services provided by the government that the beneficiary

The Supplemental Nutrition Assistance Program (SNAP), formerly known as food stamps, *helps people in need buy food. Today, recipients use a government-provided debit card that is accepted at most grocery stores.*

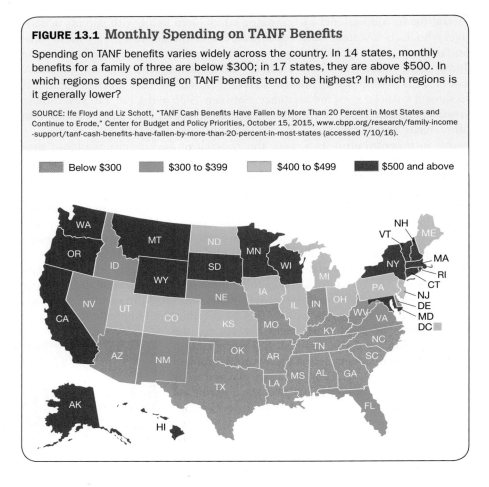

FIGURE 13.1 Monthly Spending on TANF Benefits

Spending on TANF benefits varies widely across the country. In 14 states, monthly benefits for a family of three are below $300; in 17 states, they are above $500. In which regions does spending on TANF benefits tend to be highest? In which regions is it generally lower?

SOURCE: Ife Floyd and Liz Schott, "TANF Cash Benefits Have Fallen by More Than 20 Percent in Most States and Continue to Erode," Center for Budget and Policy Priorities, October 15, 2015, www.cbpp.org/research/family-income -support/tanf-cash-benefits-have-fallen-by-more-than-20-percent-in-most-states (accessed 7/10/16).

Below $300 $300 to $399 $400 to $499 $500 and above

would otherwise have to pay for in cash. Because AFDC recipients automatically received Medicaid and food stamps, these new program created an incentive for poor Americans to establish their eligibility for AFDC.

Welfare Reform Has Dominated the Welfare Agenda in Recent Years

From the 1960s to the 1990s, opinion polls consistently showed that the public viewed welfare beneficiaries as "undeserving."[15] Underlying that judgment was the belief that welfare recipients did not want to work. These negative assessments were amplified by racial stereotypes. By 1973, 46 percent of welfare recipients were African American. Although the majority of recipients were white, media portrayals helped to create the widespread perception that the vast majority of welfare recipients were black. A careful study by Martin Gilens has shown how racial stereotypes of blacks as uncommitted to the work ethic reinforced public opposition to welfare.[16]

Despite this public opposition, it proved difficult to reform welfare, and welfare rolls reached an all-time high in 1994. Sensing continuing public frustration with welfare, when Bill Clinton was a presidential candidate he vowed "to end welfare as we know it," an unusual promise for a Democrat. Once in office, Clinton found it difficult to design a plan that would provide an adequate safety net for recipients who were unable to find work. Clinton's major achievement in the welfare field was to increase the Earned Income Tax Credit (EITC). This credit now allows working parents whose annual income falls below $53,300 (for a family of three or more) to file through their income tax return for an income supplement of up to $6,242, depending on their income and family size. The average EITC benefit in 2015 was $2,400.[17]

Congressional Republicans proposed a much more dramatic reform of welfare, which Clinton signed in 1996. The Personal Responsibility and Work Opportunity Reconciliation Act (PRWORA) repealed AFDC and replaced it with the TANF program. In place of the individual entitlement to assistance, the new law created block grants to the states and allowed states much more discretion in designing their cash-assistance programs to needy families. The new law also established time limits, restricting recipients to two years of assistance and creating a lifetime limit of five years. It imposed new work requirements on those receiving welfare, and it restricted most legal immigrants from receiving benefits. The aim of the new law was to reduce welfare caseloads, promote work, and reduce out-of-wedlock births. Notably, reducing poverty was not one of its stated objectives.

After this law was enacted, the number of families receiving assistance dropped by 60 percent nationwide, from 5.1 million families in 1994 to 1.9 million families in 2005,[18] although at least some of this drop was caused by the government moving people from SNAP to Social Security disability. The sharp decline in the number of recipients was widely hailed as a sign that welfare reform was working. Indeed, former welfare recipients have been more successful at finding and keeping jobs than many critics of the law predicted. One important indicator of how welfare has changed is the proportion of funds it provides in cash assistance. Before the 1996 reform, assistance was provided largely in the form of a cash grant. After the reform, 64 percent of welfare funds were allocated for noncash services and 36 percent for cash assistance.[19] This means that an increasing proportion of welfare funds is spent on such costs as assistance with transportation to work, temporary shelter, or onetime payments for emergencies so that people do not end up on the welfare rolls. The orientation of assistance has shifted away from subsidizing people who are not in the labor force and toward addressing temporary problems that low-income people face and providing assistance that facilitates work.[20] But critics point out that most former welfare recipients are not paid enough to pull their families out of poverty. While the 1996 law has helped reduce welfare caseloads, it has done little to reduce the underlying problem of poverty.[21]

As the economy soured in 2008 and 2009, the number of people on welfare rolls began to move upward but at a very slow rate. The American Recovery and Reinvestment Act of 2009 included the TANF Emergency Fund, which provided money for states to create subsidized jobs for low-income parents and young adults. Despite these measures, many advocates for the poor worried that the state TANF programs were not assisting enough poor families. After the Emergency

Fund expired in 2011, advocates for the poor charged that, with states making deep cuts to their budgets, TANF was not keeping pace with the growth of poverty caused by the recession. They contrasted spending on TANF to the growth of SNAP (or food stamps), which closely tracked the rise in unemployment and poverty during the recession. In 2007, before the recession took hold, approximately 26.3 million individuals a month received SNAP benefits. By 2015, that number had risen to approximately 45 million people a month, close to 15 percent of all Americans.[22]

● The Cycle of Poverty Can Be Broken by Education, Health, and Housing Policies

Describe how education, health, and housing policies try to advance equality of opportunity

The welfare state not only supplies a measure of economic security but also provides opportunity. The American belief in equality of opportunity makes such programs particularly important. Programs that provide opportunity keep people from falling into poverty, and they offer a hand up to those who are poor. At their best, opportunity policies allow all individuals to rise as high as their talents will take them. Three types of policies are most significant in opening opportunity: education policies, health policies, and housing policies.

Education Policies Provide Life Tools

Education is highly valued in the United States, a belief reflected in the fact that the vast majority of the education provided to Americans comes from public educational institutions financed through state, local, and (to a lesser extent) national government education policy. Education is an extremely important factor in shaping the distribution and redistribution of wealth and opportunity in the United States.

Compared to state and local efforts, the role of national government education policy has been limited for most of American history. Moreover, the most important national education policies have come only since World War II. The GI Bill was aimed almost entirely at postsecondary schooling; the national government did not enter the field of elementary education until after 1957.[23]

What finally brought the national government into elementary education was embarrassment over the fact that the Soviet Union had beaten the United States into space with the launching of the world's first satellite, Sputnik, in 1957. As a result, in 1958 the federal government adopted the policy under the National Defense Education Act of improving education in science and mathematics. The federal government recognized the role of education in promoting equal opportunity. In 1965 the Elementary and Secondary Education Act offered federal aid for education by allocating funds to school districts with substantial numbers of children from families who were unemployed or earning less than $2,000 a year. Today, the federal government spends $79 billion, 10 percent of all spending on K–12 education; states and localities each account for 45 percent of spending.

Over time, however, federal education funds have become less targeted on low-income districts as Congress has failed to update the formula for allocating funds.[24]

The federal role was substantially increased in 2001 by President George W. Bush's signature education act, No Child Left Behind (NCLB). Supported by Democrats and Republicans, the law sought to combine the goals of higher standards and equality of opportunity. It aimed to improve standards through stronger federal requirements for student testing and school accountability. Every child in grades 3 through 8 had to be tested yearly for proficiency in math and reading. The law aimed to promote equality of opportunity with two provisions: first, for a school to be judged a success, it had to show positive test results for all subcategories of children—minority race and ethnicity, English learners, and disability—not just overall averages. Second, parents with children in schools whose scores are poor had the right to transfer their children to a better school or to get funds for tutoring and summer programs.

NCLB soon generated considerable controversy. Many states branded it an "unfunded mandate," noting that the law placed expensive new obligations on schools to improve their performance but provided woefully inadequate resources. Teachers objected that "teaching to the test" undermined critical-thinking skills. In some states, up to half of the schools failed to meet the new standards, which resulted in a costly remedial challenge. Under the federal law, they were required to improve student performance by providing such new services as supplemental tutoring, longer school days, and additional summer school. Critics also charged that NCLB actually undermined equal opportunity because it ended up punishing underperforming schools—mostly those schools that bear the greatest burden for teaching the neediest students.[25]

Education policy is the most important means of providing equal opportunity for all Americans. In 2015, President Obama signed the Every Student Succeeds Act to replace No Child Left Behind, giving more power to the states to evaluate schools.

Faced with these conflicts, the Obama administration sought a major overhaul of NCLB. By 2015, most states had received waivers from NCLB.[26] Later that year, Congress passed a bipartisan bill replacing NCLB, creating a new program called the Every Student Succeeds Act. While maintaining a federal standardized testing schedule, it gave much more authority to the states to evaluate schools and to employ criteria other than student test scores. States will still be required to test students on math and reading in grades 3 through 8. While many people hailed the new law, others charged that it would do little to alter the achievement gap between richer and poorer schools.[27]

The Obama administration also lent its support for charter schools—publicly funded schools that are free from the bureaucratic rules and regulations of the school district in which they are located and free to design specialized curricula and to use resources in ways they think most effective. One of the Obama administration's first pieces of legislation was the American Recovery and Reinvestment Act. It included a new $4.3 billion program called Race to the Top, which offered competitive grants to state education systems. The administration awarded sizable grants to 11 states and to Washington, D.C., for proposing bold new programs for assessing teachers and overhauling failing schools.[28] Several years after the program began, however, it was clear that states had promised more than they could do in the limited time that the funds were provided.[29]

Health Policies Mean Fewer Sick Days

Until recent decades, no government in the United States—national, state, or local—concerned itself directly with individual health. But public responsibility was always accepted for *public* health. After New York City's newly created Board of Health was credited with holding down a cholera epidemic in 1867, most states created statewide public health agencies.

The U.S. Public Health Service (USPHS) has been in existence since 1798 but was only a small part of public-health policy until after World War II. The National Institutes of Health (NIH), an agency within the USPHS, was established in 1937 but little noticed for 20 years. Between 1950 and 2012, NIH expenditures by the national government increased from $160 million to $32.3 billion. NIH research on the link between smoking and disease led to one of the most visible public-health campaigns in American history. Today, the NIH's focus has turned to cancer and human immunodeficiency virus/acquired immune deficiency syndrome (HIV/AIDS). As with smoking, this work on HIV/AIDS has resulted in massive public-health education as well as new products and regulations.

Other recent commitments to the improvement of public health are the numerous laws aimed at cleaning up and defending the environment (including the creation in 1970 of the Environmental Protection Agency) and laws attempting to improve the health and safety of consumer products (regulated by the Consumer Product Safety Commission, created in 1972). Health policies aimed directly at the poor include Medicaid and nutritional programs. As Figure 13.2 shows, the government has committed large resources to health care programs. While they yield great benefits by providing health care to millions, these programs have seen their costs rise dramatically in recent years—far more than the rate of inflation—prompting growing calls for major changes in spending and funding.[30]

U.S. Education Policy: Lagging or Leading?

Much of the push for education reform including the adoption of the Common Core State Standards in most states, has been driven by the belief that American students are falling behind students in other countries. On the Program for International Student Assessment (PISA) surveys, which measure the educational performance of 15-year-old students from around the globe, American students have consistently scored lower in mathematics and science than students in many Asian and European countries.[a] For some education advocates, this trend is particularly worrisome as the United States

on average spends considerably more per student than many countries whose students scored higher on these tests.

However, some education experts point out that PISA results might not be truly comparable, as the selection of test-takers for the survey may be biased. For example, the U.S. test sample includes students from across the United States who represent many social and economic backgrounds; in contrast, Shanghai's school system (which ranked #1 on the test) excludes most migrant children and poor students whose parents come from China's rural regions.[b]

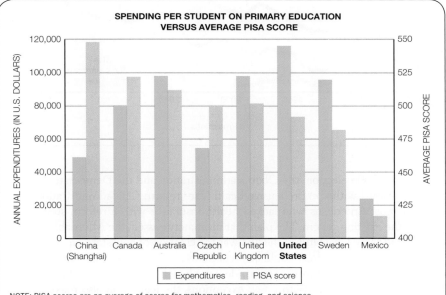

SPENDING PER STUDENT ON PRIMARY EDUCATION VERSUS AVERAGE PISA SCORE

Legend: ■ Expenditures ■ PISA score

Countries: China (Shanghai), Canada, Australia, Czech Republic, United Kingdom, **United States**, Sweden, Mexico

NOTE: PISA scores are an average of scores for mathematics, reading, and science.
SOURCES: OECD, "PISA 2012 Results in Focus," www.oecd.org/pisa/keyfindings/pisa-2012-results-overview.pdf (accessed 11/20/15); OECD, "Pisa 2012 Results: What Makes Schools Successful (Volume IV)," www.oecd-ilibrary.org/education/pisa-2012-results-what-makes-a-school-successful-volume-iv_9789264201156-en (accessed 4/22/16).

[a] Julian Ryan, "American Schools vs. the World: Expensive, Unequal, Bad at Math," *The Atlantic*, December 3, 2013, www.theatlantic.com/education/archive/2013/12/american-schools-vs-the-world-expensive-unequal-bad-at-math/281983/ (accessed 7/26/16).
[b] Brookings Institute, "Attention OECD-PISA: Your Silence on China Is Wrong," Brookings Institution, December 11, 2013, www.brookings.edu/blogs/brown-center-chalkboard/posts/2013/12/11-shanghai-pisa-scores-wrong-loveless (accessed 7/26/16).

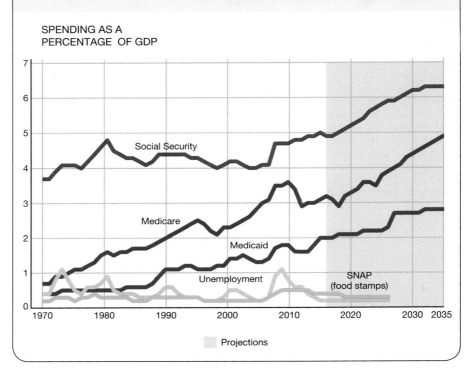

FIGURE 13.2 The Size of the Welfare State

Spending on Medicare, Medicaid, and Social Security is projected to rise as a percent of gross domestic product (GDP). Social Security, a contributory program that provides income to the elderly, is by far the largest welfare program in the United States. Which program is the smallest?

SOURCES: Congressional Budget Office, www.cbo.gov (accessed 7/16/16): and Office of Management and Budget, www.whitehouse.gov/omb/budget/Historicals (accessed 7/16/16). See endnote 30 for specific reports.

SPENDING AS A
PERCENTAGE OF GDP

Social Security

Medicare

Medicaid

Unemployment

SNAP
(food stamps)

Projections

After the 2008 election, the Obama administration and the Democratic Congress pressed forward with comprehensive health care reform. The administration aimed to cover most Americans who lacked health insurance with a reform strategy that built on the existing system. The plan that ultimately passed, the Affordable Care Act (ACA), had three key features: the first was the creation of new state-based insurance exchanges where individuals could buy health insurance, along with insurance regulation that would prohibit insurers from denying benefits for a variety of reasons such as preexisting conditions. With a few exceptions, the legislation also makes insurers cover preventive medicine in full. The second provision of the ACA, known as "the individual mandate," required uninsured individuals to purchase health insurance; those who do not have insurance are subject to a fine (scheduled to rise over time) of 1 percent of yearly household income or $95, whichever was larger. The third major provision of the ACA was a set of subsidies to help the uninsured and small businesses purchase insurance as well as an expansion of the public programs Medicaid and the State Children's Health Insurance Program (SCHIP). The Medicaid expansion made more people eligible for the program by opening it to people with incomes up to $27,724.[31] The reform also allowed working-aged adults without dependent children to qualify for the program for the first time. Figure 13.3 shows the projected number of Americans who would have insurance with and without the ACA in 2026.

Even after its enactment, the law remained highly controversial. By 2016, Republican members of the House of Representatives had voted 62 times to repeal the act, and the public remained split. In September 2016, 47 percent of those polled expressed an unfavorable opinion compared to 44 percent with favorable views. The rollout of the state insurance exchanges in 2013 reinforced negative public perceptions of the ACA. Massive initial computer problems with the main website, heathcare.gov, prevented many applications from moving forward. These problems affected applicants from the 27 states that did not set up their own insurance exchanges but relied on the federal website. Only after a major reworking of the

FIGURE 13.3 Projected Insurance Coverage with and without ACA, 2026

These projections by the Congressional Budget Office (CBO) predict that in 2026 over 20 million people would receive health insurance through the exchanges set up by the ACA. The act would also boost the number of people receiving benefits through Medicaid and the Children's Health Insurance Program. The CBO projects that the number of uninsured people will be 30 million lower with the ACA than it would be without the ACA.

SOURCES: Congressional Budget Office, Federal Subsidies for Health Insurance Coverage for People under Age 65: Tables from CBO's March 2016 Baseline, Table 1 Health Insurance Coverage for People under Age 65, Table 4 Effects of the Affordable Care Act on Health Insurance Coverage for People under Age 65, www.cbo.gov/sites/default/files /51298-2016-03-HealthInsurance.pdf (accessed 7/11/16).

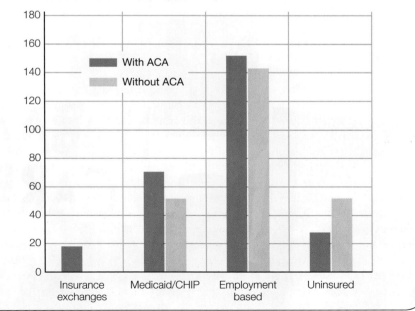

online system did the federal insurance exchanges begin to work as intended. By April 2014, the administration announced that more than 8 million people had signed up through the exchanges, a number that exceeded initial expectations.[32] Even so, the disastrous launch of the insurance exchanges represented a missed opportunity for the administration to improve public perceptions of the ACA.[33]

The new health care reform law faced challenges not only in public opinion but from state governments soon after it was enacted. Twenty-one state attorneys general filed lawsuits against the legislation on the grounds that the provision requiring individuals to purchase health insurance expanded the commerce clause beyond its constitutional limits. The states also objected to provisions that required them to expand their Medicaid programs to cover more poor people.

The Supreme Court decided these suits in 2012, ruling that most of the act was constitutional.[34] Chief Justice John Roberts, regarded as a conservative, surprised many observers by writing the decision that declared the individual mandate constitutional. However, the decision found that the mandate could not be justified as constitutional under the commerce clause, which the administration relied on in its arguments before the Court. Because the mandate regulated economic *inactivity* (i.e., failure to purchase health insurance), Roberts argued that it could not be justified under the commerce clause, which regulates economic *activity*. Instead, the Court ruled that the requirement to purchase insurance was legal under Congress's taxing powers (since, under the law, failure to purchase insurance results in a penalty). The Court also ruled that Congress did not have the power to take existing Medicaid funds away from states if they did not comply with the expansion requirements. In response, 19 states decided not to expand their Medicaid programs. In 2015 these state decisions left 3 million people who would have qualified for Medicaid without access to health care.[35]

Some Americans opposed the 2010 Affordable Care Act because they were concerned that decisions previously left to patients and their doctors would be made by the government.

The ACA survived another major challenge in 2015 when the Supreme Court upheld the law in the *King v. Burwell* decision. Conservative opponents of the ACA sued on the grounds that the language of the law prohibited the federal government from providing subsidies to beneficiaries who relied on the federal health insurance exchange. Because only 16 states had set up their own exchanges and the rest relied on the federal exchange, an estimated 6.4 million people would have lost their subsidies to purchase health insurance.[36] The Obama administration defended the law, arguing that the language in question represented nothing more than an error in drafting the legislation. The administration contended that the legislative record clearly indicated Congress's intent to make subsidies available to all who qualified, regardless of the type of health exchange they used to purchase insurance. The court sided with the administration's interpretation, agreeing that Congress intended to make subsidies available to both types of exchanges.[37]

Housing Policies Provide Residential Stability

The United States has one of the highest rates of home ownership in the world, and the central thrust of federal housing policy has been to promote home ownership. The federal government has traditionally done much less to provide housing for low-income Americans who cannot afford to buy homes. Federal housing programs were first created in the 1930s depression period, when many Americans found themselves unable to afford housing. Through public housing for low-income families, which originated in 1937 with the Wagner-Steagall National Housing Act, and subsidized private housing after 1950, the percentage of American families living in overcrowded conditions was reduced from 20 percent in 1940 to 9 percent in 1970. Federal policies made an even greater contribution to reducing "substandard" housing, defined by the U.S. Census Bureau as dilapidated houses without hot running water and without some other plumbing. In 1940, almost 50 percent of American households lived in substandard housing. By 1950, this had been reduced to 35 percent; by 1975, the figure was reduced further, to 8 percent.[38] Despite these improvements in housing standards, federal housing policy until the 1970s was largely seen as a failure. Restricted to the poorest of the poor and marked by racial segregation and inadequate spending, public housing contributed to the problems of the poor by isolating them from shopping, jobs, and urban amenities. Dilapidated high-rise housing projects stood as a symbol of the failed American policy of "warehousing the poor." By the 1980s, the orientation of housing policy had changed: most federal housing policy for low-income Americans came in the form of housing choice vouchers (formerly called *Section 8 vouchers*), which provided recipients with support to rent in the private market. While this program did not promote the same isolation of the poor, it was often useless in expensive housing markets, where the vouchers provided too little money to cover rental costs.

Beginning in 2007 and 2008, a home loan crisis presented the government with a different kind of housing problem. During the housing boom of the early 2000s, many homeowners had received loans that they later could not afford to repay. This was caused in part by the deregulation of the mortgage industry in 1999, which allowed many new mortgage companies to form, offering loans that cost little at first but required large payments from homeowners later. This "predatory lending" targeted unsophisticated buyers and made it very hard for borrowers to understand the terms of the loans. Lending standards were relaxed to the point that rising numbers of borrowers were offered "no-doc" loans, which required no documentation of the borrowers' income. As more and more Americans took out such loans, demand for housing rose; and housing prices skyrocketed. This was the housing bubble—a bubble that was bound to burst because so many borrowers would not be able to pay back their loans. As growing numbers of homeowners began to default on their loans in 2007, banks foreclosed on their houses; and the value of housing began to drop. This downward spiral set off the major recession that began in 2007. As borrowers defaulted, banks holding that debt—including the biggest banks in America—teetered on the edge of failure and threatened to destabilize the entire economy. Many of the new mortgage companies went bankrupt. As unemployment rose, more families, unable to pay their mortgages, lost their homes. Many homeowners found that their homes were "underwater," meaning that the homeowners owed more on their mortgages than the homes were now worth. By 2015 over 5 million homes had been lost to foreclosure.[39]

Social Policy Spending Benefits the Middle Class More Than the Poor

Explain how contributory and noncontributory programs benefit different groups of Americans

The two categories of social policy, contributory and noncontributory, generally serve different groups of people. We can understand much about the development of social policy by examining which constituencies benefit from different policies.

The strongest and most generous programs are those in which the beneficiaries are widely perceived as deserving of assistance and are politically powerful. Because Americans prize work, constituencies who have "earned" their benefits in some way or those who cannot work because of a disability are usually seen as most deserving of government assistance. Politically powerful constituencies are those who vote as a group, lobby effectively, and mobilize to protect the programs from which they benefit.

When we study social policies from a group perspective, we can see that senior citizens and the middle class receive the most benefits from the government's social policies and that children and the working poor receive the fewest. In addition, America's social policies do little to change the fact that minorities and women are more likely to be poor than white Americans and men.

Senior Citizens Receive over a Third of All Federal Dollars

The elderly are the beneficiaries of the two strongest and most generous social policies: old-age pensions (what we call Social Security) and Medicare (medical care for the elderly). As these programs have grown, they have provided most elderly Americans with economic security and have dramatically reduced the poverty rate among the elderly. In 1959, before very many people over the age of 65 received social insurance, the poverty rate for the elderly was 35 percent; by 2014 it had dropped to 10 percent.[40] Because of this progress, many people call Social Security the most effective antipoverty program in the United States.[41] This does not mean that the elderly are rich, however; in 2014, the median income of elderly households was $36,895, well below the national median income. The aim of these programs is to provide security and prevent poverty.[42]

Even with the success of these programs at reducing poverty among the elderly, older African Americans and Latinos are much more likely to be poor than are white seniors. In 2014 the poverty rate for African Americans and Latinos over age 65 was 18.1 percent, compared to only 7.8 percent of whites over 65. The difference is due in part to the lower wages of these groups during their working years since Social Security benefits are pegged to wages. Social Security may do less to pull immigrants out of poverty depending on the number of years they have worked in the United States.[43]

When government has tried to reform Social Security or Medicare, beneficiaries of these programs have rallied together—often successfully—in opposition.

One reason that Social Security and Medicare are politically strong is that senior citizens are widely seen as a deserving population. Because of their age, they are not expected to work. Moreover, both programs are contributory, and a work history is a requirement for receiving a Social Security pension. But these programs are also strong because they serve a constituency that has become quite powerful. The elderly are a very large group: in 2015, there were 47.8 million Americans over the age of 65. Because Social Security and Medicare are not means-tested, they are available to all former workers and their spouses over the age of 65, whether they are poor or not. The size of this group is of such political importance also because the elderly turn out to vote in higher numbers than the rest of the population.

In addition, the elderly have developed strong and sophisticated lobbying organizations that can influence policy making and mobilize elderly Americans to defend these programs against proposals to cut them. One important and influential organization is AARP (formerly the American Association of Retired Persons; it changed its name to its initials because 44 percent of its members work full- or part-time). AARP had nearly 40 million members in 2015, amounting to one-fifth of all voters. It also has a sophisticated lobbying organization in Washington that employs 55 lobbyists and a staff of 51 policy analysts.[44]

Lobbying groups for seniors are among the most powerful in the United States. They mobilize their supporters and work with legislators to block changes they believe will hurt the elderly. In the case of Medicare reform, for example, AARP had long opposed any reform that allowed private health care firms to provide Medicaid benefits. But in 2003, AARP switched its position and endorsed the Bush administration's bill to provide prescription drug benefits through the involvement of private firms. AARP's endorsement of the plan was decisive to the bill's passage. In 2005, AARP's opposition to President Bush's plan to partially privatize Social Security was decisive in killing that plan. In 2009 and 2010, AARP came out in support of health care reform, although it avoided endorsing any specific bill. Thousands of members left the organization in protest, but AARP is so large that their actions had little impact.

The Middle and Upper Classes Benefit from Social Policies

Americans don't usually think of the middle and upper classes as benefiting from social policies, but government action promotes the social welfare of these groups in a variety of ways. First, medical care and pensions for the elderly help the middle class by relieving them of the burden of caring for elderly relatives. Before these programs existed, old people were more likely to live with and depend financially on their adult children. Many middle-class families whose parents and grandparents are in nursing homes rely on Medicaid to pay nursing home bills.

In addition, the middle and upper classes benefit from what some analysts call the "shadow welfare state."[45] These are the social benefits that private employers offer to their workers—medical insurance and pensions, for example. The federal government subsidizes such benefits by not taxing the payments that employers and employees make for health insurance and pensions. These **tax expenditures**, as they are called, are an important way in which the federal government helps ensure the social welfare of the middle and upper classes. Such programs are called "tax expenditures" because the federal government helps finance them through the tax system rather than by direct spending, by providing tax deductions for private employers for amounts spent on health insurance and other benefits. Another key tax expenditure that helps those more well off is the tax exemption on mortgage interest payments: taxpayers can deduct the amount they have paid in interest on a mortgage from the income they report on their tax return. By allowing these payments to be counted as deductions, the government makes home ownership less expensive.

People often don't think of these tax expenditures as part of social policy because they are not as visible as the programs that provide direct payments or services to beneficiaries. But tax expenditures represent a significant federal investment: they cost the national treasury some $1.26 trillion a year and make it easier and less expensive for working Americans to obtain health care, save for retirement, and buy homes. These programs are very popular with the middle and upper classes, so Congress rarely considers reducing them.

The Working Poor Receive Fewer Benefits

People who are working but are poor or are just above the poverty line receive only limited assistance from government social programs. This is somewhat surprising, given that Americans value work so highly. But the working poor are typically employed in jobs that do not provide pensions or health care; often, they are renters because they cannot afford to buy homes. This means they cannot benefit from the shadow welfare state that subsidizes the social benefits enjoyed by most middle-class Americans.

Three government programs that assist the working poor are the ACA (discussed earlier), the EITC, and SNAP (formerly known as *food stamps*). The

EITC was implemented in 1976 to provide poor workers some relief from increases in the taxes that pay for Social Security. As it has expanded, the EITC has provided a modest wage supplement for the working poor, allowing them to catch up on utility bills or pay for children's clothing. Poor workers can also receive benefits from the SNAP program. To be eligible, households must earn below 130 percent of the poverty line (about $26,124 a year for a three-person family in 2016). The average monthly benefit for a family of three is $382 a month.[46] Food advocates such as Feeding America have encouraged people to take "the SNAP Challenge," in which people who do not need SNAP spend $1.50 a meal (the average for SNAP recipients) for a week. In the words of one high-profile participant, "I was hungry last week—laser-focused on how much food was left in the fridge and how many dollars were left in my wallet. I was scared about eating portions that were too big, and wasn't sure what to do if my food ran out."[47]

The working poor are more likely to be in jobs that do not provide health benefits from their employers. By expanding Medicaid to cover workers who earn up to 138 percent of the poverty line ($27,821 for a family of three in 2016), the ACA sought to ensure coverage for this group. However, the decision of 19 states to opt out of Medicaid expansion left a gap in coverage. Latinos and African Americans were more likely to be harmed by this gap than whites: 27 percent of Hispanics and 16 percent of blacks lacked access to health insurance as a result of these state decisions, but only 11 percent of whites were affected in this way.[48] Even though the working poor may be seen as deserving, they lack political power because they are not organized. There is no equivalent to AARP for the poor. Nonetheless, because work is highly valued in American society, politicians find it difficult to cut the few social programs that help the working poor.

Spending for the Nonworking Poor Is Declining

The only nonworking, able-bodied poor people who receive federal cash assistance are parents who are caring for children. The primary source of cash assistance for these families is the state-run TANF program, but they also rely on the SNAP program and Medicaid. Able-bodied adults who are not caring for children are not eligible for federal assistance other than SNAP. Many states provide small amounts of cash assistance to such individuals through programs called "general assistance," but most states have abolished or greatly reduced their general-assistance programs in an effort to encourage these adults to work. Americans don't like to subsidize adults who are not working, but they do not want to harm children.

AFDC was the most unpopular social spending program, and as a result, spending on it declined after 1980. Under TANF, states receive a fixed amount of federal funds, whether the welfare rolls rise or fall. Because the number of people on welfare has declined so dramatically since 1994—by over 50 percent—states have had generous levels of federal resources for the remaining welfare recipients. Many states, however, have used the windfall of federal dollars to cut taxes and indirectly support programs that benefit the middle class, not the poor.[49] Welfare recipients have little political power to resist cuts in their benefits. In 2016, 44.7 million people received SNAP benefits.[50]

Minorities, Women, and Children Are Most Likely to Face Poverty

Minorities, women, and children are disproportionately poor. Much of this poverty is the result of disadvantages rooted in the position of these groups in the labor market. In 2014 the poverty rate for African Americans was 26.2 percent, and for Latinos it was 23.6 percent. For non-Hispanic whites, it was 10.1 percent.[51] Much of this economic inequality stems from the fact that minority workers tend to have low-wage jobs. Minorities are also more likely to become unemployed and to remain unemployed for longer periods of time than are white Americans. African Americans, for example, typically have experienced twice as much unemployment as have other Americans. The combination of low-wage jobs and unemployment often means that minorities are less likely to have jobs that give them access to the shadow welfare state. They are more likely to fall into the precarious categories of the working poor or the nonworking poor.

Policy analysts have increasingly examined the "feminization of poverty," or the fact that women are more likely than men to be poor. This problem is particularly acute for single mothers, who are more than twice as likely as the average American to fall below the poverty line (see Figure 13.4). When the Social

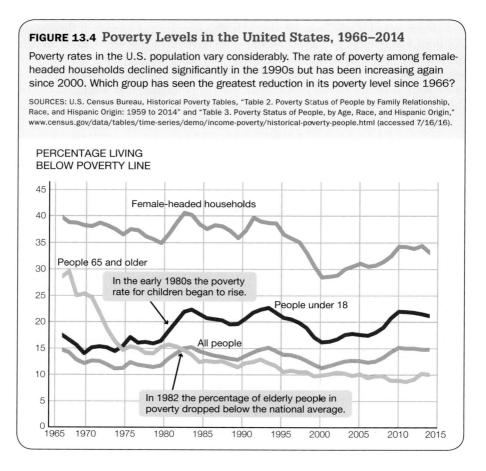

FIGURE 13.4 Poverty Levels in the United States, 1966–2014

Poverty rates in the U.S. population vary considerably. The rate of poverty among female-headed households declined significantly in the 1990s but has been increasing again since 2000. Which group has seen the greatest reduction in its poverty level since 1966?

SOURCES: U.S. Census Bureau, Historical Poverty Tables, "Table 2. Poverty Status of People by Family Relationship, Race, and Hispanic Origin: 1959 to 2014" and "Table 3. Poverty Status of People, by Age, Race, and Hispanic Origin," www.census.gov/data/tables/time-series/demo/income-poverty/historical-poverty-people.html (accessed 7/16/16).

PERCENTAGE LIVING BELOW POVERTY LINE

Female-headed households

People 65 and older

In the early 1980s the poverty rate for children began to rise.

People under 18

All people

In 1982 the percentage of elderly people in poverty dropped below the national average.

Security Act was passed in 1935, the main programs for poor women were Aid to Dependent Children (ADC) and survivors' insurance for widows. The framers of the act believed that ADC would gradually disappear as more women became eligible for survivors' insurance. The social model behind the Social Security Act was that of a male breadwinner with a wife and children. Women were not expected to work, and if a woman's husband died, ADC or survivors' insurance would help her stay at home and raise her children. The framers of Social Security did not envision today's large number of single women heading families. At the same time, they did not envision that so many women with children would also be working. This combination of changes helped make AFDC (the successor program to ADC) more controversial. Many people asked why welfare recipients shouldn't work, if the majority of women who were not on welfare worked. Such questions led to the welfare reform of 1996, which created TANF.

One of the most troubling issues related to American social policy is the number of American children who live in poverty. The rate of child poverty in 2014 was 21.1 percent—6.3 percentage points higher than that of the population as a whole. African American and Latino children experience much higher rates of poverty than do whites. In 2014 the rate of child poverty for white children was 12.3 percent, while 31.9 percent of Latino children and 37.1 percent of black children lives in poverty.[52] High rates of child poverty stem in part from the design of American social policies. Because these policies do not generously assist able-bodied adults who aren't working and because these policies offer little help to the working poor, the children of these adults are likely to be poor as well.

As child poverty has grown, several lobbying groups have emerged to represent children's interests; the best known of these is the Children's Defense Fund. But even with a sophisticated lobbying operation and although their numbers are large, poor children do not vote and therefore wield little political power.

Domestic Policy
and Your Future

Public policy encompasses many different ways for the government to achieve its objectives. All public policies are tools of government control, but the means chosen to achieve their goals can have a major effect on how the public feels about those policies. After all, who wouldn't rather be encouraged to do something by being paid to do it instead of being told that failure to do the very same thing may result in jail time? This might lead you to think that the government should do everything by relying on payments or subsidies, but for many areas of public life, this is simply not possible—not to mention incredibly expensive.

Economic policy has changed dramatically in recent decades. The American economy is now far more open to the rest of the world, and many American firms do most of their production in China and other developing economies. At the same time, the distribution of economic gains in the United States has shifted upward. As the debate about more or less government has led to a series of policy stalemates among politicians, the income of the American middle class has mostly stagnated and the gains going to the top 1 percent have soared. Some Americans think the government should do more to address income inequality through tax policy, for example by taxing the wealthy at higher rates. The "**Who Participates?**" feature on p. 433 shows taxes as a percentage of income at both the federal and state and local levels.

Social policies, established in the 1930s, have stirred up much controversy. Liberals often argue that more generous social policies are needed if the United States is truly to ensure equality of opportunity, saying that the government needs to go beyond simply providing opportunity and should ensure more equal conditions, especially where children are concerned. Conservatives, on the other hand, often argue that social policies that offer income support take the ideal of equality too far and, in the process, do for individuals what those individuals should be doing for themselves. From this perspective, social policies make the government too big, and big government is seen as a fundamental threat to Americans' liberties.

Where do average Americans fit in these debates? Americans are often said to be philosophical conservatives and operational liberals.[53] When asked about government social policy in the abstract, they say they disapprove of activist government—a conservative view. But when they must evaluate particular programs, Americans generally express support—a liberal perspective. Some programs are more popular than others. Policies in which the recipients are regarded as deserving, such as programs for the elderly, receive more support than those that assist working-age people. Programs that have a reputation for effectiveness and those that require people to help themselves through work are also viewed favorably.[54]

Yet reform is often difficult to achieve. The most pressing social policy issue in the coming decades—the rising cost of health care—has been notoriously difficult to address. The United States spends more on health care than any other advanced nation, but many Americans remain without access to care, even after the expansions in the ACA. The share of our economy devoted to health care rose from 7.2 percent in 1970 to 17.5 percent in 2014, and it appears to be growing again after a brief slowdown.[55] The causes of increasing health care costs are many, including new technology, administrative complexity, greater coverage for more people, and an aging population. Can we reap the advantages of our highly advanced health care system and reduce costs at the same time? While most Americans might prefer this outcome, it is very difficult to reach agreement on the reforms needed to attain this goal. What strategies might be used to initiate a national discussion of health care? What are the consequences of inaction for today's young adults?

Who Pays Taxes?

Taxes as a Percentage of Income, 2015

Income group	Federal taxes ↓	State and local taxes ↓
Top 1%	24%	8%
Next 9%	22%	10%
Next 10%	21%	11%
Fourth 20%	20%	11%
Middle 20%	16%	11%
Second 20%	12%	11%
Lowest 20%	7%	12%

Household income: $15,000

● Federal taxes: 7%
● State and local taxes: 12%

Income after taxes: $12,150

Household income: $310,000

● Federal taxes: 22%
● State and local taxes: 10%

Income after taxes: $210,800

SOURCE: Citizens for Tax Justice, "Who Pays Taxes in America in 2015?"
April 8, 2015, www.ctj.org/pdf/taxday2015.pdf (accessed 1/11/16).

WHAT YOU CAN DO ➡

WHAT YOU CAN DO

Compare Tax Rates

 Learn more about how tax rates vary by income, state, and local area at **www.taxfoundation.org**. Contact your representatives at the state or federal level to express your opinion.

 Compare tax rates in the United States to those paid in countries around the world at **www.businessinsider.com/america-taxes-charts-2013-1**.

☑ Learn more about your rights as a taxpayer, how to get help with your taxes, and how to avoid tax scams from the Internal Revenue Service (**www.irs.gov**).

chapterstudyguide

Practice Quiz

1. Which of the following is *not* a type of regulatory policy? *(pp. 407–9)*
   a) criminal penalties
   b) civil penalties
   c) regulatory taxation
   d) expropriation
   e) redistribution

2. Monetary policy seeks to influence the economy through *(p. 409)*
   a) taxing and spending.
   b) privatizing and nationalizing selected industries.
   c) the availability of credit and money.
   d) foreign exchange of currency.
   e) administrative regulation.

3. The most powerful institution in determining America's monetary policy is *(p. 409)*
   a) the Department of Commerce.
   b) the Department of the Treasury.
   c) the federal judiciary.
   d) the Federal Reserve Board.
   e) the president.

4. Government attempts to manipulate the economy by using its taxing and spending powers are called *(p. 410)*
   a) antitrust policies.
   b) expropriation policies.
   c) monetary policies.
   d) fiscal policies.
   e) redistributive policies.

5. The United States' welfare state was constructed initially in response to *(pp. 412–13)*
   a) the Civil War.
   b) World War II.
   c) political reforms of the Progressive era.
   d) the Great Depression.
   e) the growth of the military–industrial complex.

6. Which of the following is an example of a contributory program? *(pp. 413–14)*
   a) Medicaid
   b) Medicare
   c) Temporary Assistance for Needy Families
   d) Supplemental Nutrition Assistance Program
   e) Aid to Families with Dependent Children

7. In 1996, as part of welfare reform, Aid to Families with Dependent Children was abolished and replaced by *(p. 415)*
   a) the Earned Income Tax Credit.
   b) the DREAM Act.
   c) the Affordable Care Act.
   d) Supplemental Security Income.
   e) Temporary Assistance for Needy Families.

8. Means testing requires that applicants for welfare benefits show *(p. 415)*
   a) that they are capable of getting to and from their workplace.
   b) that they have the ability to store and prepare food.
   c) a financial need for assistance.
   d) that they have the time and resources to take full advantage of federal educational opportunities.
   e) that they are natural-born citizens who have never been convicted of a felony.

9. Which of the following are examples of in-kind benefits? *(p. 415)*
   a) Medicaid and the Supplemental Nutrition Assistance Program
   b) Social Security and the Troubled Assets Relief Program
   c) Medicare and unemployment compensation
   d) the GI Bill of Rights and the Equal Rights Amendment
   e) the Earned Income Tax Credit and No Child Left Behind

10. Which of the following was not part of the No Child Left Behind Act of 2001? *(p. 419)*
    a) a requirement that failing schools improve student performance by providing services such as supplemental tutoring, longer school days, and additional summer classes
    b) a requirement that all students be proficient in reading and math by 2014
    c) a requirement that schools show positive results for all subcategories of students and not just positive overall averages
    d) a requirement that a national test be used to evaluate every student around the country
    e) a requirement that every child in grades 3 through 8 be tested yearly for proficiency in math and reading

11. Who are the chief beneficiaries of the "shadow welfare state"? *(p. 428)*
    a) children
    b) the elderly
    c) the nonworking poor
    d) the working poor
    e) the middle class

12. Which of the following statements about poverty in the United States is most accurate? *(pp. 430–31)*
    a) African Americans have a lower poverty rate than non-Hispanic whites.
    b) Latinos have a lower poverty rate than non-Hispanic whites.
    c) Latinos have a higher poverty rate than non-Hispanic whites.
    d) The rate of child poverty is less than the rate of adult poverty.
    e) Single mothers are less likely than average Americans to fall below the poverty line.

Key Terms

contracting power *(p. 407)* the power of government to set conditions on companies seeking to sell goods or services to government agencies

contributory programs *(p. 414)* social programs financed in whole or in part by taxation or other mandatory contributions by their present or future recipients

cost-of-living adjustments (COLAs) *(p. 414)* changes made to the level of benefits of a government program based on the rate of inflation

Federal Reserve System *(p. 409)* a system of 12 Federal Reserve banks that facilitates exchanges of cash, checks, and credit; regulates member banks; and uses monetary policies to fight inflation and deflation

fiscal policy *(p. 410)* the government's use of taxing, monetary, and spending powers to manipulate the economy

indexing *(p. 414)* periodic process of adjusting of social benefits or wages to account for increases in the cost of living

in-kind benefits *(p. 415)* noncash goods and services provided to needy individuals and families by the federal government

means testing *(p. 415)* a procedure by which potential beneficiaries of a public-assistance program establish their eligibility by demonstrating a genuine need for the assistance

Medicaid *(p. 415)* a federally and state-financed, state-operated program providing medical services to low-income people

Medicare *(p. 414)* a form of national health insurance for the elderly and the disabled

monetary policies *(p. 409)* efforts to regulate the economy through the manipulation of the supply of money and credit; America's most powerful institution in this area of monetary policy is the Federal Reserve Board

noncontributory programs *(p. 414)* social programs that provide assistance to people based on demonstrated need rather than any contribution they have made

public policy *(p. 405)* a law, a rule, a statute, or an edict that expresses the government's goals and provides for rewards and punishments to promote those goals' attainment

redistribution *(p. 410)* collecting revenue in such a way as to reduce the disparities of wealth between the lowest and the highest income brackets

Social Security *(p. 414)* a contributory welfare program into which working Americans contribute a percentage of their wages and from which they receive cash benefits after retirement or if they become disabled

subsidies *(p. 405)* government grants of cash or other valuable commodities, such as land, to individuals or an organization; used to promote activities desired by the government, to reward political support, or to buy off political opposition

Supplemental Nutrition Assistance Program (SNAP) *(p. 415)* the largest antipoverty program, which provides recipients with a debit card for food at most grocery stores; formerly known as *food stamps*

tax expenditures *(p. 428)* government subsidies provided to employers and employees through tax deductions for amounts spent on health insurance and other benefits

For Further Reading

Baldwin, Robert, Martin Cave, and Martin Lodge. *Understanding Regulation*. New York: Oxford University Press, 2012.

Campbell, Andrea Louise. *How Policies Make Citizens: Senior Political Activism and the American Welfare State*. Princeton, NJ: Princeton University Press, 2005.

Cohen, David K., and Susan L. Moffitt. *The Ordeal of Equality: Did Federal Regulation Fix the Schools*? Cambridge, MA: Harvard University Press, 2009.

Edin, Kathryn J., and Luke Shafer. *$2.00 a Day: Living on Almost Nothing in America*. New York: Houghton Mifflin Harcourt, 2015.

Hacker, Jacob S. *The Great Risk Shift: Why American Jobs, Families, Health Care, and Retirement Aren't Secure—And How We Can Fight Back*. New York: Oxford University Press, 2006.

Howard, Christopher. *The Welfare State Nobody Knows: Debunking Myths about U.S. Social Policy*. Princeton, NJ: Princeton University Press, 2007.

Katz, Michael. *In the Shadow of the Poorhouse: A Social History of Welfare in America*. New York: Basic Books, 1986.

Marmor, Theodore R., Jerry L. Mashaw, and Phillip L. Harvey. *America's Misunderstood Welfare State*. New York: Basic Books, 1990.

Mettler, Suzanne. *Degrees of Inequality: How the Politics of Higher Education Sabotaged the American Dream*. New York: Basic Books, 2014.

Ravitch, Diane. *Reign of Error: The Hoax of the Privatization Movement and the Danger to America's Public Schools*. New York: Knopf, 2013.

Soss, Joe, Richard C. Fording, and Sanford F. Schramm. *Disciplining the Poor: Neoliberal Paternalism and the Persistent Power of Race*. Chicago: University of Chicago Press, 2011.

Spitzer, Robert J. *Guns across America*. New York: Oxford University Press, 2015.

Weir, Margaret, Ann Orloff, and Theda Skocpol, eds. *The Politics of Social Policy in the United States*. Princeton, NJ: Princeton University Press, 1988.

The United States spends hundreds of billions of dollars—far more than any other country—on its military and weapons. However, Americans often disagree on when and how their government should act in international affairs, especially when it comes to deploying the U.S. military.

14

Foreign Policy

WHAT GOVERNMENT DOES AND WHY IT MATTERS Ever since George Washington, in his Farewell Address, warned the American people "to have . . . as little political connection as possible" with foreign nations and to "steer clear of permanent alliances," Americans have been distrustful of foreign policy. Despite their distrust, the United States has pursued its national interests in the world through a variety of means, including diplomacy, economic policy, military action, and the sorts of entangling alliances with other nations and international organizations that would have troubled Washington.

To some college students, foreign policy may seem like a distant or abstract matter, but not too long ago tens of thousands of students were drafted and sent to serve in Korea and Vietnam. Even today, in the era of the all-volunteer military, thousands of recent college graduates (and numerous current college students) have served in America's military forces in Iraq and Afghanistan; and many others know someone who has been wounded or killed on distant battlefields.

War is only one aspect of American foreign policy, but the United States has fought many wars. Though Americans like to regard themselves as a peaceful people, since our own Civil War, American forces have been deployed abroad on hundreds of occasions for major conflicts and minor skirmishes. Writing in 1989, historian Geoffrey Perret commented that no other nation "has had as much experience of war as the United States."[1] The United States has not become less warlike in the years since Perret published his observation. The United States currently spends about $600 billion per year on its military and weapons programs—a figure that represents roughly one-third of the world's total military expenditure and three times the amount spent by the People's Republic of China, the nation that currently ranks second to the United States in overall military outlays.[2]

Foreign policy, especially military policy, is often a major political issue in the United States. An old American adage asserts that "politics stops at the water's edge." The point of this saying is that America suffers as a nation if it fails to set aside its political and partisan differences when dealing with the rest of the world. In today's world, however, the water's edge does not neatly demarcate the difference of interests between "us" and "them." As the global economic crisis that deepened in 2008 revealed, "our" economic interests and "their" economic interests are intertwined. Environmental concerns are global, not national. And even in the realm of security interests, some risks and threats are shared and require international rather than national responses. Our national government must find ways to act internationally and strike the right balance between competition and cooperation in the international arena.

In this chapter, we will first examine the main goals and purposes of American foreign policy. We will then discuss the actors and institutions that shape foreign policy. Next, we will analyze the instruments that policy makers have at their disposal to implement foreign policy.

chaptergoals

- Explain how foreign policy is designed to promote security, prosperity, and humanitarian goals (pp. 441–48)
- Identify the major players in foreign-policy making, and describe their roles (pp. 448–53)
- Describe the means the United States uses to carry out foreign policy today (pp. 453–58)

Foreign Policy Goals Are Related

Explain how foreign policy is designed to promote security, prosperity, and humanitarian goals

The term *foreign policy* refers to the programs and policies that determine America's relations with other nations and foreign entities. Foreign policy includes diplomacy, military and security policy, international human rights policies, and various forms of economic policy such as trade policy and international energy policy. Of course, foreign policy and domestic policy are not completely separate categories but are, instead, closely intertwined. Take security policy, for example. Defending the nation requires the design and manufacture of tens of billions of dollars in military hardware. The manufacture of this military equipment provides jobs in American communities where the equipment is built, while paying for it involves raising taxes or choosing not to fund other programs.

Although U.S. foreign policy has a number of purposes, three main, interrelated goals stand out. These are security, prosperity, and the creation of a better world.

Security Is Based on Military Strength

To many Americans, the chief purpose of the nation's foreign policy is protection of the U.S. security in an often hostile world. Traditionally, the United States has been concerned about threats that might emanate from other countries, such as Nazi Germany during the 1940s and then Soviet Russia until the Soviet Union's collapse in 1991. Today, American security policy is concerned not only with the actions of other nations but also with the activities of terrorist groups and other hostile **non-state actors**.[3] To protect the nation's security from foreign threats, the United States has built an enormous military apparatus and a complex array of intelligence-gathering institutions, such as the Central Intelligence Agency (CIA), charged with evaluating and anticipating challenges from abroad.[4]

During the eighteenth and nineteenth centuries, American security was based mainly on the geographic isolation of the United States. We were separated by two oceans from European and Asian powers, and many Americans thought that our security would be best preserved by remaining aloof from international power struggles. This policy of avoiding involvement in the affairs of other nations was known as **isolationism**. In his 1796 Farewell Address, President George Washington warned Americans to avoid permanent alliances with foreign powers; and in 1823, President James Monroe warned foreign powers not to meddle in the Western Hemisphere. Washington's warning and what came to be called the Monroe Doctrine were the cornerstones of the U.S. foreign policy of isolationism until the end of the nineteenth century. The United States saw itself as the dominant power in the Western Hemisphere and, indeed, believed that its "manifest destiny" was to expand from sea to sea. The rest of the world, however, should remain at arm's length.

In the twentieth century, technology made oceans less a barrier to foreign threats, and the world's growing economic interdependence meant that the nation could no longer ignore events abroad. Early in the twentieth century, the

United States entered World War I on the side of Great Britain and France when the Wilson administration concluded that a German victory would adversely affect America's economic and security interests. In 1941 the United States was drawn into World War II when Japan attacked the U.S. Pacific fleet anchored at Pearl Harbor, Hawaii. Even before the attack, the Roosevelt administration had concluded that the United States needed to act to prevent a victory by the German–Japanese–Italian Axis alliance.

Following World War II, the United States developed a new security policy known as **containment** to check or "contain" the growing power of the Soviet Union, which by the end of the 1940s had built a huge empire, enormous military forces, and nuclear weapons and intercontinental bombers capable of attacking the United States. The United States was committed to maintaining its own military might as a means of **deterrence**, to discourage the Soviets from attacking the United States or its allies. Some Americans wanted a more aggressive policy and argued that we should attack the Soviets before it was too late. Others said that we should show our peaceful intentions and attempt to placate the Soviets. This policy is called **appeasement**.

The policies that the United States adopted, deterrence and containment, could be seen as midway between aggression and appeasement. A nation pursuing a policy of deterrence, on the one hand, signals its peaceful intentions but, on the other hand, indicates its willingness and ability to fight if attacked. Thus, during the era of confrontation with the Soviet Union between the late 1940s and 1990, known as the **Cold War**, the United States frequently asserted that it had no intention of attacking the Soviet Union but at the same time built a huge military force, including a vast arsenal of nuclear weapons and intercontinental missiles, and frequently asserted that in the event of a Soviet attack it would respond with overwhelming force. The Soviet Union announced that its nuclear weapons were also intended for deterrent purposes. Eventually, the two sides possessed such enormous arsenals of nuclear missiles that each had the ability to destroy the other in the event of war. This heavily armed standoff came to be called a posture of mutually assured destruction. During the 1962 "Cuban missile crisis," the United States and the Soviet Union came to the brink of war when President Kennedy declared that the Soviet Union must remove its nuclear missiles from Cuba and threatened to use force if the Soviets refused. After an extremely intense several weeks, the crisis was defused by a negotiated compromise in which the Soviets agreed to remove their missiles in exchange for a guarantee from the United States that it would not invade Cuba. The two superpowers had come so close to nuclear war that afterward the leaders of both nations sought ways to reduce tensions. This effort led to a period of détente, in which a number of arms control agreements were signed and the threat of war was reduced.

In 1991 the Soviet Union collapsed, partly because its huge military expenditures undermined its inefficient centrally planned economy. The new Russia, though still a formidable power, posed less of a threat to the United States. Within several years, however, new security threats emerged, requiring new policy responses. The September 11, 2001, terrorist attacks demonstrated a threat against which some security scholars had long warned: that non-state actors and so-called rogue states might acquire significant military capabilities, including nuclear weapons, and would not be affected by America's deterrent capabilities.

Unlike **nation-states** (political entities consisting of a people with some common cultural experience who also share a common political authority, recognized by other sovereignties), which have governments and fixed borders, terrorist groups are non-state actors having no fixed geographic location that can be attacked. Terrorists may believe that they can attack and melt away, leaving the United States with no one against whom to retaliate. Hence, the threat of massive retaliation does not deter them. Rogue states are nations with unstable and erratic leaders who seem to pursue policies driven by ideological or religious fervor rather than careful consideration of economic or human costs. The United States considers North Korea to be a rogue state.

To counter these new security threats, the George W. Bush administration shifted from a policy of deterrence to one of **preventive war**—the willingness to strike first in order to prevent an enemy attack. The United States declared that, if necessary, it would take action to disable terrorist groups and rogue states before they could develop the ability to do it harm. This idea gained important support after the September 11 attacks. The Bush administration's "global war on terror" is an expression of this notion of prevention, as was the U.S. invasion of Iraq. The United States has also refused to rule out the possibility that it would attack North Korea or Iran if it deemed those nations' nuclear programs to be an imminent threat to American security interests. Accompanying this shift in military doctrine was a significant increase in overall U.S. military spending (see Figure 14.1).

In a 2014 speech, President Obama signaled a shift in American military policy. The president declared that U.S. policy had led to too many "military adventures." In the future, said the president, American policy would be based on collective action and restraint. While a military option would remain available if Americans

From the beginning of the Syrian civil war in 2011, the United States has backed rebels against the Bashar al-Assad regime but has increased its involvement in recent years with the aim of targeting ISIS. The United States first deployed Special Operations Forces on the ground in Syria in late 2015.

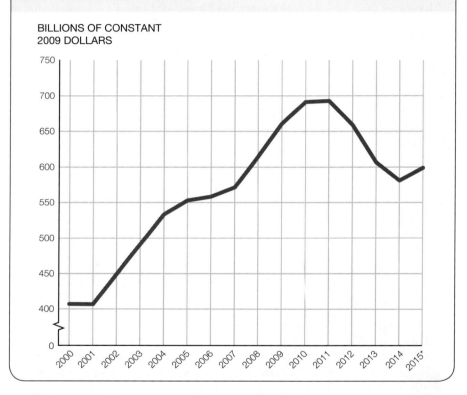

FIGURE 14.1 U.S. Spending on National Defense since 2000

During the 1990s the budget for national defense declined as the country enjoyed a "peace dividend" following the conclusion of the Cold War. After the attacks of September 11 and the commencement of the war on terrorism, however, national defense spending rose steadily; in a decade, spending increased by 70 percent. Since that time defense spending has fallen.

*Data for 2015 are estimated.
SOURCE: Office of Management and Budget, "Table 6.1—Composition of Outlays: 1940–2021," www.whitehouse .gov/omb/budget/historicals (accessed 1/7/16).

BILLIONS OF CONSTANT
2009 DOLLARS

were directly threatened, the president said that nonmilitary options, including diplomacy and economic sanctions, should always be tried first. This emphasis on diplomacy, sanctions, and collective action summarized the president's responses to major foreign policy problems, including the civil war in Syria, Russia's annexation of the Crimean area of Ukraine, the Iranian nuclear program, and the North Korean effort to build missiles capable of carrying nuclear warheads.

Since 2011, Americans have debated what to do for Syria, which has been locked in a brutal civil war waged by Syrian leader Bashar al-Assad against regime opponents. The United States has backed moderate anti-Assad rebel groups since the beginning of the war, first by sending food rations and later by providing training and funding. When a terrorist group calling itself the Islamic State of Iraq and Syria (ISIS) emerged in 2014 and proved able to overrun large portions of Iraq and Syria, the United States increased its involvement in the region. That year the United States began launching air strikes against ISIS. In 2015, President Obama deployed Special Operations Forces on the ground in Syria and halted the withdrawal of American forces from Afghanistan when it seemed likely that ISIS would increase their influence in the country after the Americans departed. Diplomacy appeared to have reached its limits. Indeed, the limits of diplomacy were underscored in 2015 when ISIS launched terror attacks in Paris and elsewhere, demonstrating its capacity to carry the war directly to its enemies.

Economic Prosperity Helps All Nations

A second major goal of U.S. foreign policy is to promote American prosperity. America's international economic policies are intended to expand employment opportunities in the United States, to maintain access to foreign energy supplies at a reasonable cost, to promote foreign investment in the United States, and to lower the prices Americans pay for goods and services.

The most important international organization for promoting free trade is the **World Trade Organization (WTO)**, established in 1995. The WTO grew out of the **General Agreement on Tariffs and Trade (GATT)**, established in 1947, which set many of the rules governing international trade. Since World War II, GATT had brought together a wide range of nations for regular negotiations designed to reduce barriers to trade. Such barriers, many believed, had contributed to the breakdown of the world economy in the 1930s and had helped cause World War II. The WTO has 159 members worldwide, including the United States. Similar policy goals are pursued in regional arrangements, such as the **North American Free Trade Agreement (NAFTA)**, a trade treaty among the United States, Canada, and Mexico to lower and eliminate tariffs among the three countries.

Working toward freer trade has been an important goal of most presidential administrations since World War II. The Obama administration, for example, reached a free-trade agreement with 12 Pacific Rim countries in 2015. Yet as globalization has advanced, concerns about free trade, and about the operation of the WTO in particular, have grown. Trade policy is complicated because most Americans benefit from a policy of free trade, which tends to reduce the cost of goods and services. One reason that consumer electronics are so inexpensive is that televisions, smartphones, and other gadgets are imported from all over the world, driving down their prices. However, many American industries and their employees are hurt by free trade if it results in factories and jobs moving abroad. Trade is an area where the line between domestic and foreign policy is blurred. Furthermore, critics believe that the WTO does not pay sufficient attention to the concerns of developing nations or to such issues as environmental degradation, human rights, and labor practices, including the use of child labor in many countries. The major problem in WTO negotiations has been conflicts between poor, developing nations and rich, developed countries.

America Seeks a More Humane World

A third goal of American policy is to make the world a better place for all its inhabitants. The main forms of policy that address this goal are international environmental policy, international human rights policy, and international peacekeeping.

Trade in Comparison

Since World War II, there has been consistent bipartisan support in the United States for promoting free trade as a way to encourage economic growth.[a] The United States played a key role in creating major international trade institutions, including the World Trade Organization. Negotiations over the Trans-Pacific Partnership (TPP), a regional trade agreement in the Asia-Pacific region, were a key priority of President Obama during his final term in office. The TPP, however, did not receive bipartisan support, with critics from both parties arguing that it would take jobs away from Americans.

Many Americans may be surprised to learn that trade plays a much smaller role in the U.S. economy than it does in most developed countries, though that percentage is increasing. According to the World Bank, while trade comprises roughly 60 percent of the GDP of most high-income countries, it makes up only about 30 percent of the U.S. economy.[b] However, given that the United States is the largest trading partner for many countries (including the European Union, Canada, China, and Mexico), those countries have a keen interest in what policies the U.S. government pursues regarding trade.

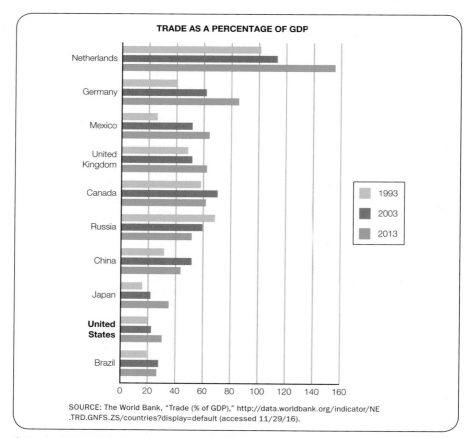

TRADE AS A PERCENTAGE OF GDP

Legend: 1993, 2003, 2013

SOURCE: The World Bank, "Trade (% of GDP)," http://data.worldbank.org/indicator/NE.TRD.GNFS.ZS/countries?display=default (accessed 11/29/16).

[a]Christopher Alessi and Robert McMahon, "Backgrounder: U.S. Trade Policy," Council on Foreign Relations, www.cfr.org/trade/us-trade-policy/p17859 (accessed 11/23/15).
[b]The World Bank measures trade as the sum of export and imports in goods and services.

One of the most basic ways that the United States promotes international humanitarian goals is by providing food, medical supplies, and other necessities to regions experiencing crises. Here, aid workers distribute food aid from the United States to refugees displaced by fighting in South Sudan.

The United States also contributes to international organizations that work for global health and against hunger, such as the World Health Organization. These policies are often seen as secondary to the other goals of American foreign policy and are forced to give way if they interfere with security or foreign economic policy. Moreover, while the United States spends billions annually on security policy and hundreds of millions on trade policy, it spends relatively little on environmental, human rights, and peacekeeping efforts. It has failed to approve the Kyoto Protocol, for example, an international agreement to reduce greenhouse gas production, and an international agreement to reduce discrimination against women. Some critics charge that the United States has the wrong priorities, spending far more to make war than to protect human rights and the global environment. Nevertheless, a number of important American foreign policy efforts are, at least in part, designed to make the world a better place.

In the realm of international environmental policy, the United States supports various international efforts to protect the environment. These include the United Nations (UN) Framework Convention on Climate Change, an international agreement to study and ameliorate harmful changes in the global environment, and the Montreal Protocol, an agreement signed by more than 150 countries to limit the production of substances potentially harmful to the world's ozone layer. Other nations have severely criticized the United States for withdrawing from the 1997 Kyoto Protocol. The United States has asserted that the Kyoto Protocol would be harmful to American economic interests. In preparation for the 2012 expiration of the Kyoto agreement, world leaders gathered in Copenhagen, Denmark, in 2009 but failed to produce a binding international agreement. In 2015, however, the United States did agree to the so-called Paris accords to reduce greenhouse gas emissions. Many Republicans, including Donald Trump, opposed the agreement. Each country agreed to reduce emissions but would set its own contribution to the effort.

The same national priorities seem apparent in the area of human rights policy. The United States has a long-standing commitment to human rights and is a party to most major international human rights agreements. These include the International Covenant on Civil and Political Rights, the UN Convention against Torture, the International Convention on the Elimination of All Forms of Racial Discrimination, and various agreements to protect children. The State Department's Bureau of Democracy, Human Rights, and Labor works cooperatively with international organizations to investigate and focus attention on human rights abuses. In 1998, the United States enacted the International Religious Freedom Act, which calls on all governments to respect religious freedom.

Another form of U.S. policy designed to improve the condition of the world is support for international peacekeeping efforts. At any point in time, a number of border wars, civil wars, and guerrilla conflicts are flaring somewhere in the world, usually in its poorer regions. These wars often generate humanitarian crises in the form of casualties, disease, and refugees. In cooperation with international agencies and other nations, the United States funds a number of efforts to keep the peace in volatile regions and to deal with the health care and refugee problems associated with conflict. In 2015, the United States provided nearly $2 billion in humanitarian assistance to help Syrian refugees displaced by the civil war in that nation and by the end of 2016 had donated over $5 billion to the cause.[5] As the world's wealthiest nation, the United States also recognizes an obligation to render assistance to nations facing crises and emergencies. In 2014, for example, the United States pledged $300 million in humanitarian aid to the people of South Sudan, a population at grave risk of famine caused by military conflict between government and rebel forces.

America's humanitarian policies are important. Without U.S. efforts and funding, many international humanitarian programs would be far less successful. Still, security and economic interests take precedence over humanitarian concerns with major trading partners such as China and Saudi Arabia, where the United States often overlooks human rights violations.

● American Foreign Policy Is Shaped by Government and Nongovernment Actors

Identify the major players in foreign-policy making, and describe their roles

As we have seen, domestic policies are made by governmental institutions and influenced by a variety of interest groups, political movements, and even the mass media. The same is true in the realm of foreign policy. The president and his chief advisers are the principal architects of U.S. foreign policy. However, the Congress, the bureaucracy, the courts, political parties, interest groups, and trade associations also play important roles in this realm. Often, the president and Congress are at odds over foreign policy.

The President Leads Foreign Policy

The Constitution assigns the president clear powers in the realm of foreign and security policy. The president is given the power to make treaties and appoint ambassadors (both with the advice and consent of the Senate), receive foreign ambassadors, and serve as commander in chief of the army and navy of the United States. Presidents have expanded upon these powers, claiming that their obligation to defend the nation serves as the basis for presidential primacy in all matters affecting America's international interests. Since World War II, presidents have declined to ask Congress for a declaration of war as required by the Constitution and have, instead, relied on congressionally enacted "authorizations of the use of military force." Such authorizations were enacted for the 1991 Persian Gulf War and the 2003 invasion of Iraq, for example. In some instances, presidents have committed American forces to foreign conflicts under their own authority.

Most American presidents have been domestic politicians who set out to make their place in history through achievements in domestic policy. President George W. Bush had virtually no foreign policy preparation prior to taking office. He had traveled very little outside the United States and had had almost no foreign experience as governor of Texas.

Nonetheless, Bush was decisive in the initiatives he took to define America's national interest for his administration. Examples include revival of the controversial nuclear missile shield ("Star Wars"); abandonment of the Anti–Ballistic Missile treaty, which alienated Russia; changes in policy priorities away from humanitarian and environmental goals and toward a far stronger emphasis on national security; and turning America's concerns away from Europe and toward an "Asia-first" policy.

September 11 and its aftermath immensely accentuated the president's role and his place in foreign policy.[6] By 2002, foreign policy was the centerpiece of the Bush administration's agenda. In a June 1 speech at West Point, the **Bush Doctrine** of preemptive war was announced. Bush argued that "our security will require all Americans . . . to be ready for preemptive action when necessary to defend our liberty and to defend our lives." Bush's statement was clearly intended to justify his administration's plans to invade Iraq, but it had much wider implications for international relations and for the central role of the American president in guiding foreign policy.

By 2010, President Barack Obama had put his own stamp on American foreign policy, altering the conduct of America's war in Afghanistan and seeking to compel the Israelis and Palestinians to accept a Middle East peace deal. Obama also sought to engage more fully America's allies, who had been miffed by the previous administration's tendency to engage in unilateral action. Thus, the United States worked closely with its NATO allies in 2011 in a successful multilateral effort to end the Libyan dictatorship of Mu'ammar Qaddafi.

Obama ended direct U.S. military involvement in Iraq in 2011 and had begun to withdraw American forces from Afghanistan. One of his triumphs was the 2011 military raid that resulted in the killing of Osama bin Laden, who had long been sought by the United States as the mastermind of the September 11 terrorist attacks. Yet President Obama faced a number of challenges as he neared the end of his presidency: Russian president Vladimir Putin upset the international order in Europe by seizing the Crimean Peninsula of Ukraine; North Korea continued to test missiles; Israel and the Palestinians fought a war in Gaza; and ISIS militants sought to win control of Iraq, Syria, and Lebanon and showed that they could strike in the hearts of European capitals. These and new problems would challenge Obama's successors. Presidents have come to dominate American foreign policy, but America's foreign policies are never able to cure the ills of the world.

The Bureaucracy Implements and Informs Policy Decisions

The major foreign policy actors in the bureaucracy are the secretaries of the departments of State, Defense, and the Treasury; the Joint Chiefs of Staff, especially the chair; and the director of the CIA. Since 1947, a separate unit in the White House has overseen the vast foreign policy establishment for the purpose of synthesizing all the messages arising out of the bureaucracy and helping the president make his own foreign policy. This is the National Security Council. It is a "subcabinet" made up of the major players just listed plus others whom each president appoints. Since the profound shake-up of September 11, two key players have been added: the secretary of the new Department of Homeland Security, created in 2002, and the director of national intelligence, established in 2005, to collate and coordinate intelligence coming in from multiple sources and to report a synthesis of all this to the president on a daily basis.

Since the creation of the CIA and the Department of Defense in 1947, the secretary of defense and the director of the CIA have often been rivals engaged in power struggles for control of the intelligence community.[7] For the most part, secretaries of defense have prevailed in these battles, and the Defense Department today controls more than 80 percent of the nation's intelligence capabilities and funds. The creation of the position of director of national intelligence to coordinate all intelligence activities set off new Washington power struggles as the "intelligence czar" faced opposition from both the CIA and the Department of Defense.

In the wake of September 11, military and law-enforcement agencies increased their role in America's foreign-policy making.[8] In recent years, American ambassadors have complained that they have been relegated to secondary status as the White House has looked to military commanders for information, advice, and policy implementation. For every region of the world, the U.S. military has assigned a "combatant commander," usually a senior general or admiral, to take charge of operations in that area. In many instances, these combatant commanders, who control troops, equipment, and intelligence capabilities, have become the real eyes, ears, and voices for American foreign policy in their designated regions.

Congress's Legal Authority Can Be Decisive

Although the Constitution gives Congress the power to declare war (see Table 14.1), Congress has exercised this power on only five occasions: the War of 1812, the Mexican War (1846), the Spanish–American War (1898), World War I (1917), and World War II (1941). For the first 150 years of American history, Congress's

TABLE 14.1

Principal Foreign Policy Provisions of the Constitution

	POWERS GRANTED	
	PRESIDENT	CONGRESS
War power	Commander in chief of armed forces	Provide for the common defense; declare war
Treaties	Negotiate treaties	Ratification of treaties by two-thirds majority (Senate)
Appointments	Nominate high-level government officials	Confirm president's appointments (Senate)
Foreign commerce	No explicit powers, but treaty negotiation and appointment powers pertain	Explicit power "to regulate foreign commerce"
General powers	Executive power; veto	Legislative power; power of the purse; oversight and investigation

role in foreign policy was limited because the United States' role in world affairs was limited. The treaty power was and is an important entrée of the Senate into foreign-policy making. But since World War II and the continual involvement of the United States in international security and foreign aid, Congress as a whole has become a major foreign-policy maker because most modern foreign policies require financing, which requires action by both the House of Representatives and the Senate. For example, Congress's first act after the September 11, 2001, attacks was to authorize the president to use "all necessary and appropriate force," coupled with a $40 billion emergency appropriations bill for homeland defense. Although President Bush believed he possessed the constitutional authority to invade Iraq, he still sought congressional approval, which he received in October 2002.

Not only does the president need Congress to provide funding for foreign and military policy initiatives but also, under the Constitution, many presidential agreements with foreign nations have to be approved by Congress. Article II, Section 2, of the Constitution declares that proposed treaties with other nations must be submitted by the president to the Senate and approved by a two-thirds vote. Because this "supermajority" is usually difficult to achieve, presidents generally prefer a different type of agreement with other nations, called an **executive agreement**. An executive agreement is similar to a treaty and has the force of law but is almost always based on authority from a prior law passed by Congress or a Senate-approved treaty.

Another aspect of Congress's role in foreign policy is the Senate's power to confirm the president's nominations of cabinet members, ambassadors, and other high-ranking officials (such as the director of the CIA but not the director of the National Security Council). A final constitutional power of Congress is the regulation of "commerce with foreign nations."

Other congressional players are the foreign policy, military policy, and intelligence committees: in the Senate, these are the Foreign Relations Committee, the Armed Services Committee, the Intelligence Committee, and the Homeland Security and Governmental Affairs Committee; in the House, these are the Foreign Affairs Committee, the Intelligence Committee, the Homeland Security Committee, and the Armed Services Committee. Usually, a few members of these committees who have spent years specializing in foreign affairs become trusted members of the foreign policy establishment and are influential makers of foreign policy. In fact, several members of Congress have left the legislature to become key foreign affairs cabinet members.

Interest Groups Pressure Foreign Policy Decision Makers

Although the president, the executive branch "bureaucracy," and Congress are the true makers of foreign policy, the "foreign policy establishment" is a much larger arena, including what can properly be called the shapers of foreign policy: a host of unofficial, informal players who possess varying degrees of influence depending on their prestige, reputation, socioeconomic standing, and, most important, the party and ideology that are dominant at a given moment.

By far the most important category of nonofficial player is the interest group—that is, the interest group to which one or more foreign policy issues are of long-standing and vital relevance. Most of these are "single-issue" economic groups, such as the tobacco industry and the computer hardware and software industries, which become most active when their particular issue is on the agenda.

Another type of interest group with a well-founded reputation for influence in foreign policy comprises people who strongly identify with their country of national origin. The interest group with the reputation for the greatest influence is Jewish Americans, whose family and emotional ties to Israel make them one of the most alert and active interest groups in all of foreign policy. In 2015, some Jewish groups lobbied heavily but ultimately unsuccessfully against the Obama administration's agreement with Iran to limit its nuclear program, which they argued posed a threat to both the United States and Israel. Similarly, Americans of Irish heritage still maintain vigilance about American policies toward Ireland and Northern Ireland. Cuban Americans have long been a powerful voice in support of maintaining sanctions against Cuba. This helps explain why relations with Cuba were not normalized until 2015. A third type of interest group is devoted to human rights. Such groups are made up of people who, instead of having self-serving economic or ethnic interests in foreign policy, are genuinely concerned about the welfare and treatment of people throughout the world—particularly those who suffer under harsh political regimes. A relatively small but often quite influential example is Amnesty International, whose exposés of human rights abuses have altered the practices of many regimes around the world. In recent years, the Christian right has been a vocal advocate for the human rights of Christians who are persecuted in other parts of the world for their religious beliefs, most notably in China.

A final actor in the realm of foreign policy is public opinion. For the most part, the public is not engaged in foreign policy issues as most Americans are concerned mainly with domestic issues. However, public opinion does begin to count when the nation is at war. Americans are often impatient with military actions that seem long and drawn out, producing costs and casualties for reasons that no longer seem clear. Fear of public opinion is one reason that presidents have favored professional military forces and technologies like drones that would reduce the immediacy of war to America's general public.

The American Israel Public Affairs Committee (AIPAC) is a powerful interest group that advocates pro-Israel policies to Congress and the president. Here, Israeli prime minister Benjamin Netanyahu speaks to the group about the White House–backed nuclear deal with Iran, against which AIPAC lobbied heavily.

Putting It Together

Three generalizations frame the remainder of this chapter. First, when an important foreign policy decision has to be made under conditions of crisis—where time is of the essence—the influence of the presidency is at its strongest. Second, within these time constraints, access to the decision is limited almost exclusively to the narrowest definition of the foreign policy establishment. The arena for participation is tiny; any discussion at all is limited to the officially and constitutionally designated players.[9] As time becomes less restricted, even when the decision to be made is of great importance, the arena of participation expands to include more government players and more nonofficial, informal players—the most concerned interest groups and the most important journalists. In other words, the arena becomes more pluralistic and, therefore, less distinguishable from the politics of domestic-policy making. Third, because there are so many other countries with power and interests on any given issue, there are severe limits on the choices the United States can make. Thus, even though foreign-policy making in noncrisis situations may closely resemble the pluralistic politics of domestic-policy making, foreign-policy making is still a narrower, more elitist arena with fewer participants.

● Tools of American Foreign Policy Include Diplomacy, Force, and Money

Describe the means the United States uses to carry out foreign policy today

We will deal here with those instruments of American foreign policy most important in the modern epoch: diplomacy, the United Nations, the international monetary structure, economic aid and sanctions, collective security, military deterrence, and arbitration.

Each of these instruments will be evaluated in this section for its utility in the conduct of American foreign policy, and each will be assessed in light of the history and development of American values.

Diplomacy Is the Master Policy Tool

We begin this treatment of instruments with diplomacy. **Diplomacy** is the representation of a government to other foreign governments. Its purpose is to promote national values or interests by peaceful means. According to Hans Morgenthau, "a diplomacy that ends in war has failed in its primary objective."[10]

Diplomacy, by its very nature, is overshadowed by spectacular international events, dramatic initiatives, and meetings among heads of state or their direct personal representatives. The traditional American distrust of diplomacy continues today, albeit in weaker form. Impatience with or downright distrust of diplomacy has been built not only into all the other instruments of foreign policy but also into the modern presidential system itself.[11] So much personal responsibility has been heaped on the presidency that it is difficult for presidents to entrust any of their authority or responsibility in foreign policy to professional diplomats in the State Department and other bureaucracies.

The significance of diplomacy and its vulnerability to politics may be better appreciated as we proceed to the other instruments. Diplomacy was an instrument more or less imposed on Americans as the prevailing method of dealing among nation-states in the nineteenth century. The other instruments to be identified and assessed below are instruments that Americans self-consciously crafted for themselves to take care of their own chosen place in the world affairs of the second half of the twentieth century and beyond. They therefore better reflect American culture and values than diplomacy does.

The United Nations Is the World's Congress

The utility of the **United Nations (UN)** to the United States as an instrument of foreign policy can be too easily underestimated because the UN is a very large and unwieldy institution with few powers and no armed forces to implement its rules and resolutions. It is an organization of nations founded in 1945 to be a channel for negotiation and a means of settling international disputes peaceably. The UN can serve as a useful forum for international discussions and an instrument for multilateral action. Most peacekeeping efforts to which the United States contributes, for example, are undertaken under UN auspices.

The UN's supreme body is the General Assembly, comprising one representative of each of the 193 member states; each member representative has one vote, regardless of the size of the country. Important issues require a two-thirds majority vote, and the annual session of the General Assembly runs only from September to December (although it can call extra sessions). The General Assembly has little organization that can make it an effective decision-making body, with only six standing committees, few tight rules of procedure, and no political parties to provide priorities and discipline. Its defenders are quick to add that although it lacks armed forces, it relies on the power of world opinion—and this is not to be taken lightly. The powers of the UN devolve mainly to the organization's "executive committee," the UN Security Council, which alone has the real power to make decisions and rulings that member states are obligated by the UN Charter to implement. The Security Council may be called into session at any time, and each member (or a designated alternate) must be present at UN headquarters in New York at all times. The council is composed of 15 members: 5 are permanent (the victors of World War II), and 10 are elected by the General Assembly for un-repeatable two-year terms. The 5 permanent members are China, France, Russia, the United Kingdom, and the United States. Each of the 15 members has only one vote, and a 9-vote majority of the 15 is required on all substantive matters. But each of the 5 permanent members also has a negative vote, a "veto"; and one veto is sufficient to reject any substantive proposal.

The International Monetary Structure Helps Provide Economic Stability

Fear of a repeat of the economic devastation that followed World War I brought the United States together with its allies (except the Soviet Union) to Bretton Woods, New Hampshire, in 1944 to create a new international economic structure for the postwar world. The result was two institutions: the International Bank for Recon-struction and Development (commonly called the World Bank) and the International Monetary Fund. The World Bank's chief mission is development aid to poor countries.

The World Bank was set up to finance long-term capital. Leading nations took on the obligation of contributing funds to enable the World Bank to make loans to capital-hungry countries. (The U.S. quota has been about one-third of the total.) The **International Monetary Fund (IMF)** was set up to provide for the short-term flow of money. It provides loans and facilitates international monetary exchanges. After the war, the dollar, instead of gold, was the chief means by which the cur-rencies of one country would be "changed into" currencies of another country for purposes of making international transactions. To permit debtor countries with no international balances to make purchases and investments, the IMF was set up to lend dollars or other appropriate currencies to such needy member countries to help them overcome temporary trade deficits.

During the 1990s the importance of the IMF increased through its efforts to reform some of the largest debtor nations and formerly communist countries, to bring them more fully into the global capitalist economy. The future of the IMF, the World Bank, and all other private sources of international investment will depend in part on extension of more credit to the developing world because credit means investment and productivity. But the future may depend even more on reducing existing debt from previous extensions of credit.

Economic Aid Has Two Sides

Every year, the United States provides nearly $30 billion in economic assistance to other nations. Some aid has a humanitarian purpose, such as helping to provide health care, shelter for refugees, or famine relief. Much American aid, however, is designed to promote American security interests or economic concerns. For ex-ample, the United States provides military assistance to a number of its allies in the form of advanced weapons or loans to help them purchase such weapons. These loans generally stipulate that the recipient must purchase the designated weapons from American firms. In this way the United States hopes to bolster its security and economic interests with one grant. The two largest recipients of American military assistance are Israel and Egypt, American allies that fought two wars against each other. The United States believes that its military assistance allows both countries to feel sufficiently secure to remain at peace with each other.

Aid is an economic carrot. Sanctions are an economic stick. Economic sanctions that the United States employs against other nations include trade embargoes, bans on investment, and efforts to prevent the World Bank or other international institutions from extending credit to a nation against which the United States has a grievance. Sanctions are most often employed when the United States seeks to weaken what it considers a hostile regime or when it is attempting to compel some particular action by another regime. In 2014, for example, the United States imposed economic sanctions against Russia in response to the Russian annexation of Crimea, which the United States regards as part of the Ukraine. The United States also uses economic sanctions to advance its international humanitarian policy goals. The United States currently has sanctions in place against a number of governments with records of serious violations of civil and political rights.[12]

Collective Security Is Designed to Deter War

In 1947, most Americans hoped that the United States could meet its world obligations through the UN and economic structures alone. But most foreign-policy makers anticipated the need for military entanglements at the time of drafting the original UN Charter by insisting on language that recognized the right of all nations to provide for their mutual defense independent of the UN. Almost immediately after enactment of the Marshall Plan, designed to promote European economic recovery, the White House and other top officials urgently requested the Senate to ratify and both houses of Congress to finance mutual defense alliances.

The Senate, at first reluctant to approve treaties providing for national security alliances, ultimately agreed with the executive branch. The first collective security agreement was the Rio Treaty (ratified by the Senate in 1947), which created the Organization of American States. This was the model treaty, anticipating all succeeding collective security treaties by providing that an armed attack against any of its members "shall be considered as an attack against all the American States," including the United States. A more significant break with U.S. tradition of avoiding peacetime entanglements came with the North Atlantic Treaty (signed in 1949), which created the **North Atlantic Treaty Organization (NATO)**. Comprising the United States, Canada, and most of Western Europe, NATO was formed to counter the perceived threat from the Soviet Union. Other collective security treaties followed. After the collapse of the Soviet Union, the importance of NATO as a military alliance seemed to wane. However, since 2014, the resurgence of Russia as a military power forced NATO members to look to one another for support.

In addition to these multilateral treaties, the United States entered into a number of **bilateral treaties** (treaties made between two nations), such as the treaty with Vietnam that resulted in ultimately unsuccessful American military action to protect that nation's government. As one author has observed, the United States has been a *producer* of security, whereas most of its allies have been *consumers* of security.[13]

This pattern has continued in the post–Cold War era, and its best illustration is the 1991 Persian Gulf War, where the United States provided the initiative, the leadership, and most of the armed forces, even though its allies reimbursed over 90 percent of the cost.

It is difficult to evaluate collective security and its treaties because the purpose of collective security as an instrument of foreign policy is prevention, and success of this kind has to be measured in terms of what has *not* happened. Critics have argued that U.S. collective security treaties posed a threat of encirclement to the Soviet Union, forcing it to produce its own collective security, particularly the Warsaw Pact.[14] Nevertheless, no one can deny the counterargument that more than 70 years have passed without a world war.

Military Force Is "Politics by Other Means"

The most visible instrument of foreign policy is, of course, military force. The United States has built the world's most imposing military, with army, navy, marine, and air force units stationed around the globe. The United States is responsible for one-third of the world's total military expenditures. The Prussian military strategist Carl von Clausewitz famously called war "politics by other means." By this he meant that nations used force or the threat of force not simply to demonstrate their capacity for violence but to achieve their foreign policy goals. Military force may be needed to protect a nation's security interests and economic concerns. Ironically, force may also be needed to achieve humanitarian goals. For example, in 2014 and 2015, international military force was required to protect tens of thousands of Yazidi refugees threatened by ISIS forces in Iraq. Without the use of military force, humanitarian assistance to the Yazidis would have been irrelevent.

Often, military efforts abroad do not turn out as the government or the public expected. Though most Americans were in favor of U.S. involvement in Iraq and Afghanistan following September 11, 2001, public opinion on the issue has shifted.

Though military force is sometimes necessary, it is generally seen as a last resort to be avoided if possible because a number of problems are commonly associated with its use. First, the use of military force is extremely costly in both human and financial terms. In the past 50 years, tens of thousands of Americans have been killed and hundreds of billions of dollars spent in America's military operations. Second, the use of military force is inherently fraught with risk. However carefully policy makers and generals plan for military operations, results can seldom be fully anticipated. For example, American policy makers expected, accurately, to defeat the Iraqi army quickly and easily in 2003. Policy makers did not anticipate, however, that American forces would still be struggling years later to defeat the insurgency that arose in the war's aftermath.

Arbitration Resolves Disputes

The final foreign policy tool is dispute arbitration. Arbitration is the resolution of a disagreement by a neutral third party. International arbitration is sometimes seen as a form of "soft power" as distinguished from military force, economic sanctions, and other coercive foreign policy instruments. The United States will occasionally turn to international tribunals to resolve disputes with other countries. For example, in 2008, the U.S. government asked the International Court of Justice to resolve a long-standing dispute with Italy over American property confiscated by the Italian government decades earlier.

Foreign Policy, Democracy,
and Your Future

The harsh realities of foreign policy often clash with the United States' history and ideals. U.S. democratic and liberal traditions lead Americans to hope for a world in which ideals rather than naked interests govern foreign policy and in which U.S. leaders follow those ideals. Traditional American values assert that our foreign policies should have a higher purpose than narrow self-interest and that America would use force only as a last resort. But the realities of foreign policy often collide with these historic ideals, leaving U.S. policy makers to struggle to explain their actions and avoid admitting to motivations that might not sit well with the public.

International events can make it difficult to pursue those ideals. The forces of globalization mean that it is easier than ever for small groups of extremists with violent intentions to travel to American shores and carry out their plans. (The "**Who Participates?**" feature on the facing page shows public opinion on security issues and reflects strong concern about international terrorism among all age groups.) On the other hand, those same forces of globalization have been the source of many positive outcomes. Greater trade reduces the price of many products for American consumers as well as for those abroad. Furthermore, many scholars believe that the increasing global economic interdependence is a force for peace: nations that trade heavily with each other are less likely to go to war with each other. What can U.S. leaders do in the future to make sure that globalization is a positive force that promotes U.S. security and prosperity?

Public Opinion on Security Issues

As we learned in this chapter, public opinion can influence foreign policy. However, many Americans are not engaged with or knowledgeable about foreign policy. Moreover, public opinion varies by age. These figures show what percentage of each age group think each issue is a critical threat.

Percentage Who Think Each Issue Is a Critical Threat

Age group   ● <25   ● 25–44   ● 45–64   ● 65+

The development of China as a world power
- 38%
- 35%
- 46%
- 48%

Islamic fundamentalism
- 25%
- 35%
- 43%
- 59%

Immigrants and refugees coming into the United States
- 24%
- 29%
- 45%
- 45%

International terrorism
- 58%
- 60%
- 68%
- 78%

SOURCE: Chicago Council Survey of American Public Opinion and U.S. Foreign Policy, 2014, www.icpsr.umich.edu/icpsrweb/ICPSR/studies/36216 (accessed 11/9/15).

WHAT YOU CAN DO ➡

WHAT YOU CAN DO

Stay Informed about International News

 Learn more about the issues above and others through coverage in major U.S. newspapers such as the New York Times (**www.nytimes.com**) and the Wall Street Journal (**www.wsj.com**).

 Check out foreign news sites for different perspectives on U.S. foreign policies and activities such as Al Jazeera English (**www.aljazeera.com**) and the BBC (**www.bbc.com**).

 For in-depth conversations about world affairs, watch videos at the World Affairs Council (**www.worldaffairs.org**) or the Council on Foreign Relations (**www.cfr.org**).

✓ Consider working with an interest group on a foreign policy issue you care about, such as Amnesty International (human rights), Move America Forward (supporting American troops), or Just Foreign Policy (equality and justice from a nonpartisan perspective).

chapterstudyguide

Practice Quiz

1. Which of the following terms best describes the American posture toward the world prior to the twentieth century? *(p. 441)*
   a) interventionist
   b) isolationist
   c) appeasement
   d) humanitarian
   e) internationalist

2. Which of the following terms describes an effort to forestall war by giving in to the demands of a hostile power? *(p. 442)*
   a) appeasement
   b) deterrence
   c) détente
   d) containment
   e) "Minuteman" theory of defense

3. *Cold War* refers to *(p. 442)*
   a) competition between the United States and Canada over Alaska.
   b) the years between World War I and World War II when the United States and Germany were hostile to one another.
   c) the long-standing conflict over which nation controls Antarctica.
   d) the period of struggle between the United States and the Soviet Union between the late 1940s and the late 1980s.
   e) the economic competition between the United States and Japan today.

4. *Bush Doctrine* refers to *(p. 449)*
   a) the idea that the United States should not allow foreign powers to meddle in the Western Hemisphere.
   b) the idea that the United States should avoid future wars by giving in to the demands of hostile foreign powers.
   c) the idea that the United States should take preemptive action against threats to its national security.
   d) the idea that the United States should never take preemptive action against threats to its national security.
   e) the idea that the United States should always secure international approval before taking any military action.

5. The Constitution assigns the power to declare war to *(p. 450)*
   a) the National Security Council.
   b) the president.
   c) the chief justice of the United States.
   d) the secretary of defense.
   e) Congress.

6. An agreement made between the president and another country that has the force of a treaty but does not require the Senate's "advice and consent" is called *(p. 451)*
   a) an executive order.
   b) an executive privilege.
   c) an executive agreement.
   d) a diplomatic decree.
   e) arbitration.

7. The making of American foreign policy during noncrisis moments is *(p. 453)*
   a) dominated entirely by the president.
   b) dominated entirely by Congress.
   c) dominated entirely by interest groups.
   d) dominated entirely by the Department of Defense.
   e) highly pluralistic, involving a large mix of both official and unofficial players.

8. Which of the following statements about the United Nations is *not* true? *(pp. 454–55)*
   a) It has a powerful army to implement its decisions.
   b) It gives every country one vote in the General Assembly.
   c) The five permanent members of the UN Security Council are China, France, Russia, the United Kingdom, and the United States.
   d) It was designed to be a channel for negotiation and a means of settling international disputes peaceably.
   e) Important issues require a two-thirds majority vote.

9. Which of the following were founded during the 1940s in order to create a new international economic structure for the postwar world? *(p. 455)*
   a) the Federal Reserve System and the Council of Economic Advisors
   b) the North Atlantic Treaty Organization and the Southeast Asia Treaty Organization
   c) the International Monetary Fund and the World Bank
   d) the International Court of Justice and the Warsaw Pact
   e) the Office of Management and Budget and the General Agreement on Tariffs and Trade

10. The North Atlantic Treaty Organization was formed in 1949 by the United States, *(p. 456)*
    a) Canada, and most of Eastern Europe.
    b) Canada, and the Soviet Union.
    c) Canada, and Mexico.
    d) Canada, and most of Western Europe.
    e) Canada, and the United Kingdom.

Key Terms

appeasement *(p. 442)* the effort to forestall war by giving in to the demands of a hostile power

bilateral treaties *(p. 456)* treaties made between two nations

Bush Doctrine *(p. 449)* foreign policy based on the idea that the United States should take preemptive action against threats to its national security

Cold War *(p. 442)* the period of struggle between the United States and the former Soviet Union lasting from the late 1940s to about 1990

containment *(p. 442)* a policy designed to curtail the political and military expansion of a hostile power

deterrence *(p. 442)* the development and maintenance of military strength as a means of discouraging attack

diplomacy *(p. 454)* the representation of a government to foreign governments

executive agreement *(p. 451)* an agreement, made between the president and another country, that has the force of a treaty but does not require the Senate's "advice and consent"

General Agreement on Tariffs and Trade *(GATT)* *(p. 445)* international trade organization, in existence from 1947 to 1995, that set many of the rules governing international trade

International Monetary Fund *(IMF)* *(p. 455)* an institution established in 1944 that provides loans and facilitates international monetary exchange

isolationism *(p. 441)* avoidance of involvement in the affairs of other nations

nation-states *(p. 443)* political entities consisting of people with some common cultural experience (nation) who also share a common political authority (state), recognized by other sovereignties (nation-states)

non-state actors *(p. 441)* groups other than nation-states that attempt to play a role in the international system; terrorist groups are one type of non-state actor

North American Free Trade Agreement *(NAFTA)* *(p. 445)* trade treaty among the United States, Canada, and Mexico to lower and eliminate tariffs among the three countries

North Atlantic Treaty Organization *(NATO)* *(p. 456)* an organization, comprising the United States, Canada, and most of Western Europe, formed in 1949 to counter the perceived threat from the Soviet Union

preventive war *(p. 443)* policy of striking first when a nation fears that a foreign foe is contemplating hostile action

United Nations *(UN)* *(p. 454)* an organization of nations founded in 1945 to be a channel for negotiation and a means of settling international disputes peaceably; the UN has had frequent successes in providing a forum for negotiation and on some occasions a means of preventing international conflicts from spreading; on a number of occasions, the UN has supported U.S. foreign policy goals

World Trade Organization *(WTO)* *(p. 445)* international organization promoting free trade that grew out of the General Agreement on Tariffs and Trade

For Further Reading

Art, Robert. *The Use of Force: Military Power and International Politics*. New York: Rowman and Littlefield, 2009.

Gaddis, John L. *The Cold War: A New History*. New York: Penguin, 2005.

Ginsberg, Benjamin. *The Worth of War*. Amherst, NY: Prometheus Books, 2014.

Hook, Steven W., and John Spanier. *American Foreign Policy since World War II*. 20th ed. Washington, DC: CQ Press, 2016.

Ikenberry, John. *American Foreign Policy*. New York: Wadsworth, 2010.

Jentleson, Bruce. *American Foreign Policy: The Dynamics of Choice in the 21st Century*. 5th ed. New York: W. W. Norton, 2013.

Mandelbaum, Michael. *The Case for Goliath: How America Acts as the World's Government in the 21st Century*. Washington, DC: Public Affairs Press, 2005.

Mearsheimer, John J., and Stephen M. Walt. *The Israel Lobby and U.S. Foreign Policy*. New York: Farrar, Straus and Giroux, 2008.

Nasr, Vali. *The Dispensable Nation: American Foreign Policy in Retreat*. New York: Anchor Books, 2014.

appendix

The Declaration of Independence

In Congress, July 4, 1776

The unanimous Declaration of the thirteen united States of America,

When in the Course of human events, it becomes necessary for one people to dissolve the political bands which have connected them with another, and to assume among the powers of the earth, the separate and equal station to which the Laws of Nature and of Nature's God entitle them, a decent respect to the opinions of mankind requires that they should declare the causes which impel them to the separation.

We hold these truths to be self-evident, that all men are created equal, that they are endowed by their Creator with certain unalienable Rights, that among these are Life, Liberty and the pursuit of Happiness.—That to secure these rights, Governments are instituted among Men, deriving their just powers from the consent of the governed.—That whenever any Form of Government becomes destructive of these ends, it is the Right of the People to alter or to abolish it, and to institute new Government, laying its foundation on such principles and organizing its powers in such form, as to them shall seem most likely to effect their Safety and Happiness. Prudence, indeed, will dictate that Governments long established should not be changed for light and transient causes; and accordingly all experience hath shewn, that mankind are more disposed to suffer, while evils are sufferable, than to right themselves by abolishing the forms to which they are accustomed. But when a long train of abuses and usurpations, pursuing invariably the same Object evinces a design to reduce them under absolute Despotism, it is their right, it is their duty, to throw off such Government, and to provide new Guards for their future security.—Such has been the patient sufferance of these Colonies; and such is now the necessity which constrains them to alter their former Systems of Government. The history of the present King of Great Britain is a history of repeated injuries and usurpations, all having in direct object the establishment of an absolute Tyranny over these States. To prove this, let Facts be submitted to a candid world.

He has refused his Assent to Laws, the most wholesome and necessary for the public good.

He has forbidden his Governors to pass Laws of immediate and pressing importance, unless suspended in their operation till his Assent should be obtained; and when so suspended, he has utterly neglected to attend to them.

He has refused to pass other Laws for the accommodation of large districts of people, unless those people would relinquish the right of Representation in the Legislature, a right inestimable to them and formidable to tyrants only.

He has called together legislative bodies at places unusual, uncomfortable, and distant from the depository of their public Records, for the sole purpose of fatiguing them into compliance with his measures.

He has dissolved Representative Houses repeatedly, for opposing with manly firmness his invasions on the rights of the people.

He has refused for a long time, after such dissolutions, to cause others to be elected; whereby the Legislative powers, incapable of Annihilation, have returned to the People at large for their exercise; the State remaining in the mean time exposed to all the dangers of invasion from without, and convulsions within.

He has endeavoured to prevent the population of these States; for that purpose obstructing the Laws for Naturalization of Foreigners; refusing to pass others to encourage their migrations hither, and raising the conditions of new Appropriations of Lands.

He has obstructed the Administration of Justice, by refusing his Assent to Laws for establishing Judiciary powers.

He has made Judges dependent on his Will alone, for the tenure of their offices, and the amount and payment of their salaries.

He has erected a multitude of New Offices, and sent hither swarms of Officers to harrass our people, and eat out their substance.

He has kept among us, in times of peace, Standing Armies without the Consent of our legislatures.

He has affected to render the Military independent of and superior to the Civil power.

He has combined with others to subject us to a jurisdiction foreign to our constitution, and unacknowledged by our laws; giving his Assent to their Acts of pretended Legislation:

For Quartering large bodies of armed troops among us:

For protecting them, by a mock Trial, from punishment for any Murders which they should commit on the Inhabitants of these States:

For cutting off our Trade with all parts of the world:

For imposing Taxes on us without our Consent:

For depriving us in many cases, of the benefits of Trial by Jury:

For transporting us beyond Seas to be tried for pretended offences:

For abolishing the free System of English Laws in a neighboring Province, establishing therein an Arbitrary government, and enlarging its Boundaries so as to render it at once an example and fit instrument for introducing the same absolute rule into these Colonies:

For taking away our Charters, abolishing our most valuable Laws, and altering fundamentally the Forms of our Governments:

For suspending our own Legislatures, and declaring themselves invested with power to legislate for us in all cases whatsoever.

He has abdicated Government here, by declaring us out of his Protection and waging War against us.

He has plundered our seas, ravaged our Coasts, burnt our towns, and destroyed the lives of our people.

He is at this time transporting large Armies of foreign Mercenaries to compleat the works of death, desolation and tyranny, already begun with circumstances of Cruelty & perfidy scarcely paralleled in the most barbarous ages, and totally unworthy the Head of a civilized nation.

He has constrained our fellow Citizens taken Captive on the high Seas to bear Arms against their Country, to become the executioners of their friends and Brethren, or to fall themselves by their Hands.

He has excited domestic insurrections amongst us, and has endeavoured to bring on the inhabitants of our frontiers, the merciless Indian Savages, whose known rule of warfare, is an undistinguished destruction of all ages, sexes and conditions.

In every stage of these Oppressions We have Petitioned for Redress in the most humble terms: Our repeated Petitions have been answered only by repeated injury. A Prince whose character is thus marked by every act which may define a Tyrant, is unfit to be the ruler of a free people.

Nor have We been wanting in attentions to our Brittish brethren. We have warned them from time to time of attempts by their legislature to extend an unwarrantable jurisdiction over us. We have reminded them of the circumstances of our emigration and settlement here. We have appealed to their native justice and magnanimity, and we have conjured them by the ties of our common kindred to disavow these usurpations, which, would inevitably interrupt our connections and correspondence. They too have been deaf to the voice of justice and of consanguinity. We must, therefore, acquiesce in the necessity, which denounces our Separation, and hold them, as we hold the rest of mankind, Enemies in War, in Peace Friends.

We, Therefore, the Representatives of the United States of America, in General Congress, Assembled, appealing to the Supreme Judge of the world for the rectitude of our intentions, do, in the Name, and by Authority of the good People of these Colonies, solemnly publish and declare, That these United Colonies are, and of Right ought to be Free and Independent States; that they are Absolved from all Allegiance to the British Crown, and that all political connection between them and the State of Great Britain, is and ought to be totally dissolved; and that as Free and Independent States, they have full Power to levy War, conclude Peace, contract Alliances, establish Commerce, and to do all other Acts and Things which Independent States may of right do. And for the support of this Declaration, with a firm reliance on the protection of divine Providence, we mutually pledge to each other our Lives, our Fortunes and our sacred Honor.

The foregoing Declaration was, by order of Congress, engrossed, and signed by the following members:

John Hancock

NEW HAMPSHIRE
Josiah Bartlett
William Whipple
Matthew Thornton

MASSACHUSETTS BAY
Samuel Adams
John Adams
Robert Treat Paine
Elbridge Gerry

RHODE ISLAND
Stephen Hopkins
William Ellery

CONNECTICUT
Roger Sherman
Samuel Huntington
William Williams
Oliver Wolcott

NEW YORK
William Floyd
Philip Livingston
Francis Lewis
Lewis Morris

NEW JERSEY
Richard Stockton
John Witherspoon
Francis Hopkinson
John Hart
Abraham Clark

PENNSYLVANIA
Robert Morris
Benjamin Rush
Benjamin Franklin
John Morton
George Clymer
James Smith
George Taylor
James Wilson
George Ross

DELAWARE
Caesar Rodney
George Read
Thomas M'Kean

MARYLAND
Samuel Chase
William Paca
Thomas Stone
Charles Carroll,
*   of Carrollton*

VIRGINIA
George Wythe
Richard Henry Lee
Thomas Jefferson
Benjamin Harrison
Thomas Nelson, Jr.
Francis Lightfoot Lee
Carter Braxton

NORTH CAROLINA
William Hooper
Joseph Hewes
John Penn

SOUTH CAROLINA
Edward Rutledge
Thomas Heyward, Jr.
Thomas Lynch, Jr.
Arthur Middleton

GEORGIA
Button Gwinnett
Lyman Hall
George Walton

Resolved, That copies of the Declaration be sent to the several assemblies, conventions, and committees, or councils of safety, and to the several commanding officers of the continental troops; that it be proclaimed in each of the United States, at the head of the army.

The Articles of Confederation

Agreed to by Congress November 15, 1777;
ratified and in force March 1, 1781

To all whom these Presents shall come, we the undersigned Delegates of the States affixed to our Names, send greeting. Whereas the Delegates of the United States of America, in Congress assembled, did, on the fifteenth day of November, in the Year of Our Lord One thousand Seven Hundred and Seventy seven, and in the Second Year of the Independence of America, agree to certain articles of Confederation and perpetual Union between the States of Newhampshire, Massachusetts-bay, Rhodeisland and Providence Plantations, Connecticut, New-York, New-Jersey, Pennsylvania, Delaware, Maryland, Virginia, North-Carolina, South-Carolina and Georgia in the words following, viz. "Articles of Confederation and perpetual Union between the states of Newhampshire, Massachusettsbay, Rhodeisland and Providence Plantations, Connecticut, New-York, New-Jersey, Pennsylvania, Delaware, Maryland, Virginia, North-Carolina, South-Carolina and Georgia.

Art. I. The Stile of this confederacy shall be "The United States of America."

Art. II. Each state retains its sovereignty, freedom and independence, and every Power, Jurisdiction and right, which is not by this confederation expressly delegated to the United States, in Congress assembled.

Art. III. The said states hereby severally enter into a firm league of friendship with each other, for their common defence, the security of their Liberties, and their mutual and general welfare, binding themselves to assist each other, against all force offered to, or attacks made upon them, or any of them, on account of religion, sovereignty, trade, or any other pretence whatever.

Art. IV. The better to secure and perpetuate mutual friendship and intercourse among the people of the different states in this union, the free inhabitants of each of these states, paupers, vagabonds and fugitives from Justice excepted, shall be entitled to all privileges and immunities of free citizens in the several states; and the people of each state shall have free ingress and regress to and from any other state, and shall enjoy therein all the privileges of trade and commerce, subject to the same duties, impositions and restrictions as the inhabitants thereof respectively, provided that such restriction shall not extend so far as to prevent the removal of property imported into any state, to any other state, of which the Owner is an inhabitant; provided also that no imposition, duties or restriction shall be laid by any state, on the property of the united states, or either of them.

If any Person guilty of, or charged with treason, felony, or other high misdemeanor in any state, shall flee from Justice, and be found in any of the united states, he shall, upon demand of the Governor or executive power, of the state from which he fled, be delivered up and removed to the state having jurisdiction of his offence.

Full faith and credit shall be given in each of these states to the records, acts and judicial proceedings of the courts and magistrates of every other state.

Art. V. For the more convenient management of the general interests of the united states, delegates shall be annually appointed in such manner as the legislature of each state shall direct, to meet in Congress on the first Monday in November, in every year, with a power reserved to each state, to recall its delegates, or any of them, at any time within the year, and to send others in their stead, for the remainder of the Year.

No state shall be represented in Congress by less than two, nor by more than seven Members; and no person shall be capable of being a delegate for more than three years in any term of six years; nor shall any person, being a delegate, be capable of holding any office under the united states, for which he, or another for his benefit receives any salary, fees or emolument of any kind.

Each state shall maintain its own delegates in a meeting of the states, and while they act as members of the committee of the states.

In determining questions in the united states, in Congress assembled, each state shall have one vote.

Freedom of speech and debate in Congress shall not be impeached or questioned in any Court, or place out of Congress, and the members of congress shall be protected in their persons from arrests and imprisonments, during the time of their going to and from, and attendance on congress, except for treason, felony, or breach of the peace.

Art. VI. No state without the Consent of the united states in congress assembled, shall send any embassy to, or receive any embassy from, or enter into any conference, agreement, or alliance or treaty with any King, prince or state; nor shall any person holding any office or profit or trust under the united states, or any of them, accept of any present, emolument, office or title of any kind whatever from any king, prince or foreign state; nor shall the united states in congress assembled, or any of them, grant any title of nobility.

No two or more states shall enter into any treaty, confederation or alliance whatever between them, without the consent of the united states in congress assembled, specifying accurately the purposes for which the same is to be entered into, and how long it shall continue.

No state shall lay any imposts or duties, which may interfere with any stipulations in treaties, entered into by the united states in congress assembled, with any king, prince or state, in pursuance of any treaties already proposed by congress, to the courts of France and Spain.

No vessels of war shall be kept up in time of peace by any state, except such number only, as shall be deemed necessary by the united states in congress assembled, for the defence of such state, or its trade; nor shall any body of forces be kept up by any state, in time of peace, except such number only, as in the judgment of the united states, in congress assembled, shall be deemed requisite to garrison the forts necessary for the defence of such state; but every state shall always keep up a well regulated and disciplined militia, sufficiently armed and accoutred, and shall provide and constantly have ready for use, in public stores, a due number of field pieces and tents, and a proper quantity of arms, ammunition and camp equipage.

No state shall engage in any war without the consent of the united states in congress assembled, unless such state be actually invaded by enemies, or shall have received certain advice of a resolution being formed by some nation of Indians to invade such state, and the danger is so imminent as not to admit of a delay, till the united states in congress asssembled can be consulted; nor shall any state grant commissions to any ships or vessels of war, nor letters of marque or reprisal, except it be after a declaration of war by the united states in congress assembled, and then only against the kingdom or state and the subjects thereof, against which war has been so declared, and under such regulations as shall be established by the united states in congress assembled, unless such state be infested by pirates; in which case vessels of war may be fitted out for that occasion, and kept so long as the danger shall continue, or until the united states in congress assembled shall determine otherwise.

Art. VII. When land-forces are raised by any state for the common defence, all officers of or under the rank of colonel, shall be appointed by the legislature of each state respectively, by whom such forces shall be raised, or in such manner as such state shall direct, and all vacancies shall be filled up by the state which first made the appointment.

Art. VIII. All charges of war, and all other expences that shall be incurred for the common defence or general welfare, and allowed by the united states in congress assembled, shall be defrayed out of a common treasury, which shall be supplied by the several states in proportion to the value of all land within each state, granted to or surveyed for any Person, as such land and the buildings and improvements thereon shall be estimated according to such mode as the united states in congress assembled, shall from time to time direct and appoint.

The taxes for paying that proportion shall be laid and levied by the authority and direction of the legislatures of the several states within the time agreed upon by the united states in congress assembled.

Art. IX. The united states in congress assembled, shall have the sole and exclusive right and power of determining on peace and war, except in the cases mentioned in the sixth article—of sending and receiving ambassadors—entering into treaties and alliances, provided that no treaty of commerce shall be made whereby the legislative power of the respective states shall be restrained from imposing such imposts and duties on foreigners, as their own people are subjected to, or from prohibiting the exportation of any species of goods or commodities whatsoever—of establishing rules for deciding in all cases, what captures on land or water shall be legal, and in what manner prizes taken by land or naval forces in the service of the united states shall be divided or appropriated—of granting letters of marque and reprisal in times of peace—appointing courts for the trial of piracies and felonies committed on the high seas and establishing courts for receiving and determining finally appeals in all cases of captures, provided that no member of congress shall be appointed a judge of any of the said courts.

The united states in congress assembled shall also be the last resort on appeal in all disputes and differences now subsisting or that hereafter may arise between two or more states concerning boundary, jurisdiction or any other cause whatever; which authority shall always be exercised in the manner following. Whenever the legislative or executive authority or lawful agent of any state in controversy with another shall present a petition to congress stating the matter in question and praying for a hearing, notice thereof shall be given by order of congress to the legislative or executive authority of the other state in controversy, and a day assigned for the appearance of the parties by their lawful agents, who shall then be directed to appoint by joint consent, commissioners or judges to constitute a court for hearing and determining the matter in question: but if they cannot agree, congress shall name three persons out of each of the united states, and from the list of such persons each party shall alternately strike out one, the petitioners beginning, until the number shall be reduced to thirteen; and from that number not less than seven, nor more than nine names as congress shall direct, shall in the presence of congress be drawn out by lot, and the persons whose names shall be so drawn or any five of them, shall be commissioners or judges, to hear and finally determine the controversy, so always as a major part of the judges who shall hear the cause shall agree in the determination: and if either party shall neglect to attend at the day appointed, without shewing reasons, which congress shall judge sufficient, or being present shall refuse to strike, the congress shall proceed to nominate three persons out of each state, and the secretary of congress shall strike in behalf of such party absent or refusing; and the judgment and sentence of the court to be appointed, in the manner before prescribed, shall be final and conclusive; and if any of the parties shall refuse to submit to the authority of such court, or to appear to defend their claim or cause, the court shall nevertheless proceed to pronounce sentence, or judgment, which shall in like manner be final and decisive, the judgment or sentence and other proceedings being in either case transmitted to congress, and lodged among the acts of congress for the security of the parties concerned: provided that every commissioner, before he sits in judgment, shall take an oath to be administered by one of the judges of the supreme or superior court of the state, where the cause shall be tried, "well and truly to hear and determine the matter in question, according to the best of his judgment, without favour, affection or hope of reward:" provided also, that no state shall be deprived of territory for the benefit of the united states.

All controversies concerning the private right of soil claimed under different grants of two or more states, whose jurisdictions as they may respect such lands, and the states which passed such grants are adjusted, the said grants or either of them being at the same time claimed to have originated antecedent to such settlement of jurisdiction, shall on the petition of either party to the congress of the united states, be finally determined as near as may be in the same manner as is before prescribed for deciding disputes respecting territorial jurisdiction between different states.

The united states in congress assembled shall also have the sole and exclusive right and power of regulating the alloy and value of coin struck by their own authority, or by that of the respective states—fixing the standard of weights and measures throughout the united states—regulating the trade and managing all affairs with the Indians, not members of any of the states, provided that the legislative right of any state within its own limits be not infringed or violated—establishing and regulating post-offices from one state to another, throughout all the united states, and exacting such postage on the papers passing thro' the same as may be requisite to defray the expences of the said office—appointing all officers of the land forces, in the service of the united states, excepting regimental officers—appointing all the officers of the naval forces, and commissioning all officers whatever in the service of the united states—making rules for the government and regulation of the said land and naval forces, and directing their operations.

The united states in congress assembled shall have authority to appoint a committee, to sit in the recess of congress, to be denominated "A Committee of the States," and to consist of one delegate from each state; and to appoint such other committees and civil officers as may be necessary for managing the general affairs of the united states under their direction—to appoint one of their number to preside, provided that no person be allowed to serve in the office of president more than one year in any term of three years; to ascertain the necessary sums of Money to be raised for the service of the united states, and to appropriate and apply the same for defraying the public expenses—to borrow money, or emit bills on the credit of the united states, transmitting every half year to the respective states an account of the sums of money so borrowed or emitted,—to build and equip a navy—to agree upon the number of land forces, and to make requisitions from each state for its quota, in proportion to the number of white inhabitants in such state; which requisition shall be binding, and thereupon the legislature of each state shall appoint the regimental officers, raise the men and cloath, arm and equip them in a soldier like manner, at the expense of the united states; and the officers and men so cloathed, armed and equipped shall march to the place appointed, and within the time agreed on by the united states in congress assembled: But if the united states in congress assembled shall, on consideration of circumstances judge proper that any state should not raise men, or should raise a smaller number than its quota, and that any other state should raise a greater number of men than the quota thereof, such extra number shall be raised, officered, cloathed, armed and equipped in the same manner as the quota of such state, unless the legislature of such state shall judge that such extra number cannot be safely spared out of the same, in which case they shall raise officer, cloath, arm and equip as many of such extra number as they judge can be safely spared. And the officers and men so cloathed, armed and equipped, shall march to the place appointed, and within the time agreed on by the united states in congress assembled.

The united states in congress assembled shall never engage in a war, nor grant letters of marque and reprisal in time of peace, nor enter into any treaties or alliances, nor coin money, nor regulate the value thereof, nor ascertain the sums and expenses necessary for the defence and welfare of the united states, or any of them, nor emit bills, nor borrow money on the credit of the united states, nor appropriate money, nor agree upon the number of vessels of war, to be built or purchased, or the number of land or sea forces to be raised, nor appoint a commander in chief of the army or navy, unless nine states assent to the same: nor shall a question on any other point, except for adjourning from day to day be determined, unless by the votes of a majority of the united states in congress assembled.

The congress of the united states shall have power to adjourn to any time within the year, and to any place within the united states, so that no period of adjournment be for a longer duration than the space of six Months, and shall publish the Journal of their proceedings monthly, except such parts thereof relating to treaties, alliances or military operations, as in their judgment require secrecy; and the yeas and nays of the delegates of each state on any question shall be entered on the Journal, when it is desired by any delegate; and the delegates of a state, or any of them, at his or their request shall be furnished with a transcript of the said Journal, except such parts as are above excepted, to lay before the legislatures of the several states.

Art. X. The committee of the states, or any nine of them, shall be authorised to execute, in the recess of congress, such of the powers of congress as the united states in congress assembled, by the consent of nine states, shall from time to time think expedient to vest them with; provided that no power be delegated to the said committee, for the exercise of which, by the articles of confederation, the voice of nine states in the congress of the united states assembled is requisite.

Art. XI. Canada acceding to this confederation, and joining in the measures of the united states, shall be admitted into, and entitled to all the advantages of this union: but no other colony shall be admitted into the same, unless such admission be agreed to by nine states.

Art. XII. All bills of credit emitted, monies borrowed and debts contracted by, or under the authority of congress, before the assembling of the united states, in pursuance of the present confederation, shall be deemed and considered as a charge against the united states, for payment and satisfaction whereof the said united states and the public faith are hereby solemnly pledged.

Art. XIII. Every state shall abide by the determinations of the united states in congress assembled, on all questions which by this confederation are submitted to them. And the Articles of this confederation shall be inviolably observed by every state, and the union shall be perpetual; nor shall any alteration at any time hereafter be made in any of them; unless such alteration be agreed to in a congress of the united states, and be afterwards confirmed by the legislatures of every state.

And Whereas it hath pleased the Great Governor of the World to incline the hearts of the legislatures we respectively represent in congress, to approve of, and to authorize us to ratify the said articles of confederation and perpetual union. Know Ye that we the undersigned delegates, by virtue of the power and authority to us given for that purpose, do by these presents, in the name and in behalf of our respective constituents, fully and entirely ratify and confirm each and every of the said articles of confederation and perpetual union, and all and singular the matters and things therein contained: And we do further solemnly plight and engage the faith of our respective constituents, that they shall abide by the determinations of the united states in congress assembled, on all questions, which by the said confederation are submitted to them. And that the articles thereof shall be inviolably observed by the states we respectively represent, and that the union shall be perpetual. In Witness whereof we have hereunto set our hands in Congress. Done at Philadelphia in the state of Pennsylvania the ninth day of July, in the Year of our Lord one Thousand seven Hundred and Seventy-eight, and in the third year of the independence of America.

The Constitution of the United States of America

We the People of the United States, in Order to form a more perfect Union, establish Justice, insure domestic Tranquility, provide for the common defence, promote the general Welfare, and secure the Blessings of Liberty to ourselves and our Posterity, do ordain and establish this Constitution for the United States of America.

Article I

SECTION 1
[LEGISLATIVE POWERS]
All legislative Powers herein granted shall be vested in a Congress of the United States, which shall consist of a Senate and House of Representatives.

SECTION 2
[HOUSE OF REPRESENTATIVES, HOW CONSTITUTED, POWER OF IMPEACHMENT]
The House of Representatives shall be composed of Members chosen every second Year by the People of the several States, and the Electors in each State shall have the Qualifications requisite for Electors of the most numerous Branch of the State Legislature.

No Person shall be a Representative who shall not have attained to the Age of twenty five Years, and been seven Years a Citizen of the United States, and who shall not, when elected, be an Inhabitant of that State in which he shall be chosen.

Representatives and *direct Taxes*[1] shall be apportioned among the several States which may be included within this Union, according to their respective Numbers, *which shall be determined by adding to the whole Number of free Persons, including those bound to Service for a Term of Years, and excluding Indians not taxed, three fifths of all other Persons.*[2] The actual Enumeration shall be made within three Years after the first Meeting of the Congress of the United States, and within every subsequent Term of ten Years, in such Manner as they shall by Law direct. The Number of Representatives shall not exceed one for every thirty Thousand, but each State shall have at Least one Representative; *and until such enumeration shall be made, the State of New Hampshire shall be entitled to chuse three, Massachusetts eight, Rhode-Island and Providence Plantations one, Connecticut five, New-York six, New Jersey four, Pennsylvania eight, Delaware one, Maryland six, Virginia ten, North Carolina five, South Carolina five, and Georgia three.*[3]

When vacancies happen in the Representation from any State, the Executive Authority thereof shall issue Writs of Election to fill such Vacancies.

The House of Representatives shall chuse their Speaker and other Officers; and shall have the sole Power of Impeachment.

---

[1]Modified by Sixteenth Amendment.

[2]Modified by Fourteenth Amendment.

[3]Temporary provision.

SECTION 3
The Senate of the United States shall be composed of two Senators from each State, *chosen by the Legislature thereof,*[4] for six Years; and each Senator shall have one Vote.

Immediately after they shall be assembled in Consequence of the first Election, they shall be divided as equally as may be into three Classes. The Seats of the Senators of the first Class shall be vacated at the Expiration of the second Year, of the second Class at the Expiration of the fourth Year, and of the third Class at the Expiration of the sixth Year, so that one third may be chosen every second Year; *and if Vacancies happen by Resignation, or otherwise, during the Recess of the Legislature of any State, the Executive thereof may make temporary Appointments until the next Meeting of the Legislature, which shall then fill such Vacancies.*[5]

No Person shall be a Senator who shall not have attained to the Age of thirty Years, and been nine Years a Citizen of the United States, and who shall not, when elected, be an Inhabitant of that State for which he shall be chosen.

The Vice President of the United States shall be President of the Senate, but shall have no Vote, unless they be equally divided.

The Senate shall chuse their other Officers, and also a President pro tempore, in the Absence of the Vice President, or when he shall exercise the Office of President of the United States.

The Senate shall have the sole Power to try all Impeachments. When sitting for that Purpose, they shall be on Oath or Affirmation. When the President of the United States is tried, the Chief Justice shall preside: And no Person shall be convicted without the Concurrence of two thirds of the Members present.

Judgment in Cases of Impeachment shall not extend further than to removal from Office, and disqualification to hold and enjoy any Office of honor, Trust or Profit under the United States: but the Party convicted shall nevertheless be liable and subject to Indictment, Trial, Judgment and Punishment, according to Law.

SECTION 4
The Times, Places and Manner of holding Elections for Senators and Representatives, shall be prescribed in each State by the Legislature thereof; but the Congress may at any time by Law make or alter such Regulations, except as to the Places of chusing Senators.

The Congress shall assemble at least once in every Year, and such Meeting shall be on the first Monday in December, unless they shall by Law appoint a different Day.[6]

SECTION 5
Each House shall be the Judge of the Elections, Returns and Qualifications of its own Members, and a Majority of each shall constitute a Quorum to do Business;

---

[4]Modified by Seventeenth Amendment.

[5]Modified by Seventeenth Amendment.

[6]Modified by Twentieth Amendment.

but a smaller Number may adjourn from day to day, and may be authorized to compel the Attendance of absent Members, in such Manner, and under such Penalties as each House may provide.

Each House may determine the Rules of its Proceedings, punish its Members for disorderly Behaviour, and, with the Concurrence of two thirds, expel a Member.

Each House shall keep a Journal of its Proceedings, and from time to time publish the same, excepting such Parts as may in their Judgment require Secrecy; and the Yeas and Nays of the Members of either House on any questions shall, at the Desire of one fifth of those Present, be entered on the Journal.

Neither House, during the Session of Congress, shall, without the Consent of the other, adjourn for more than three days, nor to any other Place than that in which the two Houses shall be sitting.

SECTION 6
[COMPENSATION, PRIVILEGES, DISABILITIES]
The Senators and Representatives shall receive a Compensation for their Services, to be ascertained by Law, and paid out of the Treasury of the United States. They shall in all Cases, except Treason, Felony and Breach of the Peace, be privileged from Arrest during their Attendance at the Session of their respective Houses, and in going to and returning from the same; and for any Speech or Debate in either House, they shall not be questioned in any other Place.

No Senator or Representative shall, during the Time for which he was elected, be appointed to any civil Office under the Authority of the United States, which shall have been created, or the Emoluments whereof shall have been encreased during such time; and no Person holding any Office under the United States, shall be a Member of either House during his Continuance in Office.

SECTION 7
[PROCEDURE IN PASSING BILLS AND RESOLUTIONS]
All Bills for raising Revenue shall originate in the House of Representatives; but the Senate may propose or concur with Amendments as on other Bills.

Every Bill which shall have passed the House of Representatives and the Senate, shall, before it become a Law, be presented to the President of the United States: If he approve he shall sign it, but if not he shall return it, with his Objections to that House in which it shall have originated, who shall enter the Objections at large on their Journal, and proceed to reconsider it. If after such Reconsideration two thirds of that House shall agree to pass the Bill, it shall be sent, together with the Objections, to the other House, by which it shall likewise be reconsidered, and if approved by two thirds of that House, it shall become a Law. But in all such Cases the Votes of both Houses shall be determined by yeas and Nays, and the Names of the Persons voting for and against the Bill shall be entered on the Journal of each House respectively. If any Bill shall not be returned by the President within ten Days (Sundays excepted) after it shall have been presented to him, the Same shall be a Law, in like Manner as if he had signed it, unless the Congress by their Adjournment prevent its Return, in which Case it shall not be a Law.

Every Order, Resolution, or Vote to which the Concurrence of the Senate and House of Representatives may be necessary (except on a question of Adjournment) shall be presented to the President of the United States; and before the Same shall take Effect, shall be approved by him, or being disapproved by him, shall be repassed by two thirds of the Senate and House of Representatives, according to the Rules and Limitations prescribed in the Case of a Bill.

SECTION 8
[POWERS OF CONGRESS]
The Congress shall have Power

To lay and collect Taxes, Duties, Imposts and Excises, to pay the Debts and provide for the common Defence and general Welfare of the United States; but all Duties, Imposts and Excises shall be uniform throughout the United States;

To borrow Money on the credit of the United States;

To regulate Commerce with foreign Nations, and among the several States, and with the Indian Tribes;

To establish an uniform Rule of Naturalization, and uniform Laws on the subject of Bankruptcies throughout the United States;

To coin Money, regulate the Value thereof, and of foreign Coin, and fix the Standard of Weights and Measures;

To provide for the Punishment of counterfeiting the Securities and current Coin of the United States;

To establish Post Offices and post Roads;

To promote the Progress of Science and useful Arts, by securing for limited Times to Authors and Inventors the exclusive Right to their respective Writings and Discoveries;

To constitute Tribunals inferior to the supreme Court;

To define and punish Piracies and Felonies committed on the high Seas, and Offences against the Law of Nations;

To declare War, grant Letters of Marque and Reprisal, and make Rules concerning Captures on Land and Water;

To raise and support Armies, but no Appropriation of Money to that Use shall be for a longer Term than two Years;

To provide and maintain a Navy;

To make Rules for the Government and Regulation of the land and naval Forces;

To provide for calling forth the Militia to execute the Laws of the Union, suppress Insurrections and repel Invasions;

To provide for organizing, arming, and disciplining, the Militia, and for governing such Part of them as may be employed in the Service of the United States, reserving to the States respectively, the Appointment of the Officers, and the Authority of training the Militia according to the discipline prescribed by Congress;

To exercise exclusive Legislation in all Cases whatsoever, over such District (not exceeding ten Miles square) as may, by Cession of particular States, and the Acceptance of Congress, become the Seat of the Government of the United States, and to exercise like Authority over all Places purchased by the Consent of the Legislature of the State in which the Same shall be, for the Erection of Forts, Magazines, Arsenals, dock-Yards, and other needful Buildings;—And

To make all Laws which shall be necessary and proper for carrying into Execution the foregoing Powers, and all other Powers vested by this

Constitution in the Government of the United States, or in any Department or Officer thereof.

SECTION 9

The Migration or Importation of such Persons as any of the States now existing shall think proper to admit, shall not be prohibited by the Congress prior to the Year one thousand eight hundred and eight, but a Tax or duty may be imposed on such Importation, not exceeding ten dollars for each Person.[7]

The Privilege of the Writ of Habeas Corpus shall not be suspended, unless when in Cases of Rebellion or Invasion the public Safety may require it.

No Bill of Attainder or ex post facto Law shall be passed.

No Capitation, or other direct, Tax shall be laid, unless in Proportion to the Census or Enumeration herein before directed to be taken.[8]

No Tax or Duty shall be laid on Articles exported from any State.

No Preference shall be given by any Regulation of Commerce or Revenue to the Ports of one State over those of another; nor shall Vessels bound to, or from, one State, be obliged to enter, clear, or pay Duties in another.

No Money shall be drawn from the Treasury, but in Consequence of Appropriations made by Law; and a regular Statement and Account of the Receipts and Expenditures of all public Money shall be published from time to time.

No Title of Nobility shall be granted by the United States: And no Person holding any Office of Profit or Trust under them, shall, without the Consent of the Congress, accept of any present, Emolument, Office, or Title, of any kind whatever, from any King, Prince, or foreign State.

SECTION 10

No State shall enter into any Treaty, Alliance, or Confederation; grant Letters of Marque and Reprisal; coin Money; emit Bills of Credit; make any Thing but gold and silver Coin a Tender in Payment of Debts; pass any Bill of Attainder, ex post facto Law, or Law impairing the Obligation of Contracts, or grant any Title of Nobility.

No State shall, without the Consent of the Congress, lay any Imposts or Duties on Imports or Exports, except what may be absolutely necessary for executing its inspection Laws: and the net Produce of all Duties and Imposts, laid by any State on Imports or Exports, shall be for the Use of the Treasury of the United States; and all such Laws shall be subject to the Revision and Control of the Congress.

No State shall, without the Consent of Congress, lay any Duty of Tonnage, keep Troops, or Ships of War in time of Peace, enter into any Agreement or Compact with another State, or with a foreign Power, or engage in War, unless actually invaded, or in such imminent Danger as will not admit of delay.

---

[7]Temporary provision.

[8]Modified by Sixteenth Amendment.

Article II

SECTION 1

The executive Power shall be vested in a President of the United States of America. *He shall hold his Office during the Term of four Years, and, together with the Vice President, chosen for the same Term, be elected, as follows*[9]

Each State shall appoint, in such Manner as the Legislature thereof may direct, a Number of Electors, equal to the whole Number of Senators and Representatives to which the State may be entitled in the Congress: but no Senator or Representative, or Person holding an Office of Trust or Profit under the United States, shall be appointed an Elector.

The electors shall meet in their respective States, and vote by ballot for two Persons, of whom one at least shall not be an Inhabitant of the same State with themselves. And they shall make a List of all the Persons voted for, and of the Number of Votes for each; which List they shall sign and certify, and transmit sealed to the Seat of the Government of the United States, directed to the President of the Senate. The President of the Senate shall, in the Presence of the Senate and House of Representatives, open all the Certificates, and the Votes shall then be counted. The Person having the greatest Number of Votes shall be the President, if such Number be a Majority of the whole Number of Electors appointed; and if there be more than one who have such Majority, and have an equal Number of Votes, then the House of Representatives shall immediately chuse by Ballot one of them for President; and if no Person have a Majority, then from the five highest on the List the said House shall in like Manner chuse the President. But in chusing the President, the Votes shall be taken by States, the Representation from each State having one Vote; A quorum for this Purpose shall consist of a Member or Members from two thirds of the States, and a Majority of all the States shall be necessary to a Choice. In every Case, after the Choice of the President, the person having the greatest Number of Votes of the Electors shall be the Vice President. But if there should remain two or more who have equal Votes, the Senate shall chuse from them by Ballot the Vice President.[10]

The Congress may determine the Time of chusing the Electors, and the Day on which they shall give their Votes; which Day shall be the same throughout the United States.

No Person except a natural born Citizen, or a Citizen of the United States, at the time of the Adoption of this Constitution, shall be eligible to the Office of President; neither shall any Person be eligible to that Office who shall not have attained to the Age of thirty five Years, and been fourteen Years a Resident within the United States.

In Case of the Removal of the President from Office, or his Death, Resignation, or Inability to discharge the Powers and Duties of the said Office, the Same shall devolve on the Vice President, and the Congress may by Law provide for the Case of Removal, Death, Resignation or Inability, both of the President and Vice President,

---

[9]Number of terms limited to two by Twenty-Second Amendment.

[10]Modified by Twelfth and Twentieth Amendments.

declaring what Officer shall then act as President, and such Officer shall act accordingly, until the Disability be removed, or a President shall be elected.

The President shall, at stated Times, receive for his Services, a Compensation, which shall neither be increased nor diminished during the Period for which he shall have been elected, and he shall not receive within that Period any other Emolument from the United States, or any of them.

Before he enter on the Execution of his Office, he shall take the following Oath or Affirmation:—"I do solemnly swear (or affirm) that I will faithfully execute the Office of President of the United States, and will to the best of my Ability, preserve, protect and defend the Constitution of the United States."

SECTION 2

[POWERS OF THE PRESIDENT]

The President shall be Commander in Chief of the Army and Navy of the United States, and of the Militia of the several States, when called into the actual Service of the United States; he may require the Opinion, in writing, of the principal Officer in each of the executive Departments, upon any Subject relating to the Duties of their respective Offices, and he shall have Power to grant Reprieves and Pardons for Offences against the United States, except in Cases of Impeachment.

He shall have Power, by and with the Advice and Consent of the Senate, to make Treaties, provided two thirds of the Senators present concur; and he shall nominate, and by and with the Advice and Consent of the Senate, shall appoint Ambassadors, other public Ministers and Consuls, Judges of the supreme Court, and all other Officers of the United States, whose Appointments are not herein otherwise provided for, and which shall be established by Law: but the Congress may by Law vest the Appointment of such inferior Officers, as they think proper, in the President alone, in the Courts of Law, or in the Heads of Departments.

The President shall have Power to fill up all Vacancies that may happen during the Recess of the Senate, by granting Commissions which shall expire at the End of their next Session.

SECTION 3

[POWERS AND DUTIES OF THE PRESIDENT]

He shall from time to time give to the Congress Information of the State of the Union, and recommend to their Consideration such Measures as he shall judge necessary and expedient; he may, on extraordinary Occasions, convene both Houses, or either of them, and in Case of Disagreement between them, with Respect to the Time of Adjournment, he may adjourn them to such Time as he shall think proper; he shall receive Ambassadors and other public Ministers; he shall take Care that the Laws be faithfully executed, and shall Commission all the Officers of the United States.

SECTION 4

[IMPEACHMENT]

The President, Vice President and all civil Officers of the United States, shall be removed from Office on Impeachment for, and Conviction of, Treason, Bribery, or other high Crimes and Misdemeanors.

Article III

SECTION 1
[JUDICIAL POWER, TENURE OF OFFICE]
The judicial Power of the United States, shall be vested in one supreme Court, and in such inferior Courts as the Congress may from time to time ordain and establish. The Judges, both of the supreme and inferior Courts, shall hold their Offices during good Behaviour, and shall, at stated Times, receive for their Services, a Compensation, which shall not be diminished during their Continuance in Office.

SECTION 2
[JURISDICTION]
The judicial Power shall extend to all Cases, in Law and Equity, arising under this Constitution, the Laws of the United States, and Treaties made, or which shall be made, under their Authority;—to all Cases affecting Ambassadors, other public Ministers and Consuls;—to all Cases of admiralty and maritime Jurisdiction;—to Controversies to which the United States shall be a Party;—to Controversies between two or more States;—*between a State and Citizens of another State;*—between Citizens of different States,—between Citizens of the same State claiming Lands under Grants of different States, *and between a State*, or the Citizens thereof, *and foreign States, Citizens or Subjects.*[11]

In all Cases affecting Ambassadors, other public Ministers and Consuls, and those in which a State shall be Party, the supreme Court shall have original Jurisdiction. In all the other Cases before mentioned, the supreme Court shall have appellate Jurisdiction, both as to Law and Fact, with such Exceptions, and under such Regulations as the Congress shall make.

The Trial of all Crimes, except in Cases of Impeachment, shall be by Jury; and such Trial shall be held in the State where the said Crimes shall have been committed; but when not committed within any State, the Trial shall be at such Place or Places as the Congress may by Law have directed.

SECTION 3
[TREASON, PROOF, AND PUNISHMENT]
Treason against the United States, shall consist only in levying War against them, or in adhering to their Enemies, giving them Aid and Comfort. No Person shall be convicted of Treason unless on the Testimony of two Witnesses to the same overt Act, or on Confession in open Court.

The Congress shall have Power to declare the Punishment of Treason, but no Attainder of Treason shall work Corruption of Blood, or Forfeiture except during the Life of the Person attainted.

Article IV

SECTION 1
[FAITH AND CREDIT AMONG STATES]

---

[11]Modified by Eleventh Amendment.

Full Faith and Credit shall be given in each State to the public Acts, Records, and judicial Proceedings of every other State. And the Congress may by general Laws prescribe the Manner in which such Acts, Records and Proceedings shall be proved, and the Effect thereof.

SECTION 2
[PRIVILEGES AND IMMUNITIES, FUGITIVES]
The Citizens of each State shall be entitled to all Privileges and Immunities of Citizens in the several States.

A Person charged in any State with Treason, Felony or other Crime, who shall flee from Justice, and be found in another State, shall on Demand of the executive Authority of the State from which he fled, be delivered up, to be removed to the State having Jurisdiction of the Crime.

No person held to Service or Labour in one State, under the Laws thereof, escaping into another, shall, in Consequence of any Law or Regulation therein, be discharged from such Service or Labour, but shall be delivered up on Claim of the Party to whom such Service or Labour may be due.[12]

SECTION 3
[ADMISSION OF NEW STATES]
New States may be admitted by the Congress into this Union; but no new State shall be formed or erected within the Jurisdiction of any other State; nor any State be formed by the Junction of two or more States, or Parts of States, without the Consent of the Legislatures of the States concerned as well as of the Congress.

The Congress shall have Power to dispose of and make all needful Rules and Regulations respecting the Territory or other Property belonging to the United States; and nothing in this Constitution shall be so construed as to Prejudice any Claims of the United States, or of any particular State.

SECTION 4
[GUARANTEE OF REPUBLICAN GOVERNMENT]
The United States shall guarantee to every State in this Union a Republican Form of Government, and shall protect each of them against Invasion; and on Application of the Legislature, or of the Executive (when the Legislature cannot be convened), against domestic Violence.

Article V
[AMENDMENT OF THE CONSTITUTION]
The Congress, whenever two thirds of both Houses shall deem it necessary, shall propose Amendments to this Constitution, or, on the Application of the Legislatures of two thirds of the several States, shall call a Convention for proposing Amendments, which, in either Case, shall be valid to all Intents and Purposes, as Part of this Constitution, when ratified by the Legislatures of three fourths of the

---

[12]Repealed by the Thirteenth Amendment.

several States, or by Conventions in three fourths thereof, as the one or the other Mode of Ratification may be proposed by the Congress; *Provided that no Amendment which may be made prior to the Year One thousand eight hundred and eight shall in any Manner affect the first and fourth Clauses in the Ninth Section of the first Article;*[13] and that no State, without its Consent, shall be deprived of its equal Suffrage in the Senate.

Article VI
[DEBTS, SUPREMACY, OATH]
All Debts contracted and Engagements entered into, before the Adoption of this Constitution, shall be as valid against the United States under this Constitution, as under the Confederation.

This Constitution, and the Laws of the United States which shall be made in Pursuance thereof; and all Treaties made, or which shall be made, under the Authority of the United States, shall be the supreme Law of the Land; and the Judges in every State shall be bound thereby, any Thing in the Constitution or Laws of any State to the Contrary notwithstanding.

The Senators and Representatives before mentioned, and the Members of the several State Legislatures, and all executive and judicial Officers, both of the United States and of the several States, shall be bound by Oath or Affirmation, to support this Constitution; but no religious Test shall be required as a Qualification to any Office or public Trust under the United States.

Article VII
[RATIFICATION AND ESTABLISHMENT]
The Ratification of the Conventions of nine States, shall be sufficient for the Establishment of this Constitution between the States so ratifying the Same.[14]

Done in Convention by the Unanimous Consent of the States present the Seventeenth Day of September in the Year of our Lord one thousand seven hundred

---

[13]Temporary provision.

[14]The Constitution was submitted on September 17, 1787, by the Constitutional Convention, was ratified by the conventions of several states at various dates up to May 29, 1790, and became effective on March 4, 1789.

and Eighty seven and of the Independence of the United States of America the Twelfth. *In Witness* whereof We have hereunto subscribed our Names,

G:⁰ *WASHINGTON—*
Presidt. and deputy from Virginia

NEW HAMPSHIRE
John Langdon
Nicholas Gilman

MASSACHUSETTS
Nathaniel Gorham
Rufus King

CONNECTICUT
Wm. Saml. Johnson
Roger Sherman

NEW YORK
Alexander Hamilton

NEW JERSEY
Wil: Livingston
David Brearley
Wm. Paterson
Jona: Dayton

PENNSYLVANIA
B Franklin
Thomas Mifflin
Robt. Morris
Geo. Clymer
Thos. FitzSimons
Jared Ingersoll
James Wilson
Gouv Morris

DELAWARE
Geo: Read
Gunning Bedford jun
John Dickinson
Richard Bassett
Jaco: Broom

MARYLAND
James McHenry
Dan of St Thos. Jenifer
Danl. Carroll

VIRGINIA
John Blair—
James Madison Jr.

NORTH CAROLINA
Wm. Blount
Richd. Dobbs Spaight
Hu Williamson

SOUTH CAROLINA
J. Rutledge
Charles Cotesworth
 Pinckney
Charles Pinckney
Pierce Butler

GEORGIA
William Few
Abr Baldwin

Amendments to the Constitution

Proposed by Congress and Ratified by the Legislatures of the Several States, Pursuant to Article V of the Original Constitution.

Amendments I–X, known as the Bill of Rights, were proposed by Congress on September 25, 1789, and ratified on December 15, 1791.

Amendment I
[FREEDOM OF RELIGION, OF SPEECH, AND OF THE PRESS]
Congress shall make no law respecting an establishment of religion, or prohibiting the free exercise thereof; or abridging the freedom of speech, or of the press; or the right of the people peaceably to assemble, and to petition the Government for a redress of grievances.

Amendment II
[RIGHT TO KEEP AND BEAR ARMS]
A well regulated Militia, being necessary to the security of a free State, the right of the people to keep and bear Arms, shall not be infringed.

Amendment III
[QUARTERING OF SOLDIERS]
No Soldier shall, in time of peace be quartered in any house, without the consent of the Owner, nor in time of war, but in a manner to be prescribed by law.

Amendment IV
[SECURITY FROM UNWARRANTABLE SEARCH AND SEIZURE]
The right of the people to be secure in their persons, houses, papers, and effects, against unreasonable searches and seizures, shall not be violated, and no Warrants shall issue, but upon probable cause, supported by Oath or affirmation, and particularly describing the place to be searched, and the persons or things to be seized.

Amendment V
[RIGHTS OF ACCUSED PERSONS IN CRIMINAL PROCEEDINGS]
No person shall be held to answer for a capital, or otherwise infamous crime, unless on a presentment or indictment of a Grand Jury, except in cases arising in the land or naval forces, or in the Militia, when in actual service in time of War or in public danger; nor shall any person be subject for the same offence to be twice put in jeopardy of life or limb; nor shall be compelled in any criminal case to be a witness against himself, nor be deprived of life, liberty, or property, without due process of law; nor shall private property be taken for public use, without just compensation.

Amendment VI
[RIGHT TO SPEEDY TRIAL, WITNESSES, ETC.]
In all criminal prosecutions, the accused shall enjoy the right to a speedy and public trial, by an impartial jury of the State and district wherein the crime shall have been committed, which district shall have been previously ascertained by law, and

to be informed of the nature and cause of the accusation; to be confronted with the witnesses against him; to have compulsory process for obtaining witnesses in his favor, and to have the Assistance of Counsel for his defence.

Amendment VII
[TRIAL BY JURY IN CIVIL CASES]
In suits at common law, where the value in controversy shall exceed twenty dollars, the right of trial by jury shall be preserved, and no fact tried by a jury, shall be otherwise reexamined in any Court of the United States, than according to the rules of the common law.

Amendment VIII
[BAILS, FINES, PUNISHMENTS]
Excessive bail shall not be required, nor excessive fines imposed, nor cruel and unusual punishments inflicted.

Amendment IX
[RESERVATION OF RIGHTS OF PEOPLE]
The enumeration in the Constitution, of certain rights, shall not be construed to deny or disparage others retained by the people.

Amendment X
[POWERS RESERVED TO STATES OR PEOPLE]
The powers not delegated to the United States by the Constitution, nor prohibited by it to the States, are reserved to the States respectively, or to the people.

Amendment XI
[PROPOSED BY CONGRESS ON MARCH 4, 1794; DECLARED RATIFIED ON JANUARY 8, 1798.]
[RESTRICTION OF JUDICIAL POWER]
The Judicial power of the United States shall not be construed to extend to any suit in law or equity, commenced or prosecuted against one of the United States by Citizens of another State, or by Citizens or Subjects of any Foreign State.

Amendment XII
[PROPOSED BY CONGRESS ON DECEMBER 9, 1803; DECLARED RATIFIED ON SEPTEMBER 25, 1804.]
[ELECTION OF PRESIDENT AND VICE PRESIDENT]
The Electors shall meet in their respective states and vote by ballot for President and Vice-President, one of whom, at least, shall not be an inhabitant of the same state with themselves; they shall name in their ballots the person voted for as President, and in distinct ballots the person voted for as Vice-President, and they shall make distinct lists of all persons voted for as President, and of all persons voted for as Vice-President, and of the number of votes for each, which lists they shall sign and certify, and transmit sealed to the seat of the government of the United States, directed to the President of the Senate;—the President of the Senate shall, in presence of the Senate and House of Representatives, open all the certificates and the votes shall then be counted;—The person having the greatest number of votes for President, shall be the President, if such number be a majority

of the whole number of Electors appointed; and if no person have such majority, then from the persons having the highest numbers not exceeding three on the list of those voted for as President, the House of Representatives shall choose immediately, by ballot, the President. But in choosing the President, the votes shall be taken by states, the representation from each state having one vote; a quorum for this purpose shall consist of a member or members from two-thirds of the states, and a majority of all the states shall be necessary to a choice. And if the House of Representatives shall not choose a President whenever the right of choice shall devolve upon them, before the fourth day of March next following, then the Vice-President shall act as President, as in the case of the death or other constitutional disability of the President.—The person having the greatest number of votes as Vice-President, shall be the Vice-President, if such number be a majority of the whole number of Electors appointed, and if no person have a majority, then from the two highest numbers on the list, the Senate shall choose the Vice-President; a quorum for the purpose shall consist of two-thirds of the whole number of Senators, and a majority of the whole number shall be necessary to a choice. But no person constitutionally ineligible to the office of President shall be eligible to that of Vice-President of the United States.

Amendment XIII
[PROPOSED BY CONGRESS ON JANUARY 31, 1865; DECLARED RATIFIED ON DECEMBER 18, 1865.]

SECTION 1
[ABOLITION OF SLAVERY]
Neither slavery nor involuntary servitude, except as a punishment for crime whereof the party shall have been duly convicted, shall exist within the United States, or any place subject to their jurisdiction.

SECTION 2
[POWER TO ENFORCE THIS ARTICLE]
Congress shall have power to enforce this article by appropriate legislation.

Amendment XIV
[PROPOSED BY CONGRESS ON JUNE 13, 1866; DECLARED RATIFIED ON JULY 28, 1868.]

SECTION 1
[CITIZENSHIP RIGHTS NOT TO BE ABRIDGED BY STATES]
All persons born or naturalized in the United States, and subject to the jurisdiction thereof, are citizens of the United States and of the State wherein they reside. No State shall make or enforce any law which shall abridge the privileges or immunities of citizens of the United States; nor shall any State deprive any person of life, liberty, or property, without due process of law; nor deny to any person within its jurisdiction the equal protection of the laws.

SECTION 2
[APPORTIONMENT OF REPRESENTATIVES IN CONGRESS]
Representatives shall be apportioned among the several States according to their respective numbers, counting the whole number of persons in each State,

excluding Indians not taxed. But when the right to vote at any election for the choice of electors for President and Vice-President of the United States, Representatives in Congress, the Executive and Judicial officers of a State, or the members of the Legislature thereof, is denied to any of the male inhabitants of such State, being twenty-one years of age, and citizens of the United States, or in any way abridged, except for participation in rebellion, or other crime, the basis of representation therein shall be reduced in the proportion which the number of such male citizens shall bear to the whole number of male citizens twenty-one years of age in such State.

SECTION 3
[PERSONS DISQUALIFIED FROM HOLDING OFFICE]
No person shall be a Senator or Representative in Congress, or elector of President and Vice-President, or hold any office, civil or military, under the United States, or under any State, who, having previously taken an oath, as a member of Congress, or as an officer of the United States, or as a member of any State legislature, or as an executive or judicial officer of any State, to support the Constitution of the United States, shall have engaged in insurrection or rebellion against the same, or given aid or comfort to the enemies thereof. But Congress may by a vote of two-thirds of each House, remove such disability.

SECTION 4
[WHAT PUBLIC DEBTS ARE VALID]
The validity of the public debt of the United States, authorized by law, including debts incurred for payment of pensions and bounties for services in suppressing insurrection or rebellion, shall not be questioned. But neither the United States nor any State shall assume or pay any debt or obligation incurred in aid of insurrection or rebellion against the United States, or any claim for the loss or emancipation of any slave; but all such debts, obligations and claims shall be held illegal and void.

SECTION 5
[POWER TO ENFORCE THIS ARTICLE]
The Congress shall have power to enforce, by appropriate legislation, the provisions of this article.

Amendment XV
[PROPOSED BY CONGRESS ON FEBRUARY 26, 1869;
DECLARED RATIFIED ON MARCH 30, 1870.]

SECTION 1
[NEGRO SUFFRAGE]
The right of citizens of the United States to vote shall not be denied or abridged by the United States or by any State on account of race, color, or previous condition of servitude.

SECTION 2
[POWER TO ENFORCE THIS ARTICLE]
The Congress shall have power to enforce this article by appropriate legislation.

Amendment XVI

[PROPOSED BY CONGRESS ON JULY 2, 1909; DECLARED RATIFIED ON FEBRUARY 25, 1913.]
[AUTHORIZING INCOME TAXES]

The Congress shall have power to lay and collect taxes on incomes, from whatever source derived, without apportionment among the several States, and without regard to any census or enumeration.

Amendment XVII

[PROPOSED BY CONGRESS ON MAY 13, 1912; DECLARED RATIFIED ON MAY 31, 1913.]
[POPULAR ELECTION OF SENATORS]

The Senate of the United States shall be composed of two Senators from each State, elected by the people thereof, for six years; and each Senator shall have one vote. The electors in each State shall have the qualifications requisite for electors of the most numerous branch of the State legislatures.

When vacancies happen in the representation of any State in the Senate, the executive authority of such State shall issue writs of election to fill such vacancies: *Provided*, That the legislature of any State may empower the executive thereof to make temporary appointments until the people fill the vacancies by election as the legislature may direct.

This amendment shall not be so construed as to affect the election or term of any Senator chosen before it becomes valid as part of the Constitution.

Amendment XVIII

[PROPOSED BY CONGRESS DECEMBER 18, 1917; DECLARED RATIFIED ON JANUARY 29, 1919.]

SECTION 1

[NATIONAL LIQUOR PROHIBITION]

After one year from the ratification of this article the manufacture, sale, or transportation of intoxicating liquors within, the importation thereof into, or the exportation thereof from the United States and all territory subject to the jurisdiction thereof for beverage purposes is hereby prohibited.

SECTION 2

[POWER TO ENFORCE THIS ARTICLE]

The Congress and the several States shall have concurrent power to enforce this article by appropriate legislation.

SECTION 3

[RATIFICATION WITHIN SEVEN YEARS]

This article shall be inoperative unless it shall have been ratified as an amendment to the Constitution by the legislatures of the several States, as provided in the Constitution, within seven years from the date of the submission hereof to the States by the Congress.[1]

---

[1] Repealed by the Twenty-First Amendment.

Amendment XIX

[PROPOSED BY CONGRESS ON JUNE 4, 1919; DECLARED RATIFIED ON AUGUST 26, 1920.]
[WOMAN SUFFRAGE]

The right of citizens of the United States to vote shall not be denied or abridged by the United States or by any State on account of sex.

Congress shall have power to enforce this article by appropriate legislation.

Amendment XX

[PROPOSED BY CONGRESS ON MARCH 2, 1932; DECLARED RATIFIED ON FEBRUARY 6, 1933.]

SECTION 1

[TERMS OF OFFICE]

The terms of the President and Vice President shall end at noon on the 20th day of January, and the terms of Senators and Representatives at noon on the 3d day of January, of the years in which such terms would have ended if this article had not been ratified; and the terms of their successors shall then begin.

SECTION 2

[TIME OF CONVENING CONGRESS]

The Congress shall assemble at least once in every year, and such meeting shall begin at noon on the 3d day of January, unless they shall by law appoint a different day.

SECTION 3

[DEATH OF PRESIDENT-ELECT]

If, at the time fixed for the beginning of the term of the President, the President elect shall have died, the Vice President elect shall become President. If a President shall not have been chosen before the time fixed for the beginning of his term, or if the President elect shall have failed to qualify, then the Vice President elect shall act as President until a President shall have qualified; and the Congress may by law provide for the case wherein neither a President elect nor a Vice President elect shall have qualified, declaring who shall then act as President, or the manner in which one who is to act shall be selected, and such person shall act accordingly until a President or Vice President shall have qualified.

SECTION 4

[ELECTION OF THE PRESIDENT]

The Congress may by law provide for the case of the death of any of the persons from whom the House of Representatives may choose a President whenever the right of choice shall have devolved upon them, and for the case of the death of any of the persons from whom the Senate may choose a Vice President whenever the right of choice shall have devolved upon them.

SECTION 5

[AMENDMENT TAKES EFFECT]

Sections 1 and 2 shall take effect on the 15th day of October following the ratification of this article.

SECTION 6
[RATIFICATION WITHIN SEVEN YEARS]
This article shall be inoperative unless it shall have been ratified as an amendment to the Constitution by the legislatures of three-fourths of the several States within seven years from the date of its submission.

Amendment XXI
[PROPOSED BY CONGRESS ON FEBRUARY 20, 1933;
DECLARED RATIFIED ON DECEMBER 5, 1933.]

SECTION 1
[NATIONAL LIQUOR PROHIBITION REPEALED]
The eighteenth article of amendment to the Constitution of the United States is hereby repealed.

SECTION 2
[TRANSPORTATION OF LIQUOR INTO "DRY" STATES]
The transportation or importation into any State, Territory, or Possession of the United States for delivery or use therein of intoxicating liquors, in violation of the laws thereof, is hereby prohibited.

SECTION 3
[RATIFICATION WITHIN SEVEN YEARS]
This article shall be inoperative unless it shall have been ratified as an amendment to the Constitution by conventions in the several States, as provided in the Constitution, within seven years from the date of the submission hereof to the States by the Congress.

Amendment XXII
[PROPOSED BY CONGRESS ON MARCH 21, 1947; DECLARED RATIFIED ON FEBRUARY 27, 1951.]

SECTION 1
[TENURE OF PRESIDENT LIMITED]
No person shall be elected to the office of President more than twice, and no person who has held the office of President or acted as President, for more than two years of a term to which some other person was elected President shall be elected to the office of the President more than once. But this Article shall not apply to any person holding the office of President when this Article was proposed by the Congress, and shall not prevent any person who may be holding the office of President, or acting as President, during the term within which this Article becomes operative from holding the office of President or acting as President during the remainder of such term.

SECTION 2
[RATIFICATION WITHIN SEVEN YEARS]
This article shall be inoperative unless it shall have been ratified as an amendment to the Constitution by the legislatures of three-fourths of the several States within seven years from the date of its submission to the States by the Congress.

Amendment XXIII

[PROPOSED BY CONGRESS ON JUNE 16, 1960; DECLARED RATIFIED ON MARCH 29, 1961.]

SECTION 1
[ELECTORAL COLLEGE VOTES FOR THE DISTRICT OF COLUMBIA]
The District constituting the seat of Government of the United States shall appoint in such manner as the Congress may direct:

A number of electors of President and Vice President equal to the whole number of Senators and Representatives in Congress to which the District would be entitled if it were a State, but in no event more than the least populous State; they shall be in addition to those appointed by the States, but they shall be considered, for the purposes of the election of President and Vice President, to be electors appointed by a State; and they shall meet in the District and perform such duties as provided by the twelfth article of amendment.

SECTION 2
[POWER TO ENFORCE THIS ARTICLE]
The Congress shall have power to enforce this article by appropriate legislation.

Amendment XXIV

[PROPOSED BY CONGRESS ON AUGUST 27, 1962; DECLARED RATIFIED ON JANUARY 23, 1964.]

SECTION 1
[ANTI-POLL TAX]
The right of citizens of the United States to vote in any primary or other election for President or Vice President, for electors for President or Vice President, or for Senator or Representative of Congress, shall not be denied or abridged by the United States or any State by reason of failure to pay any poll tax or other tax.

SECTION 2
[POWER TO ENFORCE THIS ARTICLE]
The Congress shall have power to enforce this article by appropriate legislation.

Amendment XXV

[PROPOSED BY CONGRESS ON JULY 6, 1965; DECLARED RATIFIED ON FEBRUARY 10, 1967.]

SECTION 1
[VICE PRESIDENT TO BECOME PRESIDENT]
In case of the removal of the President from office or his death or resignation, the Vice President shall become President.

SECTION 2
[CHOICE OF A NEW VICE PRESIDENT]
Whenever there is a vacancy in the office of the Vice President, the President shall nominate a Vice President who shall take the office upon confirmation by a majority vote of both houses of Congress.

SECTION 3
[PRESIDENT MAY DECLARE OWN DISABILITY]

Whenever the President transmits to the President pro tempore of the Senate and the Speaker of the House of Representatives his written declaration that he is unable to discharge the powers and duties of his office, and until he transmits to them a written declaration to the contrary, such powers and duties shall be discharged by the Vice President as Acting President.

SECTION 4
[ALTERNATE PROCEDURES TO DECLARE AND TO END PRESIDENTIAL DISABILITY]

Whenever the Vice President and a majority of either the principal officers of the executive departments, or of such other body as Congress may by law provide, transmit to the President pro tempore of the Senate and the Speaker of the House of Representatives their written declaration that the President is unable to discharge the powers and duties of his office, the Vice President shall immediately assume the powers and duties of the office as Acting President.

Thereafter, when the President transmits to the President pro tempore of the Senate and the Speaker of the House of Representatives his written declaration that no inability exists, he shall resume the powers and duties of his office unless the Vice President and a majority of either the principal officers of the executive department, or of such other body as Congress may by law provide, transmit within four days to the President pro tempore of the Senate and the Speaker of the House of Representatives their written declaration that the President is unable to discharge the powers and duties of his office. Thereupon Congress shall decide the issue, assembling within forty eight hours for that purpose if not in session. If the Congress, within twenty one days after receipt of the latter written declaration, or, if Congress is not in session, within twenty one days after Congress is required to assemble, determines by two-thirds vote of both Houses that the President is unable to discharge the powers and duties of his office, the Vice President shall continue to discharge the same as Acting President; otherwise, the President shall resume the powers and duties of his office.

Amendment XXVI
[PROPOSED BY CONGRESS ON MARCH 23, 1971; DECLARED RATIFIED ON JULY 1, 1971.]

SECTION 1
[EIGHTEEN-YEAR-OLD VOTE]

The right of citizens of the United States, who are eighteen years of age or older, to vote shall not be denied or abridged by the United States or by any State on account of age.

SECTION 2
[POWER TO ENFORCE THIS ARTICLE]

The Congress shall have power to enforce this article by appropriate legislation.

Amendment XXVII
[PROPOSED BY CONGRESS ON SEPTEMBER 25, 1789; DECLARED RATIFIED ON MAY 8, 1992.]
[CONGRESS CANNOT RAISE ITS OWN PAY]

No law varying the compensation for the services of the Senators and Representatives, shall take effect, until an election of representatives shall have intervened.

The Federalist Papers

No. 10: Madison

Among the numerous advantages promised by a well constructed Union, none deserves to be more accurately developed than its tendency to break and control the violence of faction. The friend of popular governments never finds himself so much alarmed for their character and fate, as when he contemplates their propensity to this dangerous vice. He will not fail therefore to set a due value on any plan which, without violating the principles to which he is attached, provides a proper cure for it. The instability, injustice, and confusion introduced into the public councils have, in truth, been the mortal diseases under which popular governments have everywhere perished, as they continue to be the favorite and fruitful topics from which the adversaries to liberty derive their most specious declamations. The valuable improvements made by the American constitutions on the popular models, both ancient and modern, cannot certainly be too much admired; but it would be an unwarrantable partiality to contend that they have as effectually obviated the danger on this side, as was wished and expected. Complaints are everywhere heard from our most considerate and virtuous citizens, equally the friends of public and private faith and of public and personal liberty, that our governments are too unstable, that the public good is disregarded in the conflicts of rival parties, and that measures are too often decided, not according to the rules of justice and the rights of the minor party, but by the superior force of an interested and overbearing majority. However anxiously we may wish that these complaints had no foundation, the evidence of known facts will not permit us to deny that they are in some degree true. It will be found, indeed, on a candid review of our situation, that some of the distresses under which we labor have been erroneously charged on the operation of our governments; but it will be found, at the same time, that other causes will not alone account for many of our heaviest misfortunes; and, particularly, for that prevailing and increasing distrust of public engagements and alarm for private rights which are echoed from one end of the continent to the other. These must be chiefly, if not wholly, effects of the unsteadiness and injustice with which a factious spirit has tainted our public administration.

By a faction I understand a number of citizens, whether amounting to a majority or minority of the whole, who are united and actuated by some common impulse of passion, or of interest, adverse to the rights of other citizens, or to the permanent and aggregate interests of the community.

There are two methods of curing the mischiefs of faction: the one, by removing its causes; the other, by controlling its effects.

There are again two methods of removing the causes of faction: the one, by destroying the liberty which is essential to its existence; the other, by giving to every citizen the same opinions, the same passions, and the same interests.

It could never be more truly said than of the first remedy, that it is worse than the disease. Liberty is to faction what air is to fire, an aliment without which it instantly expires. But it could not be a less folly to abolish liberty, which is essential to political life, because it nourishes faction, than it would be to wish the annihilation of air, which is essential to animal life, because it imparts to fire its destructive agency.

The second expedient is as impracticable, as the first would be unwise. As long as the reason of man continues fallible, and he is at liberty to exercise it, different opinions will be formed. As long as the connection subsists between his reason and his self-love, his opinions and his passions will have a reciprocal influence on each other; and the former will be objects to which the latter will attach themselves. The diversity in the faculties of men, from which the rights of property originate, is not less an insuperable obstacle to a uniformity of interests. The protection of these faculties is the first object of Government. From the protection of different and unequal faculties of acquiring property, the possession of different degrees and kinds of property immediately results; and from the influence of these on the sentiments and views of the respective proprietors, ensues a division of the society into different interests and parties.

The latent causes of faction are thus sown in the nature of man; and we see them everywhere brought into different degrees of activity, according to the different circumstances of civil society. A zeal for different opinions concerning religion, concerning Government, and many other points, as well of speculation as of practice; an attachment to different leaders ambitiously contending for pre-eminence and power; or to persons of other descriptions whose fortunes have been interesting to the human passions, have in turn divided mankind into parties, inflamed them with mutual animosity, and rendered them much more disposed to vex and oppress each other, than to co-operate for their common good. So strong is this propensity of mankind to fall into mutual animosities, that where no substantial occasion presents itself, the most frivolous and fanciful distinctions have been sufficient to kindle their unfriendly passions, and excite their most violent conflicts. But the most common and durable source of factions has been the various and unequal distribution of property. Those who hold and those who are without property have ever formed distinct interests in society. Those who are creditors, and those who are debtors, fall under a like discrimination. A landed interest, a manufacturing interest, a mercantile interest, a moneyed interest, with many lesser interests, grow up of necessity in civilized nations, and divide them into different classes, actuated by different sentiments and views. The regulation of these various and interfering interests forms the principal task of modern Legislation, and involves the spirit of party and faction in the necessary and ordinary operations of Government.

No man is allowed to be judge in his own cause, because his interest would certainly bias his judgment and, not improbably, corrupt his integrity. With equal, nay with greater reason, a body of men are unfit to be both judges and parties at the same time; yet what are many of the most important acts of legislation but so many judicial determinations, not indeed concerning the rights of single persons, but concerning the rights of large bodies of citizens; and what are the different classes of legislators but advocates and parties to the causes which they determine? Is a law proposed concerning private debts? It is a question to which the creditors are parties on one side and the debtors on the other. Justice ought to hold the balance between them. Yet the parties are, and must be, themselves the judges; and the most numerous party, or in other words, the most powerful faction must be expected to prevail. Shall domestic manufacturers be encouraged, and in what degree, by restrictions on foreign manufacturers? are questions which would be differently decided by the landed and the manufacturing classes, and probably by neither with a sole regard to justice and the public good. The apportionment of taxes on the various descriptions of property is an act which seems to require the most exact impartiality; yet there is, perhaps, no legislative act in which greater opportunity and temptation are given to a predominant party to trample on the rules of justice. Every shilling with which they overburden the inferior number is a shilling saved to their own pockets.

It is in vain to say that enlightened statesmen will be able to adjust these clashing interests and render them all subservient to the public good. Enlightened statesmen will not always be at the helm. Nor, in many cases, can such an adjustment be made at all without taking into view indirect and remote considerations, which will rarely prevail over the immediate interest which one party may find in disregarding the rights of another or the good of the whole.

The inference to which we are brought is that the *causes* of faction cannot be removed and that relief is only to be sought in the means of controlling its *effects*.

If a faction consists of less than a majority, relief is supplied by the republican principle, which enables the majority to defeat its sinister views by regular vote. It may clog the administration, it may convulse the society; but it will be unable to execute and mask its violence under the forms of the Constitution. When a majority is included in a faction, the form of popular government, on the other hand, enables it to sacrifice to its ruling passion or interest both the public good and the rights of other citizens. To secure the public good and private rights against the danger of such a faction, and at the same time to preserve the spirit and the form of popular government, is then the great object to which our enquiries are directed. Let me add that it is the great desideratum by which alone this form of government can be rescued from the opprobrium under which it has so long labored and be recommended to the esteem and adoption of mankind.

By what means is this object attainable? Evidently by one of two only. Either the existence of the same passion or interest in a majority at the same time must be prevented, or the majority, having such co-existent passion or interest, must be rendered, by their number and local situation, unable to concert and carry into effect schemes of oppression. If the impulse and the opportunity be suffered to coincide, we well know that neither moral nor religious motives can be relied on as an adequate control. They are not found to be such on the injustice and violence of individuals, and lose their efficacy in proportion to the number combined together, that is, in proportion as their efficacy becomes needful.

From this view of the subject it may be concluded that a pure Democracy, by which I mean a Society consisting of a small number of citizens, who assemble and administer the Government in person, can admit of no cure for the mischiefs of faction. A common passion or interest will, in almost every case, be felt by a majority of the whole; a communication and concert results from the form of Government itself; and there is nothing to check the inducements to sacrifice the weaker party or an obnoxious individual. Hence it is that such Democracies have ever been spectacles of turbulence and contention; have ever been found incompatible with personal security or the rights of property; and have in general been as short in their lives as they have been violent in their deaths. Theoretic politicians, who have patronized this species of Government, have erroneously supposed that by reducing mankind to a perfect equality in their political rights, they would at the same time be perfectly equalized and assimilated in their possessions, their opinions, and their passions.

A Republic, by which I mean a Government in which the scheme of representation takes place, opens a different prospect and promises the cure for which we are seeking. Let us examine the points in which it varies from pure Democracy, and we shall comprehend both the nature of the cure and the efficacy which it must derive from the Union.

The two great points of difference between a Democracy and a Republic are: first, the delegation of the Government, in the latter, to a small number of citizens elected by the rest; secondly, the greater number of citizens and greater sphere of country over which the latter may be extended.

The effect of the first difference is, on the one hand, to refine and enlarge the public views by passing them through the medium of a chosen body of citizens, whose wisdom may best discern the true interest of their country and whose patriotism and love of justice will be least likely to sacrifice it to temporary or partial considerations. Under such a regulation it may well happen that the public voice, pronounced by the representatives of the people, will be more consonant to the public good than if pronounced by the people themselves, convened for the purpose. On the other hand, the effect may be inverted. Men of factious tempers, of local prejudices, or of sinister designs, may, by intrigue, by corruption, or by other means, first obtain the suffrages, and then betray the interests of the people. The question resulting is, whether small or extensive Republics are most favorable to the election of proper guardians of the public weal; and it is clearly decided in favor of the latter by two obvious considerations.

In the first place it is to be remarked that however small the Republic may be, the Representatives must be raised to a certain number in order to guard against the cabals of a few; and that however large it may be they must be limited to a certain number in order to guard against the confusion of a multitude. Hence, the number of Representatives in the two cases not being in proportion to that of the Constituents, and being proportionally greatest in the small Republic, it follows that if the proportion of fit characters be not less in the large than in the small Republic, the former will present a greater option, and consequently a greater probability of a fit choice.

In the next place, as each Representative will be chosen by a greater number of citizens in the large than in the small Republic, it will be more difficult for unworthy candidates to practise with success the vicious arts by which elections are too often carried; and the suffrages of the people being more free, will be more likely to centre on men who possess the most attractive merit and the most diffusive and established characters.

It must be confessed that in this, as in most other cases, there is a mean, on both sides of which inconveniencies will be found to lie. By enlarging too much the number of electors, you render the representative too little acquainted with all their local circumstances and lesser interests; as by reducing it too much, you render him unduly attached to these, and too little fit to comprehend and pursue great and national objects. The Federal Constitution forms a happy combination in this respect; the great and aggregate interests being referred to the national, the local and particular to the State legislatures.

The other point of difference is the greater number of citizens and extent of territory which may be brought within the compass of Republican than of Democratic Government; and it is this circumstance principally which renders factious combinations less to be dreaded in the former than in the latter. The smaller the society, the fewer probably will be the distinct parties and interests composing it; the fewer the distinct parties and interests, the more frequently will a majority be found of the same party; and the smaller the number of individuals composing a majority, and the smaller the compass within which they are placed, the more easily will they concert and execute their plans of oppression. Extend the sphere and you take in a greater variety of parties and interests; you make it less probable that a majority of the whole will have a common motive to invade the rights of other citizens; or if such a common motive exists, it will be more difficult for all who feel it to discover their own strength and to act in unison with each other. Besides other impediments, it may be remarked, that where there is a consciousness of unjust or dishonorable purposes, communication is always checked by distrust in proportion to the number whose concurrence is necessary.

Hence, it clearly appears that the same advantage which a Republic has over a Democracy in controlling the effects of faction is enjoyed by a large over a small republic—is enjoyed by the Union over the States composing it. Does this advantage consist in the substitution of representatives whose enlightened views and virtuous sentiments render them superior to local prejudices and to schemes of injustice? It will not be denied that the representation of the Union will be most likely to possess these requisite endowments. Does it consist in the greater security afforded by a greater variety of parties, against the event of any one party being able to outnumber and oppress the rest? In an equal degree does the increased variety of parties comprised within the Union increase this security? Does it, in fine, consist in the greater obstacles opposed to the concert and accomplishment of the secret wishes of an unjust and interested majority? Here again the extent of the Union gives it the most palpable advantage.

The influence of factious leaders may kindle a flame within their particular States but will be unable to spread a general conflagration through the other States: a religious sect may degenerate into a political faction in a part of the Confederacy; but the variety of sects dispersed over the entire face of it must secure the national Councils against any danger from that source: a rage for paper money, for an abolition of debts, for an equal division of property, or for any other improper or wicked project, will be less apt to pervade the whole body of the Union than a particular member of it; in the same proportion as such a malady is more likely to taint a particular county or district than an entire State.

In the extent and proper structure of the Union, therefore, we behold a republican remedy for the diseases most incident to Republican Government. And according to the degree of pleasure and pride we feel in being republicans ought to be our zeal in cherishing the spirit and supporting the character of federalist.

PUBLIUS
November 22, 1787

No. 51: Madison

To what expedient, then, shall we finally resort, for maintaining in practice the necessary partition of power among the several departments as laid down in the constitution? The only answer that can be given is that as all these exterior provisions are found to be inadequate the defect must be supplied, by so contriving the interior structure of the government as that its several constituent parts may, by their mutual relations, be the means of keeping each other in their proper places. Without presuming to undertake a full development of this important idea I will hazard a few general observations which may perhaps place it in a clearer light, and enable us to form a more correct judgment of the principles and structure of the government planned by the convention.

In order to lay a due foundation for that separate and distinct exercise of the different powers of government, which to a certain extent is admitted on all hands to be essential to the preservation of liberty, it is evident that each department should have a will of its own; and consequently should be so constituted that the members of each should have as little agency as possible in the appointment of the members of the others. Were this principle rigorously adhered to, it would require that all the appointments for the supreme executive, legislative, and judiciary magistracies should be drawn from the same fountain of authority, the people, through channels having no communication whatever with one another. Perhaps such a plan of constructing the several departments would be less difficult in practice than it may in contemplation appear. Some difficulties, however, and some additional expense would attend the execution of it. Some deviations, therefore, from the principle must be admitted. In the constitution of the judiciary department in particular, it might be inexpedient to insist rigorously on the principle: first, because peculiar qualifications being essential in the members, the primary consideration ought to be to select that mode of choice which best secures these qualifications; second, because the permanent tenure by which the appointments are held in that department must soon destroy all sense of dependence on the authority conferring them.

It is equally evident that the members of each department should be as little dependent as possible on those of the others for the emoluments annexed to their offices. Were the executive magistrate, or the judges, not independent of the legislature in this particular, their independence in every other would be merely nominal.

But the great security against a gradual concentration of the several powers in the same department consists in giving to those who administer each department the necessary constitutional means and personal motives to resist encroachments of the others. The provision for defence must in this, as in all other cases, be made commensurate to the danger of attack. Ambition must be made to counteract ambition. The interest of the man must be connected with the constitutional rights of the place. It may be a reflection on human nature that such devices should be necessary to control the abuses of government. But what is government itself but the greatest of all reflections on human nature? If men were angels, no government would be necessary. If angels were to govern men, neither external nor internal controls on government would be necessary. In framing a government which is to be administered by men over men, the great difficulty lies in this: You must first enable the government to control the governed; and in the next place oblige it to control itself. A dependence on the people is, no doubt, the primary control on the government; but experience has taught mankind the necessity of auxiliary precautions.

This policy of supplying, by opposite and rival interests, the defect of better motives, might be traced through the whole system of human affairs, private as well as public. We see it particularly displayed in all the subordinate distributions of power, where the constant aim is to divide and arrange the several offices in such a manner as that each may be a check on the other; that the private interest of every individual may be a sentinel over the public rights. These inventions of prudence cannot be less requisite in the distribution of the supreme powers of the State.

But it is not possible to give to each department an equal power of self-defense. In republican government, the legislative authority necessarily predominates. The remedy for this inconveniency is to divide the legislature into different branches; and to render them, by different modes of election and different principles of action, as little connected with each other as the nature of their common functions and their common dependence on the society will admit. It may even be necessary to guard against dangerous encroachments by still further precautions. As the weight of the legislative authority requires that it should be thus divided, the weakness of the executive may require, on the other hand, that it should be fortified. An absolute negative on the legislature appears, at first view, to be the natural defense with which the executive magistrate should be armed. But perhaps it would be neither altogether safe nor alone sufficient. On ordinary occasions it might not be exerted with the requisite firmness, and on extraordinary occasions it might be perfidiously abused. May not this defect of an absolute negative be supplied by some qualified connection between this weaker branch of the stronger department, by which the latter may be led to support the constitutional rights of the former, without being too much detached from the rights of its own department?

If the principles on which these observations are founded be just, as I persuade myself they are, and they be applied as a criterion to the several State constitutions, and to the federal Constitution, it will be found that if the latter does not perfectly correspond with them, the former are infinitely less able to bear such a test.

There are, moreover, two considerations particularly applicable to the federal system of America, which place that system in a very interesting point of view.

First. In a single republic, all the power surrendered by the people is submitted to the administration of a single government; and usurpations are guarded against by a division of the government into distinct and separate departments. In the compound republic of America, the power surrendered by the people is first divided between two distinct governments, and then the portion allotted to each subdivided among distinct and separate departments. Hence a double security arises to the rights of the people. The different governments will control each other, at the same time that each will be controlled by itself.

Second. It is of great importance in a republic not only to guard the society against the oppression of its rulers, but to guard one part of the society against the injustice of the other part. Different interests necessarily exist in different classes of citizens. If a majority be united by a common interest, the rights of the minority will be insecure. There are but two methods of providing against this evil: The one by creating a will in the community independent of the majority—that is, of the society itself; the other, by comprehending in the society so many separate descriptions of citizens as will render an unjust combination of a majority of the whole very improbable, if not impracticable. The first method prevails in all governments possessing an hereditary or self-appointed authority. This, at best, is but a precarious security; because a power independent of the society may as well espouse the unjust views of the major as the rightful interests of the minor party, and may possibly be turned against both parties. The second method will be exemplified in the federal republic of the United States. Whilst all authority in it will be derived from and dependent on the society, the society itself will be broken into so many parts, interests and classes of citizens, that the rights of individuals, or of the minority, will be in little danger from interested combinations of the majority. In a free government the security for civil rights must be the same as that for religious rights. It consists in the one case in the multiplicity of interests, and in the other in the multiplicity of sects. The degree of security in both cases will depend on the number of interests and sects; and this may be presumed to depend on the extent of country and number of people comprehended under the same government. This view of the subject must particularly recommend a proper federal system to all the sincere and considerate friends of republican government: Since it shows that in exact proportion as the territory of the Union may be formed into more circumscribed Confederacies, or States, oppressive combinations of a majority will be facilitated; the best security, under the republican form, for the rights of every class of citizens, will be diminished; and consequently the stability and independence of some member of the government, the only other security, must be proportionally increased. Justice is the end of government. It is the end of civil society. It ever has been and ever will be pursued until it be obtained, or until liberty be lost in the pursuit. In a society under the forms of which the stronger faction can readily unite and oppress the weaker, anarchy may as truly be said to reign as in a state of nature, where the weaker individual is not secured against the violence of the stronger: And as, in the latter state, even the stronger individuals are prompted, by the uncertainty of their condition, to submit to a government which may protect the weak as well as themselves: So, in the former state, will the more powerful factions or parties be gradually induced, by a like motive, to wish for a government which will protect all parties, the weaker as well as the more powerful. It can be little doubted that if the State of Rhode Island was separated from the Confederacy and left to itself, the insecurity of rights under the popular form of government within such narrow limits would be displayed by such reiterated oppressions of factious majorities that some power altogether independent of the people would soon be called for by the voice of the very factions whose misrule had proved the necessity of it. In the extended republic of the United States, and among the great variety of interests, parties, and sects which it embraces, a coalition of a majority of the whole society could seldom take place on any other principles than those of justice and the general good; and there being thus less danger to a minor from the will of the major party, there must be less pretext, also, to provide for the security of the former, by introducing into the government a will not dependent on the latter, or, in other words, a will independent of the society itself. It is no less certain than it is important, notwithstanding the contrary opinions which have been entertained, that the larger the society, provided it lie within a practicable sphere, the more duly capable it will be of self-government. And happily for the *republican cause*, practicable sphere may be carried to a very great extent by a judicious modification and mixture of the *federal principle*.

PUBLIUS
February 6, 1788

The Anti-Federalist Papers

Essay by Brutus in the *New York Journal*

When the public is called to investigate and decide upon a question in which not only the present members of the community are deeply interested, but upon which the happiness and misery of generations yet unborn is in great measure suspended, the benevolent mind cannot help feeling itself peculiarly interested in the result.

In this situation, I trust the feeble efforts of an individual, to lead the minds of the people to a wise and prudent determination, cannot fail of being acceptable to the candid and dispassionate part of the community. Encouraged by this consideration, I have been induced to offer my thoughts upon the present important crisis of our public affairs.

Perhaps this country never saw so critical a period in their political concerns. We have felt the feebleness of the ties by which these United-States are held together, and the want of sufficient energy in our present confederation, to manage, in some instances, our general concerns. Various expedients have been proposed to remedy these evils, but none have succeeded. At length a Convention of the states has been assembled, they have formed a constitution which will now, probably, be submitted to the people to ratify or reject, who are the fountain of all power, to whom alone it of right belongs to make or unmake constitutions, or forms of government, at their pleasure. The most important question that was ever proposed to your decision, or to the decision of any people under heaven, is before you, and you are to decide upon it by men of your own election, chosen specially for this purpose. If the constitution, offered to your acceptance, be a wise one, calculated to preserve the invaluable blessings of liberty, to secure the inestimable rights of mankind, and promote human happiness, then, if you accept it, you will lay a lasting foundation of happiness for millions yet unborn; generations to come will rise up and call you blessed. You may rejoice in the prospects of this vast extended continent becoming filled with freemen, who will assert the dignity of human nature. You may solace yourselves with the idea, that society, in this favoured land, will fast advance to the highest point of perfection; the human mind will expand in knowledge and virtue, and the golden age be, in some measure, realised. But if, on the other hand, this form of government contains principles that will lead to the subversion of liberty—if it tends to establish a despotism, or, what is worse, a tyrannic aristocracy; then, if you adopt it, this only remaining assylum for liberty will be shut up, and posterity will execrate your memory.

Momentous then is the question you have to determine, and you are called upon by every motive which should influence a noble and virtuous mind, to examine it well, and to make up a wise judgment. It is insisted, indeed, that this constitution must be received, be it ever so imperfect. If it has its defects, it is said, they can be best amended when they are experienced. But remember, when the people once part with power, they can seldom or never resume it again but by force. Many instances can be produced in which the people have voluntarily increased the powers of their rulers; but few, if any, in which rulers have willingly abridged their authority. This is a sufficient reason to induce you to be careful, in the first instance, how you deposit the powers of government.

With these few introductory remarks, I shall proceed to a consideration of this constitution:

The first question that presents itself on the subject is, whether a confederated government be the best for the United States or not? Or in other words, whether the thirteen United States should be reduced to one great republic, governed by one legislature, and under the direction of one executive and judicial; or whether they should continue thirteen confederated republics, under the direction and controul of a supreme federal head for certain defined national purposes only?

This enquiry is important, because, although the government reported by the convention does not go to a perfect and entire consolidation, yet it approaches so near to it, that it must, if executed, certainly and infallibly terminate in it.

This government is to possess absolute and uncontroulable power, legislative, executive and judicial, with respect to every object to which it extends, for by the last clause of section 8th, article 1st, it is declared "that the Congress shall have power to make all laws which shall be necessary and proper for carrying into execution the foregoing powers, and all other powers vested by this constitution, in the government of the United States; or in any department or office thereof." And by the 6th article, it is declared "that this constitution, and the laws of the United States, which shall be made in pursuance thereof, and the treaties made, or which shall be made, under the authority of the United States, shall be the supreme law of the land; and the judges in every state shall be bound thereby, any thing in the constitution, or law of any state to the contrary notwithstanding." It appears from these articles that there is no need of any intervention of the state governments, between the Congress and the people, to execute any one power vested in the general government, and that the constitution and laws of every state are nullified and declared void, so far as they are or shall be inconsistent with this constitution, or the laws made in pursuance of it, or with treaties made under the authority of the United States.—The government then, so far as it extends, is a complete one, and not a confederation. It is as much one complete government as that of New-York or Massachusetts, has as absolute and perfect powers to make and execute all laws, to appoint officers, institute courts, declare offences, and annex penalties, with respect to every object to which it extends, as any other in the world. So far therefore as its powers reach, all ideas of confederation are given up and lost. It is true this government is limited to certain objects, or to speak more properly, some small degree of power is still left to the states, but a little attention to the powers vested in the general government, will convince every candid man, that if it is capable of being executed, all that is reserved for the individual states must very soon be annihilated, except so far as they are barely necessary to the organization of the general government. The powers of the general legislature extend to every case that is of the least importance—there is nothing valuable to human nature, nothing dear to freemen, but what is within its power. It has authority to make laws which will affect the lives, the liberty, and property of every man in the United States; nor can the constitution or laws of any state, in any way prevent or impede the full and complete execution of every power given. The legislative power is competent to lay taxes, duties, imposts, and excises;—there is no limitation to this power, unless it be said that the clause which directs the use to which those taxes, and duties shall be applied, may be said to be a limitation: but this is no restriction of the power at all, for by this clause they are to be applied to pay the debts and provide for the common defence and general welfare of the United States; but the legislature have authority to contract debts at their discretion; they are the sole judges of what is necessary to provide for the common defence, and they only are to determine what is for the general welfare; this power therefore is neither more nor less, than a power to lay and collect taxes, imposts, and excises, at their pleasure; not only [is] the power to lay taxes unlimited, as to the amount they may require, but it is perfect and absolute to raise them in any mode they please. No state legislature, or any power in the state governments, have any more to do in carrying this into effect, than the authority of one state has to do with that of another. In the business therefore of laying and collecting taxes, the idea of confederation is totally lost, and that of one entire republic is embraced. It is proper here to remark, that the authority to lay and collect taxes is the most important of any power that can be granted; it connects with it almost all other powers, or at least will in process of time draw all other after it; it is the great mean of protection, security, and defence, in a good government, and the great engine of oppression and tyranny in a bad one. This cannot fail of being the case, if we consider the contracted limits which are set by this constitution, to the late [state?] governments, on this article of raising money. No state can emit paper money—lay any duties, or imposts, on imports, or exports, but by consent of the Congress; and then the net produce shall be for the benefit of the United States: the only mean therefore left, for any state to support its government and discharge its debts, is by direct taxation; and the United States have also power to lay and collect taxes, in any way they please. Every one who has thought on the subject, must be convinced that but small sums of money can be collected in any country, by direct taxe[s], when the foederal government begins to exercise the right of taxation in all its parts, the legislatures of the several states will find it impossible to raise monies to support their governments. Without money they cannot be supported, and they must dwindle away, and, as before observed, their powers absorbed in that of the general government.

It might be here shewn, that the power in the federal legislative, to raise and support armies at pleasure, as well in peace as in war, and their controul over the militia, tend, not only to a consolidation of the government, but the destruction of liberty.—I shall not, however, dwell upon these, as a few observations upon the judicial power of this government, in addition to the preceding, will fully evince the truth of the position.

The judicial power of the United States is to be vested in a supreme court, and in such inferior courts as Congress may from time to time ordain and establish. The powers of these courts are very extensive; their jurisdiction comprehends all civil causes, except such as arise between citizens of the same state; and it extends to all cases in law and equity arising under the constitution. One inferior court must be established, I presume, in each state, at least, with the necessary executive officers appendant thereto. It is easy to see, that in the common course of things, these courts will eclipse the dignity, and take away from the respectability, of the state courts. These courts will be, in themselves, totally independent of the states, deriving their authority from the United States, and receiving from them fixed salaries; and in the course of human events it is to be expected, that they will swallow up all the powers of the courts in the respective states.

How far the clause in the 8th section of the 1st article may operate to do away all idea of confederated states, and to effect an entire consolidation of the whole into one general government, it is impossible to say. The powers given by this article are very general and comprehensive, and it may receive a construction to justify the passing almost any law. A power to make all laws, which shall be *necessary and proper*, for carrying into execution, all powers vested by the constitution in the government of the United States, or any department or officer thereof, is a power very comprehensive and definite [indefinite?], and may, for ought I know, be exercised in a such manner as entirely to abolish the state legislatures. Suppose the legislature of a state should pass a law to raise money to support their government and pay the state debt, may the Congress repeal this law, because it may prevent the collection of a tax which they may think proper and necessary to lay, to provide for the general welfare of the United States? For all laws made, in pursuance of this constitution, are the supreme lay of the land, and the judges in every state shall be bound thereby, any thing in the constitution or laws of the different states to the contrary notwithstanding.—By such a law, the government of a particular state might be overturned at one stroke, and thereby be deprived of every means of its support.

It is not meant, by stating this case, to insinuate that the constitution would warrant a law of this kind; or unnecessarily to alarm the fears of the people, by suggesting, that the federal legislature would be more likely to pass the limits assigned them by the constitution, than that of an individual state, further than they are less responsible to the people. But what is meant is, that the legislature of the United States are vested with the great and uncontroulable powers, of laying and collecting taxes, duties, imposts, and excises; of regulating trade, raising and supporting armies, organizing, arming, and disciplining the militia, instituting courts, and other general powers. And are by this clause invested with the power of making all laws, *proper and necessary*, for carrying all these into execution; and they may so exercise this power as entirely to annihilate all the state governments, and reduce this country to one single government. And if they may do it, it is pretty certain they will; for it will be found that the power retained by individual states, small as it is, will be a clog upon the wheels of the government of the United States; the latter therefore will be naturally inclined to remove it out of the way. Besides, it is a truth confirmed by the unerring experience of ages, that every man, and every body of men, invested with power, are ever disposed to increase it, and to acquire a superiority over every thing that stands in their way. This disposition, which is implanted in human nature, will operate in the federal legislature to lessen and ultimately to subvert the state authority, and having such advantages, will most certainly succeed, if the federal government succeeds at all. It must be very evident then, that what this constitution wants of being a complete consolidation of the several parts of the union into one complete government, possessed of perfect legislative, judicial, and executive powers, to all intents and purposes, it will necessarily acquire in its exercise and operation.

Let us now proceed to enquire, as I at first proposed, whether it be best the thirteen United States should be reduced to one great republic, or not? It is here taken for granted, that all agree in this, that whatever government we adopt, it ought to be a free one; that it should be so framed as to secure the liberty of the citizens of America, and such an one as to admit of a full, fair, and equal representation of the people. The question then will be, whether a government thus constituted, and founded on such principles, is practicable, and can be exercised over the whole United States, reduced into one state?

If respect is to be paid to the opinion of the greatest and wisest men who have ever thought or wrote on the science of government, we shall be constrained to conclude, that a free republic cannot succeed over a country of such immense extent, containing such a number of inhabitants, and these encreasing in such rapid progression as that of the whole United States. Among the many illustrious authorities which might be produced to this point, I shall content myself with quoting only two. The one is the baron de Montesquieu, spirit of laws, chap. xvi. vol. I [book VIII]. "It is natural to a republic to have only a small territory, otherwise it cannot long subsist. In a large republic there are men of large fortunes, and consequently of less moderation; there are trusts too great to be placed in any single subject; he has interest of his own; he soon begins to think that he may be happy, great and glorious, by oppressing his fellow citizens; and that he may raise himself to grandeur on the ruins of his country. In a large republic, the public good is sacrificed to a thousand views; it is subordinate to exceptions, and depends on accidents. In a small one, the interest of the public is easier perceived, better understood, and more within the reach of every citizen; abuses are of less extent, and of course are less protected." Of the same opinion is the marquis Beccarari.

History furnishes no example of a free republic, any thing like the extent of the United States. The Grecian republics were of small extent; so also was that of the Romans. Both of these, it is true, in process of time, extended their conquests over large territories of country; and the consequence was, that their governments were changed from that of free governments to those of the most tyrannical that ever existed in the world.

Not only the opinion of the greatest men, and the experience of mankind, are against the idea of an extensive republic, but a variety of reasons may be drawn from the reason and nature of things, against it. In every government, the will of the sovereign is the law. In despotic governments, the supreme authority being lodged in one, his will is law, and can be as easily expressed to a large extensive territory as to a small one. In a pure democracy the people are the sovereign, and their will is declared by themselves; for this purpose they must all come together to deliberate, and decide. This kind of government cannot be exercised, therefore, over a country of any considerable extent; it must be confined to a single city, or at least limited to such bounds as that the people can conveniently assemble, be able to debate, understand the subject submitted to them, and declare their opinion concerning it.

In a free republic, although all laws are derived from the consent of the people, yet the people do not declare their consent by themselves in person, but by representatives, chosen by them, who are supposed to know the minds of their constituents, and to be possessed of integrity to declare this mind.

In every free government, the people must give their assent to the laws by which they are governed. This is the true criterion between a free government and an arbitrary one. The former are ruled by the will of the whole, expressed in any manner they may agree upon; the latter by the will of one, or a few. If the people are to give their assent to the laws, by persons chosen and appointed by them, the manner of the choice and the number chosen, must be such, as to possess, be disposed, and consequently qualified to declare the sentiments of the people; for if they do not know, or are not disposed to speak the sentiments of the people, the people do not govern, but the sovereignty is in a few. Now, in a large extended country, it is impossible to have a representation, possessing the sentiments, and of integrity, to declare the minds of the people, without having it so numerous and unwieldly, as to be subject in great measure to the inconveniency of a democratic government.

The territory of the United States is of vast extent; it now contains near three millions of souls, and is capable of containing much more than ten times that number. Is it practicable for a country, so large and so numerous as they will soon become, to elect a representation, that will speak their sentiments, without their becoming so numerous as to be incapable of transacting public business? It certainly is not.

In a republic, the manners, sentiments, and interests of the people should be similar. If this be not the case, there will be a constant clashing of opinions; and the representatives of one part will be continually striving against those of the other. This will retard the operations of government, and prevent such conclusions as will promote the public good. If we apply this remark to the condition of the United States, we shall be convinced that it forbids that we should be one government. The United States includes a variety of climates. The productions of the different parts of the union are very variant, and their interests, of consequence, diverse. Their manners and habits differ as much as their climates and productions; and their sentiments are by no means coincident. The laws and customs of the several states are, in many respects, very diverse, and in some opposite; each would be in favor of its own interests and customs, and, of consequence, a legislature, formed of representatives from the respective parts, would not only be too numerous to act with any care or decision, but would be composed of such heterogenous and discordant principles, as would constantly be contending with each other.

The laws cannot be executed in a republic, of an extent equal to that of the United States, with promptitude.

The magistrates in every government must be supported in the execution of the laws, either by an armed force, maintained at the public expence for that purpose; or by the people turning out to aid the magistrate upon his command, in case of resistance.

In despotic governments, as well as in all the monarchies of Europe, standing armies are kept up to execute the commands of the prince or the magistrate, and are employed for this purpose when occasion requires: But they have always proved the destruction of liberty, and [are] abhorrent to the spirit of a free republic. In England, where they depend upon the parliament for their annual support, they have always been complained of as oppressive and unconstitutional, and are seldom employed in executing of the laws; never except on extraordinary occasions, and then under the direction of a civil magistrate.

A free republic will never keep a standing army to execute its laws. It must depend upon the support of its citizens. But when a government is to receive its support from the aid of the citizens, it must be so constructed as to have the confidence, respect, and affection of the people. Men who, upon the call of the magistrate, offer themselves to execute the laws, are influenced to do it either by affection to the government, or from fear; where a standing army is at hand to punish offenders, every man is actuated by the latter principle, and therefore, when the magistrate calls, will obey: but, where this is not the case, the government must rest for its support upon the confidence and respect which the people have for their government and laws. The body of the people being attached, the government will always be sufficient to support and execute its laws, and to operate upon the fears of any faction which may be opposed to it, not only to prevent an opposition to the execution of the laws themselves, but also to compel the most of them to aid the magistrate; but the people will not be likely to have such confidence in their rulers, in a republic so extensive as the United States, as necessary for these purposes. The confidence which the people have in their rulers, in a free republic, arises from their knowing them, from their being responsible to them for their conduct, and from the power they have of displacing them when they misbehave: but in a republic of the extent of this continent, the people in general would be acquainted with very few of their rulers: the people at large would know little of their proceedings, and it would be extremely difficult to change them. The people in Georgia and New-Hampshire would not know one another's mind, and therefore could not act in concert to enable them to effect a general change of representatives. The different parts of so extensive a country could not possibly be made acquainted with the conduct of their representatives, nor be informed of the reasons upon which measures were founded. The consequence will be, they will have no confidence in their legislature, suspect them of ambitious views, be jealous of every measure they adopt, and will not support the laws they pass. Hence the government will be nerveless and inefficient, and no way will be left to render it otherwise, but by establishing an armed force to execute the laws at the point of the bayonet—a government of all others the most to be dreaded.

In a republic of such vast extent as the United-States, the legislature cannot attend to the various concerns and wants of its different parts. It cannot be sufficiently numerous to be acquainted with the local condition and wants of the different districts, and if it could, it is impossible it should have sufficient time to attend to and provide for all the variety of cases of this nature, that would be continually arising.

In so extensive a republic, the great officers of government would soon become above the controul of the people, and abuse their power to the purpose of aggrandizing themselves, and oppressing them. The trust committed to the executive offices, in a country of the extent of the United-States, must be various and of magnitude. The command of all the troops and navy of the republic, the appointment of officers, the power of pardoning offences, the collecting of all the public revenues, and the power of expending them, with a number of other powers, must be lodged and exercised in every state, in the hands of a few. When these are attended with great honor and emolument, as they always will be in large states, so as greatly to interest men to pursue them, and to be proper objects for ambitious and designing men, such men will be ever restless in their pursuit after them. They will use the power, when they have acquired it, to the purposes of gratifying their own interest and ambition, and it is scarcely possible, in a very large republic, to call them to account for their misconduct, or to prevent their abuse of power.

These are some of the reasons by which it appears, that a free republic cannot long subsist over a country of the great extent of these states. If then this new constitution is calculated to consolidate the thirteen states into one, as it evidently is, it ought not to be adopted.

Though I am of opinion, that it is a sufficient objection to this government, to reject it, that it creates the whole union into one government, under the form of a republic, yet if this objection was obviated, there are exceptions to it, which are so material and fundamental, that they ought to determine every man, who is a friend to the liberty and happiness of mankind, not to adopt it. I beg the candid and dispassionate attention of my countrymen while I state these objections—they are such as have obtruded themselves upon my mind upon a careful attention to the matter, and such as I sincerely believe are well founded. There are many objections, of small moment, of which I shall take no notice— perfection is not to be expected in any thing that is the production of man—and if I did not in my conscience believe that this scheme was defective in the fundamental principles—in the foundation upon which a free and equal government must rest—I would hold my peace.

BRUTUS
Ocotober 18, 1787

Presidents and Vice Presidents

PRESIDENT	VICE PRESIDENT
1 George Washington *(Federalist 1789)*	John Adams *(Federalist 1789)*
2 John Adams *(Federalist 1797)*	Thomas Jefferson *(Dem.-Rep. 1797)*
3 Thomas Jefferson *(Dem.-Rep. 1801)*	Aaron Burr *(Dem.-Rep. 1801)*
	George Clinton *(Dem.-Rep. 1805)*
4 James Madison *(Dem.-Rep. 1809)*	George Clinton *(Dem.-Rep. 1809)*
	Elbridge Gerry *(Dem.-Rep. 1813)*
5 James Monroe *(Dem.-Rep. 1817)*	Daniel D. Tompkins *(Dem.-Rep. 1817)*
6 John Quincy Adams *(Dem.-Rep. 1825)*	John C. Calhoun *(Dem.-Rep. 1825)*
7 Andrew Jackson *(Democratic 1829)*	John C. Calhoun *(Democratic 1829)*
	Martin Van Buren *(Democratic 1833)*
8 Martin Van Buren *(Democratic 1837)*	Richard M. Johnson *(Democratic 1837)*
9 William H. Harrison *(Whig 1841)*	John Tyler *(Whig 1841)*
10 John Tyler *(Whig and Democratic 1841)*	
11 James K. Polk *(Democratic 1845)*	George M. Dallas *(Democratic 1845)*
12 Zachary Taylor *(Whig 1849)*	Millard Fillmore *(Whig 1849)*
13 Millard Fillmore *(Whig 1850)*	
14 Franklin Pierce *(Democratic 1853)*	William R. D. King *(Democratic 1853)*
15 James Buchanan *(Democratic 1857)*	John C. Breckinridge *(Democratic 1857)*

PRESIDENT	VICE PRESIDENT
16 Abraham Lincoln *(Republican 1861)*	Hannibal Hamlin *(Republican 1861)* Andrew Johnson *(Unionist 1865)*
17 Andrew Johnson (Unionist 1865)	
18 Ulysses S. Grant *(Republican 1869)*	Schuyler Colfax *(Republican 1869)* Henry Wilson *(Republican 1873)*
19 Rutherford B. Hayes *(Republican 1877)*	William A. Wheeler *(Republican 1877)*
20 James A. Garfield *(Republican 1881)*	Chester A. Arthur *(Republican 1881)*
21 Chester A. Arthur *(Republican 1881)*	
22 Grover Cleveland *(Democratic 1885)*	Thomas A. Hendricks *(Democratic 1885)*
23 Benjamin Harrison *(Republican 1889)*	Levi P. Morton *(Republican 1889)*
24 Grover Cleveland *(Democratic 1893)*	Adlai E. Stevenson *(Democratic 1893)*
25 William McKinley *(Republican 1897)*	Garret A. Hobart *(Republican 1897)* Theodore Roosevelt *(Republican 1901)*
26 Theodore Roosevelt *(Republican 1901)*	Charles W. Fairbanks *(Republican 1905)*
27 William H. Taft *(Republican 1909)*	James S. Sherman *(Republican 1909)*
28 Woodrow Wilson *(Democratic 1913)*	Thomas R. Marshall *(Democratic 1913)*
29 Warren G. Harding *(Republican 1921)*	Calvin Coolidge *(Republican 1921)*
30 Calvin Coolidge *(Republican 1923)*	Charles G. Dawes *(Republican 1925)*
31 Herbert Hoover *(Republican 1929)*	Charles Curtis *(Republican 1929)*

PRESIDENT	VICE PRESIDENT
32 Franklin D. Roosevelt *(Democratic 1933)*	John Nance Garner *(Democratic 1933)*
	Henry A. Wallace *(Democratic 1941)*
	Harry S. Truman *(Democratic 1945)*
33 Harry S. Truman *(Democratic 1945)*	Alben W. Barkley *(Democratic 1949)*
34 Dwight D. Eisenhower *(Republican 1953)*	Richard M. Nixon *(Republican 1953)*
35 John F. Kennedy *(Democratic 1961)*	Lyndon B. Johnson *(Democratic 1961)*
36 Lyndon B. Johnson *(Democratic 1963)*	Hubert H. Humphrey *(Democratic 1965)*
37 Richard M. Nixon *(Republican 1969)*	Spiro T. Agnew *(Republican 1969)*
	Gerald R. Ford *(Republican 1973)*
38 Gerald R. Ford *(Republican 1974)*	Nelson Rockefeller *(Republican 1974)*
39 James E. Carter *(Democratic 1977)*	Walter Mondale *(Democratic 1977)*
40 Ronald Reagan *(Republican 1981)*	George H. W. Bush *(Republican 1981)*
41 George H. W. Bush *(Republican 1989)*	J. Danforth Quayle *(Republican 1989)*
42 William J. Clinton *(Democratic 1993)*	Albert Gore, Jr. *(Democratic 1993)*
43 George W. Bush *(Republican 2001)*	Richard Cheney *(Republican 2001)*
44 Barack H. Obama *(Democratic 2009)*	Joseph R. Biden, Jr. *(Democratic 2009)*
45 Donald J. Trump *(Republican 2017)*	Michael R. Pence *(Republican 2017)*

glossary

affirmative action government policies or programs that seek to redress past injustices against specified groups by making special efforts to provide members of these groups with access to educational and employment opportunities

agency representation a type of representation in which a representative is held accountable to a constituency if he or she fails to represent that constituency properly; this is incentive for the representative to provide good representation when his or her personal backgrounds, views, and interests differ from those of his or her constituency

agenda-setting the power of the media to bring public attention to particular issues and problems

agents of socialization social institutions, including families and schools, that help to shape individuals' basic political beliefs and values

amendment a change added to a bill, law, or constitution

amicus curiae literally, "friend of the court"; individuals or groups who are not parties to a lawsuit but who seek to assist the Supreme Court in reaching a decision by presenting additional briefs

Antifederalists those who favored strong state governments and a weak national government and were opponents of the constitution proposed at the American Constitutional Convention of 1787

appeasement the effort to forestall war by giving in to the demands of a hostile power

apportionment the process, occurring after every decennial census, that allocates congressional seats among the 50 states

appropriations the amounts of money approved by Congress in statutes (bills) that each unit or agency of government can spend

Articles of Confederation America's first written constitution; served as the basis for America's national government until 1789

attitude (or opinion) a specific preference on a particular issue bandwagon effect a shift in electoral support to the candidate whom public-opinion polls report as the front-runner

authoritarian government a system of rule in which the government recognizes no formal limit but may nevertheless be restrained by the power of other social institutions

ballot initiative a proposed law or policy change that is placed on the ballot by citizens or interest groups for a popular vote

bicameral having a legislative assembly composed of two chambers or houses; distinguished from *unicameral*

bilateral treaties treaties made between two nations

bill a proposed law that has been sponsored by a member of Congress and submitted to the clerk of the House or Senate

bill of attainder a law that declares a person guilty of a crime without a trial

Bill of Rights the first 10 amendments to the Constitution, ratified in 1791; they ensure certain rights and liberties of the people

block grants federal grants-in-aid that allow states considerable discretion in how the funds are spent

briefs written documents in which attorneys explain, using case precedents, why the court should find in favor of their client

Brown v. Board of Education the 1954 Supreme Court decision that struck down the "separate but equal" doctrine as fundamentally unequal; this case eliminated state power to use race as a criterion for discrimination in law and provided the national government with the power to intervene by exercising strict regulatory policies against discriminatory actions

bureaucracy the complex structure of offices, tasks, rules, and principles of organization that are employed by all large-scale institutions to coordinate effectively the work of their personnel

Bush Doctrine foreign policy based on the idea that the United States should take preemptive action against threats to its national security

Cabinet the secretaries, or chief administrators, of the major departments of the federal government; Cabinet secretaries are appointed by the president with the consent of the Senate

categorical grants congressional grants given to states and localities on the condition that expenditures be limited to a problem or group specified by law

caucus (political) a normally closed political party business meeting of citizens to select candidates, elect officers, plan strategy, or make decisions regarding legislative matters

checks and balances mechanisms through which each branch of government is able to participate in and influence the activities of the other branches; major examples include the presidential veto power over congressional legislation, the power of the Senate to approve presidential appointments, and judicial review of congressional enactments

chief justice justice on the Supreme Court who presides over the Court's public sessions and whose official title is chief justice of the United States

citizen groups groups that claim they serve the general good rather than only their own particular interest

citizen journalism news reported and distributed by citizens, rather than professional journalists and for-profit news organizations

citizenship informed and active membership in a political community

civil law the branch of law that deals with disputes that do not involve criminal penalties

civil liberties areas of personal freedom constitutionally protected from government interference

civil rights obligation imposed on government to take positive action to protect citizens from any illegal action of government agencies and of other private citizens

"clear and present danger" test test to determine whether speech is protected or unprotected, based on its capacity to present a "clear and present danger" to society

closed primary a primary election in which voters can participate in the nomination of candidates but only of the party in which they are enrolled for a period of time prior to primary day

cloture a rule or process in a legislative body aimed at ending debate on a given bill; in the U.S. Senate, 60 senators (three-fifths) must agree in order to impose a time limit and end debate

Cold War the period of struggle between the United States and the former Soviet Union lasting from the late 1940s to about 1990

collective goods benefits, sought by groups, that are broadly available and cannot be denied to nonmembers

commander in chief the role of the president as commander of the national military and the state National Guard units (when called into service)

commerce clause Article I, Section 8, of the Constitution, which delegates to Congress the power "to regulate Commerce with foreign Nations, and among the several States and with the Indian Tribes"; this clause was interpreted by the Supreme Court in favor of national power over the economy

concurrent powers authority possessed by both state and national governments, such as the power to levy taxes

confederation a system of government in which states retain sovereign authority except for the powers expressly delegated to the national government

conference a gathering of House Republicans every two years to elect their House leaders; Democrats call their gathering the *caucus*

conference committees joint committees created to work out a compromise on House and Senate versions of a piece of legislation

conservative today this term refers to those who generally support the social and economic status quo and are suspicious of efforts to introduce new political formulae and economic arrangements; conservatives believe that a large and powerful government poses a threat to citizens' freedom

constituency the residents in the area from which an official is elected

constitutional government a system of rule in which formal and effective limits are placed on the powers of the government

containment a policy designed to curtail the political and military expansion of a hostile power

contracting power the power of government to set conditions on companies seeking to sell goods or services to government agencies

contributory programs social programs financed in whole or in part by taxation or other mandatory contributions by their present or future recipients

cooperative federalism a type of federalism existing since the New Deal era in which grants-in-aid have been used strategically to encourage states and localities (without commanding them) to pursue nationally defined goals; also known as "intergovernmental cooperation"

cost-of-living adjustments (COLAs) changes made to the level of benefits of a government program based on the rate of inflation

court of appeals a court that hears the appeals of trial court decisions

criminal law the branch of law that regulates the conduct of individuals, defines crimes, and specifies punishment for acts defined as illegal

defendant the one against whom a complaint is brought in a criminal or civil case

delegated powers constitutional powers that are assigned to one governmental agency but that are exercised by another agency with the express permission of the first

democracy a system of rule that permits citizens to play a significant part in the governmental process, usually through the election of key public officials

department the largest subunit of the executive branch; the secretaries of the 15 departments form the Cabinet

deterrence the development and maintenance of military strength as a means of discouraging attack

devolution a policy to remove a program from one level of government by delegating it or passing it down to a lower level of government, such as from the national government to the state and local governments

digital citizen a daily Internet user with high-speed home Internet access and the technology and literacy skills to go online for employment, news, politics, entertainment, commerce, and other activities

diplomacy the representation of a government to foreign governments

direct democracy a system of rule that permits citizens to vote directly on laws and policies

dissenting opinion a decision written by a justice in the minority in a particular case in which the justice wishes to express his or her reasoning in the case

divided government the condition in American government wherein the presidency is controlled by one party while the opposing party controls one or both houses of Congress

double jeopardy the Fifth Amendment right providing that a person cannot be tried twice for the same crime

dual federalism the system of government that prevailed in the United States from 1789 to 1937 in which most fundamental governmental powers were shared between the federal and state governments

due process of law the right of every citizen against arbitrary action by national or state governments

elastic clause Article I, Section 8, of the Constitution (also known as the *necessary and proper clause*), which declares that Congress can write laws needed to carry out its expressed powers, providing Congress with the authority to make all laws "necessary and proper" to do so

electoral college the electors from each state who meet after the popular election to cast ballots for president and vice president

electoral realignment the point in history when a new party supplants the ruling party, becoming in turn the dominant political force; in the United States, this has tended to occur roughly every 30 years

eminent domain the right of government to take private property for public use

equal protection clause provision of the Fourteenth Amendment guaranteeing citizens "the equal protection of the laws"; this clause has served as the basis for the civil rights of African Americans, women, and other groups

equal time rule the requirement that broadcasters provide candidates for the same political office equal opportunities to communicate their messages to the public

equality of opportunity a widely shared American ideal that all people should have the freedom to use whatever talents and wealth they have to reach their fullest potential

establishment clause the First Amendment clause that says that "Congress shall make no law respecting an establishment of religion"; this law means that a "wall of separation" exists between church and state

ex post facto laws laws that declare an action to be illegal after it has been committed

exclusionary rule the ability of courts to exclude evidence obtained in violation of the Fourth Amendment

executive agreement an agreement, made between the president and another country, that has the force of a treaty but does not require the Senate's "advice and consent"

Executive Office of the President (EOP) the permanent agencies that perform defined management tasks for the president; created in 1939, the EOP includes the OMB, the CEA, the NSC, and other agencies

executive order a rule or regulation issued by the president that has the effect and formal status of legislation

expressed powers specific powers granted by the Constitution to Congress (Article I, Section 8) and to the president (Article II)

fairness doctrine a Federal Communications Commission (FCC) requirement for broadcasters who air programs on controversial issues to provide time for opposing views; the FCC ceased enforcing this doctrine in 1985

Federal Reserve System a system of 12 Federal Reserve banks that facilitates exchanges of cash, checks, and credit; regulates member banks; and uses monetary policies to fight inflation and deflation

federal system a system of government in which the national government shares power with lower levels of government such as states

federalism a system of government in which power is divided, by a constitution, between the central (national) government and regional (state) governments

Federalist Papers a series of essays written by James Madison, Alexander Hamilton, and John Jay supporting the ratification of the Constitution

Federalists those who favored a strong national government and supported the constitution proposed at the American Constitutional Convention of 1787

fighting words speech that directly incites damaging conduct

filibuster a tactic used by members of the Senate to prevent action on legislation they oppose by continuously holding the floor and speaking until the majority backs down; once given the floor, senators have unlimited time to speak, and it requires a vote of three-fifths of the Senate to end a filibuster

fiscal policy the government's use of taxing, monetary, and spending powers to manipulate the economy

501(c)(4)s politically active nonprofits; under federal law, these nonprofits can spend unlimited amounts on political campaigns and not disclose their donors as long as their activities are not coordinated with the candidate campaigns and political activities are not their primary purpose

527 committees nonprofit independent groups that receive and disburse funds to influence the nomination, election, or defeat of candidates; named after Section 527 of the Internal Revenue Code, which defines and provides tax-exempt status for nonprofit advocacy groups

framing the power of the media to influence how events and issues are interpreted

free exercise clause the First Amendment clause that protects a citizen's right to believe and practice whatever religion he or she chooses

free riders those who enjoy the benefits of collective goods but did not participate in acquiring them

full faith and credit clause provision from Article IV, Section 1, of the Constitution requiring that the states normally honor the public acts and judicial decisions that take place in another state

gender gap a distinctive pattern of voting behavior reflecting the differences in views between women and men

General Agreement on Tariffs and Trade (GATT) international trade organization, in existence from 1947 to 1995, that set many of the rules governing international trade

general election a regularly scheduled election involving most districts in the nation or state, in which voters decide who wins office; in the United States, general elections for national office and most state and local offices are held on the first Tuesday following the first Monday in November in even-numbered years (every four years for presidential elections)

general revenue sharing the process by which one unit of government yields a portion of its tax income to another unit of government, according to an established formula; revenue sharing typically involves the national government providing money to state governments

gerrymandering the apportionment of voters in districts in such a way as to give unfair advantage to one racial or ethnic group or political party

government institutions and procedures through which a territory and its people are ruled

government corporation government agency that performs a service normally provided by the private sector

grand jury jury that determines whether sufficient evidence is available to justify a trial; grand juries do not rule on the accused's guilt or innocence

grants-in-aid programs through which Congress provides money to state and local governments on the condition that the funds be employed for purposes defined by the federal government

grassroots mobilization a lobbying campaign in which a group mobilizes its membership to contact government officials in support of the group's position

Great Compromise the agreement reached at the Constitutional Convention of 1787 that gave each state an equal number of senators regardless of its population but linked representation in the House of Representatives to population

habeas corpus a court order demanding that an individual in custody be brought into court and shown the cause for detention

home rule power delegated by the state to a local unit of government to manage its own affairs

impeachment the formal charge by the House of Representatives that a government official has committed "Treason, Bribery, or other high Crimes and Misdemeanors"

implementation the efforts of departments and agencies to translate laws into specific bureaucratic rules and actions

implied powers powers derived from the necessary and proper clause of Article I, Section 8, of the Constitution; such powers are not specifically expressed but are implied through the expansive interpretation of delegated powers

in-kind benefits noncash goods and services provided to needy individuals and families by the federal government

incumbency holding the political office for which one is running

incumbent a candidate running for re-election to a position that he or she already holds

independent agency agency that is not part of a cabinet department

indexing periodic process of adjusting of social benefits or wages to account for increases in the cost of living

informational benefits special newsletters, periodicals, training programs, conferences, and other information provided to members of groups to entice others to join

inherent powers powers claimed by a president that are not expressed in the Constitution but are inferred from it

institutional advertising advertising designed to create a positive image of an organization

interest group individuals who organize to influence the government's programs and policies

International Monetary Fund (IMF) an institution established in 1944 that provides loans and facilitates international monetary exchange

iron triangle the stable, cooperative relationships that often develop among a congressional committee, an administrative agency, and one or more supportive interest groups; not all of these relationships are triangular, but the iron triangle is the most typical

isolationism avoidance of involvement in the affairs of other nations

joint committees legislative committees formed of members of both the House and Senate

judicial activism judicial philosophy that posits that the Court should go beyond the words of the Constitution or a statute to consider the broader societal implications of its decisions

judicial restraint judicial philosophy whose adherents refuse to go beyond the clear words of the Constitution in interpreting the document's meaning

judicial review the power of the courts to review and, if necessary, declare actions of the legislative and executive branches invalid or unconstitutional; the Supreme Court asserted this power in *Marbury v. Madison* (1803)

jurisdiction the sphere of a court's power and authority

Kitchen Cabinet an informal group of advisers to whom the president turns for counsel and guidance; members of the official Cabinet may or may not also be members of the Kitchen Cabinet

laissez-faire capitalism an economic system in which the means of production and distribution are privately owned and operated for profit with minimal or no government interference

legislative initiative the president's implied power to bring a legislative agenda before Congress

libel a written statement made in "reckless disregard of the truth" that is considered damaging to a victim because it is "malicious, scandalous, and defamatory"

liberal today this term refers to those who generally support social and political reform, governmental intervention in the economy, more economic equality, the expansion of federal social services, and greater concern for consumers and the environment

libertarian someone who emphasizes freedom and believes in voluntary association with small government

liberty freedom from governmental control

limited government a principle of constitutional government; a government whose powers are defined and limited by a constitution

lobbying a strategy by which organized interests seek to influence the passage of legislation or other public policy by exerting direct pressure on members of the legislature

logrolling a legislative practice whereby agreements are made between legislators in voting for or against a bill; vote trading

majority leader the elected leader of the majority party in the House of Representatives or in the Senate; in the House, the majority leader is subordinate in the party hierarchy to the Speaker of the House

majority party the party that holds the majority of legislative seats in either the House or the Senate

majority rule/minority rights the democratic principle that a government follows the preferences of the majority of voters but protects the interests of the minority

marketplace of ideas the public forum in which beliefs and ideas are exchanged and compete

material benefits special goods, services, or money provided to members of groups to entice others to join

means testing a procedure by which potential beneficiaries of a public-assistance program establish their eligibility by demonstrating a genuine need for the assistance

media print and digital forms of communication, including television, newspapers, radio, and the Internet, intended to convey information to large audiences

Medicaid a federally and state-financed, state-operated program providing medical services to low-income people

Medicare a form of national health insurance for the elderly and the disabled

membership association an organized group in which members actually play a substantial role, sitting on committees and engaging in group projects

merit system a product of civil service reform, in which appointees to positions in public bureaucracies must objectively be deemed qualified for those positions

minority leader the elected leader of the minority party in the House or Senate

minority party the party that holds the minority of legislative seats in either the House or the Senate

Miranda rule the requirement, articulated by the Supreme Court in *Miranda v. Arizona* (1966), that persons under arrest must be informed prior to police interrogation of their rights to remain silent and to have the benefit of legal counsel

mobilization the process by which large numbers of people are organized for a political activity

monetary policies efforts to regulate the economy through the manipulation of the supply of money and credit; America's most powerful institution in this area of monetary policy is the Federal Reserve Board

nation-states political entities consisting of people with some common cultural experience (nation) who also share a common political authority (state), recognized by other sovereignties (nation-states)

necessary and proper clause provision from Article I, Section 8, of the Constitution providing Congress with the authority to make all laws necessary and proper to carry out its expressed powers

netroots grassroots online activist organizations that have redefined membership and fund-raising practices and streamlined staff structure

New Federalism attempts by presidents Nixon and Reagan to return power to the states through block grants

New Jersey Plan a framework for the Constitution, introduced by William Paterson, that called for equal state representation in the national legislature regardless of population separation of powers the division of governmental power among several institutions that must cooperate in decision making

New Politics movement a political movement that began in the 1960s and '70s, made up of professionals and intellectuals for whom the civil rights and antiwar movements were formative experiences; the New Politics movement strengthened public interest groups

niche journalism news reporting devoted to a targeted portion (subset) of a journalism market sector or for a portion of readers or viewers based on content or ideological presentation

nomination the process by which political parties select their candidates for election to public office

noncontributory programs social programs that provide assistance to people based on demonstrated need rather than any contribution they have made

non-state actors groups other than nation-states that attempt to play a role in the international system; terrorist groups are one type of non-state actor

North American Free Trade Agreement (NAFTA) trade treaty among the United States, Canada, and Mexico to lower and eliminate tariffs among the three countries

North Atlantic Treaty Organization (NATO) an organization, comprising the United States, Canada, and most of Western Europe, formed in 1949 to counter the perceived threat from the Soviet Union

open primary a primary election in which the voter can wait until the day of the primary to choose which party to enroll in to select candidates for the general election

opinion the written explanation of the Supreme Court's decision in a particular case

oral argument the stage in Supreme Court procedure in which attorneys for both sides appear before the Court to present their positions and answer questions posed by justices

original jurisdiction the authority to initially consider a case; distinguished from *appellate jurisdiction*, which is the authority to hear appeals from a lower court's decision

oversight the effort by Congress, through hearings, investigations, and other techniques, to exercise control over the activities of executive agencies

party identification an individual voter's psychological ties to one party or another

party unity vote a roll-call vote in the House or Senate in which at least 50 percent of the members of one party take a particular position and are opposed by at least 50 percent of the members of the other party

patronage the resources available to higher officials, usually opportunities to make partisan appointments to offices and to confer grants, licenses, or special favors to supporters

plaintiff the individual or organization that brings a complaint in court plea bargain a negotiated agreement in a criminal case in a which a defendant agrees to plead guilty in return for the state's agreement to reduce the severity of the criminal charge the defendant is facing

pluralism the theory that all interests are and should be free to compete for influence in the government; the outcome of this competition is compromise and moderation

pocket veto a presidential veto that is automatically triggered if the president does not act on a given piece of legislation passed during the final 10 days of a legislative session

police power power reserved to the state government to regulate the health, safety, and morals of its citizens

political action committee (PAC) a private group that raises and distributes funds for use in election campaigns

political efficacy the ability to influence government and politics

political equality the right to participate in politics equally, based on the principle of "one person, one vote"

political ideology a cohesive set of beliefs that forms a general philosophy about the role of government

political parties organized groups that attempt to influence the government by electing their members to important government offices

political socialization the induction of individuals into the political culture; learning the underlying beliefs and values on which the political system is based

politics conflict over the leadership, structure, and policies of governments

popular sovereignty a principle of democracy in which political authority rests ultimately in the hands of the people

pork-barrel legislation (or pork) appropriations made by legislative bodies for local projects that are often not needed but that are created so that local representatives can win re-election in their home districts

power influence over a government's leadership, organization, or policies

precedent prior case whose principles are used by judges as the basis for their decisions in present cases

preemption the principle that allows the national government to override state or local actions in certain policy areas; in foreign policy, the willingness to strike first in order to prevent an enemy attack

preventive war policy of striking first when a nation fears that a foreign foe is contemplating hostile action

primary elections elections within a political party to select the party's candidate for the general election

priming process of preparing the public to take a particular view of an event or political actor

prior restraint an effort by a governmental agency to block the publication of material it deems libelous or harmful in some other way; censorship; in the United States, the courts forbid prior restraint except under the most extraordinary circumstances

private bill a proposal in Congress to provide a specific person with some kind of relief, such as a special exemption from immigration quotas

privatization the transfer of all or part of a program from the public sector to the private sector

privileges and immunities clause provision, from Article IV, Section 2, of the Constitution, that a state cannot discriminate against someone from another state or give its own residents special privileges

proportional representation a multiple-member district system that allows each political party representation in proportion to its percentage of the total vote

public opinion citizens' attitudes about political issues, leaders, institutions, and events

public-opinion polls scientific instruments for measuring public opinion

public policy a law, a rule, a statute, or an edict that expresses the government's goals and provides for rewards and punishments to promote those goals' attainment

purposive benefits selective benefits of group membership that emphasize the purpose and accomplishments of the group

push polling a polling technique in which the questions are designed to shape the respondent's opinion

random digit dialing a polling method in which respondents are selected at random from a list of 10-digit telephone numbers, with every effort made to avoid bias in the construction of the sample

recall a procedure to allow voters to remove state officials from office before their terms expire by circulating petitions to call a vote

redistribution collecting revenue in such a way as to reduce the disparities of wealth between the lowest and the highest income brackets

redistricting the process of redrawing election districts and redistributing legislative representatives; this happens every 10 years to reflect shifts in population or in response to legal challenges to existing districts

referendum the practice of referring a measure proposed or passed by a legislature to the vote of the electorate for approval or rejection

regulatory agency a department, bureau, or independent agency whose primary mission is to impose limits, restrictions, or other obligations on the conduct of individuals or companies in the private sector

representative democracy (republic) a system of government in which the populace selects representatives, who play a significant role in governmental decision making

reserved powers powers, derived from the Tenth Amendment to the Constitution, that are not specifically delegated to the national government or denied to the states

revenue agency an agency responsible for collecting taxes; examples include the Internal Revenue Service for income taxes, the U.S. Customs Service for tariffs and other taxes on imported goods, and the Bureau of Alcohol, Tobacco, Firearms and Explosives for collection of taxes on the sales of those particular products

right of rebuttal a Federal Communications Commission regulation giving individuals the right to have the opportunity to respond to personal attacks made on a radio or television broadcast

roll-call vote a vote in which each legislator's yes-or-no vote is recorded as the clerk calls the names of the members alphabetically

sample a small group selected by researchers to represent the most important characteristics of an entire population

sampling error (or margin of error) polling error that arises based on the small size of the sample

select committees (usually) temporary legislative committees set up to highlight or investigate a particular issue or address an issue not within the jurisdiction of existing committees

selection bias (news) the tendency to focus news coverage on only one aspect of an event or issue, avoiding coverage of other aspects

selection bias (surveys) polling error that arises when the sample is not representative of the population being studied, which creates errors in overrepresenting or underrepresenting some opinions

selective incorporation the process by which different protections in the Bill of Rights were incorporated into the Fourteenth Amendment, thus guaranteeing citizens protection from state as well as national governments

senatorial courtesy the practice whereby the president, before formally nominating a person for a federal judgeship, seeks the indication that senators from the candidate's own state support the nomination

seniority the ranking given to an individual on the basis of length of continuous service on a committee in Congress

"separate but equal" rule doctrine that public accommodations could be segregated by race but still be considered equal

signing statements announcements made by the president when signing bills into law, often presenting the president's interpretation of the law

simple random sample (or probability sample) a method used by pollsters to select a representative sample in which every individual in the population has an equal probability of being selected as a respondent

slander an oral statement made in "reckless disregard of the truth" that is considered damaging to the victim because it is "malicious, scandalous, and defamatory"

social desirability effect the effect that results when respondents in a survey report what they expect the interviewer wishes to hear rather than what they believe

social media web-based and mobile-based technologies that are used to turn communication into interactive dialogue between organizations, communities, and individuals; social media technologies take on many different forms including blogs, Wikis, podcasts, pictures, video, Facebook, and Twitter

Social Security a contributory welfare program into which working Americans contribute a percentage of their wages and from which they receive cash benefits after retirement or if they become disabled

socialist someone who generally believes in social ownership, strong government, free markets, and reducing economic inequality

socioeconomic status status in society based on level of education, income, and occupational prestige

sociological representation a type of representation in which representatives have the same racial, gender, ethnic, religious, or educational backgrounds as their constituents; it is based on the principle that if two individuals are similar in background, character, interests, and perspectives, then one can correctly represent the other's views

solicitor general the top government lawyer in all cases before the Supreme Court in which the government is a party

solidary benefits selective benefits of group membership that emphasize friendship, networking, and consciousness-raising

Speaker of the House the chief presiding officer of the House of Representatives; the Speaker is the most important party and House leader and can influence the legislative agenda, the fate of individual pieces of legislation, and members' positions within the House

staff organization type of membership group in which a professional staff conducts most of the group's activities

standing committee a permanent committee with the power to propose and write legislation that covers a particular subject, such as finance or agriculture

stare decisis literally, "let the decision stand"; the doctrine that a previous decision by a court applies as a precedent in similar cases until that decision is overruled

states' rights the principle that the states should oppose the increasing authority of the national government; this principle was most popular in the period before the Civil War

strict scrutiny a test used by the Supreme Court in racial discrimination cases and other cases involving civil liberties and civil rights that places the burden of proof on the government rather than on the challengers to show that the law in question is constitutional

subsidies government grants of cash or other valuable commodities, such as land, to individuals or an organization; used to promote activities desired by the government, to reward political support, or to buy off political opposition

suffrage the right to vote; also called *franchise*

Supplemental Nutrition Assistance Program (SNAP) the largest antipoverty program, which provides recipients with a debit card for food at most grocery stores; formerly known as *food stamps*

supremacy clause Article VI of the Constitution, which states that laws passed by the national government and all treaties "shall be the supreme law of the land" and superior to all laws adopted by any state or any subdivision

supreme court the highest court in a particular state or in the United States; this court primarily serves an appellate function

tax expenditures government subsidies provided to employers and employees through tax deductions for amounts spent on health insurance and other benefits

term limits legally prescribed limits on the number of terms an elected official can serve

third parties parties that organize to compete against the two major American political parties

Three-Fifths Compromise the agreement reached at the Constitutional Convention of 1787 that stipulated that for purposes of the apportionment of congressional seats only three-fifths of slaves would be counted

totalitarian government a system of rule in which the government recognizes no formal limits on its power and seeks to absorb or eliminate other social institutions that might challenge it

trial court the first court to hear a criminal or civil case

turnout the percentage of eligible individuals who actually vote

two-party system a political system in which only two parties have a realistic opportunity to compete effectively for control of the government

tyranny oppressive and unjust government that employs cruel and unjust use of power and authority

unfunded mandates regulations or conditions for receiving grants that impose costs on state and local governments for which they are not reimbursed by the federal government

unitary system a centralized government system in which lower levels of government have little power independent of the national government

United Nations (UN) an organization of nations founded in 1945 to be a channel for negotiation and a means of settling international disputes peaceably; the UN has had frequent successes in providing a forum for negotiation and on some occasions a means of preventing international conflicts from spreading; on a number of occasions, the UN has supported U.S. foreign policy goals

values (or beliefs) basic principles that shape a person's opinions about political issues and events

veto the president's constitutional power to prevent a bill from becoming a law; a presidential veto may be overridden by a two-thirds vote of each house of Congress

Virginia Plan a framework for the Constitution, introduced by Edmund Randolph, that called for representation in the national legislature based on the population of each state

War Powers Resolution a resolution of Congress that the president can send troops into action abroad only by authorization of Congress or if American troops are already under attack or serious threat

whip a party member in the House or Senate responsible for coordinating the party's legislative strategy, building support for key issues, and counting votes

White House staff analysts and advisers to the president, each of whom is often given the title "special assistant"

World Trade Organization (WTO) international organization promoting free trade that grew out of the General Agreement on Tariffs and Trade

writ of certiorari a decision of at least four of the nine Supreme Court justices to review a decision of a lower court; *certiorari* is Latin, meaning "to make more certain"

writ of habeas corpus a court order that the individual in custody be brought into court and shown the cause for detention; habeas corpus is guaranteed by the Constitution and can be suspended only in cases of rebellion or invasion

endnotes

Chapter 1

1. The Pew Research Center, "Beyond Distrust: How Americans View Their Government," November 23, 2015, www.people-press.org/2015/11/23/beyond-distrust-how-americans -view-their-government/ (accessed 4/10/16).
2. Pew Research Center, "Beyond Distrust."
3. Pew Research Center, "Trust in Government Nears Record Low."
4. Joseph S. Nye, Jr., "Introduction: The Decline of Confidence in Government," in *Why People Don't Trust Government*, ed. Joseph S. Nye, Philip D. Zelikow, and David C. King (Cambridge, MA: Harvard University Press, 1999), 4.
5. Pew Research Center, "Beyond Distrust."
6. Pew Research Center, "Beyond Distrust."
7. John B. Horrigon and Lee Rainie, "Americans' Views on Open Government Data," Pew Research Center, April 21, 2015, www.pewinternet.org/2015/04/21/open-government -data/ (accessed 7/22/15).
8. Arch Puddington and Tyler Roylance, *Freedom in the World*, 2016, Essay: Democratic Breakthroughs in the Balance," Freedom House, www.freedomhouse.org/sites/default /files/FH_FITW_Report_2016.pdf (accessed 4/10/16).
9. Eugen Weber, *Peasants into Frenchmen: The Modernization of Rural France, 1870–1914* (Stanford, CA: Stanford University Press, 1976), chap. 5.
10. V. O. Key, *Politics, Parties, and Pressure Groups* (New York: Crowell, 1964), 201.
11. Harold Lasswell, *Politics: Who Gets What, When, How* (New York: Meridian Books, 1958).
12. Susan B. Carter, et al., eds., *Historical Statistics of the United States: Millennial Edition Online*, (New York: Cambridge University Press, 2006), Table Aa145–184, Population, by Sex and Race: 1790–1990, 23. Current data available at U.S. Census Bureau, www .census.gov (accessed 2/25/12).
13. Carter et al., *Historical Statistics of the United States*, Table Aa145–184, Population, by Sex and Race: 1790–1990, 23.
14. Carter et al., *Historical Statistics of the United States*, Table Aa145–184, Population, by Sex and Race: 1790–1990, 23; Table Aa2189–2215, Hispanic Population Estimates.
15. U.S. Census Bureau, "Statistical Abstract of the United States," www.census.gov (accessed 11/13/07); Claude S. Fischer and Michael Hout, *A Century of Difference: How America Changed in the Last One Hundred Years* (New York: Russell Sage Foundation, 2006), 36.
16. Carter et al., *Historical Statistics of the United States*, Table Aa22–35, Selected Population Characteristics.
17. Michael B. Katz and Mark J. Stern, *One Nation Divisible: What America Was and What It Is Becoming* (New York: Russell Sage Foundation, 2006), 16.
18. Carter et al., *Historical Statistics of the United States*, Table Aa145–184, Population, by Sex and Race: 1790–1990, 23; Karen R. Humes, Nicholas A. Jones, and Roberto R. Ramirez, "Overview of Race and Hispanic Origin: 2010. 2010 Census Briefs," no.

C210BR-02 (Washington, DC: U.S. Census Bureau, March 2011), 4, www.census.gov /prod/cen2010/briefs/c2010br-02.pdf (accessed 10/14/2011).

19. U.S. Census, "Annual Estimates of the Resident Population by Sex, Age, Race, and Hispanic Origin for the United States and States: April 1, 2010 to July 1, 2014," www .census.gov/quickfacts/table.PST045215/00#headnote-js-a (accessed 4/11/16).

20. U.S. Census Bureau, " "2014 American Community Survey 1-Year Estimates," www .census.gov/popest/data/counties/asrh/2014/PEPSR6H.html (accessed 4/11/16).

21. Michael Hoefer, Nancy Rytina, and Bryan Barker, "Estimates of the Unauthorized Immigrant Population Residing in the United States: January 2011, *Population Estimates*, Office of Immigration Statistics, Department of Homeland Security, March 2012, www.dhs.gov/sites/default/files/publications/ois_ill_pe_2011.pdf (accessed 9/25/13).

22. Pew Research Center, "2014 Religious Landscape Study," www.pewforum.org/religious -landscape-study/#religions (accessed 4/11/16).

23. Pew Research Center, "2014 Religious Landscape Study (accessed 4/11/16).

24. U.S. Census Bureau, "Demographic Trends in the 20th Century, Table 5: Population by Age and Sex for the United States: 1900 to 2000," www.census.gov/prod/2002pubs /censr-4.pdf; U.S. Census Bureau, "Annual Estimates of the Resident Population for Selected Age Groups by Sex for the United States, States, Counties, and Puerto Rico Commonwealth and Municipios: April 1, 2010 to July 1, 2014," www.census.gov /quickfacts/table/PST045215/00 (accessed 4/11/16).

25. U.S. Census Bureau, "Growth in Urban Population Outpaces Rest of Nation, Census Bureau Reports," March 26, 2012, www.census.gov/newsroom/releases/archives/2010 _census/cb12-50.html (accessed 9/25/13).

26. Thomas Piketty and Emmanuel Saez, "Income Inequality in the United States, 1913–1998," *Quarterly Journal of Economics* 18 no. 1 (2003), 1–39 (tables and figures updated to 2014, June 2015), elsa.berkeley.edu/~saez/TabFig2014prel.xls (accessed 4/11/16).

27. U.S. Census Bureau, "Income: Historical Income Data, Tables F-2, F-3, and F-6." www .census.gov/hhes/www/income/data/historical/index.html (accessed 4/12/16).

28. U.S. Census Bureau, "Historical Poverty Tables, Table 2: Poverty Status of People by Family Relationship, Race, and Hispanic Origin: 1959 to 2014," www.census.gov/hhes /www/poverty/data/historical/hstpov2.xls (accessed 4/11/16).

29. U.S. Census Bureau, "Table 1. Apportionment Population and Number of Representa- tives, by State: 2010 Census," www.census.gov/population/apportionment/files /Apportionment%20Population%202010.pdf (accessed 9/25/13).

30. Herbert McClosky and John Zaller, *The American Ethos: Public Attitudes toward Capitalism and Democracy* (Cambridge, MA: Harvard University Press, 1984), 19.

31. J. R. Pole, *The Pursuit of Equality in American History* (Berkeley: University of California Press, 1978), 19.

Chapter 2

1. Executive Office of the President of the United States, "Impacts and Costs of the October 2013 Federal Government Shutdown," November 2013, www.whitehouse .gov/sites/default/files/omb/reports/impacts-and-costs-of-october-2013-federal -government-shutdown-report.pdf (accessed 6/13/16).

2. The social makeup of colonial America and some of the social conflicts that divided colonial society are discussed in Jackson Turner Main, *The Social Structure of Revolution- ary America* (Princeton, NJ: Princeton University Press, 1965).

3. George B. Tindall and David E. Shi, *America: A Narrative History*, 8th ed. (New York: W. W. Norton, 2010), 202.

4. For a discussion of events leading up to the Revolution, see Charles M. Andrews, *The Colonial Background of the American Revolution* (New Haven, CT: Yale University Press, 1924).
5. See Carl Becker, *The Declaration of Independence* (New York: Knopf, 1942).
6. See Merrill Jensen, *The Articles of Confederation* (Madison: University of Wisconsin Press, 1970).
7. Reported in Samuel E. Morrison, Henry Steele Commager, and William Leuchtenberg, *The Growth of the American Republic*, vol. 1 (New York: Oxford University Press, 1969), 244.
8. Quoted in Morrison, Commager, and Leuchtenberg, *Growth of the American Republic*, 242.
9. Charles A. Beard, *An Economic Interpretation of the Constitution of the United States* (New York: Macmillan, 1913).
10. Max Farrand, ed., *The Records of the Federal Convention of 1787*, 4 vols., rev. ed., vol. 1 (New Haven, CT: Yale University Press, 1966).
11. Farrand, *Records of the Federal Convention of 1787*, 476.
12. Alexander Hamilton, James Madison, and John Jay, *The Federalist Papers*, ed. Clinton L. Rossiter (New York: New American Library, 1961), no. 71.
13. *The Federalist Papers*, no. 62.
14. *Marbury v. Madison*, 5 U.S. 137 (1803).
15. Max Farrand, *The Framing of the Constitution of the United States* (New Haven, CT: Yale University Press, 1962), 49.
16. Melancton Smith, quoted in Herbert J. Storing, *What the Anti-Federalists Were For* (Chicago: University of Chicago, 1981), 17.
17. *The Federalist Papers*, no. 57.
18. "Essays of Brutus," no. 15, in *The Complete Anti-Federalist*, ed. Herbert Storing (Chicago: University of Chicago Press, 1981).
19. *The Federalist Papers*, no. 10.
20. *The Federalist Papers*, no. 51.

Chapter 3

1. Brady Dennis, "Obama Administration Will Not Block State Marijuana Laws If Distribution Is Regulated," *Washington Post*, August 29, 2013, http://articles.washingtonpost.com/2013-08-29/national/41566270_1_marijuana-legalization-attorney-general-bob-ferguson-obama-administration (accessed 11/17/13).
2. ProCon.org, "35 States with Legal Gay Marriage and 15 States with Same-Sex Marriage Bans," updated November 20, 2014, http://gaymarriage.procon.org/view.resource.php?resourceID=004857 (accessed 5/11/16).
3. *United States v. Windsor*, 570 U.S. __ (2013).
4. *Obergefell v. Hodges*, 576 U.S. __ (2015); Eliott C. McLaughlin, "Most states to abide by Supreme Court's same-sex marriage ruling, but . . ." CNN, June 30, 2015, www.cnn.com/2015/06/29/us/same-sex-marriage-state-by-state/ (accessed 8/16/15).
5. *Hicklin v. Orbeck*, 437 U.S. 518 (1978).
6. *Sweeny v. Woodall*, 344 U.S. 86 (1952).
7. A good discussion of the constitutional position of local governments is in York Willbern, *The Withering Away of the City* (Bloomington: Indiana University Press, 1971). For more on the structure and theory of federalism, see Thomas R. Dye, *American Federalism: Competition among Governments* (Lexington, MA: Lexington Books, 1990), chap. 1, and Martha Derthick, "Up-to-Date in Kansas City: Reflections on American Federalism," 1992 John Gaus Lecture, *PS: Political Science and Politics* 25 (December 1992): 671–5.
8. For a good treatment of the contrast between national political stability and social instability, see Samuel P. Huntington, *Political Order in Changing Societies* (New Haven, CT: Yale University Press, 1968), chap. 2.

9. *McCulloch v. Maryland*, 4 Wheaton 316 (1819).

10. *Gibbons v. Ogden*, 9 Wheaton 1 (1824).

11. The Sherman Antitrust Act, adopted in 1890, for example, was enacted not to restrict commerce but rather to protect it from monopolies, or trusts, so as to prevent unfair trade practices and to enable the market again to become self-regulating. Moreover, the Supreme Court sought to uphold liberty of contract to protect businesses. For example, in *Lochner v. New York*, 198 U.S. 45 (1905), the Court invalidated a New York law regulating the sanitary conditions in bakeries and the hours of labor for bakers on the grounds that the law interfered with liberty of contract.

12. Kenneth T. Palmer, "The Evolution of Grant Policies," in *The Changing Politics of Federal Grants*, ed. Lawrence D. Brown, James W. Fossett, and Kenneth T. Palmer (Washington, DC: Brookings Institution Press, 1984), 15.

13. Palmer, "The Evolution of Grant Policies," 6.

14. The key case in this process of expanding the power of the national government is generally considered to be *NLRB v. Jones & Laughlin Steel Corporation*, 301 U.S. 1 (1937), in which the Supreme Court approved federal regulation of the workplace and thereby virtually eliminated interstate commerce as a limit on the national government's power.

15. *United States v. Darby Lumber Co.*, 312 U.S. 100 (1941).

16. W. John Moore, "Pleading the 10th," *National Journal*, July 29, 1996, 1940.

17. *United States v. Lopez*, 514 U.S. 549 (1995).

18. *Printz v. United States*, 521 U.S. 898 (1997).

19. Morton Grodzins, *The American System*, ed. Daniel J. Elazar (Chicago: Rand McNally, 1966).

20. See Terry Sanford, *Storm over the States* (New York: McGraw-Hill, 1967).

21. James L. Sundquist, *Making Federalism Work*, with David W. Davis (Washington, DC: Brookings Institution Press, 1969), 271. Wallace was mistrusted by the architects of the War on Poverty because he was a strong proponent of racial segregation. He believed in "states' rights," which meant that states, not the federal government, should decide what liberty and equality meant.

22. See Don Kettl, *The Regulation of American Federalism* (Baton Rouge: Louisiana State University Press, 1983).

23. Eliza Newlin Carney, "Power Grab," *National Journal*, April 11, 1998, 798.

24. Philip Rucker, "Obama Curtails Bush's Policy of 'Preemption,'" *Washington Post*, May 22, 2009, A3.

25. See Advisory Commission on Intergovernmental Relations, *Federal Regulation of State and Local Governments: The Mixed Record of the 1980s* (Washington, DC: Advisory Commission on Intergovernmental Relations, July 1993).

26. Robert Jay Dilger and Richard S. Beth, "Unfunded Mandates Reform Act: History, Impact, and Issues" (Washington, DC: Congressional Research Service, April 19, 2011), 40, http://digital.library.unt.edu/ark:/67531/metadc40084/m1/1/high_res_d/R40957 _2011Apr19.pdf (accessed 11/16/13).

27. Advisory Commission on Intergovernmental Relations, *Federal Regulation of State and Local Governments*, iii.

28. Advisory Commission on Intergovernmental Relations, *Federal Regulation of State and Local Governments*, 51.

29. Robert Frank, "Proposed Block Grants Seem Unlikely to Cure Management Problems," *Wall Street Journal*, May 1, 1995, 1.

30. Sarah Kershaw, "U.S. Rule Limits Emergency Care for Immigrants," *New York Times*, September 22, 2007, A1.

31. National Conference of State Legislatures, "2013 Report on State Immigration Laws," www.ncsl.org/research/immigration/immgration-report-august-2013.aspx (accessed 11/3/13).

32. Terry Frieden, "Justice Department Sues Utah over State Immigration Law," CNN, November 22, 2011, www.cnn.com/2011/11/22/us/utah-immigration-law/ (accessed 4/21/16).

33. *Arizona v. United States*, 567 U.S. __ (2012).

34. *United States v. Texas*, 579 U.S. __ (2016).

35. Kate Linthicum, "Obama Ends Secure Communities Program as Part of Immigration Action," *Los Angeles Times* November 21, 2014, www.latimes.com/local/california /la-me-1121-immigration-justice-20141121-story.html (accessed 8/16/15).

36. White House, Office of the Press Secretary, Memorandum for the Heads of Executive Departments and Agencies, Subject: Preemption, May 20, 2009, www.whitehouse.gov /the-press-office/presidential-memorandum-regarding-preemption (accessed 10/17/09).

37. *National Federation of Independent Businesses v. Sebelius*, 567 U.S. __ (2012). Adam Liptak, "In Health Law, Asking Where U.S. Power Stops," *New York Times*, November 14, 2011, A1.

38. *King v. Burwell*, 576 U.S. __ (2015). Robert Barnes, "Affordable Care Act Survives Supreme Court Challenge," *Washington Post*, June 25, 2015, www.washingtonpost .com/politics/courts_law/obamacare-survives-supreme-court-challenge/2015/06/25 /af87608e-188a-11e5-93b7-5eddc056ad8a_story.html (accessed 8/16/15).

Chapter 4

1. Alexander Hamilton, James Madison, and John Jay, *The Federalist Papers*, ed. Clinton Rossiter (New York: New American Library, 1961), no. 84, 513.

2. *The Federalist Papers*, no. 84, 513.

3. Let there be no confusion about the words *liberty* and *freedom*. They are synonymous and interchangeable. *Freedom* comes from the German *Freiheit*. *Liberty* is from the French *liberté*. Although people sometimes try to make them appear to be different, both of them have equal concern with the absence of restraints on individual choices of action.

4. *Barron v. Baltimore*, 7 Peters 243, 246 (1833).

5. The Fourteenth Amendment also seems designed to introduce civil rights. The final clause of the all-important Section 1 provides that no state can "deny to any person within its jurisdiction the equal protection of the laws." It is reasonable to conclude that the purpose of this provision was to obligate the state governments as well as the national government to take *positive* actions to protect citizens from arbitrary and discriminatory actions, at least those based on race.

6. For example, *The Slaughterhouse Cases*, 16 Wallace 36 (1873).

7. *Chicago, Burlington and Quincy Railroad Company v. Chicago*, 166 U.S. 226 (1897).

8. *Gitlow v. New York*, 268 U.S. 652 (1925).

9. *Near v. Minnesota*, 283 U.S. 697 (1931); *Hague v. C.I.O.*, 307 U.S. 496 (1939).

10. *McDonald v. Chicago*, 561 U.S. 3025 (2010).

11. *Palko v. Connecticut*, 302 U.S. 319 (1937).

12. *Abington School District v. Schempp*, 374 U.S. 203 (1963).

13. *Engel v. Vitale*, 370 U.S. 421 (1962).

14. *Doe v. Santa Fe Independent School District*, 530 U.S. 290 (2000).

15. *Wallace v. Jaffree*, 472 U.S. 38 (1985).

16. *Lynch v. Donnelly*, 465 U.S. 668 (1984).

17. *Van Orden v. Perry*, 545 U.S. 677 (2005).

18. *McCreary v. ACLU of Kentucky*, 545 U.S. 844 (2005).

19. *West Virginia State Board of Education v. Barnette*, 319 U.S. 624 (1943). The case it reversed was *Minersville School District v. Gobitus*, 310 U.S. 586 (1940).

20. *Holt v. Hobbs*, 574 U.S. __ (2015); *Equal Employment Opportunity Commission v. Abercrombie and Fitch Stores, Inc.*, 575 U.S. __ (2015).

21. *Abrams v. United States,* 250 U.S. 616 (1919).
22. *United States v. Carolene Products Company,* 304 U.S. 144 (1938), 4n. This footnote is one of the Court's most important doctrines. See Alfred H. Kelly, Winfred A. Harbison, and Herman Belz, *The American Constitution: Its Origins and Development,* 7th ed. (New York: W. W. Norton, 1991), 2:519–23.
23. *Schenk v. United States,* 249 U.S. 47 (1919).
24. *Hague v. Committee for Industrial Organization,* 307 U.S. 496 (1939).
25. *Stromberg v. California,* 283 U.S. 359 (1931).
26. *Texas v. Johnson,* 488 U.S. 884 (1989).
27. *Snyder v. Phelps,* 562 U.S. __ (2011).
28. For a good general discussion of "speech plus," see Louis Fisher, *American Constitutional Law* (New York: McGraw-Hill, 1990), 544–6. The case upholding the buffer zone against the abortion protesters is *Madsen v. Women's Health Center,* 512 U.S. 753 (1994).
29. *Bethel School District v. Fraser,* 478 U.S. 675 (1986).
30. *Hazelwood v. Kuhlmeier,* 484 U.S. 260 (1988).
31. *Morse v. Frederick,* 551 U.S. 393 (2007).
32. *Near v. Minnesota,* 283 U.S. 697 (1931).
33. *New York Times v. United States,* 403 U.S. 731 (1971).
34. *Branzburg v. Hayes,* 408 U.S. 656 (1972).
35. *New York Times v. Sullivan,* 376 U.S. 254 (1964).
36. See *Zeran v. America Online,* 129 F.3d 327 (4th Cir. 1997).
37. *Roth v. United States,* 354 U.S. 476 (1957).
38. Concurring opinion in *Jacobellis v. Ohio,* 378 U.S. 184 (1964).
39. *Miller v. California,* 413 U.S. 15 (1973).
40. *Reno v. American Civil Liberties Union,* 521 U.S. 844 (1997).
41. *United States v. Williams,* 553 U.S. 285 (2008).
42. *United States v. Playboy Entertainment Group,* 529 U.S. 803 (2000).
43. *Brown v. Entertainment Merchants Association,* 564 U.S. __ (2011).
44. *Chaplinsky v. State of New Hampshire,* 315 U.S. 568 (1942).
45. *Dennis v. United States,* 341 U.S. 494 (1951).
46. *Broadcasting Company v. Acting Attorney General,* 405 U.S. 1000 (1972).
47. *City Council v. Taxpayers for Vincent,* 466 U.S. 789 (1984).
48. *44 Liquormart, Inc. and Peoples Super Liquor Stores Inc., Petitioners v. Rhode Island and Rhode Island Liquor Stores Association,* 517 U.S. 484 (1996).
49. *Lorillard Tobacco v. Reilly,* 533 U.S. 525 (2001).
50. *United States v. Miller,* 307 U.S. 174 (1939).
51. *District of Columbia v. Heller,* 554 U.S. 570 (2008).
52. *McDonald v. Chicago,* 561 U.S. 3025 (2010).
53. *Horton v. California,* 496 U.S. 128 (1990).
54. *Mapp v. Ohio,* 367 U.S. 643 (1961). Although Mapp went free in this case, she was later convicted in New York on narcotics trafficking charges and served 9 years of a 20-year sentence.
55. *People v. Defore,* 242 N.Y. 13, 21, 150 N.E. 585, 587 (1926).
56. For a good discussion of the issue, see Fisher, *American Constitutional Law,* 884–9.
57. *Florida v. Jardines,* 569 U.S. __ (2013).
58. *United States v. Jones,* 565 U.S. __ (2012).
59. *Maryland v. King,* 569 U.S. __ (2013).
60. *Riley v. California,* 573 U.S. __ (2014).
61. Marjorie Cohn, "NSA Metadata Collection: Fourth Amendment Violation," JURIST, January 15, 2014, www.jurist.org/forum/2014/01/marjorie-cohn-nsa-metadata.php (accessed 4/19/16).

62. *Palko v. Connecticut*, 302 U.S. 319 (1937).

63. *Miranda v. Arizona*, 384 U.S. 436 (1966).

64. *Berghuis v. Thompkins*, 560 U.S. 370 (2010).

65. *Gideon v. Wainwright*, 372 U.S. 335 (1963). For a full account of the story of the trial and release of Clarence Earl Gideon, see Anthony Lewis, *Gideon's Trumpet* (New York: Random House, 1964). See also David O'Brien, *Storm Center*, 8th ed. (New York: W. W. Norton, 2008).

66. *Furman v. Georgia*, 408 U.S. 238 (1972).

67. *Gregg v. Georgia*, 428 U.S. 153 (1976).

68. Death Penalty Information Center, www.deathpenaltyinfo.org (accessed 11/9/16).

69. *Kennedy v. Louisiana*, 554 U.S. 407 (2008).

70. *Snyder v. Louisiana*, 522 U.S. 472 (2008).

71. *Glossip v. Gross*, 576 U.S. __ (2015).

72. *Griswold v. Connecticut*, 381 U.S. 479 (1965).

73. *Griswold v. Connecticut*, concurring opinion. In 1972 the Court extended the privacy right to unmarried women: *Eisenstadt v. Baird*, 405 U.S. 438 (1972).

74. *Roe v. Wade*, 410 U.S. 113 (1973).

75. *Lawrence v. Texas*, 539 U.S. 558 (2003).

76. *Plessy v. Ferguson*, 163 U.S. 537 (1896).

77. *Missouri ex rel. Gaines v. Canada*, 305 U.S. 337 (1938).

78. The District of Columbia case came up too, but since the District of Columbia is not a state, this case did not directly involve the Fourteenth Amendment and its "equal protection" clause. It confronted the Court on the same grounds, however—that segregation is inherently unequal. Its victory in effect was "incorporation in reverse," with equal protection moving from the Fourteenth Amendment to become part of the Bill of Rights. See *Bolling v. Sharpe*, 347 U.S. 497 (1954).

79. *Brown v. Board of Education of Topeka, Kansas*, 347 U.S. 483 (1954).

80. The Supreme Court first declared that race was a suspect classification requiring strict scrutiny in the decision *Korematsu v. United States*, 323 U.S. 214 (1944). In this case, the Court upheld President Roosevelt's executive order of 1941 allowing the military to exclude persons of Japanese ancestry from the West Coast and to place them in internment camps. It is one of the few cases in which classification based on race survived strict scrutiny.

81. For good treatments of this long stretch of the struggle of the federal courts to integrate the schools, see Paul Brest and Sanford Levinson, *Processes of Constitutional Decision-Making: Cases and Materials*, 2nd ed. (Boston: Little, Brown, 1983), 471–80; and Alfred H. Kelly, Winfred A. Harbison, and Herman Belz, *The American Constitution: Its Origins and Development*, 6th ed. (New York: W. W. Norton, 1983), 610–16.

82. Pierre Thomas, "Denny's to Settle Bias Cases," *Washington Post*, May 24, 1994, A1.

83. *Parents Involved in Community Schools v. Seattle School District No. 1*, 551 U.S. 701 (2007).

84. John A. Powell, "Segregated Schools Ruling Not All Bad: In Rejecting Seattle's Integration Bid Top Court Majority Also Held that Avoiding Racial Isolation Is a Legitimate Public Goal," *Newsday*, July 16, 2007, A33.

85. See especially *Katzenbach v. McClung*, 379 U.S. 294 (1964). Almost immediately after passage of the Civil Rights Act of 1964, a case was brought challenging the validity of Title II, which covered discrimination in public accommodations. Ollie's Barbecue was a neighborhood restaurant in Birmingham, Alabama. It was located 11 blocks away from an interstate highway and even farther from railroad and bus stations. Its table service was for whites only; there was only take-out service for blacks. The Supreme Court agreed that Ollie's was strictly an intrastate restaurant, but since a substantial

proportion of its food and other supplies were bought from companies outside the state of Alabama, there was a sufficient connection to interstate commerce; therefore, racial discrimination at such restaurants would "impose commercial burdens of national magnitude upon interstate commerce." Although this case involved Title II, it had direct bearing on the constitutionality of Title VII.

86. In 1970 this act was amended to outlaw for five years literacy tests as a condition for voting in all states.

87. See Douglas S. Massey and Nancy A. Denton, *American Apartheid: Segregation and the Making of the Underclass* (Cambridge, MA: Harvard University Press, 1993), chap. 7.

88. Michael Powell, "Bank Accused of Pushing Mortgage Deals on Blacks," *New York Times*, June 6, 2009, A16; Office of the Illinois Attorney General, "Madigan Sues Wells Fargo for Discriminatory and Deceptive Mortgage Lending Practices," press release, July 31, 2009, www.illinoisattorneygeneral.gov/pressroom/2009_07/20090731 .html (accessed 10/23/09).

89. See Jane J. Mansbridge, *Why We Lost the ERA* (Chicago: University of Chicago Press, 1986); and Gilbert Steiner, *Constitutional Inequality* (Washington, DC: Brookings Institution Press, 1985).

90. See *Frontiero v. Richardson*, 411 U.S. 677 (1973).

91. *Meritor Savings Bank v. Vinson*, 477 U.S. 57 (1986).

92. *Franklin v. Gwinnett County Public Schools*, 503 U.S. 60 (1992).

93. *United States v. Virginia*, 518 U.S. 515 (1996).

94. *Ledbetter v. Goodyear Tire and Rubber Co.*, 550 U.S. 618 (2007).

95. Claire Zillman, "Barnes & Noble Is Latest Retailer to Face Transgender Discrimination Lawsuit," *Fortune*, May 7, 2015. http://fortune.com/2015/05/07/barnes-noble -transgender-lawsuit/ (accessed 1/10/16).

96. *Lau v. Nichols*, 414 U.S. 563 (1974).

97. Dick Kirschten, "Not Black and White," *National Journal*, March 2, 1991, 497.

98. *R.A.V. v. City of St. Paul*, 506 U.S. 377 (1992).

99. *United States v. Texas*, 579 U.S. __ (2016).

100. See the discussion in Robert A. Katzmann, *Institutional Disability: The Saga of Transportation Policy for the Disabled* (Washington, DC: Brookings Institution Press, 1986).

101. For example, after pressure from the Justice Department, one of the nation's largest rental-car companies agreed to make special hand controls available to any customer requesting them. See "Avis Agrees to Equip Cars for Disabled," *Los Angeles Times*, September 2, 1994, D1.

102. For more, see Dale Carpenter, *Flagrant Conduct: The Story of* Lawrence v. Texas (New York: W. W. Norton & Co., 2012).

103. *Bowers v. Hardwick*, 478 U.S. 186 (1986).

104. Quoted in Joan Biskupic, "Gay Rights Activists Seek a Supreme Court Test Case," *Washington Post*, December 19, 1993, A1.

105. *Romer v. Evans*, 517 U.S. 620 (1996).

106. *Lawrence v. Texas*, 539 U.S. 558 (2003).

107. *United States v. Windsor*, 570 U.S. 12 (2013); *Hollingsworth v. Perry*, 570 U.S. __ (2013).

108. *Obergefell v. Hodges*, 576 U.S. __ (2015).

109. The Department of Health, Education, and Welfare (HEW) was the cabinet department charged with administering most federal social programs. In 1980, when education programs were transferred to the newly created Department of Education, HEW was renamed the Department of Health and Human Services.

110. *Regents of the University of California v. Bakke*, 438 U.S. 265 (1978).

111. *Adarand Constructors, Inc. v. Peña*, 515 U.S. 200 (1995).

112. *Grutter v. Bollinger*, 539 U.S. 306 (2003).
113. *Gratz v. Bollinger*, 539 U.S. 244 (2003).
114. *Fisher v. University of Texas*, 570 U.S. __ (2013).
115. *Fisher v. University of Texas*, No. 14-981 __ (2016).

Chapter 5

1. Larry Bartels, *Unequal Democracy: The Political Economy of the New Gilded Age* (Princeton, NJ: Princeton University Press, 2008).
2. Bernadette D. Proctor, Jessica L. Semega, and Melissa A. Kollar, "Income and Poverty in the United States: 2015," September 2016, www.census.gov/content/dam/Census /library/publications/2016/demo/p60-256.pdf (accessed 10/08/16).
3. Drew DeSilver, "5 Facts about Economic Inequality," Pew Research Center, Fact Tank, January 7, 2014, www.pewresearch.org/fact-tank/2014/01/07/5-facts-about-economic -inequality (accessed 2/13/14).
4. Bruce Stokes, "The U.S.'s High Income Gap Is Met with Relatively Low Public Concern," Pew Research Center, Fact Tank, December 6, 2013, www.pewresearch.org /fact-tank/2013/12/06/the-u-s-s-high-income-gap-is-met-with-relatively-low-public -concern (accessed 1/20/14).
5. Noam Scheiber and Dalia Sussman, "Inequality Troubles Americans across Party Lines, Times/CBS Poll Finds," June 3, 2015, *New York Times*, www.nytimes.com /2015/06/04/business/inequality-a-major-issue-for-americans-times-cbs-poll-finds.html (accessed 4/18/16).
6. Scheiber and Sussman, "Inequality Troubles."
7. M. Lodge and C. S. Taber, "Three Steps toward a Theory of Motivated Political Reasoning," in *Elements of Reason: Cognition, Choice, and the Bounds of Rationality*, ed. A. Lupia, M. McCubbins, and S. Popkin (London: Cambridge University Press, 2000); George E. Marcus, W. Russell Neuman, and Michael MacKuen, *Affective Intelligence and Political Judgment* (Chicago: University of Chicago Press, 2000); David Redlawsk, "Hot Cognition or Cool Consideration? Testing the Effects of Motivated Reasoning on Political Decision Making," *Journal of Politics* 64 (2002): 1021–44; David Redlawsk, Andrew Civettini, and Karen Emmerson, "The Affective Tipping Point: Do Motivated Reasoners Ever 'Get It'?" *Political Psychology* 31, no. 4 (2010): 563–93.
8. Marcus, Neuman, and MacKuen, *Affective Intelligence and Political Judgment*.
9. Pew Research Center, "A Year Later, U.S. Campaign against ISIS Garners Support, Raises Concerns," U.S. Politics & Policy, July 22, 2015, www.people-press.org /2015/07/22/a-year-later-u-s-campaign-against-isis-garners-support-raises-concerns/ (accessed 5/2/16).
10. See Karen Mossberger, Caroline Tolbert, and Ramona McNeal, *Digital Citizenship: The Internet, Society and Participation* (Cambridge, MA: MIT Press, 2008).
11. See Harry Holloway and John George, *Public Opinion* (New York: St. Martin's, 1986). See also Paul R. Abramson, *Political Attitudes in America* (San Francisco: Freeman, 1983).
12. Pippa Norris, ed., *Critical Citizens: Global Support for Democratic Government* (New York: Oxford University Press, 1999); Robert Putnam, *Bowling Alone: The Collapse and Revival of American Community* (New York: Simon and Schuster, 2000).
13. Todd Donovan and Shaun Bowler, *Reforming the Republic: Democratic Institutions for the New America* (New York: Prentice Hall, 2004).
14. Pew Research Center, "Beyond Distrust: How Americans View Their Government," November 23, 2015, www.people-press.org/2015/11/23/beyond-distrust-how -americans-view-their-government/ (accessed 8/11/16).
15. See Angus Campbell et al., *The American Voter* (New York: Wiley, 1960), 147.

16. Omid Aziz, Derrick McMillen, and Tony Liu, "72 Hours to Launch Celebrate Pride," https://code.facebook.com/posts/778505998932780/72-hours-to-launch-celebrate-pride/ (accessed 3/2/16).
17. Pew Research Center, "Changing Attitudes on Gay Marriage," Religion & Public Life, May 12, 2016, www.pewforum.org/2016/05/12/changing-attitudes-on-gay-marriage/ (accessed 8/11/16).
18. Jennifer A. Heerwig and Brian J. McCabe, "Education and Social Desirability Bias: The Case of a Black Presidential Candidate," *Social Science Quarterly* 90, no. 3 (2009): 674–86.
19. Raymond E. Wolfinger and Steven J. Rosenstone, *Who Votes?* (New Haven, CT: Yale University Press, 1980). See also Steven J. Rosenstone and John Mark Hansen, *Mobilization, Participation, and Democracy in America* (New York: Macmillan, 1993).
20. Katherine Tate, *Black Faces in the Mirror* (Princeton, NJ: Princeton University Press, 1993).
21. Brakkton Booker, "How Equal Is American Opportunity? Survey Shows Attitudes Vary by Race," National Public Radio, September 21, 2015, www.npr.org/sections/thetwo-way/2015/09/21/442068004/how-equal-is-american-opportunity-survey-shows-attitudes-vary-by-race (accessed 2/24/16).
22. Pew Research Center, "Across Racial Lines, More Say Nation Needs to Make Changes to Achieve Racial Equality," U.S. Politics & Policy, August 5, 2015, www.people-press.org/2015/08/05/across-racial-lines-more-say-nation-needs-to-make-changes-to-achieve-racial-equality/8-4-2015_02a/ (accessed 2/24/16).
23. Matt Barreto and Gary M. Segura, *Latino America: How America's Most Dynamic Population Is Poised to Transform the Politics of the Nation* (New York: Public Affairs, 2014).
24. Donald Green, Bradley Palmquist, and Eric Schickler, *Partisan Hearts and Minds: Political Parties and the Social Identities of Voters* (New Haven, CT: Yale University Press, 2002).
25. See Richard Lau and David Redlawsk, *How Voters Decide: Information Processing during an Election Campaign* (New York: Cambridge University Press, 2006).
26. Walter Lippmann, *Public Opinion* (New York: Harcourt, Brace and Company, 1922).
27. Cooperative Comparative Election Study 2014, Harvard University, released February 2015, http://projects.iq.harvard.edu/cces/home (accessed 12/16/15).
28. John R. Zaller, *The Nature and Origins of Mass Opinion* (New York: Cambridge University Press, 1992).
29. Carol Glynn et al., *Public Opinion*, 2nd ed. (Boulder, CO: Westview, 2004), 293. See also Michael X. Delli Carpini and Scott Keeter, *What Americans Know about Politics and Why It Matters* (New Haven, CT: Yale University Press, 1996).
30. Delli Carpini and Keeter, *What Americans Know about Politics.*
31. Adam J. Berinsky, "Assuming the Costs of War: Events, Elites and American Support for Military Conflict," *Journal of Politics* 69, no. 4 (2007): 975–97; Zaller, *Nature and Origins of Mass Opinion.*
32. Richard R. Lau and David P. Redlawsk, "Advantages and Disadvantages of Cognitive Heuristics in Political Decision Making," *American Journal of Political Science* 45 (October 2001): 951–71; Lau and Redlawsk, *How Voters Decide.*
33. For a discussion of the role of information politics, see Arthur Lupia and Matthew D. McCubbins, *The Democratic Dilemma: Can Citizens Learn What They Need to Know?* (New York: Cambridge University Press, 1998). See also Shaun Bowler and Todd Donovan, *Demanding Choices: Opinion and Voting in Direct Democracy* (Ann Arbor: University of Michigan Press, 1998). See also Samuel Popkin, *The Reasoning Voter: Communication and Persuasion in Presidential Campaigns* (Chicago: University of Chicago Press, 1991); Arthur Lupia, "Shortcuts Versus Encyclopedias: Information and Voting Behavior in California Insurance Reform Elections," *American Political Science Review* 88 (1994): 63–76; and Wendy Rahn, "The Role of Partisan Stereotypes

in Information Processing about Political Candidates," *American Journal of Political Science* 37 (1993): 472–96.

34. James Druckman, Erik Petersen, and Rune Slothuus, "How Elite Partisan Polarization Affects Public Opinion Formation," *American Political Science Review* 107, no. 1 (February 2013): 57–79.

35. Lee Rainie et al., "Social Media and Political Engagement," Pew Research Center, Internet, Science & Tech, October 19, 2012, www.pewinternet.org/2012/10/19 /social-media-and-political-engagement/ (accessed 8/14/14).

36. Tony Dokoupil, "Is the Internet Making Us Crazy? What the New Research Says," *Newsweek*, July 9, 2012, www.newsweek.com/internet-making-us-crazy-what-new -research-says-65593; Nicholas Carr, *The Shallows: What the Internet Is Doing to Our Brains* (New York: W.W. Norton, 2011).

37. Bartels, *Unequal Democracy*.

38. Benjamin Ginsberg, *The American Lie: Government by the People and Other Political Fables* (Boulder, CO: Paradigm, 2007).

39. Peter Marks, "Adept in Politics and Advertising, 4 Women Shape a Campaign," *New York Times*, November 11, 2001, B6.

40. *Roe v. Wade*, 410 U.S. 113 (1973).

41. See Gillian Peele, *Revival and Reaction* (Oxford: Clarendon, 1985). See also Connie Paige, *The Right-to-Lifers* (New York: Summit, 1983).

42. Benjamin I. Page and Robert Y. Shapiro, "Effects of Public Opinion on Policy," *American Political Science Review* 77, no.1 (1983): 175–90.

43. Page and Shapiro, "Effects of Public Opinion on Policy."

44. Pew Research Center, "Mixed Views of Economic Polices and Health Care Reform Persist," U.S. Politics & Policy, October 8, 2009, www.people-press.org/2009/10/08 /mixed-views-of-economic-policies-and-health-care-reform-persist (accessed 3/18/14).

45. Christopher Wlezien, "The Public as Thermostat: Dynamics of Preferences for Spend-ing," *American Journal of Political Science* 39, no. 4 (1995): 981–1000.

46. Malcolm E. Jewell, *Representation in State Legislatures* (Lexington: University Press of Kentucky, 1982).

47. Lawrence R. Jacobs and Robert Y. Shapiro, *Politicians Don't Pander: Political Manipulation and the Loss of Democratic Responsiveness* (Chicago: University of Chicago Press, 2000).

48. Herbert Asher, *Polling and the Public* (Washington, DC: CQ Press, 2001), 64.

49. Drew DeSilver and Scott Keeter, "The Challenges of Polling when Fewer People Are Available to Be Polled," Fact Tank, July 21, 2015, www.pewresearch.org/fact-tank /2015/07/21/the-challenges-of-polling-when-fewer-people-are-available-to-be-polled/ (accessed 3/1/16).

50. Michael Kagay and Janet Elder, "Numbers Are No Problem for Pollsters, Words Are," *New York Times*, August 9, 1992, E6.

51. See Adam Berinsky, "The Two Faces of Public Opinion," *American Journal of Political Science* 43, no. 4 (1999): 1209–30. See also Adam Berinsky, "Political Context and the Survey Response: The Dynamics of Racial Policy Opinion," *Journal of Politics* 64, no. 2 (2002): 567–84.

52. Heerwig and McCabe, "Education and Social Desirability Bias."

53. For a discussion of the growing difficulty of persuading people to respond to surveys, see John Brehm, *Phantom Respondents* (Ann Arbor: University of Michigan Press, 1993).

54. Christopher Wlezien and Stuart Soroka, "The Relationship between Public Opinion and Policy," in *Oxford Handbook of Political Behavior*, ed. Russell Dalton and Hans-Dieter Klingemann (New York: Oxford University Press, 2009), 799–817.

55. Martin Gilens, "Inequality and Democratic Responsiveness," *Public Opinion Quarterly* 69, no. 5 (2005): 778–96; Bartels, *Unequal Democracy*.

56. Ryan Claassen and Benjamin Highton, "Does Policy Debate Reduce Information Effects in Public Opinion? Analyzing the Evolution of Public Opinion on Health Care," *Journal of Politic* 68, no. 2 (2006): 410–20.

Chapter 6

1. Caroline Tolbert and Ramona McNeal, "Unraveling the Effects of the Internet on Political Participation," *Political Research Quarterly* 56, no. 2 (2003): 175–85. See also Bruce Bimber, "Information and Political Engagement in America: The Search for Effects of Information Technology at the Individual Level," *Political Research Quarterly* 54 (2001): 53–67; Bruce Bimber, *Information and American Democracy: Technology in the Evolution of Political Power* (Cambridge: Cambridge University Press, 2003); and Brian S. Krueger, "Assessing the Potential of Internet Political Participation in the United States," *American Politics Research* 30 (2002): 476–98.
2. Michael Barthel et al., "The Evolving Role of News on Twitter and Facebook." Pew Research Center. www.journalism.org/2015/07/14/the-evolving-role-of-news-on -twitter-and-facebook/ (accessed 1/14/16).
3. Julian P. Boyd et al., eds., *The Papers of Thomas Jefferson* (Princeton, NJ: Princeton University Press), press-pubs.uchicago.edu/founders/documents/amendI_speechs8 .html (accessed 5/30/14).
4. Pew Research Center, "Amid Criticism, Support for Media's 'Watchdog' Role Stands Out," U.S. Politics & Policy, August 8, 2013, www.people-press.org/2013/08/08/amid -criticism-support-for-medias-watchdog-role-stands-out/ (accessed 4/27/14).
5. Robert McChesney and John Nichols, *The Death and Life of American Journalism: The Media Revolution That Will Begin the World Again* (New York: Nation Books, 2010).
6. Darrell West, *The Next Wave: Using Digital Technology to Further Social and Political Innovation* (Washington, DC: Brookings Institution Press, 2011).
7. Pew Research Center, "Newspapers: Print and Online Ad Revenue," Source: Newspaper Association of America (2003–2013), Pew Research analysis of BIA /Kelsey data (2014), Journalism & Media, www.journalism.org/media-indicators /newspaper-print-and-online-ad-revenue/ (accessed 1/22/16).
8. Amy Mitchell, "State of the News Media 2015," Pew Research Center, Journalism & Media, April 29, 2015, www.journalism.org/2015/04/29/state-of-the-news-media -2015 (accessed 1/22/16).
9. Pew Research Center Project for Excellence in Journalism, "State of the News Media 2013, Overview," 2013, www.stateofthemedia.org/2013/overview-5/ (accessed 4/29/14).
10. Mitchell, "State of the News Media 2015," (accessed 1/14/16).
11. Pew Research Center, "The Internet's Broader Role in Campaign 2008," U.S. Politics & Policy, January 11, 2008, www.people-press.org/2008/01/11/internets-broader-role-in -campaign-2008/; Pew Research Center, "Journalism, Satire, or Just Laughs? *The Daily Show* with Jon Stewart Examined," Journalism & Media, May 8, 2008, www .journalism.org/2008/05/08/journalism-satire-or-just-laughs-the-daily-show-with -jon-stewart-examined/ (accessed 9/11/12).
12. Jonathan M. Ladd, *Why Americans Hate the Media and How It Matters* (Princeton, NJ: Princeton University Press, 2012).
13. West, *Next Wave*; Edward Glaeser, *Triumph of the City: How Our Greatest Invention Makes Us Richer, Smarter, Greener, Healthier, and Happier* (New York: Penguin Press, 2011).
14. Pew Research Center, "Internet Use Over Time," Internet, Science & Tech, 2014, www.pewinternet.org/data-trend/internet-use/internet-use-over-time/ (accessed 4/29/14).

15. Amy Mitchell, Jeffrey Gottfried, and Katerina Eva Matsa, "Facebook Top Source for Political News among Millennials," Pew Research Center, Journalism & Media, June 1, 2015, www.journalism.org/2015/06/01/facebook-top-source-for-political-news-among-millennials/ (accessed 1/14/16).
16. Aaron Smith and Maeve Duggan, "Online Political Videos and Campaign 2012," Pew Research Center, Internet, Science & Tech, November 2, 2012, www.pewinternet.org/2012/11/02/online-political-videos-and-campaign-2012/ (accessed 4/29/14).
17. Jeffrey Gottfried and Elisa Shearer, "News Use across Social Media Platforms 2016," Pew Research Center, Journalism & Media, May 26, 2016, www.journalism.org/2016/05/26/news-use-across-social-media-platforms-2016/ (accessed 6/24/16).
18. Karen Mossberger, Caroline Tolbert, and Ramona McNeal, *Digital Citizenship: The Internet, Society and Participation* (Cambridge, MA: MIT Press, 2008); Brian A. Krueger, "A Comparison of Conventional and Internet Political Mobilization," *American Politics Research* 34, no. 6 (2006): 759–76.
19. Antony Wilhelm, *Digital Nation: Toward an Inclusive Information Society* (Cambridge, MA: MIT Press, 2006); Paul DiMaggio et al., "Social Implications of the Internet," *Annual Review of Sociology* 27, no. 1 (2001): 307–36.
20. Karen Mossberger, Caroline Tolbert, and Mary Stansbury, *Virtual Inequality: Beyond the Digital Divide* (Washington, DC: Georgetown University Press, 2003); Pippa Norris, *Digital Divide: Civic Engagement, Information Poverty, and the Internet Worldwide* (New York: Cambridge University Press, 2001).
21. U.S. Census Bureau, "Nearly 8 in 10 Americans Have Access to High-Speed Internet," Newsroom, November 13, 2014, www.census.gov/newsroom/press-releases/2014/cb14-202.html (accessed 3/2/16).
22. John B. Morris, "Language and Citizenship May Contribute to Low Internet Use among Hispanics," November 17, 2015, National Telecommunications and Information Administration, U.S. Department of Commerce, www.ntia.doc.gov/blog/2015/language-and-citizenship-may-contribute-low-internet-use-among-hispanics (accessed 1/14/2016).
23. U.S. Census Bureau, "Nearly 8 in 10 Americans."
24. "Number of Monthly Active Facebook Users Worldwide as of 2nd Quarter 2016 (in Millions)," Statistica, www.statista.com/statistics/264810/number-of-monthly-active-facebook-users-worldwide/ and "Number of Facebook Users in the United States from 2014 to 2021 (in Millions)," Statistica, www.statista.com/statistics/408971/number-of-us-facebook-users/ (accessed 10/4/16).
25. Amy Mitchell, Jeffrey Gottfried, and Katerina Eva Matsa, "Political Interest and Awareness Lower among Millennials," Pew Research Center, Journalism & Media, June 1, 2015, www.journalism.org/2015/06/01/political-interest-and-awareness-lower-among-millennials/ (accessed 12/7/15).
26. W. Russell Neuman, Marion R. Just, and Ann N. Crigler, *Common Knowledge: News and the Construction of Political Meaning* (Chicago: University of Chicago Press, 1991).
27. Zoe M. Oxley, "More Sources, Better Informed Public? New Media and Political Knowledge," in *iPolitics: Citizens, Elections, and Governing in the New Media Era*, ed. Richard L. Fox and Jennifer M. Ramos (Cambridge: Cambridge University Press, 2012), 25–47.
28. Tolbert and McNeal, "Unraveling the Effects of the Internet."
29. Mossberger, Tolbert, and McNeal, *Digital Citizenship*. See Richard L. Fox and Jennifer M. Ramos, eds., *iPolitics: Citizens, Elections, and Governing in the New Media Era* (Cambridge: Cambridge University Press, 2011).
30. See Neuman, Just, and Crigler, *Common Knowledge*.

31. Cass Sunstein, *Republic.com* (Princeton, NJ: Princeton University Press, 2011). See also Mossberger, Tolbert, and McNeal, *Digital Citizenship*.
32. West, *Next Wave*; McChesney and Nichols, *Death and Life of American Journalism*.
33. Oxley, "More Sources, Better Informed Public?"
34. Doris Graber, ed., *Media Power in American Politics*, 5th ed. (Washington, DC: CQ Press, 2006).
35. Larry Bartels, *Unequal Democracy: The Political Economy of the New Gilded Age* (Princeton, NJ: Princeton University Press, 2008).
36. Shanto Iyengar and Donald R. Kinder, *News That Matters: Television and American Opinion* (Chicago: University of Chicago Press, 1987), 63.
37. *New York Times v. United States*, 403 U.S. 713 (1971).
38. Michael Massing, "The Press: The Enemy Within," *New York Review of Books*, December 15, 2005, 6.
39. *Red Lion Broadcasting Company v. Federal Communications Commission*, 395 U.S. 367 (1969).
40. United Nations General Assembly, "Report of the Special Rapporteur on the Promotion and Protection of the Right to Freedom of Opinion and Expression, 2011." www2.ohchr.org/english/bodies/hrcouncil/docs/17session/A.HRC.17.27_en.pdf (accessed 3/14/16).
41. Andrew Chadwick, *Internet Politics: States, Citizens, and New Communication Technologies* (Oxford: Oxford University Press, 2006).

Chapter 7

1. Center for Responsive Politics, "2016 Presidential Race," Center for Responsive Politics, Open Secrets, www.opensecrets.org/pres16/ (accessed 6/21/16).
2. Jeff Stein, "The 7 Trumpiest Things Donald Trump Said during His 'Counter-Debate,'" Vox.com, January 29, 2016, www.vox.com/2016/1/29/10868360/trump-quotes-counter-debate (accessed 3/10/16).
3. Alan Greenblatt, "With Major Issues Fading, Capitol Life Lures Fewer," *Congressional Quarterly Weekly Report*, October 25, 1997, 2625.
4. Daniel Galvin, *Presidential Party Building: Dwight D. Eisenhower to George W. Bush* (Princeton, NJ: Princeton, University Press, 2009).
5. For a discussion of third parties in the United States, see Daniel Mazmanian, *Third Parties in Presidential Elections* (Washington, DC: Brookings Institution Press, 1974).
6. Alex Isenstadt, "Tea Party Candidates Falling Short," *Politico*, March 7, 2010, www.politico.com/news/stories/0310/34041.html (accessed 3/11/10).
7. American National Election Studies, "Guide to Public Opinion and Electoral Behavior," www.electionstudies.org/nesguide/gd-index.htm#6 (accessed 6/24/16).
8. Jeffrey Gottfried and Elisa Shearer, "News Use across Social Media Platforms 2016," Pew Research Center, Journalism & Media, May 26, 2016, www.journalism.org/2016/05/26/news-use-across-social-media-platforms-2016/ (accessed 6/25/16).
9. Katerina Eva Matsa and Amy Mitchell, "8 Key Takeaways about Social Media and News," Pew Research Center, Journalism & Media, March 26, 2014, www.journalism.org/2014/03/26/8-key-takeaways-about-social-media-and-news/ (accessed 1/12/16).
10. Gottfried and Shearer, "News Use Across Social Media."
11. Amy Mitchell and Emily Guskin, "Twitter News Consumers Young, Mobile and Educated," Pew Research Center, Journalism & Media, November 4, 2013, www.journalism.org/2013/11/04/twitter-news-consumers-young-mobile-and-educated/ (accessed 4/12/16).
12. Pew Research Center, "The Internet News Audience Goes Ordinary," U.S. Politics & Policy, January 14, 1999, www.people-press.org/1999/01/14/the-internet-news

-audience-goes-ordinary/; Pew Research Center, "Internet Usage over Time," Internet, Science & Tech, www.pewinternet.org/data-trend/internet-use/internet-use-over-time/ (accessed 4/11/16).

13. Andrew Chadwick, *The Hybrid Media System: Politics and Power* (New York: Oxford University Press, 2012).

14. Pew Research Center, "Politics Fact Sheet," Internet, Science & Tech, November 14, 2012, www.pewinternet.org/fact-sheets/politics-fact-sheet/ (accessed 4/11/16).

15. Sidney Verba, Kay Lehman Schlozman, and Henry E. Brady, *Voice and Equality: Civic Voluntarism in American Politics* (Cambridge, MA: Harvard University Press, 1995).

16. For a discussion of the decline in voter turnout over time, see Ruy A. Teixeria, *The Disappearing American Voter* (Washington, DC: Brookings Institution Press, 1992). See also Michael McDonald and Samuel Popkin, "The Myth of the Vanishing Voter," *American Political Science Review* 95 (2001): 963–74; and Michael McDonald, "2012 November General Election Turnout Rates," United States Election Project, http://www .electproject.org/2012g (accessed 9/14/12).

17. Robert Jackman, "Political Institutions and Voter Turnout in the Democracies," *American Political Science Review* 81 (June 1987): 420.

18. Angus Campbell et al., *The American Voter* (New York: Wiley, 1960); Steven Rosenstone and John Mark Hansen, *Mobilization, Participation, and Democracy in America* (New York: Macmillan, 1993).

19. Sidney Verba and Norman H. Nie, *Participation in America: Political Democracy and Social Equality* (New York: Harper and Row, 1972).

20. Jan E. Leighley and Jonathan Nagler, "Socioeconomic Class Bias in Turnout, 1964–1988: The Voters Remain the Same," *American Political Science Review* 86, no. 3 (1992): 725–36.

21. Rosenstone and Hansen, *Mobilization, Participation, and Democracy*, 59.

22. Michael P. McDonald and John Samples, eds., *The Marketplace of Democracy: Electoral Competition and American Politics* (Washington, DC: Brookings Institution Press, 2006).

23. Mark N. Franklin, "Electoral Participation," in *Comparing Democracies: Elections and Voting in Global Perspective*, ed. Lawrence LeDuc, Richard G. Niemi, and Pippa Norris (Thousand Oaks, CA: Sage, 1996), 216–35; G. Bingham Powell, "American Voter Turnout in Comparative Perspective," *American Political Science Review* 80, no. 1 (1986): 17–43.

24. National Conference of State Legislatures, "Voter Identification Requirements," www .ncsl.org/research/elections-and-campaigns/voter-id.aspx (accessed 4/11/16).

25. Matt Barreto, Stephen Nuño, and Gabriel Sanchez, "The Disproportionate Impact of Voter-ID Requirements on the Electorate—New Evidence from Indiana," *PS: Political Science & Politics* 42 (2009): 111–16.

26. See Morris Fiorina, "Parties and Partisanship: A Forty Year Retrospective," *Political Behavior* 24, no. 2 (June 2002): 93–115.

27. On the limited polarization among ordinary voters, see Morris P. Fiorina, *Culture War? The Myth of a Polarized America*, with Samuel J. Abrams and Jeremy C. Pope (New York: Pearson Longman, 2004); on growing partisan attachment among a subset of voters, see Alan Abramowitz and Kyle Saunders, "Why Can't We Just Get Along? The Reality of a Polarized America," *The Forum* 3, no. 2 (2005): 1–22.

28. *League of United Latin American Citizens v. Wilson*, CV-94-7569 (C.D. Calif. 1995); Adam Nagourney, "Court Strikes Down Ban on Gay Marriage in California," *New York Times*, February 7, 2012, www.nytimes.com/2012/02/08/us/marriage-ban-violates -constitution-court-rules.html (accessed 8/21/12).

29. State legislatures determine the system by which electors are selected. Almost all states use this "winner-take-all" system. Maine and Nebraska, however, provide that one electoral vote goes to the winner in each congressional district and two electoral votes go to the winner statewide.
30. *Bush v. Gore*, 531 U.S. 98 (2000).
31. David Barstow, et al., "Donald Trump Tax Records Show He Could Have Avoided Taxes for Nearly Two Decades, The Times Found," *New York Times*, October 1, 2016, www .nytimes.com/2016/10/02/us/politics/donald-trump-taxes.html (accessed 11/11/16).
32. Craig Silverman, "Viral Fake Election News Outperformed Real News On Facebook In Final Months of the US Election," November 16, 2016, www.buzzfeed.com/craigsilverman /viral-fake-election-news-outperformed-real-news-on-facebook?utm term=.bvR73wjQd# .ic6olvY6V (accessed 11/18/16).
33. Center for Responsive Politics, "Behind the Candidates: Campaign Committees and Outside Groups," www.opensecrets.org/pres16/raised-summ (accessed 11/12/16).
34. *McCutcheon et al. v. Federal Election Commission*, 572 U.S. __ (2014).
35. *Citizens United v. Federal Election Commission*, 558 U.S. 50 (2010); *SpeechNow v. FEC*, 558 U.S. __ (2010).
36. *McCutcheon et al.*
37. *Buckley v. Valeo*, 424 U.S. 1 (1976).

Chapter 8

1. Alexander Hamilton, James Madison, and John Jay, *The Federalist Papers*, ed. Clinton L. Rossiter (New York: New American Library, 1961), no. 10, 83.
2. *The Federalist Papers*, no. 10.
3. The best statement of the pluralist view is in David Truman, *The Governmental Process* (New York: Knopf, 1951), chap. 2.
4. Beth L. Leech, National Survey of Governmental Relations, 2012; Center for Responsive Politics, "Political Action Committees," https://www.opensecrets.org /pacs/; Lobbyists.Info, http://www.lobbyists.info/ (accessed 12/2/15).
5. Frank R. Baumgartner et al., *Lobbying and Policy Change: Who Wins, Who Loses, and Why* (Chicago: University of Chicago Press, 2009).
6. Erika Falk, Erin Grizard, and Gordon McDonald, "Legislative Issue Advertising in the 108th Congress: Pluralism or Peril?" *Harvard International Journal of Press/Politics* 11, no. 4 (Fall 2006): 148–64.
7. Betsy Wagner and David Bowermaster, "B.S. Economics," *Washington Monthly*, November 1992, 19–21.
8. Truman, *Governmental Process*.
9. For an exploration of lower-class interest groups and social movements, see Frances Piven and Richard Cloward, *Poor People's Movements* (New York: Vintage, 1978).
10. E. E. Schattschneider, *The Semisovereign People: A Realist's View of Democracy in America* (New York: Holt, Rinehart and Winston, 1960).
11. Kay Lehman Schlozman and John T. Tierney, *Organized Interests and American Democracy* (New York: Harper and Row, 1986), 60.
12. Clay Shirky, *Here Comes Everybody: The Power of Organizing without Organizations* (New York: Penguin, 2008).
13. Mancur Olson, *The Logic of Collective Action* (Cambridge, MA: Harvard University Press, 1965).
14. John Herbers, "Special Interests Gaining Power as Voter Disillusionment Grows," *New York Times*, November 14, 1978.
15. For discussions of lobbying, see Allan J. Cigler and Burdett A. Loomis, eds., *Interest Group Politics* (Washington, DC: CQ Press, 1983). See also Jeffrey M. Berry, *Lobbying for the People* (Princeton, NJ: Princeton University Press, 1977).

16. Common Cause, "The Microsoft Playbook: A Report from Common Cause," September 25, 2000.
17. Michael Barbaro, "A New Weapon for Wal-Mart: A War Room," *New York Times*, November 1, 2005, 1.
18. Center for Responsive Politics, "Organization Profiles," www.opensecrets.org/orgs (accessed 10/13/14).
19. David Kirkpatrick, "Congress Finds Ways of Avoiding Lobbyist Limits," *Washington Post*, February 11, 2007, 1.
20. *Brown v. Board of Education of Topeka, Kansas*, 347 U.S. 483 (1954).
21. *Roe v. Wade*, 410 U.S. 113 (1973).
22. *Webster v. Reproductive Health Services*, 492 U.S. 490 (1989).
23. *Obergefell v. Hodges*, 576 U.S. __ (2015).
24. Julia Preston, "Grass Roots Roared and Immigration Bill Collapsed," *New York Times*, June 10, 2007, 1.
25. *Citizens United v. Federal Election Commission*, 558 U.S. 50 (2010).
26. Center for Responsive Politics, "2016 Outside Spending, by Super PAC," www .opensecrets.org/outsidespending/summ.php?chrt=V&type=S (accessed 11/10/16).
27. Elisabeth R. Gerber, *The Populist Paradox* (Princeton, NJ: Princeton University Press, 1999), 6.
28. Olson, *Logic of Collective Action*.

Chapter 9

1. Clinton T. Brass, *Shutdown of the Federal Government: Causes, Processes, and Effects* Congressional Research Service, September 8, 2014, www.fas.org/sgp/crs/misc /RL34680.pdf (accessed 6/11/16).
2. Spenser S. Hsu, "Waiting for Next President, Confirmations of Federal Trial Judges Stall," *Washington Post*, June 5, 2016, www.washingtonpost.com/local/public-safety /waiting-for-next-president-confirmations-of-federal-trial-judges-stall/2016/06/05 /9662 (accessed 6/11/16).
3. Jennifer E. Manning, *Membership of the 112th Congress: A Profile*, Congressional Research Service 7-5700, September 20, 2011, 2, http://fpc.state.gov/documents /organization/174246.pdf (accessed 1/23/12).
4. For some interesting empirical evidence, see Angus Campbell et al., *Elections and the Political Order* (New York: Wiley, 1966), chap. 11.
5. Partnership for a More Perfect Union at the Congressional Management Foundation, Communicating with Congress: How Citizen Advocacy Is Changing Mail Operations on Capitol Hill, Washington, DC, 2011, http://congressfoundation.org/storage/documents /CMF_Pubs/cwc-mail-operations.pdf (accessed 1/23/12).
6. John S. Saloma, *Congress and the New Politics* (Boston: Little, Brown, 1969), 184–5. A 1977 official report using less detailed categories came up with almost the same impression of Congress's workload. Commission on Administrative Review, Administrative Reorganization and Legislative Management, H.R. Doc. No. 95-232 (September 28, 1977), vol. 2, especially 17–19.
7. Ashley Parker, "Spotlighting Constituents to Buoy Congressional Candidates," *New York Times*, October 8, 2014, www.nytimes.com/2014/10/09/us/politics/out-of-the-mouths -of-constituents-candidates-find-a-message.html; Juana Summers, "Constituent Services Give Voters Something to Remember," National Public Radio, www.npr.org/2014/10/28 /359615965/constituent-services-give-voters-something-to-remember (accessed 9/14/15).
8. See Barbara C. Burrell, *A Woman's Place Is in the House: Campaigning for Congress in the Feminist Era* (Ann Arbor: University of Michigan Press, 1994); and David Broder, "Key to Women's Political Parity: Running," *Washington Post*, September 8, 1994, A17.

9. Congressional Quarterly, *Guide to the Congress of the United States*, 2nd ed. (Washington, DC: CQ Press, 1976), 229–310.

10. Mark Hugo Lopez and Paul Taylor, "The 2010 Congressional Reapportionment and Latinos," Pew Research Center, Hispanic Trends, January 5, 2011, www.pewhispanic .org/2011/01/05/the-2010-congressional-reapportionment-and-latinos (accessed 2/24/14).

11. "Did Redistricting Sink the Democrats?" *National Journal*, December 17, 1994, 2984.

12. *Miller v. Johnson*, 515 U.S. 900 (1995).

13. Bernie Becker, "Reapportionment Roundup," *New York Times*, December 24, 2009, http:// thecaucus.blogs.nytimes.com/2009/12/24/reapportionment-roundup/ (accessed 1/31/10).

14. L. Paige Whitaker, "Congressional Redistricting and the Voting Rights Act: A Legal Overview," Congressional Research Service, April 13, 2015, www.fas.org/sgp/crs/misc /R42482.pdf (accessed 7/1/16).

15. Chris Cillizza, "What the Supreme Court's Voting Rights Act Decision Means for Politics," *Washington Post*, June 25, 2013, www.washingtonpost.com/blogs/the-fix/wp/2013/06/25 /what-the-voting-rights-act-decision-means-for-politics (accessed 12/2/13).

16. Tom Hamburger and Richard Simon, "Everybody Will Know If It's Pork," *Los Angeles Times*, January 6, 2007, A1.

17. Don Seymour, "House Republicans Renew Earmark Ban for 113th Congress," website of the Speaker of the House, November 16, 2012, www.speaker.gov/general/house -republicans-renew-earmark-ban-113th-congress (accessed 12/1/13).

18. David Clarke, "Earmarks: Here to Stay or Facing Extinction?" *Congressional Quarterly* (CQ) *Weekly*, March 16, 2009, 613; Jared Allen, "Lawmakers Pushing for Earmark Reform Think Obama Boosted Their Chances," *The Hill*, January 30, 2010, thehill.com /homenews/house/78869-lawmakers-think-obama-boosted-earmark-reform (accessed 1/31/10); David S. Fallis, Scott Higham, and Kimberly Kindy, "Congressional Earmarks Sometimes Used to Fund Projects Near Lawmakers' Properties," *Washington Post*, February 6, 2012, 1.

19. Martin Frost and Tom Davis, "How to Fix What Ails Congress; Bring Back Earmarks," *Los Angeles Times*, February 8, 2015, www.latimes.com/opinion/op-ed/la-oe-frost -earmark-spending-20150209-story.html (accessed 9/14/15).

20. Associated Press, "Congress Passes Rare Private Immigration Bills," December 15, 2010, www.huffingtonpost.com/huff-wires/20101215/us-private-immigration-bills/ (accessed 2/1/12).

21. Faith Karimi, "Obama Signs Bill to Grant Nigerian Student U.S. Permanent Residency," CNN, December 29, 2012, www.cnn.com/2012/12/29/world/africa/us-nigerian-obama -law/ (accessed 11/30/13).

22. Richard Fenno, Jr., *Home Style: House Members in Their Districts* (Boston: Little, Brown, 1978).

23. Edward Epstein "Dusting Off Deliberation," CQ *Weekly*, June 14, 2010, 1436–42; Sarah Binder, "Where Have All the Conference Committees Gone?" *The Monkey Cage* (blog), December 21, 2011, themonkeycage.org/blog/2011/12/21/where-have-all-the -conference-committees-gone (accessed 2/7/12).

24. Rebecca Kimitch, "CQ Guide to the Committees: Democrats Opt to Spread the Power," *Congressional Quarterly Weekly*, April 16, 2007, 1080.

25. U.S. Senate, Senate Action on Cloture Motions, www.senate.gov/pagelayout/reference /cloture_motions/clotureCounts.htm (accessed 4/17/14).

26. Jeremy W. Peters, "Senate Vote Curbs Filibuster Power to Stall Nominees," *New York Times*, November 22, 2013, A1.

27. Burgess Everett and Daniel Strauss, "Filibuster Divides GOP 2016 Contenders," *Politico*, July 6, 2015, www.politico.com/story/2015/07/filibuster-divides-gop-2016 -contenders-119750 (accessed 9/21/15).

28. Sean Sullivan and Mike DeBonis, "Congress Averts Homeland Security Shutdown with One-Week Extension," *Washington Post*, February 28, 2015, www.washingtonpost.com/politics/house-gop-hopes-to-pass-stopgap-dhs-funding-before-midnight-shutdown/2015/02/27/22021530-be88-11e4-b274-e5209a3bc9a9_story.html (accessed 9/21/15).

29. See John W. Kingdon, *Congressmen's Voting Decisions* (New York: Harper & Row, 1973), chap. 3; and R. Douglas Arnold, *The Logic of Congressional Action* (New Haven, CT: Yale University Press, 1990).

30. Eric Lipton and Ben Protess, "Banks' Lobbyists Help in Drafting Financial Bills," *New York Times*, May 23, 2013, dealbook.nytimes.com/2013/05/23/banks-lobbyists-help-in-drafting-financial-bills/; Michael Corkery, "Citigroup Becomes the Fall Guy in the Spending Bill Battle," *New York Times*, December 12, 2014, dealbook.nytimes.com/2014/12/12/citigroup-becomes-the-fall-guy-in-the-spending-bill-battle/ (accessed 9/21/15).

31. Holly Idelson, "Signs Point to Greater Loyalty on Both Sides of the Aisle," *Congressional Quarterly Weekly Report*, December 19, 1992, 3849.

32. "2015 Vote Studies: Party Unity Remained Strong," CQ *Weekly*, February 8, 2016, https://library.cqpress.com/cqweekly/document.php?id=weeklyreport114-000004830472&type=hitlist&num=9 (accessed 6/13/16).

33. Center for Responsive Politics, Open Secrets.org, www.opensecrets.org/pacs/pacgot.php?cmte=C00525600&cycle=2016 (accessed 10/13/16).

34. Daniel Newhauser, "Three Booted from GOP Whip Team as Leaders Crack Down," June 16, 2015, www.nationaljournal.com/congress/2015/06/16/Three-Booted-From-GOP-Whip-Team-Leaders-Crack-Down (accessed 9/21/15).

35. Frank Newport, "Congressional Approval Sinks to Record Low," Gallup, Politics, November 12, 2013, www.gallup.com/poll/165809/congressional-approval-sinks-record-low.aspx (accessed 4/17/14).

36. Nick Gass, "GOP Congress Earns Low Marks from Public," Politico, August 12, 2015, www.politico.com/story/2015/08/poll-congress-approval-rating-gop-leadership-121285 (accessed 9/28/15).

37. Jonathan Weisman and Jeremy Peters, "Government Shuts Down in Budget Impasse," *New York Times*, October 1, 2013, www.nytimes.com/2013/10/01/us/politics/congress-shutdown-debate.html (accessed 12/1/13).

38. Jonathan Weisman and Ashley Parker, "Republicans Back Down, Ending Crisis over Shutdown and Debt Limit," *New York Times*, October 16, 2013, www.nytimes.com/2013/10/17/us/congress-budget-debate.html (accessed 12/1/13).

39. Molly E. Reynolds, "Speaker Ryan Meets the Realities of Governing," Brookings Institution, June 10, 2016, www.brookings.edu/blogs/fixgov/posts/2016/06/10-paul-ryan-amendments-appropriations-reynolds (accessed 6/13/16).

40. See Geoffrey C. Layman, Thomas M. Carsey, and Juliana Menasce Horowitz, "Party Polarization in American Politics: Characteristics, Causes, and Consequences," *Annual Review of Political Science* 9 (2006): 83–110.

41. Michael S. Schmidt and Maggie Haberman, "Aides for Hillary Clinton and Benghazi Committee Dispute Testimony Plan," *New York Times*, July 25, 2015, http://www.nytimes.com/2015/07/26/us/clinton-to-testify-publicly-before-house-committee-investigating-benghazi-attacks.html (accessed 9/21/15).

42. Gregory Krieg, "FBI Boss Comey's 7 Most Damning Lines on Clinton," CNN, July 5, 2016, www.cnn.com/2016/07/05/politics/fbi-clinton-email-server-comey-damning-lines/ (accessed 9/21/16).

43. Carroll J. Doherty, "Impeachment: How It Would Work," *Congressional Quarterly Weekly Report*, January 31, 1998, 222.

Chapter 10

1. These statutes are contained mainly in Title 10 of the U.S. Code, Sections 331, 332, and 333.

2. Dan Slater, "Bush Pardon Party Goes Out with a Whimper," *Wall Street Journal*, January 20, 2009, http://blogs.wsj.com/law/2009/01/20/bush-pardon-party-goes-out-with-a-whimper/ (accessed 3/20/10).

3. In *United States v. Pink*, 315 U.S. 203 (1942), the Supreme Court confirmed that an executive agreement is the legal equivalent of a treaty, despite the absence of Senate approval. This case approved the executive agreement that was used to establish diplomatic relations with the Soviet Union in 1933. An executive agreement, not a treaty, was used in 1940 to exchange "50 overage destroyers" for 99-year leases on some important military bases.

4. For a different perspective, see William F. Grover, *The President as Prisoner: A Structural Critique of the Carter and Reagan Years* (Albany: State University of New York Press, 1988).

5. There is a third source of presidential power implied from the provision for "faithful execution of the laws." This is the president's power to impound funds—that is, to refuse to spend money Congress has appropriated for certain purposes. One author referred to this as a "retroactive veto power" (Robert E. Goosetree, "The Power of the President to Impound Appropriated Funds," *American University Law Review* [January 1962]). Many modern presidents used this impoundment power freely and to considerable effect, and Congress has occasionally delegated such power to the president by statute. But in reaction to the Watergate scandal, Congress adopted the Budget and Impoundment Control Act of 1974, which was designed to circumscribe the president's ability to impound funds by requiring that the president spend all appropriated funds unless both houses of Congress consented to an impoundment within 45 days of a presidential request. Therefore, since 1974, the use of impoundment has declined significantly. Presidents have had to either bite their tongues and accept unwanted appropriations or revert to the older and more dependable but politically limited method of vetoing the entire bill.

6. For more on the veto, see Robert J. Spitzer, *The Presidential Veto: Touchstone of the American Presidency* (Albany: State University of New York Press, 1988).

7. Henry C. Black, *Black's Law Dictionary*, 6th ed. (St. Paul, MN: West Publishing, 1991), 539.

8. James G. Randall, *Constitutional Problems under Lincoln* (New York: Appleton, 1926), chap. 1.

9. Edward S. Corwin, *The President: Office and Powers*, 4th rev. ed. (New York: New York University Press, 1957), 229.

10. A substantial portion of this section is taken from Theodore J. Lowi, *The Personal President* (Ithaca, NY: Cornell University Press, 1985), 141–50.

11. All the figures since 1967, and probably 1957, are understated because additional White House staff members were on "detail" service from the military and other departments (some secretly assigned) and are not counted here because they were not on the White House payroll.

12. Article I, Section 3, provides that "The Vice-President . . . shall be President of the Senate, but shall have no Vote, unless they be equally divided." This is the only vote the vice president is allowed.

13. David Ignatius, "A Skeptical Biden's Role," RealClearPolitics.com, November 26, 2009, www.realclearpolitics.com/articles/2009/11/26/a_skeptical_bidens_role_99320.html (accessed 4/14/10).

14. Samuel Kernell, *Going Public: New Strategies of Presidential Leadership*, 3rd ed. (Washington, DC: Congressional Quarterly Press, 1997); also, Jeffrey K. Tulis, *The Rhetorical Presidency* (Princeton, NJ: Princeton University Press, 1987).
15. Tulis, *The Rhetorical Presidency*, 91.
16. Sidney M. Milkis, *The President and the Parties* (New York: Oxford University Press, 1993), 97.
17. James MacGregor Burns, *Roosevelt: The Lion and the Fox* (New York: Harcourt, Brace, 1956), 317.
18. Kernell, *Going Public*, 79.
19. Claire Cain Miller, "How Obama's Internet Campaign Changed Politics," *New York Times*, November 7, 2008; David Plouffe, *The Audacity to Win: The Inside Story and Lessons of Barack Obama's Historic Victory* (New York: Penguin, 2009).
20. Gallup, "Presidential Job Approval Center," www.gallup.com/poll/124922/presidential -approval-center.aspx (accessed 3/14/14).
21. Lowi, *The Personal President*.
22. Lowi, *The Personal President*, 11.
23. Harold W. Stanley and Richard G. Niemi, *Vital Statistics on American Politics, 2001–2002* (Washington, DC: Congressional Quarterly Press, 2001), 250–1.
24. Milkis, *The President and the Parties*, 128.
25. Milkis, *The President and the Parties*, 160.
26. The classic critique of this process is Theodore J. Lowi, *The End of Liberalism* (New York: W. W. Norton, 1969).
27. Kenneth Culp Davis, *Administrative Law Treatise* (St. Paul, MN: West Publishing, 1958), 9.
28. John M. Broder, "Powerful Shaper of U.S. Rules Quits, with Critics in Wake," *New York Times*, August 4, 2012, A1.
29. A complete inventory is provided in Harold C. Relyea, "Presidential Directives: Background and Review," Congressional Research Service Report 98-611 (Washington, DC: Library of Congress, November 9, 2001).
30. Terry M. Moe and William G. Howell, "The Presidential Power of Unilateral Action," *Journal of Law, Economics and Organization* 15, no. 1 (January 1999): 133–4.
31. *Youngstown Sheet & Tube Co. v. Sawyer*, 346 U.S. 579 (1952).
32. Peter Baker, "Obama Is Making Plans to Use Executive Power for Action on Several Fronts," *New York Times*, February 13, 2010, A12.
33. *United States v. Texas*, 579 U.S. __ (2016).
34. Mark Killenbeck, "A Matter of Mere Approval: The Role of the President in the Creation of Legislative History," *University of Arkansas Law Review* 239, no. 48 (1995).
35. Philip Cooper, *By Order of the President* (Lawrence: University Press of Kansas, 2002), 201.
36. Cooper, *By Order of the President*, 201.
37. Cooper, *By Order of the President*, 216.
38. Joyce A. Green, "Presidential Signing Statements," www.coherentbabble.com/faqs.htm (accessed 5/15/16).
39. Louis Fisher, *Congressional Abdication on War and Spending* (College Station: Texas A&M Press, 2000).

Chapter 11

1. Linda Greenhouse, "Justices Say E.P.A. Has Power to Act on Harmful Gases," *New York Times*, April 3, 2007, www.nytimes.com/2007/04/03/washington/03scotus.html?_r50 (accessed 2/15/10).

2. Environmental Protection Agency, "Regulations and Standards: Light Duty," www3.epa .gov/otaq/climate/regs-light-duty.htm#new1 (accessed 7/9/16).

3. John M. Broder, "U.S. Issues Limits on Greenhouse Gas Emissions from Cars," *New York Times*, April 2, 2010, 81.

4. Juliet Eilperin and Steve Mufson, "Everything You Need to Know about the EPA's Proposed Rule on Coal Plants," *Washington Post*, June 2, 2014, www.washingtonpost .com/national/health-science/epa-will-propose-a-rule-to-cut-emissions-from-existing -coal-plants-by-up-to-30-percent/2014/06/02/f37f0a10-e81d-11e3-afc6-a1dd9407abcf _story.html; Coral Davenport, "Court Gives Obama a Climate Change Win," *New York Times*, June 9, 2015, www.nytimes.com/2015/06/10/us/coal-epa-clean-power-plan .html (accessed 9/30/15); Amy Harder and Brent Kendall, "Obama Carbon Rules to Face Lawsuits, Congressional Tests," *Wall Street Journal*, October 23, 2015, www.wsj .com/articles/obama-carbon-rules-to-face-lawsuits-congressional-tests-1445611059 (accessed 10/29/15).

5. Margaret Cronin Fisk, Kartikay Mehrotra, Alan Katz, and Jeff Plungis, "Volkswagen Agrees to $15 Billion Diesel-Cheating Settlement," Bloomberg News, June 28, 2016, www.bloomberg.com/news/articles/2016-06-28/volkswagen-to-pay-14-7-billion-to -settle-u-s-emissions-claims (accessed 7/8/16).

6. Quoted in Leonard D. White, *The Republican Era* (New York: Free Press, 1958), 6.

7. The White House, Office of the Press Secretary, "Remarks by the President to a Joint Session of Congress on Health Care," September 9, 2009, www.whitehouse .gov/the-press-office/remarks-president-a-joint-session-congress-health-care (accessed 7/11/16).

8. Office of Personnel and Management, Data, Analysis & Documentation Federal Employment Reports, Historical Federal Workforce Tables, Total Government Employment since 1962, www.opm.gov/policy-data-oversight/data-analysis -documentation/federal-employment-reports/historical-tables/total-government -employment-since-1962/ (accessed 7/15/16).

9. Bureau of Labor Statistics, "Table B-1. Employees on Nonfarm Payrolls by Industry Sector and Selected Industry Detail," www.bls.gov/webapps/legacy/cesbtab1.htm (accepted 7/15/16).

10. There are historical reasons that American cabinet-level administrators are called "secretaries." During the Second Continental Congress and the subsequent confederal government, standing committees were formed to deal with executive functions related to foreign affairs, military and maritime issues, and public financing. The heads of those committees were called "secretaries" because their primary task was to handle all correspondence and documentation related to their areas of responsibility.

11. Environmental Protection Agency, "Understanding the Safe Drinking Water Act," August 2009, www.epa.gov/sites/production/files/2015-04/documents/epa816f04030 .pdf (accessed 1/20/14).

12. Thomas Erdbrink, Sewell Chan, and David E. Sanger, "After a U.S. Shift, Iran Has a Seat at Talks on War in Syria," *New York Times*, October 28, 2015, www.nytimes .com/2015/10/29/world/middleeast/syria-talks-vienna-iran.html (accessed 10/19/15).

13. For more detail, consult John E. Harr, *The Professional Diplomat* (Princeton, NJ: Princeton University Press, 1972), 11; and Nicholas Horrock, "The CIA Has Neighbors in the 'Intelligence Community,'" *New York Times*, June 29, 1975, sec. 4, 2. See also Roger Hilsman, *The Politics of Policy Making in Defense and Foreign Affairs*, 3rd ed. (Englewood Cliffs, NJ: Prentice Hall, 1993).

14. Charlie Savage, "Obama Curbs Secrecy of Classified Documents," *New York Times*, December 30, 2009, A19. See the comprehensive evaluation in Citizens for Responsibility and Ethics in Washington, OpenTheGovernment.org, "Measuring

Transparency under the FOIA: The Real Story behind the Numbers," December 2011, http://crew.3cdn.net/5911487fbaaa8cb0f8_9xm6bgari.pdf (accessed 1/3/12).

15. Louise Osborne, "Europeans Outraged over NSA Spying, Threaten Action," *USA Today*, October 29, 2013, www.usatoday.com/story/news/world/2013/10/28/report -nsa-spain/3284609/ (accessed 1/24/14).

16. Mary Madden and Lee Rainie, "Americans' Views about Data Collection and Security," Pew Research Center, Internet, Science & Tech, May 20, 2015, www.pewinternet.org /2015/05/20/americans-views-about-data-collection-and-security/ (accessed 9/30/15).

17. U.S. Department of the Treasury, "The Debt to the Penny and Who Holds It," www .treasurydirect.gov/NP/debt/current (accessed 7/7/16).

18. For an account of the Financial Stability Oversight Council and the passage of the Dodd-Frank financial regulatory legislation, see John T. Woolley and J. Nicholas Ziegler, "The Two-Tiered Politics of Financial Reform in the United States," in *Crisis and Control: Institutional Change in Financial Market Regulation*, ed. Renate Mayntz (Frankfurt, Germany: Campus Verlag, 2012); the council's early activities are described in Financial Stability Oversight Council, "2011 Annual Report," www.treasury.gov /initiatives/fsoc/Documents/FSOCAR2011.pdf, and in Edward V. Murphy and Michael B. Bernier, *Financial Stability Oversight Council: A Framework to Mitigate Systemic Risk* (Washington, DC: Congressional Research Service, November 15, 2011), www.llsdc.org/assets/DoddFrankdocs/crs-r42083.pdf (accessed 1/3/12).

19. Alexander Hamilton, James Madison, and John Jay, *The Federalist Papers*, ed. Clinton Rossiter (New York: New American Library, 1961), no. 51, 322.

20. The title of this section was inspired by Peri Arnold, *Making the Managerial Presidency* (Princeton, NJ: Princeton University Press, 1986).

21. For more details and evaluations, see David Rosenbloom, *Public Administration* (New York: Random House, 1986), 186–221; Charles H. Levine and Rosslyn Kleeman, "The Quiet Crisis in the American Public Service," in *Agenda for Excellence: Public Service in America*, ed. Patricia Ingraham and Donald Kettl (Chatham, NJ: Chatham House, 1992); and Patricia Ingraham and David Rosenbloom, "The State of Merit in the Federal Government," in *Agenda for Excellence*.

22. Lester Salamon and Alan Abramson, "Governance: The Politics of Retrenchment," in *The Reagan Record*, ed. John Palmer and Isabel Sawhill (Cambridge, MA: Ballinger, 1984), 40.

23. Colin Campbell, "The White House and the Presidency under the 'Let's Deal' President," in *The Bush Presidency: First Appraisals*, ed. Colin Campbell and Bert A. Rockman (Chatham, NJ: Chatham House, 1991), 185–222.

24. Vice President Gore's National Partnership for Reinventing Government, "Appendix F, History of the National Partnership for Reinventing Government: Accomplishments, 1993–2000, A Summary," http://govinfo.library.unt.edu/npr/whoweare/appendixf.html (accessed 3/28/08).

25. Michael D. Shear and Michael S. Schmidt, "Benghazi Panel Engages Clinton in Tense Session," *New York Times*, October 22, 2015, www.nytimes.com/2015/10/23/us /politics/hillary-clinton-benghazi-committee.html?_r50 (accessed 10/29/15).

26. The Office of Technology Assessment was a fourth research agency serving Congress until 1995. It was one of the first agencies scheduled for elimination by the 104th Congress. Until 1983, Congress had still another tool of legislative oversight: the legislative veto. Agencies were obliged to submit to Congress every proposed decision or rule, which would then lie before both chambers for 30 to 60 days. If Congress took no action by a one-house or two-house resolution explicitly to veto the proposed measure during the prescribed period, the measure became law. In 1983 the Supreme Court declared the legislative veto unconstitutional on the grounds that it violated the

separation of powers—that is the resolutions Congress passed to exercise its veto were not subject to presidential veto, as required by the Constitution. See *Immigration and Naturalization Service v. Chadha*, 462 U.S. 919 (1983).

Chapter 12

1. *United States v. Texas*, 579 U.S. __ (2016).
2. United States Courts, "Judicial Business 2014," www.uscourts.gov/statistics-reports/judicial-business-2014 (accessed 9/19/15).
3. Michael A. Fletcher, "Obama Criticized as Too Cautious, Slow on Judicial Posts," *Washington Post*, October 16, 2009, www.washingtonpost.com/wp-dyn/content/article/2009/10/15/AR2009101504083.html (accessed 3/1/10).
4. Russell Wheeler, "Judicial Nominations and Confirmations after Three Years—Where Do Things Stand?" Governance Studies at Brookings, January 13, 2012, www.brookings.edu/research/papers/2012/01/13-nominations-wheeler (accessed 7/11/16); United States Courts, "Judicial Vacancies," www.uscourts.gov/JudgesAndJudgeships/JudicialVacancies.aspx (accessed 9/19/2015).
5. *Arizona v. United States*, 567 U.S. __ (2012).
6. *National Federation of Independent Business v. Sebelius*, 567 U.S. __ (2012); *King v. Burwell*, 576 U.S. __ (2015).
7. Peter Wallsten and Richard Simon, "Sotomayor Nomination Splits GOP," *Los Angeles Times*, May 27, 2009, http://articles.latimes.com/2009/may/27/nation/na-court-assess27 (accessed 11/12/09); Carl Hulse, "Senate Confirms Kagan in Partisan Vote," *New York Times*, August 5, 2010, www.nytimes.com/2010/08/06/us/politics/06kagan.html (accessed 7/11/16).
8. *Marbury v. Madison*, 1 Cr. 137 (1803).
9. *National Federation of Independent Businesses v. Sebelius*, 567 U.S. __ (2012).
10. U.S. Government Printing Office, "Acts of Congress Held Unconstitutional in Whole or in Part by the Supreme Court of the United States," www.gpo.gov/fdsys/pkg/GPO-CONAN-2013/pdf/GPO-CONAN-2013-11.pdf (accessed 4/20/14).
11. *Federal Election Commission v. Wisconsin Right to Life*, 551 U.S. 449 (2007); *Citizens United v. Federal Election Commission*, 558 U.S. 310 (2010); *McCutcheon v. Federal Election Commission*, 572 U.S. __ (2014).
12. *Hamdi v. Rumsfeld*, 542 U.S. 507 (2004).
13. *Hamdan v. Rumsfeld*, 548 U.S. 557 (2006).
14. *Boumediene v. Bush*, 553 U.S. 723 (2008).
15. The Supreme Court affirmed this review power in *Martin v. Hunter's Lessee*, 1 Wheat. 304 (1816).
16. *Brown v. Board of Education*, 347 U.S. 483 (1954).
17. *Lawrence v. Texas*, 539 U.S. 558 (2003).
18. *United States v. Jones*, 567 U.S. __ (2012); *Riley v. California*, 573 U.S. __ (2014).
19. *Miller v. Alabama*, 567 U.S. __ (2012).
20. Robert Scigliano, *The Supreme Court and the Presidency* (New York: Free Press, 1971), 161. For an interesting critique of the solicitor general's role during the Reagan administration, see Lincoln Caplan, "Annals of the Law," *New Yorker*, August 17, 1987, 30–62.
21. Edward Lazarus, *Closed Chambers* (New York: Times Books, 1998), 6.
22. *Smith v. Allwright*, 321 U.S. 649 (1944).
23. Charles Krauthammer, "Why Roberts Did It," *Washington Post*, June 29, 2012, www.washingtonpost.com/opinions/charles-krauthammer-why-roberts-did-it/2012/06/28/gJQA4X0g9V_story.html (accessed 4/22/14).
24. *Roe v. Wade*, 410 U.S. 113 (1973); *Griswold v. Connecticut*, 381 U.S. 479 (1965).

25. Adam Liptak, "For Justices, Free Speech Often Means 'Speech I Agree With,'" *New York Times*, May 6, 2014, A15.
26. Alexander Hamilton, James Madison, and John Jay, *The Federalist Papers*, ed. Clinton Rossiter (New York: New American Library, 1961), no. 10, 78.

Chapter 13

1. Henry J. Kaiser Family Foundation, "Kaiser Health Tracking Poll: The Public's Views on the ACA," http://kff.org/interactive/kaiser-health-tracking-poll-the-publics-views-on -the-aca/#?response=Favorable—Unfavorable&aRange=twoYear (accessed 10/31/15).
2. *Cato Handbook for Policymakers*, 7th ed. (Washington, DC: Cato Institute, 2009), 281, http://object.cato.org/sites/cato.org/files/serials/files/cato-handbook-policymakers /2009/9/hb111-20.pdf (accessed 8/1/16).
3. James Dao, "The Nation; Big Bucks Trip Up the Lean New Army," *New York Times*, February 10, 2002, sec. 4, 5.
4. For an evaluation of the policy of withholding subsidies to carry out desegregation laws, see Gary Orfield, *Must We Bus?* (Washington, DC: Brookings Institution Press, 1978). For an evaluation of the use of subsidies to encourage work or to calm political unrest, see Frances Fox Piven and Richard Cloward, *Regulating the Poor: The Functions of Public Welfare* (New York: Random House, 1971).
5. For an evaluation of the politics of eminent domain, see Theodore J. Lowi and Benjamin Ginsberg, *Poliscide* (New York: Macmillan, 1976), especially 235 and chaps. 11 and 12, written by Julia and Thomas Vitullo-Martin.
6. Federal Reserve Board, "Open Market Operations," www.federalreserve.gov /monetarypolicy/openmarket.htm (accessed 8/1/16).
7. Ronald Reagan, "Inaugural Address," The American Presidency Project, January 20, 1981, www.presidency.ucsb.edu/ws/?pid=43130 (accessed 4/27/14).
8. Gallup, "Taxes," www.gallup.com/poll/1714/taxes.aspx (accessed 4/27/14).
9. Gallup, "Taxes."
10. Social Security Administration, "Contribution and Benefit Base," www.ssa.gov/OACT /COLA/cbb.html (accessed 12/16/15).
11. Social Security Administration, "Social Security Basic Facts," www.ssa.gov/news/press /basicfact.html (accessed 10/31/15).
12. Workers must have lost their job through no fault of their own. For a full description of the program see, Chad Stone and William Chen "Introduction to Unemployment Insurance," Center on Budget and Policy Priorities, July 30, 2014, www.cbpp.org /research/introduction-to-unemployment-insurance (accessed 11/18/15).
13. Ife Floyd and Liz Schott, "TANF Cash Benefits Have Fallen by More Than 20 Percent in Most States and Continue to Erode," Center on Budget and Policy Priorities, October 15, 2015, www.cbpp.org/research/family-income-support/tanf-cash-benefits -have-fallen-by-more-than-20-percent-in-most-states (accessed 10/31/15).
14. This poverty threshold is for a household of three persons that includes two children. Department of Health and Human Services, Office of the Assistant Secretary for Planning and Evaluation, Poverty Guidelines, January 25, 2016, http://aspe.hhs.gov /poverty-guidelines (accessed 7/10/16).
15. See Martin Gilens, *Why Americans Hate Welfare* (Chicago: University of Chicago Press, 1999), chaps. 3, 4.
16. Gilens, *Why Americans Hate Welfare*.
17. EITC and Other Refundable Credits, "Statistics for Tax Returns with EITC," www.eitc .irs.gov/EITC-Central/eitcstats (accessed 7/10/16).
18. U.S. Department of Health and Human Services, Administration for Children & Families, "Fiscal and Calendar Year 2009—TANF: Total Number of Recipients,"

May 18, 2010, www.acf.hhs.gov/programs/ofa/resource/2009-recipient-tan (accessed 8/10/16).

19. U.S. Government Accountability Office, "Temporary Assistance for Needy Families," December 2012, www.gao.gov/assets/660/650635.pdf (accessed 10/31/15).

20. Center for Law and Social Policy, "Analysis of Fiscal Year 2006 TANF and MOE Spending by States," http://clasp.org (accessed 4/9/08).

21. See the discussion of the law and the data presented in House Ways and Means Committee, *Background Material and Data on Programs within the Jurisdiction of the Committee on Ways and Means (Green Book)*, Section 7, "Temporary Assistance for Needy Families (TANF)," WMCP 106-14, http://frwebgate.access.gpo.gov (accessed 3/26/08); Rebecca M. Blank, "Evaluating Welfare Reform in the United States," *Journal of Economic Literature* 40 (December 2002): 1105–66.

22. U.S. Department of Agriculture, Food and Nutrition Service, "Supplemental Nutrition Assistance Program (SNAP)," www.fns.usda.gov/pd/34SNAPmonthly.htm (accessed 8/1/16).

23. There were a couple of minor precedents. One was the Smith-Hughes Act of 1917, which made federal funds available to the states for vocational education at the elementary and secondary levels. Another was the Lanham Act of 1940, which made federal funds available to schools in "federally impacted areas," that is, areas with an unusually large number of government employees and/or where the local tax base was reduced by large amounts of government-owned property.

24. New America Foundation, "PreK-12 Financing Overview," June 29, 2015, atlas .newamerica.org/school-finance (accessed 7/10/16).

25. David K. Cohen and Susan L. Moffitt, *The Ordeal of Equality: Did Federal Regulation Fix the Schools* (Cambridge, MA: Harvard University Press, 2009).

26. Rich Motoko, "'No Child' Law Whittled Down by White House," *New York Times*, July 6, 2012, A1; U.S. Department of Education, Elementary and Secondary Education, "ESEA Flexibility," www2.ed.gov/policy/elsec/guid/esea-flexibility/index.html (accessed 5/11/14).

27. Valerie Strauss, "The Successor to No Child Left Behind Has, It Turns Out, Big Problems of Its Own," *Washington Post*, December 7, 2015, www.washingtonpost.com/news /answer-sheet/wp/2015/12/07/the-successor-to-no-child-left-behind-has-it-turns-out -big-problems-of-its-own/ (accessed 7/11/16).

28. Sam Dillon, "Obama Proposes Sweeping Change in Education Law," *New York Times*, March 14, 2010, A1; Veronica DeVore, "'Race to the Top' Education Funds Awarded to 9 States and D.C.," August 24, 2010, www.pbs.org/newshour/rundown/2010/08 /round-two-results-announced-for-race-to-the-top.html (accessed 11/13/12).

29. Elaine Weiss, "Mismatches in Race to the Top Limit Educational Improvement: Lack of Time, Resources, and Tools to Address Opportunity Gaps Puts Lofty State Goals Out of Reach," Economic Policy Institute, September 12, 2013, www.epi.org/publication /race-to-the-top-goals/ (accessed 5/11/14).

30. Congressional Budget Office, Long-Term Budget Projections (July 2016), "Table 1. Summary Data for the Extended Baseline," www.cbo.gov/about/products/budget _economic_data (accessed 7/16/16); Congressional Budget Office, "Updated Budget Projections: 2016 to 2026," Table 4. Mandatory Outlays Projected in CBO's Baseline, www.cbo.gov/sites/default/files/114th-congress-2015-2016/reports/51384 -MarchBaseline_OneCol.pdf (accessed 7/16/16); Congressional Budget Office, Historical Budget Data (March 2016), "Table 5. Mandatory Outlays," www.cbo.gov /about/products/budget_economic_data (accessed 7/16/16); Congressional Budget Office, Baseline Projections for Selected Programs, Medicaid (Mar 2016), "Detail of

Spending and Enrollment for Medicaid for CBO's March 2016 Baseline," www.cbo
.gov/sites/default/files/51301-2016-03-Medicaid.pdf (accessed 7/16/16); Office of
Management and Budget, Historical Tables, "Table 11.3—Outlays for Payments for
Individuals by Category and Major Program: 1940-2021," www.whitehouse.gov/omb
/budget/Historicals (accessed 7/16/16).

31. Henry J. Kaiser Family Foundation, "The Coverage Gap: Uninsured Poor Adults in
States that Do Not Expand Medicaid—An Update," January 21, 2016, kff.org/health
-reform/issue-brief/the-coverage-gap-uninsured-poor-adults-in-states-that-do-not
-expand-medicaid-an-update/ (accessed 6/2/16).

32. White House, "Fact Sheet: Affordable Care Act by the Numbers," www.whitehouse.gov
/the-press-office/2014/04/17/fact-sheet-affordable-care-act-numbers (accessed 5/12/14).

33. Henry J. Kaiser Family Foundation, "Health Tracking Poll."

34. *National Federation of Independent Business v. Sebelius*, 567 U.S. __ (2012).

35. Henry J. Kaiser Family Foundation, "The Coverage Gap."

36. *King v. Burwell*, 576 U.S. __ (2015); Lena H. Sun, "6.4 million Americans Could
Lose Obamacare Subsidies, Federal Data Show," *Washington Post*, June 2, 2015, www
.washingtonpost.com/national/health-science/64-million-americans-could-lose
-obamacare-subsidies-federal-data-show/2015/06/02/fe0c87be-095a-11e5-95fd
-d580f1c5d44e_story.html (accessed 11/4/15).

37. Robert Barnes, "Affordable Care Act Survives Supreme Court Challenge," *Washington
Post*, June 25, 2015, www.washingtonpost.com/politics/courts_law/obamacare-survives
-supreme-court-challenge/2015/06/25/af87608e-188a-11e5-93b7-5eddc056ad8a
_story.html (accessed 11/4/15).

38. John E. Schwarz, *America's Hidden Success*, 2nd ed. (New York: W.W. Norton, 1988),
41–42.

39. Annamaria Andriotis, Laura Kusisto, and Joe Light, "After Foreclosures, Home Buyers
Are Back," *Wall Street Journal*, April 8, 2015, www.wsj.com/articles/after-foreclosures
-home-buyers-are-back-1428538655 (accessed 11/6/15).

40. U.S. Census Bureau, "Table 3. Poverty Status of People, by Age, Race, and Hispanic
Origin," www.census.gov/data/tables/time-series/demo/income-poverty/historical
-poverty-people.html (accessed 7/17/16).

41. See, for example, Theodore R. Marmor, Jerry L. Mashaw, and Philip L. Harvey,
America's Misunderstood Welfare State (New York: Basic Books, 1990), 156;
U.S. Census Bureau, Historical Poverty Tables.

42. U.S. Census Bureau, "Income and Poverty in the United States: 2014," www.census.gov
/content/dam/Census/library/publications/2015/demo/p60-252.pdf (accessed 7/16/16).

43. Juliette Cubanski, Giselle Casillas, and Anthony Damico, "Poverty among Seniors: An
Updated Analysis of National and State Level Poverty Rates under the Official and
Supplemental Poverty Measures," Henry J. Kaiser Family Foundation, Issue Brief, June
2015, files.kff.org/attachment/issue-brief-poverty-among-seniors-an-updated-analysis
-of-national-and-state-level-poverty-rates-under-the-official-and-supplemental-poverty
-measures (accessed 11/6/15).

44. AARP, "AARP Member Opinion Survey, Issue Spotlight: Work," December 2012,
www.aarp. org/content/dam/aarp/research/surveys_statistics/general/2012/2012
-AARP-Member-Opinion-Survey -Issue-Spotlight-Work-AARP.pdf (accessed
11/11/15); Thom File, "Who Votes? Congressional Elections and the American
Electorate: 1978–2014," U.S. Census Bureau, July 2015, www.census.gov/content
/dam/Census/library/publications/2015/demo/p20-577.pdf; AARP, "AARP Survey:
76% of People 50-Plus Pleased with Pope," September 22, 2015, www.aarp.org/about
-aarp/press-center/info-09-2015/aarp-survey-76-percent-50-plus-pleased-with-pope

.html; Open Secrets, "Profile for 2014 Election Cycle," AARP, www.opensecrets.org
/orgs/summary.php?id5D000023726&cycle5; AARP, "About the AARP Public Policy
Institute," www.aarp .org/ppi/about-ppi/#experts (accessed 11/11/15).

45. Christopher Howard, *The Hidden Welfare State: Tax Expenditures and Social Policy in
the United States* (Princeton, NJ: Princeton University Press, 1999); Jacob S. Hacker,
The Divided Welfare State: The Battle over Public and Private Benefits in the United States
(New York: Cambridge University Press, 2002).

46. U.S. Department of Agriculture, Food and Nutrition Service, "Supplemental Nutrition
Assistance Program (SNAP)," www.fns.usda.gov/snap/eligibility#Income (accessed
7/11/16); Center on Budget and Policy Priorities, "Policy Basics: Introduction to the
Supplemental Nutrition Assistance Program (SNAP)," updated March 24, 2016, www
.cbpp.org/research/policy-basics-introduction-to-the-supplemental-nutrition-assistance
-program-snap (accessed 7/11/16).

47. "Panera CEO: On Food Stamps, I Can't Eat in My Own Restaurant," September 25,
2013, https://cnneatocracy.wordpress.com/2013/09/25/panera-ceo-on-food-stamps
-i-cant-eat-in-my-own-restaurant/ (accessed 5/12/14).

48. Samantha Artiga, Anthony Damico, and Rachel Garfield, "The Impact of the Coverage
Gap for Adults in States not Expanding Medicaid by Race and Ethnicity," October 26,
2015, http://kff.org/disparities-policy/issue-brief/the-impact-of-the-coverage-gap-in
-states-not-expanding-medicaid-by-race-and-ethnicity/ (accessed 11/11/15).

49. Raymond Hernandez, "Federal Welfare Overhaul Allows Albany to Shift Money
Elsewhere," *New York Times*, April 23, 2000, 1.

50. U.S. Department of Agriculture, Food and Nutrition Service, "National and/or State
Level Monthly and/or Annual Data," April 2016, www.fns.usda.gov/pd/supplemental
-nutrition-assistance-program-snap (accessed 7/11/16).

51. U.S. Census Bureau, "Table 2. Poverty Status of People by Family Relationship, Race,
and Hispanic Origin: 1959 to 2014," www.census.gov/data/tables/time-series/demo
/income-poverty/historical-poverty-people.html (accessed 7/16/16); U.S. Census
Bureau, "Income and Poverty in the United States: 2014."

52. U.S. Census Bureau, "Table 2. Poverty Status of People by Family Relationship, Race,
and Hispanic Origin: 1959 to 2014" and "Table 3. Poverty Status of People, by Age,
Race, and Hispanic Origin."

53. L. Free and Hadley Cantril, *The Political Beliefs of Americans* (New York: Simon and
Schuster, 1968).

54. Fay Lomax Cook and Edith Barrett, *Support for the American Welfare State* (New York:
Columbia University Press, 1992); and Hugh Heclo, "The Political Foundations of
Antipoverty Policy," in *Fighting Poverty*, ed. Sheldon H. Danziger and Daniel H.
Weinberg (Cambridge, MA: Harvard University Press, 1986), 312–40.

55. Henry J. Kaiser Family Foundation, Peterson Kaiser Health System Tracker, Health
Spending Explorer, December 7, 2015, www.healthsystemtracker.org/interactive
/health-spendingexplorer/?display=As%2520a%2520%2525%2520of%2520GDP
&service=&rangeType=single&years=2014 (accessed 7 /11/16}.

Chapter 14

1. Geoffrey Perret, *A Country Made by War* (New York: Random House, 1989), 558.

2. Stockholm International Peace Research Institute, "Trends in World Military Expenditure, 2013," http://books.sipri.org/files/FS/SIPRIFS1404.pdf (accessed 6/12/14).

3. Rupert Smith, *The Utility of Force: The Art of War in the Modern World* (New York:
Vintage, 2008).

4. D. Robert Worley, *Shaping U.S. Military Forces: Revolution or Relevance in a Post–Cold
War World* (Westport, CT: Praeger Security International, 2006).

5. Better World Campaign, "How the U.S. Funds the UN," https://betterworldcampaign .org/us-un-partnership/how-the-us-funds-the-un/ (accessed 9/19/14).

6. Matthew Crenson and Benjamin Ginsberg, *Presidential Power: Unchecked and Unbalanced* (New York: W. W. Norton, 2007).

7. Benjamin Ginsberg, *The American Lie: Government by the People and Other Political Fables* (Boulder, CO: Paradigm, 2007).

8. Paul R. Pillar, *Terrorism and American Foreign Policy* (Washington, DC: Brookings Institution Press, 2003).

9. One confirmation of this is found in Theodore Lowi, *The End of Liberalism: The Second Republic of the United States*, 2nd ed. (New York: W. W. Norton, 1979), 127–30; another is found in Stephen Krasner, "Are Bureaucracies Important?" *Foreign Policy* 7 (Summer 1972): 159–79. However, it should be noted that Krasner was writing his article in disagreement with Graham T. Allison, "Conceptual Models and the Cuban Missile Crisis," *American Political Science Review* 63, no. 3 (September 1969): 689–718.

10. Hans Morgenthau, *Politics among Nations*, 2nd ed. (New York: Knopf, 1956), 505.

11. See Theodore Lowi, *The Personal President: Power Invested, Promise Unfulfilled* (Ithaca, NY: Cornell University Press, 1985), 167–9.

12. For information on current U.S. sanctions programs, visit U.S. Department of the Treasury, "Sanctions Programs and Country Information," www.treasury.gov/resource -center/sanctions/Programs/Pages/Programs.aspx (accessed 6/11/14).

13. George Quester, *The Continuing Problem of International Politics* (Hinsdale, IL: Dryden Press, 1974), 229.

14. The Warsaw Pact was signed in 1955 by Albania, Bulgaria, Czechoslovakia, Hungary, the German Democratic Republic (East Germany), Poland, Romania, and the Soviet Union. Albania later dropped out. The Warsaw Pact was terminated in 1991.

answer key

Chapter 1
1. b
2. d
3. d
4. c
5. d
6. b
7. a
8. d
9. e
10. b
11. e
12. e
13. a
14. c

Chapter 2
1. a
2. b
3. b
4. c
5. c
6. e
7. d
8. e
9. e
10. a
11. d
12. a

Chapter 3
1. b
2. c
3. c
4. e
5. a
6. a
7. d
8. c
9. b

10. d
11. b
12. d

Chapter 4
1. e
2. b
3. a
4. e
5. e
6. d
7. a
8. a
9. c
10. b
11. b

Chapter 5
1. c
2. b
3. b
4. d
5. e
6. c
7. a
8. c
9. b
10. a
11. b

Chapter 6
1. b
2. a
3. b
4. e
5. d
6. b
7. e
8. b
9. c

10. c
11. c
12. b

Chapter 7
1. a
2. c
3. d
4. e
5. d
6. e
7. d
8. c
9. b
10. d
11. c

Chapter 8
1. a
2. b
3. c
4. d
5. c
6. b
7. e
8. a
9. a
10. d
11. e
12. c

Chapter 9
1. b
2. a
3. d
4. b
5. c
6. d
7. b
8. a

9. d
10. e
11. c
12. b
13. a
14. a

Chapter 10
1. b
2. d
3. b
4. c
5. b
6. b
7. e
8. c
9. a
10. c
11. b
12. a

Chapter 11
1. d
2. b
3. b
4. b
5. e
6. c
7. d
8. a
9. d
10. d
11. a
12. d

Chapter 12
1. a
2. c
3. a
4. d

5. c

6. d

7. e

8. b

9. b

10. a

11. c

12. b

Chapter 13

1. e

2. c

3. d

4. d

5. d

6. b

7. e

8. c

9. a

10. d

11. e

12. c

Chapter 14

1. b

2. a

3. d

4. c

5. e

6. c

7. e

8. a

9. c

10. d

11. b

credits

Chapter 1: p. 2: JG Photography/Alamy; p. 5: Screenshot 2016 U.S. Department of Education Office of Federal Student Aid; p. 8: Richard B. Levine/Alamy Live News; p. 13: Rue des Archives/Granger, NYC—All rights reserved; p. 16: Jim West/Almay Stock Photo; p. 22: Don Emmert/AFP/Getty Images

Chapter 2: p. 28: Superstock/Superstock; p. 33: Bettmann/Corbis via Getty Images; p. 35: Stephen J. Boitano/LightRocket via Getty Images; p. 37: Sarin Images/Granger, NYC—All rights reserved; p. 40: Library Company of Philadelphia; p. 52: Matt Mills McKnight/Getty Images; p. 57: Rohn Engh/FPG/Getty Images

Chapter 3: p. 64: Blaine Harrington III/Getty Images; p. 69: John Moore/Getty Images; p. 75: Library of Congress; p. 76: Library of Congress; p. 82: Ilene MacDonald/Alamy Stock Photo; p. 83: AP Photo/Str; p. 86: AP Photo/Charles Dharapak

Chapter 4: p. 94: David Grossman/Alamy Live News; p. 102: Chip Somodevilla/Getty Images; p. 105: STF/AFP/Getty Images; p. 112: AP Photo/Matt York; p. 116: Tracy A. Woodward/The Washington Post via Getty Images; p. 117: Kevin Dietsch/UPI/Newscom; p. 119: Library of Congress; p. 120: Bettmann/Getty Images; p. 124: Don Emmert/AFP/Getty Images; p. 127: Leif Skoogfors/Getty Images; p. 129: Joshua Lott/The New York Times/Redux; p. 132 (left): AP Photo/Richard Drew; p. 132 (right): Drew Angerer/CNP/AdMedia/Newscom

Chapter 5: p. 142: Robert K. Chin/Alamy Stock Photo; p. 146: Newzulu/Alamy Stock Photo; p. 151: Jay Janner/MCT/Newscom; p. 152: Ed Zurga/Getty Images; p. 157 (left): Mark Wilson/Getty Images; p. 157 (right): Tom Williams/CQ Roll Call/Getty Images; p. 160: CALVIN AND HOBBES © 1994 Watterson. Reprinted with permission of UNIVERSAL UCLICK. All rights reserved.; p. 166: Bettmann/Getty Images

Chapter 6: p. 174: Brooks Kraft/Getty Images; p. 179: Vario Images GmbH & Co.KG/Alamy Stock Photo; p. 181 (left): Virginia Sherwood/NBC/NBCU Photo Bank via Getty Images; p. 181 (right): Brendan McDermid/Reuters/Newscom; p. 183: AP Photo/The Record of Bergen County, Chris Pedota; p. 186: © Julie Dermansky/Julie Dermansky/Corbis via Getty Images; p. 190: © Ryan Garza/Detroit Free Press via ZUMA Wire; p. 192: Jack Plunkett/Invision/AP; p. 194: Jeff Haynes/AFP/Getty Images

Chapter 7: p. 202: Hill Street Studios/Getty Images; p. 207: Jim West/Alamy; p. 212: Granger, NYC—All rights reserved; p. 217: EPA European Press Photo Agency B.V./Alamy Stock Photo; p. 223: © Sun-Sentinel/ZUMAPRESS.com; p. 228: Ronen Tivon/NurPhoto via Getty Images; p. 230: Richard Ellis/Alamy Stock Photo; p. 231 AP Photos/Richard Drew; p. 234: Mike Segar/Reuters/Alamy Stock Photo; p. 237: © Jay Mallin/ZUMAPRESS.com

Chapter 8: p. 244: Richard Levine/Alamy Stock Photo; p. 248: Scott Olsen/Getty Images; p. 262: Erik McGregor/Pacific Press/LightRocket via Getty Images

Chapter 9: p. 272: Jim Bourg/Reuters/Newscom; p. 278: Nicholas Kamm/AFP/Getty Images; p. 283: AP Photo/Ross D. Franklin; p. 287: AP Photo/Andrew Harnik; p. 296: Staff/Reuters/Newscom; p. 300: DPA Picture Alliance/Alamy Stock Photo

Chapter 10: p. 312: Paul Gordon/Alamy Stock Photo; p. 315 (left): AP Photo/Tim Roske; p. 315 (right): Chip Somodevilla/Getty Images; p. 318: Sven Creutzmann/Mambo Photo/Getty Images; p. 322: Joe Raedle/Getty Images; p. 328: Tom Williams/CQ Roll Call/Getty Images; p. 329: Bettmann/Getty Images; p. 333: EPA European Press Photo Agency B.V./Alamy Stock Photo; p. 336: Jewel Samad/Getty Images

Chapter 11: p. 342: Craig F. Walker/Getty Images; p. 345: AP Photo/Ben Margot; p. 350: NG Images/Alamy Stock Photo; p. 354: "Iron Triangles" republished with permission of Wadsworth, a division of Cengage Learning from *Incomplete Conquest: Governing America*, 2nd ed. by Theodore J. Lowi (New York: Holt, Rinehart and Winston, 1981), p. 139. © 1981 by CBS College Publishing; permission conveyed through Copyright Clearance Center, Inc.; p. 360: CBS/Courtesy Everett Collection; p. 362: STR/AFP/Getty Images

Chapter 12: p. 370: Bill Clark/CQ Roll Call/Getty Images; p. 373: AP Photo/Michael Tarm; p. 381: EPA European Press Photo Agency B.V./Alamy Stock Photo; p. 384: Tom Williams/CQ Roll Call/Getty Images; p. 386: AP Photo/The Decatur Daily, Clyde Stancil; p. 394: Alex Wong/Getty Images

Chapter 13: p. 402: Krista Kennell/Sipa via AP Photo; p. 410: © Michael Reynolds/EPA/Newscom; p. 413: Joseph Barnell/SuperStock; p. 415: Richard Levine/Alamy Stock Photo; p. 419: Chip Somodevilla/Getty Images; p. 424: Jewel Samad/AFP/Getty Images; p. 427: Saul Loeb/Getty Images

Chapter 14: p. 438: U.S. Navy photo by Mass Communication Specialist Seaman Kyle D. Gahlau; p. 443: Delil Souleiman/Stringer/Getty Images; p. 447: AFP/Stringer/Getty Images; p. 453: Nicholas Kamm/Getty Images; p. 457: Adek Berry/Stringer/Getty Images

index

Page numbers in *italic* refer to figures or photos.

Beard, Charles, 38
Bedford, Gunning, 39
Belgium, *133*
beliefs, 145
Berghuis v. Thompkins, 114
Berinsky, Adam, 165
Between Two Ferns, 330
biases
  in interest groups, 251
  in polling, 163
bicameralism, 42
bicameral legislature, 275
big data, bureaucracy and, 364
bilateral treaties, 456
Bill of Rights, 19, 43, 46, 48, 49. *See also*
    individual amendments
  and civil rights, 95, 97–99
  Eighth Amendment, 115–16
  Fifth Amendment, 113–14
  First Amendment, 101–9
  Fourth Amendment, 111–12
  origin of, 97, 98
  and right to privacy, 116–18
  Second Amendment, 109–11
  Sixth Amendment, 115
bills
  in conference committees, 294
  debate on, 291, 293
  private, 286
  that die in committee, 291
bin Laden, Osama, 187, 449
Bipartisan Campaign Reform Act of 2002,
    236, 264, 382, 384
Black Lives Matter movement, *94*, 122,
    154, 261, *262*
Blackmun, Harry, 389, 393
block grants, 83, 84
blogs, 175
  of Congress members, 279
  as news source, 182, 184, 185
  political knowledge from, 188
Bloomberg News, 184
Boehner, John, *287*, 299–301, *300*, 304
Boston Massacre (1770), 33
Boston Tea Party, 33, *33*
Boumediene v. Bush, 385
bourgeoisie, 10–11
Bowers v. Hardwick, 131
Brady Handgun Violence Prevention Act, 78
Brazil, *53*
  climate change issue in, *162*
  government employment in, *353*
  judicial review in, *383*
  same-sex marriage in, *133*
  trade as percentage of GDP of, *446*
  voter turnout in, *224*

Brennan, William, 107
Bretton Woods agreement, 455
Breyer, Stephen, 102
briefs, 389–90
British Broadcasting Company (BBC), 18
British taxes, 32–33
broadcast media, 179–80, 193, 194
Brown, Dwayne, *350*
Brown, Linda, 120
Brown, Michael, 154
Brown, Oliver, 120
Brown v. Board of Education, 120–21, 260,
    386
*Brown v. Entertainment Merchants Associa-
    tion*, 108
Bryan, William Jennings, 213, 216
Buckley v. Valeo, 237
budgeting, zero-base, 360
bureaucracy, 343–64
  control of, 359–63
  defined, 345
  and democracy, 364
  for economic strength, 357–58
  for efficiency improvement, 345–51
  executive branch, 350–58
  and foreign policy, 450
  getting information from, *365*, 366
  globally, 349
  merit system in, 347
  for national security, 355–57
  for the public welfare, 351–52, 354,
    354
  size of, *348*, 348–50
bureaucrats, 346–47
Bureau of Indian Affairs, 130
bureaus, federal, 350
Burger, Warren, 127
Bush, George H. W.
  bureaucracy under, 362, 363
  centralized management under, 360
  Supreme Court justices appointed by,
    371, 395
  Thomas proposed by, 381
Bush, George W.
  approval ratings for, 331
  on big government, 348
  directives to administrative agencies,
    332
  election of 2000, 167, 216
  electoral votes for, 229
  executive management under, 360, 361
  executive orders of, 333
  foreign policy initiatives of, 449
  on government secrecy, 357
  growth of government under, 85
  immigration reform bill of, 262

and invasion of Iraq, 451
legislative initiatives of, 321
and Medicare reform, 428
military budget increase under, 408
No Child Left Behind, 419
oversight under, 362
powers used by, 324
presidential pardons, 318
and regulatory role of government, 344
response to September 11 attacks, 322, 324
response to terrorism, 160, 191
and SCHIP program, 84
signing statements of, 334
Supreme Court justices appointed by, 371, 395
tax cuts of, 157–58, 410
vetoes of, 321
vice president of, 327
and war on terror, 191, 384–85
Bush, George W., administration
Americans' mistrust of, 7
EPA's authority under, 346
and illegal immigrants, 84
leaks during, 191–92
and Medicare reform, 427–28
preventive war policy of, 443
and regulatory role of government, 344
Bush Doctrine, 449
Bush v. Gore, 229

Cabinet, 325
Cable News Network (CNN), 179
Calhoun, John C., 75
California
display of Communist flag in, 104
electoral votes of, 229
gun regulations in, 109–10
Latino television channels in, 180
public accommodation settlements in, 123
recall elections in, 228
referenda in, 228
regulation of marijuana use in, 65
sale of violent video games in, 108
same-sex marriage in, 132
transgender persons in, 88
voter registration in, 223
cameras, digital, 186
campaign funds, 235–37
Canada
climate change issue in, *162*
education in, 421
federal system in, 67
government employment in, *353*
NAFTA, 445

NATO, 456
same-sex marriage in, *133*
trade as percentage of GDP, *446*
as U.S. trade partner, 446
voter turnout in, *224*
candidates
characteristics of, 226–27
media influence on perceptions of, 191
nomination of, 206
recruitment of, 206
capitalism, 20
capital punishment, 115–16
Cardozo, Benjamin, 99, 112
Carter, Jimmy, 318, 359–60
cases filed, in Supreme Court, *388*
casino gambling, 130
Castro, Raúl, *318*
categorical grants, 76
Catholics
and abortion, 159
immigrants as, 13
as proportion of Americans, 15
caucuses
congressional, *278*, 286
state, 227
CDA (Communications Decency Act), 108, 194
CEA (Council of Economic Advisers), 326
cell phones, 186, 220
censorship, 106
Central Intelligence Agency (CIA), 192, 317, 351, 441, 450
Chamber of Commerce v. Environmental Protection Agency, 390
charter schools, 420
checks and balances, 42–43, 47, *48*
Cheney, Dick, 327, 331
chief justice, 379
children, poverty among, 431
Children's Defense Fund, 431
China, 448, 455. *See also* People's Republic of China
education in, 421
media control in, 195
trade as percentage of GDP of, *446*
as U.S. trade partner, 446
Chinese Exclusion Act of 1882, 14
Christian Broadcasting Network, 159
Christian Coalition, 250
Christian right, 452–53
Christian Science Monitor, 178
CIA. *See* Central Intelligence Agency
Citadel, 128
cities
direct legislation in, 12
home rule for, 70

comedy talk shows, 180
Comey, James, 302
comity clause, 70
commander in chief, 317
commerce clause, 73
Commerce Department, 357
commercial speech, 109
committee assignments, 298
committee system (Congress), 208,
    287–89
Common Cause, 246
Communications Decency Act (CDA),
    108, 194
concurrent powers, 68
confederation, 36
conference committees, 288–89
conferences
    House, 285
    Supreme Court, 390–91
Congress, *272*, 273–304
    administrative agency delegations by,
        332
    amendments proposed by, 54
    apportionment and redistricting for,
        281–84, *282, 283*
    approval rating in 2014, 149–50
    in Articles of Confederation, 35–36
    budget approval by, 273
    bureaucracy needed by, 346
    bureaucratic responsibility of, 361–63
    committee system of, 287–89
    competition within, 205
    confirmation of judicial appointments
        by, 273–74
    and debt ceiling limit, 273
    decision making in, 295–301
    delegated powers from, 321–22
    design of, 43–44
    differences between House and Senate,
        275, 275–76
    direct patronage, 284–86
    and foreign policy, 448–52
    on government surveillance, 357
    grants-in-aid from, 79–80
    and Great Depression, 75
    immigration laws from, 13, 14
    incumbency as electoral consideration,
        279–81
    independent regulatory commissions
        established by, 351
    interest groups' access to, 258–59
    interest groups' influence on, *257*
    judicial review of acts of, 382, 384
    non-lawmaking tasks of, 301–3
    organization of, 286–89
    oversight by, 344, 361–63

parties and organization of power in,
    208
party leadership in, 286–87
party polarization in, 300–301
powers of, 45, 47–48
and the presidency, 328
presidential success on votes in, *335*
public opinion of, 303
reapportioning of seats, 16
as representatives of American people,
    275, *285*
rules of lawmaking in, 291–95
social composition of, 276–78, *277*
sociological vs. agency representation,
    276–79
sources of information on, 306
staff system of, 289
unfunded mandates of, 80, 82
waning powers of, 336
Congressional Black Caucus, *278*
Congressional Budget Office, 363
Congressional Quarterly, 184
Congressional Research Service, 363
Connecticut, 117
Connecticut Compromise, 39
conservatism, 148, 149, *149*, 394, 395, 432
conservatives, 85, 371
constituency(-ies)
    of branches of government, 47–48
    of Congress, 278–79
    and congressional decision making, 295
    defined, 275
    interventions for, 285–86
constituents, *295*
Constitution, U.S., 41–52
    Amendments to, 54–55, *56*, 57
    Annapolis Convention, 37
    Articles of Confederation vs., *42*
    balance of powers in, 41–47, *48*
    difficulties in changing, 29–30
    expressed powers from, 316–21
    foreign policy provisions of, *451*
    future of, 58
    original jurisdiction in, 377
    as plan for the country, 29
    powers of president in, 315–24, 449
    preamble of, 19
    ratification of, 46, 49–52
    rights in, 60, *97*
    and weakness of Articles of
        Confederation, 36–37
Constitutional Amendments, 54–55, *56*,
    57, *59*
Constitutional Convention of 1787, *28*,
    37–41, 382
constitutional democracies, 10

constitutional government, 10
Consumer Financial Protection Bureau, 351
Consumer Product Safety Commission, 420
containment, 442
Continental Congress
First, 34
Second, 34, 35
contract cases, 374
contracting power, 408
contributory programs, 413–14, 426
control, public policy as means of, 405–12, *406*
convenience, of new media, 187
cooperative federalism, 78–79, *79*
Copenhagen Climate Summit, 447
cost-of-living adjustments (COLAs), 415
Council of Economic Advisers (CEA), 326
Council on Environmental Quality, 326
counsel, right to, 115
court cases, 373–74
Courtney, Joe, 281
court packing, 380
court-related rights, 113–14
courts, *375*
and balance of values, 21
Congressional approval of appointments, 273–74
interest groups' use of, 260
state, 374–76
courts of appeals, 375
Covered California, 423
criminal cases, 373–74
criminal justice system, 70, 152, 154
criminal laws, 73
criminally accused, due process for, 113–16
"critical citizens," 150
cruel and unusual punishment, 115–16, *116*, *386*
Cuba, 452
media control in, 195
restored diplomatic ties with, 318, *318*, 452
Cuban missile crisis, 442
Cunningham, Randy "Duke," 284
currency, of new media, 187
cyberporn, 108
Czech Republic
education in, 421
government employment in, *353*

Daily Show, The, 180
"dark money," 236
Daschle, Tom, 297

Davie, William R., 41
Davis, Gray, 228
death-penalty laws, 115–16, *116*
debt ceiling, 273, 300
decision making, in Congress, 295–301
Declaration of Independence, 34–35, *35*
on equality, 20
inalienable rights in, 19
defendant, 373
Defense, Department of, 317
and external national security, 355–56
and foreign policy, 450
Pentagon Papers, 191
security function of, 355
Defense of Marriage Act of 1996 (DOMA), 69, 132, *132*
defense spending, *438*, 440, *444*
Delaware, 120, 386
delegated powers, 316, 321–22
Delli Carpini, Michael X., 156
democracy(-ies)
bureaucracy controlled in, 364
and campaign funding, 236–37
and conflicts among values, 21
constitutional, 10
defined, 4, 10
education on virtues of, 152
"excessive," 42
as fundamental value, 21
importance of media in, 175–77, 187, 188, 195
and inadequate political knowledge, 158
interest groups' impact on, 265–66
and liberty, 58
public opinion in, 168
representative, 12
as shared value, 147
Democratic National Committee (DNC), 208
Democratic Party. *See also* political parties
on citizenship for immigrants, 155
and congressional polarization, 301
on economic inequality, 144
on environmental protection, 155
membership of, 205
opinion on economic inequality in, 144
party-building by, 208
party identification, 218
and party system, 209–15
policy positions of, 205
and political orientation, 154–55
in 2016 presidential nominations, 203–4
roots of, 205
and second party system, 211
third parties' effects on, 216–17
trust of government among, 151

economic freedom, 19, 20
economic inequality, 143–44
economic interest groups, 248
economic interests, Kyoto Protocol and, 447
Economic Opportunity Act, 78–79
economic prosperity, foreign policy for, 445
economic sanctions, 456
economy, 45
    federal agencies maintaining, 357–58
    government intervention in, 411–12
    limited control of president over, 335
    media coverage of, 191
    role of trade in, 446
education
    gender discrimination in, 127–28
    global comparison of, 421
    and Internet access, 183
    language used in, 129
    No Child Left Behind Act, 85
    school desegregation, 123, 134
    school segregation, 120–22
    as source of public opinion, 151–52
Education, Department of, 343
Education Act of 1972, Title IX, 127
education policies, 418–21
EEOC. *See* Equal Employment Opportunity Commission
efficiency improvement, 345–51
Egypt, 456
Eighth Amendment, 115–16, 386, *386*
Eisenhower, Dwight D.
    and diplomatic ties with Cuba, 318
    and Little Rock school desegregation, 317
    on military-industrial complex, 408
    and New Deal programs, 213
EITC (Earned Income Tax Credit), 417, 428–29
Elauf, Samantha, *102*
election campaigns. *See also* presidential primary elections
    1992, 237
    1996, 237
    2008, 184
    2014, 279
    2016, 154, 158, 179, 184, 187, 188, 220, 226, 227, 235–37, 330, 362
    funding for, 204, 235–37
    future of, 238
    and incumbency, 279–81
    media's influence on, *174*
    voter mobilization in, 207, *207*, 208
election(s)
    1876, 229
    1888, 229

2000, 229
2010, 281
2012, *23*, *239*
2014, *89*, 281
2016, 216, 229–34, 281, *337*
competitiveness of, 222
and electoral college, 228–29
as hallmark of political participation, 218
incumbency advantage, 279–81
issues in, 226
in mixed regimes, 47–48
nominations, 206
online information affecting, 182
political parties' role in, 205
polling and, 166–67
third parties' effects on, 216–17, *217*
voter turnout for, 206–7, *224*, *239*, *337*
electoral college, 42, 43, 228–29, 315–16
electoral laws, 222–23
electoral politics, interest groups' use of, 263–65
electoral process
    levels and rules of, 227–29
    political parties arising from, 205
electoral realignments, *214*, 215–16
Elementary and Secondary Education Act of 1965 (ESEA), 418
elitist views, 246, 247
Ellsberg, Daniel, 191, 192
eminent domain, 114, 409
employment
    affirmative action in, 134
    in federal service, *348*, 348–50
employment discrimination, 70, 123, 128, 129
Endangered Species Act, 262
enemy combatants, 384
Energy Department, 357
energy industry, 245–46
environment, public opinion on, 155
environmental groups, 245–46
environmental policy, international, 447
Environmental Protection Agency (EPA), *342*, 343
    authority of, 346
    establishment of, 321
    as independent agency, 351
    Volkswagen charged by, 347
    water quality standards set by, 352
EOP (Executive Office of the President), 326, 331–32
EPA. *See* Environmental Protection Agency
Equal Employment Opportunity Commission (EEOC), 103, 126, 128, 131, 134

and citizenship, 8–9
comparing systems of, *53*
control of, 204
created by country's founders, 31
daily life affected by, 5, 6
defined, 4, 9
divided, 215, 216
economic interventions of, 410–11
expansion of American participation
in, 11
forms of, 9–10
functions and value of, 29–30
fundamental values underlying, 19–21
institutions and procedures of, 9–12
interest groups and expansion of,
255–56
limited, 19, 51
limits on, 10–11
and political efficacy, 7–8
and politics, 13
protection against, 98. *See also* civil
liberties
public opinion influenced by, 159
separation of church and state, 101–2
under "traditional system," 71–75
trust in, 7, 149–50
types and numbers of, *70*
government spending, 81, 408
government surveillance programs, 192,
357
grand juries, 113
grants-in-aid, 76, *77*, 79–80
Grassfire.org, 262
grassroots mobilization, 261–63
Gratz v. Bollinger, 135
Great Britain
government structure in, 31
taxes levied on colonies, 32–33
Great Compromise, 39, 41
Great Depression, 75–76, 213, 412–13, *413*
Greece, *353*
Greeks, ancient, 8
greenhouse gases, 346
Greenland, *133*
Griswold, Estelle, 117
Griswold v. Connecticut, 117, 393
Grodzins, Morton, 78
Grutter v. Bollinger, 135
Guantánamo Bay prisoners, 334
gun control debate, 111
gun ownership, 109–11, *110*
gun violence, 111, 321
Ferguson, Missouri, shooting, 154
Orlando, Florida, nightclub shooting,
188–89
school shootings, 111

habeas corpus, 97, 322, 376, 385
*Hague v. Committee for Industrial
Organization*, 104
Hamdan, Salim, 385
Hamdan v. Rumsfeld, 385
Hamdi, Yaser Esam, 384
Hamdi v. Rumsfeld, 384
Hamilton, Alexander, 43, 50, 97
Hannity, Sean, 180
Harrison, Benjamin, 229
Harrison, William Henry, 211
Hastert, Dennis, 304
"Hastert Rule," 304
hate crimes, 132
Hayes, Rutherford B., 229
Health, Education, and Welfare,
Department of, 134
Health and Human Services, Department
of, 352
health care reform, 403–4, 422–24, 432.
See also Affordable Care Act (ACA)
AARP's support of, 427–28
controversy over, *402*
health policies, 420, 422–25, 448
Hearst Corporation, 180
Here Comes Everybody (Shirky), 252
highway bills, 284
Hill, Anita, 381
Hill, The, 184
Hitler, Adolf, 10
HIV, 420
Hobbes, Thomas, 31
Holder, Eric, 86, 128
Holmes, Oliver Wendell, 103
Holt, Gregory, 103
Holt v. Hobbs, 103
Homeland Security, Department of, 87,
345
creation of, 318, 322, 344, 355
and foreign policy, 450
funding for, 294
responsibilities of, 355
security function of, 355
tax collection by, 358
home loan crisis, 425–26
home rule, 70
Hoover, Herbert, 75, 213
House Freedom Caucus, 299, 300
House of Representatives, 43. *See also*
Congress
differences between Senate and, *275*,
275–76
funding candidates' campaigns for, 206
under Great Compromise, 39
majority rule in, 21
number of representatives in, 19

oversight hearings in, 362
party unity in, *297*, 297–98
under Three-Fifths Compromise, 41
housing policies, 425–26
housing rights, 124–26
Huffington Post, 178, 182, 184
humanitarian aid, *447*, 448
humanitarian rights, 456
human rights interest groups, 452–53
human rights policy, 448
Hunter, Noelle, 279

Iceland, *133*
ideological groups, 250
ideologies, political, 148–49, *149*, 394–95
illegal immigrants, 381, *384*
IMF (International Monetary Fund), 455
immigrants
    Asians, 14
    and changes in American identity, 13
    legal citizenship for, 155
    as proportion of population, 14
    religions of, 13–15
    undocumented, 14, 84, 86, 87, 333,
        333, 384
immigration
    as 2016 campaign issue, 226
    as controversial issue, *16*
    and ethnic diversity, 13
    laws regulating, 88
    Obama's executive actions on, 294
    racial criteria for, 13–14
    state legislation on, 86, *86*
immigration laws, civil rights and, 129–30
immigration reform, *16*
Immigration Reform and Control Act of
        1986, 129
impeachment, 303
implementation of laws, 346, 347
implied powers, 67
inalienable rights, 19
income
    and Internet access, 183
    of middle class, 432
    taxes as percentage of, *434*
    in the United States, *18*
    voters compared to population by, *305*
    of voters in 2016 election, *337*
    of wealthy Americans, 432
income inequality
    public opinion on, *142*, 144
    and tax structure, 157, 158
incumbency, 280
incumbency advantage, 279–81
incumbents, 206
independent agencies, 351

Independent Petroleum Association of
        America, 245
Independent Redistricting Commission
        (Arizona), *283*
independent regulatory commissions, 351
indexing, 414
India, *53*
    climate change issue in, *162*
    judicial review in, *383*
    voter turnout in, *224*
information
    consumption of, 157
    verifying accuracy of, 187
    ways of getting/sharing, 182
information benefits (interest groups), 253,
        253
inherent powers, 321, 322, 324
Inslee, Jay, 66
Instagram, *185*
institutional advertising, 261
institutional presidency, 324–28, *325*
insurance coverage, *423*
intelligence agencies, 441, 450
interest groups, 245–66, 268
    advocation by, 247–51
    for children, 431
    and congressional decision making, *257*,
        295–96
    cultivation of access by, 258–59,
        259
    defined, 247
    direct lobbying by, 257–59
    electoral politics used by, 263–65
    and flow of cases to Supreme Court,
        389
    and foreign policy, 452–53
    in the Founding of America, 31–32
    impact on democracy, 265–66
    increasing number of, 255–56
    litigation by, 260
    lobbying expenditures of, *267*
    mobilization of public opinion by,
        261–63
    organizational components of, 251–54
    PACs vs., 245
    "pattern of cases" strategy of, 389
    pluralist and elitist views of, 247
    public opinion influenced by, 159
    for senior citizens, 427–28
    strategies used by, 256–65
Internal Revenue Service (IRS), 357, 358
international arbitration, 458
International Bank for Reconstruction and
        Development (World Bank), 455
international benefits, U.S. foreign policy
        for, 445, 447–48

International Convention on the Elimination of All Forms of Racial Discrimination, 448
International Court of Justice, 458
International Covenant on Civil and Political Rights, 448
international environmental policy, 447
international human rights policy, 448
International Monetary Fund (IMF), 455
international monetary structure, 455
international news sources, 460
international peacekeeping efforts, 448, 454
International Religious Freedom Act, 448
Internet. *See also* social media
    access to, 183, *183*, 194
    and Affordable Care Act, 423–24
    attempts to regulate content of, 194
    cyberporn on, 108
    and elections, 175
    "going public" on, 330
    and information consumption, 157
    and interest groups, 254–56
    ISIS information on, 146
    and libel laws, 107
    as news source, 181
    online news, 183–87
    and organization of interest groups, 251–52
    political participation on, 219–20
    politics changed by, 238
    politics on, 168
    public opinion surveys on, 165
    quality of information on, 188
interstate commerce, 74–75
Interstate Commerce Commission, 351
intervention, of government, 410–11
Iran, 443, 444
    and negotiations with Syria, 355
    nuclear weapons agreement with, 313, 314, 329, 452, *453*
Iraq, 444
    ISIS in, 146, 450, 457
    U.S. involvement in, *457*
Iraq War, 324, 449
    aftermath of, 458
    and Americans' mistrust of government, 7
    costs of, 349
    end of, 449
    as preventive war, 443
    public opinion on, 146
    service members in, 439
Ireland, 452
    government employment in, *353*
    same-sex marriage in, *133*
iron triangle, 259, *259*, 354, *354*
IRS (Internal Revenue Service), 357, 358

IRS Restructuring and Reform Act of 1998, 358
Islamic State of Iraq and Syria (ISIS), 146, *146*, 444–45, 450, 457
    drone strikes against, 324
    social media propaganda from, 188–89
    in Syria, 355
isolationism, 441, 442
Israel, *53*, *162*, 449, 452, 456
Italy, 458

Jackson, Andrew, 211
Jackson, Janet, *194*
Jackson, Robert H., 392
Jacksonian Democrats, *200*
Japan, 353
    government employment in, *353*
    immigrant assimilation in, 17
    judicial review in, *383*
    labor union membership in, *249*
    racial homogeneity of, 17
    trade as percentage of GDP, *446*
    voter turnout in, *224*
Jay, John, 50
Jefferson, Thomas
    and bill of rights, 97, 98
    and Declaration of Independence, 34
    and Locke's work, 31
    on newspapers, 177
    and separation of church and state, 101
Jeffersonian Republicans, 209–11, 215
Jeffersonians (Antifederalists), 205
Jehovah's Witnesses, 102
Jewish Americans, 15, 452
Jewish immigrants, 13
Johnson, Andrew, 318, 329
Johnson, Gary, *217*
Johnson, Lyndon
    election of 1964, 214
    as vice president, 327
Joint Chiefs of Staff, 450
joint committees, 288
judges
    appointed to federal courts, 380–81
    for district courts, 377
    federal, 380–81
    Supreme Court justices, 45, 372, *379*, 379–80
judicial appointments, 273–74
judicial branch, 45
judicial powers, of the president, 318
judicial restraint, 393–94
judicial review, 45, 382–86
    of acts of Congress, 382, 384
    globally, 383
    of state actions, 385–86

Literary Digest poll, 166
litigation, by interest groups, 260
Little Rock, Arkansas, school
    desegregation, 317
Little Rock Central High School, *120*
Livingston, Robert, 34
lobbies, 431. *See also* interest groups
lobbying, 268
    direct, 257–59
    expenditures on, *267*
    regulation of, 260
    by senior citizens, 427–28
local governments
    civil service laws in, 347
    and the Constitution, 70
local politics, participation in, 89, 90
Locke, John, 31, 34–35
Lockheed Martin, 408
logrolling, 299
lower federal courts, 377
Luxembourg, *133*
Lynch, Loretta, 302

Maddow, Rachel, *181*
Madison, James
    on Congress, 44
    on control of government, 359
    Federalist Papers, 50
    on interest groups, 247
    on limited government, 51, 52
    on representation, 50
    on slavery, 40
mail, voting by, *223*
majority leader, 286–87
majority party, 208
majority rule
    check on, 21
    Federalists vs. Antifederalists on, 51
    with minority rights, 21
Malik, Tashfeen, 113
managerial presidency, 359–61
manifest destiny, 441
Mapp, Dollree, 111–12
Mapp v. Ohio, 111–12
Marbury v. Madison, 45, 382
March on Washington (1963), 122
margin of error, 163
marijuana
    medical, 65, 85
    policy for use of, *64*
    recreational, 65, 85
    regulation of use of, 65–66, 88
marketplace of ideas, 103, 158
marriage, same-sex. *See* same-sex marriage
Marshall, John, 73–74
Marshall Plan, 456

Martin, Luther, 39
Maryland
    public accommodation settlements in,
        123
    slaves in, 40
Maryland v. King, 112
Massachusetts
    ban on cigarette advertising in, 109
    provincial government of, 34
    same-sex marriage in, 69
    Shays's Rebellion, 37–38
Mateen, Omar, 188, 189
material benefits (interest groups), 253, *253*
McCain, John, *129*, 167, 237
McCain-Feingold bill, 264
McClatchy Corporation, 180
McConnell, Mitch, 279
McCreary v. ACLU of Kentucky, 102
McCulloch, v. Maryland, 73, 74
McCutcheon, Shaun, *237*
*McCutcheon et al. v. Federal Election
    Commission*, 236
McDonald v. Chicago, 110
McKinley, William, 213, 216
means testing, 415
media, 175–95
    advantages of, 187
    adversarial journalism, 192–93
    and candidate characteristics, 226–27
    in a democracy, 177, 187, 188, 195
    informed consumption of, 198
    investigations by, 175, 188
    ISIS coverage by, 146
    leaked information sources, 191–92
    online news, 183–87
    ownership of, 180–82
    partisan nature of, 181, *181*, 182, 195
    political campaigns influenced by, *174*
    and political power relations, 189–94
    political role of, 175–76
    and public opinion, 159–60, 189–91
    regulation of, 193–94
    rise of new media, 182–89
    traditional, 175–82
Medicaid, 415
    as categorical grant, 76
    expansion of, 82, 422–24
    middle class benefits from, 428
    for the nonworking poor, 429
    oversight of, 352
    spending on, *422*
    for the working poor, 429
medical marijuana, 65, 85
Medicare, 414
    AARP's lobbying for, 427–28
    contributions for, 414

oversight of, 352
senior citizens' benefits from, 426, 427
spending on, *422*
Meese, Edwin, 334
Meetup.com, 220
membership associations, 252
merit system, 347
Merit Systems Protection Board, 359
Mexican War, 450
Mexico, 81, 445
climate change issue in, *162*
education in, 421
government employment in, *353*
same-sex marriage in, *133*
trade as percentage of GDP, *446*
as U.S. trade partner, 446
voter turnout in, *224*
Michigan, 135, 354
microtargeting, 207–8
middle class, 426, 428, 432
Middle East peace deal, 449
military
draft, *57*, 439
expressed powers of, 317–18
and foreign policy, 450
gays in, 134
and national security, 441–45
transgender people in, 128
Military Commissions Act, 385
military contracting, 408
military force, 457, 458
military spending, *438*, *444*
militias, 109, 110
Miller, Evan, *386*
Miller, Judith, 106
Miller v. Johnson, 283
minimum wage, public opinion on, *142*, 144
minorities, poverty among, 430
minority leader, 287
minority party, 208
minority rights, majority rule with, 21
Miranda, Ernesto, 114
Miranda rule, 114
Mississippi
child care block grant in, 84
TANF benefits in, 415
Missouri, 119–20
mixed regime, 47–48
mobilization
external, 205
in forming political parties, 205
internal, 205
and political participation, 222
by presidents, 329–31
of public opinion, 261–63

via social media, 184, 188
of voters, 207, *207*, 208
moderates, 149, *149*
monetary agencies, 358
monetary policies, 409–10
monetary structure, international, 455
money, in politics, 238
Monroe, James, 441
Monroe Doctrine, 441
Montesquieu, Baron de la Brède et de, 31, 46, 47
Montgomery bus boycott, 121
Montreal Protocol, 447
Morgenthau, Hans, 454
Morse v. Frederick, 106
mortgage crisis, 126, 425–26
mortgage interest tax exemption, 428
MSNBC, 179
MSN Latino, 180
multiracial Americans, 14
Murdoch, Rupert, 181
Murguia, Janet, *152*
Muslim, 15
mutual defense alliances, 456

NAACP. *See* National Association for the Advancement of Colored People
Nader, Ralph, 216, 251, 256
NAFTA (North American Free Trade Agreement), 445
National Aeronautics and Space Administration (NASA), *350*, 351
National Association for the Advancement of Colored People (NAACP), 120, 260, 389
National Commission on Terrorist Attacks upon the United States (9/11 Commission), 356
national debt, 7, 273, 300
National Defense Education Act of 1958, 418
National Federation of Independent Business v. Sebelius, 87
national government. *See* federal government
National Hurricane Center, 4
National Institutes of Health (NIH), 352, 420
National Journal, 184
National Opinion Research Center, University of Chicago, 163, 165
National Organization for Women (NOW), 126
national origin discrimination, 124, 129
national origin interest groups, 452
National Origins Quota System, 13

OSHA (Occupational Safety and Health Administration), 352
"outsider" candidates, 238
oversight, 302, 361–63

PACs. *See* political action committees
Page, Benjamin, 160
Palestine, 449
Palko, Frank, 113–14
Palko v. Connecticut, 113–14
Parents Involved in Community Schools v. Seattle School District No. 1, 123
Paris accords, 447
Paris terrorist attacks, 445
Parks, Rosa, 121
parliamentary system
    bicameral body vs., 303–4
    executive branch in, 323
parliaments, 11
partisan politics, 209
partisanship
    in Benghazi hearings, 362
    and congressional decision making, 299–301
    in media reporting, 181, *181*, 182, 195
    and Supreme Court, 392–95
    of voters, 225–26
Partnership to Protect Consumer Credit, 250
party identification, *214*, 218, *219*, *225*
party leadership, in Congress, 286–87
party loyalty, political participation and, 225–26
party system, 209–19, *210*
party unity votes, 296–98, *297*
Paterson, William, 39
Patient Protection and Affordable Care Act of 2010. *See* Affordable Care Act (ACA)
patronage, 284–86
Paul, Rand, 217
Paxton, Ken, 70
pay discrimination, 128
PBS (Public Broadcasting System), 179
peacekeeping efforts, 448, 454
Pelosi, Nancy, 298
Pence, Michael, *225*, 327, *328*
Pendleton Civil Service Act of 1883, 347
Pentagon Papers, 106, 160, 191
People's Republic of China, 440
Perot, Ross, 216, 237
Perret, Geoffrey, 439–40
Persian Gulf War, 449, 457
personal freedom, 19. *See also* liberty
Personal Responsibility and Work Opportunity Reconciliation Act (PRWORA), 417

Peterson, Erik, 157
petition(s)
    freedom of, 104, 105
    right of, 258
Pew Research Center, 150, 167
philosophy, political, 31
physician-assisted suicide, 118
PISA (Program for International Student Assessment), 421
plaintiff, 373
Plame, Valerie, 106
Planned Parenthood, 300
plea bargains, 376
Plessy, Homer, 119
Plessy v. Ferguson, 119, *119*
pluralism, 247
pluralist views, 247
plurality rules, in elections, 229
pocket veto, 294, 320
Poland, *249*
polarization
    of Congress, 300–301
    of politics, 156–57
police
    misconduct by, 122
    public opinion concerning, 154
police dogs, 112
police power, 68, 74
police regulation, 408
political action committees (PACs)
    and campaign finance laws, 180
    campaign funding from, 235–36
    defined, 248
    as interest group strategy, 263–64
    interest groups vs., 248
    leadership, 298
    purpose of, 205
    Super PACs, 204, 236, 264, 296
political appointments, 347
political campaigns. *See* election campaigns
political efficacy, 7–8
political environment
    as agent of political socialization, 155
    and political participation, 222
political equality, 20
political ideologies, 148–49, *149*
    conservatism, 148
    liberalism, 148
    of Supreme Court, 394–95
political knowledge
    for citizenship, 8–9
    shaping public opinion, 156–58
political mobilization, 184. *See also* mobilization
political opinions, expression of, *169*
political outlook, education and, 152

inherent powers claimed for, 322, 324
institutional, 324–28, *325*
limits on power of, 334, 336
managerial, 359–61
and party lines in Congress, 299–300
party support for, 329, *335*
popular mobilization by, 328–31
powers assigned to, 449
presidential addresses, 182
Presidential Election Campaign Fund,
236–37
presidential nominations, 168, 227
2012, 227
2016, 203–4, 206, 216, *217*, 227
presidential pardons, 318
presidential primary elections, 227
2012, 180
2016, 7, 191, 206, 236
"outsider" candidates in, 238
president(s)
actions of, and judicial review, 384–85
as chief executive, 359–61
as commander in chief, 317
and electoral college system, 228–29
expanding powers of, 336
as foreign policy leader, 449–50
political parties' support of, 208–9
powers of, 44–45
veto power of, 47, 294–95
press, freedom of, 99, 103–9, 175, 177, 195
press relations, 330
preventive war, 443
primary elections, 206, 227. *See also* presidential primary elections
priming, 191
print media, 177–79, 193
Printz v. United States, 78
Priority Enforcement Program, 87
prior restraint, 106
prisoners, freedom of worship for, 103
privacy
domestic surveillance programs, 135–36
right to, 113, 116–18, 132, 393–94
and unreasonable search, 111–13
private bills, 286
private property, 57
and eminent domain, 114, 409
state definitions of, 68
privatization, 361, 363
privileges and immunities, 70
probability sample, 161
professional associations, 248
"professional politicians," 290
Program for International Student
Assessment (PISA), 421
Progressive Party, 11, 216

Prohibition, amendment repealing, 46
propaganda, social media as, 188–89
property rights, 99, 111–12. *See also*
private property
proportional representation, 217–18
Protestants
and abortion, 159
immigrants as, 13
as proportion of Americans, 15
protests, 122, 261, 263
PRWORA (Personal Responsibility and
Work Opportunity Reconciliation
Act), 417
public accommodations, 122–23
Public Broadcasting System (PBS), 179
public health, 420, 422–24
public housing, 425
public interest groups, 250
public opinion, 143–68
on climate change, 162
defined, 145
in a democracy, 168
disapproval of Congress, 300, 303
and dominant political ideologies,
148–49, *149*
on economic inequality, 143–44
education's influence on, 151–52
and foreign policy, 453
and government policies, 160–61
government's influence on, 158–59,
191
on income inequality, *142*, 144
interest groups' mobilization of, 261–63
measuring, 161, 163–67
media's influence on, 158–60, 189–91
on minimum wage, *142*, 144
political knowledge shaping, 156–58
political socialization shaping, 150–55
private groups shaping, 159
representing attitudes about politics,
145–50
on security, *459*
shared political values, 146–47
public-opinion polls, 161, 163–67, 170
design and wording of, 163, *164*, 165
on economic inequality, 143–44
inaccurate results of, 165
samples for, 161, 163
public policy, 405. *See also* domestic
policy; foreign policy
gender and opinions about, *155*
implementation of, 346–47
as techniques of control, 405–12, *406*
public-relations strategies, 329–30
public school students, speech by, 106
public school teachers, *248*

public-sector groups, 250
purposive benefits (interest groups), *253*, 254
push polling, 167
Putin, Vladimir, 450

Qaddafi, Mu'ammar, 449

race
    and public opinion differences, 152, *153*, 154
    and redistricting, 282–84
    voters compared to population by, *305*
    of voters in 2016 election, *337*
    "whiteness," 14
Race to the Top program, 420
racial classifications in population, 14
    diversity of, 17
    global, 17
racial discrimination
    Black Lives Matter movement, *94*, 261, *262*
    and death-penalty cases, 116
    in employment, 124
    in housing, 124–26
    post–World War II, 119–21
    school segregation, 120–22
racial equality, 118–26
racial immigration criteria, 13–14
racial minorities, tolerance for, 152
racial profiling, 122
racial segregation, 79
    in public accommodations, 122–23
    in schools, 120–22
    and Southern Manifesto, 77–78
racism, 152, *153*, 154
radio news, 177, 179–81
Randolph, Edmund, 39, 41
random digit dialing, 163
ratification of the Constitution, 46, 49–52
Reagan, Ronald
    bureaucracy under, 362
    fiscal policy of, 411
    on government as a problem, 348
    New Federalism, 83–84
    Republican coalition under, 214–15
    signing statements of, 334
    Supreme Court justices appointed by, 371, 395
    and zero-base budgeting, 360
reapportionment, *282*
rebuttal, right of, 194
recall elections, 228
recession of 2008-2009, 5, 349
Reconstruction, 211–12, 329
recreational marijuana, 65, 85

reddit, *185*
redistributive policies, 409–11
redistricting, 281–84, *282, 283*
Red Lion Broadcasting Company v. FCC, 194
Reed, Stanley, 392
referenda, 12, 228
Reform Party, 216
regional population shifts, 16
Regulated Federalism, *84*
regulation
    of commerce, 74–75
    debate over scope of, 20
    of financial transactions, 295–96
    of media, 193–94
    and preemption, 80, 82
regulatory agencies, 352, 354
regulatory policies, 408–9
regulatory review, by presidents, 332
regulatory taxation, 409
Rehabilitation Act of 1973, 131
Reid, Harry, 293
religion(s), *137*
    and employment discrimination, 124
    freedom of, 101–3, 448
    free exercise of, *102*, 102–3, *105*
    of immigrants, 13–15
    and Latinos' political decisions, 154
    separation of church and state, 101–2
religiously unaffiliated, 15
religious right, 262
Reno v. ACLU, 108
representation
    in Congress, 275, *285*
    Federalists vs. Antifederalists on, 50
    and population, 19
    proportional, 217–18
    and shifts in population, 19
    sociological vs. agency, 276–79
    and writing of Constitution, 39–40
representative democracy, 12
republic, 12
Republican Party. *See also* political parties
    attacks on mainstream media, 181, 182
    on citizenship for immigrants, 155
    and congressional polarization, 301
    divisions within, 300–301
    on economic inequality, 144
    on environmental protection, 155
    external mobilization in building, 205
    fundraising by, 235
    membership of, 205
    nomination of Trump, 206
    and Obama's judicial appointments, 372, 380–81
    opinion on economic inequality in, 144

party-building by, 208
and party identification, 218
and party system, 211–15
policy positions of, 205
and political orientation, 154–55
and preemption, 80
2016 presidential nominations, 203–4,
   206
roots of, 205
Southern resentment of, 212
third parties' effects on, 216–17
as third party, 216
trust of government among, 151
and voting rights for slaves, 11
"research" lobby, 250
reserved powers, 68
revenue agencies, 358
Revolutionary War. *See* American
   Revolution (1776)
Rhode Island, 109
right(s), 60
to bear arms, 109–11
to counsel, 115
inalienable, 19
of petition, 258
to privacy, 116–18, 132, 393–94
of rebuttal, 194
right to die movement, 118
Riley v. California, 112
Rio Treaty, 456
Roberts, John, 381, 393, 424
Roberts, Pat, 293
Roe v. Wade, 117, *117*, 159, 260, 385,
   393
rogue states, 442, 443
Roll Call, 184
roll-call votes, 296–97
Romer v. Evans, 131
Romney, Mitt, 235
Roosevelt, Eleanor, 327
Roosevelt, Franklin Delano, *329*
court packing by, 379–80
election of 1932, 213
election of 1936, 166
and electoral realignment, 216
fireside chats of, 329
fiscal policy of, 411
Kitchen Cabinet of, 326
and managerial presidency, 359
New Deal, 75–76, 213
powers used by, 319
press relations of, 330
welfare system, 413
Rove, Karl, 208
rural areas, shift of population away
   from, 16

Russia, 432, 450, 455
climate change issue in, *162*
economic sanctions against, 456
media control in, 195
and negotiations with Syria, 355
as resurgent military power, 456
trade as percentage of GDP, *446*
Ryan, Paul, *287*, 301

Safe Drinking Water Act Amendments of
   1986, 334
Salon.com, 184
same-sex marriage, 69, 158, 260
nationwide legalization of, 151
states on, 69–70, 132
Supreme Court on, 69, 69–70, *132*,
   133, 151, *394*, 396
worldwide legalization of, 133, *133*
sample (survey), 161, 163
sampling error, 163
San Bernardino, California terrorist attack,
   189
sanctions, 456
Sanders, Bernie, 7, 203–4
Saudi Arabia, 448
Save Our Species Alliance, 262
Scalia, Antonin, *157*, 273, *370*, 371, 381,
   390, 395
Scalise, Steve, 299
Schattschneider, E. E., 251
SCHIP (State Child Health Insurance
   Program), 84
school desegregation, 123, 134
schools, shootings at, 111
school segregation, 120–22
search and seizure, 111–12, *112*
Seattle Post-Intelligencer, 178
Second Amendment, 109–11, *110*
Second Continental Congress, 34, 35
Second Founding, 36–41
Second Treatise of Civil Government
   (Locke), 31
secretaries, federal, 350
secrets, government, 356–57
Secure Communities program, 87
security
collective, 456–57
domestic. *See* national security
public opinion on, *459*
segregation, 77–79
housing, 124–26
school, *120*, 120–22, 134
voting, 124
Select Committee on Benghazi, 302, 362
select committees, 288
selection bias, 166–67, 190

Southern Manifesto, 77–78
South Korea, 81
Soviet Union, 10, 418, 441–43, 456, 457
Spain
　government employment in, *353*
　same-sex marriage in, *133*
Spanish-American War, 450
Speaker of the House, 208, 286
speech
　commercial, 109
　freedom of, 99, 103–9, *105*, 194
　political, 103–4
　by public school students, 106
　symbolic, 104–5
speech plus, 105
speed limit controls, *83*
spending power, 411
Spirit of the Laws, The (Montesquieu), 31,
　　47
spoils system, 347
SSI (Supplemental Security Income)
　　program, 415
staff organizations, 252
staff system (Congress), 289
Stalin, Joseph, 10
Stamp Act, 32
standing committees, 287–88
stare decisis, 374
"state, the," 9
state actions, judicial review of, 385–86
State Child Health Insurance Program
　　(SCHIP), 84
State Department
　and external national security, 355–56
　and foreign policy, 450
　and human rights abuses, 448
　security function of, 355
state governments
　and arms for militias, 109
　civil service laws, 347
　control by, 83–84
　immigration legislation of, 86, *86*
　powers of, 68
　responsibilities of, 66
　under "traditional system," 71–75
state politics, participation in, 89, 90
states
　under Articles of Confederation, 35–36
　Bill of Rights applied to, 98–99, *100*
　and cooperative federalism, 78–79
　direct legislation in, 12
　education monitoring in, 420
　electoral laws of, 222–23
　gun regulations in, 109–10, *110*
　immigration laws of, 130
　national-state balance, 84–88

obligations among, 68–69
　and power of national government, 45
　and same-sex marriage, 69–70, 132
　unemployment insurance, 414
　voter registration in, 223
states' rights, 75, *75*, 77–78, 121
Stein, Jill, *217*
Stevens, Paul, 108
Stewart, Potter, 107
Stone, Harlan F., 77, 392
strict scrutiny, 103, 121
Student Nonviolent Coordinating
　　Committee, 122
students, foreign policy and, 439
subsidies, 405, 408–9, 411, 425
Sudan, *447*, 448
suffrage, 221
Sugar Act of 1764, 32
Sundquist, James, 78–79
Sunstein, Cass, 332
Super PACs, 204, 236, 264, 296
Supplemental Nutrition Assistance
　　Program (SNAP), 415–15, 417,
　　418, 428, 429
Supplemental Security Income (SSI)
　　program, 415
supremacy clause, 46, 385
Supreme Court, *370*, 379–95
　on affirmative action, 134–35
　and Affordable Care Act, 87–88, *402*,
　　404, 424, 425
　on Alaska's employment
　　discrimination, 70
　amicus briefs, *397*, 398
　appeals to, 376–80
　appointments to, 273–74, 301
　on authority of the EPA, 346
　on Bill of Rights, 98–99
　on campaign funding, 236, 237, *237*,
　　264
　cases filed in, *388*
　and civil liberties, 95
　on Communications Decency Act, 194
　creation of, 45
　on due process, 113–16
　and end of "traditional system," 73–75
　on federal role over states, 85
　flow of cases to, 386–89
　and Fourteenth Amendment, 99
　and freedom of religion, 101–3, *102*
　on freedom of speech, 99, 103–9
　on freedom of the press, 103–9
　on gay and lesbian rights, 260
　on gender discrimination, 127–28
　on immigration, 130
　influences on decisions of, 392–95

values
   Americans' support for, *147*
   conflict of, 21
   defined, 145
   democracy, 21
   equality, 20–21
   liberty, 19–20
   political, 21–22, 145–47
   shared, 146–47
   underlying government, 4, 19–21
Van Ordern v. Perry, 102
veto power, 45, 47, 294–95, 319–21, *320*
vice presidency, 327
Vietnam War, 155, 191, 213, 456
violent broadcast content, 108
Virginia
   and Annapolis Convention, 37
   and school segregation, 120, 386
   slaves in, 40
Virginia Military Institute (VMI), 128
Virginia Plan, 39
Volcker, Paul, 410
Volkswagen, 347
voter ID laws, 124, *124*, 223
voter registration, 24, 207, 223
voter turnout, 221–22, *223*, *224*, *305*
   around the world, 224
   country comparison of, 224, *224*
   in 2012 election, *23*, *239*
   mobilization of voters, 207, *207*, 208
   parties' assistance with, 206–7
   in U.S. national elections, 224
voting, 240
   on bills, 293–94
   as building block of citizenship, 8
   and candidate characteristics, 226–27
   early, 223, *223*
   factors influencing, 222–23
   issues in, 226
   by mail, *223*
   party loyalty in, *225*, 225–26
   as political participation, 218, 220,
      222–23
voting rights
   Amendments for, *59*
   as civil right, 124, *125*
   expansion of, 11
   for Native Americans, 13–14
   state, 58
   Twenty-Sixth Amendment, *57*
   and voter ID laws, 124, *124*
Voting Rights Act amendments of 1970, 129
Voting Rights Act amendments of 1975,
   130
Voting Rights Act of 1965 (VRA), 124,
   125, 215, 284

Wagner-Steagall National Housing Act of
   1937, 425
Wales, Jimmy, 195
Wallace, George, 14, 79
Wall Street Journal, 178, 181
Wal-Mart, 258
War of 1812, 450
War on Poverty, 78–79
war on terror/terrorism, 327, 443
War Powers Resolution, 324
Warren, Earl, 379, 393
war(s), 439–40
   deterring, 456–57
   as politics by other means, 457
   power to declare, 450
   preventive, 443
   public opinion on, 453
Washington (state)
   regulation of marijuana use in, 65, 66
   and 2010 reapportionment, 281
Washington, D.C.. *See* District of
   Columbia
Washington, George, 205
   on foreign nations, 439, 441
   on Shays's Rebellion, 38
Washington Post, 160, 177, 178
Watergate, 160, 263, 362
water quality standards, 352
wealth distribution, *142*
websites, as news source, 182
Webster v. Reproductive Health Services, 260
welfare, bureaucracies promoting, 351–52,
   354, *354*
welfare reform, 416–18
welfare state, 77
welfare system, 412–18
   history of, 412–13
   reform of, 416–18
   size of, *422*
   Social Security Act of 1935, 413–16
Westboro Baptist Church demonstrations,
   104–5, *105*
*West Virginia State Board of Education v.
   Barnette*, 102
Whig Party, 211
whips, 287
whip system, 299
whistle-blowers, 191
white Americans
   as digital citizens, 183
   European Americans as proportion of
      population, 14
   Medicaid gap for, 429
   naturalized, 14
   poverty rate for, 430
   and racism, 152, *153*, 154

White House, contacting, 338
White House staff, 326
"whiteness," 14
white non-Hispanics, as digital citizens,
    183
WikiLeaks, 192
Wikipedia, 195, 252
Wilson, Darren, 154
Wilson, James, 39, 41
Wilson, Joseph, 106
Wilson, Woodrow, 441
Windsor, Edith, *132*
women
    in Congress, *275*, 290
    and gender discrimination, 126–28
    in other countries' legislatures, 290
    poverty among, 430–31
    voter support for candidacies of, 227
    voting rights for, 11
Women's Equity Action League, 126
women's rights movement, 126, *127*, 128

working poor, social benefits for,
    428–29
World Bank, 455
World Health Organization, 447
World Trade Organization (WTO), 445,
    446
World War I, 442, 450
World War II, 442, 450
writ of certiorari, 386–87
writ of habeas corpus, 376
writs, 386–87
WTO (World Trade Organization), 445,
    446
Wyoming, 109

Yates, Robert, 40, 50
Yellen, Janet, *410*
YouTube, 182
    ISIS's use of, 188
    as news source, *185*
    presidential presence on, 330

Voter Registration Information

State	Registration Deadline before Election*	Early Voting Permitted?**	Identification Required to Vote?**	More Information
Alabama	14 days	No	Photo ID requested	alabamavotes.gov
Alaska	30 days	Yes	ID requested; photo not required	elections.alaska.gov
Arizona	29 days	Yes	ID required; photo not required	azsos.gov/election
Arkansas	30 days	Yes	ID requested; photo not required	sos.arkansas.gov
California	15 days	Yes	No	sos.ca.gov
Colorado	8 days by mail or online; no in-person deadline	Yes (all voting by mail)	ID requested; photo not required	sos.state.co.us
Connecticut	14 days by mail; 7 days in person; election-day registration permitted	No	ID requested; photo not required	ct.gov/sots
Delaware	24 days	No	ID requested; photo not required	elections.delaware.gov
District of Columbia	30 days by mail or online; no in-person deadline	Yes	No	dcboee.org
Florida	29 days	Yes	Photo ID requested	dos.myflorida.com/elections
Georgia	28 days	Yes	Photo ID required	sos.ga.gov
Hawaii	30 days	Yes	Photo ID requested	hawaii.gov/elections
Idaho	25 days	Yes	Photo ID requested	idahovotes.gov
Illinois	27 days	Yes	No	elections.il.gov
Indiana	29 days	Yes	Photo ID required	in.gov/sos/elections
Iowa	10 days	Yes	No	sos.iowa.gov
Kansas	21 days	Yes	Photo ID required	kssos.org
Kentucky	29 days	No	ID requested; photo not required	elect.ky.gov
Louisiana	30 days	Yes	Photo ID requested	sos.la.gov
Maine	21 days by mail; no in-person deadline	Yes	No	maine.gov/sos
Maryland	21 days	Yes	No	elections.state.md.us
Massachusetts	20 days	No	No	www.sec.state.ma.us
Michigan	30 days	No	Photo ID requested	michigan.gov/sos
Minnesota	21 days	Yes	No	mnvotes.org
Mississippi	30 days	No	Photo ID required	sos.ms.gov
Missouri	Fourth Wednesday prior to election	No	ID requested; photo not required	sos.mo.gov
Montana	30 days by mail; no in-person deadline	Yes	ID requested; photo not required	sos.mt.gov

State	Registration Deadline before Election*	Early Voting Permitted?**	Identification Required to Vote?**	More Information
Nebraska	Third Friday prior to election by mail; second Friday prior to election in person	Yes	No	www.sos.ne.gov
Nevada	31 days by mail; 21 days in person	Yes	No	nvsos.gov
New Hampshire	10 days; election-day registration permitted	No	ID requested; photo not required	sos.nh.gov
New Jersey	21 days	Yes	No	njelections.org
New Mexico	28 days	Yes	No	sos.state.nm.us
New York	25 days	No	No	www.elections.ny.gov
North Carolina	25 days	Yes	No	ncsbe.gov
North Dakota	No voter registration required	Yes	Photo ID required	vote.nd.gov
Ohio	30 days	Yes	ID required; photo not required	sos.state.oh.us
Oklahoma	24 days	Yes	ID requested; photo not required	ok.gov/elections
Oregon	21 days	Yes (all voting by mail)	No	sos.oregon.gov
Pennsylvania	30 days	No	No	votespa.com
Rhode Island	30 days; election-day registration permitted	No	Photo ID requested	www.elections.state.ri.us
South Carolina	30 days	No	ID requested; photo not required	scvotes.org
South Dakota	15 days	Yes	Photo ID requested	sdsos.gov
Tennessee	30 days	Yes	Photo ID required	tn.gov/sos/election
Texas	30 days	Yes	Photo ID requested	votetexas.gov
Utah	30 days by mail; 7 days in person	Yes	ID requested; photo not required	elections.utah.gov
Vermont	Wednesday before the election	Yes	No	www.sec.state.vt.us/elections
Virginia	22 days	No	Photo ID required	sbe.virginia.gov
Washington	30 days by mail and online; 8 days in person	Yes (all voting by mail)	ID requested; photo not required	sos.wa.gov/elections/
West Virginia	21 days	Yes	No	sos.wv.gov
Wisconsin	20 days by mail; election-day registration permitted	Yes	Photo ID required	www.sos.state.wi.us
Wyoming	14 days; election-day registration permitted	Yes	No	soswy.state.wy.us

* Information collected from Project Vote Smart, votesmart.org/elections/voter-registration (accessed 9/1/16).
** Information collected from National Conference of State Legislatures, www.ncsl.org (accessed 9/1/16). In states where an ID is "requested," voters who do not bring ID to the polls may be required to sign an affidavit of identity, vote on a provisional ballot, have a poll worker vouch for their identity, or take additional steps after Election Day to make sure their vote is counted.